P9-DHJ-585

Property of
BRIDGEPORT PUBLIC LIBRARY
Old Mill Green Library

America's
TEST KITCHEN

Also by the Editors at America's Test Kitchen

America's Best Lost Recipes

The America's Test Kitchen Family Cookbook

The Best of America's Test Kitchen 2007, 2008

THE BEST RECIPE SERIES:
The Best International Recipe
The Best Make-Ahead Recipe
The Best 30-Minute Recipe
The Best Light Recipe
The Cook's Illustrated Guide to Grilling & Barbecue
Best American Side Dishes
The New Best Recipe
The Best Cover & Bake Recipes
The Best Meat Recipes
Baking Illustrated
Restaurant Favorites at Home
The Best Vegetable Recipes
The Best Italian Classics
The Best American Classics
The Best Soups & Stews

THE TV COMPANION SERIES:
Behind the Scenes with America's Test Kitchen
Test Kitchen Favorites
Cooking at Home with America's Test Kitchen
America's Test Kitchen Live!
Inside America's Test Kitchen
Here in America's Test Kitchen
The America's Test Kitchen Cookbook

834 Kitchen Quick Tips

PRAISE FOR THE BEST RECIPE SERIES AND OTHER AMERICA'S TEST KITCHEN TITLES

"An instant classic."
CHICAGO SUN-TIMES ON ***AMERICA'S BEST LOST RECIPES***

"This tome definitely raises the bar for all-in-one, basic, must-have cookbooks. . . . Kimball and his company have scored another hit."
PORTLAND OREGONIAN on ***THE AMERICA'S TEST KITCHEN FAMILY COOKBOOK***

"A foolproof, go-to resource for everyday cooking."
PUBLISHERS WEEKLY on ***THE AMERICA'S TEST KITCHEN FAMILY COOKBOOK***

"A timesaving tome."
THE CHICAGO TRIBUNE on ***834 KITCHEN QUICK TIPS***

"A moderate approach to lightening everyday dishes for the family."
THE CHICAGO TRIBUNE on ***THE BEST LIGHT RECIPE***

"Further proof that practice makes perfect, if not transcendent. . . . If an intermediate cook follows the directions exactly, the results will be better than takeout or Mom's."
THE NEW YORK TIMES on ***THE NEW BEST RECIPE***

"Exceptional renditions with thorough instruction . . ."
PUBLISHERS WEEKLY on ***COOKING AT HOME WITH AMERICA'S TEST KITCHEN***

"Like a mini-cooking school, the detailed instructions and illustrations ensure that even the most inexperienced cook can follow these recipes with success."
PUBLISHERS WEEKLY on ***BEST AMERICAN SIDE DISHES***

"Makes one-dish dinners a reality for average cooks, with honest ingredients and detailed make-ahead instructions."
THE NEW YORK TIMES on ***THE BEST COVER & BAKE RECIPES***

"[*The Best Meat Recipes*] conquers every question one could have about all things meat."
THE SAN FRANCISCO CHRONICLE on ***THE BEST MEAT RECIPES***

"The best instructional book on baking this reviewer has seen."
LIBRARY JOURNAL (STARRED REVIEW) on ***BAKING ILLUSTRATED***

"A must-have for anyone into our nation's cooking traditions—and a good reference, too."
LOS ANGELES DAILY NEWS on ***THE BEST AMERICAN CLASSICS***

"*Cook's Illustrated* to the rescue. . . . *The Best Vegetable Recipes* belongs on every cooking reference shelf. Here's to our health."
PITTSBURGH TRIBUNE-REVIEW on ***THE BEST VEGETABLE RECIPES***

Welcome to America's Test Kitchen

THIS BOOK HAS BEEN TESTED, WRITTEN, AND edited by the folks at America's Test Kitchen, a very real 2,500-square-foot kitchen located just outside of Boston. It is the home of *Cook's Illustrated* magazine and *Cook's Country* magazine and is the Monday-through-Friday destination for more than two dozen test cooks, editors, food scientists, tasters, and cookware specialists. Our mission is to test recipes over and over again until we understand how and why they work and until we arrive at the "best" version.

We start the process of testing a recipe with a complete lack of conviction, which means that we accept no claim, no theory, no technique, and no recipe at face value. We simply assemble as many variations as possible, test a half dozen of the most promising, and taste the results blind. We then construct our own hybrid recipe and continue to test it, varying ingredients, techniques, and cooking times until we reach a consensus. The result, we hope, is the best version of a particular recipe, but we realize that only you can be the final judge of our success (or failure). As we like to say in the test kitchen, "We make the mistakes, so you don't have to."

All of this would not be possible without a belief that good cooking, much like good music, is indeed based on a foundation of objective technique. Some people like spicy foods and others don't, but there is a right way to sauté, there is a best way to cook a pot roast, and there are measurable scientific principles involved in producing perfectly beaten, stable egg whites. This is our ultimate goal: to investigate the fundamental principles of cooking so that you become a better cook. It is as simple as that.

You can watch us work (in our actual test kitchen) by tuning in to *America's Test Kitchen* (www.americastestkitchen.com) on public television or by subscribing to *Cook's Illustrated* magazine (www.cooksillustrated.com) or *Cook's Country* magazine (www.cookscountry.com), which are each published every other month. We welcome you into our kitchen, where you can stand by our side as we test our way to the "best" recipes in America.

THE BEST CHICKEN RECIPES

A BEST RECIPE CLASSIC

THE BEST CHICKEN RECIPES

A BEST RECIPE CLASSIC

BY THE EDITORS OF

COOK'S ILLUSTRATED

PHOTOGRAPHY

KELLER + KELLER, CARL TREMBLAY, AND DANIEL J. VAN ACKERE

ILLUSTRATIONS

JOHN BURGOYNE

BROOKLINE, MASSACHUSETTS

America's Test Kitchen
17 Station Street
Brookline, MA 02445

ISBN-13: 978-1-933615-23-3
ISBN-10: 1-933615-23-0

Library of Congress Cataloging-in-Publication Data
The Editors of Cook's Illustrated

The Best Chicken Recipes: Would you roast 40 chickens to find a simple, foolproof method that results in perfectly cooked meat and beautifully browned skin every time? We did. Here are more than 300 exhaustively tested recipes for America's favorite main course.

1st Edition
ISBN-13: 978-1-933615-23-3
ISBN-10: 1-933615-23-0
(hardcover): U.S. $35 CAN $38
1. Cooking. I. Title
2008

Manufactured in the United States of America

10 9 8 7 6 5 4 3 2 1

Distributed by America's Test Kitchen, 17 Station Street, Brookline, MA 02445

Editorial Director: Jack Bishop
Associate Editors: Elizabeth Wray Emery and Rachel Toomey
Test Cook: Suzannah McFerran
Assistant Test Cook: Adelaide Parker
Design Director: Amy Klee
Art Director: Greg Galvan
Designer: Tiffani Beckwith
Staff Photographer: Daniel J. van Ackere
Additional Photography: Carl Tremblay
Food Styling: Marie Piraino and Mary Jane Sawyer
Illustrator: John Burgoyne
Production Director: Guy Rochford
Senior Production Manager: Jessica Lindheimer Quirk
Color and Imaging Specialist: Andrew Mannone
Production and Imaging Specialist: Lauren Pettapiece
Copyeditor: Jeffrey Schier
Proofreader: Holly Hartman
Indexer: Elizabeth Parson

Pictured on front of jacket: Simple Roast Chicken (page 120)

Pictured on back of jacket: Sautéed Chicken with Cherry Tomatoes, Olives, Feta, and Mint (page 305), Chicken with Spring Vegetable Risotto (page 370), Weeknight Chicken Pot Pie (page 312), Light Chicken Parmesan (page 329), Korean Fried Chicken (page 157)

CONTENTS

Preface

MY GRANDFATHER, CHARLES STANLEY, LOVED chickens. My mother, Mary Alice, loved chickens. And our family, the third generation, loves chickens as well, keeping two dozen hens on our farm for eggs. Our youngest daughter, Emily, has the job of collecting the mostly still-warm eggs in the morning and our 12-year-old son, Charlie, has to close up the coop at sunset. (He brings his pellet gun and flashlight to scare off the coyotes he thinks are lurking ominously in the shadows.) We also have more than our share of chicken memorabilia: chicken sculptures, doorstops, paintings, sketches, wastepaper baskets, and wall hangings. It must be something peculiar in the DNA.

Of course, in the kitchen, everyone likes chicken. These days, it doesn't have much flavor, so it is more of a starting point than a meal unto itself. One of our editors spent a year in Paris recently, and upon his return I asked him what was most memorable about the food. "Cucumbers and chicken," he said. To his astonishment, both had great flavor, unlike their rather pedestrian counterparts here in the States.

So, to the matter at hand. "Who needs a chicken cookbook?" Well, we all do, the reason being that, unlike the tough old coq from Coq au Vin—that stringy, chewy, but highly flavored bird used for the famous French classic—today's birds are tender, large-breasted, and on the bland side. They need help. A good cook needs to know how to infuse them with additional flavor, whether the recipe is a simple roast chicken, baked chicken parts, or a quick skillet sauté. Old-fashioned recipes that let the chicken itself do the work just don't cut it.

Of course, that means America's Test Kitchen, is probably a good bet in terms of rediscovering cooking and preparation methods for classic chicken recipes. We go back, test a variety of approaches, and then make the recipe over and over, changing variables, until we (at least hopefully) end up with a crowd-pleaser. There is no guarantee that you will love everything we do, but our promise—"Recipes That Work"—ought to be true the majority of the time. (Only if you follow the recipe, however. My favorite true story is about a reader who made one of our chicken dishes and didn't like it. Turns out that he had no chicken on hand, so he substituted shrimp!)

There is another good reason to buy and use this book. The average repertoire of chicken dishes extends through the basics—casseroles, stir-fries, and salads plus baked, roasted, and grilled—but, like with some old married couples, things get taken for granted. There is a whole wide world of chicken recipes that ask to be explored, from simple chicken enchiladas to jerk chicken to Latino-style chicken and rice to Korean fried chicken to a kitchenfull of Asian recipes. The problem with many of these recipes, of course, is that they are not suited to the American repertoire, so we have sifted through the possibilities, looking for recipes that translate well to your home, and then put them through our rigorous testing process so that they are both reliable and worth making again and again.

One of our neighbors, Dorothy, has a large map of the USA pinned to her living room wall. She has marked every state she has visited in her lifetime (she just got back from Hawaii), and now there are only three left. Each state is a bit different, to be sure, but each is familiar, sharing the essence of being American. This love of the known, coupled with a keen sense of adventure, is what makes Dorothy so interesting. It is also the essence of a good cook, one who can start with the most common ingredient and create something new each and every time.

Here at America's Test Kitchen, we love the common recipe and the common ingredient, but we never take them for granted. It's a curious mind that turns a simple chicken dinner into something special, something extraordinary.

So join us for a new look at the familiar. We hope that you enjoy the recipes, as well as the adventure.

Christopher Kimball
Founder and Editor
Cook's Illustrated and *Cook's Country*
Host, *America's Test Kitchen*

CHICKEN 101

CHICKEN 101

IN LARGE PART OWING TO ITS RELATIVELY low cost and fat content, poultry has become America's favorite meat. Plus, it's endlessly versatile, kids love it, and you can dress it up for company, cook it simply and quickly on the stovetop on busy weeknights, and use it in everything from soups and stews to sandwiches and stir-fries. But problems with preparing and cooking chicken at home abound—mostly because there are so many conflicting theories about how to handle it and cook it: Is brining really necessary? Should chicken be rinsed before cooking? And, of course, what is the best way to roast a whole bird? So—here in this primer (and throughout the book), we will take you through these issues and more, from selecting the best chicken at your market to butchering a whole chicken and chicken parts to knowing when chicken is done.

BUYING CHICKEN

EVERY GOOD CHICKEN DISH STARTS WITH high-quality, fresh chicken. But there are an overwhelming number of choices at the supermarket—how do you recognize superior poultry? We have learned over time (and plenty of tasting) that the terms "fresh," "organic," "free-range," "all-natural," and "lean" rarely indicate good flavor or texture, and neither does price. Is anything other than brand a dependable sign of quality?

Genetic and Environmental Factors

We started by identifying and investigating a long list of genetic and environmental factors that might help the consumer purchase a high-quality bird. We first looked to genetic engineering. Birds are bred to meet the goals of a particular producer. Murray's chickens, for example, are engineered for a high yield of breast meat and a low yield of fat. (Tasters found them "tough" and "dry.") Perdue chickens are bred for a high ratio of meat to bone. (We found this means big breasts but scrawny legs.) It seemed to us, at least at first pass, that few, if any, producers were engineering birds for flavor.

The older the chicken, the more distinct its flavor is. Free-range birds, whose diet is less intense and less controlled than that of indoor chickens (because free-range birds have unrestricted access to the outdoors, it is impossible to keep them from eating random grasses and insects), take longer to reach their proper weight and are older when they are processed. Yet the "free-range" moniker is no indication of superior flavor. The two free-range birds we tasted, Eberly and D'Artagnan, had both fans and critics.

How Processing Affects Flavor

Processing factors that can affect the flavor and appearance of a chicken include how the chicken was rinsed and chilled prior to packaging. Antimicrobial agents, such as sodium triphosphates, are sometimes added to the final rinse water to cut down on contamination by bacteria like salmonella. (Some tasters can detect traces of this chemical; it is usually described as "metallic.") Some rinsing methods cause excess water to build up under the skin, and this can lead to a shriveled appearance after cooking. After slaughtering and rinsing, the chickens are quickly chilled to a temperature of about 28 degrees Fahrenheit, or just above their freezing point. If the chickens are chilled too quickly, the meat can get spongy and watery. If chilled too slowly, the meat can dry out and develop an off color. None of these effects could be confirmed in our tasting because we could not be certain about how a particular bird was processed.

Our first solid clue to any possible connection between processing method and flavor emerged when we discovered that Empire, the only kosher chicken in our tasting, was also one of the best-tasting. (Murray's birds are not kosher but are processed under similar conditions in accordance with Muslim law.) Both Empire and Murray's birds are hand-slaughtered rather than killed by machine, which ensures both a clean kill and a quick and efficient "bleed-out." Industry experts indicated that machine-processed chickens are more likely to be subject to improper slaughtering, which can cause blood to clot, resulting in tough meat or a livery flavor.

Because tasters far preferred the Empire chicken to Murray's, however, it followed that more was at work here than slaughtering technique. For one thing, kosher chickens like Empire's are dunked in cold water to remove feathers after slaughter. Cold water firms both the skin and the fat layer beneath it. In contrast, most other producers scald birds in hot water to remove the feathers. The experts we talked to said that scalding can "solubilize" the chicken's fat, leading to excessive moisture loss and a wrinkled appearance in the chicken skin after cooking.

Most importantly, chickens that are processed according to kosher law are buried in salt for one hour to draw out impurities and are then rinsed in cold spring water. The combination of salt and water acts like a brine, encouraging the fiber in the meat to open and trap the salt and water, leading to a juicier, more flavorful bird. If you are going to buy a kosher chicken, Empire is our favorite. It should be noted, however, that if you are buying a kosher chicken you should not brine it, as it has already effectively been brined.

The other brand that topped our tasting was Bell & Evans. Bell & Evans does a couple of things that make its chickens stand out from the crowd. For one, the company doesn't cut costs by adjusting the feed of the chickens to take advantage of changing commodity prices. It has found what it thinks is the best feed to produce the best-tasting birds and so doesn't change the formula every week. Additionally, the company does not package its birds before shipping. Instead, the chickens are shipped loose on ice, allowing them to "weep," a process whereby blood and fluids slowly drain from the bird. The process of weeping improves the flavor of the bird because blood and fluid aren't allowed to coagulate and freeze in the bird. The result is a chicken that tastes like, well, chicken. When using a bird such as Bell & Evans, which isn't kosher, we typically recommend brining it before cooking (for more information on brining, see page 12).

It should also be noted that Tyson, a mass-produced bird priced at just $1.29 per pound, came in third in our tasting, ahead of birds costing more than twice as much. Perdue consistently finished last, with tasters describing the meat as "pithy," "chalky," and "stringy," with unpleasant sour notes as well.

Buying Boneless Breasts and Ground Chicken

If you're buying boneless, skinless breasts, you should be aware that breasts of different sizes are often packaged together, and it is usually impossible to tell what you've bought until you've opened the package. When faced with chicken breasts of varying sizes, simply pound the thicker ends of the larger pieces of chicken to match those of the smaller pieces. Some breasts will still be larger than others, but pounding will help make their thickness the same and ensure even cooking.

Finally, ground chicken is typically sold one of two ways: prepackaged or ground to order. The prepackaged variety is made from either dark or white meat. Higher-end markets and specialty markets grind their chicken to order, and therefore the choice of meat is yours. When it comes to flavor, however, tasters were unanimous—dark meat was far superior. In most of our testing, we found ground white meat chicken to be exceedingly dry and almost void of flavor. The dark meat was more flavorful and juicy due to its higher fat content.

The Bottom Line

Whether you're buying a whole chicken, chicken parts, or ground chicken, the key is to choose a reliable brand (such as Empire or Bell & Evans) and inspect the package carefully, especially if you are buying boneless breasts or chicken parts and not butchering a whole chicken yourself.

CHICKEN SAFETY AND HANDLING

GIVEN THE PREVALENCE OF BACTERIA IN THE POULTRY SUPPLY IN THIS COUNTRY, IT'S probably best to assume that the bird you buy is contaminated. That means you need to follow some simple rules to minimize the danger to you and your family.

Sell-by Dates

Cook or freeze poultry within one or two days of purchase, no matter what its sell-by date is. The sell-by date should not be considered a use-by date for the consumer, but rather a general way for the store to determine how long to display an item for sale. There are no federal regulations governing calendar dating. While some states have regulations, the dates are often determined by the processor.

Refrigerating

Keep chicken refrigerated until just before cooking. Bacteria thrive at temperatures between 40 and 140 degrees. This means leftovers should also be promptly refrigerated.

Freezing

Chicken may be frozen in its original packaging or repackaged. If freezing chicken for longer than two months, rewrap (or wrap over original packaging) with airtight foil or plastic wrap, or place inside a zipper-lock freezer bag. (Chicken can be safely frozen for many months, but it will likely start to suffer a loss in flavor and texture after one month.)

Thawing

Chicken that has been frozen should never be thawed on the countertop. This thawing method overexposes the protein to temperatures perfect for fostering the growth of bacteria. Thawing should be done in the refrigerator (about 24 hours for the average three- to four-pound chicken) or in the sink under cold running water.

Rinsing

The U.S. Department of Agriculture advises against washing poultry. Rinsing chicken will not remove or kill much bacteria, and the splashing of water around the sink can spread the bacteria found in raw chicken. That said, if you have brined your chicken (see page 12 for more information), you will need to rinse it to avoid excessively salty meat. To contain the chicken, rinse it in a colander, then pat dry while it's still in the colander. When done, simply transfer the chicken to your cooking vessel, then wash your hands and the colander with hot, soapy water.

Handling Raw Chicken

When handling chicken, make sure to wash hands, knives, cutting boards, and counters (or anything else that has come into contact with the raw bird, its juices, or your hands) with hot, soapy water. Be especially careful not to let the chicken, its juices, or your unwashed hands touch foods (like salad ingredients) that will be eaten raw.

Seasoning Raw Chicken

When seasoning raw chicken, touching the salt shaker or pepper mill once you've handled the bird can lead to cross-contamination. To avoid this, mix the necessary salt and pepper in a ramekin before handling the chicken.

Cutting Raw Chicken

Raw chicken is slippery, which makes cutting it up hazardous. Get a firmer grip by using a folded wad of paper towels in each hand to keep the chicken in place.

Cooking

The USDA recommends cooking chicken to an internal temperature of 165 degrees or higher to ensure that any bacteria have been killed.

Leftovers

Cooked chicken or leftovers should be consumed within three days.

KNOWING WHEN CHICKEN IS DONE

THE ONLY WAY TO TRULY KNOW WHEN chicken is done is to check the temperature with an instant-read thermometer. Taking a chicken's temperature can be tricky, no matter how good your thermometer is. For the most precise readings, follow the procedures at right. Also, it's important to test both breasts and both thighs in multiple spots.

White and dark meat cook at different rates. Dark meat cooks more slowly than white meat. This is partly due to the position of the bird while it is cooked, but is mainly a result of the differences in the composition of white and dark meat.

Dark meat consists of dark cells, which make up what are known as "slow-twitch" fibers, and which are necessary for long, slow, continuous activity. So the legs of chickens need both more fat and more oxygen.

White meat, on the other hand, is made up of "fast-twitch" fibers, which contain the white cells necessary for quick bursts of energy. Since fast bursts of energy can consume carbohydrates without oxygen, they do not require the stored fat and oxygen needed by "slow-twitch" fibers.

All of this contributes to why the two types of meat cook differently. Because dark meat is so dense, being extra-full of fat and proteins, it takes longer to cook than the lower-fat, "fast-twitch" breast meat. For this reason, when cooking a whole bird, we rotate the bird to protect the white meat and expose the dark meat to maximum oven heat. Also, when cooking white and dark meat parts, we often remove the breast parts early to ensure they don't dry out while the legs finish cooking.

CHECKING FOR DONENESS

WHITE MEAT

Insert the thermometer into the thickest part of the breast from the neck end, keeping it parallel to the breastbone. The white meat is done when the temperature reaches 160 to 165 degrees.

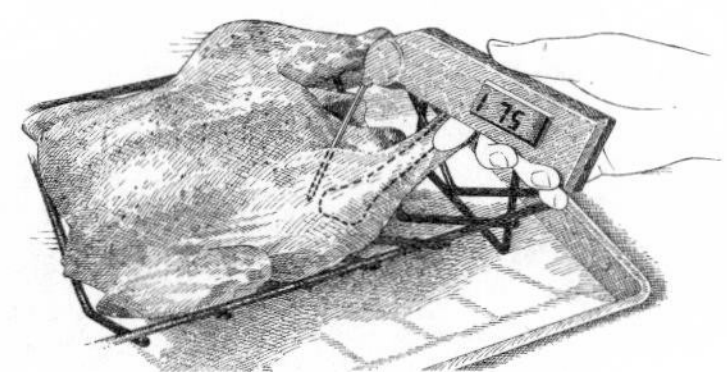

DARK MEAT

Insert the thermometer at an angle into the thickest part of the thigh—located between the drumstick and breast—taking care not to hit bone. The dark meat is done when the temperature reaches 170 to 175 degrees.

ROASTING TIMES FOR CHICKEN

The times below are guidelines based on cooking a whole chicken or chicken parts at 400 degrees, but you should gauge whether your chicken is done by checking when the breast reaches an internal temperature of 160 to 165 degrees and when the thigh registers 170 to 175 degrees.

Roasting Times for Whole Chickens

RAW CHICKEN WEIGHT	APPROXIMATE ROASTING TIME
3½ TO 4 POUNDS	50 to 55 minutes
4 TO 5 POUNDS	55 to 65 minutes
5 TO 6 POUNDS	65 to 75 minutes
6 TO 8 POUNDS	75 to 95 minutes

Roasting Times for Chicken Parts

CUT OF CHICKEN	APPROXIMATE ROASTING TIME
WHOLE BREASTS (24 ounces each)	about 50 minutes
SPLIT BREASTS (10 to 12 ounces each)	about 30 minutes
WHOLE LEGS (10 to 12 ounces each)	about 45 minutes
THIGHS (6 to 8 ounces each)	about 45 minutes
DRUMSTICKS (3 to 4 ounces each)	about 30 minutes

Preparing Boneless, Skinless Breasts

REMOVING THE TENDERLOIN

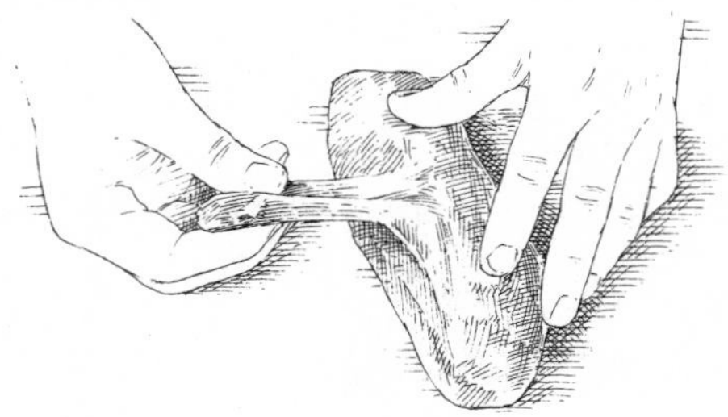

The tenderloin (the long, narrow piece of meat attached to each chicken breast) tends to fall off during pounding, so it is best removed and reserved for another use, such as a stir-fry. Simply pull it off.

TRIMMING BREASTS

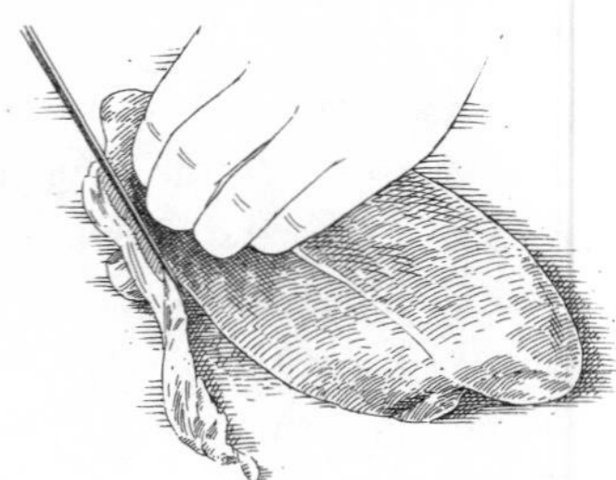

Most chicken breasts have a little yellow or white fat still attached to the breast meat. Lay each breast tenderloin-side down and smooth the top with your fingers. Any fat will slide to the edge of the breast, where it can be trimmed with a knife.

SLICING BREASTS INTO CUTLETS

Cutlets are about half the thickness of boneless, skinless breasts and are called for in many recipes. Rather than buy them already cut, we prefer to make them ourselves—store-bought cutlets are often ragged, and they vary widely in size and thickness.

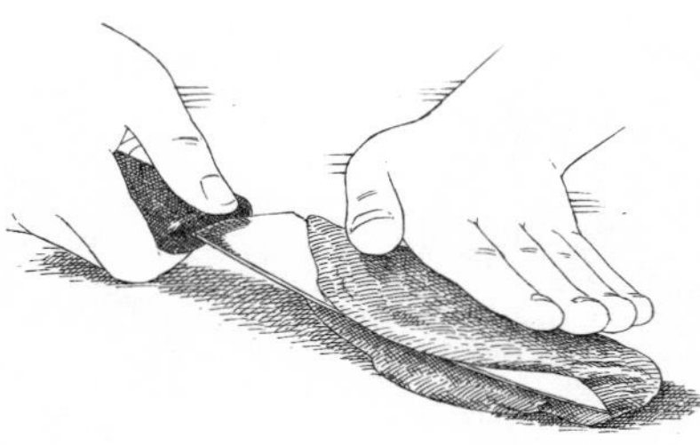

1. Lay the chicken breast flat on a cutting board, smooth side facing up. Rest one hand on top of the chicken and, using a sharp chef's knife, carefully slice the chicken in half horizontally.

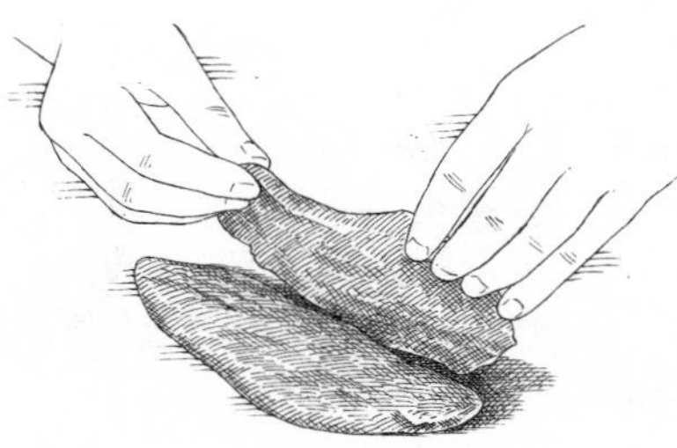

2. This will yield two thin cutlets between ⅜ and ½ inch thick.

POUNDING CUTLETS THIN

Cutlets are already thin, but to ensure that they are of even thickness (and so will cook evenly), you may need to pound them.

Place the cutlets, smooth-side down, on a large sheet of plastic wrap. Cover with a second sheet of plastic wrap and pound gently to make sure that each cutlet has the same thickness from end to end.

BUTTERFLYING THE BREAST

If making our Breaded Stuffed Chicken Breasts (page 371), you will not cut the breast all the way through (as above). Instead, you will butterfly the breast so that you can open it up like a book, creating one large cutlet.

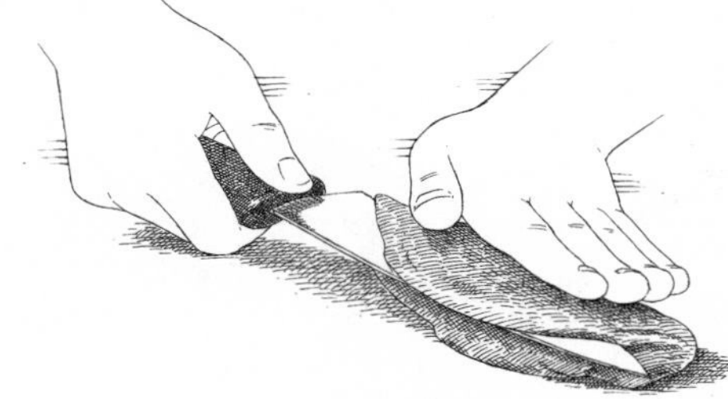

1. Starting on the thinnest side, butterfly the breast by slicing it lengthwise almost in half.

2. Open the breast up to create a single, flat cutlet.

Butchering Chicken Parts

SPLITTING WHOLE BREASTS

We typically buy breasts already split, but you may like to try doing it yourself. (When purchasing breasts that have already been split, inspect the package carefully to make sure they are of similar size and have an ample amount of skin to work with.)

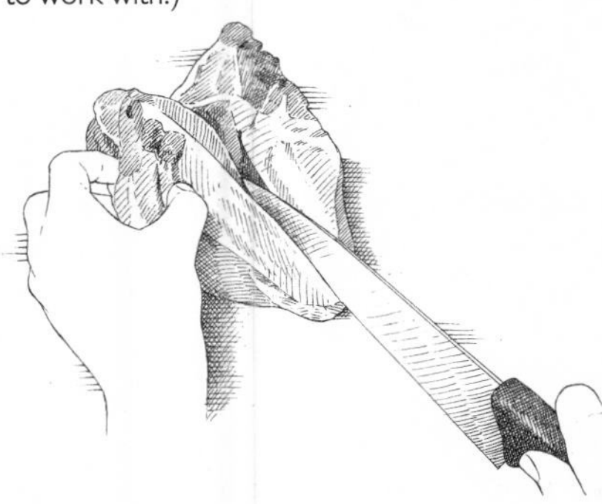

1. With the whole breast skin-side down on the cutting board, center the knife on the breastbone, then apply pressure to cut through and separate the breast into halves.

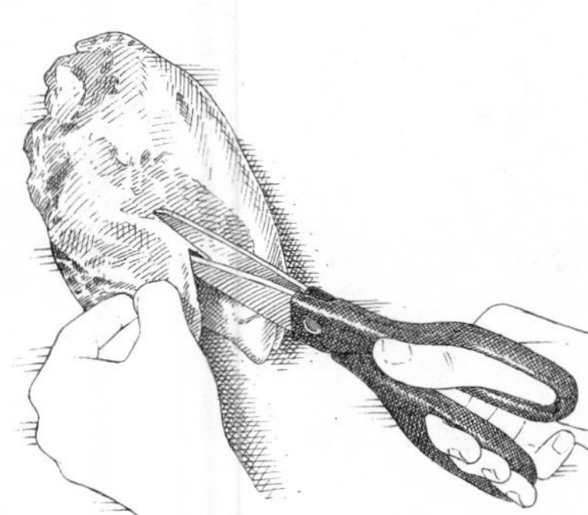

2. Note that some bone-in breasts contain a rib section, which will need to be trimmed with kitchen shears.

CUTTING UP WINGS

Wings are typically separated into two pieces—the meaty drumstick-like portion that is attached to the bird, and the double-boned section between the drumstick and the tip. (The tip is removed because it is relatively meatless.) This allows the skin to brown better and the meat to cook more evenly.

1. With a chef's knife, cut into the skin between the larger sections of the wing until you hit the joint.

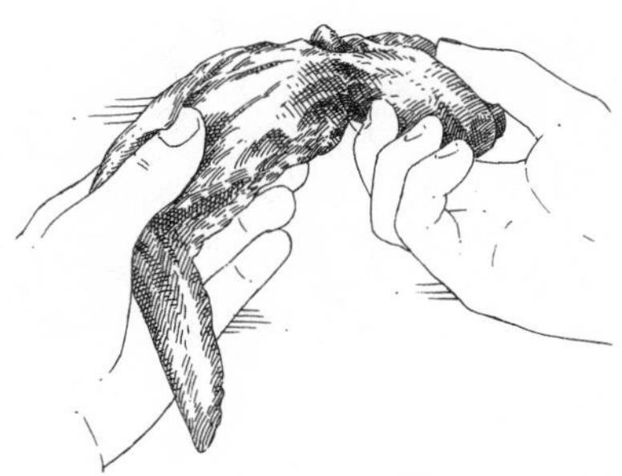

2. Bend back the two sections to pop and break the joint.

3. Cut through the skin and flesh to completely separate the two meaty portions.

4. Hack off the wingtip and discard.

TRIMMING LEG QUARTERS

Chicken legs are inexpensive and nearly impossible to overcook, and they have a rich, meaty flavor that stands up particularly well to grilling.

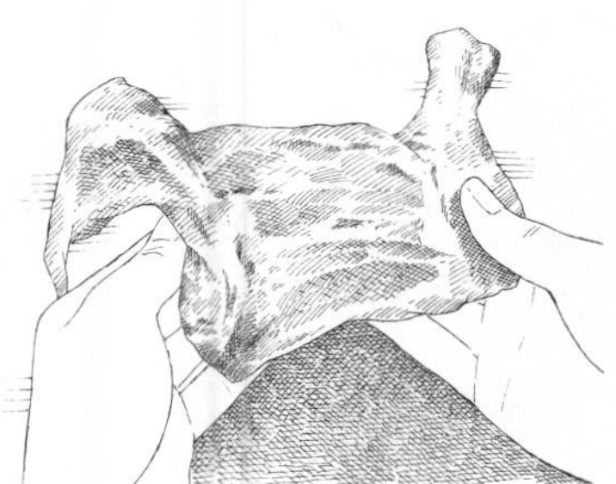

1. Carefully grasp the leg and bend the backbone section to pop the joint.

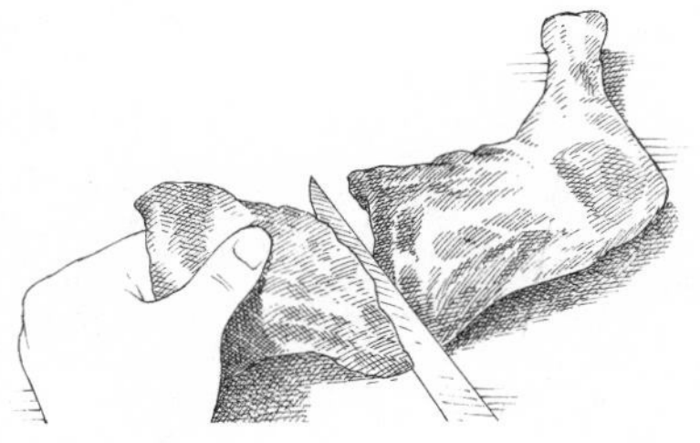

2. Using a sharp boning knife, cut the backbone section from the leg.

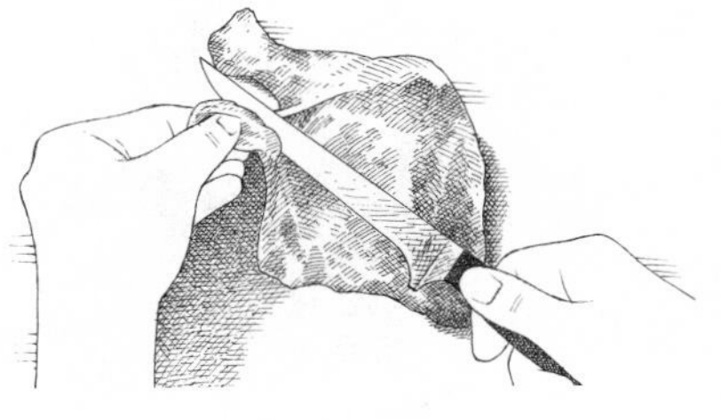

3. Trim away any large pockets of fat.

Butterflying and Splitting a Whole Chicken

PREPARING A BUTTERFLIED CHICKEN

Butterflying a chicken involves removing the backbone, then opening and flattening the bird. This method gives the thighs greater exposure to the heat, allowing them to cook at the same rate as the breast (and also allows you to cook a whole chicken in less time). And because the backbone has been removed, it is easy to add flavor under the skin with a butter or spice rub. Butterflied chicken is particularly good for roasting at high temperatures or grilling.

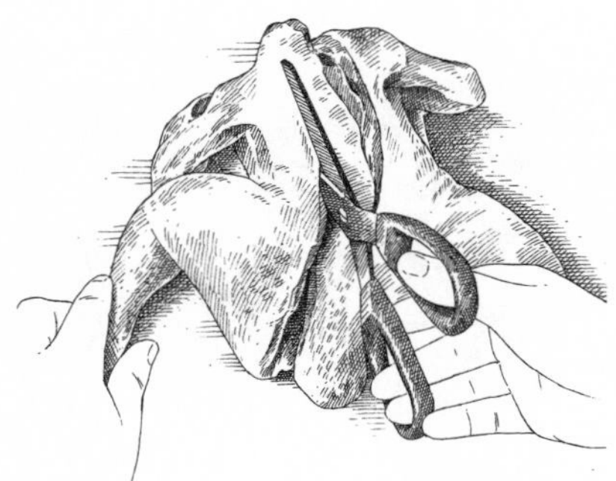

1. Using kitchen shears, cut along both sides of the backbone to remove it.

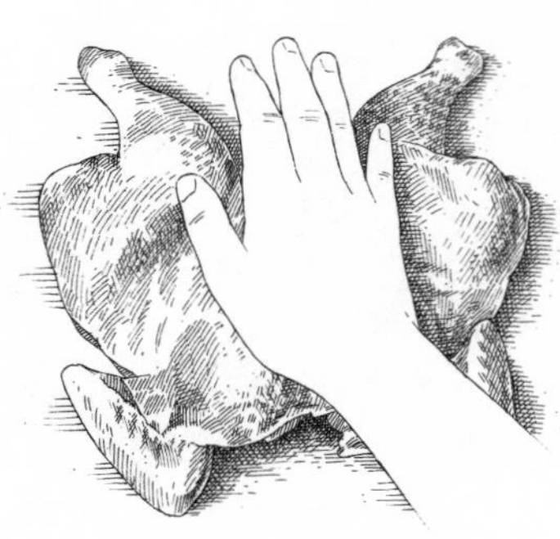

2. Flip the chicken over as shown and use the heel of your hand to flatten the breastbone.

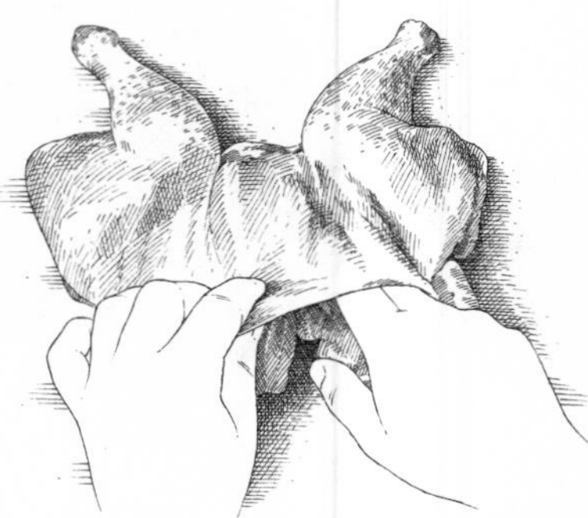

3. If using a flavored butter, slip your fingers between the skin and breast, loosening the membrane.

4. Scoop some of the butter onto a spoon, slide it under the breast skin, and push it off with your fingers.

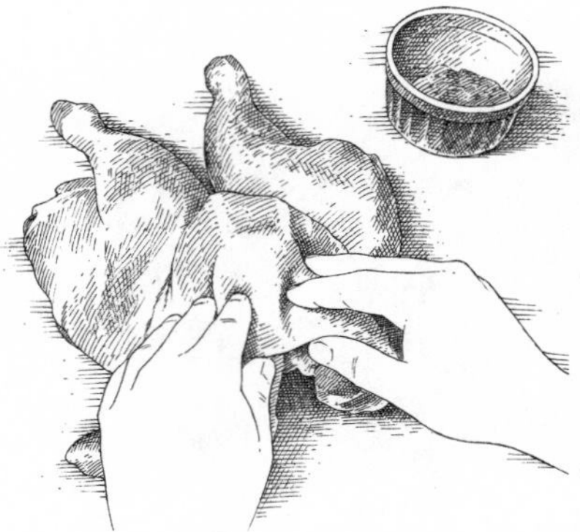

5. Gently press on the skin to distribute the butter evenly.

6. Transfer the chicken to a broiler pan rack and push each leg up to rest between the thigh and breast.

SPLITTING A WHOLE CHICKEN

Split chickens cook more quickly than whole birds and are easier to manage, particularly on the grill. Splitting a whole bird also allows you to fit more meat on the grill, as with our Alabama BBQ Chicken (page 187).

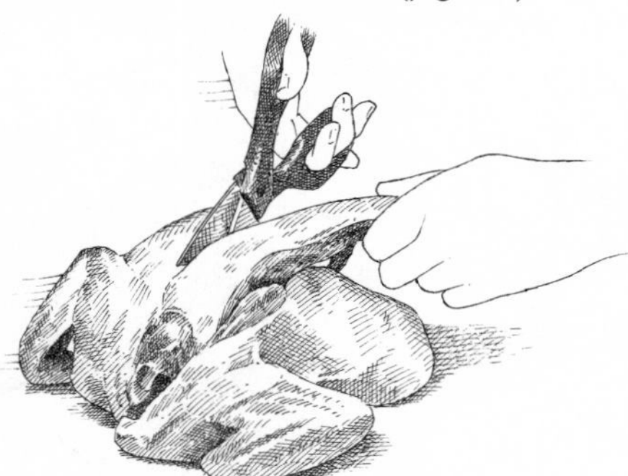

1. Using kitchen shears, cut along both sides of the backbone to remove it.

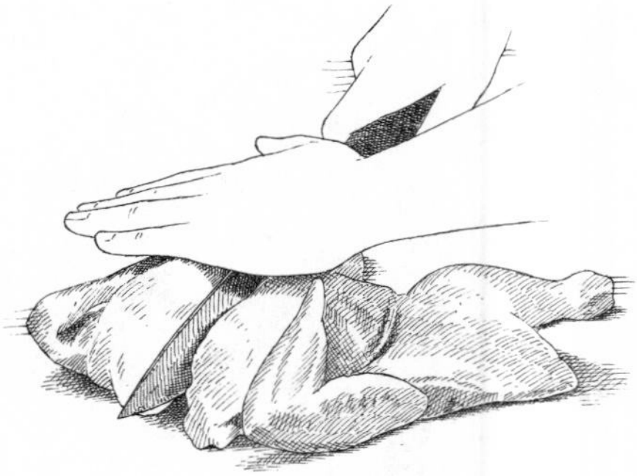

2. Using a chef's knife, split the breastbone to separate the chicken in two.

Butchering a Whole Chicken

CUTTING UP A WHOLE CHICKEN

Cutting up a whole chicken may seem like an intimidating process, but it's a handy technique to learn. For one thing, cutting up a chicken yourself is economical. For another, you may have difficulty finding packages of chicken parts that are the right size, properly butchered, and of high quality.

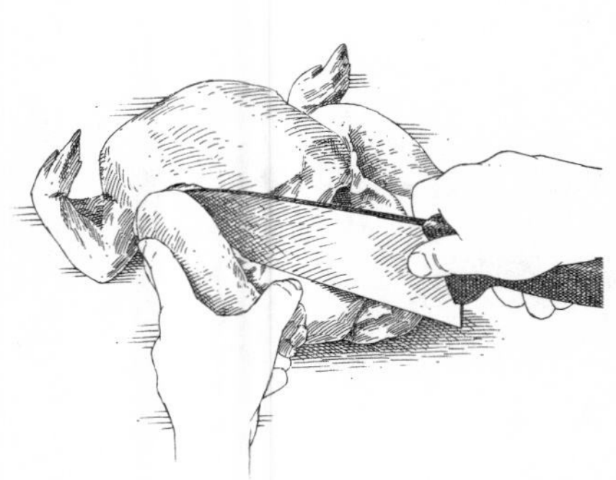

1. With a sharp chef's knife, cut through the skin around the leg where it attaches to the breast.

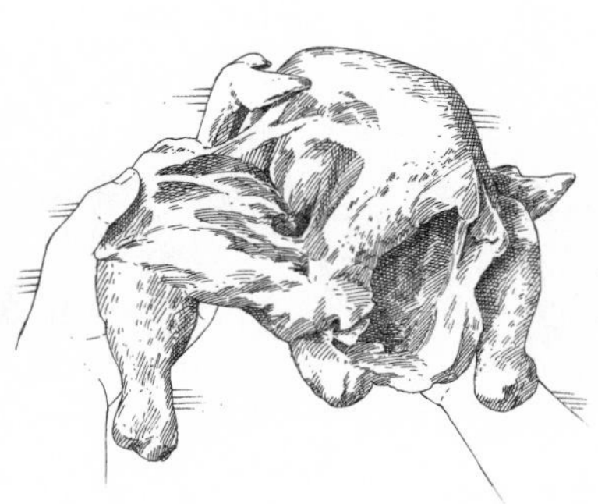

2. Using both hands, pop the leg joint out of its socket.

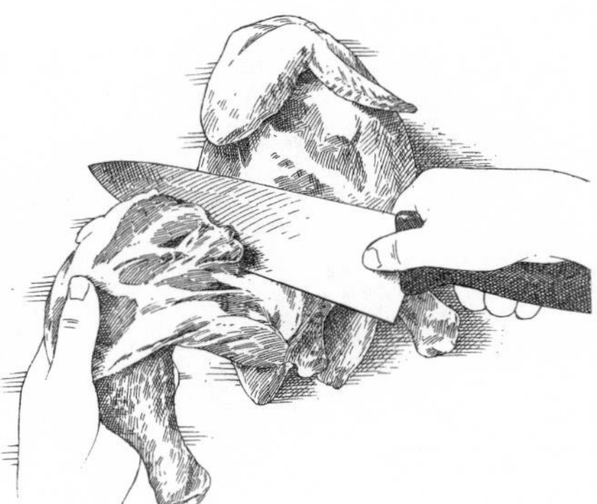

3. Use a chef's knife to cut through the flesh and skin to detach the leg from the body.

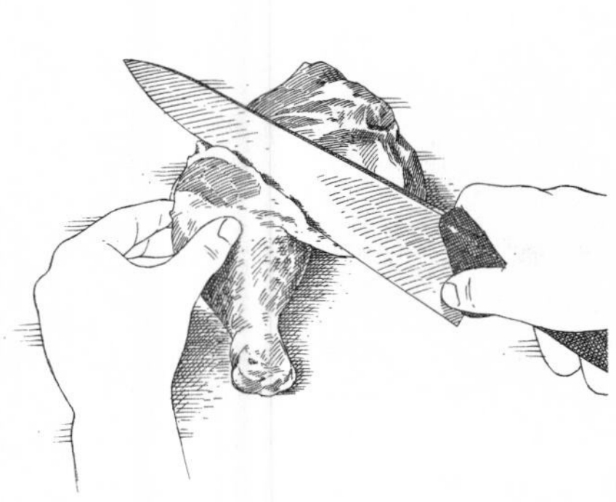

4. A line of fat separates the thigh and drumstick. Cut through the joint at this point. Repeat steps 1 through 4 with the other leg.

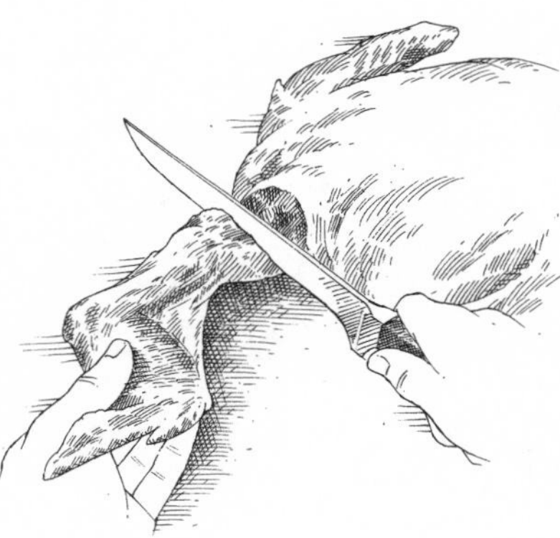

5. Bend the wing out from the breast and use a boning knife to cut through the joint. Repeat with the other wing.

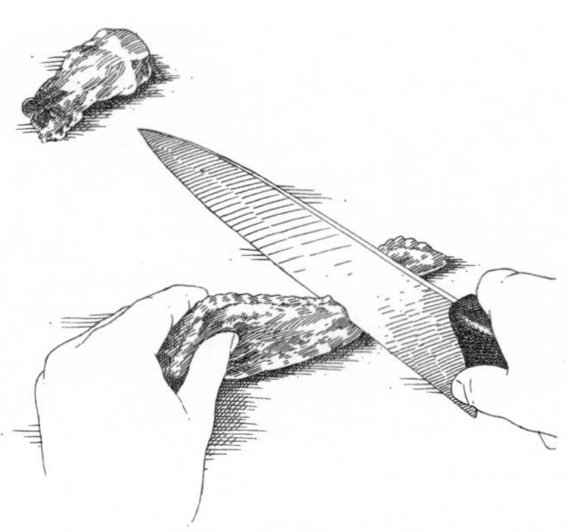

6. Cut through the cartilage around the wingtip to remove it. Discard the tip. Cut through the joint to split it. Repeat with the other wing.

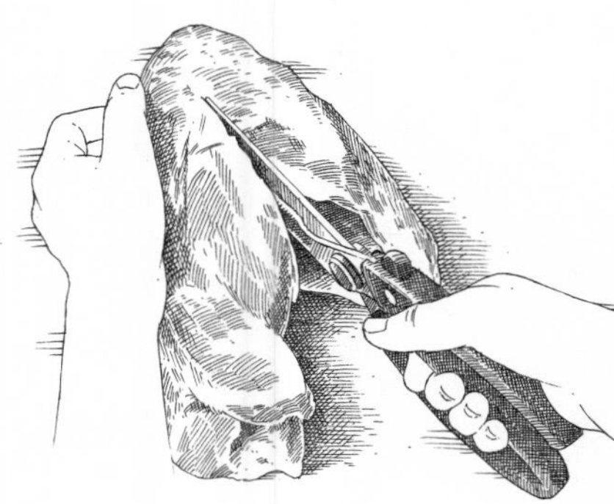

7. Using kitchen shears, cut along the ribs to completely separate the back from the breast. Discard the backbone.

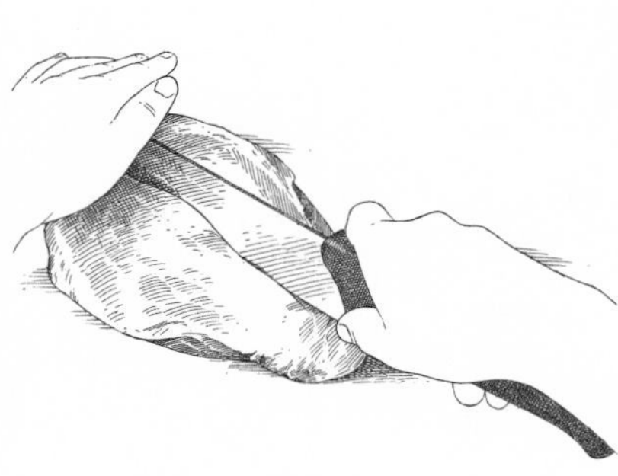

8. Place the knife on the breastbone, then apply pressure to cut through and separate the breast into halves.

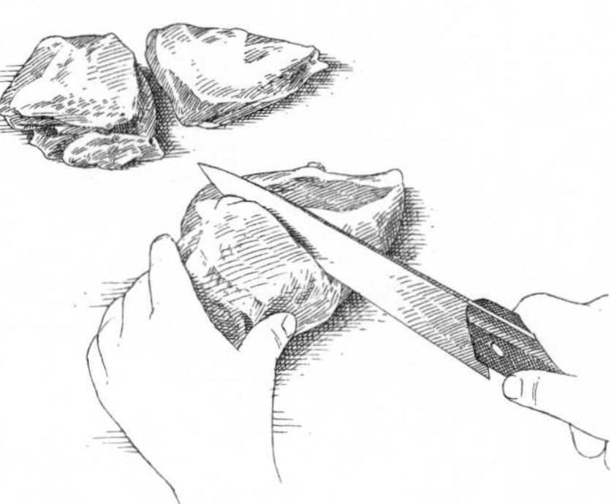

9. Cut each breast half crosswise into two pieces.

Basic Chicken Carving

CARVING BREASTS

Follow this simple technique for carving breasts when an attractive presentation is important, such as in our Chicken with Risotto (page 368).

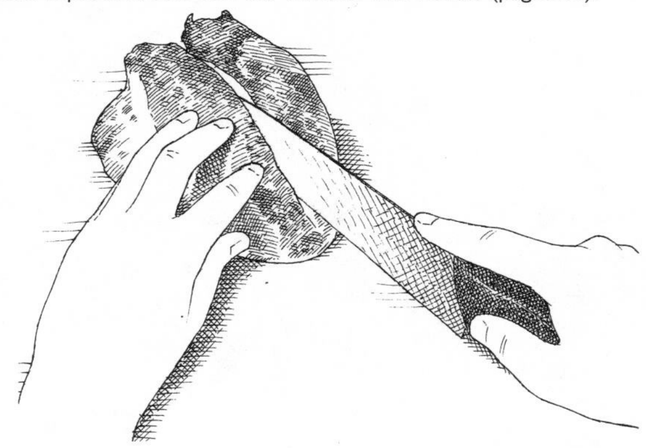

1. To remove the meat, cut straight down along one side of the breastbone.

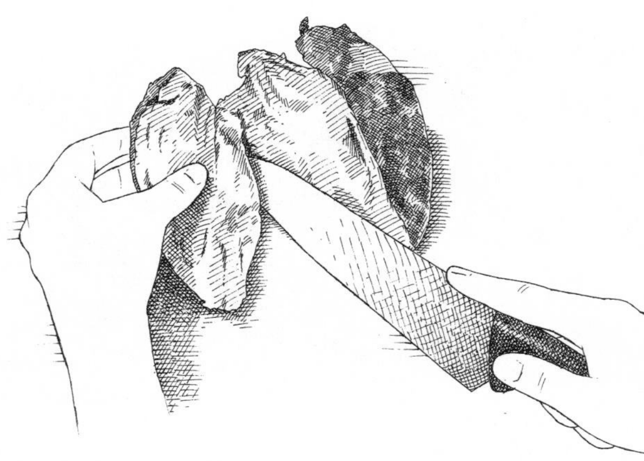

2. Run the knife down along the rib cage to remove the entire breast half.

3. Slice each breast half crosswise on the bias, making thin slices.

CARVING A BUTTERFLIED CHICKEN

A chicken that has been flattened and butterflied can be carved in just a couple steps.

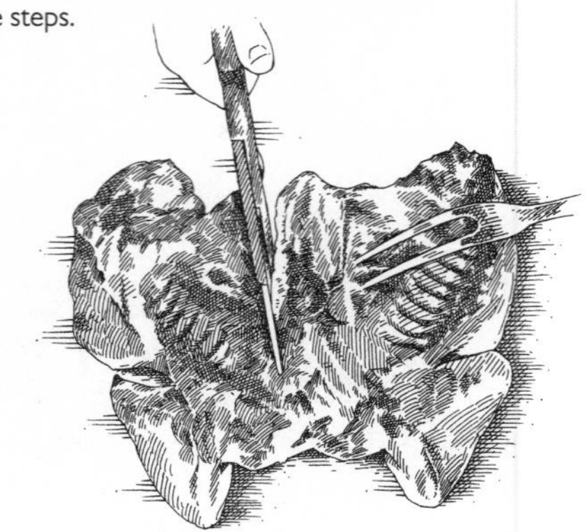

1. Place the chicken skin-side down and use kitchen shears to cut through the breastbone. (Since the breastbone is broken and the meat is flattened during pounding, this should be easy.)

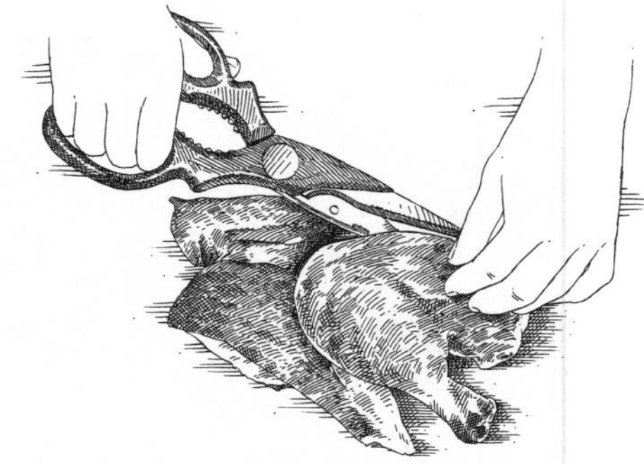

2. Once the breast has been split, only the skin is holding the portions together. Separate each leg and thigh from each breast and wing.

SHREDDING CHICKEN

Many of our soups, stews, and casseroles call for cooking the chicken and then shredding it, which helps keep the chicken moist.

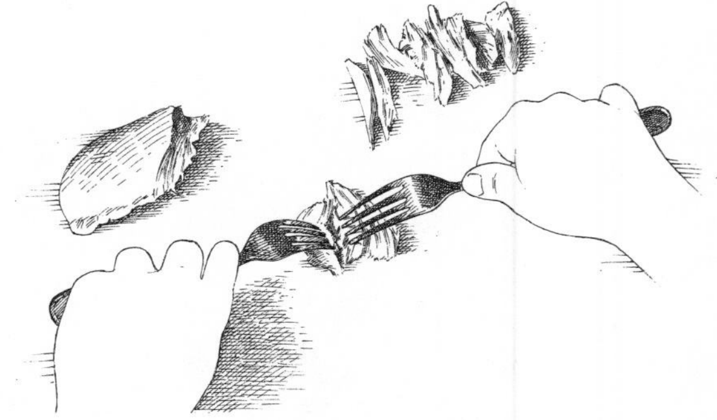

Hold a fork in each hand, with the tines facing down. Insert the tines into the chicken meat and gently pull the forks away from each other, breaking the meat apart and into long, thin strands.

CARVING A WHOLE ROASTED CHICKEN

After brining and roasting the perfect bird, you still have one last task before bringing it to the table—carving it. And while carving isn't difficult, there is definitely a way to approach it that will yield nicely portioned chicken parts and slices of boneless breast—portions that look attractive on a platter and are easy to serve. Before you start, make sure that you've let the chicken rest for 10 minutes, as this will make it easier to carve.

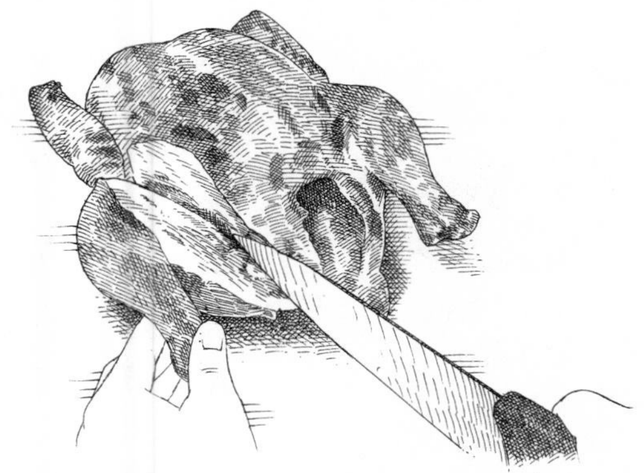

1. Cut the chicken where the leg meets the breast.

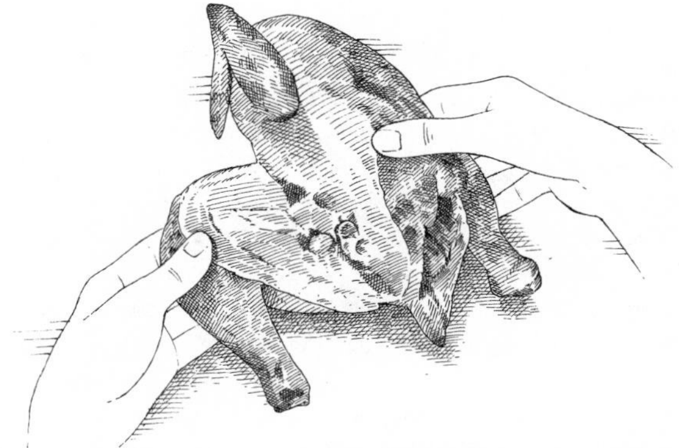

2. Pull the leg quarter away from the carcass. Separate the joint by gently pressing the leg out to the side and pushing up on the joint.

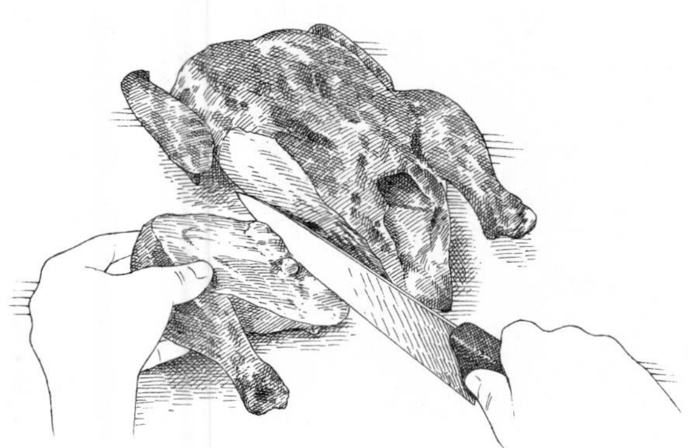

3. Carefully cut through the joint to remove the leg quarter.

4. Cut through the joint that connects the drumstick to the thigh. Repeat on the second side to remove the other leg.

5. Cut down along one side of the breastbone, pulling the breast meat away from you as you cut.

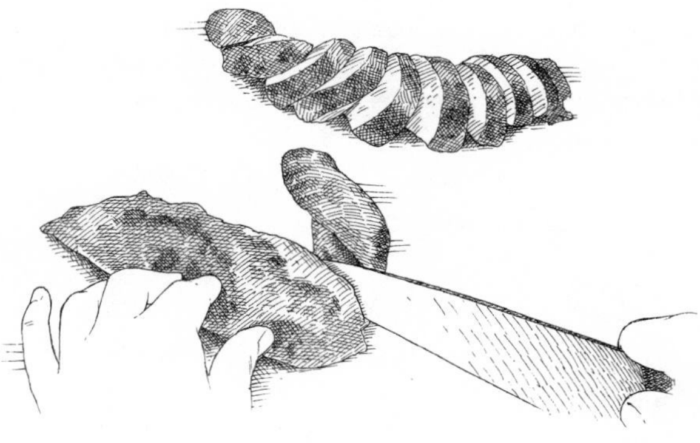

6. Remove the wing from the breast by cutting through the wing joint. Slice the breast into attractive slices.

Brining Chicken

Why are some chickens dry as sawdust while others boast meat that's firm, juicy, and well seasoned? The answer is brining. Soaking a chicken in a brine—a solution of salt (and often sugar) and a liquid (usually water)—provides it with a plump cushion of seasoned moisture that will sustain it throughout cooking. A brined bird will retain more of its weight during cooking than a bird that isn't brined. This retention translates into moist meat; the salt and sugar in the brine translate into seasoned, flavorful meat. For a complete understanding of the process, read on.

SCIENCE: WHY BRINING WORKS

Many have attributed the added juiciness of brined chicken to osmosis—the flow of water across a barrier from a place with a higher water concentration (the brine) to a place with a lower one (the chicken). We decided to test this explanation. If osmosis is, in fact, the source of the added juiciness of brined meat, we reasoned, then a bucket of pure unsalted water should add moisture at least as well as a brine, because water alone has the highest water concentration possible: 100 percent. After soaking one chicken in brine and another in water for the same amount of time, we found that both had gained moisture, about 6 percent by weight. Satisfied that osmosis was indeed the force driving the addition of moisture to meat during brining, we roasted the two birds, along with a third chicken straight out of the package. We would soon discover that osmosis was not the only reason why brined meat cooked up juicy.

During roasting, the chicken taken straight from the package lost 18 percent of its original weight, and the chicken soaked in water lost 12 percent of its presoak weight. Remarkably, the brined bird shed a mere 7 percent of its starting weight. Looking at the test results, we realized that the benefit of brining could not be explained by osmosis alone. Salt, too, was playing a crucial role by aiding in the retention of water.

Salt is made up of two ions, sodium and chloride, that are oppositely charged. Proteins, such as those in meat, are large molecules that contain a mosaic of charges, negative and positive. When proteins are placed in a solution containing salt, they readjust their shape to accommodate the opposing charges. This rearrangement of the protein molecules compromises the structural integrity of the meat, reducing its overall toughness. It also creates gaps that fill up with water. The added salt makes the water less likely to evaporate during cooking, and the result is meat that is both juicy and tender.

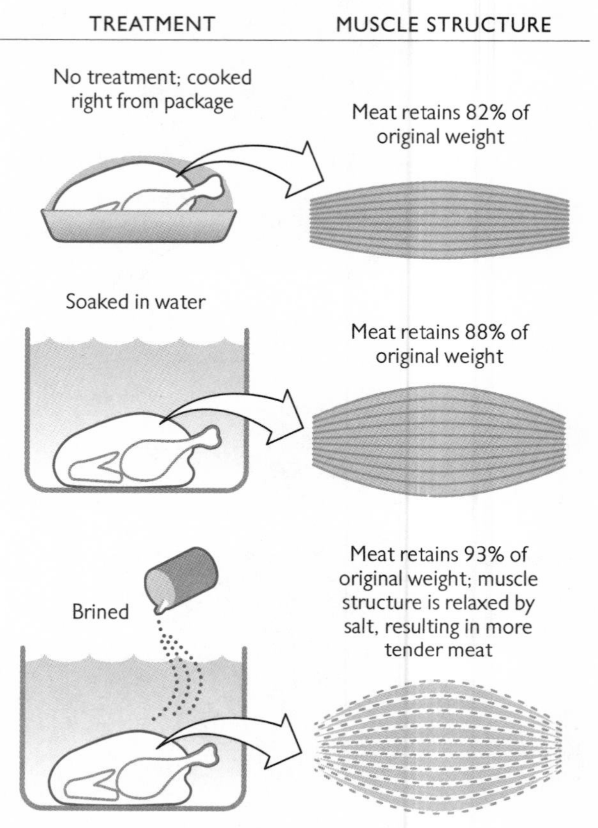

RINSING BRINED POULTRY

Chicken that has been brined should be rinsed of the excess salt on its surface. However, this step can make a soggy mess of your countertop. Placing a colander in the sink to contain the mess will streamline the process.

Place the chicken in a colander. Set the colander in an empty sink and use the sink sprayer or tap to wash off the meat. Then blot the meat dry with paper towels.

TWO TYPES OF SALT FOR BRINING

You can use either kosher or regular table salt for brining. Kosher salt is ideal because its large, airy crystals dissolve so quickly in water. Unfortunately, the salt crystals of the two major brands of kosher salt—Morton and Diamond Crystal—are not equally airy, and therefore measure differently. This inconsistency between the two brands makes precise recipe writing a challenge. Because there's no accounting for which brand of kosher salt you might have on hand, we list table salt in our brining recipes. If you use kosher salt in your brine, keep in mind the following when making the conversions from table salt in our brining recipes:

¼ cup table salt =
½ cup Diamond Crystal Kosher Salt
—or—
¼ cup plus 2 tablespoons Morton Kosher Salt

KOSHER SALT TABLE SALT

1
SALADS AND STARTERS

Salads and Starters

IF YOU ARE LIKE US, CHICKEN ISN'T ALWAYS at the front of your mind when you're choosing appetizers, nor do most of us stretch any limits of creativity when making chicken salads, but as we developed this chapter we found many surprising and creative ways to put chicken—ground, roasted, or sautéed—to work (plus, it doesn't hurt that it's inexpensive and filling, too). Furthermore, many of these recipes can be made ahead of time, making them perfect for everything from parties to summer outings on the beach.

The starters we chose here will please a crowd—from fried chicken wings (twice-fried to be super-crispy) and party chicken skewers (check out the flavoring and sauce options) to phyllo triangles stuffed with a savory mix of ground chicken, feta, and olives. Working with phyllo can be tricky, but we have come up with numerous tricks to make the process far easier (careful thawing and brushing of the layers with olive oil make phyllo easier to work with). And while these impressive-looking triangles are time-consuming to make, they can be made well ahead of time, frozen, and then simply thrown in the oven before your guests arrive. For a new spin on cocktail meatballs, we were inspired by a classic Spanish *tapas* dish with a savory tomato-saffron sauce. Here ground chicken makes a great stand-in for the usual beef and pork combination.

In addition to starters, this chapter offers several recipes for salads that are perfect for lunch or a light dinner. Chicken salad is universally loved—however, all too often it's an afterthought, a strategy for using up last night's leftovers. We set out to expand the horizon on chicken salads and develop a wide range of fresh-tasting options that would hopefully inspire intentional chicken salad making. Our salads fall into three categories: mayonnaise-based salads, vinaigrette-based salads, and composed plated salads, including the true king of all chicken salads: chicken Caesar salad.

As we developed these salads, the main question was how to cook the chicken. Roast chicken was deemed the tastiest and thereby our favorite option; our Simple Roast Chicken (page 120) is the starting point for making a great chicken salad (though in a pinch, of course, you can always use a rotisserie chicken). Using a whole roast chicken enabled us to use both white and dark meat, which tasters preferred, and it could be done ahead of time—a huge plus. For Chicken Caesar Salad (page 33) and Cobb Salad (page 36), however, we incorporated sautéed chicken breasts into each recipe, which made for the most attractive and freshest salads.

Party Chicken Skewers

CHICKEN SKEWERS ARE PERFECT COCKTAIL party fare. They're packed with flavor, and you can eat them without feeling full, getting your hands messy, or even putting your beverage down. And, as an added bonus, they are naturally low in fat.

Chicken breasts, a relatively blank canvas flavor-wise, call for a zesty marinade or highly spiced glaze. After a number of tests we learned that a more concentrated marinade, one with the least amount of oil, worked best. The flavors had more punch and clung to the chicken, while the looser marinades simply ran off the skewers as they cooked. We wanted our chicken to brown but not dry out, so we turned to marinade ingredients with a high sugar content. The sugar promotes browning, giving the chicken a lacquered look in a brief amount of time under the broiler. And, in turn, the marinade's glazy consistency helps the fresh herbs and spices stick to the chicken—a big plus.

We tested a range of marinating times for the chicken, from one hour to as long as 24 hours. While the chicken cooked after being in the marinade for one hour was good, we found that the longer the chicken marinated, the better it tasted. However, after 24 hours the texture of the chicken began to deteriorate and turn mushy.

We wanted to make enough skewers to feed a crowd, so we needed a cooking method that could produce a lot of food in little time. Grilling was an option, but the problems of hot spots, charred skewers, and sprints out to the backyard while guests are arriving nixed that idea. Broiling was a better option—it allowed us to prepare about 30 skewers at a time, keeping our guests satisfied and our sanity intact.

Because these hors d'oeuvres would be eaten by hand, tasters preferred bamboo to metal skewers; the bamboo skewers are disposable and easier to handle straight from the oven. The only downside to bamboo skewers is that they run the risk of smoldering, or even catching fire, under the broiler. To combat this issue, we lined up the meat side of the skewers on the same side of the broiler pan and protected the exposed bamboo with a strip of aluminum foil down the middle. Arranged about six inches below the broiler element, the chicken cooked through in five to seven minutes, and the skewers remained unharmed.

Skewered chicken is often served with a dipping sauce, and any dipping sauce worth its salt complements and enhances its partner. We were determined to develop individual dipping sauces for each specific marinade. We started off with a Thai-style chicken skewer with a spicy peanut dipping sauce, one of the most familiar. We then moved to a spicy chipotle skewer—which tasters really liked—paired with a creamy dipping sauce made from sour cream and mayonnaise finished with fresh cilantro and scallions. Everyone enjoyed a sweet-and-sour sauce featuring orange preserves, used for our Jamaican jerk–style skewers, and, finally, we developed a Chinese-style skewer with a hoisin-sesame sauce that won over tasters.

At last we had tender, easy-to-prepare party skewers (and dips, too) that were guaranteed to disappear at our next cocktail party.

SKEWERING THE CHICKEN

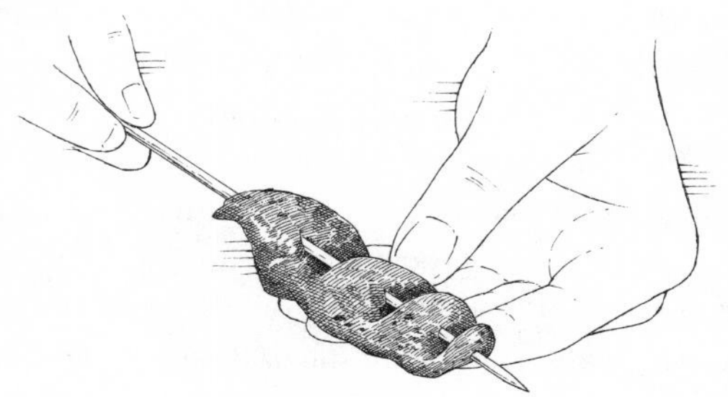

Weave the meat back and forth on the skewer until the entire strip is firmly on the skewer.

Thai-Style Chicken Skewers with Spicy Peanut Dipping Sauce

SERVES 10 TO 12
(MAKES ABOUT 30 SKEWERS)

Thirty 6-inch-long bamboo skewers are required for this recipe. Do not let the chicken marinate for longer than 24 hours or its texture will turn mushy. For the sauce, although we prefer the stronger, purer flavor of natural peanut butter here, any creamy peanut butter is fine. Depending on the sweetness of your peanut butter, you may need to season the sauce with additional sugar. For more heat, add the greater amount of red curry paste to the dipping sauce.

CHICKEN

- 1½ pounds boneless, skinless chicken breasts (about 3 large), trimmed
- ¼ cup vegetable oil
- 2 tablespoons brown sugar
- 2 tablespoons fish sauce
- 2 tablespoons minced fresh cilantro leaves
- 2 teaspoons red curry paste
- 3 medium garlic cloves, minced or pressed through a garlic press (about 1 tablespoon)
- ½ teaspoon ground turmeric
- ½ teaspoon ground coriander
- ½ teaspoon salt
- ¼ teaspoon ground black pepper

DIPPING SAUCE

- ½ cup creamy natural peanut butter (see note)
- ¼ cup hot water, plus more as needed
- 3 tablespoons juice from 2 limes
- 2 scallions, sliced thin
- 1 tablespoon fish sauce
- 1 tablespoon brown sugar, plus more as needed
- 1 tablespoon soy sauce
- 1 medium garlic clove, minced or pressed through a garlic press (about 1 teaspoon)
- ½–1 teaspoon red curry paste (see note)
- 1 tablespoon minced fresh cilantro leaves

1. FOR THE CHICKEN: Freeze the chicken for 30 minutes. Slice the chicken diagonally into ¼-inch-thick strips. In a medium bowl, whisk together all

of the marinade ingredients. Add the marinade to a large zipper-lock bag along with the chicken. Seal shut, toss to coat, and refrigerate for at least 1 hour and up to 24 hours (see note).

2. For the dipping sauce: Puree all the ingredients, except the cilantro, in a blender until smooth. If the sauce seems too thick, thin with hot water, adding a tablespoon at a time until the desired consistency is reached. Stir in the cilantro and season with brown sugar to taste. (The sauce can be refrigerated in an airtight container for up to 3 days; bring to room temperature before serving.)

3. Meanwhile, adjust an oven rack 6 inches from the broiler element and heat the broiler. Line a broiler pan bottom with foil and cover with the broiler pan top; coat the broiler pan top with nonstick cooking spray. Following the illustrations on pages 16 and 17, weave each piece of chicken onto an individual skewer, lay the skewers on the broiler pan top, and cover the skewer ends with foil, making sure not to cover the chicken. Broil until the meat is lightly browned and fully cooked through, 5 to 7 minutes. Serve with the dipping sauce.

Jamaican Jerk–Style Chicken Skewers with Spicy Orange Dipping Sauce

SERVES 10 TO 12
(MAKES ABOUT 30 SKEWERS)

Thirty 6-inch-long bamboo skewers are required for this recipe. Do not let the chicken marinate for longer than 24 hours or its texture will turn mushy. For more heat in the marinade and/or dipping sauce, include the habanero seeds and ribs when mincing.

CHICKEN

- **1½ pounds boneless, skinless chicken breasts (about 3 large), trimmed**
- **¼ cup vegetable oil**
- **2 tablespoons molasses**
- **2 scallions, sliced thin**
- **1 tablespoon minced fresh thyme leaves**
- **1 tablespoon grated zest from 1 lime**
- **1 medium garlic clove, minced or pressed through a garlic press (about 1 teaspoon)**
- **1½ teaspoons salt**
- **1 teaspoon ground allspice**
- **½ habanero chile, seeds and ribs removed, chile minced (see note)**
- **¼ teaspoon ground black pepper**

DIPPING SAUCE

- **1 cup orange marmalade**
- **¼ cup juice from 2 to 3 limes, plus more as needed**
- **3 tablespoons warm water, plus more as needed**
- **1 scallion, minced**
- **½ habanero chile, seeds and ribs removed, chile minced (see note)**
- **Salt and ground black pepper**

1. For the chicken: Freeze the chicken for 30 minutes. Slice the chicken diagonally into ¼-inch-thick strips. In a medium bowl, whisk together all of the marinade ingredients. Add the marinade to a large zipper-lock bag along with the chicken. Seal shut, toss to coat, and refrigerate for at least 1 hour and up to 24 hours (see note).

2. For the dipping sauce: Mix the marmalade, lime juice, water, scallion, habanero, ½ teaspoon salt, and ⅛ teaspoon pepper together in a small bowl. If the sauce seems too thick, thin with warm water, adding a tablespoon at a time until the desired consistency is reached. Season with lime juice, salt, and pepper to taste. (The sauce can be refrigerated in an airtight container for up to 3 days; bring to room temperature before serving.)

3. Meanwhile, adjust an oven rack 6 inches from the broiler element and heat the broiler. Line a broiler pan bottom with foil and cover with the

ARRANGING THE SKEWERS

Using a narrow strip of aluminum foil, cover the exposed portion of the skewers to prevent burning. Secure the foil by crimping it tightly at the edges.

broiler pan top; coat the broiler pan top with nonstick cooking spray. Following the illustrations on pages 16 and 17, weave each piece of chicken onto an individual skewer, lay the skewers on the broiler pan top, and cover the skewer ends with foil, making sure not to cover the chicken. Broil until the meat is lightly browned and fully cooked through, 5 to 7 minutes. Serve with the dipping sauce.

Chipotle Chicken Skewers with Creamy Cilantro Dipping Sauce

SERVES 10 TO 12
(MAKES ABOUT 30 SKEWERS)

Thirty 6-inch-long bamboo skewers are required for this recipe. Do not let the chicken marinate for longer than 24 hours or its texture will turn mushy.

CHICKEN

- 1½ pounds boneless, skinless chicken breasts (about 3 large), trimmed
- ¼ cup vegetable oil
- ¼ cup packed light brown sugar
- 2 tablespoons minced fresh cilantro leaves
- 2 teaspoons minced chipotle chile in adobo sauce
- 2 teaspoons adobo sauce
- 1 medium garlic clove, minced or pressed though a garlic press (about 1 teaspoon)
- 1½ teaspoons salt
- ½ teaspoon chili powder
- ¼ teaspoon ground black pepper

DIPPING SAUCE

- ¾ cup sour cream
- ¼ cup mayonnaise
- ¼ cup juice from 2 to 3 limes, plus more as needed
- 2 scallions, minced
- 2 tablespoons minced fresh cilantro leaves
- 1 small garlic clove, minced or pressed through a garlic press (about ½ teaspoon)
- Salt and ground black pepper

1. For the chicken: Freeze the chicken for 30 minutes. Slice the chicken diagonally into ¼-inch-thick strips. In a medium bowl, whisk together all of the marinade ingredients. Add the marinade to a large zipper-lock bag along with the chicken. Seal shut, toss to coat, and refrigerate for at least 1 hour and up to 24 hours (see note).

2. For the dipping sauce: Mix the sour cream, mayonnaise, lime juice, scallions, cilantro, garlic, ½ teaspoon salt, and ⅛ teaspoon pepper together in a medium bowl. Season with lime juice, salt, and pepper to taste. (The sauce can be refrigerated in an airtight container for up to 3 days; bring to room temperature before serving.)

3. Meanwhile, adjust an oven rack 6 inches from the broiler element and heat the broiler. Line a broiler pan bottom with foil and cover with the broiler pan top; coat the broiler pan top with nonstick cooking spray. Following the illustrations on pages 16 and 17, weave each piece of chicken onto an individual skewer, lay the skewers on the broiler pan top, and cover the skewer ends with foil, making sure not to cover the chicken. Broil until the meat is lightly browned and fully cooked through, 5 to 7 minutes. Serve with the dipping sauce.

Chinese-Style Chicken Skewers with Hoisin-Sesame Dipping Sauce

SERVES 10 TO 12
(MAKES ABOUT 30 SKEWERS)

Thirty 6-inch-long bamboo skewers are required for this recipe. Do not let the chicken marinate for longer than 24 hours or its texture will turn mushy. Be sure to use chili-garlic sauce in this recipe, and not chili-garlic paste, which is much hotter.

CHICKEN

- 1½ pounds boneless, skinless chicken breasts (about 3 large), trimmed
- 2 tablespoons sesame oil
- 2 tablespoons soy sauce
- 2 tablespoons dark brown sugar

- 2 tablespoons hoisin sauce
- 2 tablespoons minced fresh cilantro leaves
- 2 scallions, sliced thin
- 2 medium garlic cloves, minced or pressed through a garlic press (about 2 teaspoons)
- 1 tablespoon minced or grated fresh ginger
- 2 teaspoons Asian chili-garlic sauce

DIPPING SAUCE

- ½ cup hoisin sauce
- ¼ cup rice wine vinegar
- ¼ cup soy sauce
- ¼ cup vegetable oil
- 2 tablespoons minced fresh cilantro leaves
- 4 teaspoons sesame oil
- 1 teaspoon minced or grated fresh ginger
- 1 medium garlic clove, minced or pressed through a garlic press (about 1 teaspoon)

1. For the chicken: Freeze the chicken for 30 minutes. Slice the chicken diagonally into ¼-inch-thick strips. In a medium bowl, whisk together all of the marinade ingredients. Add the marinade to a large zipper-lock bag along with the chicken. Seal shut, toss to coat, and refrigerate for at least 1 hour and up to 24 hours (see note).

2. For the dipping sauce: Mix all the ingredients together in a medium bowl. (The sauce can be refrigerated in an airtight container for up to 3 days; bring to room temperature before serving.)

3. Meanwhile, adjust an oven rack 6 inches from the broiler element and heat the broiler. Line a broiler pan bottom with foil and cover with the broiler pan top; coat the broiler pan top with nonstick cooking spray. Following the illustrations on pages 16 and 17, weave each piece of chicken onto an individual skewer, lay the skewers on the broiler pan top, and cover the skewer ends with foil, making sure not to cover the chicken. Broil until the meat is lightly browned and fully cooked through, 5 to 7 minutes. Serve with the dipping sauce.

Fried Chicken Wings

When people think of fried chicken wings, they inevitably think of Buffalo wings. Conceived at the Anchor Bar in Buffalo, New York, in the 1960s, Buffalo wings are now found throughout the country at just about any bar or Super Bowl party. The odd combination of chicken wings slathered with hot sauce and dunked in blue cheese dressing may seem like a drunken concoction best forgotten the next morning, but it is actually a harmonious union. The sauce's bright heat is tamed by the soothing, creamy dip.

Because wings are such perfect party food and beloved by many, we set out to develop a variety of sauces for our wings—why not give Buffalo wings a bit of competition? Our first goal was to cook the wings to perfection; we were after a light, crispy skin. Second, we would focus on the succulent sauces in which the wings were tossed just before serving.

For fried chicken wings, the raw chicken wing itself is almost always cut in two segments, and the relatively meatless wingtip is removed. The wings come packaged as whole wings or already cut into pieces affectionately referred to as "drumettes." We found that precut wings were often poorly cut and unevenly sized, so we chose to buy whole wings and butcher them ourselves, which was easy and economical. With kitchen shears or a sharp chef's knife, the wing is halved at the main joint and the skinny tip of the wing is lopped off and discarded (or saved for stock).

While the wings were easy to butcher, cooking them proved a little trickier because of their high fat content. Wings are typically deep-fried, which renders the fat and leaves the skin crisp and golden. But deep-frying can be a daunting project in a home kitchen, with hot fat splattering about. We found that if we used a deep Dutch oven and kept the oil at a constant 350 degrees, splattering oil was minimal and cleanup easy.

The test kitchen's standard way of frying wings has always been to dredge the wings in cornstarch, which provides a thin and brittle coating, not unlike tempura, and to fry them for about 10 minutes. However, we had just developed a recipe for Korean Fried Chicken (page 157), in which we discovered a new method for frying that ensured super-crispy skin. The chicken is twice-fried, which entails frying the chicken pieces for an initial period of five minutes, followed by a five-minute rest, and concluding with an additional three to five minutes of frying until the chicken is cooked. Twice-frying, as it turns out, slows down the cooking process to allow for more moisture to evaporate and more fat to render, leaving a perfectly crisp, thin skin. We were curious if this same method would work for our wings. We headed into the kitchen, and, sure enough, it worked wonders, producing crispier, thinner-skinned chicken wings.

The other discovery made in our Korean Fried Chicken recipe pertained to the coating. After a significant amount of testing, the winning coating involved first dredging the chicken in a thin layer of cornstarch and then dipping it into a cornstarch batter before adding it to the hot oil. Again, this worked like a charm for our chicken wings. (For more information on the science behind the twice-fry method, see our story on Korean Fried Chicken on page 156.)

With our chicken wing technique squared away, we shifted our attention to our sauces. Most recipes we found agreed that authentic Buffalo wing sauce, as made at the Anchor Bar, is nothing but Frank's Louisiana Hot Sauce and butter or margarine, blended in a 2-to-1 ratio. Most recipes also suggest intensifying the sauce's heat with a bit of Tabasco or other hot pepper sauce because, on its own, Frank's is not quite spicy enough. While we liked this simple sauce, most tasters wanted something a little more dynamic. We included brown sugar to round out the flavors, and a little cider vinegar to balance out the sugar and add a pleasing sharpness.

The next sauce we developed was a honey-mustard sauce. We wanted a sauce that was not as spicy as its Buffalo counterpart. We started off with the basics, a combination of honey, Dijon mustard, butter, and Worcestershire sauce. Tasters enjoyed the flavors but felt the sauce needed some acid, to balance out the sweetness of the honey, and maybe some texture. We tried adding some whole grain mustard to the Dijon, and this was just what we were looking for—these honey-mustard wings were now disappearing at the same rate as the Buffalo wings.

Our last two sauces were Asian inspired. Our sweet soy-garlic sauce was made by combining sugar, soy sauce, water, and garlic in a saucepan and reducing it to a glaze. We balanced the sauce with a splash of rice wine vinegar and a bit of chili paste. The spicy chili-garlic sauce was also quite simple, comprising ketchup, sugar, chili-garlic sauce, and a touch of lemon juice. These two varieties were also a huge hit.

Our array of wing choices delivers close-to-foolproof and tasty recipes for a crowd-pleasing favorite.

INGREDIENTS: Hot Sauce

As often as we use hot pepper sauce in the test kitchen, we've never given much thought to brand. Considering that most are made from a basic combination of red peppers, vinegar, and salt, does brand even matter? We rounded up eight supermarket samples to find out.

First, we sprinkled each sample atop a portion of steamed white rice. Across the board, tasters deemed one sauce a knockout: Frank's won points for its "bright" and "tangy" notes and potent heat. Tasters also liked La Preferida Louisiana Hot Sauce, which was a tad hotter. Surprisingly, Tabasco, the brand most often found in restaurants and on pantry shelves (including our own), came in dead last. Why? The searing heat masked any other flavor in the sauce, and most found the thin, watery body to be unappealing. "Bitter, like pepper skin," said one taster.

To see how our winner and loser would fare in a cooked application—with other flavors in the mix—we pitted Frank's RedHot against Tabasco in a Buffalo sauce for chicken wings. Tasters once again picked Frank's RedHot as their favorite for its fuller flavor and more "luxurious" body. We'll still use Tabasco for adding heat to recipes, but when it's flavor we're after, we'll reach for Frank's.

THE BEST HOT SAUCE
Frank's RedHot is our top pick for its bright, complex flavor.

Fried Chicken Wings

SERVES 6 TO 8
(MAKES 30 TO 34 WINGS)

The chicken wings must be fried in two batches. Make sure to stir the chicken once it has been added to the oil so that the wings do not stick together.

- **3–4** quarts peanut or vegetable oil
- **1½** cups cornstarch
- **3½** pounds chicken wings, wings split and wingtips discarded (see the illustrations on page 7)
- Salt and ground black pepper
- **1** cup cold water
- **1** recipe sauce (recipes follow)

1. Adjust an oven rack to the middle position and heat the oven to 200 degrees. Measure 2 inches of the oil into a large Dutch oven and heat over medium-high heat to 350 degrees. (Use an instant-read thermometer that registers high temperatures or clip a candy/deep-fat thermometer onto the side of the pan.)

2. Sift ½ cup of the cornstarch into a shallow dish. Set a large mesh strainer over a large bowl. Pat the chicken dry with paper towels and season with salt and pepper. Working with several pieces of chicken at a time, coat the chicken thoroughly with the cornstarch, then transfer to the strainer and shake vigorously to remove all but a thin coating of cornstarch. Transfer the chicken to a wire rack set over a rimmed baking sheet.

3. Whisk the remaining 1 cup cornstarch, the water, and 1 teaspoon salt together in a large bowl to form a smooth batter. When the oil is hot, finish coating the chicken by adding half of the chicken to the batter and turn to coat well. Using tongs, remove the chicken from the batter, one piece at a time, allowing any excess batter to drip back into the bowl, and add to the hot oil.

4. Fry the chicken, stirring to prevent the pieces from sticking together and adjusting the heat as necessary to maintain an oil temperature of 350 degrees, until the chicken begins to crisp and turn slightly golden, about 5 minutes. Transfer the fried chicken wings to a clean wire rack set over a rimmed baking sheet and set aside for about 5 minutes. Meanwhile, batter and fry the remaining chicken.

5. Return the oil to 350 degrees (if necessary) over medium-high heat. Return the first batch of fried chicken wings to the oil and continue to fry until the exterior is very crisp and deep golden brown, 3 to 5 minutes. Drain briefly on a paper towel–lined plate, then transfer to a wire rack set over a rimmed baking sheet and keep warm in a 200-degree oven. Repeat with the second batch. (The unsauced fried chicken wings can be held for up to an hour in a 200-degree oven.)

6. Transfer all of the chicken wings to a large bowl, drizzle with the sauce, and gently toss until evenly coated. Transfer the chicken wings to a platter and serve.

Buffalo Sauce

MAKES ABOUT 1 CUP

Frank's RedHot Sauce is not terribly spicy. We like to combine it with a more potent hot sauce to bring up the heat. Serve with blue cheese dressing, along with carrot and celery sticks.

- **4** tablespoons (½ stick) unsalted butter
- **½** cup Frank's RedHot Sauce
- **1–2** tablespoons hot pepper sauce, plus more to taste
- **1** tablespoon dark brown sugar
- **2** teaspoons cider vinegar

Melt the butter in a small saucepan over low heat. Whisk in the hot sauces, brown sugar, and vinegar until combined; set aside until needed. (The sauce can be refrigerated in an airtight container for up to 24 hours. Rewarm and whisk to recombine before using.)

Honey-Mustard Sauce

MAKES ABOUT 1 CUP

We like to garnish these wings with minced fresh parsley leaves.

- **4** tablespoons (½ stick) unsalted butter
- **1** medium garlic clove, minced or pressed through a garlic press (about 1 teaspoon)

- ⅓ cup honey
- 2 tablespoons Dijon mustard
- 2 tablespoons whole grain mustard
- 2 tablespoons Worcestershire sauce

Melt the butter with the garlic in a small saucepan over low heat. Whisk in the honey, mustards, and Worcestershire until combined; set aside until needed. (The sauce can be refrigerated in an airtight container for up to 24 hours. Rewarm and whisk to recombine before using.)

Spicy Chili-Garlic Sauce

MAKES ABOUT 1 CUP

We like to garnish these wings with thinly sliced scallions and minced fresh cilantro leaves. Be sure to use chili-garlic sauce in this recipe and not chili-garlic paste, which is much hotter. For more heat, add the greater amount of chili-garlic sauce.

- ⅓ cup sugar
- ⅓ cup ketchup
- 3–4 tablespoons Asian chili-garlic sauce (see note)
- 2 teaspoons juice from 1 lemon

Whisk all of the ingredients together in a small bowl; set aside until needed. (The sauce can be refrigerated in an airtight container for up to 24 hours. Bring to room temperature and whisk to recombine before using.)

Sweet Soy-Garlic Sauce

MAKES ABOUT 1 CUP

We like to garnish these wings with thinly sliced scallions and minced fresh cilantro leaves.

- ½ cup sugar
- ¼ cup soy sauce
- ¼ cup water
- 3 medium garlic cloves, minced or pressed through a garlic press (about 1 tablespoon)
- 1 tablespoon rice vinegar
- 1 teaspoon Asian chili paste

Simmer all of the ingredients in a small saucepan over medium heat until syrupy, 5 to 6 minutes; set aside until needed. (The sauce can be refrigerated in an airtight container for up to 24 hours. Bring to room temperature and whisk to recombine before using.)

Phyllo Triangles

MOST TAVERNAS IN GREECE, AND CERTAINLY every Greek-American restaurant, offer some version of phyllo triangles on their menu. The most commonly known version is called spanakopita, which is filled with spinach and cheese. A less widely known alternative, called *kotopita*, is filled with chicken in place of the spinach. These savory treats are made by layering sheets of phyllo dough (see page 23) and folding them around a tasty blend of chicken, onions, and tangy feta cheese, spiked with lemon, garlic, and herbs. The triangles are then baked—each one the perfect marriage of crisp, flaky pastry and a savory filling.

Unfortunately, modern-day versions of this traditional Greek dish rarely taste as good as they sound. More often than not, the basic components of phyllo triangles don't so much combine as collide, often working at cross-purposes. A dense, dry layer of overcooked ground chicken is not enhanced by a thin crust of dried-out pastry. And scattered chunks of salty feta cheese don't do much to round out the dish. To top it off, working with store-bought phyllo dough will test anyone's patience. This can all add up to lots of labor and an often disappointing payoff—are phyllo triangles really worth it?

We wanted phyllo triangles that lived up to their billing and didn't require an army of Greek grandmothers to prepare. We focused first on perfecting the chicken and feta filling with big, bold flavors. We found that it was crucial to break the chicken meat into small pieces as it cooked. If the meat remained in large clumps it was not conducive to creating a uniform filling. Draining off the cooked chicken briefly before combining it with the other filling ingredients proved successful in warding off unwanted excess oil, which made for soggy, greasy triangles.

Tangy feta pairs well with chicken, but the marriage of flavors is ruined when big chunks of the salty cheese are found adrift in a sea of ground meat. By first crumbling up the feta, then mixing it with the eggs, we were able to distribute the cheese more evenly throughout the filling. Eggs are a standard ingredient in phyllo triangle recipes, and rightly so. They bind the filling ingredients together, add richness and flavor, and lighten the layer of chicken that otherwise gets dense when baked in the oven.

Scallions, garlic, and herbs such as mint are traditional ingredients in phyllo triangles, but are usually added in such paltry amounts that the flavors are sunk beneath the chicken and feta. We increased the quantities of each. Lemon juice and ground cayenne are included less commonly, but tasters unanimously approved. In search of a little bit more punch, we added chopped kalamata olives, which truly gave bold flavor to our ground chicken filling. We took stock: The flavors were now bright and clean, and it was time to move on to the phyllo.

The single most important thing to know when working with phyllo dough is that it needs to be at room temperature. Most problems arise when packages are hastily thawed; sheets that are still cold will crack along the folds, or they may be stuck together at the corners. Frozen phyllo dough should be thawed slowly in the refrigerator for at least eight hours or overnight. (You can also thaw it on the countertop for four to five hours.)

Phyllo is famous for its crisp, flaky layers, but it was this quality that gave us the most trouble once the triangles hit the hot oven. In every test, the papery layers curled and separated from each other as they baked. Biting into the triangles sent shattered pieces of phyllo everywhere. Looking for a solution, we tried brushing each layer with olive oil. This helped the pastry layers stick together. How much oil per layer was the next question. While one teaspoon of oil per sheet is adequate if spread carefully, we liked the added flavor and crispness of a slightly more generous amount of fat, about half a tablespoon per sheet. After many trials of assembling the triangles, we found that the best method was to use about one tablespoon of filling per triangle and fold it up as one would a flag.

Although phyllo triangles can be a lot of work, they are well worth the effort. They are ideal for entertaining because they can be assembled ahead of time. Best of all, they do not need to be thawed before baking, so, when the party starts, simply pull them straight from the freezer, place them on a parchment-lined baking sheet, brush them with a little olive oil, and bake.

INGREDIENTS: Phyllo

The most popular brand of phyllo, Athens, is available in two sizes. Both are 1-pound packages, with the larger size containing 20 sheets measuring 14 by 18 inches and the smaller containing 40 sheets measuring 14 by 9 inches—exactly half the size of the larger sheets. We developed our recipes with the smaller sheets. If using the larger sheets, simply cut them in half widthwise to make 40 (14 by 9-inch) sheets. Extra sheets can be rewrapped and kept refrigerated for one week or refrozen for two months.

THE BEST PHYLLO DOUGH

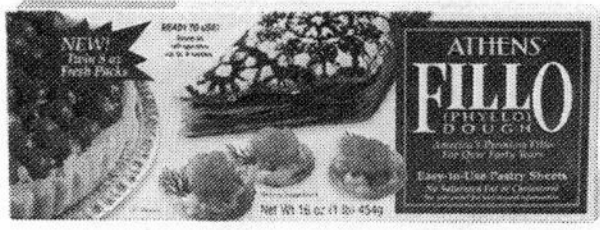

Athens Fillo is available in supermarkets nationwide.

Phyllo Triangles with Chicken, Feta, and Olives

SERVES 10 TO 12
(MAKES ABOUT 36 TRIANGLES)

Make sure that the phyllo dough is fully thawed before you attempt to work with it; don't thaw it in the microwave, but let it sit overnight in the refrigerator or on the countertop for four to five hours. Make sure the feta and cooked ground chicken are broken into very small pieces before assembling the triangles. The unbaked triangles freeze very well; freeze them on a parchment-lined baking sheet until firm, about 1 hour, then transfer them to a zipper-lock bag and freeze for up to 1 month. Do not thaw before baking; the baking time will remain the same. For more information on buying ground chicken see page 3.

FILLING

- 1 tablespoon olive oil
- 1 pound ground chicken
- 4 ounces feta cheese, crumbled into fine pieces (1 cup)
- 1 large egg, lightly beaten
- 4 scallions, sliced thin
- ¼ cup pitted kalamata olives, chopped fine
- 3 tablespoons minced fresh mint leaves
- 1½ teaspoons juice from 1 lemon
- 1 medium garlic clove, minced or pressed through a garlic press (about 1 teaspoon)
- ½ teaspoon salt
- ⅛ teaspoon ground black pepper
- ⅛ teaspoon cayenne pepper

PHYLLO LAYERS

- 1 pound (14 by 9-inch) phyllo, thawed (see note)
- Olive oil, for brushing the phyllo
- Salt and ground black pepper

1. For the filling: Heat the oil in a 12-inch skillet over medium heat until shimmering. Add the chicken and cook, breaking the meat into small pieces with a wooden spoon, until no longer pink, about 5 minutes. Transfer to a strainer and let drain, about 5 minutes. Break apart any remaining large clumps of meat with your fingers.

2. Meanwhile, mix the feta, egg, scallions, olives, mint, lemon juice, garlic, salt, pepper, and cayenne together in a large bowl. Stir in the drained chicken. (The filling can be refrigerated in an airtight container for up to 24 hours.)

3. For the phyllo layers: Adjust two oven racks to the upper- and lower-middle positions and heat the oven to 375 degrees. Unwrap and unfold the phyllo and carefully smooth it with your hands to flatten. Cover the phyllo with plastic wrap, then a damp kitchen towel. Following the illustration, lay one phyllo sheet on the counter, with the shortest end nearest you. Brush lightly but thoroughly with oil, season with salt and pepper, and top with a second sheet. Brush the second sheet with oil and cut the sheets in half lengthwise to make two 4½-inch-wide strips.

4. Place 1 generous tablespoon of filling on the bottom left-hand corner of each strip, then fold the strips of phyllo into triangles around the filling, like folding a flag (see the illustration). Brush the triangle lightly with oil. Repeat with the remaining sheets of phyllo and remaining filling, arranging the triangles, seam-side down, over 2 parchment-lined baking sheets as you work.

5. Bake until golden brown, 15 to 20 minutes, switching and rotating the baking sheets halfway through the baking time. Serve warm or at room temperature.

MAKING PHYLLO TRIANGLES

1. With the short end near you, brush a phyllo sheet with oil, season with salt and pepper, then top it with a second sheet and oil that sheet as well. Cut the sheets lengthwise to make two 4½-inch strips.

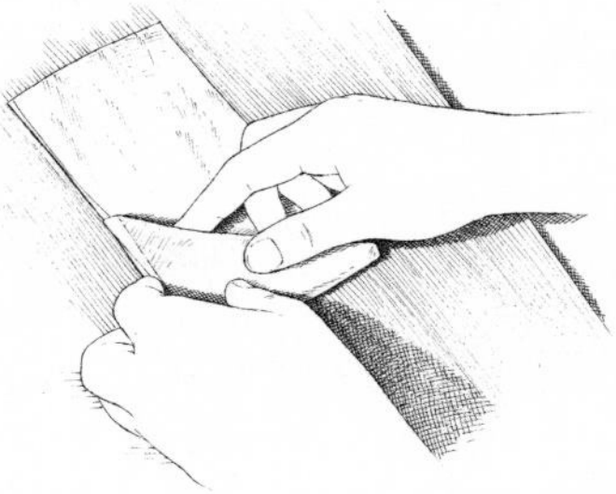

2. Place a generous 1 tablespoon of filling on the bottom left-hand corner of each strip. Fold up the phyllo to form a right-angle triangle. Continue folding up and over, as if folding a flag, to the end of the strip.

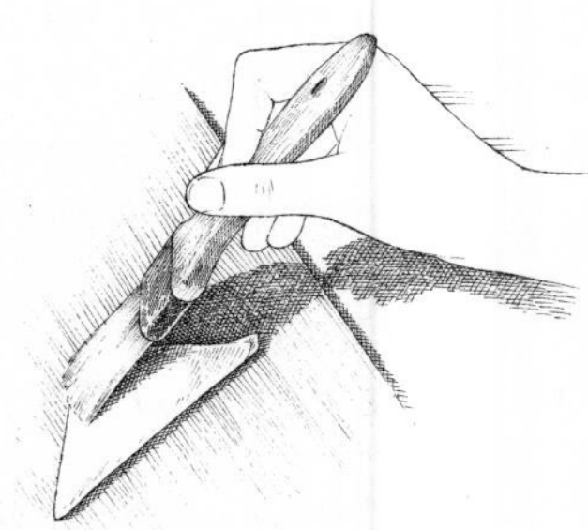

3. Brush the triangle with oil and place, seam-side down, on a parchment paper–lined baking sheet. Repeat with the remaining phyllo and filling. Bake as directed.

Asian Chicken Lettuce Cups

CONSIDERED COMMON STREET FOOD (FAST food) in Thailand, *laab gai* is as simple as a starter can get. This exotic-tasting dish consists of spicy, quickly cooked ground chicken that is eaten not with a fork but with the aid of a lettuce leaf. You spoon the ground filling onto a lettuce leaf, fold it shut, and eat it with your fingers, much as you would a small taco.

To start, we focused on the chicken. Most ground chicken is not finely ground, but rather has an unappealing stringy texture when cooked, so it often helps to smash it first with the back of a spoon before cooking. Wondering whether it would be better to mince boneless chicken breasts in the food processor or simply process store-bought ground chicken further, we gave each approach a try. The boneless chicken breasts that were processed in the food processor cooked into dry little morsels, while the ground chicken processed again in the food processor showed minimal improvement. So to keep things simple, we stuck with our smashed ground chicken and also made sure that we continued to break it into small pieces as it cooked.

Most recipes we researched called for similar flavorings, including fish sauce, lime juice, scallions, and chiles. Lime zest gave the laab gai a good punch that was nicely tempered with brown sugar and fragrant basil. Many recipes also included a surprising ingredient: toasted rice powder. We tried making laab gai without it but missed the sweet flavor that it contributed—the rice powder made the dish taste absolutely authentic. The rice powder also thickened the mixture slightly and kept it from becoming too sloppy and wet. To make rice powder, we simply toasted several tablespoons of white rice in a skillet and then ground it to a powder in a spice mill. Although any type of lettuce leaves could be used to eat the laab gai, we found the small leaf size and pronounced curvature of Boston and Bibb lettuces to work best.

Asian Chicken Lettuce Cups

SERVES 6

For serving, we found it easiest to put the chicken in a shallow serving bowl on a large plate. If you arrange the leaves of lettuce around the edge of the plate and equip everyone with a soup spoon, the platter can be placed in the center of the table and people can serve themselves. For more heat, include the seeds and ribs when mincing the chile. For more information on buying ground chicken, see page 3.

2 tablespoons long-grain white rice
2 tablespoons fish sauce
1 teaspoon grated zest plus 2 tablespoons juice from 1 lime
1 tablespoon brown sugar
1 pound ground chicken
1½ tablespoons vegetable oil
1 medium Thai red or jalapeño chile, seeds and ribs removed, chile minced (see note)
3 tablespoons chopped fresh basil leaves
2 medium scallions, sliced thin
1 head Bibb or Boston lettuce, leaves separated and left whole, washed and dried

1. Toast the rice in a 12-inch nonstick skillet over medium-high heat until golden brown and fragrant, about 3 minutes. Transfer the hot rice to a spice grinder and grind to a powder; set aside. Mix the fish sauce, lime juice, and sugar together in a small bowl and set aside.

2. In a medium bowl, mash the ground chicken, using the back of a spoon, until smooth and no strand-like pieces of meat remain.

3. With paper towels, wipe any remaining rice dust from the skillet. Add the oil and heat over medium-high heat until just smoking. Add the chicken, chile, and lime zest, reduce the heat to medium, and cook until the chicken is no longer pink, breaking the meat into small pieces with a wooden spoon, about 5 minutes.

4. Off the heat, stir in the toasted rice powder, fish sauce mixture, basil, and scallions. Transfer the chicken to a shallow serving bowl and serve alongside the lettuce leaves. Spoon some of the mixture into a lettuce leaf, fold the leaf edges up to form a taco shape, and eat with your hands.

Spanish-Style Cocktail Meatballs

INSPIRED BY A TRADITIONAL SPANISH TAPAS dish called *albondigas,* these bite-sized cocktail meatballs are served in a flavorful saffron-infused sauce. Focusing first on the meatballs, we replaced the traditional mixture of ground beef and pork with ground chicken. After reviewing several recipes, we noticed that the meatballs generally followed the same formula as traditional Italian meatballs: ground meat, along with egg yolk (for richness and structure), bread mixed with milk to form a paste (for tenderness), and seasonings such as salt, pepper, and parsley. We were concerned that a straight substitution of the leaner chicken for the fattier beef and pork could result in a drier, tougher meatball, but we thought we would give it a try. We were pleased to find that despite the leaner ground chicken, the meatballs were juicy and flavorful. The binding ingredients kept the meatballs tender, and, because they were small, the quick cooking time kept them from drying out. We forged ahead. Although the meatballs were already quite tasty, we felt the need to add a little cheese, for richness. Just a small addition of Parmesan turned out to be a huge hit.

Because these meatballs are meant to be consumed in one bite, we made them quite small—just 1 teaspoon of meatball mixture to make ½-inch-round meatballs. After browning the meatballs in a nonstick skillet (which keeps them from breaking apart), we removed them from the pan to prepare the sauce. Making use of the fond (the browned bits left behind in the pan), we started by cooking the onion and tomato in the now-empty pan, carefully scraping up the browned bits. Next we added chicken broth and white wine to the pan, along with the aromatics. At this point, the sauce was quite flavorful, so we added the meatballs back and allowed them to cook through.

We were getting close, but the sauce needed a bit more punch and some thickening. The Spanish often employ the use of a *picada*, a paste made from ground bread, almonds, and sometimes garlic and herbs, to flavor and thicken soups, stews, and sauces. For our sauce, we chose a combination of ground almonds, parsley, garlic, saffron, and paprika. Once the meatballs were cooked through, we simply stirred in this picada, which infused the sauce with vibrant flavor and an enticing aroma.

Spanish-Style Cocktail Meatballs in Tomato-Saffron Sauce

SERVES 6 TO 8
(MAKES 35 TO 40 MEATBALLS)

We like to use a nonstick skillet in this recipe because it prevents the tender meatballs from sticking to the pan and breaking apart. Serve with toothpicks or cocktail forks. For more information on buying ground chicken, *see page 3.*

MEATBALLS

- 2 slices high-quality white sandwich bread, torn into small pieces
- ⅓ cup whole milk
- 1 pound ground chicken
- ½ ounce Parmesan cheese, grated (¼ cup)
- 2 tablespoons minced fresh parsley leaves
- 1 large egg yolk
- 1 medium garlic clove, minced or pressed through a garlic press (about 1 teaspoon)
- ¾ teaspoon salt
- ⅛ teaspoon ground black pepper
- 2–3 tablespoons olive oil

SAUCE

- 1 small onion, minced
- 1 small tomato, cored, seeded, and chopped medium
- 1 cup low-sodium chicken broth
- ½ cup dry white wine
- 2 bay leaves
- 1 tablespoon minced fresh parsley leaves
- 1 tablespoon finely chopped blanched almonds
- 2 medium garlic cloves, minced or pressed through a garlic press (about 2 teaspoons)
- ¼ teaspoon saffron threads
- ¼ teaspoon paprika
- Salt and ground black pepper

1. **For the meatballs:** In a large bowl, mash the bread and milk together to form a smooth paste. Add the ground chicken, Parmesan, parsley, egg yolk, garlic, salt, and pepper to the mashed bread and mix until uniform. Shape the mixture into 1-inch-round meatballs (1 generous teaspoon per meatball; you should have 35 to 40 meatballs).

2. Heat 2 tablespoons of the oil in a 12-inch nonstick skillet over medium-high heat until shimmering. Add half of the meatballs and brown on all sides, about 5 to 7 minutes, reducing the heat if the oil begins to smoke. Transfer the meatballs to a paper towel–lined plate. Discard all but 1 tablespoon of the oil left in the skillet and repeat with the remaining meatballs. Add additional oil to the pan if needed.

3. **For the sauce:** Add the onion to the skillet and cook over medium heat, scraping up any browned bits, until softened and lightly browned, 5 to 7 minutes. Stir in the tomato and cook for 1 minute. Stir in the broth, wine, and bay leaves, then carefully return the meatballs to the skillet. Simmer just until the meatballs are cooked through and the sauce is thickened, about 10 minutes.

4. While the meatballs cook, mash together the parsley, almonds, garlic, saffron, paprika, ⅛ teaspoon salt, and a pinch of pepper. When the meatballs are cooked through, stir the parsley mixture into the sauce and season with salt and pepper to taste. Remove the bay leaves. Transfer the meatballs and sauce to a serving dish and serve immediately.

Chicken Salad

CLASSIC CHICKEN SALAD CONSISTS OF TENDER breast meat pulled apart by hand, rather than cubed with a knife, and bound loosely with mayonnaise. There's a little celery for texture, some parsley or tarragon for flavor, and a squeeze of lemon juice for freshness. We often make this salad from leftover roast or poached chicken, and we put it together intuitively, by taste and sight. But for this book we took a hard look at chicken salad, determined to find the best way to set about making it intentionally rather than simply something to do to use up leftover chicken.

Our very first question was how to cook the chicken. Although there were many choices, they basically fell into two camps—wet and dry cooking methods. The wet cooking methods included poaching, steaming, roasting in foil, and, in a method new to us, dropping the chicken into simmering aromatic water and then removing it from the heat and letting it cool to room temperature. Unfortunately, chicken cooked by each of these methods had a bland, unmistakably boiled flavor. Chicken cooked in the microwave also had that wet-cooked taste.

As for the dry-cooking methods, broiled was good, but for these salads, where we wanted the chicken to take center stage, roast chicken won hands down. Even after the skin and bones were removed, the meat tasted roasted, and the resulting chicken salad was superb. The next question was, What parts of the chicken did we want to use, or did we in fact want to use the whole bird? We did a side-by-side test of our chicken salad, one made just with roasted chicken breast meat and one made using meat from a roasted whole chicken. Tasters were unanimous; the salad made using meat from the whole roasted bird was the clear winner. The slightly richer dark meat combined with the white meat made for more complex flavors and a moister salad. It seemed just as easy to throw a whole chicken in the oven for a simple, fuss-free roast. We also determined that, if you were short on time, substituting a supermarket rotisserie chicken worked just fine, although we clearly preferred the flavors of our chicken roasted at home.

Now that we had chosen our method for cooking the chicken, we set out to develop a large range of chicken salad options, with a variety of flavor combinations to complement the classic version. Curried chicken salad was our next choice. With a dash of curry, raisins, and almonds for flavor and texture, and a touch of honey for sweetness, the classic had been transformed into something new. Waldorf chicken salad was next; we just added some sliced apple and walnuts to our classic version, and the salad was complete. Finally, we developed a spicy version featuring chipotle chile and corn, and an

Italian-inspired version with fennel, pine nuts, basil, and Parmesan.

Although mayonnaise is the go-to ingredient for chicken salad (as in the four chicken salads just described), we were in search of another angle. Mayonnaise adds luscious texture, but the creamy fat tends to dull the impact of other ingredients, no matter how aggressively you empty your spice cabinet. Instead, we thought a vinaigrette-dressed chicken—something you might serve on a bed of greens as a light dinner—would have fresh, bold flavors. We went back in the kitchen for a second round of tests.

For our new take on chicken salad, we envisioned bright, flavorful dressings paired with our shredded roast chicken, a handful of fresh vegetables, herbs, and toasted nuts. As we began our testing for the vinaigrette-dressed chicken, however, it wasn't long before we ran into trouble. Because oil and vinegar separate so easily, they cling poorly to chicken, yielding greasy, watery salads. It was clear we needed an emulsifier (a third ingredient) to help the dressing cling to the chicken and create a more cohesive salad. Rather than the standard addition of mustard, which is used in many simple vinaigrettes as the emulsifier, we went in search of other ingredients that could produce the same effect. We successfully used sun-dried tomatoes, peanut butter, roasted red peppers, and avocados as emulsifiers, creating four new vinaigrettes to dress our chicken and winning rave reviews.

Using a blender was key to creating a stable vinaigrette to dress the chicken. A mechanical blade can reduce oil to small droplets more effectively than a whisk; the smaller the droplets, the more likely they are to maintain suspension in an emulsion. With bright, creamy dressings at the ready, our chicken salads had come to life.

Classic Chicken Salad

SERVES 6

Serve the salad in rolls as sandwiches or over greens. We found that using a whole roast chicken for this salad yielded the right amount of both white and dark meat (see page 120 for our Simple Roast Chicken). For even less fuss, use a fully cooked supermarket rotisserie chicken.

- ¾ cup mayonnaise
- 2 tablespoons juice from 1 lemon
- 5 cups shredded roast chicken, at room temperature (see page 10)
- 2 celery ribs, chopped fine
- 2 scallions, minced
- 2 tablespoons minced fresh parsley or tarragon leaves
- Salt and ground black pepper

Whisk the mayonnaise and lemon juice together in a large bowl until smooth. Stir in the chicken, celery, scallions, and parsley. Season with salt and pepper to taste. Let sit at room temperature for 15 minutes before serving. (The salad can be refrigerated in an airtight container for up to 24 hours.)

Curried Chicken Salad with Raisins and Almonds

SERVES 6

Serve the salad in rolls as sandwiches or over greens. We found that using a whole roast chicken for this salad yielded the right amount of both white and dark meat (see page 120 for our Simple Roast Chicken). For even less fuss, use a fully cooked supermarket rotisserie chicken.

- ¾ cup mayonnaise
- 2 tablespoons juice from 1 lemon
- 1 tablespoon honey
- 2 teaspoons curry powder
- 5 cups shredded roast chicken, at room temperature (see page 10)
- 2 celery ribs, chopped fine
- 2 scallions, minced
- ⅓ cup golden raisins
- ¼ cup sliced almonds, toasted
- 2 tablespoons minced fresh cilantro leaves
- Salt and ground black pepper

Whisk the mayonnaise, lemon juice, honey, and curry powder together in a large bowl until smooth. Stir in the chicken, celery, scallions, raisins, almonds, and cilantro. Season with salt and pepper to taste. Let sit at room temperature for 15 minutes before serving. (The salad can be refrigerated in an airtight container for up to 24 hours.)

Waldorf Chicken Salad

SERVES 6

Serve the salad in rolls as sandwiches or over greens. We found that using a whole roast chicken for this salad yielded the right amount of both white and dark meat (see page 120 for our Simple Roast Chicken). For even less fuss, use a fully cooked supermarket rotisserie chicken.

- ¾ cup mayonnaise
- 2 tablespoons juice from 1 lemon
- 5 cups shredded roast chicken, at room temperature (see page 10)
- 2 celery ribs, chopped fine
- 2 scallions, minced
- 1 Granny Smith apple, cored and cut into ½-inch pieces
- ⅓ cup walnuts, toasted, cooled, and chopped
- 2 tablespoons minced fresh parsley leaves
- Salt and ground black pepper

Whisk the mayonnaise and lemon juice together in a large bowl until smooth. Stir in the chicken, celery, scallions, apple, walnuts, and parsley. Season with salt and pepper to taste. Let sit at room temperature for 15 minutes before serving. (The salad can be refrigerated in an airtight container for up to 24 hours.)

Spicy Chicken Salad with Chipotle Chile and Corn

SERVES 6

Serve the salad in rolls as sandwiches or over greens. We found that using a whole roast chicken for this salad yielded the right amount of both white and dark meat (see page 120 for our Simple Roast Chicken). For even less fuss, use a fully cooked supermarket rotisserie chicken.

- ¾ cup mayonnaise
- 2 tablespoons juice from 2 limes
- 2 teaspoons minced chipotle chile in adobo sauce
- 5 cups shredded roast chicken, at room temperature (see page 10)
- 2 medium scallions, minced
- 1 red bell pepper, stemmed, seeded, and chopped fine
- ⅓ cup frozen corn, thawed
- 2 tablespoons minced fresh cilantro leaves
- Salt and ground black pepper

Whisk the mayonnaise, lime juice, and chipotle chiles together in a large bowl until smooth. Stir in the chicken, scallions, bell pepper, corn, and cilantro. Season with salt and pepper to taste. Let sit at room temperature for 15 minutes before serving. (The salad can be refrigerated in an airtight container for up to 24 hours.)

Chicken Salad with Fennel, Lemon, and Parmesan

SERVES 6

Serve the salad in rolls as sandwiches or over greens. We found that using a whole roast chicken for this salad yielded the right amount of both white and dark meat (see page 120 for our Simple Roast Chicken). For even less fuss, use a fully cooked supermarket rotisserie chicken.

- ¾ cup mayonnaise
- 1 ounce Parmesan, grated (about ½ cup)
- ½ teaspoon grated zest plus 3 tablespoons juice from 1 lemon
- 5 cups shredded roast chicken, at room temperature (see page 10)
- 1 fennel bulb, trimmed, cored, and chopped fine
- 2 tablespoons minced red onion
- 2 tablespoons minced fresh basil leaves
- Salt and ground black pepper
- ¼ cup pine nuts, toasted

Whisk the mayonnaise, Parmesan, lemon juice, and lemon zest together in a large bowl until smooth. Stir in the chicken, fennel, red onion, and basil. Season with salt and pepper to taste. Let sit at room temperature for 15 minutes before serving. (The salad can be refrigerated in an airtight container for up to 24 hours.) Sprinkle with the pine nuts just before serving.

Chicken Salad with Asparagus and Sun-Dried Tomato Dressing

SERVES 6

This recipe is best served over salad greens. We found that using a whole roast chicken for this salad yielded the right amount of both white and dark meat (see page 120 for our Simple Roast Chicken). For even less fuss, use a fully cooked supermarket rotisserie chicken.

- ½ cup plus 1 tablespoon extra-virgin olive oil
- ½ pound asparagus, trimmed of tough ends and cut on the diagonal into 1-inch pieces
- Salt and ground black pepper
- ½ cup sun-dried tomatoes packed in oil, drained, rinsed, and minced
- ¼ cup red wine vinegar
- 1 small garlic clove, minced or pressed through a garlic press (about ½ teaspoon)
- 5 cups shredded roast chicken, at room temperature (see page 10)
- 1 cup chopped fresh basil leaves
- 3 ounces goat cheese, crumbled (about ¾ cup)
- ½ cup pine nuts, toasted

1. Heat 1 tablespoon of the oil in a 10-inch nonstick skillet over high heat until just smoking. Add the asparagus, ¼ teaspoon salt, and ¼ teaspoon pepper and cook until the asparagus is browned and almost tender, about 3 minutes, stirring occasionally. Transfer to a plate to cool.

2. Puree the remaining ½ cup oil, the sun-dried tomatoes, vinegar, garlic, ¼ teaspoon salt, and ¼ teaspoon pepper in a blender until smooth. Transfer to a large bowl. (The dressing can be refrigerated in an airtight container for up to 24 hours. Bring to room temperature and whisk to recombine before using.)

3. Stir the cooled asparagus, chicken, and basil into the vinaigrette. Season with salt and pepper to taste. Let sit at room temperature for 15 minutes. (The salad can be refrigerated in an airtight container for up to 24 hours.) Sprinkle with the goat cheese and pine nuts just before serving.

Thai-Style Chicken Salad with Spicy Peanut Dressing

SERVES 6

This recipe is best served over salad greens. We found that using a whole roast chicken for this salad yielded the right amount of both white and dark meat (see page 120 for our Simple Roast Chicken). For even less fuss, use a fully cooked supermarket rotisserie chicken.

- ½ cup vegetable oil
- ½ cup juice from 4 limes
- 3 tablespoons smooth peanut butter
- 2 tablespoons water
- 2 tablespoons light brown sugar
- 2 medium garlic cloves, minced or pressed through a garlic press (about 2 teaspoons)
- 2 teaspoons minced or grated fresh ginger
- 1½ teaspoons red pepper flakes
- Salt
- 5 cups shredded roast chicken, at room temperature (see page 10)
- ½ medium cucumber, peeled, seeded, and cut into 1 by ¼-inch matchsticks (about 1 cup)
- 1 carrot, peeled and grated on the large holes of a box grater (about ½ cup)
- 4 scallions, sliced thin
- 3 tablespoons minced fresh cilantro leaves
- ½ cup chopped roasted peanuts

1. Puree the oil, lime juice, peanut butter, water, sugar, garlic, ginger, red pepper flakes, and ¼ teaspoon salt in a blender until smooth. Transfer to a large bowl. (The dressing can be refrigerated in an airtight container for up to 24 hours. Bring to room temperature and whisk to recombine before using.)

2. Stir the chicken, cucumber, carrot, scallions, and cilantro into the vinaigrette. Season with salt to taste. Let sit at room temperature for 15 minutes. (The salad can be refrigerated in an airtight container for up to 24 hours.) Sprinkle with the peanuts just before serving.

Spanish-Style Chicken Salad with Roasted Red Pepper Dressing

SERVES 6

This recipe is best served over salad greens. Our two favorite brands of jarred roasted red peppers are Divina and Greek Gourmet. We found that using a whole roast chicken for this salad yielded the right amount of both white and dark meat (see page 120 for our Simple Roast Chicken). For even less fuss, use a fully cooked supermarket rotisserie chicken.

- **10 ounces jarred roasted red peppers, drained and cut into ½-inch pieces (about 1⅓ cups)**
- **½ cup extra-virgin olive oil**
- **3 tablespoons sherry or balsamic vinegar**
- **1 small garlic clove, minced or pressed through a garlic press (about ½ teaspoon)**
- **Salt and ground black pepper**
- **5 cups shredded roast chicken, at room temperature (see page 10)**
- **2 celery ribs, sliced very thin (about 1¼ cups)**
- **½ cup roughly chopped pitted green olives**
- **3 tablespoons minced fresh parsley leaves**
- **1 small shallot, minced (about 2 tablespoons)**
- **½ cup sliced almonds, toasted**

1. Puree ⅔ cup of the roasted red peppers, the oil, sherry, garlic, ¼ teaspoon salt, and ¼ teaspoon pepper in a blender until smooth. Transfer to a large bowl. (The dressing can be refrigerated in an airtight container for up to 24 hours. Bring to room temperature and whisk to recombine before using.)

2. Stir the remaining ⅔ cup roasted red peppers, the chicken, celery, olives, parsley, and shallot into the vinaigrette. Season with salt and pepper to taste. Let sit at room temperature for 15 minutes. (The salad can be refrigerated in an airtight container for up to 24 hours.) Sprinkle with the almonds just before serving.

Chicken Salad with Mango and Avocado Dressing

SERVES 6

This recipe is best served over salad greens. For more heat, include the jalapeño seeds and ribs when mincing. Queso fresco is a fresh cow's milk cheese with a moist, crumbly texture and a lightly salty, milky flavor. If you don't have queso fresco, farmer's cheese and feta make good substitutes. We found that using a whole roast chicken for this salad yielded the right amount of both white and dark meat (see page 120 for our Simple Roast Chicken). For even less fuss, use a fully cooked supermarket rotisserie chicken.

- **⅓ cup olive oil**
- **¼ cup juice from 2 limes**
- **2 medium ripe avocados, pitted, peeled, and cut into ½-inch pieces**
- **1 small garlic clove, minced or pressed through a garlic press (about ½ teaspoon)**
- **Salt and ground black pepper**
- **5 cups shredded roast chicken, at room temperature (see page 10)**
- **1 mango, peeled, pitted, and cut into ½-inch pieces**
- **¼ cup minced red onion**
- **1 jalapeño chile, seeds and ribs removed, chile minced (see note)**
- **3 tablespoons minced fresh cilantro leaves**
- **3 ounces queso fresco, crumbled (¾ cup)**

1. Puree the oil, lime juice, 1 of the avocados, the garlic, ¼ teaspoon salt, and ¼ teaspoon pepper in a blender until smooth. Transfer to a large bowl. (The dressing can be refrigerated in an airtight container for up to 24 hours. Bring to room temperature and whisk to recombine before using.)

2. Stir the remaining avocado, the chicken, mango, red onion, jalapeño, and cilantro into the vinaigrette. Season with salt and pepper to taste. Let sit at room temperature for 15 minutes. (The salad can be refrigerated in an airtight container for up to 24 hours.) Sprinkle with the cheese just before serving.

Chicken Caesar Salad

SINCE ITS DEBUT IN THE 1920s, CAESAR salad has suffered at the hands of chefs and home cooks alike. The Caesar was conceived as a salad of whole lettuce leaves cloaked with a rich dressing made from such unlikely partners as egg, Worcestershire sauce, lemon juice, garlic, and Parmesan cheese, and garnished with garlic croutons. Over time, it has been subjected to such oddball additions as chickpeas, palm hearts, and barbecued ribs.

We wanted to bring Caesar salad back to its roots. We were struck, however, by the not-inconsiderable effort required to make the salad. Given this investment of time and effort, we decided to make our Caesar not a first course but a light main dish by adding one nontraditional (but now familiar and popular) ingredient: sliced chicken breast. We wanted the chicken to add heft to the salad without disturbing the underlying magic of the dressing.

Most Caesar salad dressings have at least one of two common problems. The first is texture, which should be thick and smooth, not thin or gluey. The second is lack of balance among the dressing's key flavors—lemon, Worcestershire, and garlic (and often anchovies)—which are frequently so out of whack that they assault your palate with a biting surplus of garlic or lip-sucking profusion of lemon.

We took on texture first. The classic thickening agent in this olive oil–based dressing is egg, which is either added raw or simmered in the shell very briefly in a process called coddling. The recipes we dug up in our research also included dressings that relied on mayonnaise and sour cream for thickening, but tasters summarily rejected both, finding that the former seemed better suited to a sandwich topping, and the latter to a party dip. In side-by-side tests of raw and coddled eggs, tasters preferred the noticeably smoother consistency of the coddled-egg dressing. The brief exposure to heat caused the yolk to thicken slightly, thereby giving the dressing a creamier texture. Many tasters wanted the dressing to be thicker still, so we decided to discard the egg white, which contributed extra liquid, and to double the number of yolks to two. Keep in mind, however, that such a brief exposure to heat does not render the egg as safe as if it were cooked fully; you are still essentially consuming raw egg, which may be of concern to some diners.

A series of tests led us to a well-balanced dressing. Based on an oil quantity of ⅓ cup and our 2 coddled yolks, tasters favored just under 2 tablespoons of lemon juice and a modest teaspoon each of Worcestershire sauce and garlic. The last touch was anchovy, which tasters felt gave the dressing a welcome flavor dimension.

As for the lettuce, romaine is the standard choice. Our tasters stuck to it for its pleasantly sweet flavor and crunchy texture.

The chicken added to Caesar salad in restaurants is often dry and leathery. For our Caesar, we wanted chicken that was moist, well seasoned, and quick and easy to prepare.

Skinless, boneless breasts were the overwhelming choice of tasters, who felt that dark meat tasted out of place. With an eye toward speed and ease, we tested three cooking methods: grilling, broiling, and sautéing. Grilling was too much work for a simple salad. Broiling was a bit bland; it was quick and simple but lacked flavor. Sautéing was OK, but because it required an extra step (flouring the chicken) and (believe it or not) produced chicken that was too flavorful for this purpose, we ruled it out. We found our solution in a quick cooking method that half-sautés (with no flour required) and half-poaches boneless, skinless chicken breasts, yielding moist and flavorful meat every time. This

SLICING CHICKEN ON THE BIAS

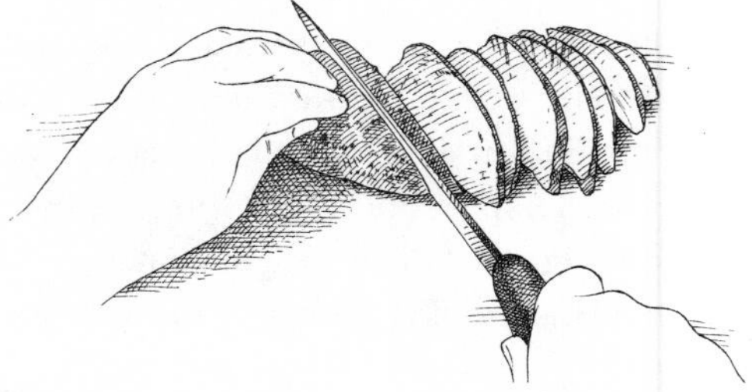

Slicing cooked chicken on the bias is a good trick to know—it looks attractive and makes the chicken easier to fork. With the knife held at an angle, slice the chicken on the bias into thin slices.

gave us what we wanted—a quick, simple cooking method and chicken that would blend right into the landscape of an already full-flavored salad.

We tried making croutons from various types of white bread and determined that any type made without sweetener tasted fine. Buy a baguette or country white loaf instead of sliced sandwich bread, as the latter usually contains added sugar. We tested three different methods of making croutons, including toasting, sautéing, and baking the bread cubes, and we tried each method with and without oil and garlic. We quickly learned that infusing olive oil with garlic flavor—rather than using minced garlic—was a key step. Whereas the minced garlic became burnt and bitter in the oven, steeping raw garlic in olive oil for 20 minutes produced a pleasantly garlicky flavor. In the end, we simply tossed raw bread cubes with the seasoned oil and baked them until crisp and golden.

Chicken Caesar Salad

SERVES 4 AS A LIGHT MAIN DISH

Both the croutons and the dressing can be made 24 hours in advance of serving. If you are unable to find romaine hearts, substitute 1 large head of romaine lettuce (about 14 to 16 ounces).

CROUTONS

- 2 medium garlic cloves, minced or pressed through a garlic press (about 2 teaspoons)
- ¼ teaspoon salt
- 3 tablespoons extra-virgin olive oil
- 1 baguette or country loaf, cut into ¾-inch cubes (about 3 cups)

DRESSING

- 2 large eggs
- 1 tablespoon plus 2 teaspoons juice from 1 lemon
- 4 anchovy fillets, rinsed and minced to a paste (about 1½ teaspoons)
- 1 medium garlic clove, minced or pressed through a garlic press (about 1 teaspoon)
- 1 teaspoon Worcestershire sauce
- Salt and ground black pepper
- ⅓ cup extra-virgin olive oil

SALAD

- 4 boneless, skinless chicken breasts (5 to 6 ounces each)
- Salt and ground black pepper
- 1 tablespoon vegetable oil
- ½ cup water
- 2 romaine hearts, washed, dried, and torn into 1½-inch pieces (about 10 cups lightly packed)
- ⅓ cup freshly grated Parmesan cheese

1. For the croutons: Adjust an oven rack to the middle position and heat the oven to 350 degrees. Mix the garlic, salt, and oil together in a small bowl; let sit for 20 minutes to infuse the flavors, then pour through a fine-mesh strainer into a medium bowl. Add the bread cubes and toss to coat. Spread the bread cubes in an even layer on a rimmed baking sheet; bake, stirring occasionally, until golden, 12 to 15 minutes. Cool on the baking sheet to room temperature. (The croutons can be stored at room temperature in an airtight container for up to 24 hours.)

2. For the dressing: Bring 2 inches water to a boil in a small saucepan over high heat. Lower the eggs into the water and cook for 45 seconds; remove with a slotted spoon. When cool enough to handle, crack the eggs open; reserve the yolks in a small bowl and discard the whites. Whisk in the lemon juice, anchovies, garlic, Worcestershire, ¼ teaspoon salt, and ⅛ teaspoon pepper until smooth. Whisking constantly, add the oil in a slow, steady stream. Season with salt and pepper to taste. (The dressing can be refrigerated in an airtight container for up to 24 hours. Bring to room temperature and whisk to recombine before using.)

3. For the salad: Pat the chicken dry with paper towels and season with salt and pepper. Heat the oil in a 12-inch nonstick skillet over medium-high heat until just smoking. Add the chicken and cook until browned on one side, about 3 minutes. Flip the chicken over, add the water, and cover. Reduce the heat to medium and continue to cook until the thickest part of the chicken registers 160 to 165 degrees on an instant-read thermometer, 5 to 7 minutes longer. Transfer to a cutting board and cool slightly. Slice the chicken on the bias following the illustrations on page 32; set aside.

4. In a large bowl, toss the lettuce, Parmesan, and about two-thirds of the dressing to coat. Divide salad among individual plates. Place the sliced chicken in the bowl used to dress the lettuce and toss with the remaining dressing. Divide the dressed chicken evenly among the plates, arranging the slices on the lettuce. Sprinkle each plate with a portion of the croutons and serve immediately.

Classic Cobb Salad

CREATED IN THE 1920s AT THE FAMOUS Hollywood hangout the Brown Derby, a classic cobb salad depends on a large supporting cast for flavor and texture—cool, crunchy greens (both mild and spicy); tender chicken; buttery avocado; juicy tomato; crisp, smoky bacon; and tangy blue cheese—to produce a vibrant salad that is substantial enough to satisfy the hankerings for a main course yet still be light and fresh-tasting.

Cobb salad's classic vinaigrette dressing is both the tie that binds the dish together and its biggest problem. Unifying the disparate elements of this salad is a lot to ask of any dressing. This notion was confirmed when we tested a half-dozen recipes, and in each case the vinaigrette didn't pass its screen test. More often than not, the flavors were dull and muted, with the salad components either drowned in inch-deep puddles of liquid or sitting high and unhappily dry. We wanted a dressing that both stood up to and integrated the cobb's multitude of flavors and textures, and a method of applying it that would season every ingredient lightly yet thoroughly.

Most of the dressing recipes we consulted called for a quartet of flavorings—garlic, lemon juice, Worcestershire sauce, and mustard—in addition to the basic red wine vinegar, olive oil, salt, and pepper. In an attempt to streamline the formula, we systematically eliminated each of the first four items, but tasters protested. Each one contributed a necessary dimension to the dressing. In fact, we ended up adding a tiny amount of sugar to help soften the double punch of the two acids—lemon juice and vinegar—and to balance the piquancy of the savory ingredients.

The recipes disagreed, however, over the particulars of those four ingredients. Recipes called for mustard in various forms, although dry was the most common choice. In side-by-side tastings of dry, spicy brown (like Gulden's) and Dijon mustards, we preferred the Dijon for its winey complexity. In addition, it is more of a staple ingredient in home kitchens than mustard powder. Another common addition that we ultimately rejected was water, which made the dressing, well, watery. The third point of contention was oil. All of the recipes specified olive oil (we liked extra-virgin best), but a number of them cut it with plain vegetable oil. Rather like the water, the vegetable oil diluted the dressing's flavor, so we skipped it. The last big question was about blue cheese, which is a standard component of the salad. Some recipes included it in the dressing, others simply added it to the salad itself. Our tasters agreed that the cheese, when incorporated in the dressing, hogged the spotlight in what should be an ensemble performance.

For the greens, we tasted four common mild salad greens—iceberg, Boston, Bibb, and romaine lettuces—and voted unanimously in favor of the romaine for its combination of flavor and crunch. That hearty crunch provided a nice backdrop for the copious toppings, so we used it in greater proportion than the spicy greens. The tasting of spicy salad greens—chicory, curly endive, arugula, and watercress—was less cut-and-dried. Each had its supporters, but watercress won out because it is the traditional choice.

Cooking the chicken with a minimum of fuss was another concern. As we did for our Chicken Caesar Salad (see page 33), we tested three cooking methods—grilling, broiling, and sautéing—and once again we reached the same conclusion. Grilling was too much work. Broiling was bland. Sautéing was OK, but because it required an extra step (flouring) and produced chicken that was actually too flavorful for this purpose, we ruled it out. The solution turned out to be a quick cooking method that half-sautés (with no flour required) and half-poaches boneless skinless chicken breasts, yielding moist and flavorful meat every time. This gave us what we wanted—a quick, simple cooking method and chicken that would blend right into the landscape of an already full-flavored salad.

We also made slight adjustments to several other ingredients. First, we switched from pale, tasteless supermarket beefsteak tomatoes to cherry tomatoes (the small, sweet, widely available grape tomatoes were our favorites), which taste better at any time but those few last weeks of summer when local tomatoes are in season. The bacon and chives, both classic cobb salad additions, remained untouched, but we doubled the quantity of another key ingredient, avocado, from one to two, because otherwise there wasn't enough to go around.

The typical blueprint for cobb salad is to lay down a bed of lettuce; arrange the chicken, tomatoes, eggs, and avocado in rows on top; sprinkle the whole arrangement with crumbled bacon, blue cheese, and chives; and toss it together at the table. It was the last step that lost us, as the individual character of each element was compromised when all were flung about in the bowl into one indistinguishable tangle. We tried drizzling the dressing over the composed salad, but that method failed to season the separate elements evenly. Tasters encountered dry spots with no dressing right next to other spots drowning in puddles of the stuff. The best method by far was to dress each ingredient independently, before arranging it on the platter. To do this without dirtying every bowl in the kitchen, we used the same one over and over, dressing and plating each ingredient as we went. This guaranteed that each morsel of each ingredient would be correctly seasoned. By dint of their delicate structures, only the eggs and avocados were exempted from this routine. Instead, we drizzled a bit of dressing evenly over them.

Perfect Hard-Cooked Eggs

MAKES 6 EGGS

You can easily scale this recipe up or down as desired; alter the pot size as needed, but do not alter the cooking time. Fresher eggs will have more centered yolks when cooked, while older eggs will produce off-centered yolks.

6 large eggs

Place the eggs in a medium saucepan, cover with 1 inch of water, and bring to a boil over high heat. As soon as the water reaches a boil, remove the pan from the heat, cover, and let sit for 10 minutes. Transfer the eggs to an ice-water bath, chill for 5 minutes, then peel.

PEELING EGGS FAST

1. After draining the hot water from the pot used to cook the eggs, shake the pot back and forth to crack the shells.

2. Add enough ice water to cover the eggs and cool. The water seeps under the broken shells, allowing them to be slipped off without a struggle.

Classic Cobb Salad

SERVES 6 AS A MAIN DISH

You'll need a large platter or wide, shallow pasta bowl to accommodate this substantial salad. Avocado discolors quickly, so prepare it at the last possible minute, just before assembling the salad. Though watercress is traditional in cobb salad, feel free to substitute an equal amount of arugula, chicory, curly endive, or a mixture thereof.

VINAIGRETTE

- ½ cup extra-virgin olive oil
- 2 tablespoons red wine vinegar
- 2 teaspoons juice from 1 lemon
- 1 teaspoon Worcestershire sauce
- 1 teaspoon Dijon mustard
- 1 medium garlic clove, minced or pressed through a garlic press (about 1 teaspoon)
- ½ teaspoon salt
- ¼ teaspoon sugar
- ⅛ teaspoon ground black pepper

SALAD

- 3 boneless, skinless chicken breasts (5 to 6 ounces each)
- Salt and ground black pepper
- 1 tablespoon vegetable oil
- ½ cup water
- 1 small head romaine lettuce, washed, dried, and torn into bite-sized pieces (about 8 cups)
- 1 bunch watercress (about 4 ounces), washed, dried, and stemmed (about 4 cups) (see note)
- 1 pint cherry or grape tomatoes (about 12 ounces), halved
- 3 hard-cooked eggs (see page 35), cut into ½-inch cubes
- 2 medium, ripe avocados, pitted, peeled, and cut into ½-inch cubes (see note) (see the illustrations on pages 52 and 53)
- 8 ounces (about 8 slices) bacon, cut crosswise into ¼-inch pieces; fried in a medium skillet over medium heat until crisp, about 7 minutes; and drained on a paper towel–lined plate
- 2 ounces blue cheese, crumbled (about ½ cup)
- 3 tablespoons minced fresh chives

1. FOR THE VINAIGRETTE: Whisk all the ingredients together in a medium bowl until well combined (alternatively, shake vigorously in a tight-lidded jar); set aside. (The dressing can be refrigerated in an airtight container for up to 24 hours. Bring to room temperature and whisk to recombine before using.)

2. FOR THE SALAD: Pat the chicken dry with paper towels and season with salt and pepper. Heat the oil in a 12-inch nonstick skillet over medium-high heat until just smoking. Add the chicken and cook until browned on one side, about 3 minutes. Flip the chicken over, add the water, and cover. Reduce the heat to medium and continue to cook until the thickest part of the chicken registers 160 to 165 degrees on an instant-read thermometer, 5 to 7 minutes longer. Transfer to a cutting board and cool slightly. Slice the chicken on the bias following the illustrations on page 32; set aside.

3. Toss the romaine and watercress with 5 tablespoons of the vinaigrette in a large bowl until coated; arrange on a very large, flat serving platter. Place the chicken in the bowl used to dress the lettuce, add ¼ cup of the vinaigrette, and toss to coat; arrange in a row along one edge of the greens. Place the tomatoes in the now-empty bowl, add 1 tablespoon of the vinaigrette, and toss gently to combine; arrange on the opposite edge of the greens. Arrange the eggs and avocados in separate rows near the center of the greens and drizzle with the remaining vinaigrette. Sprinkle the bacon, cheese, and chives evenly over the salad and serve immediately.

TESTING AVOCADOS FOR RIPENESS

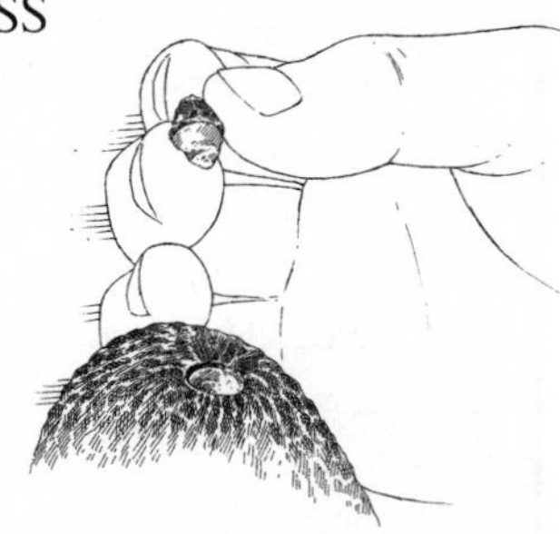

A soft avocado is sometimes bruised rather than truly ripe. To be sure, flick the small stem of the avocado. If it comes off easily and you can see green underneath it, the avocado is ripe.

2

SOUPS

Soups

NOT SURPRISINGLY, THE DIFFERENCES IN FLAVOR between chicken soup from a can and homemade chicken soup are immeasurable. What is surprising, however, is that homemade soup need not be a complicated affair. Two kinds of soup are covered in this chapter—soups that rely on homemade chicken stock, and soups that are made with store-bought, low-sodium chicken broth. How do you know which soups should be made with homemade broth and which can be made successfully with store-bought broth?

In general, we find that delicate, brothy soups that contain very few ingredients must be made with homemade stock. For instance, chicken noodle soup made with store-bought broth is not nearly as good as the same soup made with homemade broth. On the other hand, we find that soups with complex seasonings (such as Vietnamese-Style Noodle Soup with Chicken, a recipe that contains the potent flavors of star anise, fish sauce, and fresh herbs) or soups with rich and flavorful ingredients (such as Thai Chicken Soup, made with coconut milk) can be made with store-bought broth. In these cases, we have successfully devised methods for fortifying the flavor of the liquid by adding additional herbs, spices, and aromatics. Of course, you can certainly use homemade broth in these recipes; however, when we find that the quality of a soup made without homemade broth is quite high, we are happy to take this shortcut.

So first things first: What is the secret to great homemade chicken broth? We have found that the richest (and quickest) homemade chicken broth is made by lightly browning an onion and then sautéing the chicken parts (which we cut into two-inch pieces) until they are no longer pink. We then cover the pot and cook the chicken to extract as much flavor as possible before adding water and simmering the mixture. Using this technique, we were able to produce a full-flavored broth in just under an hour. We were happy to find that good homemade chicken broth does not require a full day's work in the kitchen.

In developing our soups, we learned that eking out as much flavor as possible from key ingredients was the secret to success. All of the soups in this chapter, with the exception of Italian Wedding Soup, include shredded chicken, and we found that tender breast meat is the best choice in these soups. Dark meat can be tough and gristly, and the extra fat can make the soup greasy. (Fat from dark meat isn't an issue when making broth because the broth is defatted before being used.)

We like to start by browning bone-in, skin-on chicken breasts, adding broth, and then poaching them just until cooked through. Browning the chicken adds intense chicken flavor to the broth, and poaching the chicken breasts releases their flavor into the soup; the inclusion of the skin and bones further fortifies the broth and keeps the meat from drying out. Similarly, sautéing the vegetables before adding the broth contributes an incomparable intensity of flavor.

We found that most chicken soups should be served as soon as they are ready. Chicken soups with pasta or rice certainly cannot hold, because, as they sit, the starches tend to absorb the broth, making them mushy. The broth base for most of our soups (and the shredded chicken) can be refrigerated for a day and then reheated and finished with the other ingredients and garnishes, but we find that the flavors are freshest when the soup is made and served immediately. That said, if you are making homemade broth, we do suggest that you make it at least a day in advance. That way the broth can chill in the refrigerator, making the fat easy to remove.

Lastly, all of the recipes in this chapter, full of richly flavored broth, tender shredded chicken, and a variety of vegetables, herbs, and garnishes, are hearty enough to make a meal. Though these soups are particularly satisfying on a cold winter day, they are great just about any time of year.

Homemade Stock and Soup 101

Restaurant chefs adhere to time-consuming, involved routines for making chicken and beef stocks. Bones, meat, and mirepoix (onions, carrots, and celery) are first oven-roasted or sautéed on the stovetop. A bouquet garni (a bundle of several fresh herbs) and water are added, and the stock simmers, uncovered, for hours, with the cook periodically skimming off impurities. To clarify the stock, a raft (beaten egg whites and sometimes ground meat) might then be added to trap sediment. Finally, the stock is strained, cooled, and defatted.

This method is fine for professional cooks, and it does yield rich, deeply flavored stock. But most home cooks don't want (or need) to follow such a complicated regimen. We've developed new techniques and helpful tips for making stock with great flavor—stock that requires fewer ingredients, less work, and less time than the classic method.

USING THE RIGHT EQUIPMENT

You don't need to make a huge investment in equipment to produce a good stock, but a few tools make the process easier.

Strainer: A stock made with hacked bones will contain minute bone particles and splinters and must be strained. A fine-mesh strainer is ideal for this job. Liquids must be strained into a clean bowl or pot. The sturdy, deep, relatively narrow bowl of a standing mixer is a perfect receptacle.

Dutch oven or stockpot: Stock should be made in a pot large enough to accommodate plenty of bones, meat, aromatics, and water. Whether you use a Dutch oven or stockpot, choose a lidded pot with a capacity of at least 8 quarts.

Colander: Before straining the stock, transfer the bones and large pieces of meat to a colander. This helps to prevent splashing when pouring the liquid through the strainer. Any type of colander will do—just be sure to place it over a bowl.

Meat cleaver: Hacking chicken parts into small pieces allows their flavorful juices to release quickly into the stock, significantly reducing the total simmering time. Rather than risk damaging your chef's knife, use a meat cleaver, which is designed to cut through bones.

Skimmer: A skimmer is a wide, flat, perforated spoon with a long handle. It is the best tool for skimming impurities and foam that rise to the surface of a stock as it cooks. If a skimmer is not available, a large slotted spoon works well, too.

USING THE RIGHT INGREDIENTS

CHOOSING CHICKEN

In kitchen tests, we found that stocks made with kosher or premium chickens (we like Bell & Evans) tasted better and had more body than stocks made with mass-market birds. Our advice: If you have a favorite chicken for roasting, use it for stock.

Cutting up chicken parts: Chicken hacked into small pieces with a meat cleaver will give up its flavor in record time. To cut through bone, place your hand near the far end of the meat cleaver handle, curling your fingers securely around it in a fist. Handle the cleaver the way you would a hammer, letting the weight of the blade's front tip lead the force of the chop. If you cannot chop the bone in one strike, place the cleaver in the groove of the first chop, then strike the blade's blunt edge with a heavy mallet.

THE PERFECT LADLE

You might think one ladle is the same as the next. But after dunking eight stainless steel models (plastic stains and can melt on the stovetop) into pots of soup, scattered puddles on the countertop made it clear that not all ladles are ergonomically equal. Ladles with handles shorter than nine inches simply sank in deeper pots, while more than 10 inches of grip proved cumbersome to maneuver. A large bowl is important, and a slightly offset handle is a must for cleanly transferring the ladle's contents into a bowl.

The Rösle Ladle with Pouring Rim & Hook Handle ($23.95) had everything we were looking for—including a hook handle and a drip-prevention pouring rim, which kept even wiggly noodles intact all the way to the bowl.

RÖSLE

QUICKER CHICKEN STOCK, STEP BY STEP

1. Sauté: Onions are a must for any stock, but cooking tests proved that carrots and celery aren't vital.

2. Sweat: Browning the chicken and then sweating it (cooking over low heat in a covered pot) allows the meat to release its rich, flavorful juices quickly, thus reducing the simmering time greatly.

3. Simmer: Add boiling water (to jump-start the cooking process), bay leaves (other herbs don't add much flavor), and salt.

4. Skim: Skimming away the foam that rises to the surface of chicken stock will make it clearer (though the flavor improvement is minimal).

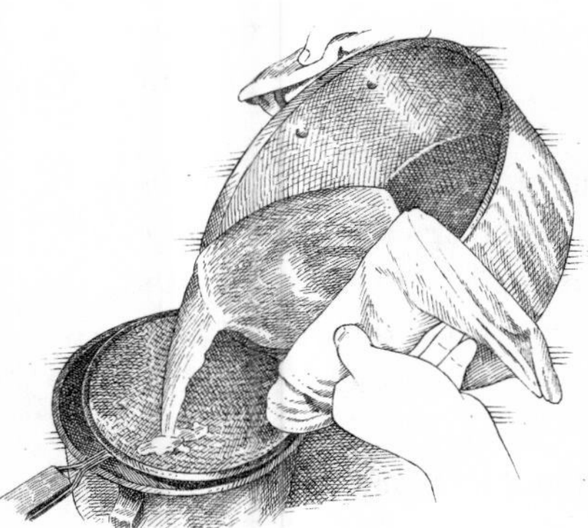

5. Strain: Once the flavor has been extracted from the stock ingredients, a skimmer or slotted spoon can be used to remove them to a colander. Then pour the stock through a fine-mesh strainer or a colander lined with cheesecloth.

6. Defat: After stock has been refrigerated, the fat hardens on the surface and is very easy to remove with a spoon. To defat hot stock, we recommend using a ladle or a fat separator.

FREEZING STOCK EFFICIENTLY

1. Ladle cooled stock into nonstick muffin tins and freeze. When the stock is frozen, twist the muffin tin just as you would twist an ice tray. Place the frozen blocks in a zipper-lock plastic bag and seal it tightly. Store the bag in the freezer.

2a. An alternative is to pour stock into a coffee mug lined with a quart-size plastic zipper-lock bag.

2b. Place the filled bags flat in a large, shallow roasting pan and freeze. Once the stock is solidly frozen, the bags can be removed from the pan and stored in the freezer.

Quick Homemade Chicken Stock

HIGH-QUALITY CHICKEN STOCK IS AN ABSOLUTE prerequisite for making a robust chicken soup. Garnished simply with vegetables, shredded chicken, and noodles, this type of soup relies on the broth for complexity, depth, and flavor. Most standard homemade stock or store-bought chicken broths are not flavorful enough for such a full-bodied chicken soup. They are fine if ladled into risotto or used in conjunction with other flavorful ingredients, but we wanted a stock that really tasted like chicken and could become the base for our chicken noodle soup recipes. We also wanted to see if we could stray from the conventional method for making stock—simmering chicken parts and aromatics, such as onions, carrots, and celery, in water for hours—and create a flavorful stock in less time.

A number of recipes that we came across promoted roasting chicken bones or parts and then using them to make broth. The theory, at least, is that roasted parts will flavor stock in minutes, not hours. We gave it a try several times, roasting chicken backs, necks, and bones—with and without vegetables. We preferred the stock made with roasted chicken parts and vegetables, but the actual chicken flavor was too tame.

Next, we tried a method we had read about in which chicken that's been hacked into small pieces is sautéed with an onion until the chicken loses its raw color. The pot is then covered, and the chicken and onion cooked over low heat until they release their rich, flavorful juices, which takes about 20 minutes. Only at that point is the water added, and the stock is simmered for just 20 minutes longer.

We knew we were onto something as we smelled the chicken and onion sautéing, and the finished stock confirmed what our noses had detected. The stock tasted pleasantly sautéed, not boiled. We had some refining to do, though. For once, we had made too strong a brew.

We substituted chicken backs and wingtips for the whole chicken and added more water. The stock was less intense, but just the right strength to make a base for some of the best chicken soup we've ever tasted. We made the broth twice more—once without onion and once with onion, celery, and carrot. The onion added a flavor dimension we liked; the extra vegetables neither added nor detracted from the final soup, so we left them out, not wanting to add an unnecessary step.

After much trial and error, we had a recipe that delivered liquid gold in just 40 minutes. While this recipe requires more hands-on work (hacking chicken parts and browning an onion, then browning chicken parts), it is ready in a fraction of the time required to make stock by more traditional methods.

So where do you find the useless chicken parts necessary for this stock? The Buffalo chicken wing fad has made wings more expensive than legs and thighs. For those who can find chicken backs, this is clearly an inexpensive way to make stock for soup. Our local grocery store usually sells them for almost nothing, but in many locations they may be difficult to find.

Luckily, we found that relatively inexpensive whole legs make an incredibly full-flavored stock for soup. In a side-by-side comparison of a stock made from backs and one made from whole legs, we found that the whole-leg stock was actually more full-flavored than the all-bone stock. Just don't try to salvage the meat from the legs. After 5 minutes of sautéing, 20 minutes of sweating, and another 20 minutes of simmering, the meat is completely void of flavor.

One note about this method: We found it necessary to cut the chicken into pieces small enough to release their flavorful juices in a short period of time. A meat cleaver, a heavy-duty chef's knife, or a pair of heavy-duty kitchen shears makes the task fairly simple. Cutting up the chicken for stock doesn't require precision. The point is to chop the pieces small enough so that they release their flavorful juices in a short period of time. Because of their larger bones, the legs and thighs can be difficult to cut. Start by splitting the leg and thigh at the joint, then hack each to yield three or four pieces.

Quick Homemade Chicken Stock

MAKES ABOUT 2 QUARTS

If you use a cleaver, you will be able to cut up the chicken parts quickly. A chef's knife or kitchen shears will also work, albeit more slowly. See the illustration and tips on page 40 for using a cleaver. This recipe can be doubled; simply cook the chicken in four batches in step 2. Remember to reserve the chicken fat for making soup, if desired.

- 1 tablespoon vegetable oil
- 1 medium onion, chopped medium
- 4 pounds chicken backs and wingtips or whole legs, hacked with a meat cleaver into 2-inch pieces (see the illustration on page 40)
- 2 quarts boiling water
- 2 teaspoons salt
- 2 bay leaves

1. Heat the oil in a large Dutch oven over medium-high heat until shimmering. Add the onion and cook until lightly browned and slightly softened, 2 to 3 minutes. Transfer the onion to a large bowl.

2. Add half of the chicken pieces to the pot and cook until no longer pink, 4 to 5 minutes. Transfer the cooked chicken to the bowl with the onion. Add the remaining chicken pieces and cook until no longer pink, 4 to 5 minutes. Return the onion and chicken pieces to the pot. Reduce the heat to low, cover, and cook until the chicken releases its juices, about 20 minutes.

3. Increase the heat to high and add the boiling water, salt, and bay leaves. Bring to a simmer, cover, and barely simmer until the stock is rich and flavorful, about 20 minutes.

4. Pour the stock through a fine-mesh strainer and discard the solids. Skim the fat and reserve for later use in soup or other recipes, if desired. (The stock can be cooled completely and refrigerated in an airtight container for up to 2 days or frozen for up to 1 month.)

Chicken Noodle Soups

STORE-BOUGHT CHICKEN BROTH IS FINE for soups with lots of other flavorings added, but for good old-fashioned chicken noodle soup, homemade stock is a must. And with homemade chicken stock on hand (see our recipe at left), making chicken noodle soup is a relatively easy proposition. Add some shredded chicken, vegetables, herbs, and noodles and you've got a great bowl of soup. We did have several questions, though. How should we cook the chicken? Which vegetables are best added to this soup? Should the vegetables be sautéed first, or can diced vegetables simply be simmered in chicken broth? As for the pasta, which kind of noodles work best, and should they be cooked in the soup or in a separate pot of boiling water? We wanted to answer all these questions, develop a basic master recipe, and then create some more unusual variations.

We tackled the chicken issue first. Tasters unanimously agreed that white meat chicken was preferable in soup, so thighs were out from the onset. Boneless, skinless breasts cooked very quickly, but they tended to dry out and offered little flavor to the broth. Bone-in, skin-on breasts, on the other hand, remained moist and tender, and had an added bonus: The skin and bones fortified the stock with chicken flavor. We browned the breasts and set them aside while the vegetables and aromatics sautéed. Then we added them back to the pot along with the stock, and simmered the mixture for just 15 minutes. The result was perfectly cooked breast meat ready to be boned, skinned, and shredded when cool, and stirred into the finished soup. (We tried dicing the chicken, but tasters thought it was reminiscent of canned soup.)

Next, we tested a wide range of vegetables, including onions, carrots, celery, leeks, potatoes, zucchini, tomatoes, and mushrooms. We concluded that the classic mirepoix ingredients (onions, carrots, and celery) should be part of a basic chicken noodle soup. Other vegetables are fine choices, but we decided that they are more appropriate for variations. For instance, tomatoes and zucchini give chicken noodle soup an Italian character, and mushrooms are a natural choice with wild rice and barley.

To settle the issue of how to cook the vegetables, we prepared two batches of soup. For the first batch, we sautéed the onions, carrots, and celery in a little vegetable oil until softened and then added the chicken stock. For the second batch, we simply simmered the sliced vegetables in broth. As might be expected, we found that sautéing brought out flavors in the vegetables and made a big difference in the finished soup.

We saw a few recipes that suggested saving chicken fat skimmed from homemade stock and using this fat as a cooking medium for the vegetables. We tested this and found that chicken fat does in fact add another level of chicken flavor to the soup. Although not essential, it makes sense to use chicken fat if you have planned ahead and saved what you skimmed from the surface of your broth.

In addition to the vegetables, we found that thyme and parsley brightened the flavors. We added thyme (fresh or dried) early on in the cooking to give it time to soften and permeate the broth. To preserve its freshness, the parsley was best added just before serving.

The noodles were the last (and the most important) element that we needed to investigate. Dried egg noodles are the most common choice, and they were tasters' favorite. We decided to next clarify the issue of how to cook them. We simmered egg noodles in the soup as well as in a separate pot of salted water. The noodles cooked in the soup pot shed some starch that somewhat clouded the soup. In contrast, noodles cooked in a separate pot and then added to the stock left the finished soup completely clear.

The effect on the soup, however, paled in comparison to the effect on the noodles. Noodles cooked separately tasted bland and did not meld with the soup. The noodles cooked in the soup absorbed some of the chicken broth, giving them a rich, well-rounded flavor. We concluded that you must cook the noodles in the soup.

While the recipes that follow are adaptable, we have carefully timed the addition of vegetables, noodles, grains, and other ingredients to make sure that each item is perfectly cooked—not overcooked. You can make adjustments if you keep in mind general cooking times for additional ingredients or substitutions.

Classic Chicken Noodle Soup

SERVES 4 TO 6

When making the chicken stock, remember to reserve the fat so that you can use it for browning the chicken.

- **1½ pounds bone-in, skin-on split chicken breasts (about 2 split breasts), trimmed**
- **Salt and ground black pepper**
- **2 tablespoons reserved chicken fat or vegetable oil**
- **1 medium onion, minced**
- **1 carrot, peeled and sliced ¼ inch thick**
- **1 celery rib, sliced ¼ inch thick**
- **1 teaspoon minced fresh thyme leaves or ½ teaspoon dried**
- **2 quarts Homemade Chicken Stock (page 43)**
- **2 cups (3 ounces) wide egg noodles**
- **¼ cup minced fresh parsley leaves**

1. Pat the chicken dry with paper towels and season with salt and pepper. Heat the reserved fat in a large Dutch oven over medium-high heat until just smoking. Brown the chicken on both sides, 5 to 8 minutes per side, reducing the heat if the pan begins to scorch. Transfer the chicken to a plate and set aside.

2. Add the onion, carrot, celery, thyme, and ½ teaspoon salt to the fat left in the pot and cook over medium-low heat until softened, about 5 minutes. Stir in the stock, scraping up any browned bits. Add the chicken and bring to a simmer. Reduce the heat to low, cover, and cook until the thickest part of the breast registers 160 to 165 degrees on an instant-read thermometer, 10 to 15 minutes.

3. Transfer the chicken to a cutting board. When the chicken is cool enough to handle, remove the meat from the bones and shred into bite-sized pieces (see the illustration on page 10); discard the skin and bones. (Up to this point, the stock and chicken can be cooled and refrigerated in separate airtight containers for up to 24 hours. Return the broth to a simmer before proceeding with the recipe.) Stir the noodles into the soup and cook over medium heat until the noodles are just tender, about 5 minutes.

4. Return the shredded chicken to the soup and continue to cook until heated through, about 2 minutes. Stir in the parsley, season with salt and pepper to taste, and serve.

Chicken Soup with Orzo and Spring Vegetables

SERVES 4 TO 6

When making the chicken stock, remember to reserve the fat so that you can use it for browning the chicken.

- 1½ pounds bone-in, skin-on split chicken breasts (about 2 split breasts), trimmed
- Salt and ground black pepper
- 2 tablespoons reserved chicken fat or vegetable oil
- 1 medium leek, white and light green parts only, quartered lengthwise, sliced ¼ inch thick, and rinsed thoroughly (see the illustrations at right)
- 1 carrot, peeled and sliced ¼ inch thick
- 1 celery rib, sliced ¼ inch thick
- 1 teaspoon minced fresh thyme leaves or ½ teaspoon dried
- 2 quarts Homemade Chicken Stock (page 43)
- ½ cup orzo
- ¼ pound asparagus, trimmed and cut into 1-inch lengths
- ¼ cup fresh or frozen peas
- 2 tablespoons minced fresh tarragon leaves

1. Pat the chicken dry with paper towels and season with salt and pepper. Heat the reserved fat in a large Dutch oven over medium-high heat until just smoking. Brown the chicken on both sides, 5 to 8 minutes per side, reducing the heat if the pan begins to scorch. Transfer the chicken to a plate and set aside.

2. Add the leek, carrot, celery, thyme, and ½ teaspoon salt to the fat left in the pot and cook over medium-low heat until softened, about 5 minutes. Stir in the stock, scraping up any browned bits. Add the chicken and bring to a simmer. Reduce the heat to low, cover, and cook until the thickest part of the breast registers 160 to 165 degrees on an instant-read thermometer, 10 to 15 minutes.

3. Transfer the chicken to a cutting board. When the chicken is cool enough to handle, remove the meat from the bones and shred into bite-sized pieces (see the illustration on page 10); discard the skin and bones. (Up to this point, the stock and chicken can be cooled and refrigerated in separate airtight containers for up to 24 hours. Return the broth to a simmer before proceeding with the recipe.) Stir the orzo, asparagus, and peas into the soup and cook over medium heat until the orzo is just tender, about 5 minutes.

4. Return the shredded chicken to the soup and continue to cook until heated through, about 2 minutes. Stir in the tarragon, season with salt and pepper to taste, and serve.

PREPARING LEEKS

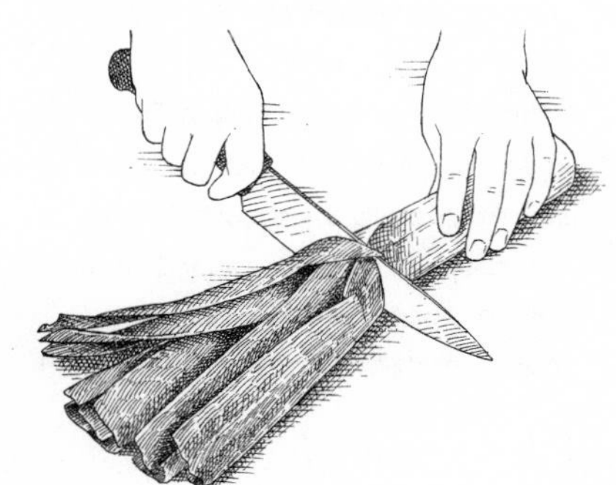

1. Trim and discard the roots and the dark green leaves.

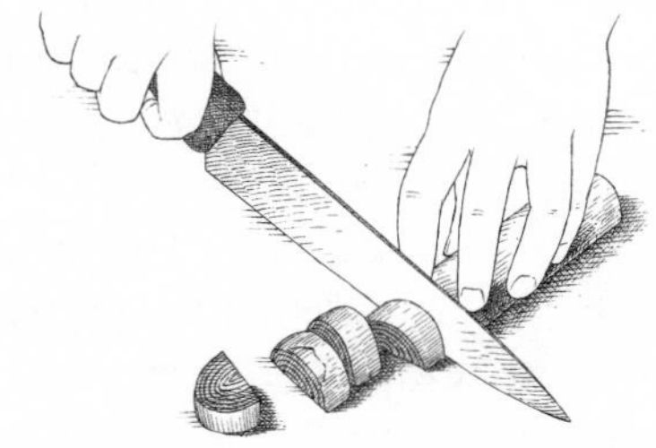

2. Slice the trimmed leek in half or quarters lengthwise (depending on the recipe), then cut into ¼- to ½-inch pieces (depending on the recipe).

3. Rinse the cut leeks thoroughly to remove dirt and sand.

Chicken Soup with Shells, Zucchini, and Tomatoes

SERVES 4 TO 6

When making the chicken stock, remember to reserve the fat so that you can use it for browning the chicken.

- 1½ pounds bone-in, skin-on split chicken breasts (about 2 split breasts), trimmed
- Salt and ground black pepper
- 2 tablespoons reserved chicken fat or olive oil
- 1 medium onion, minced
- 1 carrot, peeled and sliced ¼ inch thick
- 1 celery rib, sliced ¼ inch thick
- 1 teaspoon minced fresh thyme leaves or ½ teaspoon dried
- 2 quarts Homemade Chicken Stock (page 43)
- 1 zucchini, cut into ½-inch pieces
- 1 cup small shells or macaroni
- ½ cup chopped fresh or canned tomatoes
- ¼ cup chopped fresh basil leaves
- Freshly grated Parmesan (for serving)

1. Pat the chicken dry with paper towels and season with salt and pepper. Heat the reserved fat in a large Dutch oven over medium-high heat until just smoking. Brown the chicken on both sides, 5 to 8 minutes per side, reducing the heat if the pan begins to scorch. Transfer the chicken to a plate and set aside.

2. Add the onion, carrot, celery, thyme, and ½ teaspoon salt to the fat left in the pot and cook over medium-low heat until softened, about 7 minutes. Stir in the stock, scraping up any browned bits. Add the chicken and bring to a simmer. Reduce the heat to low, cover, and cook until the thickest part of the breast registers 160 to 165 degrees on an instant-read thermometer, 10 to 15 minutes.

3. Transfer the chicken to a cutting board. When the chicken is cool enough to handle, remove the meat from the bones and shred into bite-sized pieces (see the illustration on page 10); discard the skin and bones. (Up to this point, the stock and chicken can be cooled and refrigerated in separate airtight containers for up to 24 hours. Return the stock to a simmer before proceeding with the recipe.) Stir the zucchini, shells, and tomatoes into the soup and cook over medium heat until the shells are tender, about 5 minutes.

4. Return the shredded chicken to the soup and continue to cook until heated through, about 2 minutes. Stir in the basil and season with salt and pepper to taste. Serve, passing the Parmesan separately.

Chicken Soup with Wild Rice, Leeks, and Mushrooms

SERVES 4 TO 6

Wild rice and mushrooms lend a woodsy flavor to this luxurious take on basic chicken noodle soup. When making the chicken stock, remember to reserve the fat so that you can use it for browning the chicken.

- 1½ pounds bone-in, skin-on split chicken breasts (about 2 split breasts), trimmed
- Salt and ground black pepper
- 2 tablespoons reserved chicken fat or vegetable oil
- 1 medium leek, white and light green parts only, quartered lengthwise, sliced ¼ inch thick, and rinsed thoroughly (see the illustrations on page 45)
- 1 carrot, peeled and sliced ¼ inch thick
- ½ pound white mushrooms, wiped clean, trimmed, and sliced ¼ inch thick
- 1 teaspoon minced fresh thyme leaves or ½ teaspoon dried
- 2 quarts Homemade Chicken Stock (page 43)
- 1 cup water
- ½ cup wild rice
- ½ ounce dried porcini mushrooms, rinsed and minced
- ¼ cup minced fresh parsley leaves

1. Pat the chicken dry with paper towels and season with salt and pepper. Heat the reserved fat in a large Dutch oven over medium-high heat until just smoking. Brown the chicken on both sides, 5 to 8 minutes per side, reducing the heat if the pan begins to scorch. Transfer the chicken to a plate and set aside.

2. Add the leek, carrot, white mushrooms, thyme, and ½ teaspoon salt to the fat left in the pot, cover,

and cook over medium-low heat, stirring often, until the mushrooms have released their liquid, 8 to 10 minutes. Stir in the stock and water, scraping up any browned bits. Add the chicken and bring to a simmer. Reduce the heat to low, cover, and cook until the thickest part of the breast registers 160 to 165 degrees on an instant-read thermometer, 10 to 15 minutes.

3. Transfer the chicken to a cutting board. When the chicken is cool enough to handle, remove the meat from the bones and shred into bite-sized pieces (see the illustration on page 10); discard the skin and bones. (Up to this point, the broth and chicken can be cooled and refrigerated in separate airtight containers for up to 24 hours. Return the broth to a simmer before proceeding with the recipe.) Stir the rice and dried mushrooms into the soup and cook over low heat, partially covered, until the rice is tender, about 1 hour.

4. Return the shredded chicken to the soup and continue to cook until heated through, about 2 minutes. Stir in the parsley, season with salt and pepper to taste, and serve.

Chicken Soup with Barley and Mushrooms

SERVES 4 TO 6

When making the chicken stock, remember to reserve the fat so that you can use it for browning the chicken.

- 1½ pounds bone-in, skin-on split chicken breasts (about 2 split breasts), trimmed
- Salt and ground black pepper
- 2 tablespoons reserved chicken fat or vegetable oil
- 1 medium onion, minced
- 1 carrot, peeled and sliced ¼ inch thick
- ½ pound white mushrooms, wiped clean, trimmed, and sliced ¼ inch thick
- 1 teaspoon minced fresh thyme leaves or ½ teaspoon dried
- 2 quarts Homemade Chicken Stock (page 43)
- 1 cup water
- ½ cup barley
- ½ ounce dried porcini mushrooms, rinsed and minced
- ¼ cup minced fresh parsley leaves

1. Pat the chicken dry with paper towels and season with salt and pepper. Heat the reserved fat in a large Dutch oven over medium-high heat until just smoking. Brown the chicken on both sides, 5 to 8 minutes per side, reducing the heat if the pan begins to scorch. Transfer the chicken to a plate and set aside.

2. Add the onion, carrot, white mushrooms, thyme, and ½ teaspoon salt to the fat left in the pot, cover, and cook over medium-low heat, stirring often, until the mushrooms have released their liquid, 8 to 10 minutes. Stir in the stock and water, scraping up any browned bits. Add the chicken and bring to a simmer. Reduce the heat to low, cover, and cook until the thickest part of the breast registers 160 to 165 degrees on an instant-read thermometer, 10 to 15 minutes.

3. Transfer the chicken to a cutting board. When the chicken is cool enough to handle, remove the meat from the bones and shred into bite-sized pieces (see the illustration on page 10); discard the skin and bones. (Up to this point, the stock and chicken can be cooled and refrigerated in separate airtight containers for up to 24 hours. Return the broth to a simmer before proceeding with the recipe.) Stir the barley and dried mushrooms into the soup and cook over low heat, partially covered, until the barley is just tender, about 45 minutes.

4. Return the shredded chicken to the soup and continue to cook until heated through, about 2 minutes. Stir in the parsley, season with salt and pepper to taste, and serve.

Vietnamese-Style Noodle Soup with Chicken

A GOOD VIETNAMESE NOODLE SOUP, OR *pho*, starts with a long-simmered broth flavored with Asian spices and sauces. The broth is rich but not heavy and is filled with fettuccine-width rice noodles, some shredded chicken (or thinly sliced beef), scallion slices, crisp bean sprouts, and lots of whole fresh mint, basil, and/or cilantro leaves. This mix of raw and cooked, and hot and cold, makes this soup unique, and it provides a terrific strategy for an everyday, home-cooked, one-pot meal that tastes anything but ordinary.

From past tastings, we knew that store-bought low-sodium chicken broth is a great alternative to homemade broth when fortified with the herbs, sauces, and spices that are customary in this Vietnamese broth. Starting with low-sodium chicken broth, we added chopped onions, garlic, and fresh ginger and simmered it for 20 minutes. The flavor of the broth was immeasurably improved, but we wanted to do less work. So instead of chopping, we merely quartered the onions and crushed medallions of ginger and whole garlic cloves with the side of a chef's knife before simmering them in the broth; the result tasted just as good.

With this base to build on, we experimented with other ingredients to try to get the authentic taste we were looking for. We found that soy and fish sauces added much-needed body and depth of flavor to our broth. Fish sauce brought just the right combination of salt and a musky sweetness, while soy sauce lent richness. Cloves and star anise are other common additions and are particularly nice flavorings when paired with chicken, so we included them in the mix. Lastly, we added a pinch of sugar, which balanced out the salt and acidity from the sauces.

Satisfied with the broth, we turned our attention to the noodles. We found that boiled rice noodles had a tendency to get mushy and, if left in the hot soup for any length of time, break apart. Ultimately, we settled on soaking the noodles in boiling water—a fine distinction that did not overcook them. We drained the noodles when they had softened to the point that they were tender but still had tooth.

Next, we looked at what cut of chicken to use. We had success in our other chicken soup recipes browning bone-in, skin-on chicken breasts, poaching them in the broth and then shredding the meat and returning it to the finished soup. And this recipe was no different—the shredded white meat was perfectly moist and well seasoned.

With all the components in place, all that was left were the finishing touches: a handful of bean sprouts, fresh herbs and scallions, a squeeze of fresh lime juice, and sliced chile for heat.

SLICING SCALLIONS ON THE BIAS

Slicing the scallions on the bias makes for an attractive presentation. Simply hold the scallion at an angle, then slice it thin.

INGREDIENTS: Fish Sauce

Fish sauce, or *nam pla* or *nuoc cham,* is a salty, amber-colored liquid made from salted, fermented fish. It is used both as an ingredient and a condiment in Southeast Asia. Used in very small amounts, it adds a well-rounded, salty flavor to sauces, soups, and marinades. We tasted six brands of fish sauce—one from Vietnam, one from the Philippines, and the rest from Thailand. Tasters had preferences among the sauces, but those preferences varied greatly from taster to taster. With such a limited ingredient list—most of the brands contained some combination of fish extract, water, salt, and sugar—the differences among sauces were minimal. If you are a fan of fish sauce and plan to use it often, you might want to make a special trip to an Asian market to buy a rich, dark sauce, like Tiparos fish sauce (below left), that is suitably pungent. Because most supermarkets don't carry a wide selection of fish sauce, we recommend buying whatever is available. That will most likely be Thai Kitchen (below right), an Americanized brand found in most supermarkets, which was the lightest-colored (and flavored) brand we tasted.

THE BEST FISH SAUCES

Tiparos is a dark and pungent sauce, while Thai Kitchen has a milder flavor but is more widely available.

TIPAROS

THAI KITCHEN

Vietnamese-Style Noodle Soup with Chicken

SERVES 4 TO 6

This recipe is great made with store-bought low-sodium chicken broth, but feel free to make your own homemade stock (see page 43).

BROTH AND CHICKEN

- 1½ pounds bone-in, skin-on split chicken breasts (about 2 split breasts), trimmed
- Salt and ground black pepper
- 2 tablespoons vegetable oil
- 2 quarts low-sodium chicken broth (see note)
- 2 cups water
- ⅓ cup fish sauce
- 2 tablespoons soy sauce
- 2 tablespoons sugar
- 2 medium onions, quartered
- 4 medium garlic cloves, smashed and peeled
- 1 (5-inch) piece fresh ginger, peeled, cut into ⅛-inch rounds, and smashed
- 4 star anise pods
- 4 whole cloves

NOODLES AND GARNISH

- 8 ounces (¼-inch-wide) dried flat rice noodles
- 2 cups bean sprouts
- ½ cup fresh basil leaves
- ½ cup fresh cilantro leaves
- 2 scallions, sliced thin on the bias (see the illustration at left)
- 1 jalapeño chile, sliced thin crosswise
- 1 lime, cut into wedges (for serving)

1. For the broth and chicken: Pat the chicken dry with paper towels and season with salt and pepper. Heat the oil in a large Dutch oven over medium-high heat until just smoking. Brown the chicken on both sides, 5 to 8 minutes per side, reducing the heat if the pan begins to scorch. Transfer the chicken to a plate and set aside.

2. Stir in the remaining broth ingredients, scraping up any browned bits. Add the chicken and bring to a simmer. Reduce the heat to low, cover, and cook until the thickest part of the breast registers 160 to 165 degrees on an instant-read thermometer, 10 to 15 minutes.

3. Transfer the chicken to a cutting board. Pour the broth through a fine-mesh strainer, discarding the solids. (Do not wash the pot.) When the chicken is cool enough to handle, remove the meat from the bones and shred into bite-sized pieces (see the illustration on page 10); discard the skin and bones. (Up to this point, the broth and chicken can be cooled and refrigerated in separate airtight containers for up to 24 hours.) Return the strained broth to the Dutch oven.

4. For the noodles and garnish: Meanwhile, bring 2 quarts of water to a boil in a medium saucepan. Off the heat, add the rice noodles and let stand, stirring occasionally, until tender, 10 to 15 minutes. Drain and distribute the noodles, the shredded chicken, and bean sprouts among individual bowls.

5. Arrange the basil, cilantro, scallions, jalapeño, and lime wedges attractively on a large serving platter and set aside. Return the broth to a simmer; ladle the soup into the individual bowls and serve, passing the garnishes separately.

Thai Chicken Soup

ONE OF OUR FAVORITE THINGS TO EAT AT A Thai restaurant is a bowl of *tom khaa gai,* or the easier-to-pronounce translation: Thai chicken soup. It doesn't look like much—a creamy, pale broth laced with chicken, mushrooms, and cilantro—but what it lacks in looks it makes up for in flavor. Sweet and sour components balance the richness of coconut milk infused with lemon grass and lime, and this, in turn, tempers a slow-building chile burn.

This classic Thai soup is relatively easy to make, if you can find all of the proper ingredients, which may not be easy. Its complex flavor is largely derived from such exotica as galangal, kaffir lime leaves, lemon grass, and bird's eye chiles. We'd be hard-pressed to find most of these ingredients at our local market. That said, we aimed to make the most authentic version possible with widely available ingredients.

We found a handful of "simplified" or "Americanized" Thai chicken soup recipes that, while largely informative regarding substitutions, mostly missed the mark. Each lacked the taut balance of hot, sour, salty, and sweet components that makes Thai cooking so compelling. (Appropriately enough, that balance, in Thai, is called *yum.*) So for the time being, at least, we stuck with the classic recipes. We'd address substitutions once we knew how best to prepare the soup.

Variation in Thai chicken soup recipes tends to center on two basic components: broth and garnishes. Traditionally, recipes typically prepare the broth in one of two methods. The first involves poaching a whole chicken in water with aromatics, after which the broth is blended with coconut milk and further seasoned; the chicken—now shredded—is stirred in with the mushrooms. In the second approach, chicken broth and coconut milk are simmered with the aromatics, after which thin-sliced raw chicken and the remaining ingredients and seasonings are added. Both methods have their merits, so we decided to try something in between (that also worked for our other chicken soup recipes). We browned bone-in, skin-on chicken breasts and simmered them in chicken broth, coconut milk, and aromatics until cooked through, and then shredded the meat and returned it to the finished soup. The chicken bones helped to fortify the broth, and the meat picked up flavor as well.

How long did the broth and aromatics need to simmer for the best results? We cobbled together a working recipe from the best we had tried—a blend of chicken broth, coconut milk, lemon grass, shallots, galangal, and cilantro. A scant 15 minutes after the broth had come to a simmer proved perfect—the chicken cooked through and the broth was flavorful. Much longer and the broth tasted bitter, vegetal, and over-extracted.

After preparing a few more batches with varying ratios of chicken broth and coconut milk, we settled on equal parts of each. Rich-tasting without being cloying, and definitely chicken flavored, the blend was perfectly balanced. We also tried a technique we had come across in a couple of recipes. The coconut milk was added in two parts: half at the beginning and the remainder just before serving. What seemed fussy made a big difference, as the coconut flavor came through most clearly.

Now came the hard part: making substitutions. We tried everything from lemon grass to kaffir lime leaf substitutes, but they all felt like distant seconds. It was a bad trend. Replacing the authentic ingredients was not working as well as hoped, as the soup did not taste nearly as good as we hoped. Perhaps authentic flavor really wasn't possible without the proper ingredients. Then we found our magic bullet. At one tasting postmortem, a colleague suggested red curry paste, an ingredient we hadn't considered to that point. While it is never added to traditional Thai chicken soup, the curry paste includes all the exotic ingredients for which we were trying so hard to find acceptable substitutions. We whisked a small spoonful of the paste into the soup in front of us and were struck by the surprising transformation from boring to—dare we say?—authentic.

Curry paste is usually added early on in cooking to mellow its potent flavor, but we found that this

MINCING LEMON GRASS

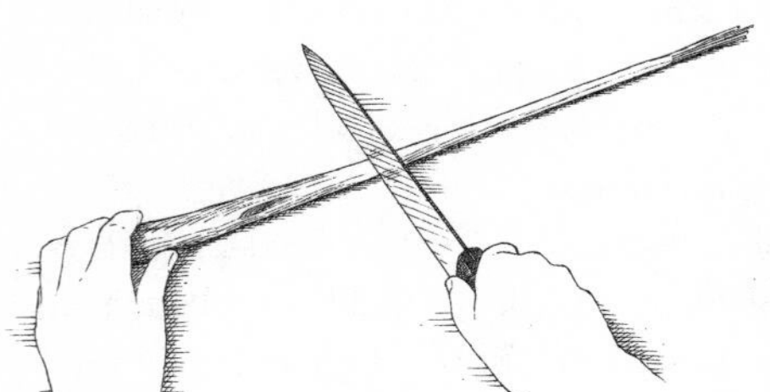

1. Trim all but the bottom 5 inches of the lemon grass stalk.

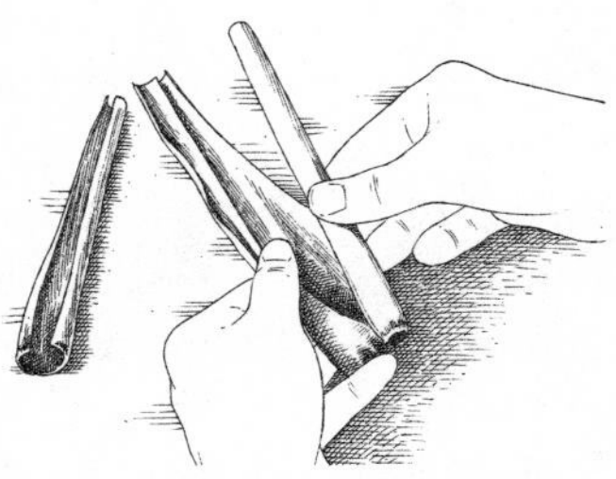

2. Remove the tough outer sheath from the trimmed lemon grass. If the lemon grass is particularly thick or tough, you may need to remove several layers to reveal the tender inner portion of the stalk.

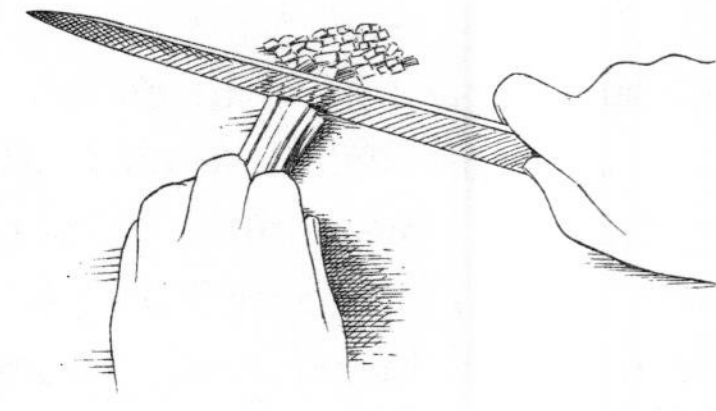

3. Cut the trimmed and peeled lemon grass in half lengthwise, then slice thin crosswise.

flattened the flavors too much. Adding a dollop at the very end of cooking—whisked together with pungent fish sauce and tart lime juice—allowed the sharpness of the galangal, the fragrance of the kaffir lime leaves, and the bright heat of the chiles to come through loud and clear. Out went the mediocre substitutes ginger and lime zest, and in went two teaspoons of easy-to-find red curry paste.

With the broth tasting great, we could finally tackle the mushrooms. Oyster mushrooms are traditional but hard to find and expensive. Supermarket options like cremini, shiitake, and white mushrooms each had their merits, but the latter proved to be the closest match to the mild flavor and chewy texture of oyster mushrooms. Sliced thin and submerged in the broth, they quickly softened and absorbed the soup's flavors like a sponge.

A sprinkling of cilantro usually suffices as a finishing touch, but tasters wanted more. The clean, bright heat of thin-sliced Thai chiles and the sharp bite of scallions did the trick. With 20-odd minutes of cooking and a minimum of hands-on effort, we had Thai chicken soup that tasted every bit as good as that served at Thai restaurants.

Thai Chicken Soup

SERVES 4 TO 6

This recipe is great made with store-bought low-sodium chicken broth, but feel free to make your own homemade stock (see page 43). Although we prefer the richer, more complex flavor of regular coconut milk, light coconut milk can be substituted for one or both cans. Don't be tempted to use jarred or dried lemon grass—its flavor is characterless. For a spicier soup, add additional red curry paste to taste.

- **1½ pounds bone-in, skin-on split chicken breasts (about 2 split breasts), trimmed**
- **Salt and ground black pepper**
- **2 tablespoons vegetable oil**
- **3 stalks lemon grass, bottom 5 inches only, trimmed and sliced thin (see note) (see the illustrations at left)**
- **4 medium shallots, chopped coarse (about ¾ cup)**
- **8 sprigs fresh cilantro, chopped coarse**
- **3 tablespoons fish sauce**
- **4 cups low-sodium chicken broth (see note)**
- **2 (14-ounce) cans coconut milk (see note)**
- **½ pound white mushrooms, wiped clean, trimmed, and sliced ¼ inch thick**
- **1 tablespoon sugar**
- **3 tablespoons juice from 2 limes**
- **2 teaspoons Thai red curry paste (see note)**

GARNISH

- **½ cup fresh cilantro leaves**
- **2 fresh Thai, serrano, or jalapeño chiles, seeds and ribs removed, chiles minced**
- **2 scallions, sliced thin on the bias (see the illustration on page 48)**
- **1 lime, cut into wedges (for serving)**

1. Pat the chicken dry with paper towels and season with salt and pepper. Heat the oil in a large Dutch oven over medium-high heat until just smoking. Brown the chicken on both sides, 5 to 8 minutes per side, reducing the heat if the pan begins to scorch. Transfer the chicken to a plate and set aside.

2. Add the lemon grass, shallots, cilantro sprigs, and 1 tablespoon of the fish sauce to the fat left in the pot and cook over medium-low heat until softened but not browned, 2 to 5 minutes. Stir in the chicken broth and 1 can of the coconut milk, scraping up any browned bits. Add the chicken and bring to a simmer. Reduce the heat to low, cover, and cook until the thickest part of the breast registers 160 to 165 degrees on an instant-read thermometer, 10 to 15 minutes.

3. Transfer the chicken to a cutting board. Pour the broth through a fine-mesh strainer, discarding the solids. (Do not wash the pot.) When the chicken is cool enough to handle, remove the meat from the bones and shred into bite-sized pieces (see the illustration on page 10); discard the skin and bones. (Up to this point, the broth and chicken can be cooled and refrigerated in separate airtight containers for up to 24 hours.) Return the strained broth to the Dutch oven.

4. Stir in the remaining can coconut milk, the mushrooms, and sugar and cook over medium heat

until the mushrooms are almost tender, about 3 minutes. Return the shredded chicken to the soup and cook until heated through, about 2 minutes.

5. Meanwhile, whisk the lime juice, curry paste, and remaining 2 tablespoons fish sauce together. Off the heat, whisk the mixture into the soup. Ladle the soup into individual bowls, garnish with the cilantro, chiles, and scallions, and serve, passing the lime wedges separately.

Tortilla Soup

A MEAL IN A BOWL, THIS SPICY CHICKEN-tomato broth, overflowing with garnishes (fried tortilla strips, crumbled cheese, diced avocado, and lime wedges), always satisfies with its intensely rich flavors and contrasting textures. In essence, it's a turbo-charged, south-of-the-border chicken soup. But as we rounded up recipes for this soup, our enthusiasm began to fade. Cotija? Epazote? Crema? Authentic recipes called for at least one, if not several, uniquely Mexican ingredients, none of which we were going to find at our local market. In addition, the time required to make homemade chicken broth and to fry tortilla strips seemed beyond the pale for a weeknight soup.

Just to get our bearings, we did make a few of these authentic recipes (after a long hunt for ingredients). They tasted great, but the preparation was arduous at best. Yet when we cooked up a few "Americanized" recipes, we ended up with watery brews of store-bought chicken broth and canned tomatoes topped with stodgy, off-the-shelf tortilla chips. Quick, but definitely not what we would call great-tasting.

We started anew and broke the soup into its three classic components: a flavor base made with fresh tomatoes, garlic, onion, and chiles; chicken broth; and an array of garnishes, including fried tortilla strips. We zeroed in on the flavor base first, recalling that the best of the soups we had made called for a basic Mexican cooking technique in which the vegetables are charred on a *comal,* or griddle, then pureed and fried to create a concentrated paste that flavors the soup.

Lacking a comal in the test kitchen, we used a cast-iron skillet for charring, and the results were superb, even with mediocre supermarket tomatoes. The downside was that it took 25 attentive minutes to complete the task. We wondered if we could skip charring altogether by adding smoke-flavored dried chiles to a puree of raw tomatoes, onion, and garlic. (We used guajillo chiles, which are often used to spice up tortilla soup.) The answer was yes, but toasting and grinding these hard-to-find chiles didn't bring us any closer to a quick and easy recipe. Chipotle chiles (smoked jalapeños) seemed like a more practical choice. Canned in a vinegary tomato mixture called adobo sauce, chipotles pack heat, roasted smoky flavor, and, more important, convenience. We also found that aggressively frying the raw tomatoes, onion, and chipotle puree over high heat forced all of the water out of the mixture and further concentrated its flavor.

With the vegetable-charring step eliminated, we moved on to the chicken broth. Yes, the test kitchen does have an excellent recipe for homemade stock (see page 43), but we were hoping to

PITTING AN AVOCADO

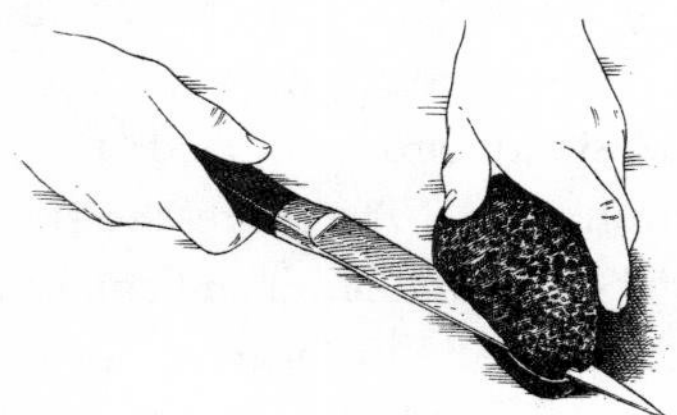

1. Start by slicing around the pit and through both ends with a chef's knife. With your hands, twist the avocado to separate the two halves.

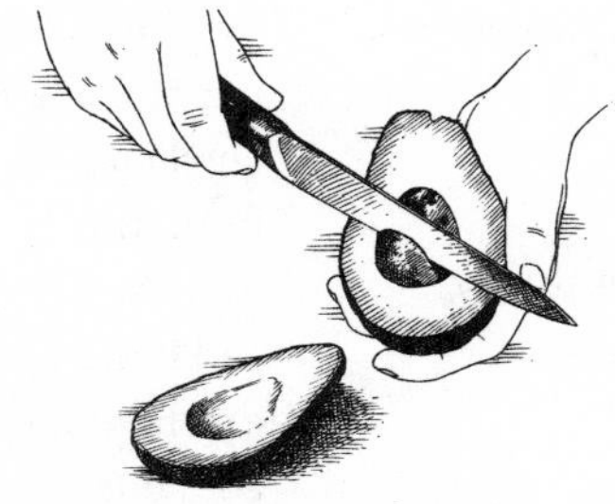

2. Stick the blade of the chef's knife sharply into the pit. Lift the knife, twisting the blade to loosen and remove the pit.

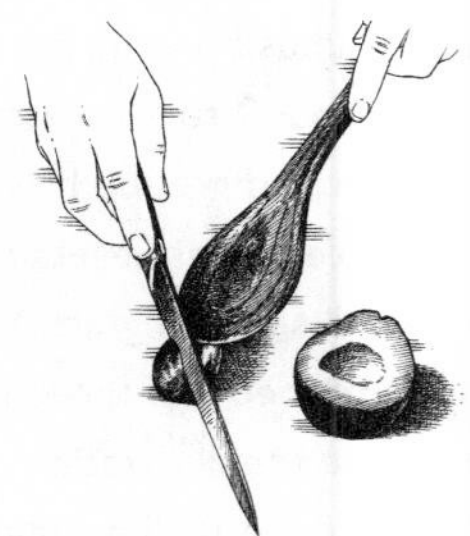

3. Don't pull the pit off the knife with your hands. Instead, use a large wooden spoon to pry the pit safely off the knife.

move this recipe into the express lane. The obvious alternative was to doctor store-bought low-sodium chicken broth (as we did in many of our other recipes), especially since this soup is awash with so many other vibrant flavors. Like our other chicken soup recipes, we browned the chicken and poached it in store-bought broth bolstered with onion and garlic. Cooked this way, the chicken flavored the broth and retained its juiciness and tender texture.

Every authentic recipe for tortilla soup calls for fresh epazote, a common Mexican herb that imparts a heady, distinctive flavor and fragrance to the broth. Unfortunately, while epazote is widely available in the American Southwest, it is virtually nonexistent in other parts of the country. Still, we managed to track some down for testing purposes. Its wild, pungent flavor is difficult to describe, but after careful tasting we decided that it most closely resembles fresh cilantro, mint, and oregano. Using a broth steeped with epazote as a control, we sampled broths made with each of these herbs. The winner was a pairing of strong, warm oregano with pungent cilantro. It was not identical to the flavor of epazote, but it scored highly for its intensity and complexity. We now had deeply flavored broth that, when stirred together with the tomato mixture, made for a soup that was starting to taste like the real thing.

Flour tortillas, whether fried or oven-baked, tasted fine on their own but quickly disintegrated in hot soup. That left us with corn tortillas. The classic preparation is frying, but cooking up two or three batches of corn tortilla strips took more time and attention than we wanted to muster. Tasters flatly rejected the notion of raw corn tortillas—a recommendation we found in more than one recipe—as they rapidly turned gummy and unpalatable when added to the hot soup. Corn tortillas require some sort of crisping. After much testing, we came across a technique in a low-fat cookbook that was both fast and easy: Lightly oiled tortilla strips are simply toasted in the oven. The result? Chips that are just as crisp, less greasy, and much less trouble to prepare than their fried cousins.

As for the garnishes, we worked through the list one ingredient at a time. Lime added sharp, fresh notes to an already complex bowl, as did cilantro leaves and minced jalapeño. Avocado was another no-brainer. Thick, tart Mexican crema (a tangy, cultured cream) is normally swirled into individual soup bowls. If it's unavailable, sour cream is a natural stand-in. Crumbled cotija or queso fresco cheese is great but may be hard to find. If you can't find either, use a mild cheddar cheese or Monterey Jack, which melts nicely.

DICING AN AVOCADO

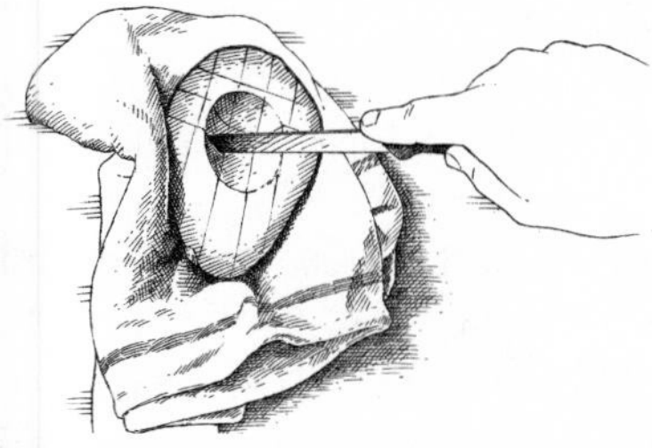

1. Use a dish towel to hold the avocado steady. Make ½-inch cross-hatch incisions in the flesh of each avocado half with a dinner knife.

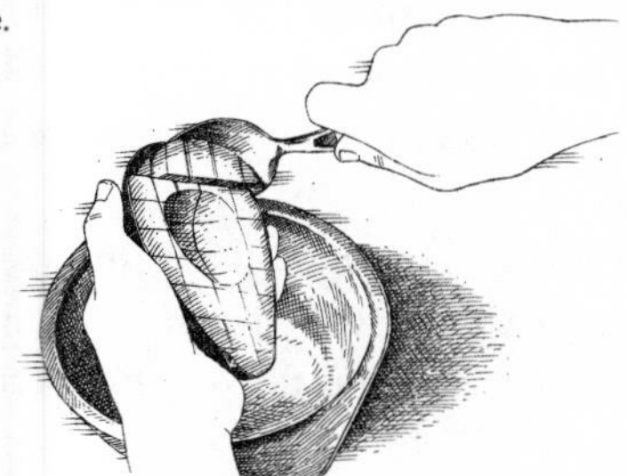

2. Using a spoon inserted between the skin and the flesh, separate the diced flesh from the skin and gently scoop out the avocado cubes.

Tortilla Soup

SERVES 4 TO 6

This recipe is great made with store-bought low-sodium chicken broth, but feel free to make your own homemade stock (see page 43). If you desire a soup with mild spiciness, trim the ribs and seeds from the jalapeño (or omit the jalapeño altogether) and use the minimum amount of chipotle in adobo sauce. Look for thin corn tortillas—we found that thicker tortillas baked up chewy rather than crisp.

1½ pounds bone-in, skin-on split chicken breasts (about 2 split breasts), trimmed
Salt and ground black pepper
¼ cup vegetable oil

- 2 quarts low-sodium chicken broth (see note)
- 1 very large white onion (about 1 pound), root end trimmed, quartered, and peeled
- 4 medium garlic cloves, peeled
- 2 large sprigs fresh epazote, or 8 to 10 sprigs fresh cilantro plus 1 sprig fresh oregano
- 8 (6-inch) corn tortillas, cut into ½-inch-wide strips (see note)
- 2 medium tomatoes, cored and quartered
- ½ medium jalapeño chile, seeded if desired (see note)
- 1½–4 teaspoons minced chipotle chile in adobo sauce (see note)

GARNISHES

- 1 Haas avocado, diced fine
- 1 lime, cut into wedges
- 8 ounces cotija cheese, crumbled, or Monterey Jack cheese, diced fine
- Cilantro leaves
- Minced jalapeño chile
- Mexican crema or sour cream

1. Pat the chicken dry with paper towels and season with salt and pepper. Heat 2 tablespoons of the oil in a large Dutch oven over medium-high heat until just smoking. Brown the chicken on both sides, 5 to 8 minutes per side, reducing the heat if the pan begins to scorch. Transfer the chicken to a plate and set aside.

2. Stir in the broth, 2 of the onion quarters, 2 of the garlic cloves, the epazote (or cilantro and oregano), and ½ teaspoon salt, scraping up any browned bits. Add the chicken and bring to a simmer. Reduce the heat to low, cover, and cook until the thickest part of the breast registers 160 to 165 degrees on an instant-read thermometer, 10 to 15 minutes.

3. Transfer the chicken to a cutting board. Pour the broth through a fine-mesh strainer, discarding the solids; set the broth aside. (Do not wash the pot.) When the chicken is cool enough to handle, remove the meat from the bones and shred into bite-sized pieces (see the illustration on page 10); discard the skin and bones. (Up to this point, the broth and chicken can be cooled and refrigerated in separate airtight containers for up to 24 hours.)

4. Meanwhile, adjust an oven rack to the middle position and heat the oven to 425 degrees. Toss the tortilla strips with 1 tablespoon of the oil, spread them out over a rimmed baking sheet, and bake, stirring occasionally, until crisp and dark golden, about 14 minutes. Season with salt and transfer to a paper towel–lined plate.

5. Puree the tomatoes, 2 remaining onion quarters, 2 remaining garlic cloves, the jalapeño, 1½ teaspoons of the chipotle, and ⅛ teaspoon salt in a food processor until smooth. Heat the remaining tablespoon oil in the now-empty Dutch oven over high heat until shimmering. Add the pureed mixture and cook, stirring frequently, until the mixture has darkened in color, about 10 minutes. Stir in the strained broth and bring to a boil, then reduce the heat to low and simmer to blend the flavors, about 15 minutes.

6. Return the shredded chicken to the soup and continue to cook until heated through, about 2 minutes. Season with salt, pepper, and the remaining chipotle to taste. Distribute the tortilla strips among individual bowls, ladle the soup over the top, and serve, passing the garnishes separately.

MULLIGATAWNY

MULLIGATAWNY IS A PUREED VEGETABLE soup that originated in India during the British Raj. The soup is mildly spicy but not hot. There should be a faint sweetness as well, usually from coconut, and it is often served garnished with chicken or lamb. (For this book, of course, we used chicken.) At its best, mulligatawny is silky and elegant, with potent yet balanced spices and aromatics. But very often this soup falls far short of expectations, with poorly incorporated, raw-tasting spices and an overly thin base. We wanted to reclaim this soup's once velvety texture and deep, complex flavor.

We decided to start with the question of the liquid base, and we quickly found out that chicken broth was the ideal base for the competing spices and vegetables. Water made a soup that was not quite as rich as the versions made with chicken broth, but it was still acceptable.

Curry powder, a blend of spices sold in this

country, is a central ingredient in most mulligatawny soups. We wondered whether to use a prepackaged blend or make our own. After experimenting with homemade curry powders and spice blends, we found that the end product was not worth the effort of toasting and grinding spices. If we had homemade curry powder on hand we would use it, but commercial curry powder is just fine with some modifications. After some tinkering, we were happy with a blend of curry powder and garam masala, another Indian spice blend containing cinnamon, cardamom, cumin, coriander, black pepper, and, sometimes, cloves. We found it best to sauté the spices with the aromatics in order to bloom their flavor.

We focused next on the aromatics: garlic, ginger, and coconut. After testing various amounts of garlic and ginger, we noted that we liked equal amounts of both. Coconut gives mulligatawny its distinctive sweet flavor. Some recipes asked for coconut milk, others for fresh coconut meat, and still others added dried coconut, both sweetened and unsweetened. The coconut milk gave the soup a silky consistency, but the coconut flavor tended to dominate the dish. Fresh coconut was not flavorful enough, and in any case was much too troublesome to prepare. Dried coconut was the best option, adding enough flavor to the soup without taking it over. Unsweetened shredded coconut worked fine, but sweetened shredded coconut gave us the balance that we were looking for. We cooked the coconut with the onions and spices to allow it to toast and develop its flavor before the rest of the ingredients were added.

With our aromatics and spices under control, it was time to test the vegetables and legumes, which would give the soup flavor, bulk, and color when pureed. We tested onions, carrots, celery, cauliflower, spinach, peas, and lentils. Not surprisingly, we found that onions were a must in the soup. Carrots added color and sweetness, and the celery provided a cool flavor that contrasted nicely with the warm spices. Cauliflower was rejected for the cabbage-like flavor it gave to the soup. Spinach and peas did little to enhance the soup's flavor, and they imparted an undesirable color when pureed.

Several recipes suggested using pureed rice or lentils to thicken the soup, and while tasters didn't oppose their flavor (in fact, they liked the additional flavor of the lentils), they didn't like the thick, porridge-like texture that each produced when pureed. After a bit more testing, we found that sprinkling a little flour over the sautéed aromatics (to make a roux) gave the soup a thickened yet velvety consistency—silky and substantial but

INGREDIENTS: Supermarket Chicken Broth

Which chicken broth should you reach for when you haven't got time for homemade? We recommend choosing a mass-produced, lower-sodium brand and checking the label for evidence of mirepoix ingredients (carrots, celery, onion, and herbs). In a tasting of all the widely available brands, Swanson Certified Organic was a clear winner. And if you don't mind adding water, Better Than Bouillon Chicken Base came in a very close second and was the favorite of several tasters. Swanson's less-expensive Natural Goodness Chicken Broth was just about as good as the winner, though some tasters thought it tasted "overly roasted."

THE BEST CHICKEN BROTHS

SWANSON CERTIFIED ORGANIC FREE RANGE CHICKEN BROTH
Swanson's newest broth won tasters over with "very chickeny, straightforward, and honest flavors," a hearty aroma, and restrained "hints of roastiness."

BETTER THAN BOUILLON CHICKEN BASE
We're not ready to switch to a concentrated base for all our broth needs (you have to add water), but the 18-month refrigerator shelf life means it's a good replacement for dehydrated bouillon.

SWANSON NATURAL GOODNESS CHICKEN BROTH
Swanson's standard low-sodium broth was full of chicken flavor, but several tasters noted an out-of-place, overly roasted flavor.

not heavy. Although a few sources said that pureeing the soup was optional, we think that the broth of mulligatawny must be smooth and refined—the only solids that should be allowed to float upon this sophisticated soup are purposeful garnishes, such as lentils, chicken, and fresh herbs.

Returning to the idea of adding lentils to the soup—leaving them whole rather than pureeing them as a thickener—we experimented with adding them after the soup was pureed, and tested several lentil varieties. Chana dal, a smaller cousin to chickpeas, also known as yellow split peas, imparted an overly earthy, vegetal flavor that didn't meld with the flavor of the soup—and took over an hour to cook. Red lentils all but disintegrated in the soup, leaving a grainy texture. We finally settled on standard brown lentils (or the small green French lentils know as lentils du puy), which held their shape when cooked and readily absorbed the surrounding flavors. A finishing dollop of yogurt and shower of cilantro is all that is needed to finish this deeply flavorful and elegant soup. Traditionally, mulligatawny is served over basmati rice, although this version can certainly stand on its own as either a main course or an appetizer.

Mulligatawny

SERVES 4 TO 6

This recipe is great made with store-bought low-sodium chicken broth, but feel free to make your own homemade stock (see page 43). French green lentils (lentils du puy) will also work well here; the cooking time will remain the same. Do not use red lentils, because they turn very soft when cooked and will disintegrate in the soup. Garam masala is a flavorful spice blend popular in Indian cooking; it is available in the spice aisle of most supermarkets.

- 1½ pounds bone-in, skin-on split chicken breasts (about 2 split breasts), trimmed
- Salt and ground black pepper
- 2 tablespoons vegetable oil
- 2 medium onions, minced
- ½ cup sweetened shredded or flaked coconut
- 1 tablespoon garam masala (see note)
- 1 tablespoon curry powder
- 4 medium garlic cloves, minced or pressed through a garlic press (about 4 teaspoons)
- 4 teaspoons minced or grated fresh ginger
- 1 teaspoon tomato paste
- ¼ cup unbleached all-purpose flour
- 7 cups low-sodium chicken broth (see note)

INGREDIENTS: Garam Masala

Though there are countless variations of garam masala, the warm flavors (*garam* means "warm" or "hot" and *masala* means "spice blend") dominating this Indian spice blend are consistent: coriander, black pepper, dried chiles, cardamom, and cinnamon are staples, while nutmeg, cloves, mace, fennel, and cumin frequently turn up as supporting players. Garam masala is commonly sprinkled on finished dishes, but we find this method results in harsh flavors. Instead, we prefer it bloomed in oil or butter at the outset of a dish.

Concocting this complex spice blend at home can add a great deal of time to recipe preparation—not to mention how it can crowd your pantry with jars of seldom-used ingredients, running up a hefty shopping tab in the process. In search of a good-tasting commercial garam masala, we tested a few of the top brands.

Tasters disliked the bitter and overwhelming flavors of Spice Islands and Zamouri garam masalas. Spice Barn garam masala was dubbed one-dimensional. Penzeys Punjabi Style garam masala combined the basic coriander-cardamom-cinnamon-pepper-chile combination with a few exotic additions that tasters found warm, floral, and tangy.

But tasters' favorite was McCormick Gourmet Collection garam masala for its ability to both assimilate into dishes and also round out their acidic and sweet notes. Tasters also liked the slightly pungent hits of coriander and the subtle warmth of cardamom, cinnamon, and cloves. Widely available in supermarkets, McCormick won praise from tasters for adding a mellow, well-balanced aroma to most dishes.

THE BEST GARAM MASALA

Sticking with mostly core garam masala ingredients won this supermarket brand top ratings with tasters.

- 2 carrots, peeled and chopped medium
- 1 celery rib, chopped medium
- ½ cup brown lentils, rinsed and picked over (see note)
- 2 tablespoons minced fresh cilantro leaves
- Plain yogurt (for serving)

1. Pat the chicken dry with paper towels and season with salt and pepper. Heat the oil in a large Dutch oven over medium-high heat until just smoking. Brown the chicken on both sides, 5 to 8 minutes per side, reducing the heat if the pan begins to scorch. Transfer the chicken to a plate and set aside.

2. Add the onions, coconut, garam masala, and curry powder to the fat left in the pot and cook over medium-low heat until the onions are softened, 5 to 7 minutes. Stir in the garlic, ginger, and tomato paste and cook until fragrant, about 30 seconds. Stir in the flour until evenly combined, about 1 minute. Gradually whisk in the chicken broth, scraping up any browned bits. Add the carrots, celery, and chicken breasts and bring to a simmer. Reduce the heat to low, cover, and cook until the thickest part of the breast registers 160 to 165 degrees on an instant-read thermometer, 10 to 15 minutes.

3. Transfer the chicken to a cutting board. When the chicken is cool enough to handle, remove the meat from the bones and shred into bite-sized pieces (see the illustration on page 10); discard the skin and bones. Puree the soup in a blender in batches until smooth, then return to a clean pot. Stir in the lentils and bring to a simmer over medium-high heat. Cover, reduce the heat to medium-low, and cook until the lentils are just tender, about 40 minutes. (Up to this point, the soup and chicken can be cooled and refrigerated in separate airtight containers for up to 24 hours. Return the soup to a simmer before proceeding with the recipe.)

4. Return the shredded chicken to the soup and continue to cook until heated through, about 2 minutes. Season with salt and pepper to taste. Ladle the soup into individual bowls, sprinkle with the cilantro, and dollop with yogurt before serving.

Italian Wedding Soup

ITALIAN WEDDING SOUP HAS AN INTERESTING history that actually has nothing to do with matrimony. The recipe is based on a centuries-old southern Italian meat and vegetable soup called *minestra maritata;* the "marriage" (maritata) is of flavors and ingredients—in this case, meatballs and greens. Our goal was to develop a recipe for this classic soup—with a flavorful broth, tender meatballs (chicken, of course), hearty pasta, and earthy greens—that was balanced and harmonious (just like a good marriage) in flavors and textures.

Wedding soup is traditionally made with a slow-simmered homemade chicken broth (*brodo* in Italian). Since it takes so much time to make the meatballs, we decided to streamline our recipe by leaving out the broth-making step and using store-bought low-sodium broth instead. Our first step was to doctor the broth. Cooking garlic and red pepper flakes in extra-virgin olive oil before adding the broth was the obvious way to build better flavor. And while some recipes suggest cooking the meatballs separately and then adding them to the soup, we found that poaching the raw meatballs directly in the broth added more depth and richness to the broth, and it saved time (and dirty dishes).

Our next focus was the meatballs. Usually the meat is ground beef or a combination of pork and beef. For our recipe we wanted to use ground chicken, and we found that we needed to boost this leaner meat with seasonings like garlic, parsley, oregano, salt, and pepper. To keep the meatballs tender, we mashed bread with milk and mixed in this paste with the chicken. We also found it best to add a little egg yolk (not a whole egg as some sources suggested) to help bind the filling ingredients and add richness. While cheese isn't completely necessary in these meatballs, tasters felt that the addition enriched the ground chicken. Because these meatballs are meant to be eaten in just one bite from a spoon, we made them quite small—just 1 teaspoon of the mixture to make 1-inch-round meatballs.

Next, the greens proved to be a challenge. Most

recipes call for stirring chopped spinach or escarole into the soup just before serving. But our tasters found these greens too bland and too delicate (they dissolved in the soup). After testing several different types of hearty greens, we settled on earthy-flavored chopped kale. It added great flavor and texture and was hearty enough to withstand the hot broth.

Our last area of investigation was pasta. Our tests showed that smaller shapes were best in this soup. Larger shapes crowded out the other ingredients and soaked up too much liquid. Ditalini (small tubes), tubettini (very small tubes), or orzo (rice-shaped pasta) were all options. Of these, tasters preferred the slender pieces of orzo, which easily fit on a soup spoon. As with our other chicken soup recipes, we found that the orzo gained flavor when cooked in the soup—plus, we had one less pot to clean.

Lastly, for a complete, authentic experience, it is important to garnish the soup with grated Parmesan and a splash of fruity extra-virgin olive oil just before serving; the cheese's nuttiness and the oil's fruitiness bring out and heighten the flavors in the soup.

Italian Wedding Soup

SERVES 6 TO 8

Serve with extra Parmesan cheese and a drizzle of extra-virgin olive oil. This recipe is great made with store-bought low-sodium chicken broth, but feel free to make your own homemade stock (see page 43). For more information on buying ground chicken, see page 3.

MEATBALLS

- 2 slices high-quality white sandwich bread, torn into small pieces
- ⅓ cup whole milk
- 1 pound ground chicken
- 1 ounce Parmesan cheese, grated (about ½ cup)
- 3 tablespoons minced fresh parsley leaves
- 3 medium garlic cloves, minced or pressed through a garlic press (about 1 tablespoon)
- 1 large egg yolk
- ¾ teaspoon salt
- ½ teaspoon ground black pepper
- ½ teaspoon dried oregano

SOUP

- 1 tablespoon extra-virgin olive oil, plus more for serving
- 2 medium garlic cloves, minced or pressed through a garlic press (about 2 teaspoons)
- ¼ teaspoon red pepper flakes
- 3 quarts low-sodium chicken broth (see note)
- 1 pound kale (1 small bunch), stemmed and leaves chopped (about 12 cups)
- 1 cup orzo
- 3 tablespoons minced fresh parsley leaves
- Salt and ground black pepper
- Freshly grated Parmesan cheese (for serving)

1. For the meatballs: In a large bowl, mash the bread and milk together to form a smooth paste. Add the ground chicken, Parmesan, parsley, garlic, egg yolk, salt, pepper, and oregano to the mashed bread and mix until uniform. Shape the mixture into 1-inch balls (1 teaspoon per meatball) and arrange on a rimmed baking sheet. Cover with plastic wrap and refrigerate until firm, at least 30 minutes. (The meatballs can be made up to 24 hours in advance.)

2. For the soup: Heat the oil, garlic, and red pepper flakes in a large Dutch oven over medium-high heat until fragrant, about 1 minute. Add the broth and kale and bring to a simmer; cook until the kale is tender, 10 to 15 minutes.

3. Stir in the meatballs and orzo and simmer until the meatballs are cooked through and the orzo is tender, about 10 minutes.

4. Stir in the parsley and season with salt and pepper to taste. Ladle into individual bowls and serve, passing extra-virgin olive oil and Parmesan separately.

HANDLING KALE

Hold each leaf at the base of the stem over a bowl filled with water and use a sharp knife to slash the leafy portion from either side of the thick stem. Discard the stems and then wash and dry the leaves. Chop as directed.

3 CHILIS, STEWS, AND BRAISES

Chilis, Stews, and Braises

CHILIS, STEWS, AND BRAISES MADE WITH chicken are great because they cook relatively quickly in comparison to other meat stews, making them a terrific choice for a weeknight meal. And, for the most part, the ingredients go into one pot to cook, and then the finished dish can be served from the same pot. With little-to-no last-minute preparation, these recipes are also ideal for entertaining.

This chapter includes a variety of chilis, stews, and braises—from an All-American Chicken Chili made with ground chicken instead of beef, and a lighter White Chicken Chili made with shredded chicken, to an array of braises and curries. For most of these dishes, with the curries and the ground meat chili being the exceptions, we found that bone-in, skin-on chicken parts were the best choice, as they allowed us to build the most flavor into the dish while offering the home cook a choice of dark or light meat.

For the ground chicken chili, we found that to create the perfect balance of flavor, while at the same time keeping some of the meat in larger pieces, it was important to add half of the meat to the cooked vegetables and the other half after the chili had simmered for an hour. When adding the second half of the meat to the chili, we packed the meat into a ball and then broke off pieces to add to the simmering chili. This prevented the meat from cooking in long strands (see the illustration on page 63).

For most of the dishes in this chapter, we found that the chicken absolutely had to be browned first—otherwise the flavors were lackluster. Deglazing the pan after browning and scraping up all the browned bits left behind gives stews and braises a depth of flavor that just cannot be infused any other way. That said, there were several recipes in this chapter that were obvious exceptions: the Indian and Thai curries and chicken mole were so intensely flavored that browning the chicken simply did not matter.

To determine whether stews and braises cook best on the stovetop or in the oven, we tried both, simmering a basic braise on the stovetop over low heat and in a moderate oven. Both methods worked fine, but simmering our chilis, braises, and stews right on the stovetop worked best—we were able to easily monitor the heat and adjust the burner to maintain a gentle simmer.

A final note about our choice of liquids for use in chicken stews. If you have homemade chicken broth on hand, you can certainly use it in these recipes. However, we have found that the differences between chicken stews or braises made with homemade chicken broth and those made with store-bought chicken broth are minimal, so the latter is a fine option (see page 55 for more information on low-sodium chicken broth).

All-American Chicken Chili

CHICKEN CHILI IS A GREAT ALTERNATIVE TO beef chili. Unfortunately, many chicken chili recipes yield a pot of raw-tasting spices, dry meat, and under-flavored sauce. Our goal was to develop a no-fuss chicken chili that would rival its beef counterpart—rich, meaty, and thick, with just the right amount of spices.

Most recipes for basic chicken chili begin by sautéing onions and garlic. Tasters liked red bell peppers added to these aromatics but rejected other options, including green bell peppers, celery, and carrots. After this first step, things became less clear. The most pressing concern was the spices (how much and what kind). Also to be considered were the cooking liquid (what kind, if any) and the proportions of meat, tomatoes, and beans.

Addressing the spices first, we started with a basic formula of 2 pounds ground chicken, 4 tablespoons chili powder, 2 teaspoons ground cumin, and a little dried oregano and red pepper flakes. While many recipes add the spices to the pot after the chicken has been browned, we found that the ground spices added in this manner were harsh and bitter. We preferred to add the spices with the aromatics—they developed their flavors fully when they had direct contact with the hot cooking oil.

To find the perfect balance of spices and heat level, we used chili powder—typically 80 percent ground dried red chiles, with the rest a mix of garlic powder, onion powder, oregano, ground cumin, and salt—and supplemented it with more cumin and oregano, and tossed in some cayenne for heat. We also tried other spices, such as cinnamon, allspice, and coriander, but only the coriander was welcomed as part of our working recipe—cinnamon and allspice were both out of place.

Two pounds of ground chicken seemed ideal when paired with two 15-ounce cans of beans. The meat remained moist and juicy, yet tasters complained that the chili was visually unappealing. Since the meat is stirred into the pot with the cooked vegetables and then simmered for over an hour, it breaks down dramatically—looking more like a fine meat sauce, like Bolognese, than thick meat chili. We tried adding the meat at a later stage, which helped visually, but the chili then lacked a cohesive flavor. By adding half of the meat to the cooked vegetables and the other half after the chili had simmered for an hour, we were able to create the perfect balance of flavor while at the same time keeping some of the meat in larger pieces. We did find that, when adding the second pound of meat to the chili, it is important to pack the meat into a ball and then break off pieces to add to the simmering chili. This prevents the meat from cooking in long strands (see the illustration at right).

For the liquid component, we tried beer, water, chicken broth, wine, and no liquid at all except for that in the tomatoes—the last resulting in the best-tasting chili by far. The added liquids seemed to dilute the other flavors. Since we knew that tomatoes were definitely going into our chili, we first added two small (14.5-ounce) cans of diced tomatoes. Not only was this clearly not enough, the tomatoes were also too chunky, and they were floating in a thin sauce. We then tried two 28-ounce cans of diced tomatoes, pureeing the contents of one can to reduce the chunkiness and thicken the sauce. The chunkiness was reduced, but the sauce was still watery. Next we tried one can of tomato puree and one can of diced tomatoes, and tasters unanimously preferred the thicker consistency of this combination.

Our attention now turned to the beans. Two 15-ounce cans proved to be the right amount, and tasters liked dark red kidney beans or black beans because both keep their shape better than light red kidney beans, the other common choice. As for when to add the beans, many chili recipes do so at the end of cooking, with the goal of letting them heat through without causing them to fall apart. We found that this method makes for tasteless beans floating in an extremely flavorful chili. We prefer to add the beans with the tomatoes. We found that the more time the beans spent in the pot, the better they tasted.

We tried cooking the chili with the lid on, with the lid off, and with the lid on in the beginning and off at the end. The chili cooked with the lid on was too soupy; that cooked with the lid off too dense. Keeping the lid on for half of the cooking time and then removing it was ideal—the consistency was rich but not too thick. One hour and 40 minutes of gentle simmering was sufficient to meld the flavors. Our chili, basically complete, required little more than lime wedges, passed separately at the table, which both brightened the flavor of the chili and accentuated the heat of the spices.

INGREDIENTS: Chili Powder

While there are numerous applications for chili powder, its most common use is in chili. Considering that most chili recipes rely so heavily on chili powder (ours uses a whopping ¼ cup), we thought it was necessary to gather up as many brands as possible to find the one that made the best chili. To focus on the flavor of the chili powder, we made a bare-bones version of our chili and rated each chili powder for aroma, depth of flavor, and level of spiciness. Tasters concluded that Spice Islands Chili Powder was the clear winner. This well-known supermarket brand was noted by one taster as having "a big flavor that stands out among the others."

THE BEST CHILI POWDER

Spice Islands Chili Powder is our favorite chili powder, with its perfect balance of chili flavor and spiciness.

All-American Chicken Chili

SERVES 6 TO 8

Serve with lime wedges, diced fresh tomatoes, diced avocado, sliced scallions, chopped red onion, minced cilantro, sour cream, and/or shredded Monterey Jack or cheddar cheese. If you like, you can substitute black beans for the kidney beans. For more information on buying ground chicken, see page 3.

- 2 tablespoons vegetable oil
- 2 medium onions, minced
- 1 red bell pepper, stemmed, seeded, and cut into ½-inch pieces
- 6 medium garlic cloves, minced or pressed through a garlic press (about 2 tablespoons)
- ¼ cup chili powder
- 1 tablespoon ground cumin
- 2 teaspoons ground coriander
- 1 teaspoon dried oregano
- ½ teaspoon red pepper flakes
- ¼ teaspoon cayenne pepper
- Salt
- 2 pounds ground chicken
- 2 (15-ounce) cans dark red kidney beans, drained and rinsed (see note)
- 1 (28-ounce) can diced tomatoes
- 1 (28-ounce) can tomato puree
- Water, as needed

1. Heat the oil in a large Dutch oven over medium heat until shimmering. Add the onions, bell pepper, garlic, chili powder, cumin, coriander, oregano, pepper flakes, cayenne, and 1 teaspoon salt and cook, stirring often, until the vegetables are softened, about 10 minutes.

2. Increase the heat to medium-high. Stir in half of the chicken, about ½ pound at a time, and cook while breaking up the chunks with a wooden spoon until no longer pink, about 3 minutes per ½ pound.

3. Stir in the beans, tomatoes, and tomato puree and bring to a boil. Cover and simmer over low heat, stirring occasionally, for 1 hour. Following the illustration below, pack the remaining chicken together into a ball, then pinch off teaspoon-sized pieces and stir them into the chili.

4. Uncover and continue to simmer, stirring occasionally, until the chicken is tender and the chili is dark, rich, and thickened slightly, about 40 minutes. (If the chili begins to stick to the bottom of the pot, stir in ½ cup water and continue to simmer.) Season with salt to taste. Serve. (The chili can be cooled completely and refrigerated in an airtight container for up to 2 days or frozen for up to 1 month. If frozen, thaw completely in the refrigerator. Reheat over medium-low heat, adding water as needed to adjust the consistency.)

GETTING THE RIGHT TEXTURE FROM GROUND CHICKEN

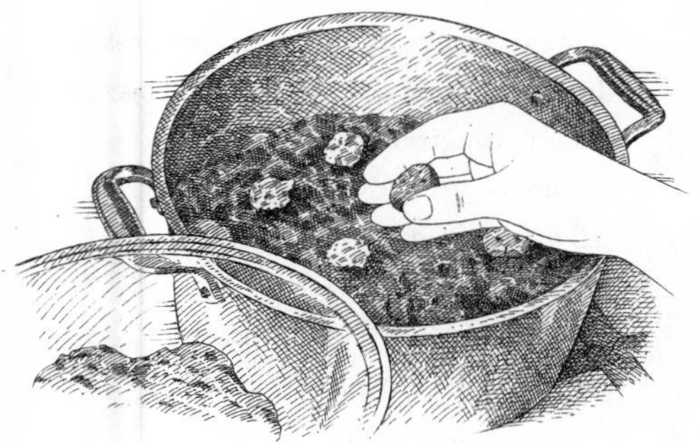

Pack the meat into a ball, then pinch off teaspoon-sized pieces of meat and stir them into the chili. This technique makes the ground chicken appear crumbled, rather than stringy.

White Chicken Chili

A LIGHTER COUNTERPART TO TRADITIONAL ground meat and bean chili, white chicken chili contains a chicken and white bean base simmered in chicken broth and, depending on the recipe, a wide range of ingredients, including diced tomatoes, green salsa, pickled chiles, and chili powder. White chili is a fairly recent creation, which is good news because it allowed us free rein in somewhat new territory, without any risk of breaking the rules. We wanted to develop the ultimate recipe for white chicken chili.

White chicken chili is typically made with either diced or ground chicken. We started with ground chicken. Tasters were not sold—they wanted more substance and a meatier texture. We then prepared a batch with diced chicken breast that we simmered in chicken broth. This was certainly an improvement, but the cubed meat was reminiscent of the tasteless, dry meat floating in canned chicken soup. Instead, we browned bone-in, skin-on chicken breasts, simmered them in chicken broth just until they were cooked through, and then shredded the meat and returned it to the mix at the end. Tasters raved about the flavor the meat contributed to the chili, and the shredded meat was hearty and moist. But obstacles still remained.

The first few batches we made contained the requisite onions and garlic, but also red bell peppers, tomato paste, diced tomatoes, and chili powder—ingredients found in several of the recipes we researched. The flavor these ingredients contributed was welcomed, but some of our tasters rejected all things red from the start, under the premise that white chili should have nothing in common with red chili. This left us with no flavor base.

We thought about adding green bell peppers but agreed that we wanted something that packed a little more punch. We settled on a combination of poblano, Anaheim, and jalapeño chiles. The dark blackish-green poblanos and the long green Anaheims provided sweetness and depth, while the jalapeños imparted richness and heat. To save ourselves from having to dice lots of onions and chiles, we pulsed them in the food processor until chunky.

Sautéing the onions and chiles before simmering them in the chili contributed an excellent green-chile flavor, but tasters complained that the broth was too thin. We decided to remove a portion of the cooked chiles and puree them with an equal amount of beans and chicken broth. The chiles and beans that were pureed not only added body to the broth, they also melded with the other ingredients and intensified the flavors of the chili. At the same time, the chiles that remained in the chili and the whole beans that were added imparted a nice contrast in texture.

The backbone was in place, but we still needed to iron out the details of seasonings. We knew that we would need to add some spices at the beginning of the cooking process in order to build flavor, yet the chili would also benefit from some bright, fresh flavors added just before serving. Using a generous hand with ground cumin and ground coriander produced a mellow yet complex effect on the chili, while scallions, cilantro, oregano, and lime juice, along with a little raw minced jalapeño for heat, provided the perfect finish.

This white chili pleased even the skeptics and self-proclaimed chili aficionados in the test kitchen. Some still refused to categorize it as "chili," preferring to refer to it as a chicken stew, but they gobbled it up nevertheless.

White Chicken Chili

SERVES 6 TO 8

For more heat, include the jalapeño seeds and ribs when mincing. If Anaheim chiles cannot be found, add an additional poblano and jalapeño to the chili. Serve with sour cream, tortilla chips, and lime wedges.

- 3 pounds bone-in, skin-on split chicken breasts (about 4 split breasts), trimmed
- Salt and ground black pepper
- 2 tablespoons vegetable oil, plus more as needed
- 3 poblano chiles, seeds and ribs removed, chiles chopped coarse
- 3 Anaheim chiles, seeds and ribs removed, chiles chopped coarse (see note)
- 2 jalapeño chiles, seeds and ribs removed, chiles chopped coarse (see note)
- 2 medium onions, chopped coarse
- 6 medium garlic cloves, minced or pressed through a garlic press (about 2 tablespoons)
- 1 tablespoon ground cumin
- 1½ teaspoons ground coriander
- 2 (15-ounce) cans cannellini beans, drained and rinsed
- 4 cups low-sodium chicken broth
- ¼ cup minced fresh cilantro leaves
- 4 scallions, sliced thin
- 3 tablespoons juice from 3 limes
- 1 tablespoon minced fresh oregano leaves
- 1 jalapeño chile, seeds and ribs removed, chile minced

EASIER CITRUS PRESSING

A citrus press can be a handy tool, but using one to press the juice from several lemons or limes can be a pain. Try cutting the fruit into quarters rather than halves. Juicing a quarter is not only easier than juicing a half, but it also yields more juice.

1. Pat the chicken dry with paper towels and season with salt and pepper. Heat the oil in a large Dutch oven over medium-high heat until just smoking. Brown the chicken on both sides, 5 to 8 minutes per side, reducing the heat if the pan begins to scorch. Transfer the chicken to a plate and set aside.

2. While the chicken is browning, pulse the chiles (except the minced jalapeño) and the onions in 2 batches in a food processor to the consistency of chunky salsa, 10 to 12 one-second pulses, stopping to scrape down the sides of the workbowl as needed.

3. Pour off all but 1 tablespoon fat from the pot. (Add additional oil to equal 1 tablespoon, if needed.) Add the processed chile-onion mixture, garlic, cumin, coriander, and 1 teaspoon salt and cook over medium heat, stirring occasionally, until the vegetables are softened, about 10 minutes. Remove the pot from the heat and transfer 1 cup of the chile mixture to the food processor.

4. Process the chile mixture with 1 cup of the beans and 1 cup of the broth until smooth, about 20 seconds. Add the chile-bean mixture and the remaining 3 cups broth to the pot and stir, scraping up any browned bits.

5. Nestle the chicken, along with any accumulated juices, into the pot and bring to a simmer. Cover, turn the heat to medium-low, and simmer until the thickest part of the breast registers 160 to 165 degrees on an instant-read thermometer, about 20 minutes.

6. Transfer the chicken to a cutting board. Stir the remaining beans into the chili and cook over medium heat until the beans are heated through and the chili has thickened slightly, about 10 minutes. When the chicken is cool enough to handle, remove the meat from the bones and shred into bite-sized pieces (see the illustrations on page 10); discard the skin and bones. Return the shredded chicken to the chili and continue to cook until heated through, about 2 minutes. (Up to this point, the chili can be cooled completely and refrigerated in an airtight container for up to 2 days or frozen for up to 1 month. If frozen, thaw completely in the refrigerator. Reheat over medium-low heat, adding water as needed to adjust the consistency.)

7. Stir the cilantro, scallions, lime juice, oregano, and minced jalapeño into the chili. Season with salt and pepper to taste. Serve.

Chicken and Dumplings

DESPITE AMERICA'S ONGOING LOVE AFFAIR with comfort food, chicken and dumplings, unlike its baked cousin, chicken pot pie, hasn't made a comeback. After making several dozen batches of dumplings, we think we know why.

As tricky as it can be to make pie pastry or biscuits for pot pie, dumplings are far more temperamental. With pot pie, dry oven heat and a rich sauce camouflage minor flaws in biscuits or pastry, whereas moist, steamy heat highlights gummy or leaden dumplings. What's more, pot pie, with its meat, vegetables, bread, and sauce, is a complete meal. Chicken and dumplings is, well, chicken and dumplings. A few hearty vegetables would make it a complete meal—just the selling point to attract today's busy cook.

Our mission in developing a recipe for chicken and dumplings was twofold. First, we wanted a recipe that was as foolproof and complete as that for a good chicken pot pie. Second, we wanted a dumpling that was light yet substantial, tender yet durable. But which style of dumpling to explore?

In different parts of the country, dumplings come in different shapes. They may be rolled thin and cut into strips, rolled thick and stamped out like biscuits, or simply dropped into the stew in rounds. Most flour-based dumplings are made of flour, salt, and one or more of the following: butter, eggs, milk, and baking powder. Depending on the ingredient list, dumplings are usually mixed in one of three ways. The most common is a biscuit or pastry style in which cold butter is cut into the dry ingredients, then cold milk and/or eggs are stirred in just until mixed. Other dumplings are made by simply mixing wet into dry ingredients. Many of the eggier dumplings are made pâte-à-choux style (a type of French pastry used to make cream puffs), adding flour to hot water and butter, then whisking in eggs one at a time.

We spent a full day making batch after batch of dumplings in some combination of the ingredients and three mixing methods outlined above. By the end of the day, after sampling dumplings that ranged from tough and chewy to fragile and disintegrated, we had a method for producing light and fluffy dumplings that held up beautifully during cooking. To make these dumplings, we cut butter into a mix of flour, baking powder, and salt. Then, instead of adding cold liquid to the dry ingredients, we added hot liquid to the flour-butter mixture. This type of dumpling is a success because hot liquids, unlike cold ones, expand and set the starch in the flour, keeping it from absorbing too much of the cooking liquid. We took the process a step further—instead of cutting the butter into the flour, we simply melted it and mixed it into the dry ingredients with the warm liquid. These were the firm yet tender dumplings we were looking for, and they were easy to make.

Although we were pretty sure that dumplings made with vegetable shortening wouldn't taste as good as those made with butter, we had high hopes for the ones made with chicken fat. After a side-by-side test of dumplings made with butter, shortening, and chicken fat, we selected those made with chicken fat (butter was a close second). The shortening dumpling tasted flat, like cooked flour and chicken broth, while the ones made with chicken fat tasted chickeny and rich. Liquids were simple. Dumplings made with chicken broth, much like those made with chicken fat, tasted too similar to the stewing liquid. Those made with water were dull. Because buttermilk tends to separate and even curdle when heated, buttermilk dumplings felt wrong. Whole milk dumplings were tender, with a rich flavor—our first choice.

With the dough resolved, we tested the formula by shaping it. After fussing with a rolling pin, biscuit cutters, and the like, we decided that the simpler route of dropping spoonfuls of dough into the stew actually yielded better-textured dumplings.

We now turned our energies to updating the chicken part of the dish. To make the dish clean and sleek, we left the chicken pieces on the bone, cut the vegetables into long, thin strips, and thickened the stewing liquid only slightly. As we ate the finished product, we realized that we needed a knife (to cut the chicken off the bone), a fork (to eat the vegetables, dumplings, and meat), and a spoon (for the liquid). Although we wanted the dish to look beautiful, it had to be eater-friendly. This meant that the chicken had to come off the bone, the vegetables needed to be cut a little smaller, and the liquid would have to be reduced and thickened. As the dish evolved, we worked toward making it not only a one-dish, but also a one-utensil, meal.

We browned bone-in chicken pieces (the meat stayed more moist and tender when cooked on the bone), and then sautéed the vegetables in butter before adding flour to make a roux (paste) to thicken the liquid, which we added next. A combination of chicken broth, milk, and dry sherry did the trick, producing a deeply flavored, slightly creamy stew. We then poached the browned chicken in the liquid, shredded the meat, and returned it to the stew, along with peas and parsley, to make the dish beautiful before adding the dumplings.

Not only was our final dish eye-catching and palate-pleasing, it was simple to make. Best of all, we could eat it with a fork.

Old-Fashioned Chicken and Dumplings

SERVES 6 TO 8

The breasts and thighs/drumsticks do not cook in the same amount of time; if using both, note that the breast pieces are added partway through the cooking time. Don't use low-fat or nonfat milk for this dish. After pouring the fat from the pan in step 2, you should have 3 tablespoons for making the dumplings; if there is not enough fat, supplement, as needed, with butter. Also, make the dumpling dough only when you're ready to top the stew with the dumplings.

STEW

- 4 pounds bone-in, skin-on chicken pieces (split breasts cut in half, drumsticks, and/or thighs), trimmed
- Salt and ground black pepper
- 2 tablespoons vegetable oil
- 4 tablespoons (½ stick) unsalted butter
- 4 carrots, peeled and sliced ¼ inch thick
- 2 celery ribs, sliced ¼ inch thick
- 1 medium onion, minced
- 6 tablespoons unbleached all-purpose flour
- 4½ cups low-sodium chicken broth
- ¼ cup whole milk
- ¼ cup dry sherry
- 1 teaspoon minced fresh thyme leaves or ½ teaspoon dried
- 2 bay leaves
- 1 cup frozen peas
- 3 tablespoons minced fresh parsley leaves

DUMPLINGS

- 2 cups (10 ounces) unbleached all-purpose flour
- 1 tablespoon baking powder
- 1 teaspoon salt
- 1 cup whole milk
- 3 tablespoons reserved chicken fat or unsalted butter

1. For the stew: Pat the chicken dry with paper towels and season with salt and pepper. Heat the oil in a large Dutch oven over medium-high heat until just smoking. Brown half of the chicken on both sides, 5 to 8 minutes per side, reducing the heat if the pan begins to scorch. Transfer the chicken to a plate, leaving the fat in the pot. Return the pot with the fat to medium-high heat and repeat with the remaining chicken; transfer the chicken to the plate.

2. Pour off any chicken fat and reserve. Add the butter, carrots, celery, onion, and ¼ teaspoon salt to the pot and cook over medium heat, stirring occasionally, until softened, 5 to 7 minutes. Stir in the flour and cook for 1 minute. Whisk in the broth, milk, sherry, thyme, and bay leaves, scraping up any browned bits.

3. Nestle the chicken, along with any accumulated juices, into the pot and bring to a simmer. Cover, turn the heat to medium-low, and simmer until the chicken is fully cooked and tender, about 20 minutes for the breasts (160 to 165 degrees on an instant-read thermometer) or 1 hour for the thighs and drumsticks (170 to 175 degrees on an instant-read thermometer). (If using both types of chicken, simmer the thighs and drumsticks for 40 minutes before adding the breasts.)

4. Transfer the chicken to a cutting board. When the chicken is cool enough to handle, remove the meat from the bones and shred into bite-sized pieces (see the illustrations on page 10); discard the skin and bones. Remove and discard the bay leaves. Skim as much fat as possible off the surface of the sauce. (Up to this point, the stew can be cooled completely and refrigerated in an airtight container for up to 24 hours. Reheat over medium-low heat.)

5. For the dumplings: Stir the flour, baking powder, and salt together in a large bowl. Microwave the milk and reserved chicken fat in a microwave-safe bowl until just warm (do not overheat), about 1 minute. Stir the warmed milk mixture into the flour mixture with a wooden spoon until incorporated and smooth.

6. Return the stew to a simmer, stir in the peas and parsley, and season with salt and pepper to taste. Following the illustrations on page 68, drop golf-ball-sized dumplings into the stew, leaving about ¼ inch of space around each dumpling (you should have about 18 dumplings). Reduce the heat to low, cover, and cook until the dumplings have doubled in size, 15 to 18 minutes. Serve.

VARIATION

Chicken and Dumplings with Leeks and Tarragon

Follow the recipe for Old-Fashioned Chicken and Dumplings, substituting 2 leeks, white and light green parts only, halved lengthwise, sliced 1-inch thick, and rinsed thoroughly (see the illustrations on page 45), for the carrots and celery, and minced fresh tarragon leaves for the parsley.

MAKING THE DUMPLINGS

1. Gather a golf-ball-sized portion of the dumpling batter onto a soup spoon, then push the dumpling into the stew using a second spoon.

2. Cover the stew with the dumplings, leaving about ¼ inch of space around each dumpling to allow room to expand. Cover the pot and cook for 15 to 18 minutes.

3. When fully cooked, the dumplings will have doubled in size.

Braised Chicken

WE'VE CERTAINLY MADE OUR SHARE OF braised chicken here in the test kitchen, from stovetop-only braises to braises that start on the stovetop and then cook long and slow in the oven. And we've also made some shortcut braises, jump-starting them in the microwave. But for this book, we were looking for a simple formula for a stovetop braise that could be varied to create a wide array of recipes—from classics like Chicken Provençal and Chicken Cacciatore to more imaginative and unusual ones.

Many braised chicken recipes start with a whole chicken, but we wanted our recipes to be a bit simpler, so we opted for quicker-cooking, more convenient chicken parts. We chose bone-in, skin-on parts—the bone keeps the meat moist, and the skin helps to contribute flavor to the sauce from the browning process.

Using chicken parts also allowed us to customize the dish depending on whether we wanted white meat, dark meat, or both. Not surprisingly, we found that the breasts cooked in a third of the time as the thighs and drumsticks, so we would have to stagger the cooking. Once the liquid was simmering and ready for the chicken, we added only the thighs and drumsticks and cooked them for 40 minutes. At that point we added the breast meat and cooked the entire dish for an additional 20 minutes. All the meat was perfectly cooked, and it was time to focus on the cooking liquid.

Although some braises use water as the liquid base, we found that chicken broth and some type of wine gave our dishes a nice acidity and depth of flavor. In general, we determined that 1½ cups of chicken broth and ½ cup of wine (the type depended on the flavor profile of a given dish) yielded the right balance of chickeny richness and bright flavors.

After browning the chicken and before poaching it in the broth and wine, we set it aside on a plate while we cooked the aromatics—the other ingredients important to a braised chicken dish—in the pan. In most cases, onions or leeks and garlic were all that were needed. Spices and herbs were also incorporated at this point, and while the type and amounts varied from recipe to recipe, bay leaves were a constant, adding a depth of flavor that isn't obvious but is missed when omitted from most recipes.

EQUIPMENT: Dutch Ovens

A good Dutch oven (variously called a stockpot, round oven, or casserole by manufacturers) is absolutely a kitchen essential. They are heavier and thicker than a real stockpot, allowing them to retain and conduct heat more effectively, and deeper than a skillet, so they can handle large cuts of meat and cooking liquid. Dutch ovens are the best choice for braises, pot roasts, stews, and chilis, as they can go on the stovetop to sear foods and then into the oven to finish with steady, slow cooking. Their tall sides also make them useful for deep-frying, and many cooks press Dutch ovens into service for jobs like boiling pasta. But with prices for these kitchen workhorses ranging from $40 on the low end to six times as much at the other end of the spectrum, we wondered if more money buys you a better pot. We rounded up nine Dutch ovens and brought them into the test kitchen to find out.

For our first test, we prepared a beef stew that starts on the stovetop and then moves to the oven. In each pan we browned cubes of beef in batches and observed whether the pan heated evenly and consistently without burning the drippings. After the long, slow cooking in the oven, we tasted the stew to see if the meat had become fork-tender and the broth had reduced to an intense flavor. Of all the tests we did, this was the most important, because it focused on the unique abilities of Dutch ovens. As expected, the pricey All-Clad and Le Creuset pots sailed through with flying colors. Surprisingly, so did a few of the others.

We noticed a few trends. Our favorite pots from All-Clad and Le Creuset measure 9¾ inches across, enabling them to brown 3½ pounds of beef in three batches, something narrower pots couldn't do—the narrowest one required five batches of browning, a serious flaw. A couple of the pots were also too light and browned the meat unevenly.

Next we tested heat transfer and retention by frying a pound of frozen French fries. The best pans retain heat well enough to prevent the temperature of the oil from dropping too precipitously when food is added. Those whose oil temperature dropped too much or took too long to recover produced soggy, greasy fries. An unexpected issue emerged during this test. Fries cooked in the cast iron pans tasted rusty. Cast iron is a great choice for a Dutch oven because it holds heat so well. But cast iron will react with many foods. Some manufacturers (such as Le Creuset, Tramontina, and Mario Batali) coat their cast iron with a layer of enamel to avoid this.

For our last test, we steamed a triple batch of white rice in each Dutch oven to see how they simmered on very low heat. All but one pot made fluffy rice with intact grains.

When all the smoke and steam and sizzling fry oil cleared, the most expensive pots came out on top. Other than price, it's hard to argue with the pots made by All-Clad and Le Creuset. (Some of our test cooks prefer the sturdiness of the latter, while others opt for the lighter, easier-to-manage All-Clad pot.)

Although we weren't surprised by our winners, we were shocked at their narrow margin of victory. The $40 Tramontina 6.5 quart Cast Iron Dutch Oven held its own and kept up with the winners in almost every test. While our test cooks are not ready to trade in their favorite Dutch ovens, the Tramontina is a real find for budget-minded cooks.

If you're willing to spend $100 on a Dutch oven, and you have the biceps to handle it, the Mario Batali pot is comparable in size to the Le Creuset and All-Clad pots and performs nearly as well. Yes, the browning wasn't perfect, but that seems like a minor quibble that most cooks would never notice. These are two other good choices, and both reasonably priced. Now that's good news.

THE BEST DUTCH OVENS

The All-Clad Stainless 8-quart Stockpot ($260) and the 7¼-quart Le Creuset Round French Oven ($230) are our top choices. (The All-Clad is the best choice for cooks who prefer a lighter pot.) For those looking for a less-expensive alternative, the Tramontina Cast Iron Dutch Oven ($40) and the Mario Batali Italian Essentials Pot by Copco ($100) are both solid choices and are our best buys.

ALL-CLAD STAINLESS

LE CREUSET ROUND FRENCH OVEN

TRAMONTINA CAST IRON DUTCH OVEN

MARIO BATALI ITALIAN ESSENTIALS POT BY COPCO

After sautéing the aromatics, we added the flour to thicken the cooking liquid to a proper sauce-like consistency. Once the broth and wine were added, we scraped the fond from the bottom of the pan. Then we placed the chicken back in the pan and covered it to finish cooking. (At this point, many recipes transfer the entire pot to the oven to finish cooking, but we found this extra step to be unnecessary.) When the chicken was cooked through, we transferred it to a serving platter and tented it with foil while we finished the sauce.

Some recipes required only the simple addition of fresh herbs and/or peas, while others benefited from the addition of heavy cream (Braised Chicken with Fennel, Leeks, and Prunes) or sour cream (Chicken Paprikash). Still others were more complex: Spanish-Style Braised Chicken with Almonds and Pine Nuts wasn't complete until hard-cooked eggs and a Spanish-style picada—a combination of ground almonds, pine nuts, garlic, parsley, and saffron—was stirred in to add unmistakable body and flavor to the sauce. Once the sauce returned to a simmer, we cooked it until thickened, which took just a few minutes, then poured it directly over the chicken.

We were pleased that we had developed the perfect formula for eight juicy, flavorful, and diversely flavored braised chicken dishes that are easy enough to make during the week yet special enough to serve to company.

Braised Chicken with White Wine and Herbs

SERVES 4 TO 6

If using both chicken breasts and thighs/drumsticks, we recommend cutting the breast pieces in half so that each serving can include both white and dark meat. The breasts and thighs/drumsticks do not cook at the same rate; if using both, note that the breast pieces are added partway through the cooking time. Serve with Easy Mashed Potatoes (page 138).

- **4 pounds bone-in, skin-on chicken pieces (split breasts cut in half, drumsticks, and/or thighs), trimmed**
- **Salt and ground black pepper**
- **2 tablespoons vegetable oil, plus more as needed**
- **1 medium onion, minced**
- **2 medium garlic cloves, minced or pressed through a garlic press (about 2 teaspoons)**
- **1 tablespoon unbleached all-purpose flour**
- **1½ cups low-sodium chicken broth**
- **½ cup white wine**
- **2 bay leaves**
- **1 tablespoon minced fresh thyme leaves or 1 teaspoon dried**
- **2 tablespoons minced fresh tarragon leaves**
- **2 tablespoons minced fresh parsley leaves**
- **2 teaspoons juice from 1 lemon**

1. Pat the chicken dry with paper towels and season with salt and pepper. Heat the oil in a large Dutch oven over medium-high heat until just smoking. Brown half of the chicken on both sides, 5 to 8 minutes per side, reducing the heat if the pan begins to scorch. Transfer the chicken to a plate, leaving the fat in the pot. Return the pot to medium-high heat and repeat with the remaining chicken; transfer the chicken to the plate.

2. Pour off all but 1 tablespoon of the fat from the pot. (Add additional oil to equal 1 tablespoon, if needed.) Add the onion and ¼ teaspoon salt to the pot and cook over medium heat, stirring occasionally, until softened, 5 to 7 minutes. Stir in the garlic and cook until fragrant, about 30 seconds. Stir in the flour and cook for 1 minute. Whisk in the broth, wine, bay leaves, and thyme, scraping up any browned bits.

3. Nestle the chicken, along with any accumulated juices, into the pot and bring to a simmer. Cover, turn the heat to medium-low, and simmer until the chicken is fully cooked and tender, about 20 minutes for the breasts (160 to 165 degrees on an instant-read thermometer) or 1 hour for the thighs and drumsticks (170 to 175 degrees on an instant-read thermometer). (If using both types of chicken, simmer the thighs and drumsticks for 40 minutes before adding the breasts.)

4. Transfer the chicken to a serving dish, tent loosely with foil, and let rest while finishing the sauce. Remove and discard the bay leaves. Skim as much fat as possible off the surface of the sauce and return to a simmer until the sauce has thickened slightly, 4 to 6 minutes. Off the heat, stir in the tarragon, parsley, and lemon juice and season with salt and pepper to taste. Pour the sauce over the chicken and serve.

Simple Polenta

SERVES 4 TO 6

Be sure to use medium- or coarse-ground cornmeal, or cornmeal labeled as "polenta"; finely ground cornmeal will cook up to a much different texture. If you do not have a heavy-bottomed saucepan, you may need to use a flame tamer to manage the heat (see below for information on making one with aluminum foil). It's easy to tell whether a flame tamer is necessary; if the polenta bubbles or sputters at all after the first 10 minutes, this means that the heat is too high and hence you do need one. Properly heated polenta will do little more than release wisps of steam. When stirring the polenta, scrape the sides and bottom of the pan to ensure even cooking.

- **6** **cups water**
- **Salt**
- **1½** **cups polenta, or evenly ground medium- or coarse-ground cornmeal**
- **1½** **ounces Parmesan cheese (¾ cup)**
- **3** **tablespoons unsalted butter, cut into large chunks**
- **Ground black pepper**

1. Bring the water to a boil in a heavy-bottomed 4-quart saucepan over medium-high heat. Once boiling, add 1½ teaspoons salt and pour the polenta from a measuring cup into the water in a very slow stream, all the while stirring in a circular motion with a wooden spoon, following the illustration above.

2. Reduce the heat to the lowest possible setting and cover. Cook, vigorously stirring the polenta once every 5 minutes, making sure to scrape clean the bottom and corners of the pot, until the polenta has lost its raw cornmeal taste and becomes soft and smooth, about 30 minutes. Stir in the Parmesan and butter, and season with salt and pepper to taste. Serve immediately.

MAKING POLENTA

When the water comes to a boil, add the salt, then pour the polenta from a measuring cup into the water in a very slow stream, all the while stirring in a circular motion with a wooden spoon to prevent clumping.

MAKING A FLAME TAMER

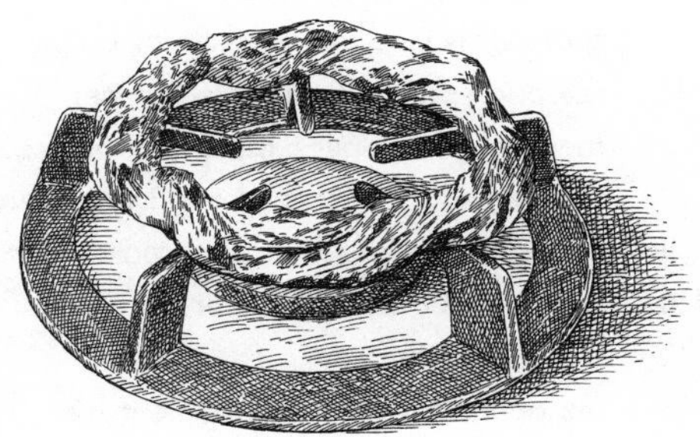

A flame tamer (or heat diffuser) is a metal disk that can be fitted over a burner (electric or gas) to reduce the heat transfer. (It costs less than $10 and is stocked at most kitchenware stores.) This device is especially useful when trying to keep a pot at the barest simmer. If you don't own a flame tamer, you can fashion one from aluminum foil. Take a long sheet of foil and shape it into a 1-inch-thick ring that will fit on your burner. Make sure that the ring is an even thickness so that a pot will rest flat on it. The foil ring achieves the same effect as a flame tamer by elevating the pot slightly above the flame or electric coil, allowing you to keep a pot of polenta at the merest simmer.

Braised Chicken with Leeks and Saffron

SERVES 4 TO 6

If using both chicken breasts and thighs/drumsticks, we recommend cutting the breast pieces in half so that each serving includes both white and dark meat. The breasts and thighs/drumsticks do not cook at the same rate; if using both, note that the breast pieces are added partway through the cooking time. Saffron gives this stew a yellow-orange hue and a rich, earthy flavor. Buy saffron threads (not powder) and crumble them yourself for the best flavor. Serve with Easy Mashed Potatoes (page 138) or Basic Pilaf-Style Rice (page 114).

- 4 pounds bone-in, skin-on chicken pieces (split breasts cut in half, drumsticks, and/or thighs), trimmed
- Salt and ground black pepper
- 2 tablespoons vegetable oil, plus more as needed
- 2 large leeks, white and light green parts only, halved lengthwise, sliced thin, and rinsed thoroughly (see the illustrations on page 45)
- ¼ teaspoon saffron threads (see note)
- 2 medium garlic cloves, minced or pressed through a garlic press (about 2 teaspoons)
- 1 tablespoon unbleached all-purpose flour
- 1½ cups low-sodium chicken broth
- ½ cup white wine
- 1½ teaspoons minced fresh thyme leaves or ½ teaspoon dried
- 2 bay leaves
- 2 teaspoons juice from 1 lemon
- ¼ cup minced fresh parsley leaves

1. Pat the chicken dry with paper towels and season with salt and pepper. Heat the oil in a large Dutch oven over medium-high heat until just smoking. Brown half of the chicken on both sides, 5 to 8 minutes per side, reducing the heat if the pan begins to scorch. Transfer the chicken to a plate, leaving the fat in the pot. Return the pot to medium-high heat and repeat with the remaining chicken; transfer the chicken to the plate.

2. Pour off all but 1 tablespoon fat from the pot. (Add additional oil to equal 1 tablespoon, if needed.) Add the leeks, saffron, and ¼ teaspoon salt to the pot and cook over medium heat, stirring occasionally, until the leeks are softened, 5 to 7 minutes. Stir in the garlic and cook until fragrant, about 30 seconds. Stir in the flour and cook for 1 minute. Whisk in the broth, wine, thyme, and bay leaves, scraping up any browned bits.

3. Nestle the chicken, along with any accumulated juices, into the pot and bring to a simmer. Cover, turn the heat to medium-low, and simmer until the chicken is fully cooked and tender, about 20 minutes for the breasts (160 to 165 degrees on an instant-read thermometer) or 1 hour for the thighs and drumsticks (170 to 175 degrees on an instant-read thermometer). (If using both types of chicken, simmer the thighs and drumsticks for 40 minutes before adding the breasts.)

4. Transfer the chicken to a serving dish, tent loosely with foil, and let rest while finishing the sauce. Remove and discard the bay leaves. Skim as much fat as possible off the surface of the sauce and return to a simmer until the sauce has thickened slightly, 4 to 6 minutes. Off the heat, stir in the lemon juice and season with salt and pepper to taste. Pour the sauce over the chicken, sprinkle with the parsley, and serve.

Braised Chicken with Fennel, Leeks, and Prunes

SERVES 4 TO 6

If using both chicken breasts and thighs/drumsticks, we recommend cutting the breast pieces in half so that each serving can include both white and dark meat. The breasts and thighs/drumsticks do not cook at the same rate; if using both, note that the breast pieces are added partway through the cooking time. While half a cup of brandy may seem like a lot for this recipe, we recommend using an inexpensive brand and not skimping on the amount—it provides just the right balance of flavors. Serve with buttered egg noodles or Basic Pilaf-Style Rice (page 114).

- 4 pounds bone-in, skin-on chicken pieces (split breasts cut in half, drumsticks, and/or thighs), trimmed
- Salt and ground black pepper
- 2 tablespoons vegetable oil, plus more as needed

- 1 large leek, white and light green parts only, halved lengthwise, sliced ¼ inch thick, and rinsed thoroughly
- 1 large fennel bulb (about 1 pound), trimmed of stalks, cored, and cut into ¼-inch-thick strips (see the illustrations on page 100)
- 2 medium garlic cloves, minced or pressed through a garlic press (about 2 teaspoons)
- 1 tablespoon unbleached all-purpose flour
- 1½ cups low-sodium chicken broth
- ½ cup brandy (see note)
- 2 bay leaves
- 1 cup heavy cream
- 1 cup pitted prunes, halved
- 2 tablespoons minced fresh tarragon leaves
- 2 tablespoons minced fresh parsley leaves
- 1 tablespoon juice from 1 lemon

1. Pat the chicken dry with paper towels and season with salt and pepper. Heat the oil in a large Dutch oven over medium-high heat until just smoking. Brown half of the chicken on both sides, 5 to 8 minutes per side, reducing the heat if the pan begins to scorch. Transfer the chicken to a plate, leaving the fat in the pot. Return the pot to medium-high heat and repeat with the remaining chicken; transfer the chicken to the plate.

2. Pour off all but 1 tablespoon fat from the pot. (Add additional oil to equal 1 tablespoon, if needed.) Add the leek, fennel, and ¼ teaspoon salt to the pot and cook over medium heat, stirring occasionally, until softened, 5 to 7 minutes. Stir in the garlic and cook until fragrant, about 30 seconds. Stir in the flour and cook for 1 minute. Whisk in the broth, brandy, and bay leaves, scraping up any browned bits.

3. Nestle the chicken, along with any accumulated juices, into the pot and bring to a simmer. Cover, turn the heat to medium-low, and simmer until the chicken is fully cooked and tender, about 20 minutes for the breasts (160 to 165 degrees on an instant-read thermometer) or 1 hour for the thighs and drumsticks (170 to 175 degrees on an instant-read thermometer). (If using both types of chicken, simmer the thighs and drumsticks for 40 minutes before adding the breasts.)

4. Transfer the chicken to a serving dish, tent loosely with foil, and let rest while finishing the sauce. Remove and discard the bay leaves. Skim as much fat as possible off the surface of the sauce and return to a simmer until the sauce has thickened slightly, 4 to 6 minutes. Off the heat, stir in the cream and prunes, cover, and let sit for 5 minutes. Stir in the tarragon, parsley, and lemon juice. Season with salt and pepper to taste. Pour the sauce over the chicken and serve.

Chicken Paprikash

SERVES 4 TO 6

If using both chicken breasts and thighs/drumsticks, we recommend cutting the breast pieces in half so that each serving can include both white and dark meat. The breasts and thighs/drumsticks do not cook at the same rate; if using both, note that the breast pieces are added partway through the cooking time. Be sure to add the sour cream just before serving, especially if making the dish in advance. Serve with buttered egg noodles, Basic Pilaf-Style Rice (page 114), or Easy Mashed Potatoes (page 138).

- 4 pounds bone-in, skin-on chicken pieces (split breasts cut in half, drumsticks, and/or thighs), trimmed
- Salt and ground black pepper
- 2 tablespoons vegetable oil, plus more as needed
- 1 medium onion, halved and sliced thin
- 1 red bell pepper, stemmed, seeded, and sliced into ¼-inch-wide strips
- 1 green bell pepper, stemmed, seeded, and sliced into ¼-inch-wide strips
- 3½ tablespoons sweet paprika
- 1 tablespoon unbleached all-purpose flour
- 1½ cups low-sodium chicken broth
- ½ cup dry white wine
- 1 (14.5-ounce) can diced tomatoes, drained
- ¼ teaspoon dried marjoram
- ⅓ cup sour cream
- 2 tablespoons minced fresh parsley leaves

1. Pat the chicken dry with paper towels and season with salt and pepper. Heat the oil in a large Dutch oven over medium-high heat until just smoking. Brown half of the chicken on both sides, 5 to 8 minutes per side, reducing the heat if the pan begins to scorch. Transfer the chicken to a

plate, leaving the fat in the pot. Return the pot to medium-high heat and repeat with the remaining chicken; transfer the chicken to the plate.

2. Pour off all but 1 tablespoon fat from the pot. (Add additional oil to equal 1 tablespoon, if needed.) Add the onion, bell peppers, and ¼ teaspoon salt to the pot and cook over medium heat, stirring occasionally, until softened, 8 to 10 minutes. Stir in 3 tablespoons of the paprika and the flour and cook for 1 minute. Stir in the broth, wine, tomatoes, and marjoram, scraping up any browned bits.

3. Nestle the chicken, along with any accumulated juices, into the pot and bring to a simmer. Cover, turn the heat to medium-low, and simmer until the chicken is fully cooked and tender, about 20 minutes for the breasts (160 to 165 degrees on an instant-read thermometer), or 1 hour for the thighs and drumsticks (170 to 175 degrees on an instant-read thermometer). (If using both types of chicken, simmer the thighs and drumsticks for 40 minutes before adding the breasts.)

4. Transfer the chicken to a serving dish, tent loosely with foil, and let rest while finishing the sauce. Skim as much fat as possible off the surface of the sauce and return to a simmer until the sauce has thickened slightly, 4 to 6 minutes. Off the heat, stir the remaining 1½ teaspoons paprika and ¼ cup of the sauce into the sour cream to temper, then stir the sour cream mixture into the pot. Season with salt and pepper to taste. Pour the sauce over the chicken, sprinkle with the parsley, and serve.

Chicken Provençal

SERVES 4 TO 6

If using both chicken breasts and thighs/drumsticks, we recommend cutting the breast pieces in half so that each serving can include both white and dark meat. The breasts and thighs/drumsticks do not cook at the same rate; if using both, note that the breast pieces are added partway through the cooking time. This dish is often served with rice or crusty bread, but Simple Polenta (page 71) is also a good accompaniment. Herbes de Provence, a blend of dried herbs such as rosemary, basil, marjoram, bay leaves, thyme, and lavender, is available in the spice aisle of well-stocked supermarkets or specialty stores.

- 4 pounds bone-in, skin-on chicken pieces (split breasts cut in half, drumsticks, and/or thighs), trimmed
- Salt and ground black pepper
- 2 tablespoons vegetable oil, plus more as needed
- 1 medium onion, minced
- 6 medium garlic cloves, minced or pressed through a garlic press (about 2 tablespoons)
- 2 tablespoons tomato paste
- 1 anchovy fillet, minced (about 1 teaspoon)
- ⅛ teaspoon cayenne pepper
- 1 tablespoon unbleached all-purpose flour
- 1½ cups low-sodium chicken broth
- ½ cup dry white wine
- 1 (14.5-ounce) can diced tomatoes, drained
- 1 tablespoon minced fresh thyme leaves
- 1 teaspoon minced fresh oregano leaves
- 1 teaspoon herbes de Provence (optional) (see note)
- 2 bay leaves
- 1½ teaspoons grated zest from 1 lemon
- ½ cup niçoise olives, pitted (see note) (see the illustration on page 101)
- 1 tablespoon minced fresh parsley leaves
- 1 tablespoon extra-virgin olive oil

1. Pat the chicken dry with paper towels and season with salt and pepper. Heat the oil in a large Dutch oven over medium-high heat until just smoking. Brown half of the chicken on both sides, 5 to 8 minutes per side, reducing the heat if the pan begins to scorch. Transfer the chicken to a plate, leaving the fat in the pot. Return the pot to medium-high heat and repeat with the remaining chicken; transfer the chicken to the plate.

2. Pour off all but 1 tablespoon fat from the pot. (Add additional oil to equal 1 tablespoon, if needed.) Add the onion and ¼ teaspoon salt to the pot and cook over medium heat, stirring occasionally, until softened, 5 to 7 minutes. Stir in the garlic, tomato paste, anchovy, and cayenne and cook until fragrant, about 30 seconds. Stir in the flour and cook for 1 minute. Whisk in the broth, wine, tomatoes, thyme, oregano, herbes de Provence (if using) and bay leaves, scraping up any browned bits.

3. Nestle the chicken, along with any accumulated juices, into the pot and bring to a simmer.

Cover, turn the heat to medium-low, and simmer until the chicken is fully cooked and tender, about 20 minutes for the breasts (160 to 165 degrees on an instant-read thermometer) or 1 hour for the thighs and drumsticks (170 to 175 degrees on an instant-read thermometer). (If using both types of chicken, simmer the thighs and drumsticks for 40 minutes before adding the breasts.)

4. Transfer the chicken to a serving dish, tent loosely with foil, and let rest while finishing the sauce. Remove and discard the bay leaves. Skim as much fat as possible off the surface of the sauce, stir in 1 teaspoon of the lemon zest, and return to a simmer until the sauce has thickened slightly, 4 to 6 minutes. Off the heat, stir in the olives, cover, and let sit for 5 minutes. Season with salt and pepper to taste. Combine the remaining ½ teaspoon lemon zest with the parsley. Pour the sauce over the chicken, sprinkle with the parsley mixture, drizzle with extra-virgin olive oil, and serve.

Chicken Cacciatore with Portobellos and Sage

SERVES 4 TO 6

If using both chicken breasts and thighs/drumsticks, we recommend cutting the breast pieces in half so that each serving can include both white and dark meat. The breasts and thighs/drumsticks do not cook at the same rate; if using both, note that the breast pieces are added partway through the cooking time. The addition of the Parmesan cheese rind is optional, but we highly recommend it for the robust, savory flavor it lends the dish. An equal amount of minced fresh rosemary leaves can be substituted for the sage. Serve with crusty bread or Simple Polenta (page 71).

- 4 pounds bone-in, skin-on chicken pieces (split breasts cut in half, drumsticks, and/or thighs), trimmed
- Salt and ground black pepper
- 2 tablespoons olive oil, plus more as needed
- 6 ounces (about 3 medium) portobello mushroom caps, wiped clean and cut into ¾-inch chunks
- 1 medium onion, minced
- 4 medium garlic cloves, minced or pressed through a garlic press (about 4 teaspoons)
- 1 tablespoon unbleached all-purpose flour
- 1½ cups low-sodium chicken broth
- ½ cup dry red wine
- 1 (14.5-ounce) can diced tomatoes, drained
- 2 teaspoons minced fresh thyme leaves or ½ teaspoon dried
- 2 bay leaves
- 1 Parmesan cheese rind, about 4 by 2 inches (optional) (see note)
- 2 teaspoons minced fresh sage leaves (see note)

1. Pat the chicken dry with paper towels and season with salt and pepper. Heat the oil in a large Dutch oven over medium-high heat until just smoking. Brown half of the chicken on both sides, 5 to 8 minutes per side, reducing the heat if the pan begins to scorch. Transfer the chicken to a plate, leaving the fat in the pot. Return the pot to medium-high heat and repeat with the remaining chicken; transfer the chicken to the plate.

2. Pour off all but 1 tablespoon fat from the pot. (Add additional oil to equal 1 tablespoon, if needed.) Add the mushrooms, onion, and ¼ teaspoon salt to the pot, cover, and cook over medium heat, stirring occasionally, until the mushrooms have released their liquid, 8 to 10 minutes. Stir in the garlic and cook until fragrant, about 30 seconds. Stir in the flour and cook for 1 minute. Whisk in the broth, wine, tomatoes, thyme, and bay leaves, scraping up any browned bits.

3. Nestle the Parmesan rind, if using, and chicken, along with any accumulated juices, into the pot and bring to a simmer. Cover, turn the heat to medium-low, and simmer until the chicken is fully cooked and tender, about 20 minutes for the breasts (160 to 165 degrees on an instant-read thermometer) or 1 hour for the thighs and drumsticks (170 to 175 degrees on an instant-read thermometer). (If using both types of chicken, simmer the thighs and drumsticks for 40 minutes before adding the breasts.)

4. Transfer the chicken to a serving dish, tent loosely with foil, and let rest while finishing the sauce. Remove and discard the bay leaves and cheese rind. Skim as much fat as possible off the surface of the sauce and return to a simmer until the sauce has thickened slightly, 4 to 6 minutes. Stir in the sage and season with salt and pepper to taste. Pour the sauce over the chicken and serve.

VARIATION

Chicken Cacciatore with White Wine and Tarragon

Follow the recipe for Chicken Cacciatore with Portobellos and Sage, substituting 3 large shallots, minced (¾ cup), for the onion, 10 ounces white mushrooms, wiped clean and halved, for the portobellos, dry white wine for the red wine, and tarragon for the sage.

Spanish-Style Braised Chicken with Almonds and Pine Nuts

SERVES 4 TO 6

If using both chicken breasts and thighs/drumsticks, we recommend cutting the breast pieces in half so that each serving can include both white and dark meat. The breasts and thighs/drumsticks do not cook at the same rate; if using both, note that the breast pieces are added partway through the cooking time. Be sure to choose a sherry labeled "fino," which means it's dry. The picada, a mixture of ground nuts, garlic, parsley, and saffron, thickens the sauce, so this recipe does not use flour. It is easiest to grind the picada into a paste in the food processor or with a mortar and pestle, but it can also be chopped by hand. Basic Pilaf-Style Rice (page 114) makes a good accompaniment to this dish.

PICADA

- 2 tablespoons chopped almonds
- 2 tablespoons chopped pine nuts
- 2 medium garlic cloves, minced or pressed through a garlic press (about 2 teaspoons)
- 1 tablespoon minced fresh parsley leaves
- ⅛ teaspoon saffron threads
- 1 hard-cooked egg, minced (see page 35)

CHICKEN AND SAUCE

- 4 pounds bone-in, skin-on chicken pieces (split breasts cut in half, drumsticks, and/or thighs), trimmed
- Salt and ground black pepper
- 2 tablespoons olive oil, plus more as needed
- 1 medium onion, minced
- 1½ cups low-sodium chicken broth
- ½ cup dry sherry
- 1 (14.5-ounce) can diced tomatoes, drained
- 2 bay leaves
- Pinch ground cinnamon

1. FOR THE PICADA: Process the nuts, garlic, parsley, and saffron in a food processor until paste-like, 12 to 15 seconds (see note). Transfer to a small bowl, stir in the egg, and set aside.

2. FOR THE CHICKEN AND SAUCE: Pat the chicken dry with paper towels and season with salt and pepper. Heat the oil in a large Dutch oven over medium-high heat until just smoking. Brown half of the chicken on both sides, 5 to 8 minutes per side, reducing the heat if the pan begins to scorch. Transfer the chicken to a plate, leaving the fat in the pot. Return the pot to medium-high heat and repeat with the remaining chicken; transfer the chicken to the plate.

3. Pour off all but 1 tablespoon fat from the pot. (Add additional oil to equal 1 tablespoon, if needed.) Add the onion and ¼ teaspoon salt to the pot and cook over medium heat until softened, 5 to 7 minutes. Stir in the broth, sherry, tomatoes, bay leaves, and cinnamon, scraping up any browned bits.

4. Nestle the chicken, along with any accumulated juices, into the pot and bring to a simmer. Cover, turn the heat to medium-low, and simmer until the chicken is fully cooked and tender, about 20 minutes for the breasts (160 to 165 degrees on an instant-read thermometer) or 1 hour for the thighs and drumsticks (170 to 175 degrees on an instant-read thermometer). (If using both types of chicken, simmer the thighs and drumsticks for 40 minutes before adding the breasts.)

5. Transfer the chicken to a serving dish, tent loosely with foil, and let rest while finishing the sauce. Remove and discard the bay leaves. Skim as much fat as possible off the surface of the sauce and return to a simmer until the sauce has thickened slightly, 4 to 6 minutes. Stir the picada into the sauce and return to a simmer for 4 minutes longer. Pour the sauce over the chicken and serve.

Chicken Tagine

TAGINES ARE A NORTH AFRICAN SPECIALTY—exotically spiced, assertively flavored stews slow-cooked in earthenware vessels of the same name. They can include all manner of meats, vegetables, and fruit, though our hands-down favorite combines chicken with richly flavored figs and fragrant honey.

While we love tagine, it's not a dish we ever thought was suited for American home-cooking. Why? The few traditional recipes we had seen required time-consuming, labor-intensive cooking methods, a special pot (the tagine), and hard-to-find ingredients. We're usually game for a day in the kitchen or a hunt for exotica, but isn't tagine, at its most elemental level, just stew?

A little research proved that we weren't the first to take a stab at making tagine more accessible. While most of the recipes we tried lacked the depth of an authentic tagine, they did hold promise, proving that a Western cooking method (braising in a Dutch oven) was a serviceable substitution for stewing for hours in a tagine. We also discovered that the flavors we associated with Moroccan cooking weren't necessarily "exotic"—they were a strategic blending of ingredients we already had in our cupboard.

EQUIPMENT: Tagines

Tagines (the cooking vessel, not the stew) have lately enjoyed a fashionable comeback in cookware catalogs and food magazines. A shallower take on the Dutch oven, a tagine has a distinctive conical lid that makes for a dramatic presentation at the dinner table. According to tradition, the conical shape helps cooking performance as well: As steam rises during cooking, it condenses in the tip of the relatively cool lid (it's farther from the heat source than are most lids) and drips back into the stew, conserving water in the process. Less steam loss means you can start off with less liquid and thus end up with more concentrated flavors. Or so the story goes.

To put this theory to the test, we brought equal amounts of water to a simmer in three tagines—a traditional terra-cotta model ($34) and modern versions from All-Clad ($199) and Le Creuset ($119.99)—put the lids on, and let the water "cook" over low heat. We included our favorite Dutch ovens (also All-Clad and Le Creuset; see page 69 for more information) for comparison. After one hour, we measured the water left in each of the pots, and it was clear that the tagine's conical shape was not such an advantage after all. The big losers—literally—were the All-Clad Dutch oven and the traditional terra-cotta tagine, which lost 16 percent and 30 percent of their water, respectively. (By contrast, the others lost only 8 to 9 percent.) More important than the shape of the pot were the lid's weight and fit: the leaky All-Clad Dutch oven had the lightest lid, while the base and lid of the handmade terra-cotta tagine simply didn't fit together as precisely as their machine-made counterparts.

What does all this loss mean when it's more than water cooking? Not much, said our tasters, after sampling five batches of chicken tagine. Although the amount of liquid left behind in the stews varied, that variance translated to little discernible flavor difference. If you're a stickler for tradition, try to choose a tagine with a heavy, tight-fitting lid or be ready to add more liquid if the sauce begins to dry out during cooking.

THE BEST TAGINES

TRADITIONAL
The handmade lid of this traditional terra-cotta tagine ($34) let steam leak out, but it made a decent tagine, isn't very expensive, and looks good on the table.

TOP TAGINE
All-Clad's tagine ($199) made a great Moroccan braise, but with such limited use it's hard to say if it's worth the hefty price tag.

A FINE OPTION
A Dutch oven produces a tasty tagine—and its usefulness doesn't stop there.

Almost all of the recipes we collected specified a whole chicken, broken into pieces, and we soon found out why. Batches made entirely with white meat lacked the depth and character of those made with a blend of dark and white. But when we cooked the white and dark meat in the same way—simmered partially submerged in broth—the white meat turned dry and stringy.

Noting that the dark meat—drumsticks and thighs—takes roughly one hour of simmering time to become tender, we found that the breasts (cut in half for easier serving) took only 20 minutes. Giving the dark meat a 40-minute head start in the pot took care of the different cooking times and ensured that all of the chicken was perfectly cooked and ready at the same time.

Some recipes called for rubbing the chicken with lemon and salt and letting the meat marinate before cooking; others employed salt alone or salt blended with spices. We found that adding spices at this point resulted in a muddy-flavored broth.

Some carrots, a large sliced onion, and a few minced garlic cloves rounded out the basic flavors of the stew, and we finally felt ready to tackle the defining ingredients: spices, figs, and honey. Many recipes called for a spice blend called ras el-hanout, which translates loosely as "top of the shop" and may contain upward of 30 spices. We experimented with a broad range of spices until we landed on a blend that was short on ingredients but long on flavor. Cumin and ginger lent depth, cinnamon brought warmth that tempered a little cayenne heat, and coriander boosted the stew's lemon flavor. Paprika added sweetness but, perhaps more important, colored the broth a deep, attractive red. Thoroughly blooming the spices in hot oil brought out the full depth of their flavors.

Finding the right fig proved harder than we anticipated. Sweet, fresh, juicy figs were the obvious choice for the stew, but they are seasonal and thus a rarity at our local markets. Other options included dried figs, and, after tasting several varieties in the tagine, we concluded that Turkish figs were our favorite type. But when we added the dried figs to the stew too soon, they lost some of their deep flavor and turned mushy. Stirring in the figs just a few minutes before serving proved a better approach, as they retained their flavor and softened only slightly.

The lemon flavor in authentic tagines comes from preserved lemon, a long-cured Moroccan condiment that's hard to find outside of specialty stores. "Quick" preserved lemons can be produced at home in a few days, but we wanted to keep our recipe as simple as possible. Part tart citrus, part pickled brine, traditional preserved lemon has a unique flavor that's tough to imitate. So we chose not to try; instead, we aimed for a rich citrus backnote in the dish. We added a few broad ribbons of lemon zest along with the onions, and the high heat coaxed out the zest's oils and mellowed them. Adding a lemon's worth of juice just before serving reinforced the bright flavor.

For the honey, we found that adding it with the broth balanced things out. Chopped cilantro leaves freshened the flavors of the stew, but we felt it still lacked a certain spark. A last-minute addition of raw garlic, finely chopped lemon zest, and a spoonful of honey seemed to clinch it, as the sharpness and sweetness brought out the best in each of the stew's components.

Chicken Tagine with Dried Figs and Honey

SERVES 4 TO 6

Use a vegetable peeler to remove wide strips of zest from the lemon before juicing it (see the illustration at left); be sure to trim away the bitter-tasting white pith from the zest before using. The breasts and thighs/drumsticks do not cook at the same rate; if using both, note that the breast pieces are added partway through the cooking time. Serve with Perfect Couscous (page 80). Most markets carry three types of dried figs: Turkish, Calimyrna (a California-grown variety of Turkish Smyrna figs), and Mission. After trying each, we most preferred the softer, silkier texture of the Turkish or its close cousin, Calimyrna.

- 5 medium garlic cloves, minced or pressed through a garlic press (about 5 teaspoons)
- 1¼ teaspoons sweet paprika
- ½ teaspoon ground cumin
- ¼ teaspoon ground ginger
- ¼ teaspoon ground coriander

- ¼ teaspoon ground cinnamon
- ⅛–¼ teaspoon cayenne pepper
- 3 (2-inch-long) strips lemon zest from 1 to 2 lemons (see note)
- 2 tablespoons honey
- 4 pounds bone-in, skin-on chicken pieces (split breasts cut in half, drumsticks, and/or thighs), trimmed
- Salt and ground black pepper
- 2 tablespoons olive oil, plus more as needed
- 1 large onion, halved and sliced ¼ inch thick
- 2 medium carrots, peeled and cut crosswise into ½-inch-thick coins, very large pieces cut into half-moons (about 2 cups)
- 2 cups low-sodium chicken broth
- 1 cup dried Turkish figs, stemmed and quartered (see note)
- 2 tablespoons minced fresh cilantro leaves
- 3 tablespoons juice from 1 to 2 lemons

1. Combine 4 teaspoons of the garlic, the paprika, cumin, ginger, coriander, cinnamon, and cayenne together in a small bowl; set aside. Mince 1 strip of the lemon zest and mix with the remaining teaspoon of minced garlic and 1 tablespoon of the honey in a separate small bowl; set aside.

2. Pat the chicken dry with paper towels and season with salt and pepper. Heat the oil in a large Dutch oven over medium-high heat until just smoking. Brown half of the chicken on both sides, 5 to 8 minutes per side, reducing the heat if the pan begins to scorch. Transfer the chicken to a plate, leaving the fat in the pot. Return the pot to medium-high heat and repeat with the remaining chicken; transfer the chicken to the plate.

3. Pour off all but 1 tablespoon fat from the pot. (Add additional oil to equal 1 tablespoon, if needed.) Add the onion, the remaining 2 lemon zest strips, and ¼ teaspoon salt to the pot and cook over medium heat, stirring occasionally, until softened, 5 to 7 minutes. Stir in the garlic-spice mixture and cook until fragrant, about 30 seconds. Stir in the carrots, broth, and the remaining 1 tablespoon honey, scraping up any browned bits.

4. Nestle the chicken, along with any accumulated juices, into the pot and bring to a simmer. Cover, turn the heat to medium-low, and simmer until the chicken is fully cooked and tender, about 20 minutes for the breasts (160 to 165 degrees on an instant-read thermometer) or 1 hour for the thighs and drumsticks (170 to 175 degrees on an instant-read thermometer). (If using both types of chicken, simmer the thighs and drumsticks for 40 minutes before adding the breasts.)

5. Transfer the chicken to a serving dish, tent loosely with foil, and let rest while finishing the sauce. Skim as much fat as possible off the surface of the sauce, add the figs, and return to a simmer until the sauce has thickened slightly and the carrots are tender, 4 to 6 minutes. Stir in the garlic/lemon-zest/honey mixture, cilantro, and lemon juice. Season with salt and pepper to taste. Pour the sauce over the chicken and serve.

VARIATIONS

Chicken Tagine with Saffron and Mint

Follow the recipe for Chicken Tagine with Dried Figs and Honey, substituting ¼ teaspoon saffron threads, crumbled, for the cumin, ginger, coriander, cinnamon, and cayenne pepper, and orange zest for the lemon zest. Omit the honey. Substitute ½ cup Moroccan oil-cured olives, pitted, for the figs, mint for the cilantro, and ⅓ cup orange juice for the lemon juice.

Chicken Tagine with Dates and Yogurt

Follow the recipe for Chicken Tagine with Dried Figs and Honey, substituting pitted dates, halved, for the dried figs and ½ cup plain whole milk yogurt for the lemon juice. Omit the honey.

REMOVING LARGE STRIPS OF CITRUS ZEST

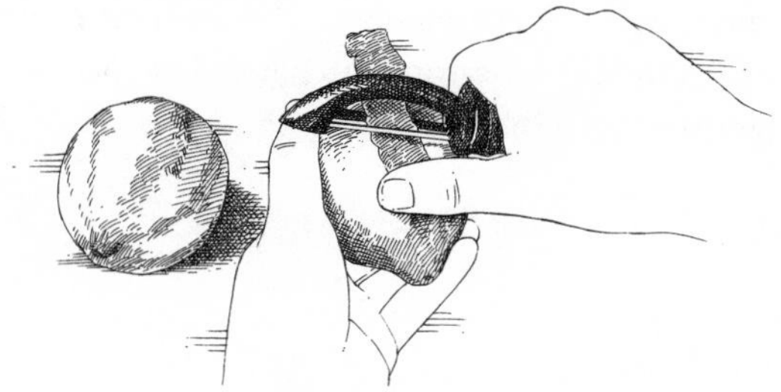

Run a vegetable peeler from pole to pole to remove long, wide strips of zest.

Perfect Couscous

SERVES 4 TO 6

For the fluffiest texture, use a large fork to fluff the grains; a spoon or spatula can mush its light texture. Specialty markets may carry couscous of varying sizes (such as large pearl Israeli-style couscous), but stick to the basic fine-grained variety, as the other sizes require different cooking methods. The simple flavors of this couscous pair well with a wide variety of poultry dishes, including Chicken Tagine (pages 78–79).

- 4 tablespoons (½ stick) unsalted butter
- 2 cups couscous (see note)
- 1 small onion, minced
- Salt
- 2 cups water
- 1¾ cups low-sodium chicken broth
- 1½ teaspoons juice from 1 lemon
- Ground black pepper

1. Melt 2 tablespoons of the butter in a large skillet over medium-high heat. Add the couscous and cook, stirring frequently, until some of the grains are just beginning to brown, about 3 minutes. Transfer the couscous to a large heatproof bowl.

2. Add the remaining 2 tablespoons butter, the onion, and ¾ teaspoon salt to the skillet and cook, stirring occasionally, until softened, 5 to 7 minutes. Stir in the water and broth and bring to a boil.

3. Pour the boiling liquid over the toasted couscous, cover tightly with plastic wrap, and let sit until the couscous is tender, about 12 minutes. Remove the plastic wrap, fluff the grains with a fork (see note), and gently stir in the lemon juice. Season with salt and pepper to taste and serve immediately.

Red-Cooked Chicken

RED-COOKED CHICKEN—PIECES OF TENDER chicken gently simmered in dark soy sauce, rice wine, ginger, scallions, and star anise until stained a deep mahogany—is as dramatic as it is delicious. A soothing dish akin to comfort food, red-cooked chicken is also often referred to as a "rice-sending dish" because the sauce is said to stimulate the appetite for rice.

Red cooking is a Chinese cooking technique that is also called Chinese stewing, red stewing, or red braising and is linked to Shanghai and other parts of eastern China that are known for the premium quality of their soy sauce and rice wine. We were lucky enough to stumble across this dish at our local Chinese restaurant and knew we wanted it in our repertoire of recipes. So with some recipes in hand, we headed to the test kitchen to try to replicate red-cooked chicken.

We've braised a lot of chicken in the test kitchen, and whether it contains wine, broth, or soy sauce, there are some similarities. All braises start by browning the chicken to yield a fond that enriches the braising liquid, then aromatics are added, followed by the braising liquid. Finally, it all simmers together until the meat is fall-apart tender. The tricky part for us was that we were unfamiliar with using dark soy sauce—the defining ingredient in red-cooked dishes—as part of the braise. Different than the soy sauce we see in supermarkets, dark soy sauce is a darker, slightly thicker soy sauce that is aged longer and contains added molasses to give it its distinctive appearance and slightly bitter flavor. Our inexperience showed in the earliest versions, which are now referred to as "the red-cooked clunkers." But the memory of the restaurant version propelled us back into the test kitchen to get it right.

As with any braise, this dish begins with the meat. We tried using a whole bird cut into manageable pieces, but as with our other braises, we found the extra work unnecessary and ultimately decided on chicken pieces. Dark meat is the most forgiving part of the bird when braising, as it's difficult to overcook, but white meat also works well in this braise as long as it's removed from the pot when it reaches 160 degrees (otherwise it dries out).

Our next, and most challenging, focus was the sauce. Once the chicken was browned, we added our sauce ingredients—equal amounts of dark soy sauce and chicken broth formed the base of the sauce. Chinese rice cooking wine or dry sherry (we found that either one works well in this dish) added a little acid, and a generous 3 tablespoons of sesame oil rounded out the flavors. Unfortunately, the resulting sauce was thinner and more bitter than we wanted. Simply decreasing the chicken broth from ½ cup to ⅓ cup helped remedy that problem, but not enough. With the slightly bitter quality of the dark soy sauce, the flavor of the sauce was still not quite right—we would need something to counter the bitterness. Sugar was our most likely savior, and, after trying granulated, light brown, and dark brown, we found that 3 tablespoons of light brown sugar added enough rich sweetness to bring this sauce back into balance.

Next, we turned our attention to aromatics. Ginger and garlic are typically used in recipes for red-cooked dishes, and a generous 2 tablespoons of each was perfect. Spices traditional to the flavor of this dish are star anise and five-spice powder. We found that three pieces of star anise added a delicate licorice flavor to the sauce that didn't overpower, while the five-spice powder made the sauce a bit gritty. Instead, we singled out one of the spices in five-spice powder—Sichuan peppercorns, adding just 1 teaspoon to the mix for its alluring heat.

With our recipe for red-cooked chicken near completion, we headed back into the kitchen for one last test. In our early research we had come across a few recipes that included hard-cooked eggs alongside the chicken. Although tasters weren't initially sold on the idea, just one test changed their minds. The eggs, which are hard-cooked first, cooled, and then peeled, are added to the braise alongside the browned chicken. In the finished dish, the outsides of the eggs are stained a deep mahogany, yet the interiors remain snowy white and bright yellow. But it was the combination of the rich, earthy eggs alongside the moist, meaty chicken that had everyone sold. This simple extra step turned this Chinese classic into a test kitchen favorite.

Red-Cooked Chicken

SERVES 4 TO 6

Dark soy sauce, available at Asian markets, gives this dish its characteristic red color and deep, fruity flavor; you can substitute regular soy sauce, but the color will not be very dark, and the flavor will be blander. Sichuan peppercorns are available at Asian markets. If using both chicken breasts and thighs/drumsticks, we recommend cutting the breast pieces in half so that each serving can include both white and dark meat. The breasts and thighs/drumsticks do not cook at the same rate; if using both, note that the breast pieces are added partway through the cooking time. Serve with Simple White Rice (page 386).

- 4 pounds bone-in, skin-on chicken pieces (split breasts cut in half, drumsticks, and/or thighs), trimmed
- 2 tablespoons vegetable oil, plus more as needed
- 6 medium garlic cloves, minced or pressed through a garlic press (about 2 tablespoons)
- 2 tablespoons minced or grated fresh ginger
- 1 teaspoon Sichuan peppercorns (see note)
- 3 star anise
- ½ cup dark soy sauce (see note)
- ⅓ cup low-sodium chicken broth
- ¼ cup Chinese rice cooking wine or dry sherry
- 3 tablespoons toasted sesame oil
- 3 tablespoons light brown sugar
- 4 hard-cooked eggs, peeled (see page 35)

1. Pat the chicken dry with paper towels. Heat the oil in a large Dutch oven over medium-high heat until just smoking. Brown half of the chicken on both sides, 5 to 8 minutes per side, reducing the heat if the pan begins to scorch. Transfer the chicken to a plate, leaving the fat in the pot.

Return the pot to medium-high heat and repeat with the remaining chicken; transfer the chicken to the plate.

2. Pour off all but 1 tablespoon fat from the pot. (Add additional oil to equal 1 tablespoon, if needed.) Add the garlic, ginger, Sichuan peppercorns, and star anise to the pot and cook over medium heat until fragrant, about 30 seconds. Stir in the soy sauce, chicken broth, rice wine, sesame oil, and brown sugar, scraping up any browned bits.

3. Nestle the hard-cooked eggs and chicken, along with any accumulated juices, into the pot and bring to a simmer. Cover, turn the heat to medium-low, and simmer until the chicken is fully cooked and tender, about 20 minutes for the breasts (160 to 165 degrees on an instant-read thermometer) or 1 hour for the thighs and drumsticks (170 to 175 degrees on an instant-read thermometer), turning over the chicken and eggs halfway through cooking to ensure even coloring from the sauce. (If using both types of chicken, simmer the thighs and drumsticks for 40 minutes before adding the breasts.)

4. Transfer the chicken and eggs to a serving dish, tent loosely with foil, and let rest while finishing the sauce. Remove and discard the star anise. Skim as much fat as possible off the surface of the sauce. Pour the sauce over the chicken and eggs and serve.

Indian-Style Chicken Curries

THE TERM "CURRY" IS DERIVED FROM THE Tamil word *kari*, which simply means sauce or gravy. We tend to think of curry as a spiced yellow-colored meat and vegetable stew typically served over rice. But a curry can be most any type of stew, and as a result there are hundreds, perhaps thousands, of ways to make curry. We wanted to develop a recipe for yellow chicken and vegetable curry and set out to discover what separates good curry from bad curry while sticking as close to tradition as possible.

Chicken and vegetable curries can be complicated affairs, with lengthy ingredient lists and fussy techniques meant to yield perfectly cooked chicken, vegetables, and sauce. But we wanted something simpler—a curry we could make on a weeknight in less than an hour. Most streamlined recipes we tried, however, were uninspired. A few attempted to make up for the flavor deficit by overloading the dish with spices, and the results were harsh and overpowering. We had our work cut out for us.

While some curries are made with exotic whole and ground spices (fenugreek, asafetida, dried rose petals, and so on), we decided to limit ourselves to everyday ground spices such as cumin, cloves, cardamom, cinnamon, and coriander. Our testing dragged on for days, and it was hard to reach consensus in the test kitchen. Frankly, most of the homemade spice mixtures we tried were fine.

We had been reluctant to use store-bought curry powder, assuming its flavor would be inferior to a homemade blend, but it seemed worth a try. We were surprised when tasters liked the curry powder nearly as well as a homemade mixture made with seven spices. It turns out that store-bought curry powder contains some of the exotic spices we had dismissed at the outset. As long as we used enough, our recipe had decent flavor.

Looking for ways to improve the flavor of the curry powder, we tried toasting the spices in a skillet until their seductive aroma emerged. This simple step took just one minute and turned commercial curry powder into a flavor powerhouse. Why was toasting so beneficial? When added to a simmering sauce, spices can be heated to only 212 degrees. In a dry skillet, temperatures can exceed 500 degrees, causing flavors to explode.

With the spices settled, we turned to building the rest of our flavor base. Many classic recipes begin with a generous amount of sautéed onion, which adds depth and body to the sauce, and we followed suit. Ghee (clarified butter) is traditionally used to sauté the onions. It adds terrific richness, though we found that vegetable oil was a fine substitute. Almost all curry recipes add equal amounts of garlic and ginger to the onions, and we found no reason to stray from this well-balanced tradition. Wanting to take our sauce to the next level, we stirred in a minced fresh chile for heat and a spoonful of tomato paste for sweetness. The latter ingredient was decidedly inauthentic, but we found it really helped. We then added the toasted curry powder to the pan and let it dissolve. Creating a supercharged base for our curry took just 15 minutes.

With the sauce set, we decided to focus on the chicken and vegetables. First, we investigated whether it was essential to sear the chicken before it was simmered in the sauce—some recipes that we found did this, while others did not. In a side-by-side test of chicken curry made with seared and unseared chicken, we found that it was nearly impossible to distinguish between them. The assertive flavors and color of the spices made searing unnecessary.

As for the chicken, we preferred boneless, skinless chicken breasts because they required just 15 to 20 minutes of simmering in order to cook through. We then removed them from the sauce and easily shredded the meat, stirring it back into the curry before serving. The shredded chicken not only looked far more appealing than cubes, but the shreds soaked up the sauce better.

For the vegetables, we settled on the classic pairing of cauliflower and peas (although we also came up with variations using chickpeas and raisins, and potatoes and green beans). The combination of textures and colors was good, and the vegetables picked up flavor from the sauce. Next, we determined that a combination of water and pureed canned tomatoes, along with a splash of cream or coconut milk, allowed the delicate vegetables, tender, shredded chicken, and fragrant spices to shine.

Lastly, we experimented with garam masala, a spice blend often sprinkled onto Indian dishes before serving. Like curry powder, garam masala varies among cooks but usually includes warm spices such as black pepper, cinnamon, coriander, and cardamom (its name means "hot spice blend" in Hindi). Following our success with the curry powder, we decided to buy a jar of commercial garam masala. But when we added a few pinches to the curry postcooking, the result was raw and harsh-tasting. What if we first toasted the garam masala along with the curry powder? Lightning did strike twice, as the garam masala mellowed into a second wave of flavor that helped the curry reach an even more layered complexity. Here was a robust, satisfying chicken and vegetable curry that relied on supermarket staples.

Indian-Style Chicken Curry with Cauliflower and Peas

SERVES 4 TO 6

For more heat, include the serrano ribs and seeds when mincing. Serve with plain yogurt, mango chutney, and Basic Pilaf-Style Rice (page 114), if desired.

- 2 tablespoons sweet or mild curry powder
- 1 teaspoon garam masala
- ¼ cup vegetable oil
- 2 medium onions, minced
- Salt
- 3 medium garlic cloves, minced or pressed through a garlic press (about 1 tablespoon)
- 1 tablespoon minced or grated fresh ginger
- 1 serrano chile, seeds and ribs removed, chile minced (see note)
- 1 tablespoon tomato paste
- 1¼ cups low-sodium chicken broth
- 1 (14.5-ounce) can diced tomatoes, pulsed in a food processor until nearly smooth, with ¼-inch pieces visible
- ½ medium head cauliflower, trimmed, cored, and cut into 1-inch florets (about 4 cups)
- 1½ pounds boneless, skinless chicken breasts (about 4 medium), trimmed
- 6 ounces frozen peas (about 1 cup)
- ¼ cup heavy cream or coconut milk
- 2 tablespoons minced fresh cilantro leaves

1. Toast the curry powder and garam masala in a small skillet over medium-high heat, stirring constantly, until fragrant, about 1 minute. Transfer to a small bowl and set aside.

2. Heat 3 tablespoons of the oil in a large Dutch

oven over medium-high heat until shimmering. Add the onions and ¼ teaspoon salt and cook, stirring occasionally, until caramelized, about 10 minutes, reducing the heat if the onions begin to darken too quickly.

3. Reduce the heat to medium, stir in the remaining 1 tablespoon oil, the garlic, ginger, chile, tomato paste, and toasted spices and cook until fragrant, about 30 seconds. Stir in the broth and tomatoes, scraping up any browned bits.

4. Add the cauliflower, then nestle the chicken breasts into the pot and bring to a simmer. Cover, turn the heat to medium-low, and simmer just until the cauliflower is tender and the thickest part of the breast registers 160 to 165 degrees on an instant-read thermometer, 10 to 15 minutes.

5. Transfer the chicken to a cutting board. When the chicken is cool enough to handle, shred into bite-sized pieces (see page 10). Return the shredded chicken to the sauce with the peas and cream and continue to cook until heated through, about 2 minutes longer. Stir in the cilantro, season with salt to taste, and serve.

VARIATIONS

Indian-Style Chicken Curry with Chickpeas and Raisins

Follow the recipe for Indian-Style Chicken Curry with Cauliflower and Peas, substituting 1 (15-ounce) can chickpeas, drained and rinsed, for the cauliflower, and ½ cup raisins for the peas.

Indian-Style Chicken Curry with Potatoes and Green Beans

Follow the recipe for Indian-Style Chicken Curry with Cauliflower and Peas, adding 12 ounces red potatoes (about 5 small), scrubbed and cut into ½-inch chunks, with the onion in step 2, and substituting 8 ounces green beans, stem ends trimmed and cut into 1-inch lengths, for the cauliflower in step 4. Omit the peas.

Thai-Style Chicken Curries

LIKE MOST THAI FOOD, THAI CURRIES EMBRACE a delicate balance of tastes, textures, temperatures, and colors that come together to create a harmonious whole. Thai curries almost always contain coconut milk, which not only blends and carries flavors but also forms the backbone of the sauce, and some type of protein, like chicken (which we were using in our recipe), tofu, shrimp, or pork. The balance is tilted toward aromatics, which are added in the form of a paste and usually consist of garlic, ginger, shallots, lemon grass, kaffir lime leaves, shrimp paste, and chiles. These curry pastes can be quite involved and may require an hour of preparation. The curries themselves come together rather quickly and simmer gently for a short amount of time.

We set out to explore the two most common types of Thai curries: green curry and red curry. We wanted to understand the basic structure of these dishes and figure out ways that they could be made accessible to the American home cook. In doing so, we would need to find substitutes for some ingredients, such as kaffir lime leaves and shrimp paste, which are not readily available in most American supermarkets.

Our work was divided into three neat areas: developing recipes for the pastes, cooking the pastes to draw out their flavor, and incorporating the chicken into the curry. We started with the pastes.

Traditionally, the ingredients for Thai curries are pounded together using a mortar and pestle to form a smooth paste. Since this process can take up to an hour and requires a tool most American cooks don't own, we turned to a blender. To facilitate blending, we found that we had to add some liquid to the paste. Oil worked well—it didn't compete with the other curry flavors—but we had to use a fair amount to achieve a smooth paste. We determined that by also adding some water, about ⅓ cup, we were able to reduce the amount of oil to 2 tablespoons, resulting in a less greasy sauce.

With the method down, we focused first on the chiles. For the green curry paste, we noted that fresh tiny green Thai chiles are most commonly called for. They can be difficult to find, so we tested several substitutions and found that serranos and jalapeños are the best candidates. Red curry paste relies on dried red Thai chiles, rather than fresh. (Though dried red Thai chiles are traditional, japonés and de árbol chiles work well, too.) The dried chiles are usually soaked in hot water until softened. We found that we could get more flavor out of the chiles if we toasted them and then tossed them in the blender dry instead of soaking (they rehydrate with the moisture in the blender). Because the dried chiles lacked body, we supplemented them with fresh red jalapeños.

Shallots, garlic, and ginger are constants in most curry pastes. And toasted and ground coriander seeds, as well as fresh coriander root, are other common additions. We found that cilantro leaves (the name commonly used for the leaves of the coriander plant) are too moist and floral to use as a substitute for the roots, but that cilantro stems are fine.

Lemon grass is an essential ingredient to Thai curry, and we were happy to discover that it is relatively easy to find. We did find a substitute for galangal, a rhizome related to ginger that's both peppery and sour: A combination of fresh ginger and lime juice added the necessary hot and sour notes in its place. We found that adding the lime juice directly to the finished curry, rather than to the curry paste, best preserves its flavor.

Kaffir lime leaves have a clean, floral aroma. Many tasters compare it with lemon verbena, and we found that lime zest approximates this flavor.

Shrimp paste—a puree of salted, fermented shrimp and other seasonings—adds a salty, fishy note to Thai curry pastes. Since this ingredient can be hard to find, we searched for substitutes. Anchovy paste was a reasonable solution, but adding fish sauce directly to the curry is traditional and adds the same kind of subtle fishy flavor.

Moving on, we considered the other components of the dish—the chicken and vegetables. Common Thai additions for vegetables include pea eggplant, breadfruit, bamboo shoots, young jackfruit, banana blossoms, and pumpkin tendrils. All except the bamboo shoots were far too difficult for us to find, and none of us were keen on the addition of canned bamboo shoots. We had noted that it wasn't unusual to have a curry with just protein and no vegetable, especially with such a hefty amount of fresh herbs added at the end. Indeed, tasters liked the simplicity of the chicken-only curries.

Next, we focused on the chicken. We decided to use boneless, skinless chicken breasts, as we did in our Indian-style curries (see pages 83–84). We cooked the curry paste in a skillet and then added water (along with a little fish sauce and brown sugar). This formed a sauce and created enough liquid in which to poach the chicken breasts. We tested different ways to cut the chicken, but tasters unanimously preferred shredded chicken. This was simple enough to achieve; we removed the chicken once it was fully cooked, and set it aside to cool before shredding it. Then we returned the chicken to the sauce, finishing it with coconut milk for a luxuriously smooth texture.

Once the curry was finished, a final Thai garnish of fresh basil, cilantro, and lime juice completed the dish. Thai curries are saucy and hot and require a nice cushion of rice. Jasmine rice is the most traditional option, but regular long-grain rice works fine.

Thai-Style Green Curry with Chicken

SERVES 4 TO 6

We strongly prefer the flavor of Thai chiles here; however, serrano and jalapeño chiles are decent substitutions. For more heat, include the chile ribs and seeds when mincing. Serve with Simple White Rice (page 386).

CURRY PASTE

- **⅓ cup water**
- **12 Thai, serrano, or jalapeño chiles, seeds and ribs removed, chiles minced (see note)**
- **8 medium garlic cloves, peeled**
- **3 medium shallots, peeled and quartered**
- **2 stalks lemon grass, bottom 5 inches only, trimmed and sliced thin (see the illustrations on page 50)**
- **2 tablespoons minced fresh cilantro stems**
- **2 tablespoons grated zest from 2 limes**
- **2 tablespoons vegetable oil**
- **1 tablespoon minced or grated fresh ginger**
- **2 teaspoons ground coriander**
- **1 teaspoon ground cumin**
- **1 teaspoon salt**

CHICKEN

- 1¼ cups water
- 2 tablespoons fish sauce
- 1 tablespoon light brown sugar
- 1½ pounds boneless, skinless chicken breasts (about 4 medium), trimmed
- 1 (14-ounce) can coconut milk
- ½ cup loosely packed fresh basil leaves
- ½ cup loosely packed fresh cilantro leaves
- 2 tablespoons juice from 1 lime

1. FOR THE CURRY PASTE: Puree all of the curry paste ingredients together in a blender to a fine paste, about 3 minutes, stopping to scrape down the sides as needed.

2. FOR THE CHICKEN: Cook the curry paste in a large nonstick skillet over medium-high heat, stirring often, until the paste begins to sizzle and no longer smells raw, about 2 minutes. Stir in the water, fish sauce, and sugar, then nestle the chicken into the skillet and bring to a simmer. Cover, turn the heat to medium-low, and simmer until the thickest part of the breast registers 160 to 165 degrees on an instant-read thermometer, 10 to 15 minutes.

3. Transfer the chicken to a cutting board. Stir the coconut milk into the skillet and return to a simmer until the sauce has thickened slightly, about 8 minutes. When the chicken is cool enough to handle, shred into bite-sized pieces (see the illustrations on page 10).

4. Return the shredded chicken to the sauce and continue to cook until heated through, about 2 minutes. Off the heat, stir in the basil, cilantro, and lime juice and serve.

Thai-Style Red Curry with Chicken

SERVES 4 TO 6

We recommend wearing gloves when handling the toasted chiles; they are very spicy and might burn your skin. If you can't find fresh red jalapeño chiles, you can substitute green jalapeño chiles, but the color of the sauce will be slightly muddy. For more heat, include the jalapeño ribs and seeds when mincing. Serve with Simple White Rice (page 386).

CURRY PASTE

- 8 small, dried red chiles, such as Thai, japonés, or de árbol, brushed clean
- ⅓ cup water
- 4 medium shallots, peeled and quartered
- 2 stalks lemon grass, bottom 5 inches only, trimmed and sliced thin (see the illustrations on page 50)
- 6 medium garlic cloves, peeled
- 1 medium red jalapeño chile, seeds and ribs removed, chile minced (see note)
- 2 tablespoons minced fresh cilantro stems
- 2 tablespoons vegetable oil
- 1 tablespoon grated zest from 1 lime
- 2 teaspoons ground coriander
- 1 teaspoon ground cumin
- 1 teaspoon minced or grated fresh ginger
- 1 teaspoon tomato paste
- 1 teaspoon salt

CHICKEN

- 1¼ cups water
- 2 tablespoons fish sauce
- 1 tablespoon light brown sugar
- 1½ pounds boneless, skinless chicken breasts (about 4 medium), trimmed
- 1 (14-ounce) can coconut milk
- ½ cup loosely packed fresh basil leaves
- ½ cup loosely packed fresh cilantro leaves
- 2 tablespoons juice from 1 lime

1. FOR THE CURRY PASTE: Adjust an oven rack to the middle position and heat the oven to 350 degrees. Place the dried red chiles on a rimmed baking sheet and toast in the oven until fragrant and puffed, about 5 minutes. Remove the chiles from the oven and let cool. When cool enough to handle, seed and stem the chiles, then break into small pieces.

2. Puree the toasted chile pieces and the remaining curry paste ingredients together in a blender to a fine paste, about 3 minutes, stopping to scrape down the sides as needed.

3. FOR THE CHICKEN: Cook the curry paste in a large nonstick skillet over medium-high heat, stirring often, until the paste begins to sizzle and no longer smells raw, about 2 minutes. Stir in the

water, fish sauce, and sugar, then nestle the chicken into the skillet and bring to a simmer. Cover, turn the heat to medium-low, and simmer until the thickest part of the breast registers 160 to 165 degrees on an instant-read thermometer, 10 to 15 minutes.

4. Transfer the chicken to a cutting board. Stir the coconut milk into the skillet and return to a simmer until the sauce has thickened slightly, about 8 minutes. When the chicken is cool enough to handle, shred into bite-sized pieces (see the illustrations on page 10).

5. Return the shredded chicken to the sauce and continue to cook until heated through, about 2 minutes. Off the heat, stir in the basil, cilantro, and lime juice and serve.

Chicken Mole

MOLE, FROM THE AZTEC WORD FOR "SAUCE," is a rich blend of chiles, nuts, spices, fruit, and sometimes chocolate, and is considered the national dish of Mexico. The popular mole rojo (red mole) and mole poblano are distinguished from other moles by their inclusion of chocolate and are the style of mole you're apt to find on most restaurant menus. Chicken and turkey are commonly stewed in mole until tender and flavorful; mole is also used as a sauce ladled over enchiladas, tamales, rice, and potatoes.

An authentic mole has complex layers of flavor, but these exotic flavors come with a price: a laundry list of ingredients and a notoriously long and complicated cooking method. Our goal was to translate mole for American home cooks without sacrificing the dish's traditional flavor.

We began by testing three red and two poblano mole recipes uncovered in our research. Moles are generally made by sautéing all of the individual ingredients in an ample amount of oil. This step acts to bloom each item, bringing it to its peak of flavor. Next, all the ingredients are brought together in a large pot with the addition of broth or water and simmered. The mixture is then pureed and returned to the pot to continue cooking until the flavors meld—depending on the mole and the number of ingredients, this could take as long as three hours.

All of the moles we tried tasted a bit different from one another—some were sweeter, others were a bit spicier, and a few had a thicker consistency—but they all featured deep, rich, exotic flavors. Because there are so many different styles of mole, there is a lot of room for interpretation—which was perfect, as it gave us a little breathing room for developing our own recipe.

To start, we cobbled together a simple working recipe—sautéing some basic aromatics (onion and garlic), then adding the remaining ingredients, such as nuts, seeds, dried fruit, and chocolate. At this point, the mixture was simmered with added chicken broth and then pureed. With this basic recipe in hand, we set out to test the variables.

Dried chiles are a key ingredient in mole, so we thought it would be an appropriate place for us to start. Most authentic mole recipes call for several (up to five or six) different types of chiles (such as mulatos, guajillos, pasillas, anchos, and chipotles), but these chiles are used to add flavor only and are in no way meant to bring heat to the sauce. We sought out and tested all of these chiles in various sauces and were pleased to find that we could come up with a delicious mole using just two of the most common: anchos and chipotles. Two ancho chiles laid down a full, mild base of chile flavor, while just half a chipotle added a more intense chile flavor and a hint of heat.

As with the dried chiles for our Thai curry (see page 84), we found that toasting the chiles in the oven until fragrant and puffed—a clear indication that they are perfectly toasted but not burned—brought out the best flavor. We then broke the toasted chiles into small pieces and added them right to the simmering sauce.

Most mole recipes call for some combination of toasted almonds, pumpkin seeds, peanuts, and sesame seeds. We found that we liked the rich, creamy flavors of toasted peanuts and sesame seeds. Unfortunately, the peanuts remained grainy even after blending. We solved this problem by using peanut butter instead, and were pleased to find that the butter also gave the sauce a luxurious, velvety texture.

For the chocolate, Mexican chocolate (which contains cinnamon and sometimes almonds and vanilla) is traditional, but we found that semisweet and bittersweet tasted great as well—we noticed little difference among them.

Cinnamon and cloves, along with some raisins, helped to add complexity to our sauce. Adding canned diced tomatoes also helped to round out the flavor and deepened the sauce's color.

As the construction of our mole finally came to an end, we turned our attention to incorporating the chicken into the dish. Having had success with boneless, skinless chicken breasts in both our Indian and Thai curries, we followed suit here. The chicken poached in the flavorful sauce—it was moist and tender, but it also cooked quickly and was easy to shred and return to the silky smooth sauce.

Served with rice or even wrapped up in tortillas, this chicken mole is a simplified version of the authentic dish.

Chicken Mole

SERVES 4 TO 6

Ancho chiles are poblano chiles that have been dried, and chipotle chiles are jalapeño chiles that have been dried and smoked. We recommend wearing gloves when handling the toasted chiles; they are very spicy and might burn your skin. The flavor of mole made with whole ancho chiles is superior to mole made with ground ancho powder, but, if necessary, substitute 2 tablespoons ground ancho powder for the fresh; skip step 1 and add the powder with the cinnamon in step 2. Feel free to substitute ½ teaspoon ground chipotle powder, or ½ teaspoon minced chipotle in adobo sauce, for the chipotle chile and add with the cinnamon in step 2. For less heat, use only 1½ ancho chiles and ¼ chipotle chile. Serve with Simple White Rice (page 386) or warm corn tortillas.

- 2 ancho chiles, brushed clean (see note)
- ½ chipotle chile, brushed clean (see note)
- 3 tablespoons vegetable oil
- 1 medium onion, minced
- Salt
- 1 ounce bittersweet, semisweet, or Mexican chocolate, chopped coarse
- ½ teaspoon ground cinnamon
- ⅛ teaspoon ground cloves
- 2 medium garlic cloves, minced or pressed through a garlic press (about 2 teaspoons)
- 2 cups low-sodium chicken broth
- 1 (14.5-ounce) can diced tomatoes, drained
- ¼ cup raisins
- 2 tablespoons sesame seeds, toasted, plus more for serving
- ¼ cup peanut butter
- Ground black pepper
- Sugar
- 1½ pounds boneless, skinless chicken breasts (about 4 medium), trimmed

1. Adjust an oven rack to the middle position and heat the oven to 350 degrees. Place the ancho and chipotle chiles on a baking sheet and toast in the oven until fragrant and puffed, about 6 minutes. Remove the chiles from the oven and let cool. When cool enough to handle, seed and stem the chiles and break into small pieces.

2. Heat the oil in a large skillet over medium heat until shimmering. Add the onion and ¼ teaspoon salt and cook until softened, 5 to 7 minutes. Stir in the toasted chile pieces, the chocolate, cinnamon, and cloves and cook until the spices are fragrant and the chocolate is melted and bubbly, about 2 minutes. Stir in the garlic and cook until fragrant, about 30 seconds. Stir in the broth, tomatoes, raisins, sesame seeds, and peanut butter and cook, stirring occasionally, until the sauce has thickened slightly and measures about 2½ cups, about 10 minutes.

3. Transfer the chile mixture to a blender (or food processor) and process until smooth, about 20 seconds. Season with salt, pepper, and sugar to taste. (Up to this point, the sauce can be cooled completely and refrigerated in an airtight container for up to 3 days.) Return the sauce to the skillet.

4. Nestle the chicken into the skillet and bring to a simmer. Cover, turn the heat to medium-low, and simmer until the thickest part of the breast registers 160 to 165 degrees on an instant-read thermometer, 10 to 15 minutes.

5. Transfer the chicken to a cutting board. Return the sauce to a simmer until thickened slightly, 4 to 6 minutes. When the chicken is cool enough to handle, shred into bite-sized pieces (see the illustration on page 10). Return the shredded chicken to the sauce and continue to cook until heated through, about 2 minutes. Sprinkle with sesame seeds and serve.

4
ROASTED, BAKED, AND BROILED

Roasted, Baked, and Broiled

WHEN YOU DO NOT HAVE TIME TO ROAST A whole bird (see Chapter 5 for recipes), roasting, baking, or broiling chicken parts is a fast and simple solution. Not only is the bird already cut up for you (with only minimal trimming required), you can more easily cater to individual preferences for white or dark meat. But we have all had more than our share of bland, dry, roasted chicken breasts or wings and thighs with flabby skin. We set out to restore roasted and broiled chicken parts to their proper status. We wanted moist, well-seasoned meat paired with crisp, golden brown skin—and we didn't want these results to require too much work on a weeknight.

Brining, which involves soaking the chicken in a solution of water, salt, and sometimes sugar (see page 12 for more information on brining), is a technique that we often use in the test kitchen when cooking whole chickens or chicken parts that are exposed to the high heat of the broiler or grill. Brining ensures that the meat is seasoned through to the bone and also adds moisture that is retained when the chicken is cooked, resulting in a more flavorful, juicy piece of meat. However, as we cooked our way through these recipes, we discovered that brining is not always necessary when cooking chicken parts—instead, we found some interesting alternatives to ensure moist, flavorful meat.

One of those alternatives is salting, a technique we use in both our Spice-Rubbed Picnic Chicken (page 96) and Chicken Tikka Masala (page 113) with great success. Salting works by initially drawing moisture out of the meat; then, after several hours, that moisture is pulled back into the meat, taking some of the salt along with it and resulting in juicy, flavorful meat. The glaze on our glazed chicken breasts (see page 97) provides a protective barrier from the heat, keeping the meat juicy and tender. We also applied butter rubs and cheese-based stuffings to our Roasted Chicken Breasts (page 93) and our Easy Stuffed Chicken Breasts (page 105). The butter and cheese baste the breasts as they cook, again keeping the meat moist and juicy. Finally, we marinate the breasts in our chicken bakes (see page 99), adding simple but flavorful vegetables to the mix to create a one-dish meal. We did find one exception to our no-brining policy in this chapter: the broiled chicken thighs. Here the heat is so high that we found a brine to be essential for keeping the meat from drying out.

Oven temperature was another key element to factor into the equation. In general, when roasting parts, higher is better. After testing temperatures ranging from 350 degrees up to 500 degrees, we found that 450 degrees produced the best results. The skin became nice and crisp and the interior of the meat cooked through without the exterior drying out. The one problem with higher temperatures is that the pan drippings can burn, causing the oven to smoke—not ideal if you are expecting guests. We found a broiler pan to be the perfect solution—the drippings wind up on the bottom of the pan, protected from the high heat.

Air circulation proved to be essential for ensuring crisp skin and an evenly cooked piece of chicken. Lifting the chicken out of its juices and up onto a rack further helped the cause, as did carefully separating the skin from the meat, allowing more air to circulate underneath the skin.

Broiling chicken parts presented a new set of challenges. Broiling is a great year-round alternative to grilling. With broiling, the oven temperature is extremely high and, therefore, the placement of the pan in the oven becomes crucial to the success of perfectly browned, crispy skin and meat that is cooked through in a relatively short time. Slashing the skin in a few places allows the melting fat to escape as it cooks, enabling the skin to render beautifully. We found thighs to be ideal for broiling, as they are less likely than breast meat to dry out and are small enough that they can cook all the way through before the skin burns.

With these recipes you can find a host of ways to transform plain old chicken into a flavorful and satisfying meal, any night of the week.

Roasted Chicken Breasts

ROASTED BONE-IN, SKIN-ON CHICKEN BREASTS can be the ultimate simple-yet-elegant main course, and when done right the result is moist, tender, well-seasoned meat and crisp, golden-brown skin. But the simplest dishes can also be the hardest to get right—dry, chalky meat and rubbery, flaccid skin are all too often the norm. Despite the demand for this simple dish, recipes for plain roasted chicken breasts are in short supply, and we wondered why. Research showed that even the most basic recipes included flavoring ingredients. Minimalists add herbs, lemon, or mustard; others enhance with olives, capers, sesame, or honey. We tested a half-dozen recipes, and it was clear that most of them use these potent ingredients in an attempt to disguise the bland, dry meat. The skin on all of the breasts proved equally disappointing. Hints of crispness were overshadowed by mostly fatty, rubbery skin. Our goal was to create a simple recipe for plain roasted chicken breasts that would yield perfectly cooked meat and skin, along with a few flavorful variations. We envisioned a quick and easy recipe, perfect for a weeknight meal.

We started by simply splitting the breasts (you can also purchase them already split) and roasting them in the oven. We tried roasting them at a range of heat levels, from 350 degrees all the way up to 500 degrees, but the meat emerged bone-dry every time. We then wondered if cutting the breasts before roasting them was even a good idea. We split two raw breasts and roasted them along with two unsplit breasts. We were shocked by the results. This simple technique—roasting whole instead of split breasts—dramatically improved the juiciness of the meat. The explanation? Whole breasts retain more of their juices than cut breasts, which have more avenues for moisture loss. But waiting to cut through the breastbone until after cooking presented problems: uneven halves, unattractive pieces, and chicken that was not easy to eat. Carving the meat entirely off the bones and serving it fanned on the plate was a simpler, more attractive alternative.

In terms of oven temperature, the visual difference was glaring when the breasts emerged from the oven. The skin on the breasts roasted at 350 degrees was pale yellow and rubbery looking; the skin roasted at 500 degrees was completely charred. Neither tasted great, though breasts from the hotter ovens were definitely better. In the end, 450 degrees proved best. The meat was still juicy and the skin color improved, but the skin still wasn't as crisp as we wanted. And, occasionally, fat dripped from the chicken into the baking pan, smoking up the kitchen.

PREPARING THE CHICKEN FOR ROASTING

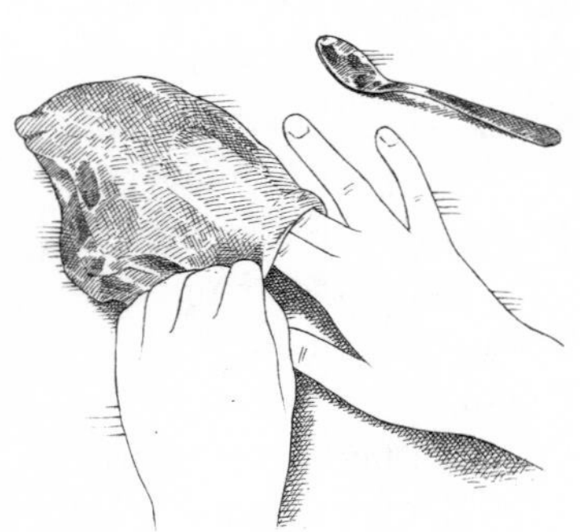

1. Gently lift the skin at the bottom of the breast to create a small pocket for the butter.

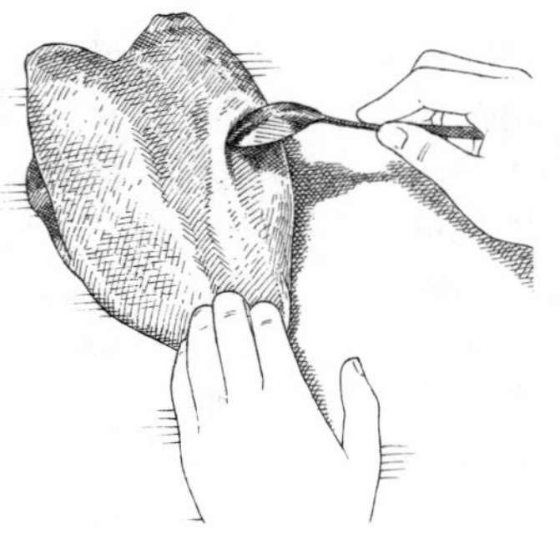

2. Using your fingers or a small spoon, place half of the butter in the center of each breast. Gently press on the skin to spread the butter over the meat.

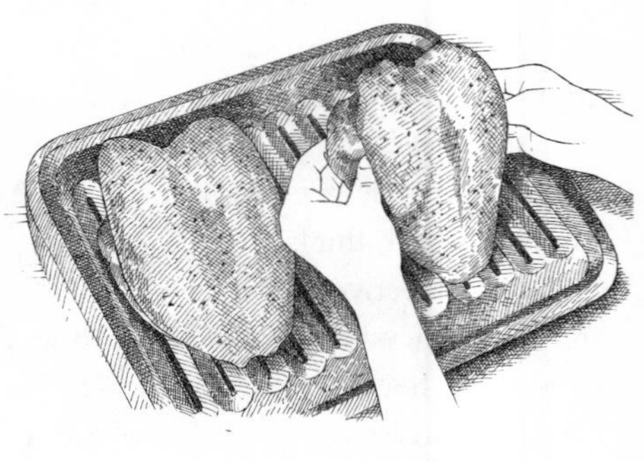

3. Gently pull out the rib cage from each side of the breast to create a stable base.

To solve the problem of smoking, we switched from our 13 by 9-inch Pyrex pan to a stainless roasting pan fitted with a rack. Still, a shallow layer of fat formed, causing some smoke. The good news was that we had unwittingly discovered another secret of perfectly baked chicken. By getting the breasts up off the pan bottom, the rack allowed heat to circulate underneath them. The result was more even, quicker-cooking, and juicier meat. Inspired by the rack, we tried creating a natural rack by pulling out the rib cage on each side of the whole breast so that it could stand up on its own. It worked! Instead of curling under the breast, the edges of the breast now fanned outward, allowing for better air circulation. But the smoke still ensued. We tried again, this time using a broiler pan. Bingo—the fat dripped below the rack, which shielded it from the heat. Roasting was now smoke-free, the meat was juicier, and the broiler pan was easy to clean up as long as we covered the bottom of it with foil.

One problem, however, remained: Our chicken breasts still had mediocre skin. We knew from earlier tests that separating the skin from the meat allows hot air to circulate more freely under the skin, renders more fat, and produces crispier skin. We tried several different approaches, including slashing the skin and severing it everywhere but along the breastbone, before determining that a one-sided, pocket opening worked best. Using our fingers, we gently pulled apart the bottom edge and used a spoon to open up a cavity. This method minimized skin shrinkage and allowed the skin to roast to a deep golden brown. Now the color of the skin was appealing, but a crispy texture still remained elusive.

We had been rubbing oil on the skin, as it helped with browning and crisping. Now we tried rubbing some under the skin as well. The results were even better. Next we tried butter instead of oil. This was the best approach yet, as the butter helped to keep the delicate breast meat juicy and moist while adding flavor. We tried rubbing softened butter on top of the skin too, but the cold skin caused the butter to seize up, making spreading difficult. So we stayed with the oil on top of the skin.

Up to this point we had been seasoning the outer breasts liberally with salt and pepper. We now tried salting under the skin, and this produced meat that was well seasoned and juicy. As we were already rubbing on butter, we tried adding the salt to the butter to make the seasoning easier. This worked perfectly.

At last we had perfectly roasted chicken breasts. And our recipe was just as easy as—and even quicker than—some of the simplest recipes we had tested. Here was the secret formula: Roast a whole breast, use a very hot oven, allow air to circulate under the breastbone and under the skin, and use modest amounts of oil, butter, salt, and pepper. This technique also made it easy to add flavors by simply flavoring the butter—as long as we avoided sugar and honey, which made the skin burn, or too much ground spice (more than a teaspoon), which created a gritty texture. Best of all, we now had a simple recipe that produces white meat so good that even lovers of dark meat may take notice.

Roasted Chicken Breasts

SERVES 4

To ensure that the breasts cook at the same rate, purchase two similarly sized whole breasts (not split breasts), with their skin fully intact. Whole chicken breasts weighing about 1½ pounds each work best in this recipe because they require a cooking time long enough to ensure that the skin will brown and crisp nicely. If you do not own a broiler pan, use a roasting pan fitted with a flat wire rack. This recipe can easily be doubled—just make certain not to crowd the chicken breasts on the pan, as this will impede the browning and crisping of the skin.

- **2 tablespoons unsalted butter, at room temperature**
- **Salt and ground black pepper**
- **2 whole bone-in, skin-on chicken breasts, trimmed (about 1½ pounds each)**
- **Vegetable oil**

1. Adjust an oven rack to the middle position and heat the oven to 450 degrees. Line a broiler-pan bottom with foil and cover with the broiler-pan top; set aside.

2. Mix together the butter, ½ teaspoon salt, and ¼ teaspoon pepper. Pat the chicken dry with paper towels. Following the illustrations on page 92, use your fingers to gently loosen the center portion of skin covering each breast. Place the butter (about 1 tablespoon per breast) under the skin, directly on the meat in the center of each breast. Gently press on the skin to distribute the butter evenly over the meat. Rub the top of the skin with oil and season with salt and pepper.

3. Place the chicken breasts on the prepared broiler pan, propping up the breasts on their rib bones (see the illustration on page 92). Roast until the thickest part of the breast registers 160 to 165 degrees on an instant-read thermometer, 35 to 40 minutes. Transfer the chicken to a cutting board and let rest for 5 minutes. Following the illustrations on page 10, remove the meat from the bones and slice on the bias. Serve.

VARIATIONS

Roasted Chicken Breasts with Chipotle, Cumin, and Cilantro

Follow the recipe for Roasted Chicken Breasts, mixing 2 teaspoons minced chipotle chile in adobo, 2 teaspoons minced fresh cilantro leaves, and 1 teaspoon ground cumin into the softened butter with the salt and pepper.

INGREDIENTS: Chipotle Chiles

Smoky, sweet, and moderately spicy, chipotle chiles are jalapeño chiles that have been smoked over aromatic wood and dried. They are sold as is—wrinkly, reddish-brown, and leathery—or canned in adobo, a tangy, oily, tomato- and herb-based sauce. We recommend purchasing canned chipotles because they are already reconstituted by the adobo and, consequently, are easier to use. Most recipes call for just a chile or two, as they are so potent, but the remaining chiles keep indefinitely if stored in an airtight container in the refrigerator, or they may be frozen. Cans of chipotles in adobo are readily available in the Mexican food section of most supermarkets.

REHYDRATING DRIED PORCINI MUSHROOMS

When soaking dried porcini mushrooms, most of the sand and dirt will fall to the bottom of the bowl. Use a fork to lift the rehydrated mushrooms from the liquid without stirring up the sand. If the mushrooms still feel gritty, rinse them briefly under cool running water.

Roasted Chicken Breasts with Herbs and Porcini Mushrooms

In a small bowl, cover 2 tablespoons dried porcini mushrooms with boiling water; let sit until softened, about 15 minutes. Using a fork, lift the mushrooms from the liquid and chop fine (you should have about 4 teaspoons). Follow the recipe for Roasted Chicken Breasts, mixing the porcini, 1 teaspoon minced fresh thyme leaves, and 1 teaspoon minced fresh rosemary into the softened butter with the salt and pepper.

Roasted Chicken Breasts with Olives, Parsley, and Lemon

Follow the recipe for Roasted Chicken Breasts, mixing 1 tablespoon finely chopped pitted kalamata olives, 2 teaspoons minced fresh parsley leaves, and 1 teaspoon grated zest from 1 lemon into the softened butter with the salt and pepper.

Roasted Chicken Breasts with Garlic, Rosemary, and Lemon

Follow the recipe for Roasted Chicken Breasts, mixing 2 medium garlic cloves, minced or pressed through a garlic press (about 2 teaspoons), 2 teaspoons minced fresh rosemary, and 1 teaspoon grated zest from 1 lemon into the softened butter with the salt and pepper.

Picnic Chicken

COLD BARBECUED CHICKEN IS A PICNIC classic. Maybe because picnics offer so much more than food (fresh air, a nice view), most people don't care that this recipe often doesn't make culinary sense. Covered with sticky sauce, the chicken is hard to eat with a fork and impossibly messy when eaten using your hands. And because the chicken has been cooked and then chilled, the skin is flabby and the meat is so dry it squeaks. We wanted picnic chicken good enough to serve at our dining room table.

For starters, great picnic chicken ought to have moist, tender meat. We decided we also wanted the robust, spicy, and slightly sweet flavor of barbecue. On the other hand, we didn't want to have to light the grill for a dish that would be going straight into the fridge. The oven is a much easier option for a make-ahead recipe. After sampling several mediocre recipes from various cookbooks, we knew we had our work cut out for us: Turning this dish into something that was a lot better than worse-for-the-wear leftovers was going to be a tall order.

The first advance we made was as quick as it was dramatic. About 90 percent of the recipes we found called for slathering roasted, skin-on chicken with barbecue sauce and letting it sit overnight. Given that the main problem was soggy skin, this approach seemed counterintuitive. The few remaining recipes went the dry-rub route, relying on dried spices to provide traditional barbecue flavor. Although most got the flavor wrong—and were plagued by the same bland-meat problem as the wet-sauced versions—the skin was noticeably less soggy the next day. So dry rubs were in, sticky sauces were out.

Trying some simple combinations of chili powder, black pepper, paprika, cayenne, and a little brown sugar for that trademark barbecue sauce sweetness, we fiddled with the proportions until we were able to replicate the flavors of a good sauce. By rubbing the spice mixture all over the chicken, even under the skin, we achieved the robust barbecue flavor we had thought only barbecue sauce

SCIENCE: Salting: Better than Brining?

In the test kitchen, we're strong advocates of brining—soaking meat in a solution of salt and water (and sometimes sugar) before cooking. The meat absorbs water as well as salt, with the latter helping the meat retain moisture as it cooks. With our Spice-Rubbed Picnic Chicken, however, brining made the skin soggy. To solve this problem, we turned to salting the chicken overnight, which helped the meat retain moisture as it cooked—and didn't harm the skin.

Chicken naturally contains some salt and lots of water, which coexist in a happy balance. In coating the chicken with salt, we threw off that balance. To restore order, or equilibrium, water in the meat moved to the surface, where it dissolved the salt.

But wouldn't drawing all that water out of the chicken make the situation worse, causing the meat to dry out? It certainly did—until we figured out the timing. When we tried cooking chicken that had been salted for three hours, the chicken cooked up drier than if we hadn't salted it. (The juices that had made it to the exterior simply evaporated in the oven.) But when we cooked the chicken after six hours, the story changed entirely. By that point, the exterior salt had pulled so much water to the surface that the balance of the salt concentration had changed. To restore equilibrium, the water simply changed directions, flowing back into the meat. But this time—and here's the key—the dissolved salt went along for the ride. Essentially, we had "brined" the chicken using its own juices instead of a bucket of water.

Once we successfully tapped into this means of delivering salt to the interior, we wondered if it was possible to deliver other flavors the same way. As it turns out, it all comes down to whether the flavoring agent is water-soluble (like salt) or fat-soluble. With the rub we used for our Spice-Rubbed Picnic Chicken, the salt and brown sugar, which dissolve easily in water, flowed right in, as did some of the distinguishing flavor compounds of the black pepper, cayenne, chili powder, and paprika. But the spiciness was waylaid at the surface. Capsaicin, the compound that gives chile peppers their spicy heat, is soluble only in fat, so it was unable to join the caravan.

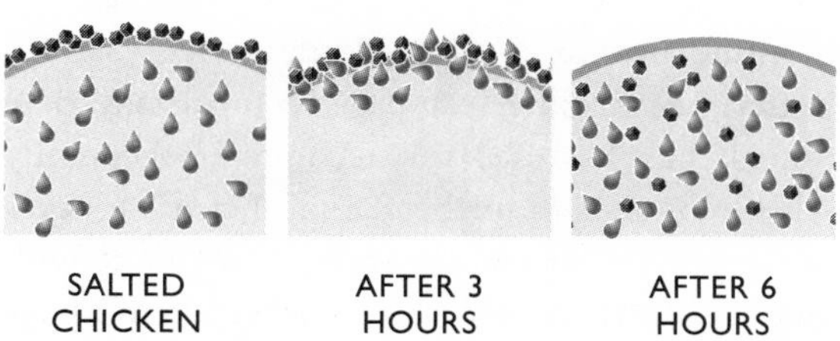

SALTED CHICKEN | AFTER 3 HOURS | AFTER 6 HOURS

could deliver. When tasters sampled the chicken the next day, it drew raves for flavor, and there were no sticky fingers in sight. Unfortunately, the skin was still flabby.

Clearly, we needed to spend more time trimming the fat before cooking the chicken. The breast and, especially, the thighs possess some excess fat that never quite renders properly, no matter how long the chicken cooks. Right out of the oven, that fat is mildly annoying; the coagulated mess you bite into the next day is disgusting.

The solution came in two parts. First, a simple but diligent trimming of the chicken pieces yielded improved results and took just a modicum of effort and time. Second, by slitting the skin with a sharp knife (and being careful not to cut into the flesh), we provided escape hatches for the melting fat during roasting; with a final blast of heat (we went all the way to 500 degrees) in the few last minutes, the skin was nicely rendered. The next day we found not tough, flabby skin but a thinner, flavorful coat on each piece of chicken. Although this skin was still less than crisp, we were making serious headway.

We always brine whole birds and sometimes chicken parts if cooked at particularly high heat (such as grilling or broiling). Brining involves soaking the meat in a solution of water, salt, and sometimes sugar, which helps flavor the meat and keep it moist. But when roasting chicken parts, we found that the added moisture also makes for flabby skin. Perhaps we could find a way to get the salt into the meat without the water. Back in our research library, we came across a technique used by Judi Rodgers, chef of San Francisco's Zuni Café. She salts all of her meat, vegetables, and even fish for up to three days depending on the size of the product. The salt is thought to draw moisture out of the product initially; then, after a few hours, the reverse happens, and the salt and moisture flow back into the flesh (see "Salting: Better than Brining?" on page 95 for details). The test kitchen has used this technique successfully with some recipes for beef, a meat that we never brine, but we had never thought to try it with chicken. Curious, we salted the chicken pieces, being careful not to under- or overseason, and then placed them in a covered dish in the refrigerator overnight.

The next morning, we added our spices and roasted the chicken. Tasters waited patiently as we allowed the chicken to cool to room temperature (after all, this dish wasn't going to be served hot). It was worth the wait. The chicken was well seasoned throughout and the meat very moist. Best of all, the skin was flavorful, delicate, and definitely not flabby. The salting had worked exactly as hoped, both seasoning the meat and keeping it moist, even during high-heat roasting. With the chicken where we wanted it to be, we worked on streamlining the recipe. We combined the spice rub with the salt and applied it at the same time, saving a step. We also placed the chicken pieces directly on the rack they'd be cooked on so that they would be oven-ready the next morning.

The final surprise—a completely unexpected bonus—was that after an overnight stay in the fridge, some of the spice flavor had penetrated the meat along with the salt. Not only had we come up with a great recipe for picnic chicken, but we had stumbled across a fascinating alternative to brining, one that could produce moist meat that was also deeply flavored by means of a spice rub.

Spice-Rubbed Picnic Chicken

SERVES 6 TO 8

If you do not own a broiler pan, use a roasting pan fitted with a flat wire rack. If you plan to serve the chicken later in the same day that you cook it, refrigerate it immediately after it has cooled, then let it come back to room temperature before serving. For more heat, use the larger amount of cayenne pepper.

- **3 tablespoons brown sugar**
- **2 tablespoons kosher salt**
- **2 tablespoons chili powder**
- **2 tablespoons sweet paprika**
- **2 teaspoons ground black pepper**
- **¼–½ teaspoon cayenne pepper (see note)**
- **5 pounds bone-in, skin-on chicken pieces (split breasts cut in half, drumsticks, and/or thighs), trimmed and skin slashed (see the illustration on page 108)**

1. Line a broiler-pan bottom with foil and cover with the broiler-pan top; set aside. Combine the sugar, salt, and spices in a small bowl. Coat the chicken pieces with the spices, gently lifting the skin to distribute the spice rub underneath but leaving it attached to the chicken. Place the chicken, skin-side up, on the prepared broiler pan, lightly tent with foil, and refrigerate for at least 6 hours and up to 24 hours.

2. Adjust an oven rack to the middle position and heat the oven to 425 degrees. Roast the chicken until the thickest part of the smallest piece registers 140 degrees on an instant-read thermometer, 15 to 20 minutes. Increase the oven temperature to 500 degrees and continue roasting until browned and crisp and the thickest part of the breast registers 160 to 165 degrees on an instant-read thermometer, 5 to 8 minutes longer, removing the pieces from the oven and transferring them to a wire rack once they finish cooking. Continue to roast the thighs and/or drumsticks, if using, until the thickest part of the meat registers 170 to 175 degrees on an instant-read thermometer, about 5 minutes longer.

3. Transfer the chicken to the wire rack and cool completely before refrigerating or serving.

Glazed Chicken Breasts

ON A RECENT FLIGHT TO PARIS, ONE OF our test kitchen colleagues chose the glazed chicken meal option. The flight attendant set down a plastic tray displaying a pale chicken breast with flabby skin smothered in a cloying glaze. He made it through two bites. That evening he found himself at an upscale restaurant ordering the house specialty: duck à l'orange. A silver platter arrived bearing carved duck pieces clad with deep-amber skin coated in a shiny, glazy sauce. The meat was perfectly moist, and each bite revealed the satisfying combination of roasted poultry and a citrus sauce balanced by sweet and sour flavors.

These contrasting experiences got us thinking about glazed chicken's status in the American culinary repertoire. Although this weeknight dinner is typically a humdrum affair, we set out to develop a glazed chicken breast with moist meat and perfectly rendered skin sufficiently coated with a complexly flavored glaze: a main course worthy of fine china, but still something we could make after work on a Tuesday night.

Most of the recipes for glazed chicken breasts uncovered in our research were simple "dump-and-bake" versions. The instructions: Pour a jar of fruit preserves over raw chicken breasts and bake. We were not surprised when our attempt at one of these recipes emerged from the oven looking much like an airplane meal. Despite the dump-and-bake recipe's dismal results—flabby, pale skin and a candylike glaze that pooled at the bottom of the pan—we did have to admire its simplicity. Browning the skin was an easy fix. We could brown the chicken in an ovensafe skillet on the stovetop before transferring the skillet to the oven to finish cooking. Then we could add a glaze to the pan just after the chicken breasts were sufficiently browned.

But first we needed to fix the glaze. Every recipe we dug up in our research used a good deal of sticky, sweet ingredients for the base: fruit preserves, molasses, maple syrup, and brown sugar. Our colleague had described his duck à l'orange sauce in Paris as glazy yet not cloying, and we wondered how this was achieved. Our hunch was that it was some sort of reduction sauce. Flipping through French cookbooks, we found our answer: reduced orange juice. Orange juice is sticky, and its acidity helps balance the sugar—another key ingredient in the duck sauce. We were not interested in creating a recipe for chicken à l'orange, but using orange juice in our glaze seemed like a good place to start.

The recipes we found for classic orange sauce offered us enough guidance to piece together a working glaze. After browning some chicken breasts, we transferred the meat to a plate while we reduced a mixture of orange juice and sugar until glazy. We then returned the chicken breasts to the skillet, rolled them in the glaze, and finished them off in the oven. Tasters complained that the glaze was "too thin" and "unbearably sweet," and that it "did not adhere to the chicken." Sugar would have been the ideal solution to the textural issue, but was inappropriate for a glaze that was already too sweet.

Then we remembered a technique a test kitchen colleague used for her cake frosting recipe. She mixed in a small amount of light corn syrup to add luster and body but, curiously, not sweetness. We had always assumed corn syrup was super-sweet, but when we tasted a lineup of sugar, brown sugar, maple syrup, and honey against corn syrup, we discovered just the opposite. Nutrition labels on the sweeteners confirmed our finding: Corn syrup contains half (and sometimes less than half) as much sugar as other sweeteners.

Excited by the prospect that corn syrup might help our cause, we immediately trimmed some chicken breasts, heated a skillet, and whipped up a new batch of glaze. Not only did this corn-syrup-enhanced glaze cook up perfectly, the meat seemed juicier—especially surprising, since the glaze without the corn syrup had already been keeping our chicken breasts quite moist. A quick call to our science editor revealed that the concentrated glucose in corn syrup has a high affinity for water, which means it helps to hold moisture in the glaze, making the overall dish seem juicier. That same glucose also thickens and adds a gloss to the glaze.

However, as much as tasters liked the glaze's clean flavor, they now thought it wasn't sweet enough. A little honey instead of sugar gave the glaze just the right level of sweetness, and minced shallot, vinegar, Dijon mustard, and a pinch of pepper flakes created complexity.

Despite these improvements, there was still one complaint: We wanted the glaze to cling even better to the chicken. From past tests, we knew that adding cornstarch or flour to the sauce only made it gloppy. Maybe the problem wasn't with the glaze but with the chicken. What if we added a thin layer of flour to the outside of the meat before browning it? In the test kitchen, we don't typically coat meat with flour before browning it, but it gave the chicken breasts a thin, crispy crust that served as a good grip for the glaze. (Cornstarch also held the glaze, but it turned the skin a bit slimy.) To ensure that the flour didn't brown too much before the chicken skin adequately rendered, we found it necessary to use a lower flame.

We added a small amount of orange juice just before serving to brighten the glaze flavors even further. This finishing touch made all the difference. Now we had elevated glazed chicken to an elegant new height—far beyond 30,000 feet.

Orange-Honey Glazed Chicken Breasts

SERVES 4

When reducing the sauce in step 5, remember that the skillet handle will be hot; use an oven mitt. If the glaze looks dry during baking, add up to 2 tablespoons of juice to the pan. If your skillet is not ovensafe, brown the chicken breasts and reduce the glaze as instructed, then transfer the chicken and glaze to a 13 by 9-inch baking dish and bake (but don't wash the skillet). When the chicken is fully cooked, transfer the chicken to a plate to rest and scrape the glaze back into the skillet to be further reduced.

- 1½ cups plus 2 tablespoons orange juice
- ⅓ cup light corn syrup
- 3 tablespoons honey
- 1 tablespoon Dijon mustard
- 1 tablespoon distilled white vinegar
- ⅛ teaspoon red pepper flakes
- Salt and ground black pepper
- ½ cup unbleached all-purpose flour
- 4 bone-in, skin-on split chicken breasts (10 to 12 ounces each), trimmed
- 2 tablespoons vegetable oil
- 1 medium shallot, minced (about 3 tablespoons)

1. Adjust an oven rack to the middle position and heat the oven to 375 degrees. Whisk 1½ cups of the orange juice, the corn syrup, honey, mustard, vinegar, pepper flakes, ⅛ teaspoon salt, and ⅛ teaspoon pepper together in a medium bowl. Set aside. Place the flour in a shallow dish. Pat the chicken dry with paper towels and season with salt and pepper.

Working with one chicken breast at a time, coat the chicken with flour, shaking off the excess.

2. Heat the oil in an ovensafe 12-inch skillet over medium-high heat until just smoking (see note). Brown the chicken on both sides, 5 to 8 minutes per side, reducing the heat if the pan begins to scorch. Transfer the chicken to a plate.

3. Pour off all but 1 teaspoon of fat from the pan. Return the pan to medium heat, add the shallot, and cook until softened, about 1½ minutes. Increase the heat to high and add the orange juice mixture. Simmer, stirring occasionally, until syrupy and reduced to about 1 cup, 6 to 10 minutes. Remove the skillet from the heat and tilt it to one side so that the glaze pools in the corner of the pan. Using tongs, roll each chicken breast in pooled glaze to coat evenly and place, skin-side down, in the skillet.

4. Transfer the skillet to the oven and bake until the thickest part of the breast registers 160 to 165 degrees on an instant-read thermometer, 25 to 30 minutes, turning the chicken skin-side up halfway through cooking. Transfer the chicken to a platter and let rest for 5 minutes.

5. Meanwhile, return the skillet to high heat (the handle will be very hot) and cook the glaze, stirring constantly, until thick and syrupy, about 1 minute. Remove the pan from the heat and whisk in the remaining 2 tablespoons orange juice. Spoon 1 teaspoon of the glaze over each breast and serve, passing the remaining glaze separately.

➢ VARIATIONS

Apple-Maple Glazed Chicken Breasts

Follow the recipe for Orange-Honey Glazed Chicken Breasts, substituting apple cider for the orange juice and 2 tablespoons maple syrup for the honey.

Pineapple–Brown Sugar Glazed Chicken Breasts

Follow the recipe for Orange-Honey Glazed Chicken Breasts, substituting pineapple juice for the orange juice and 2 tablespoons brown sugar for the honey.

Chicken and Vegetable Bakes

BAKED CHICKEN IS AN OLD STANDBY FOR easy weeknight meals, but it is typically met with little excitement when it appears on the dinner table—overcooked, dry, and just plain bland are the descriptions that come to mind. We wanted to turn simple baked chicken into a meal, complete with tender, flavorful vegetables and a zesty sauce to accompany the moist, well-seasoned meat. This dish would stand on its own for dinner, perhaps with the lone addition of crusty bread to sop up the extra sauce.

We started our kitchen tests by choosing the type of chicken. Bone-in, skin-on breasts were tasters' favorite because the bone and skin protected the meat from drying out in the oven, keeping it moist and tender. (That said, boneless, skinless breasts can be substituted, but the baking time will be slightly shorter.) Next, we had to figure out how to get flavor into the chicken.

Simply brushing the chicken with butter and adding a sprinkling of herbs wasn't giving us the flavor impact we wanted. We turned to marinating instead, hoping to incorporate some of the marinade into a flavorful sauce at the end. The only problem, however, is that most marinades contain some sort of acidic component—such as lemon juice, vinegar, or yogurt—that breaks down the meat, resulting in mealy, mushy chicken when marinated for any length of time. As a solution to this problem, we used an acid-free marinade. After mixing the marinade, we reserved about ⅓ cup, spiked it with a little lemon juice, and poured it over the chicken after it emerged from the oven. This technique was perfect for this recipe—the chicken was moist, tender, and thoroughly permeated by the flavors of the marinade, while the acid that was incorporated at the end added a sharp, fresh dimension. Since we hoped to add a variety of vegetables to our baked chicken, we chose a garlic and herb marinade for its bright but neutral flavors.

It was now time to turn our attention to the vegetables. We wanted vegetables that required minimal prep and could be thrown right into the baking dish with the chicken. Cherry tomatoes seemed like an obvious choice. First we tried them cut in half, but found that they broke down too much in the oven. Left whole, the tomatoes softened beautifully, and some even burst, releasing their flavorful juices into the pan to make a sauce while still maintaining their presence in the dish.

Searching for other vegetables that would complement the tomatoes, we thought of the flavors of the Mediterranean and chose fennel for its sweet anise flavor and kalamata olives for their brininess. To ensure that the fennel cooked at the same rate as the chicken and tomatoes, we found that it was important to slice it thin.

Tasters were happy with this trio of vegetables but wanted a bit more flavor. Instead of chopping more shallots, garlic, and herbs, we simply tossed the vegetables with a couple tablespoons of the reserved marinade we were using to finish the chicken. The marinade heightened the flavor of the vegetables and pooled in the baking dish with the juice from the tomatoes to make a tasty sauce. From previous tests, we knew 450 degrees was the ideal temperature for our chicken bake, and a 45-minute stint in the oven ensured that the chicken was cooked all the way through yet still remained moist and tender. A sprinkle of fresh basil just before serving was the perfect finishing touch.

Encouraged by the success of our first chicken bake, we ventured on to create a few other vegetable combinations to vary the dish. After numerous tests, we settled on three other options. One incorporates fennel again, but swaps out the tomatoes and kalamata olives for oranges and oil-cured olives. The next variation is inspired by early spring and consists of a mixture of asparagus and artichokes. The final combination is a heartier one, pairing green bell peppers with chorizo and cherry tomatoes.

We were happy with how far we had taken a simple baked chicken dish. With moist, tender chicken, fresh vegetables, and a flavorful but virtually effortless sauce, we'll never look at baked chicken the same way again.

PREPARING FENNEL

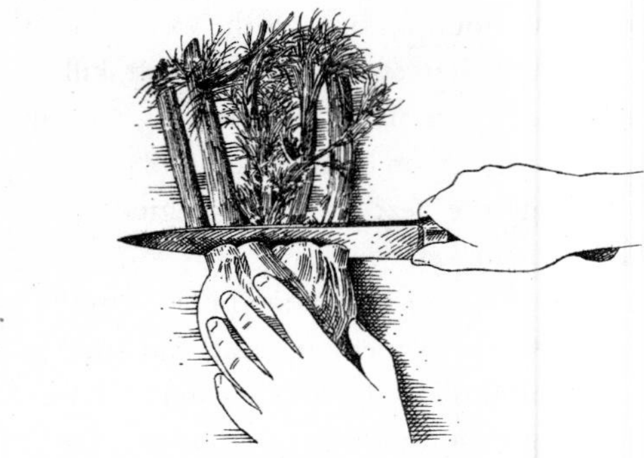

1. Cut off the stems and feathery fronds. (The fronds can be minced and used for a garnish, if desired.)

2. Trim a very thin slice from the base and remove any tough or blemished outer layers from the bulb.

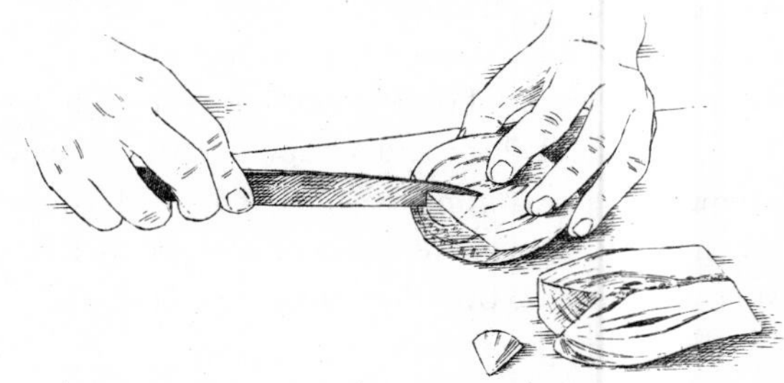

3. Cut the bulb in half through the base. Use a small, sharp knife to remove the pyramid-shaped core.

4. Place the cored fennel on a work surface and, with the knife blade parallel to the cutting board, cut the fennel in half crosswise. With the knife blade perpendicular to the cutting board, cut the fennel pieces lengthwise into thin strips.

Baked Chicken with Fennel, Tomatoes, and Olives

SERVES 4

If you choose to use boneless, skinless breasts, note that the cooking time will be slightly shorter—start checking for doneness about 10 minutes earlier than you would for bone-in, skin-on breasts.

CHICKEN AND MARINADE

- ½ cup extra-virgin olive oil
- ¼ cup water
- ¼ cup minced fresh basil leaves
- 1 medium shallot, minced (about 3 tablespoons)
- 6 medium garlic cloves, minced or pressed through a garlic press (about 2 tablespoons)
- 1 teaspoon salt
- ¼ teaspoon ground black pepper
- 4 bone-in, skin-on split chicken breasts (10 to 12 ounces each), trimmed

VEGETABLES

- 2 medium fennel bulbs (about 1½ pounds), trimmed of stalks, cored, and sliced thin (see the illustrations on page 100)
- 1 pint cherry tomatoes (10 to 12 ounces)
- ½ cup kalamata olives, pitted (see the illustration at right)
- ½ teaspoon salt
- ¼ teaspoon ground black pepper
- 2 tablespoons juice from 1 lemon
- 3 tablespoons chopped fresh basil leaves

1. For the chicken and marinade: In a medium bowl, whisk together all the ingredients except the chicken until well combined. Transfer ⅓ cup of the marinade to an airtight container and set aside. Add the remaining marinade to a large zipper-lock bag along with the chicken breasts. Seal shut, toss to coat, and refrigerate for at least 1 hour and up to 24 hours. (If you marinate the chicken for more than 1 hour, refrigerate the reserved marinade until you are ready to cook the chicken; bring to room temperature before using.)

2. For the vegetables: Adjust an oven rack to the middle position and heat the oven to 450 degrees. In a large bowl, combine 2 tablespoons of the reserved marinade with the fennel, tomatoes, olives, salt, and pepper and toss to coat. Transfer the vegetables to a 13 by 9-inch baking dish.

3. Remove the chicken breasts from the zipper-lock bag and lay them, skin-side up, on top of the vegetables. Bake until the thickest part of the breast registers 160 to 165 degrees on an instant-read thermometer, about 45 minutes. Meanwhile, stir the lemon juice into the reserved marinade.

4. Transfer the chicken and vegetables to a serving platter along with the cooking juices from the pan. Pour the reserved marinade mixture over the chicken and let rest for 5 minutes. Sprinkle with the chopped basil and serve.

VARIATIONS

Baked Chicken with Fennel, Oranges, and Oil-Cured Olives

If the fennel retains a slight crunch when the chicken is cooked through, return the vegetables to the oven while the chicken rests.

CHICKEN AND MARINADE

- ½ cup extra-virgin olive oil
- ¼ cup water
- ¼ cup minced fresh cilantro leaves
- 1 medium shallot, minced (about 3 tablespoons)

PITTING OLIVES QUICKLY

Removing pits from olives by hand is not all that quick and easy. To speed things up a bit, cover a cutting board with a clean kitchen towel and spread the olives on top, spacing them about 1 inch apart. Place a second clean towel over the olives. Using a mallet, pound all of the olives firmly, being careful not to split the pits. Remove the top towel and, using your fingers, press the pit out of each olive.

- 6 medium garlic cloves, minced or pressed through a garlic press (about 2 tablespoons)
- 1 teaspoon salt
- ¼ teaspoon ground black pepper
- ⅛ teaspoon cayenne pepper
- 4 bone-in, skin-on split chicken breasts (10 to 12 ounces each), trimmed

VEGETABLES

- 2 medium fennel bulbs (about 1½ pounds), trimmed of stalks, cored, and sliced thin (see the illustrations on page 100)
- 2 oranges, peeled, quartered lengthwise, and sliced crosswise into ½-inch-thick wedges (see the illustrations below)
- ½ cup oil-cured black olives, pitted (see the illustration on page 101)
- ½ teaspoon salt
- ¼ teaspoon ground black pepper
- 2 tablespoons juice from 1 lemon
- 3 tablespoons minced fresh cilantro leaves

CUTTING CITRUS

Here is how to cut up an orange—or any citrus fruit—into bite-sized pieces that don't fall apart when cooked.

1. Cut away the rind and pith from the orange using a paring knife.

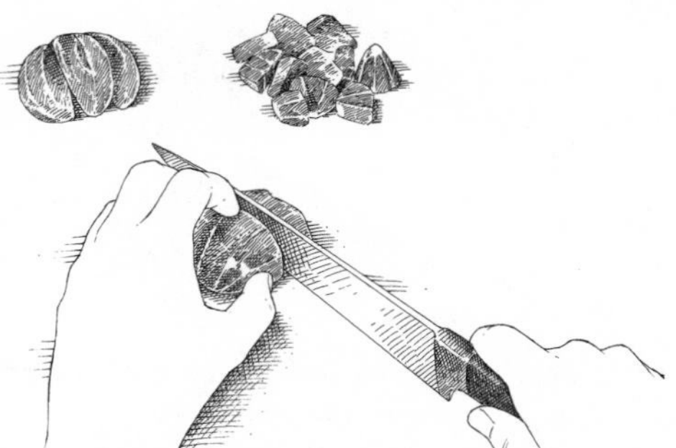

2. Quarter the peeled orange, then slice each quarter crosswise in ½-inch-thick wedges.

1. FOR THE CHICKEN AND MARINADE: In a medium bowl, whisk together all the ingredients except the chicken until well combined. Transfer ⅓ cup of the marinade to an airtight container and set aside. Add the remaining marinade to a large zipper-lock bag along with the chicken breasts. Seal shut, toss to coat, and refrigerate for at least 1 hour and up to 24 hours. (If you marinate the chicken for more than 1 hour, refrigerate the reserved marinade until you are ready to cook the chicken; bring to room temperature before using.)

2. FOR THE VEGETABLES: Adjust an oven rack to the middle position and heat the oven to 450 degrees. In a large bowl, combine 2 tablespoons of the reserved marinade with the fennel, oranges, olives, salt, and pepper and toss to coat. Transfer the vegetables to a 13 by 9-inch baking dish.

3. Remove the chicken breasts from the zipper-lock bag and lay them, skin-side up, on top of the vegetables. Bake until the thickest part of the breast registers 160 to 165 degrees on an instant-read thermometer, about 45 minutes. Meanwhile, stir the lemon juice into the reserved marinade.

4. Transfer the chicken and vegetables to a serving platter along with the cooking juices from the pan. Pour the reserved marinade mixture over the chicken and let rest for 5 minutes. Sprinkle with the minced cilantro and serve.

Baked Chicken with Spring Vegetables, Capers, and Lemon

Be sure to buy thick asparagus for this recipe—pencil-thin asparagus will overcook. Thaw the artichokes completely and carefully pat them dry before roasting or else they won't brown and might also prevent the other vegetables from browning.

CHICKEN AND MARINADE

- ½ cup extra-virgin olive oil
- ¼ cup water
- ¼ cup minced fresh tarragon leaves
- 1 medium shallot, minced (about 3 tablespoons)
- 6 medium garlic cloves, minced or pressed through a garlic press (about 2 tablespoons)
- 1 teaspoon salt

- ¼ teaspoon ground black pepper
- 4 bone-in, skin-on split chicken breasts (10 to 12 ounces each), trimmed

VEGETABLES

- 1 (9-ounce) box frozen artichokes, thawed and patted dry
- 1 pound asparagus (about 1 bunch), tough ends trimmed, cut in half
- ¼ cup capers, rinsed
- ½ lemon, sliced ¼ inch thick, end pieces discarded
- ½ teaspoon salt
- ¼ teaspoon ground black pepper
- 2 tablespoons juice from 1 lemon
- 3 tablespoons minced fresh tarragon leaves

1. FOR THE CHICKEN AND MARINADE: In a medium bowl, whisk together all the ingredients except the chicken until well combined. Transfer ⅓ cup of the marinade to an airtight container and set aside. Add the remaining marinade to a large zipper-lock bag along with the chicken breasts. Seal shut, toss to coat, and refrigerate for at least 1 hour and up to 24 hours. (If you marinate the chicken for more than 1 hour, refrigerate the reserved marinade until you are ready to cook the chicken; bring to room temperature before using.)

2. FOR THE VEGETABLES: Adjust an oven rack to the middle position and heat the oven to 450 degrees. In a large bowl, combine 2 tablespoons of the reserved marinade with the artichokes, asparagus, capers, lemon slices, salt, and pepper and toss to coat. Transfer the vegetables to a 13 by 9-inch baking dish.

3. Remove the chicken breasts from the zipper-lock bag and lay them, skin-side up, on top of the vegetables. Bake until the thickest part of the breast registers 160 to 165 degrees on an instant-read thermometer, about 45 minutes. Meanwhile, stir the lemon juice into the reserved marinade.

4. Transfer the chicken and vegetables to a serving platter along with the cooking juices from the pan. Pour the reserved marinade mixture over the chicken and let rest for 5 minutes. Sprinkle with the tarragon and serve.

Baked Chicken with Green Peppers and Chorizo

If you cannot find chorizo, substitute linguiça or smoked kielbasa.

CHICKEN AND MARINADE

- ½ cup extra-virgin olive oil
- ¼ cup water
- ¼ cup minced fresh parsley leaves
- 1 medium shallot, minced (about 3 tablespoons)
- 6 medium garlic cloves, minced or pressed through a garlic press (about 2 tablespoons)
- 1 teaspoon salt
- ¼ teaspoon ground black pepper
- 4 bone-in, skin-on split chicken breasts (10 to 12 ounces each), trimmed

VEGETABLES

- 2 green bell peppers, stemmed, seeded, and sliced thin
- 1 pint cherry tomatoes (about 12 ounces)
- 4 ounces chorizo (see note), sliced ¼ inch thick, then cut into half-moons
- ½ teaspoon salt
- ¼ teaspoon ground black pepper
- 2 tablespoons sherry vinegar
- 3 tablespoons minced fresh parsley leaves

1. FOR THE CHICKEN AND MARINADE: In a medium bowl, whisk together all the ingredients except the chicken until well combined. Transfer ⅓ cup of the marinade to an airtight container and set aside. Add the remaining marinade to a large zipper-lock bag along with the chicken breasts. Seal shut, toss to coat, and refrigerate for at least 1 hour and up to 24 hours. (If you marinate the chicken for more than 1 hour, refrigerate the reserved marinade until you are ready to cook the chicken; bring to room temperature before using.)

2. FOR THE VEGETABLES: Adjust an oven rack to the middle position and heat the oven to 450 degrees. In a large bowl, combine 2 tablespoons of the reserved marinade with the bell peppers, tomatoes, chorizo, salt, and pepper and toss to coat. Transfer the vegetables to a 13 by 9-inch baking dish.

3. Remove the chicken breasts from the zipper-lock bag and lay them, skin-side up, on top of the vegetables. Bake until the thickest part of the breast registers 160 to 165 degrees on an instant-read thermometer, about 45 minutes. Meanwhile, stir the vinegar into the reserved marinade.

4. Transfer the chicken and vegetables to a serving platter along with the cooking juices from the pan. Pour the reserved marinade mixture over the chicken and let rest for 5 minutes. Sprinkle with the parsley and serve.

Easy Stuffed Chicken Breasts

WHILE WE LOVE OUR BREADED AND STUFFED chicken breasts (see page 370), sometimes we yearn for an easier approach—one that can be assembled quickly on a weeknight rather than saved for a special-occasion dinner. This would mean no-fuss fillings and a simple method for stuffing the chicken—without butterflying and pounding chicken breasts or even breading them.

Turning first to boneless, skinless breasts, we wondered if we could construct a filling that we could place on top of, instead of inside, the chicken. Cheese seemed like the obvious starting point—it is a common filling for stuffed chicken, and we thought it would adhere nicely to the top of the chicken breasts. We tried both shredded and sliced, but both forms tended to slide off the breasts and burn on the baking sheet. Although some of the cheese did adhere, tasters still wanted a creamier filling. A plain chicken breast with cheese melted over the top simply wasn't going to cut it.

Though we wanted a simpler approach than our breaded and stuffed chicken breasts, we wondered if we could still borrow a couple of basics. We whipped up a simple mixture of cream cheese and goat cheese seasoned with lemon zest, garlic, and herbs—easy enough and no cooking required. Then we simply packed the mixture on top of the chicken breasts, and into the oven they went. As the chicken baked, the stuffing became molten and, like the cheese we'd tried before, slid right off the breasts. The stuffing that did remain on the chicken, however, basted the breasts, keeping them moist and creating a creamy, flavorful sauce. We were onto something. If only we could find a better way to get the mixture to adhere to the chicken.

A little research led us to change gears and try bone-in, skin-on chicken breasts. We had come across several recipes that called for cutting a pocket into the breasts just above the bone, and others that stuffed the filling under the skin. First, we tried cutting a pocket into the breast and packing the filling inside. The results were decent, but a significant amount of the filling oozed out, and cutting a pocket into the breasts was a bit more effort than we wanted.

With high hopes, we tried the under-skin option—after all, there is already a natural pocket in place. Working carefully, we loosened the skin and fit about 1½ tablespoons of the cheese mixture underneath. The skin held the filling in place, and when the chicken emerged from the oven it was tender, with a creamy, tangy, saucelike filling. Better yet, the creamy filling basted the breasts as they cooked, keeping the meat perfectly moist and juicy. Our results were the best yet, but one large problem remained—the skin was flabby and inedible.

We wondered if increasing the oven temperature would help to crisp up the skin. All along we had been baking the chicken breasts at 375 degrees. We tried cooking the chicken at 400 degrees, 425 degrees, and 450 degrees. The skin on the chicken cooked at 450 degrees was golden brown and crisp, and the meat was perfectly cooked. Success! With our basic filling recipe in place, we tried adding a variety of ingredients. We quickly found that melting cheeses like cheddar and Gruyère, even when mixed with cream cheese, ooze out from under the skin, and that chutney burns. In all of our tests, the potent ingredients—like black olives, blue cheese, and Parmesan cheese—mixed into a creamy base made the most flavorful stuffings, and they all stayed in place under the skin.

A final note: When shopping for bone-in, skin-on chicken breasts, it is important that the skin be intact to secure the stuffing. If possible, hand-select the chicken breasts from your butcher's case, rather than buying packaged sets of chicken breasts.

Easy Stuffed Chicken Breasts with Cheese Filling

SERVES 4

It is important to buy chicken breasts with skin still attached and intact; otherwise the stuffing will leak out. If you do not own a broiler pan, use a roasting pan fitted with a flat wire rack. Serve with lemon wedges, if desired.

- **4** **bone-in, skin-on split chicken breasts (10 to 12 ounces each), trimmed**
- **1** **recipe cheese filling (pages 105–106)**
- **Olive oil**
- **Salt and ground black pepper**

1. Adjust an oven rack to the middle position and heat the oven to 450 degrees. Line a broiler-pan bottom with foil and cover with the broiler-pan top; set aside.

2. Pat the chicken dry with paper towels. Following the illustrations below, use your fingers to gently loosen the center portion of skin covering each breast. Place a quarter of the filling under the skin, directly on the meat in the center of each breast half. Gently press on the skin to distribute the filling over the meat. Rub the skin with oil and season with salt and pepper.

3. Place the chicken breasts skin-side up on the prepared broiler pan. Bake until the thickest part of the breast registers 160 to 165 degrees an instant-read thermometer, 30 to 35 minutes. Let the chicken rest for 5 minutes before serving.

FILLING EASY STUFFED CHICKEN BREASTS

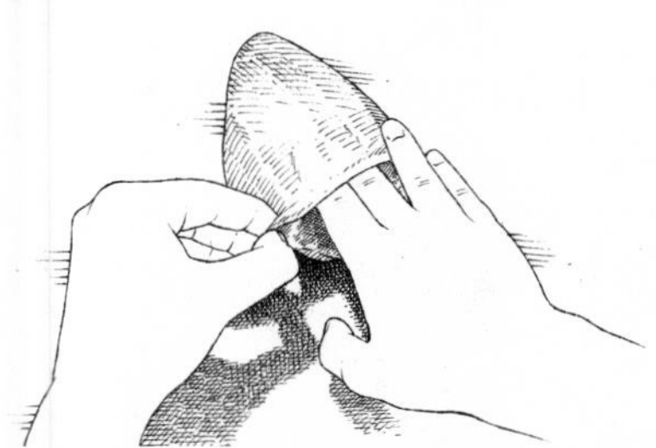

1. Using your fingers, gently loosen the center portion of the skin covering each breast, making a pocket for the filling.

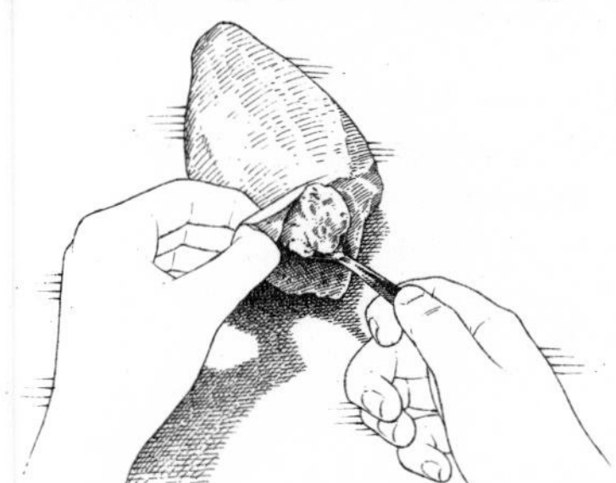

2. Using your fingers or a small spoon, place a quarter of the filling under the loosened skin, directly on the meat in the center of each breast half. Gently press on the skin to distribute the filling over the meat.

Lemon and Goat Cheese Filling

MAKES ENOUGH TO STUFF 4 BONE-IN, SKIN-ON SPLIT CHICKEN BREASTS

- **3** **ounces goat cheese, softened (about ¾ cup)**
- **2** **ounces cream cheese, softened (about ¼ cup)**
- **2** **teaspoons minced fresh thyme leaves**
- **1** **small garlic clove, minced or pressed through a garlic press (about ½ teaspoon)**
- **¼** **teaspoon grated zest from 1 lemon**
- **⅛** **teaspoon salt**
- **⅛** **teaspoon ground black pepper**

Mix all the ingredients together until uniform and spread 1½ tablespoons per chicken breast under the skin as directed in the recipe.

Olive and Goat Cheese Filling

MAKES ENOUGH TO STUFF 4 BONE-IN, SKIN-ON SPLIT CHICKEN BREASTS

- **3** **ounces goat cheese, softened (about ¾ cup)**
- **2** **ounces cream cheese, softened (about ¼ cup)**
- **¼** **cup pitted kalamata olives, chopped fine**
- **2** **teaspoons minced fresh oregano leaves**
- **1** **small garlic clove, minced or pressed through a garlic press (about ½ teaspoon)**
- **⅛** **teaspoon salt**
- **⅛** **teaspoon ground black pepper**

Mix all the ingredients together until uniform and spread 1½ tablespoons per chicken breast under the skin as directed in the recipe.

Blue Cheese and Scallion Filling

MAKES ENOUGH TO STUFF 4 BONE-IN, SKIN-ON SPLIT CHICKEN BREASTS

- 3 ounces blue cheese, softened (about ¾ cup)
- 2 ounces cream cheese, softened (about ¼ cup)
- 1 scallion, minced
- 1 small garlic clove, minced or pressed through a garlic press (about ½ teaspoon)
- ⅛ teaspoon salt
- ⅛ teaspoon ground black pepper

Mix all the ingredients together until uniform and spread 1½ tablespoons per chicken breast under the skin as directed in the recipe.

Parmesan and Basil Filling

MAKES ENOUGH TO STUFF 4 BONE-IN, SKIN-ON SPLIT CHICKEN BREASTS

- 2 ounces Parmesan cheese, grated (about 1 cup)
- 2 ounces cream cheese, softened (about ¼ cup)
- ¼ cup minced fresh basil leaves
- 2 tablespoons extra-virgin olive oil
- 1 small garlic clove, minced or pressed through a garlic press (about ½ teaspoon)
- ⅛ teaspoon salt
- ⅛ teaspoon ground black pepper

Mix all the ingredients together until uniform and spread 1½ tablespoons per chicken breast under the skin as directed in the recipe.

Skillet Green Beans

SERVES 4

This is a great way to use older, end-of-season green beans. It is a departure from most green bean recipes; a slow braising process infuses the beans with flavor and leaves them meltingly tender.

- 1 tablespoon olive oil
- 1 medium shallot, minced (about 3 tablespoons)
- ¾ cup low-sodium chicken broth
- ½ teaspoon minced fresh thyme leaves
- 1 pound green beans, trimmed (see the illustration)
- Salt and ground black pepper

Heat the oil in a 12-inch skillet over medium heat until shimmering. Add the shallot and cook until lightly browned, about 4 minutes. Stir in the broth and thyme, then add the beans. Cover, reduce the heat to low, and simmer until the beans are tender, 15 to 20 minutes. Season with salt and pepper to taste and serve.

PREPPING GREEN BEANS

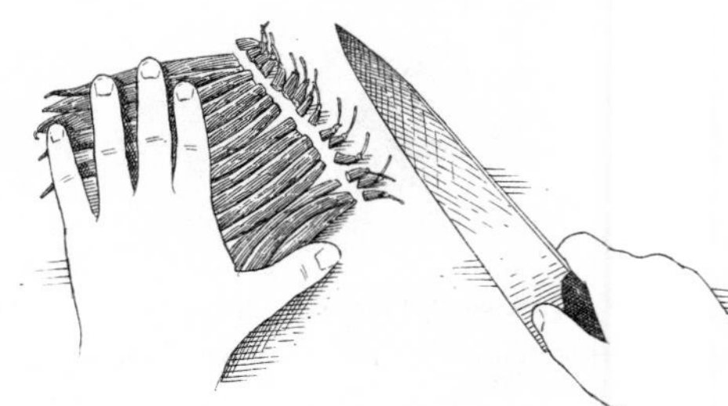

To make the task of preparing green beans for cooking less tedious, try this easy technique. Line the beans up in a row and trim off the inedible stem ends with just one cut.

Broiled Chicken

BROILING IS A GREAT YEAR-ROUND ALTERnative to grilling. When properly prepared, broiled chicken parts are moist and well seasoned, with a lovely caramelized flavor and crisp skin. Broiled chicken can also be made quickly and inexpensively, requiring little attention and the most basic of ingredients, making it the ultimate weeknight dinner.

The difficulties with broiling chicken relate directly back to the level of heat, which is obviously high. If food is placed too close to the heating element, it can easily char on the outside long before it is cooked through at the center. Achieving crisp skin can be hard if it is not given time to slowly render its fat. To avoid these problems, we would have to figure out the optimal distance between the oven rack and the heat source. In addition, we wanted to determine which parts of the chicken are best suited to broiling, and the best way to season the meat.

Starting with the chicken itself, we chose to broil only bone-in, skin-on chicken parts for two reasons. First, we like the contrast of crisp skin with juicy, tender meat, and we know that the skin helps to keep the meat from drying out. Second, chicken cooked with the bone in seems to have a better, meatier flavor.

After a number of tests, we ultimately chose chicken thighs as the most appropriate chicken part for broiling. They are small enough that they can cook all the way through without the skin burning, and they are less likely to dry out than breasts. If you really like white meat, breasts are doable as well, and we have included a variation for cooking them. If your family has lovers of both dark and white meat, we have a recipe for cooking them together, which simply requires removing the breasts from the oven earlier than the thighs to prevent them from overcooking and drying out.

From prior discoveries in the test kitchen, we knew that brining the chicken (soaking it in a solution of water, salt, and sometimes sugar) was crucial for simple broiled chicken. Brining helps add moisture to the chicken—especially important when cooking chicken at such high temperatures—and results in well-seasoned meat.

With the type of chicken and preparation in place, we moved on to finding the best way to broil it. We decided to limit ourselves to the modern-style oven broilers, in which the distance from the heat can be controlled. Many recipes we found said to broil the bird four to eight inches away from the heating element. This distance resulted in chicken with thick, charred, rubbery skin and meat that was not always cooked through. We tried broiling chicken at every rack level in the oven, starting with the highest position (closest to the heating element) and moving all the way down to the lowest position. We found that chicken cooked on the bottom shelf, about 13 inches from the top of the oven, was best, staying moist and tender. To caramelize the chicken even more after it was almost completely cooked, we moved it up to the second shelf from the top for the final minute or two of broiling. This approach gave us chicken that closely resembled grilled chicken in both appearance and depth of meaty flavor.

Although the skin was now well browned, we still found it a touch too thick for our taste. Remembering a technique used in cooking duck, we tried slashing the skin a few times before placing it in the oven to broil. This worked quite well. The skin rendered just a little more fat, because of the extra surface area exposed to the heat of the broiler. We also discovered that starting the chicken skin-side down was key to getting a thin, crisp skin. This way, we could finish the chicken skin-side up so that it could crisp under the direct heat of the broiler.

All this chicken needed now was a rub for a burst of flavor. Garlic, lemon, and rosemary add just the right notes, and we offer a couple of flavor variations so that you can mix things up. You can also add barbecue sauce (see page 209 for our recipe) in the last few minutes of the cooking process (the high sugar content in most sauces will burn under the heat of the broiler if the sauce is put on at the beginning).

Broiled Chicken Thighs with Garlic, Lemon, and Rosemary Rub

SERVES 4

If using kosher chicken, skip the brining process. To use kosher salt in the brine, see page 12 for conversion information and more tips on brining. If you do not own a broiler pan, use a roasting pan fitted with a flat wire rack. This recipe will work only in broilers with adjustable racks, not in fixed-height broilers.

CHICKEN

- ½ cup table salt
- ½ cup sugar
- 8 bone-in, skin-on chicken thighs (5 to 6 ounces each), trimmed
- Ground black pepper

GARLIC, LEMON, AND ROSEMARY RUB

- 5 medium garlic cloves, minced or pressed through a garlic press (about 5 teaspoons)
- 2 teaspoons grated zest and ¼ cup juice from 2 lemons
- 1 tablespoon minced fresh rosemary
- Pinch ground black pepper
- 3 tablespoons extra-virgin olive oil

1. Dissolve the salt and sugar in 2 quarts cold water in a large container. Submerge the chicken in the brine, cover, and refrigerate for 30 minutes. Meanwhile, combine the garlic, lemon zest, rosemary, and pepper in a small bowl. Whisk the lemon juice and oil together in another small bowl.

2. Remove the chicken from the brine, rinse well, and pat dry with paper towels. Spread about 1½ teaspoons of the garlic mixture under the skin. Following the illustration at right, make three diagonal slashes in the skin.

3. Meanwhile, adjust one oven rack to the lowest position and the other rack to the upper-middle position (the top rack should be about 6 inches from the broiler element; the bottom rack should be 13 inches from it); heat the broiler. Line a broiler-pan bottom with foil and cover with the broiler-pan top. Season the chicken pieces with pepper and place, skin-side down, on the prepared broiler pan.

4. Broil the chicken on the bottom rack of the oven until just beginning to brown, 12 to 16 minutes. Using tongs, turn the chicken skin-side up and continue to broil on the bottom rack until the skin is slightly crisp and the thickest part of the thigh registers 170 to 175 degrees on an instant-read thermometer, about 15 minutes. Brush the chicken with the lemon juice and oil mixture and move the pan to the upper rack; broil until the chicken is dark spotty brown and the skin is thin and crisp, about 1 minute. Serve.

VARIATIONS

Shallot, Orange, and Thyme Rub

MAKES ABOUT ⅓ CUP, ENOUGH FOR 1 RECIPE BROILED CHICKEN

- 1 medium shallot, minced (about 3 tablespoons)
- 2 teaspoons grated zest and ¼ cup juice from 1 orange
- 1 tablespoon minced fresh thyme leaves
- Pinch ground black pepper
- 3 tablespoons extra-virgin olive oil

Combine the shallot, orange zest, thyme, and pepper in a small bowl. Whisk the orange juice and oil together in another small bowl. Follow the recipe for Broiled Chicken Thighs with Garlic, Lemon, and Rosemary Rub, substituting the shallot mixture for the garlic mixture, and the orange juice and oil mixture for the lemon juice and oil mixture.

ENSURING CRISP SKIN

Make three diagonal slashes in the skin of each chicken piece to help render the fat.

Ginger, Lime, and Cilantro Rub

MAKES ABOUT ⅓ CUP, ENOUGH FOR 1 RECIPE BROILED CHICKEN

- 2 tablespoons minced or grated fresh ginger
- 2 teaspoons grated zest and ¼ cup juice from 3 limes
- 2 tablespoons minced fresh cilantro leaves
- Pinch ground black pepper
- 3 tablespoons extra-virgin olive oil

Combine the ginger, lime zest, cilantro, and pepper in a small bowl. Whisk the lime juice and oil together in another small bowl. Follow the recipe for Broiled Chicken Thighs with Garlic, Lemon, and Rosemary Rub, substituting the ginger mixture for the garlic mixture, and the lime juice and oil mixture for the lemon juice and oil mixture.

Broiled Chicken Breasts

Follow the recipe for Broiled Chicken Thighs, substituting 4 bone-in, skin-on split chicken breasts (about 12 ounces each) for the chicken thighs. Broil the chicken breasts, skin-side down, on the bottom rack until just beginning to brown, 12 to 16 minutes. Using tongs, turn the chicken skin-side up and continue to broil on the bottom rack until the skin is slightly crisp and the thickest part of the breast registers 160 to 165 degrees on an instant-read thermometer, about 10 minutes. Move the pan to the upper rack; broil until the chicken is dark spotty brown and the skin is thin and crisp, about 1 minute.

Broiled Chicken Thighs and Breasts

Follow the recipe for Broiled Chicken Thighs, substituting 2 bone-in, skin-on split chicken breasts (about 12 ounces each) for 4 of the chicken thighs. Broil the chicken breasts and thighs, skin-side down, on the bottom rack until the thickest part of the breast registers 160 to 165 degrees on an instant-read thermometer (flipping the breasts and thighs skin-side up after the initial 12 to 16 minutes of broiling), 22 to 26 minutes total; transfer the breasts to a plate and cover with foil to keep warm. Continue to broil the thighs on the bottom rack until the thickest part of the thigh registers 170 to 175 degrees on an instant-read thermometer, about 5 minutes longer. Return the breasts, skin-side up, to the pan and move the pan to the upper rack; broil until the chicken is dark spotty brown and the skin is thin and crisp, about 1 minute.

Chicken Teriyaki

WHEN THE FISH ISN'T FRESH AND THE SOBA'S just so-so, you can usually count on chicken teriyaki as a reliable standby at most Japanese restaurants. But with so many lackluster Americanized adaptations out there—including everything from skewered chicken chunks shellacked in a corn-syrupy sauce to over-marinated, preformed chicken breast patties—what is the real deal? Traditionally, chicken teriyaki is pan-fried, grilled, or broiled, with the sauce added during the last stages of cooking. In fact, the Japanese term teriyaki can be translated as *teri,* meaning "shine" or "luster"—referring to the glossy sauce—and *yaki,* meaning "to broil." Tired of food-court chicken teriyaki wannabes, we were determined to develop a simple but authentic recipe.

In Japan, the chicken is most often served off the bone and cut into thin strips. The sauce itself—unlike most bottled versions—consists of just three basic ingredients: soy sauce, sugar, and either mirin (a sweet Japanese rice wine) or sake.

The half-dozen test recipes we assembled were, for the most part, disappointing. The most promising recipes had one thing in common: The skin was left on. Despite minor complaints about the sauce being too watery, tasters seemed to like a marinated and broiled version best, followed by one in which the chicken was pan-fried and simmered in sauce during the final minutes of cooking. While the skin kept the meat tender and moist, it also had a major flaw: its chewing-gum-like texture. If we were going to leave the skin on, we had to come up with a way to keep it crisp, even with the addition of sauce. A skillet or broiler—or perhaps a tag-team effort employing both—would be integral to getting us there.

Chicken thighs were clearly preferred by tasters over chicken breasts. Whether the chicken breasts were seared and broiled, solely broiled, marinated, or left plain and sauced at the end, they always ended up unappealingly dry, bland, and even a little rubbery around the edges compared with the thigh meat. The deeper, meatier taste of the thighs stood up nicely to the salty profile of the teriyaki sauce, while the breast meat acted as not much more than a one-dimensional backdrop, contributing little flavor of its own.

With the thighs now an established standard, the questions of bone in or bone out, and skin on or skin off, begged to be answered. The skin seemed to create a protective barrier against the heat source, keeping the meat moist, so it would have to be left on. Because most skin-on chicken thighs are sold with the bone attached, we would have to bone them ourselves if we wanted to serve the meat in easy-to-eat strips. Even with a sharp paring knife and a straightforward technique, it took kitchen novices a few tries before they felt completely comfortable with the procedure, but the effort was well worth it. Not only did boning the chicken thighs allow the meat to cook faster, it also made cutting the pieces of hot chicken into strips much easier.

Because most of the recipes we came across in our research called for marinating the meat to infuse it with as much flavor as possible, all of our initial efforts began with this step; but whether we pricked the skin with a fork or slashed it with a knife, marinating the thighs in the teriyaki sauce caused the skin to become flabby. A combination of searing the thighs and then finishing them under the broiler yielded the most promising results, but once the meat received its final dredge in a reduced portion of the marinade to get that glazy shine, the skin always slipped back into sogginess.

Exhausted at the thought of having to refine a long-winded process of boning, marinating, searing, reducing, and broiling that didn't seem to work, we solicited the advice of our colleagues in the test kitchen. One suggested something so simple, so obvious, that we wondered why we hadn't thought of it sooner. "Why not just broil the chicken without marinating it and spoon the sauce on at the end?" she asked. We had gotten so caught up with trying to infuse the meat with flavor that we had all but forgotten a main principle of traditional teriyaki: apply the sauce at the end.

PREPARING CHICKEN THIGHS FOR TERIYAKI

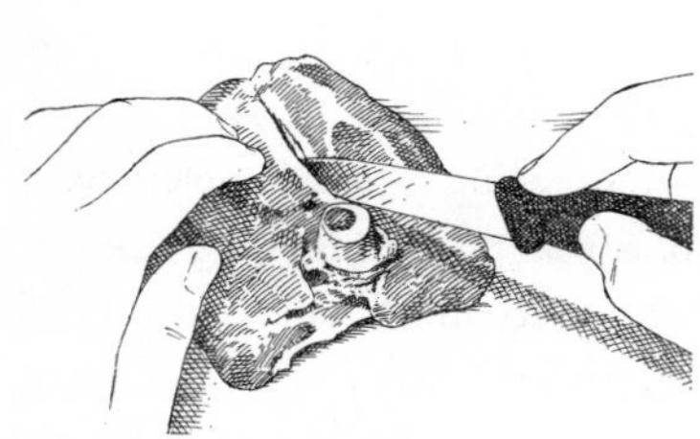

1. After trimming the excess skin and fat (leaving enough skin to cover the meat), cut a slit along the white line of fat from one joint to the other joint to expose the bone.

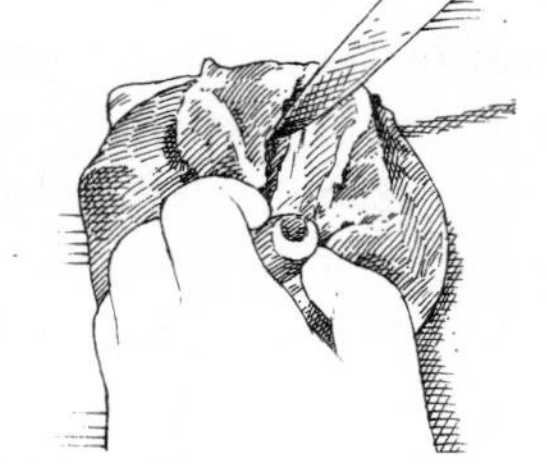

2. Using the tip of a knife, cut/scrape the meat from the bone at both joints.

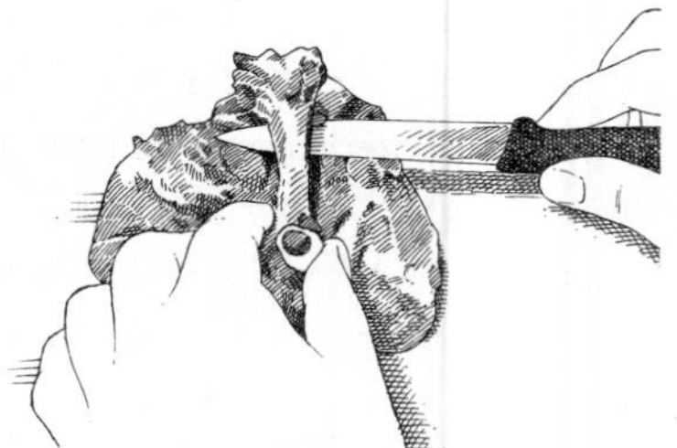

3. Slip the knife under the bone to separate the meat completely from the bone.

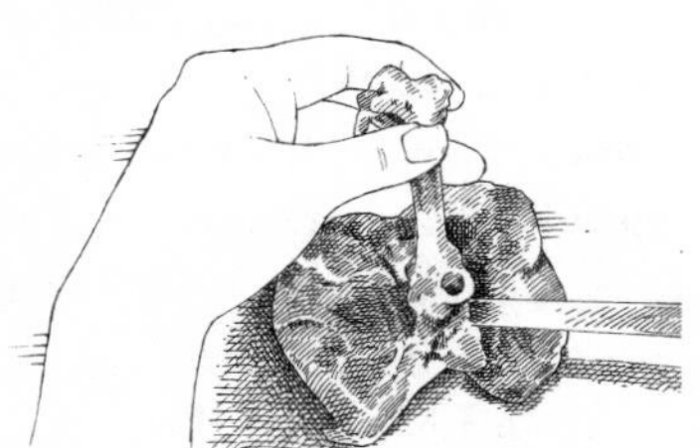

4. Discard the bone. Trim any remaining cartilage from the thigh.

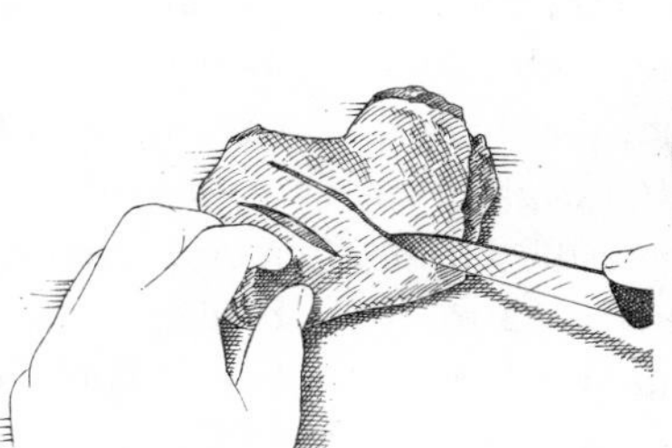

5. Cut three diagonal slashes in the skin. Do not cut into the meat.

6. Tuck the meat under the skin and lightly flatten the thigh to an even thickness.

For our Broiled Chicken Thighs recipe (page 108), which cooked the chicken thighs bone in and skin on, we found that the best broiling method was to start the chicken on the lower rack of the oven and then move it to the upper rack for the final few minutes. This was not the case with boneless thighs. Because the thighs were boned, the cooking time was dramatically reduced, and it was therefore unnecessary to start the chicken on the lower rack. We found that placing the rack in the middle (about eight inches from the heat source) provided the most consistent level of browning and crispness for the boneless thighs. On the middle rack, the skin turned almost as crisp as a potato chip, and the meat cooked perfectly and remained juicy, but there were still some spots where the fat didn't render completely. To remedy this problem, we slashed the skin, which allowed the heat to penetrate more easily, and tucked the exposed edges of meat underneath the skin while smoothing out the tops, which reduced the occurrence of dips and bumps where small pockets of fat had gotten trapped.

As for brining, we found this step unnecessary as well—brined thighs that were broiled and then coated with the flavorful teriyaki sauce (which includes soy sauce) were simply too salty.

With the chicken taken care of, it was time to concentrate on the sauce. Bottled teriyaki sauce was uniformly rejected in favor of a homemade sauce, which took just five minutes to prepare. Working with various amounts of soy sauce, sugar, and mirin (which tasters preferred to sake), we found that the best balance of sweetness and saltiness was achieved with equal amounts of soy sauce and sugar (½ cup) and with a smaller amount of mirin (2 tablespoons), which added a slightly sweet, wine flavor. In terms of consistency, getting the sauce glazy (but neither as thick as molasses nor as thin as water) was difficult. No matter how carefully we watched the sauce simmer, it either was too thin or became tacky while the soy sauce burned, producing what one person called a "strangely bologna-like" flavor. A minimal amount of cornstarch (2 teaspoons) quickly solved this problem.

Although the sauce was now clean and balanced, it needed more depth, which was achieved through the addition of some grated ginger and minced garlic. With at-once crisp and moist, sweet and salty glazed chicken now available at home, we would never have to eat food-court teriyaki again.

Chicken Teriyaki

SERVES 4

If you do not own a broiler pan, use a roasting pan fitted with a flat wire rack. This recipe will work only in broilers with adjustable racks, not in fixed-height broilers. Mirin, a sweet Japanese rice wine, is best in this recipe, although 2 tablespoons white wine plus 1 teaspoon sugar can be substituted if mirin is unavailable. Serve with Simple White Rice (page 386).

- **8 bone-in, skin-on chicken thighs (5 to 6 ounces each), trimmed, boned, and skin slashed (see the illustrations on page 110)**
- **Ground black pepper**
- **½ cup soy sauce**
- **½ cup sugar**
- **2 tablespoons mirin (see note)**
- **2 teaspoons cornstarch**
- **1 medium garlic clove, minced or pressed through a garlic press (about 1 teaspoon)**
- **½ teaspoon minced or grated fresh ginger**

1. Adjust an oven rack about 8 inches from the broiler element and heat the broiler. Line a broiler-pan bottom with foil and cover with the broiler-pan top; set aside. Pat the chicken dry with paper towels, season with pepper, and place, skin-side up, on the prepared broiler pan. Tuck any exposed meat under the skin and lightly flatten the thighs to an even thickness (see the illustration on page 110).

2. Broil the chicken until the skin is crisp and golden brown and the thickest part of the thigh registers 170 to 175 degrees on an instant-read thermometer, 8 to 14 minutes, rotating the pan halfway through the cooking time.

3. Meanwhile, bring the soy sauce, sugar, mirin, cornstarch, garlic, and ginger to a simmer in a small saucepan over medium-high heat, then reduce the heat to low and cook, stirring occasionally, until the sauce is a thick, syrupy glaze and measures about ¾ cup, about 5 minutes. Transfer the sauce to a small bowl, cover, and set aside.

4. Transfer the chicken to a cutting board and let rest for about 3 minutes. Slice the chicken thighs into ½-inch-wide strips, then transfer the chicken to a serving platter. Drizzle about half of the sauce over the top and serve, passing the remaining sauce separately.

Chicken Tikka Masala

IT IS SAID THAT IN THE 1970s A PLATEFUL of overcooked chicken tikka—boneless, skinless chicken chunks skewered and cooked in a tandoor oven—was sent back to the kitchen of a London curry house by a disappointed patron. The Bangladeshi chef in charge acted quickly, heating canned tomato soup with cream, sprinkling in Indian spices, and pouring it over the chicken before sending it back out to the dining room. His inventive creation of chicken tikka masala satisfied the demanding customer, and, as the recipe was perfected, diners worldwide (including those in India) fell in love with the tender, moist pieces of chicken napped in a lightly spiced tomato cream sauce.

Despite its popularity in restaurants, recipes for chicken tikka masala were absent from some of our favorite Indian cookbooks, a testament to its lack of authenticity in Indian cuisine. The recipes we did find had much in common. They all called for marinating chicken breast chunks in yogurt, often for 24 hours, then skewering them, kebab-style, for cooking. The tandoor oven was replaced with a broiler or grill. The masala ingredients varied, and the sauces were all as easy to prepare as a quick Italian tomato sauce. But the similarities didn't end there: In all of the recipes, the chicken was either mushy or dry and the sauces were unbearably rich and overspiced. The good news is that these problems did not seem impossible to overcome, and the promise of a new way to cook chicken with exotic flavors held plenty of appeal. We just needed a decent recipe.

We wanted a four-season dish, so we chose the broiler as our cooking medium and began to analyze the yogurt marinade for the chicken. The marinade is meant to tenderize the meat and infuse it with the essence of spices and aromatics. While overnight marinades did adequately flavor the chicken, they also made the texture too tender, bordering on mushy. Given enough time, the lactic acid in yogurt breaks down the protein strands in meat.

Using shorter marinating times, we embarked on a series of tests intended to improve the texture of the chicken, including marinating in heavily salted yogurt, lightly salted yogurt, watered-down yogurt, and yogurt flavored with spices. Most of the chicken we produced still missed the mark. Two or three hours of marinating desiccated the outer layer of the chicken, while really short marinades didn't do much at all.

Cooking the boneless breasts whole and cutting them into pieces only after they were broiled was a step in the right direction. The larger pieces of chicken didn't dry out as quickly under the searing heat of the broiler, and we no longer had to contend with the fussy step of skewering raw, slippery chicken pieces. Unfortunately, the chicken still wasn't juicy enough.

We were not having much luck with the yogurt marinade and were tempted to abandon it altogether, but yogurt is so fundamental to this recipe that excluding it felt like a mistake. Could we find a different way to use it? We first considered brining the chicken and then dunking it in the yogurt. While the results were better, the moisture from the brining was preventing the chicken from getting a good char on the outside, and, furthermore, we were not able to incorporate the other spices to season the meat.

We then turned to salting, a technique we have used for steaks, roasts, chicken parts, and whole turkeys. Salt initially draws moisture out of protein; then, the reverse happens and the salt and moisture flow back in. What if we salted the chicken first, then dipped it in yogurt right before cooking? We rubbed the chicken with a simple mixture of salt and everyday spices common in Indian cookery: coriander, cumin, and cayenne. We waited 30 minutes, which gave us time to prepare the masala sauce, then dunked the chicken in yogurt and broiled it. The result was the best tikka yet, nicely seasoned with spices and tender but not soft. In just half an hour's time, the salt rub had done its job of flavoring the chicken and keeping it moist, and the yogurt mixture acted as a protective barrier, shielding the lean meat from the powerful heat of the broiler.

We didn't stop there. To encourage gentle charring on the chicken, we fattened up the yogurt by adding two tablespoons of oil. We also took advantage of the yogurt's thick texture, mixing it with minced garlic and freshly grated ginger. The aromatics clung to the chicken as it cooked, producing tikka that was good enough to eat on its own.

Having perfected the chicken, we shifted our focus to the sauce. *Masala* means "spice mixture," and the ingredients in a masala sauce depend largely on the whims of the cook. When the masala is to be served as part of chicken tikka masala, however, tomatoes and cream always form the base. Working with a mixture of sautéed aromatics (onion, ginger, garlic, and chile) simmered with tomatoes (crushed tomatoes were favored over diced canned or fresh because of their smooth consistency) and cream, we tested combination after combination of spices. With plenty of winners and no real losers, we eventually settled on the simplest choice of all: commercial garam masala. Garam masala blends warm spices such as cardamom, black pepper, cinnamon, and coriander in one jar. To bloom the flavor of the garam masala, we sautéed it in oil along with the aromatics instead of adding it to the simmering sauce, as some recipes suggest. There was just one problem: Many commercially prepared masala sauces contain tartrazine, an artificial coloring. Without it, the spices lent our sauce an unappealing gray cast. A tablespoon of tomato paste easily restored a pleasant shade of red.

Most versions of chicken tikka masala call for a cup or more of cream, but tasters wanted us to scale back the amount. After experimenting with heavy cream, half-and-half, and even yogurt, we decided on ⅔ cup heavy cream, which was luxurious but not so rich that it was impossible to finish a whole serving.

At this point, our recipe was getting rave reviews, but we had the nagging feeling that something was missing. We made a mental scan through a flavor checklist: Salt? No. Acidity? No. Heat? No. Sweetness? That was it. We stirred a teaspoon of sugar into the pot, and then another. Our work was done, the sugar having successfully rounded out the flavors of the sauce. When we spooned the chicken over basmati rice and sprinkled it with fresh cilantro, we knew we had a dish worth staying home for.

Chicken Tikka Masala

SERVES 4

This dish is best when prepared with whole-milk yogurt, but low-fat yogurt can be substituted. If you do not own a broiler pan, use a roasting pan fitted with a flat wire rack. For more heat, include the serrano ribs and seeds when mincing. Serve with Basic Pilaf-Style Rice (page 114).

CHICKEN TIKKA

- 1 teaspoon salt
- ½ teaspoon ground cumin
- ½ teaspoon ground coriander
- ¼ teaspoon cayenne pepper
- 4 boneless, skinless chicken breasts (5 to 6 ounces each), trimmed
- 1 cup plain whole-milk yogurt (see note)
- 2 tablespoons vegetable oil
- 1 tablespoon minced or grated fresh ginger
- 2 medium garlic cloves, minced or pressed through a garlic press (about 2 teaspoons)

MASALA SAUCE

- 3 tablespoons vegetable oil
- 1 medium onion, minced
- Salt
- 1 serrano chile, ribs and seeds removed, chile minced (see note)
- 1 tablespoon garam masala
- 1 tablespoon tomato paste
- 2 medium garlic cloves, minced or pressed through a garlic press (about 2 teaspoons)
- 2 teaspoons minced or grated fresh ginger
- 1 (28-ounce) can crushed tomatoes
- 2 teaspoons sugar
- ⅔ cup heavy cream
- ¼ cup minced fresh cilantro leaves
- Ground black pepper

1. FOR THE CHICKEN: Combine the salt, cumin, coriander, and cayenne in a small bowl. Pat the chicken dry with paper towels and sprinkle with the spice mixture, pressing gently so that the mixture adheres. Place the chicken on a plate, cover with plastic wrap, and refrigerate for 30 to 60 minutes. Whisk the yogurt, oil, ginger, and garlic together in a large bowl; set aside.

2. FOR THE SAUCE: Heat the oil in a large Dutch oven over medium heat until shimmering. Add the onion and ¼ teaspoon salt and cook until softened, 5 to 7 minutes. Stir in the chile, garam masala, tomato paste, garlic, and ginger and cook until fragrant, about 30 seconds. Add the tomatoes and sugar and bring to a boil. Reduce the heat to medium-low, cover, and simmer for 15 minutes, stirring occasionally. Stir in the cream and return to a simmer. Remove the pan from the heat and cover to keep warm. (Up to this point, the sauce can be cooled and refrigerated in an airtight container for up to 4 days; rewarm before using.)

3. While the sauce simmers, adjust an oven rack about 6 inches from the broiler element and heat the broiler. Line a broiler-pan bottom with foil and cover with the broiler-pan top. Using tongs, dip the chicken into the yogurt mixture (the chicken should be coated with a thick layer of yogurt) and arrange on the prepared broiler pan. Discard the excess yogurt mixture. Broil until the thickest part of the breast registers 160 to 165 degrees on an instant-read thermometer and the exterior is lightly charred in spots, 10 to 18 minutes, flipping over the chicken halfway through cooking.

4. Transfer the chicken to a cutting board and let sit for 5 minutes. Cut the chicken into 1-inch chunks and stir into the warm sauce (do not simmer the chicken in the sauce). Stir in the cilantro, season with salt and pepper to taste, and serve.

Basic Pilaf-Style Rice

SERVES 4

Olive oil can be substituted for the butter depending on what you are serving with the pilaf. For the most evenly cooked rice, use a wide-bottomed saucepan with a tight-fitting lid.

- 2½ cups water
- 1½ teaspoons salt
- ⅛ teaspoon ground black pepper
- 3 tablespoons unsalted butter (see note)
- 1 small onion, minced
- 1½ cups basmati or long-grain rice, rinsed

1. Bring the water to a boil, covered, in a small saucepan over medium-high heat. Add the salt and pepper; cover to keep hot. Meanwhile, melt the butter in a large saucepan over medium heat. Add the onion and cook until softened, about 4 minutes. Stir in the rice and cook until the edges of the grains begin to turn translucent, about 3 minutes. Stir the hot, seasoned water into the rice. Return to a boil, then reduce the heat to low, cover, and simmer until all the water is absorbed, 16 to 18 minutes.

2. Off the heat, remove the lid and place a clean kitchen towel folded in half over the saucepan (see the illustration); replace the lid. Let stand for 10 minutes; fluff the rice with a fork and serve.

STEAMING RICE

After the rice is cooked, cover the pan with a clean kitchen towel, replace the lid, and allow the pan to sit for 10 minutes.

5 THE WHOLE BIRD

The Whole Bird

A WHOLE ROASTED CHICKEN REPRESENTS everything good about home cooking: It's simple, satisfying, and perfect for a weeknight family meal or Sunday supper. When it's done right, golden, burnished skin gives way to moist, juicy, and flavorful meat, with every part cooked to perfection. But what should be simple often isn't, and problems with roasting a whole bird abound—tough, chewy skin, dry white meat, and underdone dark meat are all too often the result. High temperatures and relatively long cooking times lead to burned drippings and a smoky kitchen. We set out to uncover the secrets of achieving perfect roast chicken every time.

After roasting dozens of chickens, we were happy to find that the process can indeed be a simple affair, and many of the steps commonly associated with cooking a whole chicken aren't necessary. Two steps you don't need? Trussing and basting. With our Simple Roast Chicken (page 120), we found that trussing actually slows down the cooking of the chicken thighs because less of the thigh is exposed to the heat. The result is breast meat that is dried out by the time the thighs have finished cooking. Basting proved to be unnecessarily fussy as well—simply brushing the skin with oil once, before the chicken goes into the oven, still results in great color and crisp texture. (A little butter under the skin doesn't hurt, either, providing both flavor and additional moisture for the delicate breast meat.)

One step we did find essential is flipping the chicken not once, but twice during cooking to ensure an evenly cooked bird. We further found that tucking the wings behind the back was important to prevent them from burning.

As we have done for years in the test kitchen, we opted for brining the chicken (soaking it in a solution of water, salt, and sometimes sugar) before roasting it. Brining ensures that the meat is seasoned through to the bone and also adds moisture that is retained when the chicken is cooked, resulting in a more flavorful, juicy piece of meat.

We have included a primer on brining (see page 12), which explains the science behind the brining technique as well as providing some useful information on the steps involved and the equipment needed to make the process as easy as possible.

We also offer simple instructions for roasting two chickens so that you can save one for a meal later in the week—all you need is a larger roasting pan and rack to hold both chickens. You can then turn to our chapter "Starting with Leftovers" on page 393, which gives you lots of ideas for taking leftover chicken and transforming it into something new.

Roast chicken with vegetables (see page 124) is classic Sunday supper fare, but who knew that the best way to make this dish was to cook the chicken and vegetables separately? We found that you can prevent soggy, greasy vegetables by roasting them while the chicken rests: Simply place them in the same roasting pan used to cook the chicken, and add the defatted cooking juices to the vegetables to infuse them with rich chicken flavor—without the grease.

Butterflying chicken (removing the backbone and flattening the bird) is another technique that we found helps the breast and thighs cook quickly and evenly. But the high heat we use in our High-Roast Butterflied Chicken (page 132) to get ultra-crisp skin can also mean burned drippings and billowing smoke. To solve this problem, we placed potatoes in the bottom of a broiler pan and placed the chicken on the broiler-pan top. The potatoes soak up the drippings, preventing them from burning and creating a tasty side dish in the process. And for our "Stuffed" Roast Butterflied Chicken (page 135), we came up with another inventive technique—placing the stuffing in a bowl made of aluminum foil, with the butterflied chicken placed on top. Unconventional, yes, but eliminating the problems of either not enough stuffing or stuffing that never reaches a safe temperature, we think, is worth the results.

Finally, we explored a cooking technique new to us here in the test kitchen, but one used commonly in France—casserole-style roasting. The chicken is placed whole in a pot with a tight-fitting lid and roasted in the oven. The result was humbling—some of the most moist and tender chicken we had ever tasted. The main difference was the skin—while not super-crisp, it was perfectly rendered—and tasters were also won over by the juiciest meat they had ever experienced.

This chapter provides you with a range of recipes for roasting chicken. Some are simple and some are a bit more involved, but all allow you to enjoy roast chicken any night of the week.

EQUIPMENT: Roasting Racks

A roasting rack (also known as a V-rack) raises poultry and roasts out of the drippings, while giving the oven's heat easy access to the whole surface—a good start toward a well-rendered exterior and even cooking. We recommend purchasing a fixed V-rack (as opposed to an adjustable one) because we've found that the adjustable V-racks are not as sturdy as the fixed ones and are prone to collapse, especially after turning the bird. But which brand of V-rack is best? We brought several into the test kitchen to find out.

Right away, we noted that not all V-racks are actually V-shaped. The slight bend on the Progressive V Shape Non-Stick Roasting Rack ($3.49) barely qualifies as a "V" and leaves no room for roasting vegetables underneath. The innovative Cuisipro Roast and Serve ($28.95) is shaped like a trough with a hinge at the center. Remove the dowel from the hinge and the rack comes apart, dropping the roast onto a platter or cutting board. While it worked fine, this rack was another that didn't elevate the roast enough, and its size (15 inches by 11½ inches) makes it a tight squeeze in all but the largest pans.

In addition to shape, handles were a decisive factor. Tall, vertical handles make removing the rack easy, even with bulky oven mitts. Horizontal handles, or no handles at all, make removal nearly impossible. In our tests, we also noticed that handle position matters. When located on the short sides of a rectangular rack, they can get in the way of the roasting pan's handles. We prefer handles positioned on the long side of the rack.

The All-Clad Nonstick Roasting Rack ($24.95) is our top choice. It's large enough to hold two small chickens and has the features we like. With its handles on the short side, the Norpro ($9.75) is a distant runner-up. If you're also in the market for a new roasting pan, you should consider our favorite roaster, the Calphalon Contemporary Stainless Steel Roasting Pan ($100), which includes a rack that's just as good as the All-Clad model.

THE BEST ROASTING RACK

ALL-CLAD

All-Clad's Nonstick Roasting Rack is our favorite for its large capacity and easy-to-grasp handles.

Simple Roast Chicken

COOKING A WHOLE CHICKEN AT HOME appears to be a simple task. Yet the results are often wildly inconsistent, with meat that's either overcooked and bone-dry or underdone and practically raw on the inside. To solve this problem once and for all, we decided to set our sights on devising a foolproof recipe for roast chicken that would give us perfectly crisp and well-seasoned skin, juicy and tender white meat with just a hint of chew, and fully cooked dark meat—all the way to the bone.

To begin, we developed a series of tests based on a few simple observations. First, chicken is made up of two totally different types of meat, white and dark, which cook at different rates. The white meat is inevitably overcooked and dry even as the dark meat is still little more than raw next to the bone. Second, chicken has skin that should be nicely browned and crisp. As we found during the testing process, crisp skin is not always consistent with perfectly cooked meat. Finally, chicken is an odd amalgam of meat and bones. The drumsticks and wings stick out, the thigh meat is on the side of the bird, and the breast meat is on the top. The home cook is dealing with a complex structure, quite different from a brisket or a pot roast. In search of a solution, we roasted chickens 14 different ways.

We started our tests with the most pertinent question: What is the best oven temperature for roasting a chicken? Our first bird went into a 450-degree oven and cooked for 45 minutes. When it emerged, the skin was dark and crisp, but we encountered the classic problem with high-heat cooking: While the dark meat was fine, the outer portion of the white meat was overcooked and on the tough side. We then went to the other extreme and tested a bird roasted in a 275-degree oven for an hour and 35 minutes, raising the heat to 425 degrees for the last 10 minutes to crisp the skin. The white meat was not quite as juicy as the dark, but not dry, either. The skin, however, was a light gold, not a rich sienna, and it was chewy, not crisp.

We then took the middle road: We roasted the bird at 375 degrees for one hour. The skin was golden and slightly crisp, and the breast meat was still juicy by the time the thighs had cooked through. But we wanted the skin to be crispier still. We tried preheating the oven to the higher temperature of 450 degrees and turning the heat down to 350 degrees upon putting in the chicken. The bird cooked in just over 50 minutes, and the skin was pale gold and slightly chewy. Next, we roasted a bird at 375 degrees for 30 minutes, then raised the heat to 450 degrees for the remainder of the cooking time. This method delivered the best results—perfectly cooked meat and crisp skin.

We were happy with these results, but there remained a couple of techniques often recommended for roasting chicken that we wanted to test. The first was basting. We started with butter and basted every 15 minutes. The results were appalling. Despite a nice brown color, the skin was chewy and greasy. The next bird was basted with oil, which turned out a crispier skin that was more of a golden-brown color. We then tried simply brushing the bird with olive oil before roasting and letting it cook undisturbed in the oven without any further basting. This was the best method—great color and great crisp texture, with minimal fuss.

We also knew from earlier tests that separating the skin from the meat allows hot air to circulate more freely under the skin, renders more fat, and produces crispier skin. We had further learned in our Roasted Chicken Breasts (page 93) that applying butter under the skin helped to keep the delicate breast meat juicy while adding flavor. We applied the same method here and met with success.

Trussing is another technique that is often recommended when roasting a whole bird, as it is said to promote more even cooking. We trussed a bird according to the best French method and found that

EQUIPMENT: Roasting Pans

Though most cooks haul out their roasting pan infrequently, when you do need this large pan, nothing else will do. A roasting pan is a must for cooking whole birds. A roasting pan should promote deep, even browning of food. It should be easy to maneuver in and out of the oven. And it should be able to travel from oven to stovetop, so that you can deglaze the pan and loosen drippings.

Roasting pans can be made from stainless steel, enameled steel, nonstick-coated aluminum, or anodized aluminum, all of which we tested. We decided not to test pans lined with copper, which are prohibitively expensive; cast-iron pans, which when loaded with food are too heavy to lift; and pans made from Pyrex, ceramic, or stoneware, all of which seem better suited to lasagna and casseroles because they can't be used on top of the stove.

We tested eight roasting pans and preferred the materials we like in other cookware—stainless steel and anodized aluminum. These materials are heavy (though not prohibitively so) and produce good browning. Although nonstick coatings made cleanup easier, roasting racks slid around in these pans.

Roasting pans generally come in two different styles—upright handles and side handles. Upright handles tend to be square in shape, while side handles are generally oval loops. We found upright handles to be easier to grip. The problem with side handles is that their position, coupled with the large size of the pan, can cause you to bring your forearms perilously close to the hot oven walls. We tested one pan without handles, which was by far the most difficult to take out of the oven.

We tested pans ranging in length from 16 to 20 inches and in width from 11 to 14 inches. We preferred pans that measured about 16 inches long and 12 to 14 inches across. Larger pans made for an awkward fit in the oven and, because of their large surface area, tended to burn pan drippings more easily.

Our favorite pan is the Calphalon Contemporary Stainless Steel Roasting Pan ($100). It had all the features of more expensive pans (including its own V-rack). It's hefty enough for even the biggest bird, easy to get into and out of the oven, and widely available.

THE BEST ROASTING PAN

CALPHALON

The Calphalon Contemporary Stainless Steel Roasting Pan ($100) is sturdy enough to support the weight of a large bird, has easy-to-grip upright handles, and a bottom that is heavy enough to prevent burning.

it took one and a half hours to cook. The white meat was overcooked, but the dark meat was just right. It was also interesting to note that the cooking time was so long. We concluded that trussing makes it more difficult to cook the inner part of the thigh properly—because it is less exposed to the heat, it needs more oven time. The result is white meat that is overcooked by the time the dark meat is done. An untrussed bird took only one hour to cook, and the white and dark meat were both nicely roasted.

Having figured out that continuous basting and trussing were both unnecessary, we were hoping to find that the bird need not be turned, either. But even cooking is crucial when roasting a whole bird, and we quickly discovered that turning the chicken was essential. We focused our attention on finding the easiest method.

First, we roasted a bird for 15 minutes on each side and then put it on its back. This chicken, weighing close to 3½ pounds, took just 50 minutes to cook. The skin was golden and crunchy, the white and dark meat perfectly cooked, and the overall presentation superb. To make this process a bit easier, we tried roasting another bird breast-side down for 20 minutes and then turned it breast-side up. This chicken was good, but the skin was less crisp, and, at the point at which the white meat was perfect, the dark meat was a bit undercooked. Thus, we learned that two turns are crucial.

After we had roasted half a dozen birds according to our basic method (375 degrees for 30 minutes, then 450 degrees for the rest of the cooking time, with two turns for even cooking), we made an interesting discovery. The thigh that was facing up during the first 15 minutes of roasting ended up higher in temperature than the thigh that started off facing down. Why? The thigh that started off facedown in the roasting pan was in a cold pan that reflected little heat, and therefore it cooked more slowly at first. By the time the thigh that started faceup was turned facedown, the pan was hot and radiating plenty of heat. To even things out, we decided to preheat the roasting pan.

Now that we had our method in place, we did have one final question: Could we get away with roasting the chicken at one temperature, rather than raising it partway through? We did a side-by-side test of one chicken roasted by the method we had arrived at, and one roasted at 400 degrees from start to finish. When tasting the chicken, the difference was barely recognizable. Remembering our goal of "simple" roast chicken, we opted to cook the bird at an even 400 degrees—one less thing to remember, and it turned out just as good.

After 14 chickens, the agreed-upon best method: Roast the untrussed chicken on its side at 400 degrees in a preheated pan, turning it on its other side after 15 minutes. After another 15 minutes, turn the chicken breast-side up and continue to cook until the thigh has reached an internal temperature of 170 to 175 degrees and the breast registers 160 to 165 degrees. Easy, straightforward, and guaranteed to produce a truly satisfying, simple roast chicken.

To spruce things up a bit, we developed two recipes using our simple roast chicken method, adding some flavor to our butter that goes under the skin, and creating a simple but flavorful jus, or sauce, using the chicken juices left in the roasting pan.

Simple Roast Chicken

SERVES 2 TO 3

We recommend using a V-rack (see page 118) to roast the chicken. If you don't have a V-rack, set the bird on a regular roasting rack and use balls of aluminum foil to keep the roasting chicken propped up on its side. If using a kosher bird, skip the brining process. To use kosher salt in the brine, see page 12 for conversion information and more tips on brining.

- ½ cup table salt
- ½ cup sugar
- 1 (3½- to 4-pound) whole chicken, giblets discarded
- 2 tablespoons unsalted butter, softened
- 1 tablespoon olive oil
- Ground black pepper

1. Dissolve the salt and sugar in 2 quarts cold water in a large container. Submerge the chicken in the brine, cover, and refrigerate for 1 hour.

2. Adjust an oven rack to the lower-middle position, place a roasting pan on the rack, and heat the oven to 400 degrees. Coat a V-rack with

nonstick cooking spray and set aside (see note). Remove the chicken from the brine, rinse well, and pat dry with paper towels.

3. Following the illustrations at right, use your fingers to gently loosen the center portion of skin covering each side of the breast. Place half of the butter (1 tablespoon) under the skin, directly on the meat in the center of each side. Gently press on the skin to distribute the butter over the meat. Following the illustration on page 123, tuck the wings behind the back. Rub the skin with the oil, season with pepper, and place the chicken, wing-side up, on the prepared V-rack. Place the V-rack in the preheated roasting pan and roast for 15 minutes.

4. Remove the roasting pan from the oven and, using 2 large wads of paper towels, rotate the chicken so that the opposite wing side is facing up. Return the roasting pan to the oven and roast for another 15 minutes.

5. Using 2 large wads of paper towels, rotate the chicken so that the breast side is facing up and continue to roast until the thickest part of the breast registers 160 to 165 degrees and the thickest part of the thigh registers 170 to 175 degrees on an instant-read thermometer, about 20 to 25 minutes longer. Transfer the chicken to a cutting board and let rest for 10 minutes. Carve the chicken following the illustrations on page 11 and serve.

Rosemary-Garlic Roast Chicken with Jus

SERVES 2 TO 3

We recommend using a V-rack (see page 118) to roast the chicken. If you don't have a V-rack, set the bird on a regular roasting rack and use balls of aluminum foil to keep the roasting chicken propped up on its side. If using a kosher bird, skip the brining process. To use kosher salt in the brine, see page 12 for conversion information and more tips on brining.

CHICKEN AND BRINE

- ½ cup table salt
- ½ cup sugar
- 1 (3½- to 4-pound) whole chicken, giblets discarded
- 2 teaspoons minced fresh rosemary
- 2 medium garlic cloves, minced or pressed through a garlic press (about 2 teaspoons) plus 10 medium garlic cloves, unpeeled
- Ground black pepper
- 2 tablespoons unsalted butter, softened
- 1 tablespoon olive oil
- 1 cup low-sodium chicken broth

JUS

- ½ cup low-sodium chicken broth
- ½ cup dry vermouth or dry white wine
- 2 bay leaves
- 1 fresh rosemary sprig
- 2 tablespoons unsalted butter, cut into 2 pieces and chilled
- Salt and ground black pepper

APPLYING THE BUTTER

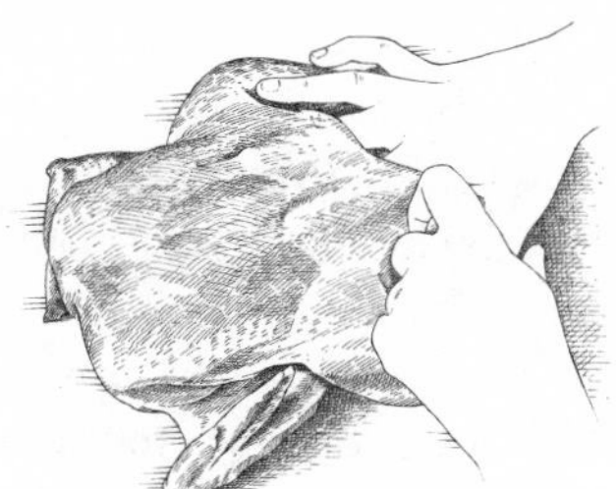

1. With your fingers, carefully loosen the skin over the breast.

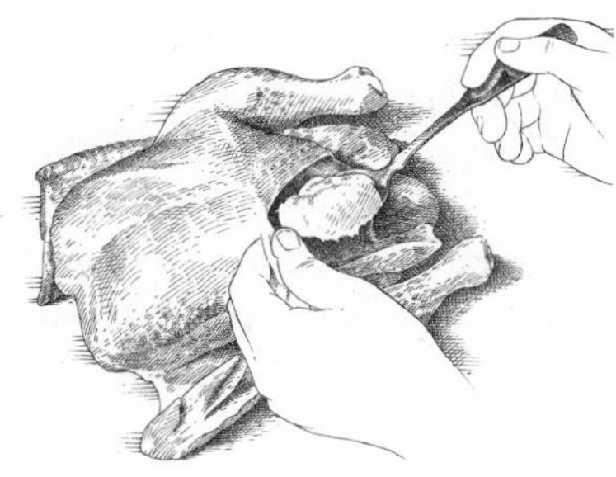

2. Spoon half of the butter under the skin on each side of the breast.

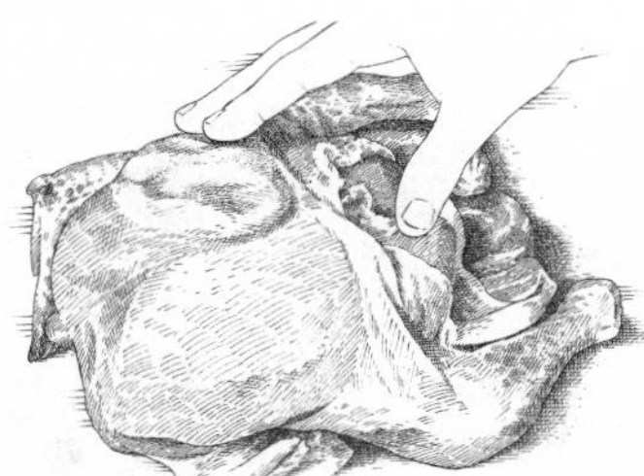

3. With your fingers on top of the skin, work the butter to distribute it evenly over the breast.

1. FOR THE CHICKEN AND BRINE: Dissolve the salt and sugar in 2 quarts cold water in a large container. Submerge the chicken in the brine, cover, and refrigerate for 1 hour. Mix the rosemary, minced garlic, and ⅛ teaspoon of pepper into the softened butter in a small bowl; set aside.

2. Adjust an oven rack to the lower-middle position, place a roasting pan on the rack, and heat the oven to 400 degrees. Coat a V-rack with nonstick cooking spray and set aside (see note). Remove the chicken from the brine, rinse well, and pat dry with paper towels.

3. Following the illustrations on page 121, use your fingers to gently loosen the center portion of skin covering each side of the breast. Place half of the butter mixture (about 1½ tablespoons) under the skin, directly on the meat in the center of each side. Gently press on the skin to distribute the butter mixture over the meat. Following the illustration on page 123, tuck the wings behind the back. Rub the skin with the oil, season with pepper, and place the chicken, wing-side up, on the prepared V-rack. Place the V-rack in the preheated roasting pan and roast for 15 minutes.

4. Remove the roasting pan from the oven and, using 2 large wads of paper towels, rotate the chicken so that the opposite wing side is facing up. Scatter the unpeeled garlic in the bottom of the roasting pan. Return the roasting pan to the oven and roast for another 15 minutes.

5. Using 2 large wads of paper towels, rotate the chicken so that the breast side is facing up. Add the chicken broth and continue to roast until the thickest part of the breast registers 160 to 165 degrees and the thickest part of the thigh registers 170 to 175 degrees on an instant-read thermometer, about 20 to 25 minutes longer. Tip the chicken to let the juices flow from the cavity into the roasting pan, then transfer the chicken to a cutting board and let rest while making the jus. Remove the garlic cloves from the roasting pan and peel. Place the garlic in a small bowl and mash to a paste with a fork; set aside.

6. FOR THE JUS: While the chicken rests, using a wooden spoon, scrape up any browned bits in the roasting pan. Pour the cooking juices into a fat separator and set aside to settle, about 3 minutes. Pour the defatted juices into a medium saucepan, stir in the broth, vermouth, bay leaves, and rosemary sprig, and simmer over medium-high heat until the liquid has reduced to about 1 cup, about 10 minutes. Strain the sauce and return it to the saucepan, discarding the solids. Off the heat, whisk in the reserved garlic paste and butter. Season with salt and pepper to taste. Cover and set aside to keep warm until serving. Carve the chicken following the illustrations on page 11 and serve, passing the jus separately.

Lemon-Thyme Roast Chicken with Jus

SERVES 2 TO 3

We recommend using a V-rack (see page 118) to roast the chicken. If you don't have a V-rack, set the bird on a regular roasting rack and use balls of aluminum foil to keep the roasting chicken propped up on its side. If using a kosher bird, skip the brining process. To use kosher salt in the brine, see page 12 for conversion information and more tips on brining.

CHICKEN AND BRINE

- ½ cup table salt
- ½ cup sugar
- 1 (3½- to 4-pound) whole chicken, giblets discarded
- 2 teaspoons minced fresh thyme leaves
- 1 teaspoon zest from 1 lemon
- Ground black pepper
- 2 tablespoons unsalted butter, softened
- 1 tablespoon olive oil
- 1 cup low-sodium chicken broth

JUS

- ½ cup low-sodium chicken broth
- ½ cup dry vermouth or dry white wine
- 2 bay leaves
- 2 large shallots, minced (about ½ cup)
- 1 fresh thyme sprig
- 2 tablespoons juice from 1 lemon
- 2 tablespoons unsalted butter, cut into 2 pieces and chilled
- Salt and ground black pepper

1. FOR THE CHICKEN AND BRINE: Dissolve the salt and sugar in 2 quarts cold water in a large container. Submerge the chicken in the brine, cover, and refrigerate for 1 hour. Mix the thyme, lemon zest, and ⅛ teaspoon of pepper into the softened butter in a small bowl; set aside.

2. Adjust an oven rack to the lower-middle position, place a roasting pan on the rack, and heat the oven to 400 degrees. Coat a V-rack with nonstick cooking spray and set aside (see note). Remove the chicken from the brine, rinse well, and pat dry with paper towels.

3. Following the illustrations on page 121, use your fingers to gently loosen the center portion of skin covering each side of the breast. Place half of the butter mixture (about 1½ tablespoons) under the skin, directly on the meat in the center of each side. Gently press on the skin to distribute the butter mixture over the meat. Following the illustration below, tuck the wings behind the back. Rub the skin with the oil, season with pepper, and place the chicken, wing-side up, on the prepared V-rack. Place the V-rack in the preheated roasting pan and roast for 15 minutes.

4. Remove the roasting pan from the oven and, using 2 large wads of paper towels, rotate the chicken so that the opposite wing side is facing up. Return the roasting pan to the oven and roast for another 15 minutes.

5. Using 2 large wads of paper towels, rotate the chicken so that the breast side is facing up. Add the chicken broth and continue to roast until the thickest part of the breast registers 160 to 165 degrees and the thickest part of the thigh registers 170 to 175 degrees on an instant-read thermometer, about 20 to 25 minutes longer. Tip the chicken to let the juices flow from the cavity into the roasting pan, then transfer the chicken to a cutting board and let rest while making the jus.

6. FOR THE JUS: While the chicken rests, using a wooden spoon, scrape up any browned bits in the roasting pan. Pour the cooking juices into a fat separator and set aside to settle, about 3 minutes. Pour the defatted juices into a medium saucepan, stir in the broth, vermouth, bay leaves, shallots, and thyme, and simmer over medium-high heat until the liquid has reduced to about 1 cup, about 10 minutes. Strain the sauce and return it to the saucepan, discarding the solids. Off the heat, whisk in the lemon juice and butter. Season with salt and pepper to taste. Cover and set aside to keep warm until serving. Carve the chicken following the illustrations on page 11 and serve, passing the jus separately.

TWO ROAST CHICKENS

AN EXTRA ROAST CHICKEN PROVIDES A HOST of possibilities for second meals. Sure, you can pick up a rotisserie chicken at the supermarket, but why not roast a second chicken while you're already roasting one for dinner? Plus, home-roasted chicken is going to taste far better than anything you could buy at the market. See page 393 for our chapter "Starting with Leftovers," in which we have developed inspired recipes to transform leftover chicken in appealing and interesting ways.

After testing, we found that the only difference between roasting one chicken and two is the equipment (and a slightly higher oven temperature). In early tests, we found that chickens crowded together in a small roasting pan won't roast evenly, so when roasting two chickens you need a large roasting pan (or a disposable pan supported by a baking sheet) and a large, turkey-sized V-rack. What more could we ask for? We had one old-fashioned roasted chicken to enjoy one day and enough leftovers so that we could create a fresh-flavored dinner for a second meal.

PROTECTING THE WINGS

Tucking the wings under the bird will prevent the wingtips from burning.

Two Roast Chickens

SERVES 6

If using kosher birds, skip the brining process. To use kosher salt in the brine, see page 12 for conversion information and more tips on brining. You will need a turkey-sized V-rack and a large roasting pan to fit both chickens. If you are reserving some of the chicken for leftovers, pull the meat from the bone and keep in an airtight container for up to 2 days.

- 1 cup table salt
- 1 cup sugar
- 2 (3½- to 4-pound) whole chickens, giblets discarded
- 4 tablespoons unsalted butter, softened
- 2 tablespoons olive oil
- Ground black pepper

1. Dissolve the salt and sugar in 1 gallon cold water in a large container. Submerge the chickens in the brine, cover, and refrigerate for 1 hour.

2. Adjust an oven rack to the lower-middle position, place a roasting pan on the rack, and heat the oven to 450 degrees. Coat a turkey-sized V-rack with nonstick cooking spray and set aside. Remove the chickens from the brine, rinse well, and pat dry with paper towels.

3. Following the illustrations on page 121, use your fingers to gently loosen the center portion of skin covering each side of each breast. Place one-quarter of the butter (1 tablespoon) under the skin, directly on the meat in the center of each side of each breast. Gently press on the skin to distribute the butter over the meat. Following the illustration on page 123, tuck the wings behind the backs. Rub the skin of each chicken with 1 tablespoon of the oil and season with pepper. Place the chickens, wing-side up, on the prepared V-rack. Place the V-rack in the preheated roasting pan and roast for 25 minutes.

4. Remove the roasting pan from the oven and, using 2 large wads of paper towels, rotate the chickens so that the opposite wing sides are facing up. Return the roasting pan to the oven and roast for another 25 minutes.

5. Using 2 large wads of paper towels, rotate the chickens so that the breast sides are facing up. Add ½ cup water to the bottom of the pan to prevent the drippings from burning and continue to roast until the thickest part of the breasts registers 160 to 165 degrees and the thickest part of the thighs registers 170 to 175 degrees on an instant-read thermometer, about 25 to 30 minutes longer. Transfer the chickens to a cutting board and let rest for 10 minutes. Carve the chickens following the illustrations on page 11 and serve, reserving some as desired for leftovers (see note).

Roast Chicken with Vegetables

ROASTING CHICKEN AND VEGETABLES together is far more appealing in theory than in practice. It's a tempting proposition: With a chicken perched atop a roasting rack dripping flavorful juices into the empty expanse below, it seems a shame not to toss in a few vegetables to soak up all that yummy, chickeny goodness. A bonus side dish—no fuss or forethought required.

Unfortunately, when it comes to chicken and vegetables, killing two birds with one stone usually means victimizing the veggies. They may be chock-full of chicken flavor, but they are also awash in greasy schmaltz and overcooked to a mushy consistency. Our goal was to come up with a recipe that gives each component the attention it deserves—not just the chicken. We wanted juicy meat, crisp-thin skin, and vegetables infused with chicken flavor, not just with chicken fat.

Even though the vegetables were no doubt the true victims here, the chicken had a few grievances of its own. Most roast chicken recipes in the test kitchen call for a 3½-pound bird. That's fine for two or three people (or four on a diet), but we wanted enough chicken to feed a hungry family. So we opted for the big birds in our supermarket's poultry case—specifically, the "oven-stuffer roasters." Weighing in at 6 to 8 pounds, these chickens can easily serve six.

Now that we were in big-bird territory, however, we had a new set of problems. First, while we planned to follow the test kitchen's usual

Buttered Peas with Thyme

SERVES 4 TO 6

- 2 tablespoons unsalted butter
- 1 shallot, minced
- 1 medium garlic clove, minced or pressed through a garlic press (about 1 teaspoon)
- 2 teaspoons sugar
- 1 pound frozen peas (do not thaw)
- 1 teaspoon minced fresh thyme leaves
- Salt and ground black pepper

Melt the butter in a large nonstick skillet over medium-high heat. Add the shallot, garlic, and sugar; cook until softened, about 2 minutes. Stir in the peas and cook, stirring often, until just heated through, about 2 minutes. Off the heat, stir in the thyme and season with salt and pepper to taste.

VARIATIONS

Peas with Feta and Mint

Follow the recipe for Buttered Peas with Thyme, substituting 1 tablespoon minced fresh mint leaves for the thyme. Just before serving, crumble 3 ounces feta cheese (about ¾ cup) over the peas.

Peas with Bacon, Shallot, and Sherry Vinegar

Fry 6 ounces chopped bacon in a nonstick skillet until crisp, about 5 minutes. Using a slotted spoon, transfer the bacon to a paper towel–lined plate and pour off all but 2 tablespoons of the fat. Follow the recipe for Buttered Peas with Thyme, substituting the bacon fat for the butter. Off the heat, add 2 teaspoons sherry vinegar and the bacon to the pan along with the thyme.

Peas with Pearl Onions and Lemon

Follow the recipe for Buttered Peas with Thyme, omitting the shallot and garlic. After melting the butter, add 8 ounces frozen pearl onions and ½ cup water to the skillet. Cover the pan and cook, shaking occasionally, until the onions are tender, about 5 minutes. Uncover the pan and simmer until the water has evaporated and the onions have browned, about 5 minutes, then add the frozen peas and cook, stirring often, until just heated through, about 2 minutes. Off the heat, add 2 teaspoons lemon juice to the pan along with the thyme.

Peas with Tarragon Cream

Follow the recipe for Buttered Peas with Thyme, substituting 1 tablespoon minced fresh tarragon leaves for the thyme. Before adding the peas to the skillet, pour ½ cup heavy cream into the pan, bring to a simmer, and cook until almost clotted and the mixture measures about ⅓ cup. Add the frozen peas and cook until they have heated through and the cream has loosened to form a sauce.

chicken-roasting procedure—brining (to season the meat and keep it moist) and flipping (for even cooking)—we would have to adjust the times for this larger bird. Second, because mass-produced chickens generally taste bland, the test kitchen tends to splurge on chickens from boutique poultry purveyors, which offer superior flavor in exchange for slightly steeper prices. Unfortunately, these "boutique birds" mostly come in petite sizes; the big chickens in our supermarket are almost exclusively of the bland, mass-produced variety.

We tackled brining first. The test kitchen's standard formula for brining poultry is ½ cup of table salt and ½ cup of sugar in 2 quarts of water. With a 3½-pound chicken, it takes an hour for the brine to penetrate the meat fully. With an 18-pound turkey, it takes about six hours. We figured the brining time for our 6- to 8-pound roaster would fall somewhere in between. Sure enough, a few tests told us that the magic number was just under four hours. While that kind of wait may be OK for a once-a-year holiday feast, it seemed like overkill for a typical Sunday-night supper. Trying out various amounts of salt and sugar, we found that upping the concentration to 1½ cups of each, per gallon of water, gave us a fully seasoned chicken in just two hours.

Next, we tried adapting the "small bird" kitchen-tested roasting method for this large chicken: basically, one wing faceup for 15 minutes, the other wing faceup for 15 minutes, then breast faceup until done (about 20 to 25 minutes more). An additional 15 minutes or so for each step yielded evenly cooked white and dark meat. We experimented with various combinations of oven temperatures but found that the best method was also the easiest: 400 degrees from start to finish. This chicken had juicy, seasoned meat and crisp, well-rendered skin.

Turning our attention to the vegetables, we stuck with the usual suspects—carrots, onions, parsnips, and potatoes. We knew from experience that roasting the cut-up vegetables right along with the chicken was problematic. The sheer volume of greasy juices overwhelms them, if overcooking doesn't kill them off first. We tried pouring off all the juices from the roasting pan when the chicken was mostly done, adding the vegetables to a virtually fat-free pan. While this was a big improvement, the chicken continued to render fat as it finished cooking, making the vegetables too greasy still.

At this point, we were beginning to wonder whether grease-free, chicken-infused veggies were but a pipe dream. After all, the test kitchen had

EQUIPMENT: Instant-Read Thermometers

In the test kitchen, we always use an instant-read thermometer to determine when poultry is optimally cooked. (We also use it to check the temperature of meat, bread, caramel sauce, and candy, and to test the temperature of oil when frying.) Our favorite instant-read thermometer is the ThermoWorks Super-Fast Thermapen, a test kitchen workhorse that quickly provides accurate readings across a broad range of temperatures. But at $85, the Thermapen isn't cheap. And, in the past, the only inexpensive instant-read thermometers available were mediocre dial-face models. Dial-face thermometers are hard to read, and their sensors are in the wrong place—more than an inch up the stem. In contrast, digital instant-read thermometers have their sensors on the very tip of the probe, making them easy to use in both shallow liquids and deep roasts.

But in recent years, cheaper digital instant-read thermometers have become available. Could any of them approach the performance of our trusty Thermapen? We purchased eight digital instant-read thermometers, all priced under $25, and put them through their paces in the kitchen.

Three of the models we tested (Cooper-Atkins, CDN Candy, and Polder 363-90) weren't totally accurate in boiling water and/or ice water. What's more, none of the offenders featured a calibrating function.

In our next test—taking the temperature of hot oil (where you want a reading as soon as possible), testers' hands became uncomfortably hot with the slower models. Fast response time proved to be an especially important factor in our ratings.

Does the size of the thermometer make a difference? Bigger is better, but only to a point. With its mammoth 8¼-inch probe, the CDN Candy thermometer had no trouble finding the center of our biggest roast, but it was cumbersome with smaller items. At the other end of the spectrum, the probes on the CDN Q2-450, Cooper-Atkins, and Polder 371 were too short (just 2¾ inches) to reach the center of a big roast. The ideal probe length is 4 to 5 inches.

Some of the thermometers include "extra" features—such as auto shutoff and minimum/maximum temperature memory—but these were deemed nonessential. Testers did value thermometers that could be calibrated. They also liked thermometers that registered a wide range of temperatures, from below zero (for frozen items) to 400 degrees.

What did we find? None of our cheap contenders could match the speed, temperature range, or accuracy of the Thermapen, but the CDN ProAccurate Quick Tip Digital Cooking Thermometer came pretty close, and for a fraction of the price.

THE BEST INSTANT-READ THERMOMETERS

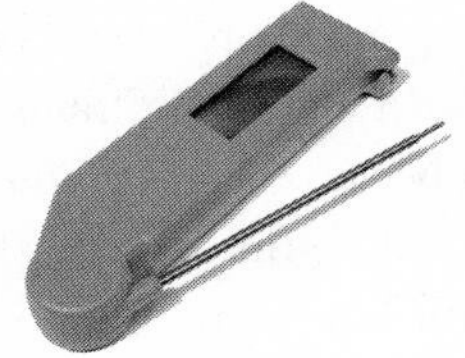

THERMOWORKS

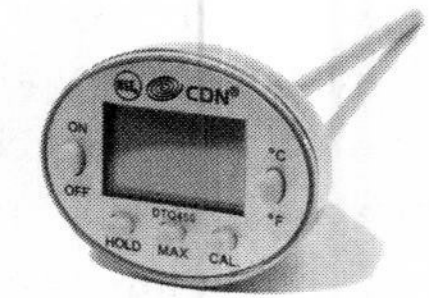

CDN PROACCURATE

The ThermoWorks Super-Fast Thermapen 211-476 is fast, accurate, and easy to use. The Thermapen also has the widest temperature range (−58 to 572 degrees), but note its hefty price tag—$85. The CDN ProAccurate Quick Tip Digital Cooking Thermometer DTQ450 was not quite as fast as the mighty Thermapen, but fast enough, and its low price, $17.95, puts it in reach of most cooks.

already figured out the secret to perfectly caramelized vegetables—tossing them with some oil and salt and roasting them in a pan. In a separate pan, that is: Maybe the secret to great roast chicken and vegetables was to keep the chicken and vegetables as far away from each other as possible.

That's when we made our first real breakthrough. If we roasted the vegetables separately, we figured, we could control precisely how much fat mingled with them. Our idea was to use the test kitchen's existing recipe for roast vegetables, replacing the oil with an equal amount of chicken fat. Even better, if we timed things so that the vegetables roasted during the chicken's half-hour rest (a step that helps redistribute juices throughout the meat), we could serve them piping hot along with the chicken.

With new hope, we plopped yet another chicken into the roasting pan, our cut-up vegetables at the ready. As soon as the chicken was finished cooking, we moved it to a cutting board to rest and tossed the vegetables with 3 tablespoons of chicken fat salvaged from the pan, transferring them to a baking sheet and into the oven. Thirty minutes later, disappointment loomed: The vegetables were greasy and poorly browned. Even worse, they barely tasted like chicken at all.

The browning problem we solved easily, by cranking up the heat from 400 degrees to 500 degrees. But the greasiness lingered, as did the puzzling lack of chicken flavor. Dejected, we were packing it in for the day (literally and figuratively) when we noticed the dark, sticky fond (browned bits) encrusted on the bottom of the roasting pan. It was at that moment that we realized the error of our ways. Of course! It wasn't the chicken fat that contained all the flavor, but the chicken fond—the building block of flavor for every pan sauce we had ever made. By adding some store-bought chicken broth to the pan partway through cooking, we were able to preserve the fond and prevent it from becoming too hardened or just plain burned.

Once the chicken was fully cooked (and safely removed from the pan), we poured the pan contents into a fat separator. We tossed the fat altogether, opting for the cleaner taste of olive oil, but how were we going to introduce the defatted drippings—the sole agent of chicken flavor—to the vegetables? Added too early, the liquid hindered browning, giving us ultra-chickeny but utterly soggy vegetables. Experimenting with times and amounts, we got the best results when adding ½ cup of the defatted drippings to the vegetables after 20 to 25 minutes, then cranking up the oven to the broil setting for 10 minutes to get the veggies good and glazed, stirring them once partway through.

This carefully composed version of roast chicken and vegetables had been transformed into a sophisticated meal fit for company, not just our forgiving families. Who would have thought that the secret to ultra-chickeny chicken and vegetables is to make sure the chicken and vegetables never meet at all—at least not until they hit the plate?

Inspired by our findings, we improvised a bit more and developed two variations on the vegetables. Spring vegetables were our first thought, substituting asparagus, artichokes, and shallots for their winter vegetable counterparts. We simply added the asparagus and artichokes to the pan just before broiling; otherwise, they became grossly overcooked. Finally, we developed a version with just potatoes, because sometimes that is all you want. We kept the shallots with the potato version, as their sweet roasted flavor complemented the potatoes.

Roast Chicken with Root Vegetables

SERVES 6

We prefer a large, traditional (not nonstick) roasting pan for this recipe; if using a nonstick roasting pan, or if your broiler doesn't accommodate a roasting pan, refrain from turning up the oven to broil when cooking the vegetables and continue to cook them at 500 degrees, stirring every 5 to 7 minutes to ensure they don't become too dark. You can substitute the following seasonal vegetables for any of those in the recipe: turnips, rutabagas, fennel bulbs, celery root, and beets; peel these vegetables (except for the fennel) and cut them into 2-inch pieces. If using a kosher bird, skip the brining process. To use kosher salt in the brine, see page 12 for conversion information and more tips on brining.

CHICKEN AND BRINE

- 1½ cups table salt
- 1½ cups sugar
- 1 (6- to 8-pound) whole chicken, giblets discarded
- 3 tablespoons unsalted butter, softened
- 1½ tablespoons olive oil
- Ground black pepper
- 1 cup low-sodium chicken broth, plus more as needed

VEGETABLES

- 1 pound small red potatoes (about 6), scrubbed and quartered
- 1 pound carrots (about 6 medium), peeled and cut into 2-inch pieces
- 3 parsnips, peeled and cut into 2-inch pieces
- 3 small onions, peeled, root end left intact, and quartered
- 3 tablespoons olive oil
- ½ teaspoon salt
- ⅛ teaspoon ground black pepper

1. FOR THE CHICKEN AND BRINE: Dissolve the salt and sugar in 1 gallon cold water in a large container. Submerge the chicken in the brine, cover, and refrigerate for 2 hours.

2. Adjust an oven rack to the lower-middle position, place a large roasting pan on the rack, and heat the oven to 400 degrees. Coat a V-rack with nonstick cooking spray and set aside. Remove the chicken from the brine, rinse well, and pat dry with paper towels.

3. Following the illustrations on page 121, use your fingers to gently loosen the center portion of skin covering each side of the breast. Place half of the butter (1½ tablespoons) under the skin, directly on the meat in the center of each side. Gently press on the skin to distribute the butter over the meat. Following the illustration on page 123, tuck the wings behind the back. Rub the skin with the oil, season with pepper, and place the chicken, wing-side up, on the prepared V-rack. Place the V-rack in the preheated roasting pan and roast for 30 minutes.

4. Remove the roasting pan from the oven and, using 2 large wads of paper towels, rotate the chicken so that the opposite wing side is facing up. Return the roasting pan to the oven and roast for another 30 minutes.

5. Using 2 large wads of paper towels, rotate the chicken so that the breast side is facing up. Add the chicken broth and continue to roast until the thickest part of the breast registers 160 to 165 degrees and the thickest part of the thigh registers 170 to 175 degrees on an instant-read thermometer, 30 to 40 minutes longer. (If necessary, add more broth to maintain a thin layer of liquid on the bottom of the roasting pan.) Tip the chicken to let the juices flow from the cavity into the roasting pan, then transfer the chicken to a cutting board and let rest while roasting the vegetables.

6. FOR THE VEGETABLES: While the chicken rests, adjust an oven rack to the middle position and increase the oven temperature to 500 degrees. Using a wooden spoon, scrape up any browned bits in the roasting pan. Pour the cooking juices into a fat separator and set aside to settle, about 3 minutes. Return the now-empty roasting pan to the oven and heat until the oven reaches 500 degrees, about 5 minutes.

7. Toss the vegetables with the oil, salt, and pepper. Scatter the vegetables in a single layer in the roasting pan, arranging the potatoes and onions cut-side down. Roast the vegetables, without stirring, for 20 to 25 minutes.

8. While the vegetables are roasting, pour off ½ cup of the defatted juices from the fat separator; discard the remaining juices and fat. Remove the roasting pan from the oven and heat the broiler. Drizzle the reserved juices over the vegetables and broil, without stirring, for 5 minutes. Stir the vegetables, coating well with the juices, and continue to broil until tender and deep golden brown, about 5 minutes longer. Transfer the vegetables to a serving platter. While the vegetables are broiling, carve the chicken following the illustrations on page 11. Transfer to the platter with the vegetables and serve.

Roast Chicken with Spring Vegetables

SERVES 6

We prefer a large, traditional (not nonstick) roasting pan for this recipe; if using a nonstick roasting pan, or if your broiler doesn't accommodate a roasting pan, refrain from turning up the oven to broil when cooking the vegetables and continue to cook them at 500 degrees, stirring every 5 to 7 minutes to ensure they don't become too dark. If using a kosher bird, skip the brining process. To use kosher salt in the brine, see page 11 for conversion information and more tips on brining.

CHICKEN AND BRINE

- 1½ cups table salt
- 1½ cups sugar
- 1 (6- to 8-pound) whole chicken, giblets discarded
- 3 tablespoons unsalted butter, softened
- 1½ tablespoons olive oil
- Ground black pepper
- 1 cup low-sodium chicken broth, plus more as needed

VEGETABLES

- 1 pound small red potatoes (about 6), scrubbed and quartered
- ½ pound shallots (about 6 medium), peeled, root end left intact, and halved
- 3 tablespoons olive oil
- ½ teaspoon salt
- ⅛ teaspoon ground black pepper
- 1 pound asparagus (about 1 bunch), tough ends trimmed, cut into 2-inch lengths
- 1 (9-ounce) box frozen artichokes, thawed and patted dry

1. For the chicken and brine: Dissolve the salt and sugar in 1 gallon cold water in a large container. Submerge the chicken in the brine, cover, and refrigerate for 2 hours.

2. Adjust an oven rack to the lower-middle position, place a large roasting pan on the rack, and heat the oven to 400 degrees. Coat a V-rack with nonstick cooking spray and set aside. Remove the chicken from the brine, rinse well, and pat dry with paper towels.

3. Following the illustrations on page 121, use your fingers to gently loosen the center portion of skin covering each side of the breast. Place half of the butter (1½ tablespoons) under the skin, directly on the meat in the center of each side. Gently press on the skin to distribute the butter over the meat. Following the illustration on page 123, tuck the wings behind the back. Rub the skin with the oil, season with pepper, and place the chicken, wing-side up, on the prepared V-rack. Place the V-rack in the preheated roasting pan and roast for 30 minutes.

4. Remove the roasting pan from the oven and, using 2 large wads of paper towels, rotate the chicken so that the opposite wing side is facing up. Return the roasting pan to the oven and roast for another 30 minutes.

5. Using 2 large wads of paper towels, rotate the chicken so that the breast side is facing up. Add the chicken broth and continue to roast until the thickest part of the breast registers 160 to 165 degrees and the thickest part of the thigh registers 170 to 175 degrees on an instant-read thermometer, 25 to 35 minutes longer. (If necessary, add more broth to maintain a thin layer of liquid on the bottom of the roasting pan.) Tip the chicken to let the juices flow from the cavity into the roasting pan, then transfer the chicken to a cutting board and let rest while roasting the vegetables.

6. For the vegetables: While the chicken rests, adjust an oven rack to the middle position and increase the oven temperature to 500 degrees. Using a wooden spoon, scrape up any browned bits in the roasting pan. Pour the cooking juices into a fat separator and set aside to settle, about 3 minutes. Return the now-empty roasting pan to the oven and heat until the oven reaches 500 degrees, about 5 minutes.

7. Toss the potatoes and shallots with 1½ tablespoons of the oil, ¼ teaspoon of the salt, and a pinch of pepper. Scatter the potatoes and shallots in a single layer in the roasting pan, arranging them cut-side down. Roast, without stirring, for 15 to 20 minutes. Meanwhile, toss the asparagus and artichokes with the remaining 1½ tablespoons oil, ¼ teaspoon salt, and pepper; set aside.

8. While the vegetables are roasting, pour off ½ cup of the defatted juices from the fat separator; discard the remaining juices and fat. Remove the roasting pan from the oven and heat the broiler. Add the asparagus and artichokes to the pan. Drizzle the reserved juices over the vegetables and broil, without stirring, for 5 minutes. Stir the vegetables, coating well with the juices, and continue to broil until tender and deep golden brown, about 5 minutes longer. Transfer the vegetables to a serving platter. While the vegetables are broiling, carve the chicken following the illustrations on page 11. Transfer to the platter with the vegetables and serve.

Roast Chicken with Potatoes

SERVES 6

We prefer a large, traditional (not nonstick) roasting pan for this recipe; if using a nonstick roasting pan, or if your broiler doesn't accommodate a roasting pan, refrain from turning up the oven to broil when cooking the vegetables and continue to cook them at 500 degrees, stirring every 5 to 7 minutes to ensure they don't become too dark. If using a kosher bird, skip the brining process. To use kosher salt in the brine, see page 12 for conversion information and more tips on brining.

CHICKEN AND BRINE

- 1½ cups table salt
- 1½ cups sugar
- 1 (6- to 8-pound) whole chicken, giblets discarded
- 3 tablespoons unsalted butter, softened
- 1½ tablespoons olive oil
- Ground black pepper
- 1 cup low-sodium chicken broth, plus more as needed

VEGETABLES

- 2½ pounds small red potatoes (about 15), scrubbed and quartered
- ½ pound shallots (about 6 medium), peeled, root end left intact, and halved
- 3 tablespoons olive oil
- ½ teaspoon salt
- ⅛ teaspoon ground black pepper

1. For the chicken and brine: Dissolve the salt and sugar in 1 gallon cold water in a large container. Submerge the chicken in the brine, cover, and refrigerate for 2 hours.

2. Adjust an oven rack to the lower-middle position, place a large roasting pan on the rack, and heat the oven to 400 degrees. Coat a V-rack with nonstick cooking spray and set aside. Remove the chicken from the brine, rinse well, and pat dry with paper towels.

3. Following the illustrations on page 121, use your fingers to gently loosen the center portion of skin covering each side of the breast. Place half of the butter (1½ tablespoons) under the skin, directly on the meat in the center of each side. Gently press on the skin to distribute the butter over the meat. Following the illustration on page 123, tuck the wings behind the back. Rub the skin with the oil, season with pepper, and place the chicken, wing-side up, on the prepared V-rack. Place the V-rack in the preheated roasting pan and roast for 30 minutes.

4. Remove the roasting pan from the oven and, using 2 large wads of paper towels, rotate the chicken so that the opposite wing side is facing up. Return the roasting pan to the oven and roast for another 30 minutes.

5. Using 2 large wads of paper towels, rotate the chicken so that the breast side is facing up. Add the chicken broth and continue to roast until the thickest part of the breast registers 160 to 165 degrees and the thickest part of the thigh registers 170 to 175 degrees on an instant-read thermometer, 30 to 40 minutes longer. (If necessary, add more broth to maintain a thin layer of liquid on the bottom of the roasting pan.) Tip the chicken to let the juices flow from the cavity into the roasting pan, then transfer the chicken to a cutting board and let rest while roasting the potatoes.

6. For the vegetables: While the chicken rests, adjust an oven rack to the middle position and increase the oven temperature to 500 degrees. Using a wooden spoon, scrape up any browned bits in the roasting pan. Pour the cooking juices into a fat separator and set aside to settle, about 3 minutes. Return the now-empty roasting pan to the oven and heat until the oven reaches 500 degrees, about 5 minutes.

7. Toss the potatoes and shallots with the oil,

salt, and pepper. Scatter the potatoes and shallots in a single layer in the roasting pan, arranging them cut-side down. Roast the vegetables, without stirring, for 20 to 25 minutes.

8. While the vegetables are roasting, pour off ½ cup of the defatted juices from the fat separator; discard the remaining juices and fat. Remove the roasting pan from the oven and heat the broiler. Drizzle the reserved juices over the vegetables and broil, without stirring, for 5 minutes. Stir the vegetables, coating well with the juices, and continue to broil until tender and deep golden brown, about 5 minutes longer. Transfer the vegetables to a serving platter. While the vegetables are broiling, carve the chicken following the illustrations on page 11. Transfer to the platter with the vegetables and serve.

High-Roast Chicken

AT THE PINNACLE OF SIMPLE FOOD IS ROAST chicken—the easy answer to any weeknight-cooking conundrum. Our Simple Roast Chicken (page 120) fits that bill of fare perfectly. But occasionally we want something different. High-roasting is a technique in which the bird is roasted at temperatures in excess of 450 degrees, producing a crisp skin tanned to a deep golden hue. Sounds good, but we were pretty certain the breast meat would overcook at such high temperatures. Still, we thought this technique was worth a shot.

In her book *Roasting: A Simple Art* (Morrow, 1995), Barbara Kafka suggests roasting a 5- to 6-pound bird at 500 degrees for about an hour. While cooking a chicken in that manner seemed to verge on pyromaniacal, we had heard several people swear by the method, so, along with roasting birds at 425 and 450 degrees, we gave it a go. However, we decided to use 3½- to 4-pound birds because they are the size most commonly found in grocery stores.

When the birds came out of the oven, the differences among them were marked. The 500-degree bird was a looker, with beautiful, deep brown, crisp skin. The other two were splotchy and only mildly attractive. Of course, however, the inevitable had occurred: The breast meat on all the birds had been torched; as the thighs sauntered up to the finish line, the more delicate breast meat overcooked. Worst of all, with 450- and 500-degree oven temperatures, we chased everyone, coughing and hacking, out of the kitchen, which had filled with billows of smoke.

To remedy the uneven cooking, we tried several adjustments, from preheated roasting pans to different configurations of oven temperatures, all to no avail. The obvious solution was to rotate the bird so that the breast would spend some time shielded from the intense oven heat, while the thighs would receive the exposure they needed to catch up. After trying this technique, however, we vetoed it. We were after deep browning and crisp skin, neither of which was produced by this method. For that, the bird needs to spend all or at least most of the roasting time breast up.

We suspected that the fix lay in butterflying the chicken—that is, removing the backbone, then opening and flattening the bird. This method would give the thighs greater exposure to the heat, increasing the odds that they would cook at the same rate as the breast. In addition, all areas with skin would be faceup to facilitate even browning and crisping. We tried it, and it worked like a charm. The thighs actually raced ahead of the breast meat and finished cooking first. For the best-browned, most crisp, and nicest-looking bird, 500 degrees was the optimal temperature.

There was still that smoking problem. We tried putting water in the pan under the bird (set on a rack), but this steamed the chicken and prevented the skin from crisping. We tried bread slices, soaked wood chips, and even uncooked rice to catch the drippings, but they all turned to charcoal before the chicken was done. Then we tried potatoes. They burned in spots, dried out in others, and stuck to the pan, but they also showed mouthwatering potential; tasters lined up for any morsel of crisp potato that could be salvaged. Even better, by creating a buffer and absorbing some of the drippings, the potatoes kept the fat from hitting the hot pan bottom, where it would normally sizzle and burn on contact. We knew that with some finessing, the answer to the smoking problem could also provide a great side dish.

We assumed that the potatoes would need some

protection as they cooked to keep them from burning and drying out. A broiler pan came to the rescue. With its slotted top and its ample bottom pan, which nicely accommodated the potatoes, it was just what the chicken and potatoes ordered. The potatoes in the broiler pan had turned a deep brown and were as crisp as potato chips, but far tastier. A foil lining on the pan bottom helped with potato removal and cleanup, and that was that. Not surprisingly, the potatoes won their own fans, who, waiting for the daily potato call, began to regard the chicken as the side dish.

The other step in preparation for roasting that makes a significant improvement in the flavor and texture of the bird is brining. The salt in the brine permeates the chicken so that the meat is evenly seasoned and full-flavored. Brining also keeps the breast meat moist and tender, providing a cushion if it overcooks a bit (though there's little chance of that happening with a butterflied bird).

With technique resolved, we wanted to work flavorings into the roast chicken. Clearly, anything on the surface of the chicken would burn at 500 degrees. Instead, garlic, herbs, and other bold flavors mixed with some softened butter and placed under the chicken skin before roasting added subtle, welcome flavor, not only to the chicken but to the potatoes below as well. In addition, the butter helps to keep the breast meat moist.

When all was said and done, we had roasted four dozen chickens and more than 60 pounds of potatoes, but we had accomplished what we had set out to do: We had four-star, perfectly browned roast chicken with spectacular skin—and potatoes, too.

High-Roast Butterflied Chicken with Potatoes

SERVES 2 TO 3

If using a kosher bird, skip the brining process. To use kosher salt in the brine, see page 12 for conversion information and more tips on brining. Because you'll be cooking the chicken under high heat, it's important that you rinse it thoroughly before proceeding—otherwise, the sugar remaining on the skin from the brine will caramelize and ultimately burn. For this cooking technique, russet potatoes offer the best potato flavor, but Yukon Golds develop a beautiful color and retain their shape better after cooking. Either works well in this recipe. A food processor makes quick and easy work of slicing the potatoes.

EQUIPMENT: Kitchen Shears

A pair of kitchen shears is not an essential kitchen implement. But when you need to butterfly or trim chicken, there is no tool better suited to the task. To test their versatility, we also used kitchen shears to cut lengths of kitchen twine, trim pie dough, and cut out parchment paper rounds. We found two pairs to recommend.

Wüsthof Kitchen Shears ($34.95) made easy, smooth cuts even through small chicken bones and completed all tasks flawlessly. The size and proportion of the shears felt ideal—the blades could open wide for large jobs and to achieve more forceful cutting, but the shears were also suited to smaller, more detailed tasks, such as snipping pieces of twine. These shears boasted heft, solid construction, and textured handles that were comfortable even when wet and greasy. They were also suitable and comfortable for left-handed users.

Messermeister Take-Apart Kitchen Shears ($23.99) were also great performers, though the blades didn't have quite the spread of those on the Wüsthof. These shears, too, made clean, easy cuts and accomplished all tasks without hesitation. The soft, rubberlike handles proved extremely comfortable, but lefties take note: These scissors were clearly designed for right-handed users.

THE BEST KITCHEN SHEARS

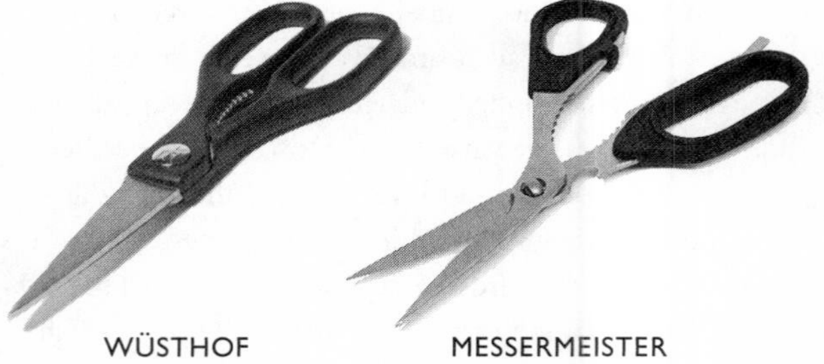

WÜSTHOF MESSERMEISTER

Wüsthof Kitchen Shears performed flawlessly in all tests. Messermeister Take-Apart Kitchen Shears are less expensive than the Wüsthof, and they worked nearly as well; however, left-handed testers were less enthused with this model.

CHICKEN AND BRINE

- ½ cup table salt
- ½ cup sugar
- 1 (3½- to 4-pound) whole chicken, giblets discarded
- 1 recipe flavored butter (recipes follow)
- 1 tablespoon olive oil
- Ground black pepper

POTATOES

- 2½ pounds russet or Yukon Gold potatoes (4 or 5 medium), peeled and sliced ⅛ to ¼ inch thick (see note)
- 1 tablespoon olive oil
- ½ teaspoon salt
- ⅛ teaspoon ground black pepper

1. For the chicken and brine: Dissolve the salt and sugar in 2 quarts cold water in a large container. Submerge the chicken in the brine, cover, and refrigerate for 1 hour.

2. Adjust an oven rack to the lower-middle position and heat the oven to 500 degrees. Line a broiler-pan bottom with foil. Remove the chicken from the brine, rinse well, and pat dry with paper towels. Following illustrations 1 and 2 on page 8, butterfly the chicken and flatten the breastbone, then tuck the wings behind the back.

3. Following illustrations 3 through 6 on page 8, use your fingers to gently loosen the center portion of skin covering each side of the breast. Place half of the butter mixture (about 1½ tablespoons) under the skin, directly on the meat in the center of each side. Gently press on the skin to distribute the butter over the meat. Rub the skin with the oil and season with pepper. Place the chicken on the broiler-pan top and push each leg up to rest between the thigh and breast.

4. For the potatoes: Toss the potatoes with the oil, salt, and pepper. Spread the potatoes in an even layer in the prepared broiler-pan bottom. Place the broiler-pan top with the chicken on top.

5. Roast the chicken until just beginning to brown, about 20 minutes. Rotate the pan and continue to roast until the skin is crisped and deep brown and the thickest part of the breast registers 160 to 165 degrees and the thickest part of the thigh registers 170 to 175 degrees on an instant-read thermometer, 20 to 25 minutes longer. Transfer the chicken to a cutting board and let rest for 10 minutes.

6. While the chicken rests, remove the broiler-pan top and, using paper towels, soak up any excess grease from the potatoes. Transfer the potatoes to a serving platter. Carve the chicken following the illustrations on page 10, transfer to the platter with the potatoes, and serve.

Chipotle Butter with Lime and Honey

MAKES ABOUT 3 TABLESPOONS, ENOUGH FOR 1 RECIPE HIGH-ROAST BUTTERFLIED CHICKEN WITH POTATOES

- 2 tablespoons unsalted butter, softened
- 2 teaspoons minced chipotle chile in adobo sauce
- 1 medium garlic clove, minced or pressed through a garlic press (about 1 teaspoon)
- 1 teaspoon honey
- 1 teaspoon grated zest from 1 lime

Mash all of the ingredients together in a small bowl.

Mustard-Garlic Butter with Thyme

MAKES ABOUT 3 TABLESPOONS, ENOUGH FOR 1 RECIPE HIGH-ROAST BUTTERFLIED CHICKEN WITH POTATOES

- 2 tablespoons unsalted butter, softened
- 1 tablespoon Dijon mustard
- 1 medium garlic clove, minced or pressed through a garlic press (about 1 teaspoon)
- 1 teaspoon minced fresh thyme leaves
- Pinch ground black pepper

Mash all of the ingredients together in a small bowl.

"Stuffed" Roast Chicken

STUFFED ROAST CHICKEN SHOULD BE THE culinary equivalent of a power couple, each partner bringing a lot to the table, at least in theory. The stuffing elevates the roast chicken beyond common everyday fare, while the chicken lends flavor and moisture to what would otherwise be dry bread crumbs. Unlike roast turkey, its bigger and more complicated cousin, stuffed roast chicken should be simple, but often it doesn't deliver. What you get instead is either a perfectly cooked bird filled with lukewarm stuffing (hello, salmonella!) or safe-to-eat stuffing packed in parched poultry. We also wanted more than a few tablespoons of stuffing per person, a problem given the small cavity of a roasting chicken, even one weighing in at more than 5 pounds. No wonder most home cooks ask for a trial separation when it comes to this everyday recipe.

We've roasted literally thousands of chickens in the test kitchen and have made more than our fair share of stuffing. It will come as no surprise, then, that we immediately decided to brine the bird before stuffing and roasting it. This was the only way to ensure moist, flavorful white meat. Next, we were on to the stuffing, and our initial tests revolved around the traditional stuff-'n-truss method used in turkey preparation. This technique was an abject failure. When we packed the chicken loosely with stuffing, we ended up with a miserly 1½ cups. We then packed the chicken until it nearly burst (about 3 cups), first heating the stuffing to 145 degrees in a microwave to give it a head start. But the stuffing still did not reach the safe temperature of 165 degrees by the time the meat was done. Apparently, fully cooked stuffing meant overcooked breast meat.

Having perfected a method for high-roast chicken (see page 131) that starts with a butterflied bird (the backbone is removed and the bird is flattened and then roasted at 500 degrees), we figured that attempting to somehow incorporate stuffing was worth a try. We began with a flattened, brined bird and placed it on a broiler-pan top with 3 cups of stuffing directly beneath the chicken and another 5 cups in the boiler-pan bottom. After an hour, the skin on the chicken was crisp and evenly browned and the meat mostly moist. Finally, we had enough stuffing (at a safe 165 degrees) to feed a crowd, but now it suffered from a dual identity. The stuffing underneath the cavity was cohesive, while its counterpart in the bottom of the pan was dry and crunchy. When we tried placing all of the stuffing in the bottom of the pan, not directly beneath the chicken, it became greasy. In addition, the chicken (technically speaking) was not stuffed.

For our next test, we replaced the broiler pan with a traditional roasting pan and piled a mound of stuffing into it before placing a splayed butterflied chicken on top. After about an hour at

STUFFING BUTTERFLIED CHICKEN

1. Stack two 12-inch squares of foil on top of each other. Fold the edges to construct an 8 by 6-inch bowl.

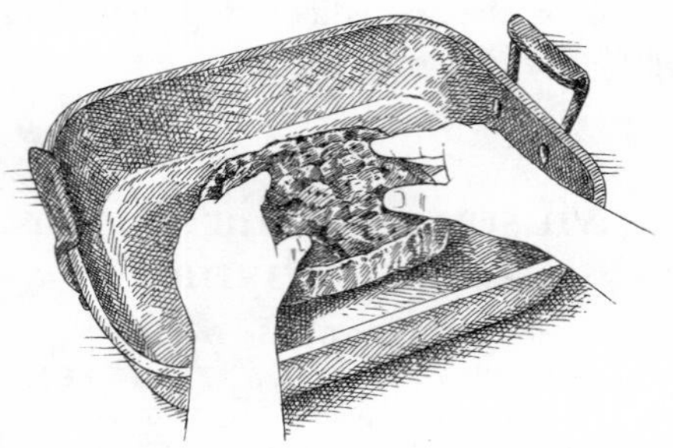

2. Coat the inside of the foil bowl with nonstick cooking spray and pack the stuffing into the bowl.

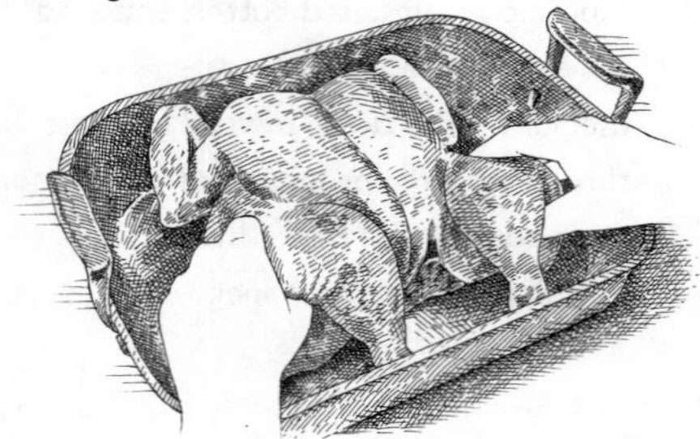

3. Position the chicken over the stuffing. Adjust the edges of the foil bowl to fit the shape of the chicken cavity.

500 degrees, the chicken was slightly dry and the stuffing had many burnt bits. At 425 degrees, the chicken skin browned less evenly, but the stuffing was moist and cohesive. Tasters agreed that 450 degrees yielded the best results, although the stuffing was still charred in some areas and was greasy from the rendered fat.

To solve these two problems, we began a series of tests that eventually culminated in a strange version of culinary origami. First, we placed the stuffing inside an 8-inch square baking dish upon which the butterflied chicken perched; the whole thing then went into a roasting pan. Because the splayed chicken extended partially over the top of the baking dish, we hoped most of the fat from the skin would drip into the roasting pan rather than into the stuffing, but this was not the case. Next, we turned to aluminum foil, creating a packet around the stuffing and poking holes into the foil so that the chicken juices could irrigate the dry contents. Sure, this stuffing was moist, but it lacked color and texture because it was shielded from the oven's dry heat. Finally, we made an aluminum foil bowl, mounded the stuffing into it, and placed the chicken on top, snugly encasing the stuffing. After about an hour of roasting, with a single pan rotation in between, the stuffing was browned and chewy on the bottom as well as moist and flavorful throughout from the juices. The fat from the skin was deposited directly into the roasting pan, never even touching the stuffing. And even though the roasting pan was hot, we could easily grab the foil bowl with our bare hands and dump the stuffing in one fell swoop into a serving bowl. Good technique and cleanup, all in one!

It was time to get serious about the stuffing itself. An informal poll in the test kitchen revealed that most people wanted a jazzed-up version of a traditional bread stuffing. We obliged by replacing the typical onion with thinly sliced leek, adding the requisite celery, and throwing in some chopped mushrooms for additional texture and substance. A dose of minced garlic, fresh sage and parsley, and chicken broth finished our recipe.

With a roasting technique and stuffing recipes now in place, we had finally managed to turn stuffed roast chicken into a successful marriage.

"Stuffed" Roast Butterflied Chicken

SERVES 4 TO 6

Use a traditional (not nonstick) roasting pan to prepare this recipe. When arranging the chicken over the stuffing, it should extend past the edges of the bowl so that most of the fat renders into the roasting pan. If using a kosher bird, skip the brining process. To use kosher salt in the brine, see page 12 for conversion information and more tips on brining.

- ½ cup table salt
- ½ cup sugar
- 1 (5- to 6-pound) whole chicken, giblets discarded
- 1 tablespoon olive oil
- Ground black pepper
- 1 recipe Mushroom-Leek Bread Stuffing with Herbs (recipe follows)

1. Dissolve the salt and sugar in 2 quarts cold water in a large container. Submerge the chicken in the brine, cover, and refrigerate for 1½ hours.

2. Adjust an oven rack to the lower-middle position and heat the oven to 450 degrees. Remove the chicken from the brine, rinse well, and pat dry with paper towels. Following illustrations 1 and 2 on page 8, butterfly the chicken and flatten the breastbone, then tuck the wings behind the back. Rub the skin with the oil and season with pepper.

3. Following the illustrations on page 134, construct a foil bowl, coat the inside of the bowl with nonstick cooking spray, and place the bowl in a roasting pan. Gently mound and pack the stuffing into the foil bowl and position the chicken over the stuffing. Roast the chicken until just beginning to brown, about 30 minutes. Rotate the pan and continue to roast until the skin is crisped and deep golden brown and the thickest part of the breast registers 160 to 165 degrees and the thickest part of the thigh registers 170 to 175 degrees on an instant-read thermometer, about 25 to 35 minutes longer. Transfer the chicken to a cutting board and let rest for 10 minutes.

4. While the chicken rests, transfer the stuffing to a serving bowl and fluff. Cover the stuffing with foil to keep warm. Carve the chicken following the illustrations on page 10 and serve with the stuffing.

Mushroom-Leek Bread Stuffing with Herbs

The dried bread cubes for this stuffing can be stored in an airtight container for up to 1 week.

- 6 slices high-quality white sandwich bread, cut into ¼-inch cubes
- 2 tablespoons unsalted butter
- 1 leek, white and light green parts only, halved lengthwise, sliced ⅛ inch thick, and rinsed thoroughly (see the illustrations on page 45)
- 1 celery rib, chopped fine
- 8 ounces white mushrooms, wiped clean and chopped medium
- ¼ cup minced fresh parsley leaves
- 2 medium garlic cloves, minced or pressed through a garlic press (about 2 teaspoons)
- ½ teaspoon minced fresh sage leaves or ¼ teaspoon dried
- ½ teaspoon minced fresh thyme leaves or ¼ teaspoon dried
- ½ cup plus 2 tablespoons low-sodium chicken broth
- 1 large egg
- ½ teaspoon salt
- ½ teaspoon ground black pepper

1. Adjust an oven rack to the middle position and heat the oven to 250 degrees. Spread the bread cubes in a single layer on a rimmed baking sheet. Bake until thoroughly dried but not browned, about 30 minutes, stirring halfway through the baking time.

2. Meanwhile, melt the butter in a 12-inch skillet over medium-high heat. Add the leek, celery, and mushrooms and cook, stirring occasionally, until the vegetables begin to brown, 6 to 8 minutes. Stir in the parsley, garlic, sage, and thyme and cook until fragrant, about 30 seconds.

3. Whisk the broth, egg, salt, and pepper together in a large bowl. Add the bread cubes and leek-mushroom mixture and toss gently until evenly moistened and combined. Use as directed.

French-Style Chicken in a Pot

WE FIRST ENCOUNTERED *POULET EN COCOTTE* in a Parisian bistro. Recommended to us by the waiter as a specialty of the house, the dish featured a whole chicken baked with a smattering of root vegetables in a covered pot. It was just the kind of homey comfort food we were craving. At first glance, the chicken was nothing to rave about—it had pale, soft skin very unlike the crisp exterior of the roasted poultry we were used to—but its deep aroma was better than that of any roast chicken we could remember. Our first bite confirmed that the dish was very special indeed—the meat was incredibly tender and juicy, with a rich, soul-satisfying flavor.

The basic method for poulet en cocotte is simple: Place a seasoned chicken in a pot, scatter in a small handful of chopped vegetables, cover, and bake. Unlike braising, little or no liquid is added to the pot, resulting in a drier cooking environment. Many of the recipes we found called for auxiliary ingredients such as bacon, mushrooms, or tomatoes. But when we tried these extras, we found they served only to cover up what we were really after: great chicken flavor, pure and simple. We would stick with the chunks of potatoes, onions, and carrots we remembered from our meal in Paris.

As we continued to experiment with different recipes in the test kitchen, we realized the bistro had described their dish as a "specialty of the house" with good reason: Nothing we made could compare. Though most recipes did nothing to the chicken except season it before placing it in the pot to bake, we decided extra measures were necessary. We tried basting the bird, but going to the oven every 20 minutes was a hassle that had little impact on the taste. Next, we tried lightly browning the top and bottom of the chicken on the stovetop before baking. Now we were getting somewhere—the flavor was beginning to deepen. But how could we get even more intense chicken flavor? We remembered earlier tests in which we had added a splash of wine or broth to the pot at the start of cooking. These versions resulted in meat that was very juicy, but the steamier environment created a washed-out flavor. What if we actually decreased the humidity inside the pot?

Eager for answers, we prepped a new chicken and a batch of vegetables, drying each thoroughly with paper towels before adding them to the pot. This had little effect. And then it dawned on us that the vegetables were releasing liquid and making the pot too steamy. To create something close to a one-pot meal, we had been using more vegetables and in larger chunks than we remembered from our bistro dish. But we'd gladly sacrifice the veggies if it meant a bird with better flavor.

For our next go-round, we cooked a chicken with nothing more than a little oil to prevent it from sticking. When we pulled the pot from the oven and removed the lid, a tiny puff of steam emerged—not the great whoosh that had been escaping from the tests with vegetables. This was a bird with great flavor that won over tasters. And with no vegetables to soak them up, the flavorful juices remained in the pot. After defatting the liquid, we had a simple, richly flavored jus to accompany our chicken—a huge bonus. Still, the bird was not quite perfect. Tasters complained that the breast meat was a tad tough and fibrous, and we had to agree. We wondered what a lower oven temperature would do.

Setting up a half dozen chickens in pots, we tested a range of oven temperatures below 400 degrees. To account for pots with poorly fitting lids, we sealed each with foil before adding the top, ensuring that as much of the chicken juices as possible would stay inside. Temperatures from 300 to 375 degrees produced better results, but even lower temperatures—between 250 and 300 degrees—yielded chickens with incredibly tender breast meat. And while these birds took much longer than average to cook (about an hour and a half—all walk-away time, mind you), tasters raved about the meat's rich, concentrated flavor, which was all thanks to the technique: slow-cooking the chicken in nothing more than its own juices.

The last cooking hurdle to clear was the matter of the dark meat not cooking quickly enough. By the time the breast meat was perfectly cooked to 160 degrees, the dark meat (which needs to be cooked to 175 degrees) still wasn't ready. Placing the rack on the lowest position to situate the bird closer to the heat source, combined with browning the dark meat for an extra minute or two, solved the problem.

With the cooking process under control, it was time to finesse the flavors. Two teaspoons of kosher salt was enough to season the chicken without making the jus too salty. And we discovered that we could get away with adding a small amount of potently flavored aromatic vegetables—chopped onion and celery and whole garlic cloves—to the pot. Lightly browning them along with the chicken helped wick away any excess moisture; the caramelization added rich color and flavor to the jus. Stirring in a little fresh lemon juice to finish the jus brightened and balanced all of its flavors.

This French-style chicken in a pot will never place first in a beauty contest, of course, if a browned roast bird is the standard. But its tender, juicy, intensely flavored meat is sure to be a winner every time.

French-Style Chicken in a Pot

SERVES 4

We developed this recipe to work with a 5- to 8-quart Dutch oven with a tight-fitting lid. If you choose not to serve the skin with the chicken, simply remove it before carving. The amount of jus will vary depending on the size of the chicken; for every ¼ cup jus, season it with about ¼ teaspoon lemon juice.

- **1 (4½- to 5-pound) whole chicken, giblets discarded**
- **Salt and ground black pepper**
- **1 tablespoon olive oil**
- **1 small onion, chopped medium (about ½ cup)**
- **1 small celery rib, chopped medium (about ¼ cup)**
- **6 medium garlic cloves, peeled and trimmed**
- **2 bay leaves**
- **1 sprig fresh rosemary (optional)**
- **½–1 teaspoon juice from 1 lemon**

1. Adjust an oven rack to the lowest position and heat the oven to 250 degrees. Pat the chicken dry with paper towels and season with the salt and pepper. Following the illustration on page 123, tuck the wings behind the back.

2. Heat the oil in a large Dutch oven over medium heat until just smoking. Add the chicken,

breast-side down; scatter the onion, celery, garlic, bay leaves, and rosemary (if using) around the chicken. Cook until the breast is lightly browned, about 5 minutes. Using 2 large wads of paper towels, flip the chicken breast-side up and cook until the chicken and vegetables are well browned, 6 to 8 minutes.

3. Remove the Dutch oven from the heat; place a large sheet of foil over the pot and cover tightly with the lid. Transfer the pot to the oven and bake until the thickest part of the breast registers 160 to 165 degrees and the thickest part of the thigh registers 170 to 175 degrees on an instant-read thermometer, about 1½ hours.

4. Transfer the chicken to a carving board, tent loosely with foil, and let rest 20 minutes. Meanwhile, strain the chicken juices from the pot through a fine-mesh strainer into a fat separator, pressing on the solids to extract as much liquid as possible; discard the solids (you should have about ¾ cup juices). Allow the liquid to settle for about 5 minutes, then pour into a small saucepan and set over low heat.

5. Following the illustrations on page 11, carve the chicken, adding any accumulated juices to the saucepan. Stir the lemon juice into the jus to taste. Serve the chicken, passing the jus separately at the table.

EQUIPMENT: Clay Cookers

Clay pot roasters have garnered fame for coaxing remarkable flavor from few ingredients and minimal work: You simply soak the cooker in water for 15 minutes, add the raw ingredients, and place the covered pot in a cold oven. You then crank the heat up to at least 400 degrees. Theoretically, the steam released from the water-soaked clay and the gradual temperature increase should yield tender, juicy meat.

Can a clay cooker outperform a Dutch oven? To find out, we compared two batches of our French-Style Chicken in a Pot, one cooked in a Dutch oven and the other adapted for a clay roaster. We preferred the Dutch oven method. Though both chickens cooked up equally moist and fall-apart tender, clay cookers are not stovetop-safe, so we needed to brown the chicken in a skillet before transferring it to the clay pot. We'll stick with the Dutch oven for low-heat roasting.

Easy Mashed Potatoes

SERVES 4

For smooth, velvety mashed potatoes, add the butter first, then the half-and-half—and make sure both are warm.

- **2 pounds russet potatoes (4 medium), peeled and cut into 1-inch chunks**
- **8 tablespoons (1 stick) unsalted butter, melted**
- **1 cup half-and-half, warmed**
- **Salt and ground black pepper**

1. Cover the potatoes by 1 inch of water in a large saucepan and bring to a boil. Reduce to a simmer and cook until a dinner fork can be slipped easily into the center of the potatoes, about 15 minutes.

2. Drain the potatoes, tossing them to remove excess water. Wipe the saucepan dry. Add the potatoes back into the pot and mash to a uniform consistency (or process through a food mill or ricer back into the pot).

3. Using a flexible rubber spatula, fold the melted butter into the potatoes until just incorporated. Fold in ¾ cup of the half-and-half, adding the remaining ¼ cup as needed to adjust the consistency. Season with salt and pepper to taste. Serve immediately.

VARIATIONS

Scallion and Horseradish Mashed Potatoes

Fold ¼ cup drained, prepared horseradish and 3 minced scallions into the potatoes with the half-and-half in step 3.

Smoky Cheddar and Grainy Mustard Mashed Potatoes

Fold 2 tablespoons whole-grain mustard and 1 cup shredded smoked cheddar into the potatoes with the half-and-half in step 3.

Blue Cheese Mashed Potatoes

Fold 1 cup crumbled blue cheese into the potatoes with the half-and-half in step 3.

6

BREADED, BATTERED, AND FRIED

Breaded, Battered, and Fried

FEW OF US CAN RESIST A CRISP BREADED chicken breast or a properly fried piece of chicken. Whether served on its own, adorned with a spritz of lemon juice, or piled high with fixings on a sandwich, the juicy, tender meat is perfectly accented by the crisp crunch of the crust.

But pan-frying and deep-frying, the techniques required to produce such chicken, can feel intimidating to the home cook. Perhaps the idea of working with a pot of bubbling oil seems daunting, or the few extra steps required for breading the chicken seem like too much bother to most. In any case, pan-frying and deep-frying needn't be a chore. We'll show you how to prepare a variety of breaded, battered, and fried chicken with minimal fuss.

While we've developed these recipes using straightforward cooking methods, accommodations will need to be made depending upon the cut of chicken. Cuts of chicken vary—boneless, skinless breasts cook differently than bone-in, skin-on thighs—each requiring slightly different handling. But although the technique may vary slightly from one recipe to another, the ultimate goals in this chapter are the same—a piece of chicken with a well-browned, crisp exterior and a moist, juicy interior.

What did we learn from our testing? A few steps are key to even cooking and browning. First, when working with boneless, skinless chicken breasts or cutlets, we found that it is essential to pound them to an even thickness (½ inch in most cases is ideal) so that each piece cooks at the same rate and finishes cooking by the time the crust has browned. Similarly, for bone-in, skin-on chicken pieces, we like to cut the larger breast pieces in half so that they are closer in size to the thighs and drumsticks.

Using enough oil and ensuring that the oil is the right temperature (see specific recipes for oil temperatures) are also important. If you've ever eaten a cutlet with a sodden crust, or a greasy piece of fried chicken, you can bet the cooking oil hadn't been hot enough.

Next, it's important to allow enough space around the pieces of chicken in the pan. If the pan is too crowded, the chicken pieces will steam, rather than fry, which prevents a crisp crust from forming. That's why most of our recipes cook the chicken in two batches (holding the first batch warm in a 200-degree oven while the second batch is cooking).

When it comes to specific recipes, we found that homemade bread crumbs are essential to breaded chicken cutlets—dried bread crumbs taste unpalatably stale. Not surprisingly, mild-flavored crispy breaded chicken breasts can play host to a variety of flavors. So, in addition to classic crispy breaded chicken, we've included variations—one seasoned with Parmesan cheese, one with garlic and oregano, and another with Dijon mustard and Worcestershire sauce.

In addition to breaded chicken breasts, we have developed a recipe for Parmesan-crusted chicken cutlets (see page 148). These cutlets are coated entirely with Parmesan (no bread crumbs in sight). The result? A cheesy crust that is undeniably rich with nutty Parmesan.

Nut-crusted chicken breasts offer another alternative to bread crumbs. We like nut-crusted chicken served with simple fruit relishes and chutneys for a quick burst of flavor. Almond-Crusted Chicken Breasts with Cranberry-Orange Relish, Pistachio-Crusted Chicken Breasts with Peach Chutney, and Macadamia-Crusted Chicken Breasts with Pineapple Relish (pages 150–152) are surefire ways to keep your meals interesting.

And as for fried chicken—this chapter has recipes for both Southern-style fried chicken (see page 155) and its cousin, Korean Fried Chicken (page 157). Both types of fried chicken use bone-in, skin-on chicken pieces, but the similarities stop there. Southern fried chicken sports an extra-crunchy coating achieved through buttermilk and seasoned flour, while Korean style gets its paper-thin crisp skin from being fried twice. After frying, Korean-fried chicken is also coated with a sweet soy-based sauce.

We've also included Firecracker Chicken (page 159)—similar to chicken tenders, these addictive strips of boneless, skinless crunchy fried chicken are served with a fiery homemade hot sauce. The sauce performs triple duty—in addition to serving the sauce with the finished chicken, a portion is used as a marinade for the strips, and more sauce is used to season the flour coating. Exceedingly spicy, this chicken has a real flavor bang.

The best thing about this chapter is that most of these recipes come together quickly, making them a great choice for a weeknight dinner.

BREADED CHICKEN BREASTS

A TENDER BONELESS CHICKEN BREAST, PAN-fried with a cloak of mild-flavored crumbs, has universal appeal. Almost every cuisine has such a dish. Though simple, this dish can fall prey to a host of problems. The chicken itself may be rubbery and tasteless, and the coating—called a bound breading, and arguably the best part of the dish—often ends up uneven, greasy, pale, or even burnt.

First, we started with the chicken. Throughout the first series of tests, we noticed that the thin tip of the breast and the opposite end, which is more plump, cooked at different rates. This problem was a cinch to fix; all we had to do was pound the chicken breasts gently to an even ½-inch thickness with a meat pounder or the bottom of a small saucepan. To promote even cooking, we also found it best to remove the floppy tenderloin from the underside of each breast before pounding. (Set aside the tenderloin to use in stir-fries or another dish.)

The ideal bread-crumb coating should be crisp but not greasy. To explore the possibilities, we pan-fried breasts coated with fresh bread crumbs (made from fresh sliced white sandwich bread ground in the food processor) and with dry bread crumbs. The dry bread crumbs had a disappointingly stale flavor. The fresh bread crumbs swept the test, with a mild, subtly sweet flavor and a light, crisp texture.

MAKING FRESH BREAD CRUMBS

Tear pieces of high-quality white sandwich bread (including the crusts) into quarters and pulse in a food processor to coarse crumbs, about 16 pulses. One slice of high-quality white sandwich bread will yield about ½ cup of fresh bread crumbs.

We then went on to test crumbs made from different styles of white bread, pitting the high-quality white sandwich bread used in our first test against Italian, French, and country-style breads. The sandwich bread was the sweetest and appealed to tasters in this recipe. That said, fresh crumbs made from any of these breads were good.

During the crumb testing, we made several important observations about the breading process. Our standing breading method proceeds as follows: dry breasts are coated with flour, then dipped in beaten egg, and finally dredged in bread crumbs. From our tests, we learned that the breasts had to be thoroughly dry before beginning. If the breasts were even slightly moist, the breading would peel off the cooked chicken in sheets. Dry breasts also encouraged the thinnest possible coating of flour, preventing any gumminess in the finished dish. We also learned that we could not dispense with the coating of flour that went onto the chicken before the egg wash and crumbs. When we took this shortcut, we found ourselves with an identical problem—breading that simply didn't adhere through the cooking process.

Once the breasts are lightly floured, they're quickly dipped in beaten egg. But the beaten egg is typically thick and viscous and has a tendency to stick in clumps on the meat, giving the breading an overly thick, indelicate texture. Thinning the egg with oil, water, or both is a common practice that allows any excess to slide off the meat more easily, leaving a thinner, more delicate coating. We tried all three practices, and we honestly couldn't detect much difference in the flavor or texture of the finished breading. In repeated tests, we did notice that the breading made with oil-thinned egg wash seemed to brown a little more deeply than that made with water-thinned wash, so we added a tablespoon of oil to our two beaten eggs and moved on.

As for the bread crumbs, we found that it was essential to press the crumbs onto the breasts to ensure an even, thorough coat. Once breaded, the breasts should rest for about five minutes before frying. This short rest period further helps bind the breading to the meat.

With our chicken ready to pan-fry, we got out

our skillet. In any breaded preparation, the oil in the pan should reach one-third to one-half of the way up the food for thorough browning. To ensure that the breading doesn't overbrown or burn before the meat is done, the oil should be heated just until shimmering (but not smoking). We prefer neutral-flavored vegetable oil for pan-frying. For the chicken breasts to brown evenly and become crisp, there must be ample space around them in the pan. Otherwise, the chicken will steam and turn soggy rather than crisp. For this reason, we cook our chicken breasts in two batches—holding the first batch in a 200-degree oven to keep warm. The result is chicken with a crisp, well-browned crust every time.

Crispy Breaded Chicken Breasts

SERVES 4

When coating the breasts with the bread-crumb mixture, use your hands to pat a thorough, even coating onto the chicken to make sure the crumbs adhere. While homemade bread crumbs taste best, you can substitute 2 cups panko (ultra-crisp Japanese-style bread crumbs). See the illustrations at right for tips on breading chicken breasts.

- **4** boneless, skinless chicken breasts (5 to 6 ounces each), tenderloins removed and breasts trimmed (see the illustrations on page 6)
- Salt and ground black pepper
- **3–4** slices high-quality white sandwich bread, torn into quarters
- **¾** cup unbleached all-purpose flour
- **2** large eggs
- **1** tablespoon plus ¾ cup vegetable oil
- Lemon wedges (for serving)

1. Adjust an oven rack to the middle position and heat the oven to 200 degrees. Following the illustrations on page 6, pound each breast between 2 sheets of plastic wrap to a uniform ½-inch thickness. Pat the chicken dry with paper towels and season with salt and pepper.

2. Pulse the bread in a food processor to coarse crumbs, about 16 pulses. (You should have about 2 cups.) Place the bread crumbs in a shallow dish. Combine the flour, ½ teaspoon salt, and ¼ teaspoon

BREADING CHICKEN BREASTS AND CUTLETS

1. Dredge the breasts or cutlets lightly but thoroughly in the flour mixture, shaking off the excess.

2. Using tongs, dip both sides of the breasts or cutlets in the egg mixture, taking care to coat them thoroughly and allowing the excess to drip back into the dish to ensure a very thin coating. Tongs keep the egg from coating your fingers.

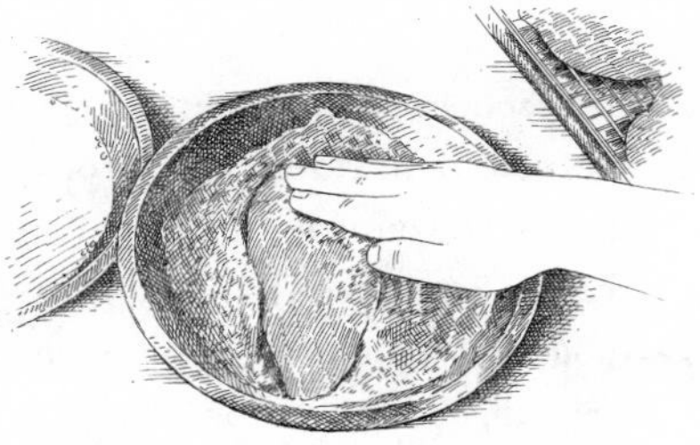

3. Dredge both sides of the breasts or cutlets in the bread crumbs, pressing the crumbs in place with your fingers to form an even, cohesive coat.

4. Place the breaded breasts or cutlets in a single layer on a wire rack set over a baking sheet and allow the coating to dry for about 5 minutes. This drying time stabilizes the breading so that it can be sautéed without sticking to the pan or falling off.

pepper in a second shallow dish and whisk the eggs and 1 tablespoon of the oil in a third shallow dish. Working with 1 chicken breast at a time, dredge in the flour mixture, shaking off the excess, then coat with the egg mixture, allowing the excess to drip off. Finally, coat with the bread crumbs, pressing gently so that the crumbs adhere. Place the breaded chicken in a single layer on a wire rack set over a rimmed baking sheet and let sit for 5 minutes.

3. Meanwhile, heat 6 tablespoons of the remaining oil in a 12-inch nonstick skillet over medium-high heat until shimmering. Add two of the chicken breasts and cook until deep golden brown and crisp on both sides, 4 to 6 minutes in total. Drain the chicken briefly on paper towels, then transfer to a clean wire rack set over a rimmed baking sheet and keep warm in the oven.

4. Discard the oil and wipe out the skillet with paper towels. Repeat with the remaining 6 tablespoons oil and breaded chicken. Serve with the lemon wedges.

Sautéed Tender Greens

SERVES 4

Quick to prepare and satisfying, sautéed tender greens make a great accompaniment to our breaded chicken breasts—as well as to a variety of chicken dishes. To stem spinach or beet greens, simply pinch off the leaves where they meet the stems. A thick stalk runs through each Swiss chard leaf, so it must be handled differently; see the illustration on page 58 for information on this technique. The greens should be moist but not soaking when they go into the pot.

- 3 tablespoons olive oil
- 2 medium garlic cloves, minced or pressed through a garlic press (about 2 teaspoons)
- 2 pounds damp tender greens, such as spinach, beet greens, or Swiss chard, stemmed, washed, shaken to remove excess water, and chopped coarse
- Salt and ground black pepper
- Lemon wedges (optional)

Heat the oil and garlic in a large Dutch oven over medium-high heat until the garlic sizzles and turns golden, 1 to 2 minutes. Add the greens, cover, and cook, stirring occasionally, until the greens wilt completely, 2 to 3 minutes. Uncover and season with salt and pepper to taste. Raise the heat to high and cook until the liquid evaporates, 2 to 3 minutes. Serve, passing the lemon wedges separately (if desired).

VARIATIONS

Crispy Chicken Milanese

Follow the recipe for Crispy Breaded Chicken Breasts, replacing ¼ cup of the bread crumbs with ½ ounce Parmesan cheese, grated (about ¼ cup).

Crispy Chicken with Garlic and Oregano

Follow the recipe for Crispy Breaded Chicken Breasts, whisking 3 tablespoons minced fresh oregano leaves and 6 medium garlic cloves, minced or pressed through a garlic press (about 2 tablespoons), into the egg mixture in step 2.

Crispy Deviled Chicken

Follow the recipe for Crispy Breaded Chicken Breasts, seasoning the chicken with ⅛–¼ teaspoon cayenne pepper in addition to the salt and ground black pepper in step 1, and whisking 3 tablespoons Dijon mustard, 1 tablespoon Worcestershire sauce, and 2 teaspoons minced fresh thyme leaves into the egg mixture in step 2.

Crispy Chicken Fingers

Homemade chicken fingers are much tastier (and cheaper) than the frozen versions you can buy at the supermarket. For convenience, try making a big batch all at once, then freeze them in single-serving zipper-lock freezer bags, where they will keep for up to a month. Simply reheat them in a 425-degree oven until hot and crisp, about 15 minutes, flipping them once halfway through.

Follow the recipe for Crispy Breaded Chicken Breasts, using chicken breasts cut into strips or 1½-inch pieces, then breading and frying as directed in steps 2 through 4. Serve with your favorite honey-mustard or barbecue sauce.

CHICKEN PARMESAN

CHICKEN PARMESAN—BREADED CHICKEN breasts topped with cheese and tomato sauce—is beloved by many American families. Although the dish has its roots in Italy, the execution and, often, the excess are purely American. The chicken, if not prepared properly, can be soggy or greasy—especially under the weight of too much sauce and cheese. Serving the chicken on top of a big pile of spaghetti is another typical shortcoming. We aimed to revamp this hearty dish with an eye toward restraint.

We made several decisions at the outset. First, we would cover the chicken with a modest amount of cheese and tomato sauce. You spend a lot of time breading and cooking the chicken; why bury it under a mountain of molten cheese and sauce? We also wanted to avoid a problem common with this dish: a soggy crust.

Based on our experience with Crispy Breaded Chicken Breasts (page 143), we knew the best way to bread and cook a chicken breast. However, we wondered if sautéing would be the right route here, as the cheese that coats the cooked breasts would be melted under the broiler or in the oven. We figured it was worth trying to cook the chicken under the broiler and save a step. Unfortunately, broiling resulted in an inconsistent and unimpressively browned crust. In contrast, sautéing produced a beautiful, deep golden color and rich, satisfying flavor.

At this point, some recipes we found in our research instruct the cook to cover the chicken with tomato sauce and cheese and then return it to the oven to melt the cheese. However, this method is flawed, as the sauce quickly turns the crust soggy. Instead, we decided to hold off on the sauce until serving and simply sprinkle the cooked breasts with mozzarella and Parmesan (3 tablespoons mozzarella and 1 tablespoon Parmesan per breast were sufficient). We then broiled the cheese-topped breasts until the cheeses melted and turned spotty brown.

As for the sauce, we wanted a smooth, thick sauce that comes together quickly. We also wanted our recipe to make enough sauce to toss with pasta. A 28-ounce can of crushed tomatoes was just right, and it yielded the perfect amount of sauce. In the test kitchen, we prefer to crush our own tomatoes because the consistency of canned varies so much from brand to brand; we simply pulsed a 28-ounce can of diced tomatoes in the food processor until crushed.

All it took was a little olive oil, garlic, red pepper flakes, tomato paste, and basil to enliven the flavor of the sauce, while keeping the recipe simple. We spooned just 2 tablespoons of the sauce over part of each chicken breast after broiling and passed the remaining sauce at the table. Tasters dug into the juicy chicken with gusto, savoring the moist meat, crisp crust, gooey cheese, and bright tomato sauce—an unbeatable combination.

Chicken Parmesan

SERVES 4

If you are tight on time, you can omit step 1 and substitute 3 cups of your favorite plain tomato sauce. This recipe makes enough sauce to serve over pasta—we like spaghetti or linguine.

TOMATO SAUCE

- 1 (28-ounce) can diced tomatoes
- 2 tablespoons olive oil
- 4 medium garlic cloves, minced or pressed through a garlic press (about 4 teaspoons)
- 1 tablespoon tomato paste
- ⅛ teaspoon red pepper flakes
- 1 tablespoon minced fresh basil leaves
- Salt and ground black pepper

CHICKEN

- 1 recipe Crispy Breaded Chicken Breasts (page 143)
- 3 ounces mozzarella cheese, shredded (about ¾ cup)
- ½ ounce Parmesan cheese, grated (about ¼ cup), plus more for serving
- 1 tablespoon chopped fresh basil leaves

1. FOR THE SAUCE: Pulse the tomatoes with their juices in a food processor until mostly smooth, about 10 pulses; set aside. Cook the oil, garlic, tomato paste, and pepper flakes in a medium saucepan over medium heat until the tomato paste begins to brown, about 2 minutes. Stir in the

pureed tomatoes and cook until the sauce is thickened and measures 3 cups, about 20 minutes. Off the heat, stir in the basil and season with salt and pepper to taste. Cover and set aside until needed.

2. Meanwhile, adjust an oven rack to the upper-middle position (the top rack should be about 6 inches from the broiler element) and heat the broiler. After cooking the chicken breasts in steps 3 and 4 of the recipe on page 144, transfer them to a clean wire rack set over a rimmed baking sheet.

3. Top each breast with 3 tablespoons of the mozzarella and 1 tablespoon of the Parmesan. Broil until the cheeses melt and are spotty brown, about 3 minutes.

4. Transfer the chicken breasts to a serving platter or individual plates. Spoon 2 tablespoons sauce over part of each breast and sprinkle with the basil. Serve, passing the remaining sauce and additional Parmesan separately.

Parmesan-Crusted Chicken

WHEN IT COMES TO ITALIAN-STYLE CHICKEN breasts, most people are familiar with two classic recipes: Chicken Milanese (pan-fried chicken breasts with a Parmesan-accented breading; page 144) and Chicken Parmesan (breaded chicken breasts topped with melted cheese and tomato sauce; page 145). Although both offer some degree of Parmesan flavor, they're undeniably more focused on the bread crumbs. So it comes as no surprise that cookbook authors and food magazines have recently begun devising Italian-inspired chicken recipes that put the spotlight on the cheese.

In place of the traditional thick layer of breading, Parmesan-crusted chicken offers a thinner, crisp yet chewy, waferlike sheath of Parmesan cheese. With short ingredient lists, including only chicken breasts and Parmesan cheese, plus one or two adherents such as eggs or flour, the recipes we found for this dish seemed straightforward and promising. But variations in cooking technique yielded samples that were far cries from their beautiful descriptions. A baked version was pale, wet, and gummy. And while several pan-fried recipes were nicely browned, their soft coatings were marred by bald spots, and they tasted surprisingly bitter and burnt. To come up with a superior dish, we'd have to conquer the problems of weak Parmesan flavor and mushy, patchy crusts.

We also had to figure out what was causing the acrid flavor in so many recipes. After all, what good is a picture-perfect cutlet if it tastes like a charcoal briquette? After some initial tests, we knew a few things for sure. First, the chicken would have to be pan-fried, not baked. While baking simply melted the cheese, pan-frying showed the potential to deliver the crisp crust we were after. Second, the chicken would have to be cooked in a nonstick skillet to keep the crust from fusing to the bottom of the pan, and it would have to be cooked quickly to prevent the cheese from burning. Boneless, skinless chicken breasts, therefore, were a given, and they had to be fairly thin. We found that by cutting large chicken breasts (8 ounces each) in half into cutlets and pounding them to a ¼-inch thickness, they would cook through in just four to six minutes.

For the coating, we began with the breading procedure for classic chicken Milanese (coating the cutlets in flour, followed by beaten egg, followed by bread crumbs), swapping grated Parmesan for both the flour and bread crumb layers. Unfortunately, the grated cheese didn't provide the smooth, dry base necessary for the beaten egg to cling to, producing an uneven crust with soft, eggy patches. After reintroducing flour as the base layer, the egg and cheese adhered more neatly to the cutlet. But the crust still had a slightly souffléed texture. Omitting the yolks greatly improved matters. The whites clung to the flour and acted like flavorless glue that helped the cheese stick to the chicken.

Now coated with flour, egg whites, and a thin layer of Parmesan, the chicken tasted only faintly of cheese. Looking for big cheese flavor, we tried adding a handful of grated Parmesan to the egg whites. Although cheesier, the mixture was thick, sludgy, and difficult to handle. Adding cheese to the dry base layer of flour was much more successful. Ultimately, we found that equal parts flour and grated cheese kept the binding qualities of the flour intact while contributing a powerful Parmesan boost. Now the coating had two distinct layers of cheese: a fresh, tangy base and a toastier exterior. But the crust was still a little thin and spotty for our liking.

To this point, we'd been using the smallest holes on the box grater to transform the Parmesan into a fine, powdery consistency, which was perfect for whisking into the flour but less impressive when it came to providing a significant outer crust—it was too delicate and lacy. It struck us that the thicker, coarser texture of shredded—rather than finely grated—cheese would provide the bulkier layer we were looking for.

With ½ cup of shredded cheese per cutlet, the chicken finally had a substantial crust. The key to crispness was revealed during a side tasting of preshredded supermarket Parmesan cheese. We noticed that while the flavor of the preshredded cheese was inferior to authentic Parmigiano-Reggiano, it produced chicken that was much crispier and less chewy. Knowing that many of these packaged tub cheeses include starches to prevent caking, we wondered if adding flour to our Parmesan would do the same thing. The answer was yes: Tossing a mere tablespoon of flour with the outermost layer of shredded cheese filled in any gaps between the cheese and egg white layers, creating a crispier exterior.

Our recipe was coming along, but we still had a problem—a major problem. Whenever we cooked the chicken until it looked gorgeous—a deep, dark brown—it tasted burnt. When we underbrowned the chicken (a counterintuitive move), it tasted fine.

EQUIPMENT: Box Graters

Owing to conveniently pouched grated cheeses, bagged hash browns, and jarred preminced aromatics, box graters have been steadily losing their edge—and it's no wonder. Not only do these unwieldy stainless steel blocks occupy precious cabinet space, but rare is the home cook who can say that he or she has never sliced a knuckle while painstakingly shredding potatoes or a block of cheddar. True, food processors may shred pounds of cheese or vegetables more swiftly, but lugging out the hefty appliance for a handful of mozzarella or a pair of russet potatoes seems impractical. Surely one of the seven box graters we tested would do.

Mozzarella fared well on almost all of the graters; even the teeth on Best's wobbly Box Grater ($16.95) and Progressive's equally unsteady ProGrip Large Tower Grater ($12.99) required little pressure for a firm bite into the semisoft cheese. Rubber grips on the corner feet of the latter tripodlike model, however, failed to maintain stability when it came to shredding spuds; in fact, too much potato-grating pressure over time caused one of the feet to come unglued. Nonskid bases on Anolon's Box Grater ($24.95), KitchenAid's KG300 Box Grater ($19.99), and OXO's Good Grips Box Grater ($14.99), while not an unwelcome feature, only marginally improved the graters' stability and could not compensate for those fitted with thicker, blunter blades. Besides, once the plastic-bottomed measuring cup attachments were in place on the Anolon and KitchenAid models, these rubber bases were irrelevant.

Save for a handful of other minor bells and whistles, the only feature that significantly distinguished one shred of potato or Parmigiano-Reggiano from another was blade quality. Six of the eight graters, including Cuisipro's excessively comprehensive 6-Sided Grater ($25.89), featured traditionally deep punctures—fine for semisoft cheeses and softer vegetables, but no match for the shallower, razor-sharp edges on Microplane's 34005 Better Box Grater ($24.95). Dry Parmesan shreds, which occasionally chipped and flaked on the other models, fell lithely from these exceptionally sharp blades. In conjunction with its poorly designed knuckle guard, however, Microplane's unusually short (under five inches) shredding plane disqualified it from the top ranks. Meanwhile, with its sharp blades and clear, marked container, the OXO delivered on all fronts, and the second-to-lowest price tag of all the graters made it not only a sharp but a smart choice as well.

THE BEST BOX GRATER

An all-around good tool, our winning box grater, the OXO Good Grips Box Grater ($14.99), features sharp blades, a slim body, and a clear, marked container for easy storage and cleanup.

OXO GOOD GRIPS

After some head scratching, we traced the problem back to the Maillard reaction. This chemical effect occurs when amino acids (building blocks for proteins) and sugars in foods are heated, causing them to combine and form new flavor compounds. Most cheeses undergo very little of this reaction when heated, because they don't contain much sugar. Parmesan cheese, however, contains fairly high levels of the sugar galactose, which undergoes the reaction quite readily. As the galactose reacts with sizable amounts of glutamic acid (an amino acid), the formation of bitter-tasting substances happens as soon as the cheese starts to brown. Cooking the cutlets over medium heat kept browning at bay and allowed the chicken and cheese to cook through without tasting burnt.

We were confident that this Parmesan-crusted chicken, with a perfectly moist, tender interior and a crisp, flavorful cheese crust, could finally live up to its name. By emptying the serving platter in a flash, our tasters agreed without saying a word.

Parmesan-Crusted Chicken Cutlets

SERVES 4

To make slicing the chicken easier, freeze it for 15 minutes. Note that 6 ounces of the Parmesan are shredded on the largest holes of the box grater (see the photos at right), and the remaining ½ ounce of Parmesan is grated on the smallest holes of a box grater (or Microplane rasp grater). We like the flavor that authentic Parmigiano-Reggiano lends to this recipe. A less-expensive cheese, such as Boar's Head Parmesan cheese, can also be used, but the resulting cheese crust will be slightly saltier and chewier. Although the portion size (1 cutlet per person) might seem small, these cutlets are rather rich due to the cheese content. To make 8 cutlets, double the ingredients and cook the chicken in 4 batches, transferring the cooked cutlets to a warm oven and wiping out the skillet after each batch.

- 2 large boneless, skinless chicken breasts (about 8 ounces each), tenderloins removed and breasts trimmed (see the illustrations on page 6)
- Salt and ground black pepper
- 6 ounces Parmesan cheese, shredded (about 2 cups) (see note)
- 5 tablespoons unbleached all-purpose flour
- ½ ounce Parmesan cheese, grated (about ¼ cup) (see note)
- 3 large egg whites
- 2 tablespoons minced fresh chives (optional)
- 4 teaspoons olive oil
- Lemon wedges (for serving)

1. Adjust an oven rack to the middle position and heat the oven to 200 degrees. Following the illustrations on page 6, slice each chicken breast in half horizontally and pound each cutlet between 2 sheets of plastic wrap to a uniform ¼-inch thickness. Pat the chicken dry with paper towels and season with salt and pepper.

2. Combine the 2 cups shredded Parmesan and 1 tablespoon of the flour in a shallow dish. Whisk the remaining ¼ cup flour and the ¼ cup grated Parmesan together in a second shallow dish and whisk the eggs and chives (if using) in a medium bowl until slightly foamy. Working with 1 chicken cutlet at a time, dredge in the flour mixture, shaking off the excess, then coat with the egg white mixture, allowing the excess to drip off. Finally, coat with the shredded Parmesan mixture, pressing gently so that the cheese adheres. Place the coated cutlets in a single layer on a wire rack set over a rimmed baking sheet.

TWO WAYS TO CUT THE PARMESAN

GRATED

SHREDDED

An ideal crust requires cheeses of two different textures. A base layer of finely grated Parmesan cut on the smallest holes of a box or Microplane grater is paired with an exterior layer of coarsely shredded Parmesan cut on the largest holes of a box grater.

3. Heat 2 teaspoons of the oil in a 12-inch nonstick skillet over medium heat until shimmering. Add 2 of the cutlets and cook until pale golden brown on both sides, 4 to 6 minutes in total. (While the chicken is cooking, use a thin nonstick spatula to gently separate any cheesy edges that have melted together.) Transfer to a clean wire rack set over a rimmed baking sheet and keep warm in the oven. Wipe out the skillet with paper towels. Repeat with the remaining 2 teaspoons oil and chicken. Serve with lemon wedges.

Sautéed Cherry Tomatoes

SERVES 4

If the cherry tomatoes are especially sweet, you may want to reduce or omit the sugar. Don't toss the tomatoes with the sugar before cooking or they will release too much of their juice.

- 1 tablespoon olive oil
- 4 cups cherry tomatoes, halved
- 2 teaspoons sugar
- 1 medium garlic clove, minced or pressed through a garlic press (about 1 teaspoon)
- 2 tablespoons shredded fresh basil leaves
- Salt and ground black pepper

Heat the oil in a 12-inch skillet over medium-high heat until shimmering. Add the tomatoes and sugar and cook, tossing frequently, until the tomatoes are hot, about 1 minute. Stir in the garlic and cook until fragrant, about 30 seconds. Off the heat, stir in the basil and season with salt and pepper to taste. Serve.

➢ VARIATION

Sautéed Cherry Tomatoes with Curry and Mint

Add 1½ teaspoons curry powder to the skillet with the garlic. Substitute 1 tablespoon shredded mint leaves for the basil. Stir in 2 tablespoons plain yogurt just before serving.

Nut-Crusted Chicken Breasts

A SIMPLE BREADED CHICKEN BREAST CAN be quickly transformed into a richer dish with the addition of nuts to the breading. Too bad this easy-sounding recipe is so problematic. Ground nuts don't readily adhere to the chicken, and, when they do, they usually burn long before the chicken is cooked through. For the transformation from straight bread crumbs to nuts to be a success, we had to uncover a few key tricks.

Using boneless, skinless chicken breasts, we began by adapting our standard breading technique: dredging the chicken in flour and then an egg wash, and, finally, bread crumbs. We first tried replacing the bread crumbs with sliced almonds, but the thin almond slices refused to stick to the chicken. We had more success when the almonds were processed into fine crumbs in the food processor, but even then the crust tasted dense, oily, and sodden after it was cooked or, worse, they burned to an inedible mess.

Unlike bread-crumb crusts, which need a fair amount of time in a hot skillet to crisp up, nut crusts brown quickly because of their high oil content. Some recipes solve this burning issue by baking the coated chicken breasts, but no one in the test kitchen liked the pallid, soggy results. For a really crisp coating, pan-frying seemed to be our only option.

To keep the nuts from burning, and to cut their somewhat dense nature, we tried mixing them with some fresh bread crumbs. Their flavor was neutral (other options, such as crushed crackers and cereal, were too distracting) and the crumbs did indeed help to keep the nuts from burning. Testing various ratios of nuts to bread crumbs, we landed on equal parts freshly ground nuts and crumbs. We found that light Japanese-style bread crumbs, called panko, worked especially well. And a teaspoon of moisture-absorbing cornstarch further ensured an ultra-crisp crust.

As for flavor, we were surprised to find that the nut crust tasted relatively mild. To spruce it up, we added potent Dijon mustard and minced garlic to the eggs. We also found that flavoring the nuts with 2 teaspoons cinnamon was an easy and effective way to bring out their character.

Cooking the chicken turned out to be fairly straightforward. The important factors were to not overcrowd the skillet (a 12-inch skillet allowed us to comfortably fit two chicken breasts at a time, so we cooked the chicken in two batches) and to use enough oil to reach one-third to one-half of the way up the breasts for even browning.

While the chicken was delicious on its own, some tasters felt that a brightly flavored chutney or relish was in order to balance the richness of the nutty crust, so we developed an easy cranberry-orange relish to serve alongside. Holding the chicken warm in a 200-degree oven, we simply wiped the oil out of the pan and returned it to the stove to make a quick relish. All of the ingredients are simply added to the pan and simmered together—no sautéing aromatics or long simmering times required.

EQUIPMENT: Meat Pounders

The key to quick-cooking cutlets and easily rolled chicken breasts is a uniformly thin breast. But do you need to buy one of those fancy meat pounders to do the job, or is there something in your kitchen that will work just as well? We gathered several styles of meat pounders, as well as a sauté pan, a mallet, and a rolling pin, to find the best tool for pounding chicken (and pork).

What we found was that the best pounders were relatively lightweight, with a large flat surface. We also preferred a pounder with a disk shape, because there were no sharp edges to poke into the meat. The winner of our testing was the Norpro Offset Pounder ($14.99). This pounder quickly and efficiently transformed breasts into cutlets, and its offset handle meant no more bruised knuckles. Rather not spend money on a meat pounder? Our runner-up turned out to be a small skillet. Using the bottom of the skillet and pounding gently, we were able to achieve completely satisfactory results. While it's not a very elegant substitution, it certainly works in a pinch.

THE BEST MEAT POUNDER

The offset handle and light weight makes the Norpro Offset Pounder easy to manage.

NORPRO

Noticing how good the nut-crusted chicken tasted with fruit, we decided to come up with some variations. We paired pistachio-crusted, curry-scented chicken with a zesty peach chutney, and a macadamia-crusted chicken with a spicy, tropical pineapple relish. Tasters had mixed reactions—while they raved about all of the combinations we had developed, they were frustrated that we had made it so difficult for them to decide which recipe to make.

Almond-Crusted Chicken Breasts with Cranberry-Orange Relish

SERVES 4

Don't process the nuts longer than directed or they will turn pasty and oily. Regular store-bought dried bread crumbs taste very disappointing here; if you cannot find panko, process 2 slices of high-quality white sandwich bread to coarse crumbs in a food processor, then spread them out on a baking sheet and let them dry in a 250-degree oven for about 20 minutes.

CHICKEN

- 4 boneless, skinless chicken breasts (5 to 6 ounces each), tenderloins removed and breasts trimmed (see the illustrations on page 6)
- Salt and ground black pepper
- 3/4 cup sliced almonds (see note)
- 3/4 cup panko (Japanese bread crumbs) (see note)
- 2 teaspoons ground cinnamon
- 1 teaspoon cornstarch
- 1 cup (5 ounces) unbleached all-purpose flour
- 2 large eggs
- 4 teaspoons Dijon mustard
- 3 medium garlic cloves, minced or pressed through a garlic press (about 1 tablespoon)
- 3/4 cup vegetable oil

RELISH

- 3/4 cup dried cranberries
- 1/2 cup orange marmalade
- 1/2 cup orange juice
- 2 tablespoons minced fresh chives
- 1 teaspoon juice from 1 lemon
- Salt and ground black pepper

1. For the chicken: Adjust an oven rack to the middle position and heat the oven to 200 degrees. Following the illustrations on page 6, pound each breast between 2 sheets of plastic wrap to a uniform ½-inch thickness. Pat the chicken dry with paper towels and season with salt and pepper.

2. Process the almonds in a food processor to fine crumbs, about 10 seconds (do not overprocess). Toss the nuts with the panko, cinnamon, and cornstarch in a shallow dish. Combine the flour, ½ teaspoon salt, and ¼ teaspoon pepper in a second shallow dish and whisk the eggs, mustard, and garlic in a third shallow dish. Working with 1 chicken breast at a time, dredge in the flour mixture, shaking off the excess, then coat with the egg mixture, allowing the excess to drip off. Finally, coat with the nut mixture, pressing gently so that the crumbs adhere. Place the breaded chicken in a single layer on a wire rack set over a rimmed baking sheet and let sit for 5 minutes.

3. Meanwhile, heat 6 tablespoons of the oil in a 12-inch nonstick skillet over medium heat until shimmering. Add 2 of the chicken breasts and cook until browned on both sides, 4 to 6 minutes total. Drain the chicken briefly on a paper towel–lined plate, then transfer to a clean wire rack set over a rimmed baking sheet and keep warm in the oven. Discard the oil and wipe out the skillet with paper towels. Repeat with the remaining 6 tablespoons oil and nut-crusted chicken.

4. For the relish: Discard the oil and wipe out the skillet with paper towels. Add the cranberries, marmalade, and orange juice to the skillet and simmer over medium-high heat until thick and glossy, 3 to 5 minutes. Off the heat, stir in the chives and lemon juice and season with salt and pepper to taste. Serve, passing the cranberry relish separately.

➢ VARIATIONS

Pistachio-Crusted Chicken Breasts with Peach Chutney

Don't process the nuts longer than directed or they will turn pasty and oily. Regular store-bought dried bread crumbs taste very disappointing here; if you cannot find panko, process 2 slices of high-quality white sandwich bread to coarse crumbs in a food processor, then spread them out on a baking sheet and let them dry in a 250-degree oven for about 20 minutes.

CHICKEN

- 4 boneless, skinless chicken breasts (5 to 6 ounces each), tenderloins removed and breasts trimmed (see the illustrations on page 6)
- Salt and ground black pepper
- ¾ cup shelled pistachios (see note)
- ¾ cup panko (Japanese bread crumbs) (see note)
- 2 teaspoons curry powder
- 1 teaspoon cornstarch
- 1 cup (5 ounces) unbleached all-purpose flour
- 2 large eggs
- 4 teaspoons Dijon mustard
- 3 medium garlic cloves, minced or pressed through a garlic press (about 1 tablespoon)
- ¾ cup vegetable oil

CHUTNEY

- ¾ cup peach preserves
- ½ cup raisins
- ½ cup water
- 1 teaspoon minced or grated fresh ginger
- ⅛ teaspoon cayenne pepper
- 2 tablespoons minced fresh cilantro leaves
- 2 teaspoons white vinegar
- Salt and ground black pepper

1. For the chicken: Adjust an oven rack to the middle position and heat the oven to 200 degrees. Following the illustrations on page 6, pound each breast between 2 sheets of plastic wrap to a uniform ½-inch thickness. Pat the chicken dry with paper towels and season with salt and pepper.

2. Process the pistachios in a food processor to fine crumbs, about 25 seconds (do not overprocess). Toss the nuts with the panko, curry powder, and cornstarch in a shallow dish. Combine the flour, ½ teaspoon salt, and ¼ teaspoon pepper in a second shallow dish and whisk the eggs, mustard, and garlic in a third shallow dish. Working with 1 chicken breast at a time, dredge in the flour mixture, shaking off the excess, then coat with the egg mixture, allowing the excess to drip off. Finally, coat with the nut mixture, pressing gently so that the crumbs adhere. Place the nut-crusted chicken in a single layer on a wire rack set over a rimmed baking sheet and let sit for 5 minutes.

3. Meanwhile, heat 6 tablespoons of the oil in a 12-inch nonstick skillet over medium heat until shimmering. Add 2 of the chicken breasts and cook until browned on both sides, 4 to 6 minutes total. Drain the chicken briefly on a paper towel–lined plate, then transfer to a clean wire rack set over a rimmed baking sheet and keep warm in the oven. Discard the oil and wipe out the skillet with paper towels. Repeat with the remaining 6 tablespoons oil and nut-crusted chicken.

4. For the chutney: Discard the oil and wipe out the skillet with paper towels. Add the peach preserves, raisins, water, ginger, and cayenne to the skillet and simmer over medium-high heat until thick and glossy, 3 to 5 minutes. Off the heat, stir in the cilantro and vinegar and season with salt and pepper to taste. Serve, passing the peach chutney separately.

Macadamia-Crusted Chicken Breasts with Pineapple Relish

For more heat, include the jalapeño seeds and ribs when mincing. Don't process the nuts longer than directed or they will turn pasty and oily. Regular store-bought dried bread crumbs taste very disappointing here; if you cannot find panko, process 2 slices of high-quality white sandwich bread to coarse crumbs in a food processor, then spread them out on a baking sheet and let them dry in a 250-degree oven for about 20 minutes.

CHICKEN

- 4 boneless, skinless chicken breasts (5 to 6 ounces each), tenderloins removed and breasts trimmed (see the illustrations on page 6)
- Salt and ground black pepper
- ¾ cup macadamia nuts (see note)
- ¾ cup panko (Japanese bread crumbs) (see note)
- 1 teaspoon cornstarch
- ¼ teaspoon ground allspice
- 1 cup (5 ounces) unbleached all-purpose flour
- 2 large eggs
- 4 teaspoons Dijon mustard
- 3 medium garlic cloves, minced or pressed through a garlic press (about 1 tablespoon)
- ¾ cup vegetable oil

RELISH

- 1 (20-ounce) can crushed pineapple, packed in juice
- 2 tablespoons packed brown sugar
- 1 jalapeño chile, seeds and ribs removed, chile minced (see note)
- 2 tablespoons minced fresh mint leaves
- 2 teaspoons juice from 1 lime

1. For the chicken: Adjust an oven rack to the middle position and heat the oven to 200 degrees. Following the illustrations on page 6, pound each breast between 2 sheets of plastic wrap to a uniform ½-inch thickness. Pat the chicken dry with paper towels and season with salt and pepper.

2. Process the macadamia nuts in a food processor to fine crumbs, about 15 seconds (do not overprocess). Toss the nuts with the panko, cornstarch, and allspice in a shallow dish. Combine the flour, ½ teaspoon salt, and ¼ teaspoon pepper in a second shallow dish and whisk the eggs, mustard, and garlic in a third shallow dish. Working with 1 chicken breast at a time, dredge in the flour mixture, shaking off the excess, then coat with the egg mixture, allowing the excess to drip off. Finally, coat with the nut mixture, pressing gently so that the crumbs adhere. Place the nut-crusted chicken in a single layer on a wire rack set over a rimmed baking sheet and let sit for 5 minutes.

3. Meanwhile, heat 6 tablespoons of the oil in a 12-inch nonstick skillet over medium heat until shimmering. Add 2 of the chicken breasts and cook until browned on both sides, 4 to 6 minutes total. Drain the chicken briefly on a paper towel–lined plate, then transfer to a clean wire rack set over a rimmed baking sheet and keep warm in the oven. Discard the oil and wipe out the skillet with paper towels. Repeat with the remaining 6 tablespoons oil and nut-crusted chicken.

4. For the relish: Discard the oil and wipe out the skillet with paper towels. Add the pineapple with its juice, brown sugar, and jalapeño to the skillet and simmer over medium-high heat until thick, 3 to 5 minutes. Off the heat, stir in the mint and lime juice and season with salt and pepper to taste. Serve, passing the pineapple relish separately.

Fried Chicken

WHAT MAKES FRIED CHICKEN GREAT? THERE'S no doubt about it: the crust. Crisp and crackling with flavor, the crust must cleave to the chicken itself, not balloon away or flake off in chips like old radiator paint. In addition, it should carry a deep, uniform mahogany color, without spots or evidence of greasiness. As for the chicken itself, tender, moist, and flavorful are the descriptors of the day. Served hot, the chicken should be demonstrably juicy; served at room temperature, it should be moist. On no account should it be agonizingly dry or require a saltshaker as a chaperone.

The truth is that frying chicken at home can be a daunting task, a messy tableau of buttermilk dip and breading, hot fat, and splatters one hopes will end at the stove's edge. The results are often tantamount to the mess: greasy, peeling chicken skin and dry, unseasoned meat that's a long way from Grandma's.

In our first stove-side excursion, we fried up several batches of chicken with different coatings, oils, and so on. But at this stage our real interest resided beneath the skin: Half of the chickens had been brined for two hours; the other half had not. A brine is at minimum a mixture of salt and water; sugar is often added as well. When soaked in brine, chicken (as well as other poultry and meat) absorbs some of the salt and some of the water, thereby becoming more flavorful and more juicy once cooked. The tasting results bore out these benefits of brining: However glorious the crust, however perfectly fried the piece, the unbrined chicken earned marks far below its brined competition. Who wants to bite through a crisp, rich, seasoned crust only to hit dry, white Styrofoam? Another benefit of brining presented itself during cooking. Our brined chicken parts fried at equal rates, relieving us of the need to babysit the white meat or pull the wings out of the fat early.

While brining per se may not be common practice when preparing fried chicken, soaking the chicken pieces in some kind of liquid—particularly

EQUIPMENT: Candy/Deep-Fry Thermometers

Candy thermometers are designed for stovetop recipes where close monitoring of temperature is key—especially candy making and deep-frying. The thermometer stays in the liquid during cooking. But which brand is best? To find out, we brought 13 models into the test kitchen and made multiple batches of caramel and our Crispy Fried Chicken.

Thermometers with the simplest style—a plain glass tube—worked fine, but they are also fragile and the gradations were hard to read. What's more, a few models had a tendency to slide down and touch the bottom of the pan, giving a false reading. Similar thermometers with a metal "foot" to keep the thermometer off the pan bottom didn't work in a small (shallow) batch of caramel or oil and were also hard to read. Dial-face thermometers required as much as 2½ inches of liquid—a rarity when making candy.

The best of the bunch were the digital models, which have easy-to-read consoles and alarm features that warn the cook when the caramel is done or the oil is hot enough. But they tend to be top-heavy, with a precarious grip on the saucepan. Testers wanted something similar to our favorite thermometer for roasts, the Polder Digital Cooking Timer/Thermometer, in which a long wire separates the "brains" from the business end. We'd use the Polder for candy or frying but couldn't find a way to secure the probe to the side of the pot. Then we found the CDN Digital Cooking Thermometer and Timer. It's similar to the Polder but comes with a mounting clip that lets you attach the probe to your pan. An on/off switch would be nice (to save batteries over time), but it still gets our top recommendation for its clip-on ease.

THE BEST CANDY/DEEP-FRY THERMOMETER

CDN

The CDN Digital Cooking Thermometer and Timer ($24.95) is our top choice for candy making and deep-frying.

buttermilk—is traditional. This process is thought to tenderize the meat (a mistaken assumption) and add flavor. We examined a number of soaking solutions and found the bright acidic taste and clinging viscosity of buttermilk to produce the best flavor accents and richest browning during cooking.

Appreciating the tang of a buttermilk soak but unwilling to forgo the succulence of brined chicken, we found ourselves whispering "buttermilk brine." Plus, instead of soaking the chicken in buttermilk alone, why not add the saline blast of a brine, doubling the rewards and minimizing the number of steps? And to get even more of a leg up, we made it a flavored brine, adding a mountain of crushed garlic, a couple of crumbled bay leaves, and some sweet paprika.

This remarkable "twofer" won high marks indeed, well above those garnered by a unilateral soak or brine. The buttermilk and paprika showed spirit, the garlic and bay leaves crept into the crust, and the meat was tender and seasoned. We also spiked the brine with ¼ cup of sugar—not enough to sweeten but enough to bring other flavors out of hiding.

Fried foods taste irresistibly good when dressed in crumbs or flour, not only because they are protected from damaging temperatures, but also because hot, enveloping fat performs minor miracles on the flavor of the flour or crumbs. But what kind of coating is best?

To find out, we tested straight flour against a panoply of contenders: matzo crumbs, ground saltines, cornflakes, Melba toast, cornmeal, and panko (Japanese-style bread crumbs). In the end, plain flour, which necessitated no seasoning whatsoever because the chicken had been brined, surpassed all other options for the integrity and lightness of the crust it produced.

Many fried chicken recipes use a single breading process in which the chicken is dipped first into beaten egg, then into flour or crumbs. A double, or bound, breading dips the chicken into flour first, then into egg, and finally into flour or crumbs. In side-by-side tests, we found that the double breading offered a superior base coat that was more tenacious in its grip and more protective in its bearing, without being overly thick or tough.

Another practice that has made its way into many fried chicken recipes is that of air-drying the breaded chicken before frying it. Rather than becoming soggy in the refrigerator, as might be expected, the breading toughens up over time to produce a fried chicken of superior crispness.

We were also curious about the effect of air-drying on unbreaded chicken. We have come to favor the laser-crisp and taut skin of roasted birds that have been air-dried and wanted to see if an analogous effect could be achieved by refrigerating our brined, unbreaded chicken on a rack for a couple of hours. We were reasonably confident this would allow the buttermilk to dry just enough and the chicken to bread nicely without first being dabbed or dried, frying up dry and crisp.

We tested the effects of air-drying the chicken either before or after breading and compared the results with chicken that underwent no air-drying. Both air-dried versions were superior in terms of crust, but each was distinctly different from the other. The chicken that was breaded and then air-dried had a heartier, more toothsome crust—crunchy to some, hard to others. The chicken that was air-dried and then breaded was lighter and crispier—flaky, more shattery. We preferred this traditionally Southern crust. Though it initially seemed ideal, we noticed that its delicate crispness succumbed to sandiness and porosity over the course of a few hours. This was not acceptable.

The memory of a particularly light but resilient crust on a chicken-fried steak we had made persuaded us to add baking soda and baking powder to an egg wash bolstered with buttermilk. We hoped the sandiness in the crust that developed over time might thus be offset. Stirred into the wash, 1 teaspoon of baking powder and ½ teaspoon of baking soda produced just enough lift to lighten the breading to perfection. Not only did it bronze to a shattery filigree in the hot fat, it also remained crisp as it cooled.

One of the most important requirements of fat as a frying medium is that it offer nothing of its own flavor—in fact, it should have none to offer in the first place. This means that the oil must be refined—in other words, cleansed and sanitized. Another requirement is that the oil perform at temperatures below its smoke point (the temperature at which it emits smoke and acrid odors) to maintain thermal stability. With the relatively moderate temperatures required by our recipe, all refined vegetable oils stayed well below their smoke points. In the end, peanut oil edged out vegetable oil and Crisco shortening by virtue of its marginally more neutral and clean flavor, but all are decent choices.

A cast-iron Dutch oven covered during the first half of the frying reduced splatters to a fine spray, maintained the oil temperature impeccably, and fried the chicken through in about 15 minutes total versus the 20 minutes per side recommended in many recipes.

Drying the gleaming, bronzed statuettes was the most satisfying test. Paper bags are simply not porous enough to keep the chicken out of a gathering pool of grease. We found that paper towels absorbed excess fat quickly and that placing the drained pieces onto a bare rack thereafter kept them crisp.

Crispy Fried Chicken

SERVES 4 TO 6

If using a kosher bird, skip the brining process. To use kosher salt in the brine, see page 12 for conversion information and more tips on brining. Maintaining an even oil temperature is key. After the chicken is added to the pot, the temperature will drop dramatically, and most of the frying will be done at about 325 degrees. Use an instant-read thermometer with a high upper range; a clip-on candy/deep-fry thermometer is fine, too, though it can be clipped to the pot only for the uncovered portion of frying.

CHICKEN

- **½ cup table salt (see note)**
- **¼ cup sugar**
- **2 tablespoons paprika**
- **7 cups buttermilk**
- **3 medium garlic heads, cloves separated and smashed**
- **3 bay leaves, crumbled**
- **4 pounds bone-in, skin-on chicken pieces (split breasts cut in half, drumsticks, and/or thighs), trimmed**
- **3–4 quarts peanut oil or vegetable oil**

COATING

- **4 cups (20 ounces) unbleached all-purpose flour**
- **1 large egg**
- **1 teaspoon baking powder**
- **½ teaspoon baking soda**
- **1 cup buttermilk**

1. FOR THE CHICKEN: Dissolve the salt, sugar, and paprika in the buttermilk in a large container. Add the garlic and bay leaves, submerge the chicken in the brine, cover, and refrigerate for 2 to 3 hours.

2. Remove the chicken from the brine, shake off the excess brine, and place in a single layer on a wire rack set over a rimmed baking sheet. Refrigerate uncovered for 2 hours. (Up to this point, the chicken can be covered with plastic wrap and refrigerated for up to 6 more hours.)

3. Adjust an oven rack to the middle position and heat the oven to 200 degrees. Measure 2 inches of oil into a large Dutch oven and heat over medium-high heat to 375 degrees.

4. FOR THE COATING: Place the flour in a shallow dish. Whisk the egg, baking powder, and baking soda together in a medium bowl, then whisk in the buttermilk (the mixture will bubble and foam). Working with 3 chicken pieces at a time, dredge in the flour, shaking off the excess, then coat with the egg mixture, allowing the excess to drip off. Finally, coat with flour again, shake off the excess, and return to the wire rack.

5. When the oil is hot, add half of the chicken pieces to the pot, skin-side down, cover, and fry until deep golden brown, 7 to 11 minutes, adjusting the heat as necessary to maintain an oil temperature of about 325 degrees. (After 4 minutes, check the chicken pieces for even browning and rearrange if some pieces are browning faster than others.) Turn the chicken pieces over and continue to cook until an instant-read thermometer inserted into the center of the chicken registers 160 to 165 degrees for breasts, or 170 to 175 degrees for thighs or drumsticks, 6 to 8 minutes. Drain the chicken briefly on a paper towel–lined plate, then transfer to a clean wire rack set over a rimmed baking sheet and keep warm in the oven.

6. Return the oil to 375 degrees (if necessary) over medium-high heat and repeat with the remaining chicken pieces. Serve.

Korean Fried Chicken

FRIED CHICKEN HAS, UNTIL RECENTLY, ALWAYS been considered a Western delicacy. But in recent years, as Western culture migrates to the East, so has its penchant for convenience and fast food, including fried chicken. The Koreans, however, have completely transformed the thick-crusted fried chicken of the American South into chicken with a paper-thin, crisp coating—each piece painted with a tangy, saucy glaze.

While we love Southern-style fried chicken (who doesn't?), we wanted to find out what all the hype surrounding Korean fried chicken was about. Korean-style fried chicken is purportedly twice-fried to give it a super-crisp and thin skin. Twice-frying involves frying the chicken pieces for an initial period, typically 3 to 5 minutes, removing the chicken from the oil and allowing it to rest for about 5 to 7 minutes, then returning it to the oil to finish cooking. We were curious to see how well this technique actually worked, so we built a recipe from existing information gathered from Korean cookbooks and headed into the test kitchen.

With paper-thin, crisp skin as our goal, we began by testing twice-fried chicken against our conventional fried chicken. For these initial tests, we left off any coating so that we could fully judge the results of the frying method. The twice-fried chicken had an initial fry time of 5 minutes, followed by a 5 minute rest, and concluded with a 3- to 5-minute fry until the chicken was cooked. The conventional fried chicken was fried straight through for 7 to 11 minutes until cooked.

After tasting both versions side-by-side, it was clear that the twice-fried method resulted in a crispier, thinner-skinned chicken (irrelevant to our traditional Southern fried chicken recipe, which is all about its crunchy exterior). But why does twice-frying yield crispier chicken? We consulted our science editor for the answer.

Our science editor explained that chicken skin is composed of 50 percent water and 40 percent fat, with the remaining 10 percent consisting of connective tissue and other matter. When the chicken is fried, the meat cooks, the moisture in the skin begins to evaporate, and the fat begins to melt, or render. But by the time the chicken is cooked through, there is still a significant amount of water remaining in the skin, as well as fat. In order to crisp the skin, one could continue to fry the chicken, but then the meat would overcook and the skin would start to burn. Twice-frying, however, slows down the cooking process to allow more moisture to evaporate and more fat to render. Here's how it works.

In the first fry, the meat begins to cook, the moisture in the skin—specifically the outer layer of the skin—begins to evaporate, and the fat begins to render. The chicken is then removed from the oil

---

EQUIPMENT: Garlic Presses

A defiantly sticky and undeniably stinky job, hand-mincing garlic is a chore many cooks avoid by pressing the cloves through a garlic press. The question for us was not whether garlic presses work, but which of the many available models works best. After squeezing our way through 12 different models, the unanimous winner was Kuhn Rikon's 2315 Epicurean Garlic Press. Solidly constructed of stainless steel, it has an almost luxurious feel, with ergonomically curved handles that are comfortable to squeeze and a hopper that smoothly and automatically lifts out for cleaning as you open the handles. It passed all our kitchen tests with flying colors. At $35, however, it is also quite expensive. Also doing well in our tests was the Trudeau Garlic Press—with a solid construction, it is sturdy and easy to use, and is our best buy at a reasonable $11.99.

THE BEST GARLIC PRESSES

The Kuhn Rikon 2315 Epicurean Garlic Press produces a very fine mince, good yield, and great paste consistency, making it the all-around winner. The Trudeau Garlic Press is a solid and reliable choice for those looking to spend a little less and is our best buy.

and allowed to rest, which brings down the temperature of both the meat and the skin. This resting period serves two purposes: First, it allows time for more moisture to evaporate from the skin; second, it helps prevent the meat from overcooking. In the second fry, the relatively dry outer layer of skin can quickly become very hot and crisp, while retaining moisture within the deepest layers of skin and the meat. During this process, more fat is rendered, providing an ultra-thin, crisp skin. With a clear explanation of the twice-frying process, we moved on to determining whether or not we should brine, and what would be the best coating for the chicken.

We immediately found that, unlike traditional fried chicken, twice-fried chicken did not benefit from a soak in a brine (a mixture of salt, water, and sometimes sugar that seasons the meat and makes it more juicy once cooked). The moisture from the brine inhibited the skin's ability to brown; with the flavorful sauce that would ultimately coat the crisp chicken, dry meat and lack of flavor was not a concern. Moving on, we turned to the coating.

Many of the recipes we found called for dusting the chicken with cornstarch before frying, while other recipes took it a step further and dipped the chicken into a thin mixture of cornstarch and water, or into a batter of eggs, cornstarch, and water. We tested our fried chicken with all three techniques: cornstarch only, a batter of cornstarch and water, and a batter of cornstarch, water, and eggs. The chicken that was coated with only cornstarch fried up crispier than without the coating, gaining a golden brown color. But the skin was only moderately crisp, and the cornstarch seemed to weigh the skin down in some spots. The two batter tests yielded lackluster results, as both slid immediately off the chicken when it hit the hot oil. It was clear that we needed to prepare the surface of the chicken in a manner that would allow the batter to stick. The obvious solution was to coat the chicken pieces with a thin layer of cornstarch before dipping them into the batter.

Now that the batter was adhering to the chicken, we tried our test again. The egg batter turned into a heavy, dense crust. The cornstarch batter, however, yielded chicken with a light, crisp, and beautifully golden crust. This was unlike any fried chicken we'd ever eaten.

With our chicken fried, we shifted our attention to our sauce. Proper Korean fried chicken is coated very lightly with a pungent sauce. But before you think along the lines of Buffalo wings, think again—the coating is very light, not a thick slather. A popular Korean fried chicken sauce is a sweet soy-garlic sauce. We made our sweet soy-garlic sauce by combining sugar, soy sauce, water, and garlic in a saucepan and reducing it to a glaze. We balanced the sauce with a splash of rice wine vinegar and a shot of hot sauce. Once the chicken was fried, we tossed it lightly with the sauce until coated and sprinkled it with sliced scallions and minced cilantro. Tasters grabbed plenty of napkins before stepping up to enjoy this fried chicken feast.

Korean Fried Chicken

SERVES 4

The chicken must be fried in two batches. To make the best use of your time, batter the second batch of chicken while the first batch is having its initial fry. If using both light and dark meat (breasts and thighs and/or drumsticks), we suggest dividing them into corresponding batches, since the dark meat requires a few extra minutes to cook through on the second fry in step 6.

SAUCE

- ½ cup sugar
- ¼ cup soy sauce
- ¼ cup water
- 3 medium garlic cloves, minced or pressed through a garlic press (about 1 tablespoon)
- 1 tablespoon rice vinegar
- 1 teaspoon Asian chili-garlic sauce

CHICKEN AND COATING

- 3–4 quarts peanut or vegetable oil
- 1½ cups cornstarch
- 3½ pounds bone-in, skin-on chicken pieces (split breasts cut in half, drumsticks, and/or thighs)
- Salt and ground black pepper
- 1 cup water
- 2 scallions, sliced thin on the bias (see the illustration on page 48)
- 1 tablespoon minced fresh cilantro leaves

1. For the sauce: Simmer all of the ingredients in a small saucepan over medium heat until syrupy, 5 to 6 minutes; set aside. (The sauce can be refrigerated in an airtight container for up to 24 hours. Bring to room temperature and whisk to recombine before using.)

2. For the chicken and coating: Adjust an oven rack to the middle position and heat the oven to 200 degrees. Measure 2 inches of oil into a large Dutch oven and heat over medium-high heat to 350 degrees. (Use an instant-read thermometer that registers high temperatures, or clip a candy/deep-fat thermometer onto the side of the pan.)

3. Sift ½ cup of the cornstarch into a shallow dish. Set a large mesh strainer over a large bowl. Pat the chicken dry with paper towels and season with salt and pepper. Working with several pieces of chicken at a time, coat the chicken thoroughly with the cornstarch, then transfer to the strainer and shake vigorously to remove all but a thin coating of cornstarch. Transfer the coated chicken to a wire rack set over a rimmed baking sheet.

4. Whisk the remaining 1 cup cornstarch, the water, and 1 teaspoon salt together in a large bowl to form a smooth batter. When the oil is hot, finish coating the chicken by adding half of the chicken to the batter and turn to coat well. Using tongs, remove the chicken from the batter, 1 piece at a time, allowing any excess batter to drip back into the bowl, and add to the hot oil.

5. Fry the chicken, stirring to prevent the pieces from sticking together and adjusting the heat as necessary to maintain an oil temperature of 350 degrees, until the chicken begins to crisp and turn slightly golden, and registers about 90 degrees on an instant-read thermometer, about 5 minutes. Transfer the fried chicken to a clean wire rack set over a rimmed baking sheet and set aside for about 5 minutes. Meanwhile, batter and fry the remaining chicken.

6. Return the oil to 350 degrees (if necessary) over medium-high heat. Return the first batch of fried chicken to the oil and continue to fry until the exterior is very crisp and deep golden brown, and an instant-read thermometer inserted into the center of the chicken registers 160 to 165 degrees for breasts, or 170 to 175 degrees for thighs or drumsticks, 3 to 6 minutes. Drain briefly on a paper towel–lined plate, then transfer to a wire rack set over a rimmed baking sheet and keep warm in a 200-degree oven. Repeat with the second batch. (The unsauced fried chicken can be held for up to an hour in a 200-degree oven.)

7. Transfer all of the chicken to a large bowl, drizzle with the sauce, and gently toss until evenly coated. Transfer the chicken to a platter, sprinkle with the scallions and cilantro, and serve.

Firecracker Chicken

All recipes for firecracker chicken have one thing in common—tongue-tingling heat capable of satisfying any chile-head's cravings for fire. Most recipes marinate boneless chicken breasts in hot sauce; the chicken is then breaded, pan-fried, and served with more hot sauce. Our first question was simple: Did we have to make our own hot sauce, or could we just use bottled sauce?

Commercial hot sauce wasn't bad, but our tasters wanted something fresher and more interesting—and something different than Buffalo wing sauce. The recipes we tested agreed on the chiles, but there was little consensus on the other base ingredients for the spicy marinade/finishing sauce. After testing numerous condiments in our fridge, we settled on an unlikely foundation for our sauce.

Yellow (aka "hot dog") mustard has a bright flavor and color as well as a welcome pungency, and its consistency helped it cling nicely to the fried chicken. As for the spice, tasters liked habanero chiles for their unapologetic burn, but they wanted a more complex heat. We added pickled banana peppers (plus some of their pickling juices) for a nice acidic tang, and dry mustard for its sinus-clearing heat. It was time to move on to the chicken.

We found that pounding the chicken breasts to a ½-inch thickness and then slicing each breast in half lengthwise produced chicken strips that were just the right size—enough of a ratio of tender interior to crisp exterior, and they could be eaten with a knife and fork, unlike smaller chicken fingers. When it came to marinating, it took at least 30 minutes for the flavors of the hot sauce to penetrate the chicken strips, although any amount of time up to two hours sufficed (after two hours, the acid and chiles in the sauce began to break down the chicken and turn it mushy).

The next consideration was the coating. In classic fried chicken, the coating adheres to the cut-up chicken parts because the skin is very tacky. But we were using strips of boneless, skinless breasts and encountered problems from the start. We began by testing standard breading (flour, egg wash, and bread crumbs), as well as the simple method of dredging the chicken, still wet from the marinade, into flour.

Tasters complained that the chicken strips coated in bread crumbs were too chicken finger–like. While we love chicken fingers, they simply weren't what we wanted from this recipe. Just plain flour didn't provide enough crunch, so we looked to other ingredients. Crushed Melba toast gave the chicken some crunch, but the crumbs browned too quickly and did not adhere to the chicken very well, leaving more coating in the oil than on the chicken. Cornmeal was another candidate that didn't fare well. Its fine grains left the coating with a gritty sandiness that was hardly popular in the test kitchen.

During testing, a funny thing happened. We noticed that the coating on the pieces of chicken dredged last was thicker than the coating on those dredged first. What was going on? It seems that each time a piece was dredged, the flour absorbed some of the marinade from the chicken. By the time we got around to the last couple of pieces, the flour was almost sticky. This resulted in chicken with a crunchier, thicker coating. The obvious next test was to add some of the sauce straight to the flour. We simply dredged the chicken pieces in the combined mixture, and the chicken fried up with a sturdy, crunchy coating.

Unfortunately, the coating still wasn't sticking to the chicken. We eventually figured out the problem. The chicken had soaked up enough of the firecracker marinade to cause it to steam when it hit the hot oil; the extra liquid steamed the coating right off. Two things helped—letting the coated chicken dry in the refrigerator for 15 minutes, and adding baking powder and cornstarch to the coating (to absorb moisture and encourage browning).

The coating was now more clingy, but still not quite clingy enough. The proteins in eggs can "glue" coatings onto countless foods, so we dried the marinated chicken with paper towels, dipped it in beaten eggs, and then rolled it in the moistened flour coating. Sure enough, this chicken fried up beautifully, with a crisp, crunchy coating that adhered to the chicken. But now tasters didn't like the "eggy flavor" this method added! Taking a cue from our Parmesan-crusted chicken recipe, we used just egg whites to reduce the egg flavor, but the whites were so thin that they didn't hold the coating, and we didn't want to add any other ingredients for fear of imparting flavors that would take away from the hot sauce. After we mulled over different ways to thicken the egg whites, it hit us—why not just beat the egg whites? The foamy egg whites held on to a ton of coating.

Our firecracker chicken finally packed a crunch—and a kick—that was worthy of its name.

Firecracker Chicken

SERVES 6

For more heat, include the habanero seeds and ribs when mincing. For even more heat, add an additional habanero; if you are spice-averse, substitute a jalapeño for the habanero. We like to drizzle the sauce over the chicken strips just before serving, but the sauce is just as good served on the side for dipping.

FIRECRACKER SAUCE

- **½ cup sliced pickled banana peppers, chopped fine, plus ¼ cup pickling liquid**
- **¼ cup juice from 2 lemons**
- **¼ cup vegetable oil**
- **¼ cup yellow mustard**

- 3 tablespoons dry mustard
- 2 tablespoons chili sauce
- 2 tablespoons brown sugar
- 3 medium garlic cloves, minced or pressed through a garlic press (about 1 tablespoon)
- 1 habanero chile, seeds and ribs removed, chile minced (see note)
- 4 scallions, sliced thin

CHICKEN

- 6 boneless, skinless chicken breasts (5 to 6 ounces each), tenderloins removed and breasts trimmed (see the illustrations on page 6)
- 2 cups (10 ounces) unbleached all-purpose flour
- ½ cup cornstarch
- 1 tablespoon salt
- 1 teaspoon baking powder
- 4 large egg whites
- 1 cup vegetable oil

1. FOR THE SAUCE: Whisk the ingredients together in a large bowl; set aside.

2. FOR THE CHICKEN: Following the illustrations on page 6, pound each breast between 2 sheets of plastic wrap to a uniform ½-inch thickness. Slice each breast in half lengthwise and transfer to a large zipper-lock bag with ¼ cup of the sauce. Seal shut, toss to coat, and refrigerate for at least 30 minutes or up to 2 hours.

3. Meanwhile, combine the flour, cornstarch, salt, and baking powder in a large bowl. Add 6 tablespoons of the sauce and, using your hands, combine until the mixture resembles wet sand.

4. Whisk the egg whites in a large bowl until foamy. Remove the chicken from the marinade and pat dry with paper towels. Working with 1 chicken strip at a time, coat with the egg whites, then dredge in the flour mixture, pressing gently so that the flour adheres. Place the coated chicken pieces on a wire rack set over a rimmed baking sheet and refrigerate for at least 15 minutes or up to 4 hours.

5. Adjust an oven rack to the middle position and heat the oven to 200 degrees. Heat the oil in a 12-inch skillet over medium-high heat until shimmering. Add half of the chicken strips and cook until golden brown on both sides, 5 to 7 minutes total. Drain briefly on a paper towel–lined plate and transfer to a clean wire rack set over a rimmed baking sheet and keep warm in the oven. Repeat with the remaining chicken strips. Transfer the chicken to a serving platter, drizzle with the remaining sauce, and serve.

SEEDING FRESH CHILES

Using a knife to remove the seeds and ribs from a hot chile pepper takes a very steady hand. Fortunately, there is a safer and equally effective alternative.

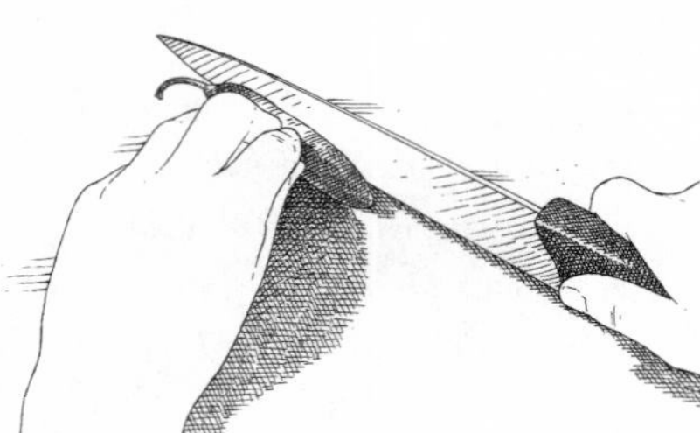

1. Cut the pepper in half lengthwise with a knife.

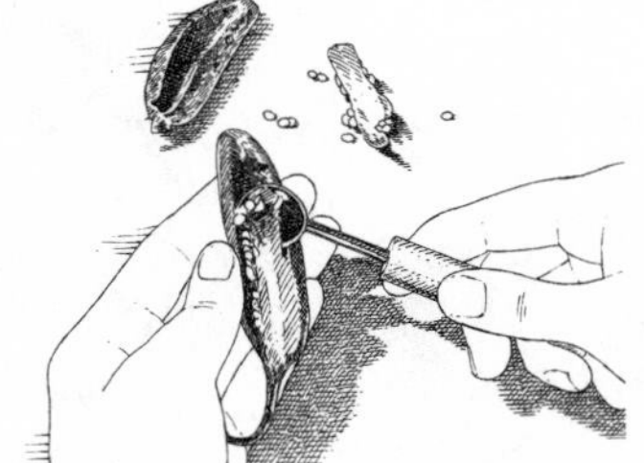

2. Starting opposite the stem end, run the edge of a small melon baller down the inside of the pepper, scraping up the seeds and ribs.

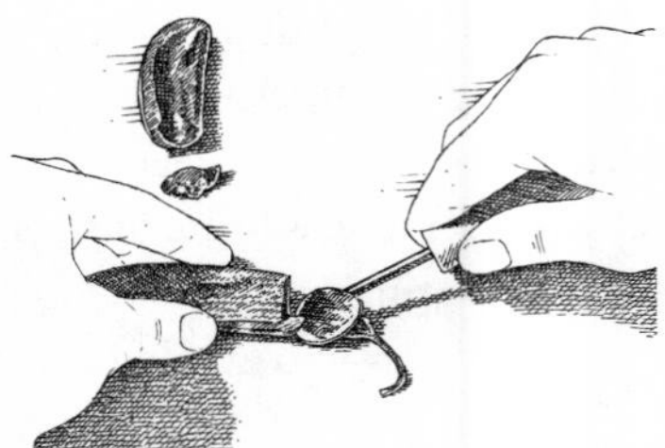

3. Cut off the core with the scoop.

7 BACKYARD CHICKEN

Backyard Chicken

CHICKEN IS ONE OF THE MOST POPULAR items for grilling. Because it takes well to numerous seasonings and can be served in so many forms—parts, whole birds, and breasts—it need never taste or appear to be quite the same from one meal to another. But the problems with grilling chicken are substantial: Inevitably the chicken chars on the outside before it is even close to cooked through on the inside or, if the interior is cooked sufficiently, the meat is bone-dry and void of any flavor. Luckily, these challenges aren't insurmountable, and through countless hours outside we have found some techniques to ensure moist, flavorful, and perfectly grilled chicken every time.

The first lesson we learned is that not all chicken can be grilled the same way, with the same fire and amount of heat. Thin pieces such as the cutlets in our Chicken Fajitas (page 168) can withstand the heat of a hot fire, because they cook through in such a short period of time and so don't have a chance to dry out. On the other hand, whole birds (and bigger parts such as leg quarters and split breasts) would blacken on the outside and remain raw on the inside if grilled solely over high heat. For recipes such as our Grill-Roasted Whole Chicken (page 200), we keep the chicken over the cooler part of the grill the entire time, allowing it to cook through at a slow, steady pace. With these longer cooking times, you can also toss in wood chunks or chips so that the meat picks up true smoky flavor. And finally, we discovered that many recipes—from Chicken Wings (page 176) to Tandoori Chicken (page 192)—require two levels of heat. These recipes start with the chicken on the cooler part of the grill to cook through slowly without drying out and to allow the fat to render (without the risk of dangerous flare-ups that could char the skin). The pieces are then moved to the hotter part of the grill to finish cooking through and to develop a crisp, browned crust.

As in many of the other chapters in this book, brining plays an essential role in keeping chicken moist and well-seasoned. This is particularly important on the grill, where extremely high heat or long cooking times make chicken particularly prone to drying out. There were a few exceptions. Our Barbecued Pulled Chicken (page 188) uses only dark meat—which is not as susceptible as white meat to drying out—and, when we combined this with low, slow cooking, we found that brining wasn't essential. And with Lemon-Parsley Chicken Breasts (page 166) and Chicken Kebabs (page 170), we went with quick marinades to infuse the meat with moisture and flavor. (The thinner or smaller pieces in these recipes could become much too salty if left to brine for an hour.) By reserving some of the unused marinade to add to the chicken after it comes off the grill, its bold flavors are reinforced, brightening the overall dish. Spice rubs are another natural option and even easier than marinades. Rubs, after being spread on the chicken, meld and become complex, seasoning the meat throughout.

Finally, if you are new to grilling or just need a refresher on the basics, we have put together a primer. It includes tips on setting up the grill and how to arrange the charcoal in the grill to produce varying heat levels, as well as advice to help you avoid common problems when grilling.

Grilled Chicken Breasts

LEFT TO THEIR OWN DEVICES, BONELESS, skinless breasts don't stand a chance on the backyard grill. Because they have no skin and little fat, untreated chicken breasts invariably turn out dry and leathery, with a mild—some might say bland—flavor. A quick and easy "solution" that millions of outdoor cooks commonly resort to is soaking the breasts in a store-bought marinade. Nice idea, but in a taste test we couldn't find one brand we could stomach, let alone recommend. These Italian-style marinades suffer from viscous, gelatinous consistencies and tart, fake flavors. Taking a few minutes to make our own marinade would yield much better results.

We knew that nothing else mattered if we couldn't produce a perfectly grilled chicken breast—moist, tender, and able to stand on its own, flavor-wise. We also wanted to keep things as simple as possible, without having to pound the chicken breasts or remove the tenderloin. However, we knew we'd have to make one compromise in our quest for simplicity: Because boneless, skinless breasts are prone to drying out, they would need to be brined before grilling.

Cooked as most recipes suggest—that is, over a hot, single-level fire—the breasts did what we expected: The outsides turned into black shoe leather by the time the internal temperature reached 160 degrees. When we cooked them solely over indirect heat on the cooler side of a modified two-level fire (all the coals banked on one side of the grill), the interiors were noticeably moister, but the tough exteriors lacked color and true grilled flavor. Although first searing the meat over the hotter side of the grill offered a slight improvement, the chicken still wasn't where we wanted it to be.

Were our conventional methods holding us back? Several test cooks suggested using a "hobo pack": wrapping the chicken in a tight foil pouch to keep it moist while cooked over the grill. But without periodically opening the foil and risking a steam burn, we had no way of knowing when the chicken was ready. And even when it was cooked through, it still lacked grilled texture and flavor. We needed a gentler cooking method. Since stovetop poaching does wonders for chicken, we wondered if we could make it work on the grill. We placed a disposable aluminum pan filled halfway with chicken broth over the cooking grate, let it reach a simmer, and added the chicken breasts. Once they came up to 140 degrees, we finished them on the hot grates. Tasters complained that the texture was neither poached nor grilled, but "weird."

Had we gone too far? Maybe not, if we looked at things from a different perspective. Suppose we inverted the disposable pan over the chicken to trap the heat? (We don't use the lid on a charcoal grill unless we're cooking over relatively low heat.) Would creating less temperature fluctuation allow the breasts to cook more evenly? Would they retain more moisture if exposed to less dry heat? We started by searing the breasts on the hotter side of the grill, then we moved them to the cooler side, where we covered them with the pan (flipping them halfway through). Tasters noticed improved flavor and texture. We were closer to what we wanted, but still no cigar. What if we tried reversing the cooking order—starting the covered breasts on the cooler side of the grill until they were nearly done (140 degrees), then giving them a quick sear afterward? The result was perfectly cooked boneless, skinless chicken breasts.

We could now pursue our original goal of injecting some real flavor into the breasts by creating a marinade that could take the place of the brining. Lemon and garlic immediately came to mind, so we mixed together a combination of a few tablespoons of olive oil, lemon juice, garlic, salt, and pepper. We added some sugar to cut the acidity and help with browning. We quickly found that too much lemon juice caused the exterior of the chicken breasts to turn white. No good—we weren't cooking ceviche. But cutting the lemon juice down to 1 tablespoon made the interior bland and dry.

We knew from past brining experiences that, without enough liquid, osmosis—the flow of water across a barrier from a place with a higher water concentration (the brine or marinade) to a place with a lower one (the chicken)—couldn't take place properly. The liquid moving into the chicken should have carried with it some of the dissolved salt and flavor, but these molecules were too concentrated to penetrate the tissue. Adding 2 tablespoons of water diluted the concentration of salt and flavor molecules in the marinade enough for the dissolved molecules to flow in and out of the chicken. A 30-minute marinade did the trick.

We thought we were finished, but tasters weren't ready to let us off the hook. We wanted to keep things simple, but they wanted a sauce. No problem: We could use the essential ingredients from the marinade—plus chopped parsley for color and Dijon mustard for extra flavor and emulsification—to spoon over the cooked chicken. This new complementary sauce added more moisture as well as another layer of flavor. These grilled chicken breasts were easy enough to make on a weeknight and special enough to serve to guests at our next dinner party.

Charcoal-Grilled Lemon-Parsley Chicken Breasts

SERVES 4

This chicken can be served with a simply prepared vegetable for a light dinner. It can also be used in a sandwich or tossed with greens for a salad. If using as part of a salad, transfer the chicken to a large bowl and toss with reserved sauce instead of drizzling the individual breasts with sauce. You will need a disposable 13 by 9-inch aluminum roasting pan for this recipe. For more information on setting up a grill, see page 180.

- 6 tablespoons olive oil
- 2 tablespoons juice from 1 lemon
- 1 tablespoon minced fresh parsley leaves
- 1¼ teaspoons sugar
- 1 teaspoon Dijon mustard
- Salt and ground black pepper
- 2 tablespoons water
- 3 medium garlic cloves, minced or pressed through a garlic press (about 1 tablespoon)
- 4 large boneless, skinless chicken breasts (about 8 ounces each), trimmed

1. Whisk 3 tablespoons of the oil, 1 tablespoon of the lemon juice, the parsley, ¼ teaspoon of the sugar, the mustard, ¼ teaspoon salt, and ¼ teaspoon pepper together in a small bowl; set aside.

2. In a separate bowl, whisk the remaining 3 tablespoons oil, 1 tablespoon lemon juice, and 1 teaspoon sugar together with the water, garlic, 1½ teaspoons salt, and ½ teaspoon pepper. Transfer the marinade to a large zipper-lock bag along with the chicken breasts. Seal shut, toss to coat, and refrigerate for at least 30 minutes and up to 1 hour.

3. Meanwhile, light a large chimney starter filled with charcoal (about 6 quarts) and allow to burn until the coals are fully ignited and partially covered with a thin layer of ash, 20 to 25 minutes. Open the bottom vent on the grill. Build a modified two-level fire by arranging all the coals over half of the grill, leaving the other half empty (see the illustration on page 181). Set the cooking grate in place, cover the grill with the lid, and let the grate heat up, about 5 minutes. Use a grill brush to scrape the cooking grate clean. Dip a wad of paper towels in oil; holding the wad with tongs, oil the cooking grate.

EQUIPMENT: Tongs

It is hard to imagine grilling—or much cooking at all, for that matter—without the benefit of kitchen tongs. A large fork pierces foods and causes some loss of fluids. A spatula is useless with flank steak or chicken parts. A pair of tongs, however, is ideal for turning foods as they cook. But today it's possible to find tongs in a wide array of styles. The handles may be ergonomic or the tongs may telescope or fold in half. Are these newfangled versions any better than basic, old-school models?

Testing all manner of tongs, we groped and grabbed kebabs, asparagus, chicken drumsticks, and 3-pound slabs of ribs and found that tong performance differs dramatically. The business end of a pair of tongs, the pincers, can be smooth or scalloped, and we found that those with scalloped edges get a better grip on food. But that's not the end of the story. The shape of the scalloping can vary. Our tests showed that edges with deep, sharp scalloping were more likely to break delicate foods, rip thin-skinned items, or shred meat fibers. We preferred the gentler touch of wide, shallow scalloping. And pincers that were slightly concave, or cupped, did a good job of grasping hard, irregularly shaped, and large objects.

The winner was a pair of 12-inch locking tongs made of stainless steel and santoprene by OXO. They missed a perfect score only because one picky tester thought the pincers bruised cooked asparagus. A minor complaint indeed—and a flawless performance otherwise.

THE BEST TONGS

The OXO Good Grips 12-inch Locking Tongs ($10.99) has soft cushioning on the arms, keeping hands comfortable, firmly planted, and cool.

OXO GOOD GRIPS

4. Remove the chicken from the zipper-lock bag, allowing the excess marinade to drip off. Place the chicken in the center of the cooler side of the grill, smooth-side down, with the thicker part facing the coals. Cover with a disposable aluminum pan and grill until the bottom of the chicken just begins to develop light grill marks and is no longer translucent, 6 to 9 minutes. Flip the chicken and rotate so that the thinner side faces the coals. Cover with the aluminum pan and continue to grill until the chicken is opaque and firm to the touch and the thickest part of the breast registers 140 degrees on an instant-read thermometer, 6 to 9 minutes longer.

5. Move the chicken to the hotter side of the grill and grill on both sides, uncovered, until dark grill marks appear and the thickest part of the breast registers 160 to 165 degrees on an instant-read thermometer, 1 to 2 minutes per side. Transfer the chicken to a cutting board and let rest for 5 minutes. Slice each breast on the bias into ¼-inch-thick slices (see the illustrations on page 10) and transfer to individual plates. Drizzle with the reserved sauce and serve.

VARIATIONS

Gas-Grilled Lemon-Parsley Chicken Breasts

Follow the recipe for Charcoal-Grilled Lemon-Parsley Chicken Breasts through step 2. Turn all the burners to high and heat the grill with the lid down until very hot, about 15 minutes. Use a grill brush to scrape the cooking grate clean. Dip a wad of paper towels in oil; holding the wad with tongs, oil the cooking grate. Leave the primary burner on high and turn off the other burner(s). Proceed with the recipe from step 4, grilling with the lid down. Increase the browning times in step 5 by 1 to 2 minutes.

Grilled Chipotle-Lime Chicken Breasts

Follow the recipe for Charcoal- or Gas-Grilled Lemon-Parsley Chicken Breasts, substituting lime juice for the lemon juice, 1 teaspoon minced

GRILLING BONELESS, SKINLESS CHICKEN BREASTS

1. Place the chicken on the cooler side of the grill, with the thicker parts facing the coals.

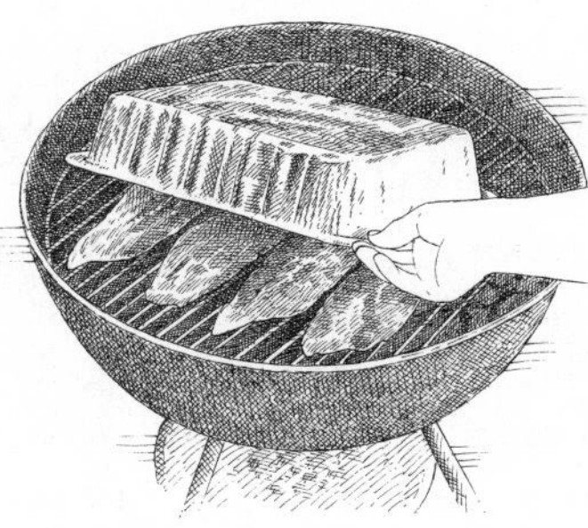

2. Cover with a disposable aluminum roasting pan and cook for 6 to 9 minutes.

3. Flip the chicken so that the thinner parts face the coals and continue grilling, covered, for 6 to 9 minutes.

4. Finish the chicken directly over the coals until dark grill marks appear, 1 to 2 minutes each side.

chipotle chile in adobo sauce for the mustard, and cilantro for the parsley.

Grilled Orange-Tarragon Chicken Breasts

Follow the recipe for Charcoal- or Gas-Grilled Lemon-Parsley Chicken Breasts, substituting orange juice for the lemon juice and tarragon for the parsley. Add ¼ teaspoon grated orange zest to the sauce in step 1.

Chicken Fajitas

WITH OR WITHOUT THE SIZZLING CAST-IRON skillet, what passes for chicken fajitas in most restaurants these days is about as authentic as Belgian toaster waffles. Dry, stringy chicken breasts and limp, tasteless vegetables desperately need a truckload of toppings, and so guacamole, sour cream, and salsa are slathered on in a weak attempt to mask the bland, soggy flavors of the underlying ingredients. We wanted to go back to the basics, a simple combination of smoky grilled vegetables and strips of chicken, wrapped up at the table in warm flour tortillas. Fajitas are a complete meal from the grill, but each component needs special handling.

While the skirt steak in classic beef fajitas has no need for a marinade to add juiciness or flavor, boneless chicken breasts need all the help they can get. Starting with a mixture of lime juice, vegetable oil, garlic, salt, and pepper as our base, we tried several marinating methods. Grilling the chicken plain and tossing the cooked strips into the marinade (now really a sauce) left the chicken with only superficial flavor. Brining—soaking in a saltwater solution—seasoned the chicken and kept it juicy, but tasters found the meat too moist—waterlogged, even. "It might as well have been poached," said one. Making a "brinerade" (a cross between a brine and a marinade) by adding the marinade to a concentrated 2-cup brine only weakened the final flavors.

Up to this point, soaking the chicken breasts directly in the marinade yielded the best results: tender browned chicken with bright, unadulterated tang. The high-acid mixture (⅓ cup lime juice and 4 tablespoons oil) not only added fresh citrus flavor notes but also reduced the marinating time to a mere 15 minutes—any longer and the meat started to "cook" in the acid, like a "chicken ceviche" of sorts. Although moving in the right direction, the marinade still lacked smokiness and depth. After trying numerous (and unsuccessful) flavor additions, we finally hit upon Worcestershire sauce, an unlikely candidate for chicken but one that has some of the characteristics of umami, an overused and little-understood culinary term that refers to a fifth taste sensation beyond the familiar sweet, sour, bitter, and salty. (Some simply liken it to "meaty," while many think of umami as an unusual, sophisticated juxtaposition of flavors that provides a unique taste experience.) A mere tablespoon of Worcestershire was plenty to add another layer of saltiness and smoke without revealing its true identity. A bit of brown sugar helped round out the salty flavors, and minced jalapeño and cilantro added freshness.

Both green and red bell peppers gave the fajitas some needed contrast, not just in terms of color but also in their bitter and sweet flavors. Quartering the peppers allowed them to lie flat on the grill and cook evenly on both sides. Onion wedges cooked unevenly, while rounds were both pretty and practical. We quickly discovered that whereas the chicken needed blazing-hot coals, the vegetables, which are more prone to burning, required more moderate heat. Placing them over medium-hot coals helped them brown nicely as well as cook through without burning. To allow the chicken and vegetables to cook side by side at slightly different heat levels, we created a simple two-level fire. We started with a full chimney of ignited coals and then spread a third of them in a single layer on half the grill and piled the rest high on the other side, creating two cooking zones. Once the cooking grate was in place, the chicken cooked for 8 to 12 minutes on the hotter side of the grill, while the vegetables cooked safely on the cooler side.

As for the flour tortillas, 8- to 10-inch rounds yielded too much excess tortilla; small (but not dainty) 6-inch tortillas were the perfect size. Heating each side of the tortillas for a brief 20 seconds on the cooler side of the grill allowed them to puff up and lose their raw, gummy texture. Quickly wrapping the warmed tortillas in a clean kitchen towel or foil prevented them from becoming dry and brittle. With the warm tortillas steaming in the wrapper, and the requisite toppings ready to go, all that was left to do was to separate the onion into rings and slice the bell peppers and chicken breasts into strips. But something was still missing. By tossing just a small amount of unused reserved marinade back in with the chicken strips and vegetables, we were able to give them a burst of fresh flavor. It wasn't until we had eaten our way through half of the chicken fajitas that we realized we'd forgotten to add any condiments.

Charcoal-Grilled Chicken Fajitas

SERVES 4

For more heat, include the jalapeño seeds and ribs when mincing. When you head outside to grill, bring along a clean kitchen towel or a large piece of foil in which to wrap the tortillas and keep them warm as they come off the grill. Guacamole (page 210), Tomato Salsa (page 211), sour cream, shredded cheddar or Monterey Jack cheese, and lime wedges make great accompaniments to the fajitas. For more information on setting up a grill, see page 180.

- 6 tablespoons vegetable oil
- ⅓ cup juice from 2 to 3 limes
- 1½ tablespoons minced fresh cilantro leaves
- 3 medium garlic cloves, minced or pressed through a garlic press (about 1 tablespoon)
- 1 tablespoon Worcestershire sauce
- 1½ teaspoons brown sugar
- 1 jalapeño chile, seeds and ribs removed, chile minced (see note)
- Salt and ground black pepper
- 1½ pounds boneless, skinless chicken breasts (about 3 large), trimmed
- 1 large red onion, peeled and cut into ½-inch-thick rounds (do not separate the rings)
- 1 large red bell pepper, stemmed, seeded, and quartered
- 1 large green bell pepper, stemmed, seeded, and quartered
- 8–12 (6-inch) flour tortillas

1. Whisk 4 tablespoons of the oil, the lime juice, cilantro, garlic, Worcestershire, brown sugar, jalapeño, 1 teaspoon salt, and ¾ teaspoon pepper together in a medium bowl. Reserve ¼ cup of the marinade and set aside. Add 1 more teaspoon salt to the remaining marinade. Transfer the marinade to a large zipper-lock bag along with the chicken breasts. Seal shut, toss to coat, and refrigerate for 15 minutes. Brush both sides of the onion rounds and peppers with the remaining 2 tablespoons oil and season with salt and pepper; set aside.

2. Meanwhile, light a large chimney starter filled with charcoal (about 6 quarts) and allow to burn until the coals are fully ignited and partially covered with a thin layer of ash, 20 to 25 minutes. Open the bottom vent on the grill. Build a two-level fire by arranging one-third of the coals in a single layer over half the grill and piling the remaining coals over the other half (see the illustration on page 181). Set the cooking grate in place, cover the grill with

INGREDIENTS:
Supermarket Flour Tortillas

It's no surprise that the best flour tortillas are freshly made to order. But those of us without a local tortilleria must make do with the packaged offerings at the local supermarket. To find out which ones taste best, we rounded up every 6-inch flour tortilla we could find (usually labeled "fajita size") and headed into the test kitchen to taste them.

Tasters immediately zeroed in on texture, which varied dramatically from "doughy and stale" to "thin and flaky." The thinner brands were the hands-down winners. Most brands had a mild, pleasantly wheaty flavor, but two of the doughier brands, Olé and La Banderita (both made by the same company), were panned for sour off-notes. Our advice is simple: Get the thinnest tortillas you can find at your local market.

THE BEST SUPERMARKET TORTILLAS
Thin, flaky Tyson Mexican Original Flour Tortillas, Fajita Style, were tasters' clear favorite.

the lid, and let the grate heat up, about 5 minutes. Use a grill brush to scrape the cooking grate clean. Dip a wad of paper towels in oil; holding the wad with tongs, oil the cooking grate.

3. Remove the chicken from the zipper-lock bag, allowing the excess marinade to drip off. Place the chicken on the hotter side of grill, smooth-side down. Place the onion rounds and peppers (skin-side down) on the cooler side of the grill. Grill, uncovered, until the chicken is well browned, 4 to 6 minutes. Flip the chicken and continue grilling until the thickest part of the breast registers 160 to 165 degrees on an instant-read thermometer, 4 to 6 minutes longer.

4. Meanwhile, grill the peppers until spottily charred and crisp-tender, 8 to 10 minutes, turning once or twice as needed. Grill the onions until tender and charred on both sides, 10 to 12 minutes, turning every 3 to 4 minutes. When the chicken and vegetables are done, transfer to a large plate and tent loosely with foil.

5. Working in 2 to 3 batches, place the tortillas in a single layer on the cooler side of the now-empty grill and grill until warm and lightly browned, about 20 seconds per side (do not grill too long or the tortillas will become brittle). As the tortillas are done, wrap them in a kitchen towel or a large sheet of foil.

6. Separate the onions into rings and place in a medium bowl. Slice the bell peppers lengthwise into ¼-inch strips and place in the bowl with the onions. Toss 2 tablespoons of the reserved marinade with the vegetables. Slice the chicken into ¼-inch strips and toss with the remaining 2 tablespoons reserved marinade in a separate bowl. Arrange the chicken and vegetables on a large platter and serve with the warmed tortillas and other accompaniments (if using).

➢ VARIATION

Gas-Grilled Chicken Fajitas

Follow the recipe for Charcoal-Grilled Chicken Fajitas through step 1. Turn all the burners to high, close the lid, and heat the grill until very hot, about 15 minutes. Use a grill brush to scrape the cooking grate clean. Dip a wad of paper towels in oil; holding the wad with tongs, oil the cooking grate. Leave the primary burner on high and turn the other burner(s) to medium. Proceed with the recipe from step 3, grilling with the lid down. In step 5, when the grill is empty, set all the burners to medium. Working in batches, if necessary, place the tortillas in a single layer on the cooking grate and grill until warm and lightly browned, about 20 seconds per side. As they are done, wrap the tortillas in a kitchen towel or large sheet of foil. Proceed as directed in step 6.

Grilled Chicken Kebabs

CHICKEN AND FRESH VEGETABLE KEBABS grilled to juicy perfection make great summer fare, either as appetizers or as the main course. The best grilled chicken kebabs are succulent, well-seasoned, and really taste like they've been cooked over an open fire. They are complemented by fruits and vegetables that are equally satisfying—grill-marked but juicy, cooked all the way through but neither shrunken nor incinerated.

When we started our testing, we figured it would be simple. After all, skewered chicken is simple food, a standby of every street-corner grill cook from here to China. But we quickly ran into a few difficulties. When we simply threaded the chicken and veggies on skewers, brushed them with a little oil, and sprinkled them with salt and pepper, we were always disappointed. Sometimes the components cooked at different rates, resulting in dry meat and undercooked vegetables. Even when nicely grilled, quick-cooking kebabs didn't absorb much flavor from the fire and were bland. White meat seemed to lose moisture as it cooked, so that by the time it had reached a temperature zone that made it safe to eat, it was too dry to enjoy. With its extra fat, dark meat was invariably juicier than white meat, but it still needed a considerable flavor boost before it could be called perfect. Sticking with dark meat, we decided to attack the flavor problem first, reasoning that once we could produce well-seasoned, juicy chicken chunks, we'd work out the kinks of cooking fruits and vegetables at the same time.

Wanting to add a little moisture as well as flavor, we turned to marinades. We mixed together a simple marinade of lemon juice, olive oil, garlic, and herbs and soaked the chicken in it for three hours, the recommended time for skin-on chicken parts. We liked the glossy, slightly moist grilled crust that the marinade produced and the way the garlic and herb flavors penetrated the meat. But we found the flavor of the lemon juice to be overpowering on these small chunks. More of a problem, however, was the way the acid-based marinade "tenderized" the chicken. When chicken parts are bathed in this solution, the skin protects the meat, which grills up juicy and firm. Even with shorter marinating times (we tried one hour and half an hour), the skinless chunks were mushy after cooking.

Was there a way to season the chicken all the way through and keep it moist on the grill without the acid? We ruled out brining because it would make the small, skinless chicken chunks much too salty. But we wanted to get the juiciness and flavor that brining imparts. Figuring that soaking the chicken in a lightly salted marinade (rather than the large quantities of water and salt called for in brining) might work, we prepared two batches of acid-free olive oil marinade, one with salt and one without, and let the chunks sit in the marinade for three hours before grilling. The results were what we had hoped for: The salted marinade produced plump, well-seasoned chunks of chicken. The chicken marinated without salt was drier and seemed to have absorbed less flavor from the garlic and herbs.

One small problem remained. What if we wanted a little bit of lemon flavor on our chicken without sacrificing texture? We made up a batch of our marinade and added just a teaspoon of lemon juice to see what would happen. After just half an hour with such a small amount of juice, the chicken chunks had turned white, indicating that they had been partially cooked by the acid. When cooked, they exhibited the same softening as chicken marinated for a longer time in a much more acidic solution. Instead, we reserved some of the marinade before adding the chicken, spiked it with a little lemon or lime juice, and poured the mixture over the kebabs as they came off the grill. This gave the kebabs the final boost of fresh flavor that we were after.

After fine-tuning the method, we settled on 1 teaspoon salt (this quantity seasons the chicken without making it overly salty) for 2 pounds of chicken, and a marinating time of at least three hours (during testing, chicken marinated for less time did not absorb enough flavor). Because there is no acid in the marinade and thus no danger of it breaking down the texture of the meat, it can be combined

EQUIPMENT: Skewers

When we first got the assignment to conduct an equipment test on skewers, we figured our editor had finally lost it. How much "performance" difference could there really be between one pointed stick and another? Once we'd surveyed the field, our attitude changed—it really is possible to buy bad skewers.

First of all, forget what most grilling books say: If you're cooking over very high heat, bamboo skewers will burn and break apart—no matter how long you soak them in water beforehand. We had better luck with metal skewers. They may cost more, but they're reusable and they can handle the heartiest kebabs without bending or breaking.

Not all metal skewers are created equal, however. We had a tough time flipping food on round skewers—the skewer itself turned just fine, but the food stayed in place. Flat skewers proved much more effective. Double-pronged skewers turned the food, but some were flimsy and most had a tendency to twist out of their parallel configuration. Other models took the sturdy concept too far, with bulky skewers that severed delicate pieces of meat.

Our choice: any flat, thin metal skewer will do. We particularly liked Norpro's 12-inch stainless steel skewers (six skewers for $10), which are just 3/16 inch thick.

THE BEST SKEWER

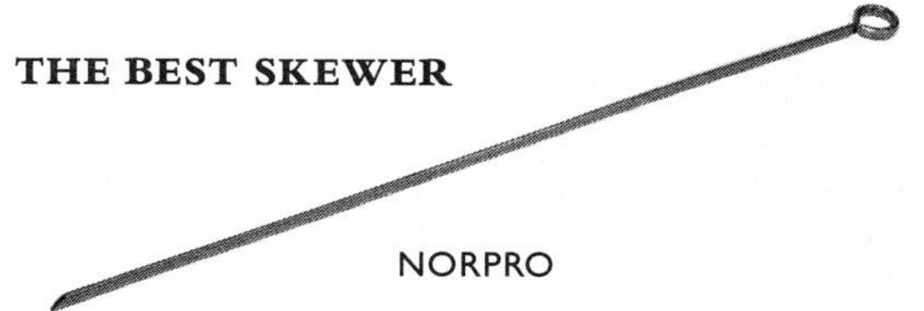

With the flat metal surface of Norpro's 12-inch stainless steel skewers, the food turns along with the skewer.

with the chicken up to 24 hours before cooking.

As for the fire, we found medium-hot to be best. A hotter fire chars the outside before the inside is done; a cooler fire won't give you those appetizing grill marks and may dry out the chicken as it cooks. For the juiciest chicken with the strongest grilled flavor, skewers should be cooked for eight to 10 minutes. Check for doneness by cutting into one of the pieces with a small knife as soon as the chicken looks opaque on all sides. Remove it from the grill as soon as there is no sign of pink at the center.

After experimenting with various sizes and shapes, we chose 1½-inch chunks, small enough for easy eating but big enough to get some good grilled flavor before they have to come off the fire. With smaller chunks and thin strips, there's no margin for error; a few seconds too long on the grill and you'll wind up with a dry-as-dust dinner. A final note on skewering—we found that chicken pieces skewered on a round skewer tended to spin when we lifted them from the grill, inhibiting even cooking. A flat skewer worked best and proved more effective at holding the meat in place (see page 171 for our testing of skewers).

It was clear early on that cooking chicken and vegetables together enhances the flavor of both. Therefore, we needed to figure out how to prepare the vegetables so that they would cook at the same rate as the chicken. We eliminated items like potatoes and yams, which take more time than chicken to cook through on the grill. Because the chicken was so highly flavored from the marinade, and because we did not like the way some vegetables and fruits began to lose their characteristic flavor after just a short dip, we decided against marinating them. We found that simply tossing the fruits and vegetables with a little olive oil, salt, and pepper produced the best-textured and best-flavored chunks.

In general, resilient (but not rock-hard) vegetables fared well. When cut in proper sizes, onions, zucchini, eggplant, mushrooms, and bell peppers cook thoroughly but stay moist and lend good flavor and crunch to chicken skewers. Cherry tomatoes, on the other hand, cook too quickly and tend to disintegrate by the time the chicken is done.

Firm-textured fruits like apples, pears, and pineapples grill beautifully, holding their shape while cooking all the way through. Fruits that tend toward softness when overripe, like peaches and nectarines, work fine if still firm. Softer fruits like mangoes or grapes turn to mush after 10 minutes over the fire, no matter their size.

PREPARING ONIONS FOR KEBABS

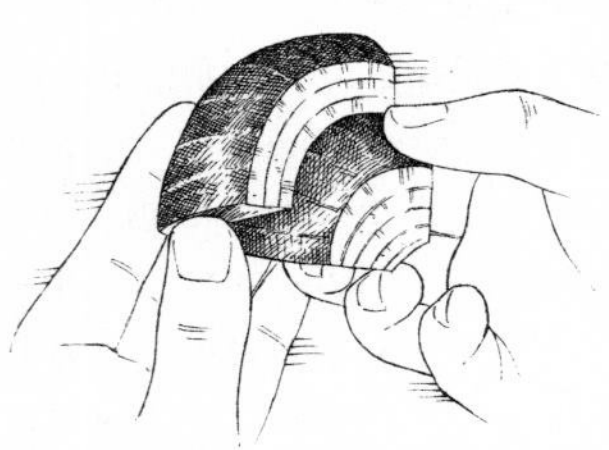

1. Trim off the stem and root ends, cut the onion into quarters, and peel. Remove the three outer layers of the onion from the core.

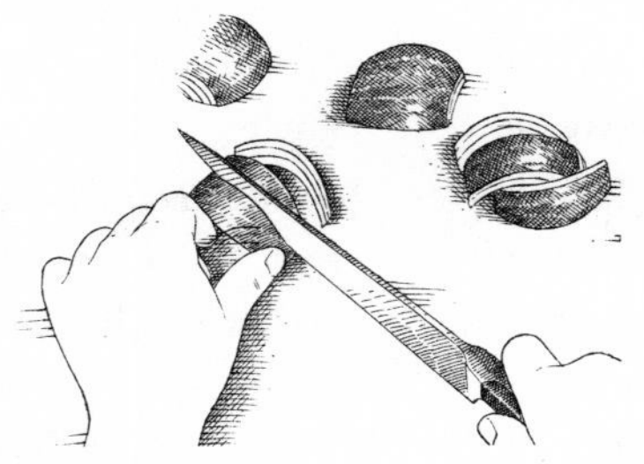

2. Working with the outer layers only, cut each quarter—from pole to pole—into three equal strips.

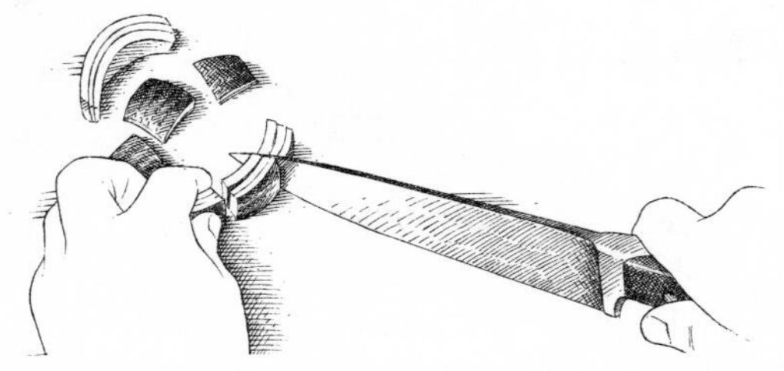

3. Cut each of the 12 strips crosswise into three pieces. You should have thirty-six 3-layer stacks of separate pieces of onion.

Charcoal-Grilled Chicken Kebabs

SERVES 4

You will need eight 12-inch skewers for this recipe. Although white breast meat can be used, we prefer the juicier, more flavorful dark thigh meat for these kebabs. Whichever you choose, do not mix white and dark meat on the same skewer, since they cook at different rates. For more information on setting up a grill, see page 180.

CHICKEN AND MARINADE

- ½ **cup extra-virgin olive oil**
- ¼ **cup minced fresh mint leaves**
- 1½ **teaspoons chopped fresh rosemary**
- 3 **medium garlic cloves, minced or pressed through a garlic press (about 1 tablespoon)**
- 1½ **teaspoons grated zest plus 2 tablespoons juice from 1 lemon**
- 1 **teaspoon salt**
- ⅛ **teaspoon ground black pepper**
- 2 **pounds boneless, skinless chicken thighs (about 8 thighs), trimmed and cut into 1½-inch chunks**

VEGETABLES

- 3 **yellow, red, or orange bell peppers, stemmed, seeded, and cut into 1-inch pieces**
- 1 **large red onion, prepared according to the illustrations on page 172**
- 2 **tablespoons extra-virgin olive oil**
- ½ **teaspoon salt**
- ¼ **teaspoon ground black pepper**
- 1 **lemon, cut into wedges (for serving)**

1. For the chicken and marinade: Whisk the olive oil, mint, rosemary, garlic, lemon zest, salt, and pepper together in a medium bowl. Transfer ¼ cup of the marinade to an airtight container, stir in the lemon juice, and set aside. Add the remaining marinade to a large zipper-lock bag along with the chicken. Seal shut, toss to coat, and refrigerate for at least 3 hours and up to 24 hours. (If you marinate the chicken for more than 3 hours, refrigerate the reserved marinade until you are ready to cook the chicken; bring to room temperature before using.)

2. Meanwhile, light a large chimney starter filled with charcoal (about 6 quarts) and allow to burn until the coals are fully ignited and partially covered with a thin layer of ash, 20 to 25 minutes. Open the bottom vent on the grill. Build a single-level fire by arranging the coals evenly over the bottom of the grill (see the illustration on page 181). Set the cooking grate in place, cover the grill with the lid, and let the grate heat up, about 5 minutes. Use a grill brush to scrape the cooking grate clean. Dip a wad of paper towels in oil; holding the wad with tongs, oil the cooking grate.

3. For the vegetables: Meanwhile, toss the vegetables with the olive oil, salt, and pepper; set aside.

4. Remove the chicken chunks from the zipper-lock bag, allowing the excess marinade to drip off. Using eight 12-inch skewers, thread each skewer with 2 pieces of pepper, 3 pieces of onion, and 1 cube of chicken. Repeat this sequence 2 more times on each skewer.

5. Grill the kebabs, uncovered, turning each kebab one-quarter turn every 2 minutes, until the chicken and vegetables are lightly browned and the meat is fully cooked, 8 to 10 minutes. Transfer the kebabs to a platter, pour the reserved marinade–lemon juice mixture over the top, and let rest for 5 to 10 minutes before serving with the lemon wedges.

VARIATION

Gas-Grilled Chicken Kebabs

Follow the recipe for Charcoal-Grilled Chicken Kebabs through step 1. Turn all the burners to high, close the lid, and heat the grill until very hot, about 15 minutes. Use a grill brush to scrape the cooking grate clean. Dip a wad of paper towels in oil; holding the wad with tongs, oil the cooking grate. Proceed with the recipe as directed from step 3, grilling with the lid down.

Charcoal-Grilled Caribbean Chicken Kebabs with Black Bean and Mango Salsa

SERVES 4

You will need eight 12-inch skewers for this recipe. Although white breast meat can be used, we prefer the juicier, more flavorful dark thigh meat for these kebabs. Whichever you choose, do not mix white and dark meat on the same skewer, since they cook at different rates. For more information on setting up a grill, see page 180.

CHICKEN AND MARINADE

- ½ **cup extra-virgin olive oil**
- ¼ **cup minced fresh parsley leaves**
- 3 **medium garlic cloves, minced or pressed through a garlic press (about 1 tablespoon)**
- 1½ **teaspoons grated zest plus 2 tablespoons juice from 1 lime**
- 1 **teaspoon ground cumin**

1 teaspoon chili powder
½ teaspoon ground allspice
¼ teaspoon ground cinnamon
1 teaspoon salt
½ teaspoon ground black pepper
2 pounds boneless, skinless chicken thighs (about 8 thighs), trimmed and cut into 1½-inch chunks

VEGETABLES
3 large onions, cut into ½-inch-thick wedges
2 tablespoons extra-virgin olive oil
½ teaspoon salt
¼ teaspoon ground black pepper
1 recipe Black Bean and Mango Salsa (page 212)

1. For the chicken and marinade: Whisk the olive oil, parsley, garlic, lime zest, cumin, chili powder, allspice, cinnamon, salt, and pepper together in a medium bowl. Transfer ¼ cup of the marinade to an airtight container, stir in the lime juice, and set aside. Add the remaining marinade to a large zipper-lock bag along with the chicken. Seal shut, toss to coat, and refrigerate for at least 3 hours and up to 24 hours. (If you marinate the chicken for more than 3 hours, refrigerate the reserved marinade until you are ready to cook the chicken; bring to room temperature before using.)

2. Meanwhile, light a large chimney starter filled with charcoal (about 6 quarts) and allow to burn until the coals are fully ignited and partially covered with a thin layer of ash, 20 to 25 minutes. Open the bottom vent on the grill. Build a single-level fire by arranging the coals evenly over the bottom of the grill (see the illustration on page 181). Set the cooking grate in place, cover the grill with the lid, and let the grate heat up, about 5 minutes. Use a grill brush to scrape the cooking grate clean. Dip a wad of paper towels in oil; holding the wad with tongs, oil the cooking grate.

3. For the vegetables: Meanwhile, toss the onions with the olive oil, salt, and pepper; set aside.

4. Remove the chicken chunks from the zipper-lock bag, allowing the excess marinade to drip off. Using eight 12-inch skewers, thread each skewer with 1 wedge of onion and 1 cube of chicken. Repeat this sequence 4 more times on each skewer.

5. Grill the kebabs, uncovered, turning each kebab one-quarter turn every 2 minutes, until the chicken and onions are lightly browned and the meat is fully cooked, 8 to 10 minutes. Transfer the kebabs to a platter, pour the reserved marinade–lime juice mixture over the top, and let rest for 5 to 10 minutes before serving with the Black Bean and Mango Salsa.

VARIATION

Gas-Grilled Caribbean Chicken Kebabs with Black Bean and Mango Salsa

Follow the recipe for Charcoal-Grilled Caribbean Chicken Kebabs with Black Bean and Mango Salsa through step 1. Turn all the burners to high, close the lid, and heat the grill until very hot, about 15 minutes. Use a grill brush to scrape the cooking grate clean. Dip a wad of paper towels in oil; holding the wad with tongs, oil the cooking grate. Proceed with the recipe as directed from step 3, grilling with the lid down.

Charcoal-Grilled Curry Chicken Kebabs with Yogurt-Mint Cucumber Sauce

SERVES 4

You will need eight 12-inch skewers for this recipe. Although white breast meat can be used, we prefer the juicier, more flavorful dark thigh meat for these kebabs. Whichever you choose, do not mix white and dark meat on the same skewer, since they cook at different rates. For more information on setting up a grill, see page 180.

CHICKEN AND MARINADE
½ cup extra-virgin olive oil
¼ cup minced fresh mint or cilantro leaves
3 medium garlic cloves, minced or pressed through a garlic press (about 1 tablespoon)
1½ teaspoons grated zest plus 2 tablespoons juice from 1 lemon
1 teaspoon curry powder
1 teaspoon salt
½ teaspoon ground black pepper
2 pounds boneless, skinless chicken thighs (about 8 thighs), trimmed and cut into 1½-inch chunks

VEGETABLES AND FRUIT

- 1 small pineapple, peeled, cored, and cut into 1-inch cubes
- 1 large red onion, prepared according to the illustrations on page 172
- 2 tablespoons extra-virgin olive oil
- ½ teaspoon salt
- ¼ teaspoon ground black pepper
- 1 recipe Yogurt-Mint Cucumber Sauce (page 212)

1. FOR THE CHICKEN AND MARINADE: Whisk the olive oil, mint, garlic, lemon zest, curry, salt, and pepper together in a medium bowl. Transfer ¼ cup of the marinade to an airtight container, stir in the lemon juice, and set aside. Add the remaining marinade to a large zipper-lock bag along with the chicken. Seal shut, toss to coat, and refrigerate for at least 3 hours and up to 24 hours. (If you marinate the chicken for more than 3 hours, refrigerate the reserved marinade until you are ready to cook the chicken; bring to room temperature before using.)

2. Meanwhile, light a large chimney starter filled with charcoal (about 6 quarts) and allow to burn until the coals are fully ignited and partially covered with a thin layer of ash, 20 to 25 minutes. Open the bottom vent on the grill. Build a single-level fire by arranging the coals evenly over the bottom of the grill (see the illustration on page 181). Set the cooking grate in place, cover the grill with the lid, and let the grate heat up, about 5 minutes. Use a grill brush to scrape the cooking grate clean. Dip a wad of paper towels in oil; holding the wad with tongs, oil the cooking grate.

3. FOR THE VEGETABLES AND FRUIT: Meanwhile, toss the pineapple and onion with the olive oil, salt, and pepper; set aside.

4. Remove the chicken chunks from the zipper-lock bag, allowing the excess marinade to drip off. Using eight 12-inch skewers, thread each skewer with 2 pieces of pineapple, 3 pieces of onion, and 1 cube of chicken. Repeat this sequence 3 more times on each skewer.

5. Grill the kebabs, uncovered, turning each kebab one-quarter turn every 2 minutes, until the chicken, onion, and pineapple are lightly browned and the meat is fully cooked, 8 to 10 minutes. Transfer the kebabs to a platter, pour the reserved marinade–lemon juice mixture over the top, and let rest for 5 to 10 minutes before serving with the Yogurt-Mint Cucumber Sauce.

VARIATION

Gas-Grilled Curry Chicken Kebabs with Yogurt-Mint Cucumber Sauce

Follow the recipe for Charcoal-Grilled Curry Chicken Kebabs with Yogurt-Mint Cucumber Sauce through step 1. Turn all the burners to high, close the lid, and heat the grill until very hot, about 15 minutes. Use a grill brush to scrape the cooking grate clean. Dip a wad of paper towels in oil; holding the wad with tongs, oil the cooking grate. Proceed with the recipe as directed from step 3, grilling with the lid down.

Charcoal-Grilled Southwestern Chicken Kebabs with Red Pepper–Jícama Relish

SERVES 4

For more heat, include the jalapeño ribs and seeds when mincing. You will need eight 12-inch skewers for this recipe. Although white breast meat can be used, we prefer the juicier, more flavorful dark thigh meat for these kebabs. Whichever you choose, do not mix white and dark meat on the same skewer, since they cook at different rates. For more information on setting up a grill, see page 180.

CHICKEN AND MARINADE

- ½ cup extra-virgin olive oil
- ¼ cup minced fresh cilantro leaves
- 3 medium garlic cloves, minced or pressed through a garlic press (about 1 tablespoon)
- 1½ teaspoons grated zest plus 2 tablespoons juice from 1 lime
- 1 teaspoon ground cumin
- 1 teaspoon chili powder
- 1 teaspoon ground turmeric
- 1 jalapeño chile, seeds and ribs removed, chile minced (see note)
- ½ teaspoon salt
- ⅛ teaspoon ground black pepper

2 pounds boneless, skinless chicken thighs (about 8 thighs), trimmed and cut into 1½-inch chunks

VEGETABLES

2 green bell peppers, stemmed, seeded, and cut into 1-inch pieces
1 large onion, prepared according to the illustrations on page 172
10 ounces white mushrooms, wiped clean and stems removed
2 tablespoons extra-virgin olive oil
½ teaspoon salt
¼ teaspoon ground black pepper
1 recipe Red Pepper–Jícama Relish (page 210)

1. For the chicken and marinade: Whisk the olive oil, cilantro, garlic, lime zest, cumin, chili powder, turmeric, jalapeño, salt, and pepper together in a medium bowl. Transfer ¼ cup of the marinade to an airtight container, stir in the lime juice, and set aside. Add the remaining marinade to a large zipper-lock bag along with the chicken. Seal shut, toss to coat, and refrigerate for at least 3 hours and up to 24 hours. (If you marinate the chicken for more than 3 hours, refrigerate the reserved marinade until you are ready to cook the chicken; bring to room temperature before using.)

2. Meanwhile, light a large chimney starter filled with charcoal (about 6 quarts) and allow to burn until the coals are fully ignited and partially covered with a thin layer of ash, 20 to 25 minutes. Open the bottom vent on the grill. Build a single-level fire by arranging the coals evenly over the bottom of the grill (see the illustration on page 181). Set the cooking grate in place, cover the grill with the lid, and let the grate heat up, about 5 minutes. Use a grill brush to scrape the cooking grate clean. Dip a wad of paper towels in oil; holding the wad with tongs, oil the cooking grate.

3. For the vegetables: Meanwhile, toss the vegetables with the olive oil, salt, and pepper; set aside.

4. Remove the chicken chunks from the zipper-lock bag, allowing the excess marinade to drip off. Using eight 12-inch skewers, thread each skewer with 1 piece of pepper, 3 pieces of onion, 1 mushroom, and 1 cube of chicken. Repeat this sequence 2 more times on each skewer.

5. Grill the kebabs, uncovered, turning each kebab one-quarter turn every 2 minutes, until the chicken and vegetables are lightly browned and the meat is fully cooked, 8 to 10 minutes. Transfer the kebabs to a platter, pour the reserved marinade–lemon juice mixture over the top, and let rest for 5 to 10 minutes before serving with the Red Pepper–Jícama Relish.

VARIATION

Gas-Grilled Southwestern Chicken Kebabs with Red Pepper–Jícama Relish

Follow the recipe for Charcoal-Grilled Southwestern Chicken Kebabs with Red Pepper–Jícama Relish through step 1. Turn all the burners to high, close the lid, and heat the grill until very hot, about 15 minutes. Use a grill brush to scrape the cooking grate clean. Dip a wad of paper towels in oil; holding the wad with tongs, oil the cooking grate. Proceed with the recipe as directed from step 3, grilling with the lid down.

Grilled Chicken Wings

CHICKEN WINGS ARE GREAT COOKED ON the grill—their fat is rendered and falls away onto the coals. Cooked in the oven, the wings rest in their own fat and turn out flabby. But grill wings incorrectly and you get greasy meat, surrounded by a charred, rubbery, thick coating of skin that is hardly appealing. We wanted to develop a grilling technique that was foolproof and that would produce wings with crisp, thin, caramelized skin; tender and moist meat; and smoky grilled flavor that was well seasoned throughout. Furthermore, we wanted the wings to be eater-friendly; eating them should not be a chore.

Wings are made up of three parts: the meaty, drumstick-like portion that is closest to the breast section of the bird, the two-boned center portion that is surrounded by a band of meat and skin, and the small, almost meatless wingtip. After cutting and grilling wings several different ways, we concluded that wingtips are not worth grilling. They offer almost no meat and char long before the other two parts are even close to being cooked through.

Now that we had the wingtips discarded, we pushed the meat up the bones of the remaining, meatier parts to replicate the lollipop-shaped wings favored by traditional chefs. This took too much time and effort. We then decided that the best method for preparing wings is to separate the two usable portions at the joint. The pieces are small enough to be eaten as finger food and are less awkward to eat than a whole wing.

Our first round of tests was disappointing. Grilling the wings directly over the coals at temperatures ranging from high heat to low heat produced wings that were mediocre at best. Those cooked over medium-high and high heat charred quickly, and the skin remained thick and tough. Grilling the wings over medium and medium-low heat produced better wings; the skin was crispier and thinner, but the wings still lacked the great caramelized crust that we desired.

At this point we decided to try a two-level fire (not modified), in which two-thirds of the coals are stacked on one side of the grill and the remaining third of the coals is placed in a single layer on the other side. We started the wings over the cooler side to cook low and slow and then moved them to the hotter side to finish. This method was what we were looking for, rendering more fat from the skin and thereby producing a thin, delicate crust.

Prompted by past experience, we felt that brining might improve the flavor as well as the texture of our chicken wings. We used a brining solution in which equal amounts of sugar and salt are added to water. Tasting the wings as they came off the grill, we happily discovered not only that the brined chicken wings were tasty and well seasoned throughout, but that brining had produced some unexpected bonuses. The brined chicken meat was noticeably plumper before grilling and more tender after, and the wings developed a crispier, more caramelized skin than those that had not been brined.

Charcoal-Grilled Chicken Wings

SERVES 4 TO 6 (MAKES 20 TO 24 WINGS)

Make sure your grill is large enough to hold all the wings over roughly one half of the grate surface. If using kosher chicken, skip the brining process. To use kosher salt in the brine, see page 12 for conversion information and more tips on brining. For more information on setting up a grill, see page 180.

- **6 tablespoons table salt (see note)**
- **6 tablespoons sugar**
- **2½ pounds chicken wings, wingtips discarded and wings split (see the illustrations on page 7) (see note)**
- **Ground black pepper**
- **1 recipe sauce for chicken wings (see pages 21–22)**

1. Dissolve the salt and sugar in 1 quart cold water in a large container. Submerge the chicken in the brine, cover, and refrigerate for 30 minutes. Remove the chicken from the brine, rinse well, and pat dry with paper towels. Season with pepper.

2. Meanwhile, light a large chimney starter filled with charcoal (about 6 quarts) and allow to burn until the coals are fully ignited and partially covered with a thin layer of ash, 20 to 25 minutes. Open the bottom vent on the grill. Build a two-level fire by arranging one-third of the coals in a single layer over half the grill and piling the remaining coals over the other half (see the illustration on page 181). Set the cooking grate in place, cover the grill with the lid, and let the grate heat up, about 5 minutes. Use a grill brush to scrape the cooking grate clean. Dip a wad of paper towels in oil; holding the wad with tongs, oil the cooking grate.

3. Place the chicken over the cooler side of the grill. Grill, uncovered, turning once, until the wings are spotty light brown, the skin has thinned, and the fat has rendered, 8 to 10 minutes.

4. Move the chicken to the hotter side of the grill. Continue to grill, turning often to prevent charring, and brushing with the sauce, until the

wings are spotty dark brown and the skin has crisped, 2 to 3 minutes longer. Transfer the chicken to a platter and serve, passing the remaining sauce separately, if using.

VARIATION

Gas-Grilled Chicken Wings

Chicken wings require a lot of space on the grill. Rather than regulating the burners to create two heat levels, both burners are turned to medium heat for the initial phase of cooking and then turned to high to finish the process.

Follow the recipe for Charcoal-Grilled Chicken Wings through step 1. Turn all the burners to high, close the lid, and heat the grill until very hot, about 15 minutes. Use a grill brush to scrape the cooking grate clean. Dip a wad of paper towels in oil; holding the wad with tongs, oil the cooking grate. Turn all the burners down to medium. Proceed with step 3 in the recipe and cook the chicken, larger drumettes toward the back of the grill (where the heat is usually more intense), with the grill lid down, turning once, until the color is spotty light brown, the skin has thinned, and the fat has rendered, 12 to 14 minutes. In step 4, turn all the burners up to high. Continue to grill, turning often to prevent charring, and brushing with the sauce, until the wings are spotty dark brown and the skin has crisped, 3 to 4 minutes longer. Transfer the chicken to a platter and serve, passing the remaining sauce separately, if using.

EQUIPMENT: Gas Grills

Although cooking over a live fire may thrill, gas grills deliver what 21st-century Americans prize most: ease. Turn on the gas, hit the ignition switch, and voilà—an instant fire of whatever intensity you need for tonight's recipe. It really is, or at least it really should be, a no-brainer.

We selected some of the most promising models, based on a combination of cooking area and price (which fell into three categories: less than $500, $500 to $1,000, and more than $1,000), and performed a battery of cooking tests. By grilling our way through almost $1,000 worth of groceries over high, medium, and low heat, we learned which designs and features affect performance the most.

Mention that you're firing up the grill and the first thing to pop into most people's minds is steak—sizzling, fragrant, grill-marked, and caramelized to a rich red-brown hue. You'll need plenty of heat to bring that image to life, and, on this count, all of the grills in our group delivered. Average high temperature readings were consistently in the range of roughly 600 to 800 degrees.

Our high-heat cooking tests, searing both steaks and chicken thighs, put these numbers in perspective. What did we find? That you don't need enough heat to launch a rocket to give steak or chicken a good sear. Even grills with below-average heat output produced well-marked, heavily crusted steaks. Even heat distribution is another important feature, which we tested by covering the entire grilling surface with 1-inch-thick planks of eggplant and cooking them over medium-high heat.

Because gas grills allow precise heat control, they are especially well suited to barbecuing and grill-roasting. These techniques require low, indirect heat (in the range of 250 degrees to 350 degrees) and long cooking times to cook through large cuts of meat, fish, or whole fowl. Most of the grills performed acceptably in this respect, maintaining the temperature at or near the target, with minimal adjustment, for 1 hour and 15 minutes to 1 hour and 30 minutes.

Melted fat that drips from hot food down onto the burners causes both excessive smoke and flare-ups that can give food an unwelcome, slightly burnt off-flavor. The fatty chicken thighs and steaks that we cooked were reliable indicators of which grills tended to flare. Effective design for fat drainage limits this problem.

Our favorite gas grill is the Weber Spirit E-310. Gas grills aren't cheap, but at $499 it is the best grill for the money. So what made it stand apart from the competition? It has all the features you need without the useless bells and whistles that drive up the cost of fancier grills. Three burners give you maximum flexibility, whether searing steaks on high or slowly barbecuing chicken on low. The cooking surface is an ample 424 square inches, and the thermometer in the lid reads real temperatures. Weber grills have excellent fat drainage systems, with V-shaped bars that channel grease into drainage trays and prevent flare-ups.

EQUIPMENT: Charcoal Grills

Despite being fairly simple pieces of equipment, charcoal grills seem to come in all shapes, sizes, and styles. There's everything from bare-bones kettles to backyard-dominating behemoths with all the bells and whistles. We chose six different grills of various prices and sizes and put them through their paces.

Grilling a veritable mountain of food over two weeks revealed very little difference in the performance of the six grills. Each developed a fire hot enough to sear the food, which is what charcoal grilling is all about. Each also offered vents to control airflow—and thereby the intensity of the fire—but we were not able to detect any advantages or disadvantages based on the number or position of the vents.

It was possible, however, to identify two important design factors: the size of the grill and the depth of the grill cover. The bigger the grill, the better. It is all too easy to fill up a cooking grate, whether cooking for a crowd or simply grilling side dishes or extras for tomorrow's lunch. The Bar-B-Chef has a whopping 585 square inches of cooking grate, close to double the area of the five other grills we tested.

While the test kitchen generally doesn't use the grill's cover for direct-heat grilling, it is used for grill-roasting large cuts, such as a whole chicken or turkey or prime rib. The test kitchen recommends a 12- to 14-pound turkey for grill-roasting, and only the Bar-B-Chef and Patio Classic grills could close over a 14-pound turkey; the rest, except for one particularly small model, fit over a 12-pounder.

In the end, we found that all of the grills tested would do the job, but it's the extras that can make the process easier and more enjoyable. So which ones really matter? An attached table makes a huge difference, and two are better than one. Only one grill, the Weber One Touch Gold, lacked at least one, though an aftermarket add-on table is available. If you plan to barbecue or grill-roast, some means of adding additional fuel to the fire is essential. While the Bar-B-Chef offered a perfect solution—a door to the charcoal grate, which made it a breeze to add coals—our other favorites had hinged cooking grates.

Our advice is to buy the largest, best-outfitted grill your budget will allow. The Bar-B-Chef isn't cheap, but it's built to last and offers everything you could ever need or want in a grill. Our two other favorites, the Patio Classic and Weber One Touch Gold, worked nearly as well, though they are smaller and lack the frills.

THE BEST CHARCOAL GRILLS

BAR-B-CHEF

The Bar-B-Chef Charcoal Barbecue on Cart ($449) has all the bells and whistles to match its steep price tag: enormous size, bombproof construction, smart design, and every extra you could dream of.

PATIO CLASSIC

We also liked the Patio Classic 3500 Series ($219)—it has a user-friendly design, except for its large cooking grate "trap door," which necessitates removing much of the cooking food to add fuel to the fire.

WEBER

The Weber One Touch Gold ($139) is a classic kettle grill that offers a few important well-designed extras (a large ash-catch system and a hinged grate); it is our best buy.

The Basics of Charcoal Grilling

CHOOSING A CHARCOAL GRILL

Grilling over charcoal provides exceptional browning and searing that a gas grill simply can't replicate. Besides searing, charcoal adds another distinct advantage—smoke flavor.

Inside a standard covered kettle grill are two separate grates (or racks)—one for holding the lit charcoal, the other for cooking the food. There's plenty of room between these two grates (at least six inches), so you can build a hot fire with a lot of charcoal. The grill is covered with a domed lid that is tall enough to accommodate a large roast or turkey. Both the grill and lid have adjustable air vents that let you control the rate at which the fuel burns. Some charcoal grill grates have hinged sections that make it much easier to add coals during cooking. If you have a choice, buy a grill with this feature. For the results from our testing of charcoal grills, see page 179.

CHOOSING A TYPE OF CHARCOAL

Lump hardwood charcoal, also known as charwood, is more expensive than the ubiquitous briquette but is our preferred product for most direct grilling chores because it puts out so much heat. We also like the fact that this product is 100 percent hardwood and contains no additives.

But does charcoal type influence flavor? To find out, we grilled steaks and zucchini over three fires built with the following: hardwood charcoal, regular charcoal briquettes, and Match Light, a Kingsford product infused with lighter fluid to guarantee rapid ignition. The flavor differences in the steaks were nearly imperceptible, but the delicate zucchini was a different story; the zucchini grilled over Match Light tasted oddly bitter. In separate tests with delicate foods—chicken, fish, and vegetables—grilled over fires started with lighter fluid, tasters also detected harsh, acrid flavors. Consequently, we like to steer clear of both Match Light and lighter fluid. Hardwood charcoal is the best choice for grilling because it burns hot and fast, while slower-burning briquettes are optimal for grill-roasting and barbecuing.

MEASURING CHARCOAL

Many recipes call for a particular volume of charcoal, such as 4 quarts. An easy way to measure it is to use an empty half-gallon milk or juice carton. Just wash the carton thoroughly and store it with the charcoal. Each full carton equals roughly two quarts.

LIGHTING A CHARCOAL GRILL

We find that a chimney starter (also called a flue starter) is the best way to light charcoal. (See the illustration below.) A chimney starter is foolproof, and it eliminates the need for lighter fluid (which can impart harsh, acrid flavors to food). We strongly recommend that you visit a hardware store (or other shop that sells grilling equipment) and purchase this indispensable device.

To use a chimney starter, place several sheets of crumpled newspaper in the lower chamber and set the starter on the bottom grate of a kettle grill (where the charcoal will eventually go); the top cooking grate should not be in place. Fill the upper chamber with the requisite amount of charcoal. Light the newspaper through the holes in the side of the chimney starter and wait until the coals at the top of the pile are covered with fine gray ash. (This will take about 20 minutes.) Dump the lit charcoal in the bottom of the grill and arrange as directed. (For additional firepower, add more unlit charcoal and wait until it has caught fire before grilling.) You can then set the cooking grate in place, allow it to heat up, and then clean it. After that, you are ready to grill.

Note that after you empty the lit charcoal into the grill, the starter will still be very hot. Don't put it down on the lawn—it will burn the grass. Instead, set the starter on a concrete or stone surface away from any flammable objects and allow it to cool off for at least half an hour. Make sure you choose a spot away from children and pets.

CHIMNEY STARTER

LIGHTING A FIRE WITHOUT A STARTER

If you don't have access to a chimney starter, use this method as a last resort.

1. Place eight crumpled sheets of newspaper beneath the rack on which the charcoal sits.

2. With the bottom air vents open, pile the charcoal on the rack and light the paper. After about 20 minutes, the coals should be covered with fine gray ash and ready for cooking.

BUILDING THE RIGHT CHARCOAL FIRE

Instead of just turning dials and pressing buttons to manipulate heat as you would with an oven, it is necessary to arrange lit coals according to what type of food you are grilling.

SINGLE-LEVEL FIRE

Delivers direct, moderate heat. Use with fairly thin foods that cook quickly, such as fruits, vegetables, fish and shellfish, hamburgers, and chicken kebabs.

To Prepare: Arrange all the lit charcoal in an even layer.

TWO-LEVEL FIRE

Allows the cook to sear foods over a very hot section of the grill and to finish the cooking over a cooler section so that the exterior doesn't char. Use for bone-in chicken legs and thighs.

To Prepare: Arrange some lit coals in a single layer on half of the grill. Leave the remaining coals in a pile.

MODIFIED TWO-LEVEL FIRE

Ideal for foods that are susceptible to burning but require a long cooking time. A modified two-level fire can also be used to create an especially hot fire when grilling small, thin cuts of meat. Use for bone-in chicken breasts, boneless chicken breasts, and thighs.

To Prepare: Pile all the lit coals onto one side of the grill, leaving the other side empty. We often cover foods on the cooler side of the grill with a disposable aluminum pan to trap the heat and create an ovenlike cooking environment.

DOUBLE-BANKED FIRE

Ideal for bone-in, skin-on chicken pieces, butterflied chicken, and whole roasted chicken. This creates intense heat on opposite sides of the grill and a moderate level of indirect heat in the center. It also allows the fat from chicken skin to render and crisp without causing flare-ups.

To Prepare: Steeply bank the coals on opposite sides of the grill, leaving the center of the grill empty.

FIVE TIPS FOR BETTER CHARCOAL GRILLING

1. Use enough charcoal. There's no sense spending a lot of money on meat and then letting it steam over an inadequate fire. The size of your grill, the amount of food being cooked, and the desired intensity of the fire are all factors in deciding how much charcoal to use. In the end, you want a fire that is slightly larger than the space on the cooking grate occupied by the food. The higher you pile the charcoal (and therefore the closer it is to the cooking grate), the more intense the fire will be.

2. Always make sure to open the bottom vent completely before adding the charcoal.

3. Make sure the coals are partially covered with fine gray ash before you start to grill. Fine gray ash is a sign that the coals are fully lit and hot.

4. Once the coals are ready, set the cooking grate in place and let it heat up for five minutes. Once the grate is hot, scrape it clean with a grill brush.

5. Don't use the cover when grilling. (Exceptions to this are grill-roasting and barbecuing, in which case the lid of the grill should be down, with the vents open. See page 183 for more information on these methods of indirect cooking.) If you need to trap heat to cook something through, like a boneless, skinless chicken breast, we suggest covering the food with a disposable aluminum roasting pan or pie plate.

ADDING MORE COALS TO A LIT CHARCOAL FIRE

We recommend that you buy a charcoal grill with a hinged cooking grate. This feature allows you to lift up the edge of the grate and add more unlit charcoal as needed. If your grill doesn't have this feature, you must transfer foods to a tray, lift up the grate with fireproof gloves, and then add coals. A hinged cooking grate allows foods to stay in place as you add coals.

The Basics of Gas Grilling

CHOOSING A GAS GRILL

While we favor charcoal grills for the better browning and smoky flavor they provide, gas grills are more convenient. And a gas grill is consistent, delivering the same results day in and day out. But gas grills can be roughly three times more expensive than charcoal grills, so it pays to shop carefully.

Several features and design elements separate a good gas grill from a poor one. A built-in thermometer that registers real numbers (not just low, medium, and hot) is essential. A gauge that tells you how much gas is left in the tank is also a plus. As you might expect, a large grill offers the cook more possibilities. In addition to size, the number of burners is critical. It's not possible to cook by indirect heat on a grill with only one burner, because the burner is usually positioned in the center of the grill, so the cooler parts of the grill are too small to accommodate most foods. Indirect cooking requires a grill with at least two burners. With one burner on and one burner off, at least half of the grill will be cool enough for slow cooking.

The heat should be evenly distributed across the entire surface of the grill. We found that most gas grills are plenty hot. The problem is that gas grills are often unable to sustain temperatures low enough for barbecuing. After extensive tests of eight models, we highly recommend the Weber Spirit E-310 ($499).

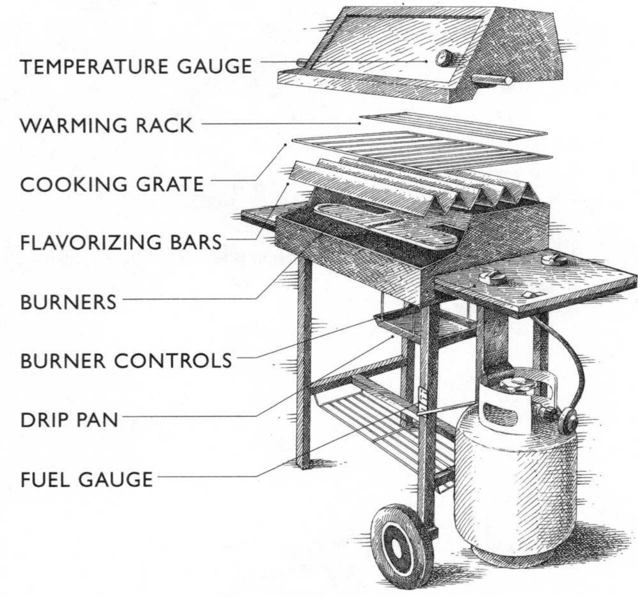

LIGHTING A GAS GRILL

Lighting a gas grill is remarkably easy. Just make sure to read your owner's manual and to follow directions regarding the order in which the burners must be lit. In most instances, an electric igniter will light the burners. Electric igniters can fail occasionally, though, especially in windy conditions. Most models have a hole for lighting the burners with a match. Read all the directions carefully and make sure to wait several minutes (or as directed) between attempts at lighting the grill. This waiting time allows excess gas to dissipate and is an important safety measure.

THREE TIPS FOR BETTER GAS GRILLING

1. Remove the warming rack before lighting the grill unless you know you are going to need it. On most grills, the rack is very close to the cooking surface, and it can be hard to reach foods on the back of the grill without burning your hands on the hot metal.
2. Heat the grill with all the burners turned to high (even if you plan on cooking over low heat), and keep the lid down for at least 15 minutes. Once the grill is hot, scrape the grate clean with a grill brush and then adjust the burners as desired.
3. Whether cooking by direct or indirect heat, keep the lid down. With charcoal grills, residue from the briquettes can build up on the inside of the lid and give quickly cooked foods an off-flavor, but this isn't a problem with gas grills, because gas burns cleanly. Keeping the lid down concentrates the heat when searing and keeps the temperature steady when slow-cooking.

CHECKING THE FUEL LEVEL IN A GAS TANK

There's nothing worse than running out of fuel halfway through grilling. If your grill doesn't have a gas gauge, use this technique to estimate how much gas is left in the tank.

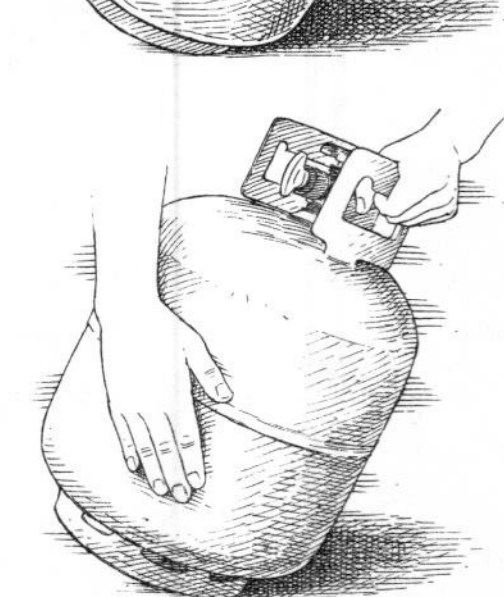

1. Bring a cup or so of water to a boil in a small saucepan or glass measuring cup (if using the microwave). Pour the water over the side of the tank.

2. Feel the metal with your hand. Where the water has succeeded in warming the tank, it is empty; where the tank remains cool to the touch, there is still propane inside.

ADJUSTING A GAS GRILL TO MEET YOUR NEEDS

It's quite simple to regulate the heat on a gas grill—just adjust the burners.

FOR A SINGLE-LEVEL FIRE

Adjust the burners to high for a hot fire, or turn the burners to medium after heating.

FOR A TWO-LEVEL FIRE

Leave one burner on high or medium-high and turn the other(s) to medium or medium-low.

FOR A MODIFIED TWO-LEVEL FIRE

Leave one burner on high and turn the other(s) off.

FOR A DOUBLE-BANKED FIRE

Leave one burner on high and turn the other(s) off.

The Basics of Indirect Cooking

A whole roast chicken cannot be grilled—the exterior would be charred well before the interior could cook through. The solution is indirect cooking. With indirect cooking, the lid of the grill is down (the lid is up when grilling over direct heat with charcoal). This traps heat and creates a regulated cooking environment much like that of an oven. While grilling calls for filling the grill with charcoal or lighting all the gas burners, indirect cooking involves a smaller fire. The lit coals are banked on one side of the grill, or one of the gas burners is turned off. Foods are placed over the cooler part of the grill. Since there is no direct heat, the food cooks evenly, without flare-ups. Indirect cooking is generally divided into two categories: grill-roasting, in which food is cooked relatively quickly over moderate heat, and barbecuing, in which food is cooked quite slowly at low temperatures. Wood chips or chunks are often used to add smoky flavor.

INDIRECT COOKING ON A CHARCOAL GRILL

1. Dump hot coals onto the charcoal grate, piling the coals to one side. Place soaked and drained wood chunks or a foil packet filled with wood chips on the coals. Set the cooking grate in place, heat, and scrape clean. Place the food on the cooler side of the grill, cover, and open the air vents as directed.

2. A grill thermometer inserted through the vents on the grill lid can tell you if the fire is too hot or if it has cooled off to the point that you need to add more charcoal. Because you want to know the temperature at the spot where the food is being cooked, rotate the lid so that the thermometer is close to the food.

INDIRECT COOKING ON A GAS GRILL

Remove part or all of the cooking grate. Place a foil tray with soaked wood chips on top of the primary burner. Replace the cooking grate. Light all the burners and cover the grill. When the grill is smoking heavily (after about 20 minutes), turn off the burner (or burners) without chips and place the food over it (or them). Cover the grill.

MAKING A FOIL PACKET FOR WOOD CHIPS ON A CHARCOAL GRILL

Place the amount of wood chips called for in the recipe in the center of an 18-inch square of heavy-duty aluminum foil. Fold in all four sides of the foil to encase the chips. Turn the foil packet over. Use a fork to poke about six large holes (each about the size of a quarter) through the top of the foil packet to allow smoke to escape.

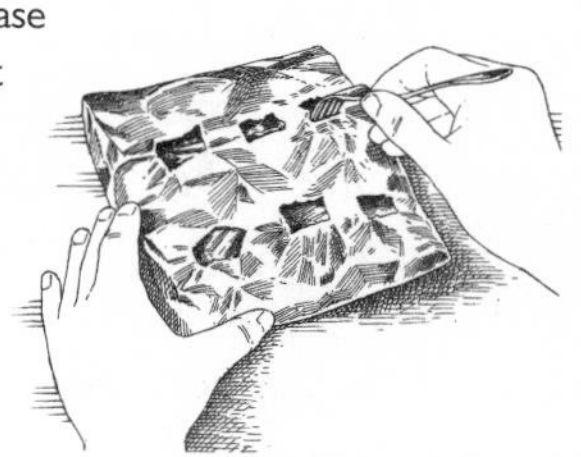

WOOD CHIPS AND CHUNKS 101

Charcoal itself has some flavor (gas adds none), but the real smoky flavor of good ribs or brisket comes from wood chunks or chips. Chips will work on either a charcoal or a gas grill, but chunks are suited to charcoal fires only, since to work they must rest in a pile of lit coals. Chips and chunks come from the same source—trees. The only difference between them is size. Chunks are usually the size of lemons; chips are thinner shards, similar to mulch. The most common choices are hardwoods like hickory, mesquite, and alder, although some stores may also carry cherry or oak. Ideally, the chunks should smolder slowly, releasing smoke for as long as possible. We found that wood chunks should be soaked in water to prevent the wood from catching fire as soon as it hits the coals, while chips are placed in a foil packet or tray for protection.

MAKING A FOIL TRAY FOR WOOD CHIPS ON A GAS GRILL

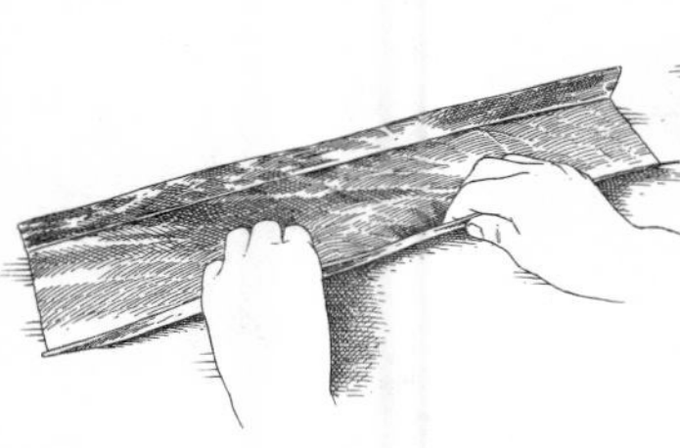

1. Make a 1-inch fold on one long side of an 18 by 12-inch piece of heavy-duty aluminum foil. Fold three more times to create a 1-inch-high side. Repeat on the other long side.

2. With a short side facing you, fold in both corners as if wrapping a gift.

3. Turn up the inside inch or so of each triangular fold to match the rim on the long sides of the foil tray.

4. Fold the triangle over the rim to seal. Repeat on the other short side. The tray can now be filled with soaked and drained wood chips.

Classic Barbecued Chicken

SMOKY GRILLED CHICKEN SMOTHERED IN A thick barbecue sauce is one of America's favorite summer meals. But despite its popularity, this recipe causes backyard grillers plenty of headaches. Who hasn't served barbecued chicken that was nearly black on the outside yet bloody near the bone? Chicken is hard enough to grill, because the skin cooks faster than the meat. Adding barbecue sauce just makes the problem worse. Our goal in developing a foolproof recipe for barbecued chicken was to produce perfectly cooked meat that boasted intense flavor from both the grill and the liberal application of tangy-sweet barbecue sauce. We decided to start with the cooking technique and get to the sauce later.

Most recipes call for searing the chicken quickly over high heat to render the fat in the skin, and then finishing it over lower heat to gently cook the interior. But we've found that placing raw chicken over a hot (or even medium-hot) fire causes too many flare-ups, resulting in burnt skin. The test kitchen has had much better luck starting chicken over lower heat to render the fat slowly and completely without the danger of flare-ups.

Following this method, we spread the coals in an even layer on one side of the grill, added the chicken, skin-side down, to the other side, and covered the grill. Thirty minutes later, we had tender chicken that was almost cooked throughout. In an effort to fit more chicken easily on the grill, we followed a similar indirect cooking method that we use for our whole roasted chickens: We created a double-banked fire, which piles the coals evenly on both sides of the grill, leaving the center empty. This had the advantage of facilitating a larger cool zone for the grill, with even heat coming from both sides. We added another round of chicken, skin-side down, to the center of the grill and covered it—the results were superb. We were then able to move the chicken out over the hot coals to give them a final sear, which added nice char in the final stages of grilling.

The only problem was, the chicken didn't have much flavor. We've always been told to never, ever add barbecue sauce to anything until just before it was ready to be pulled off the grill—otherwise the sugar in the sauce will burn. But since our grill-roasted parts weren't cooked directly over a flame, we wondered if we could sauce them at the outset. We couldn't: The sauce turned black and bitter. How could we get deep layers of barbecue flavor without saucing earlier?

EQUIPMENT: Grill Brushes

Eventually, all grill grates become sticky and dirty. All that barbecue sauce, marinade, and burnt chicken turn into an intractable layer resembling creosote. A heavy-duty grill brush seems like the tool for the job, but how do you know which one to buy? We purchased seven different brushes to find out.

To put the brushes through their paces, we concocted a gooey "paint" of honey, molasses, mustard, and barbecue sauce. We slathered it thickly onto brand-new cooking grates and baked it into a thick layer approximating a well-used, very dirty grate.

The brushes came in a variety of shapes and sizes and materials. Size mattered: the short-handled brushes sometimes led to burnt knuckles. The handle needs to be long enough to scrape the grate while hot, which is the ideal time to clean it.

Long or short wasn't the end of it; material also made a huge difference. The stainless steel handle on one model quickly became too hot to grasp, and plastic proved too flexible to scrub effectively. All but one of the brushes had brass bristles, and, no matter how thick or thin the bristles were, they all eventually bent and clogged up with grime.

In the end, only one brush successfully was able to scrape the grills clean of the tenacious "paint"—the Grill Wizard. The Grill Wizard may look unusual, but it's incredibly effective because there are no brass bristles to bend, break, or clog with unwanted grease and grime. Instead, this brush comes equipped with two large woven mesh stainless steel "scrubbie" pads that are detachable, washable, and replaceable.

THE BEST GRILL BRUSH

The Grill Wizard BBQ Brush ($10.99) cleans like a pro and is built to last (replaceable scrubbing pads help out here).

GRILL WIZARD

Brining the chicken, then seasoning it with a mixture of pepper and cayenne before it went on the grill, added some flavor, but not enough. Then it occurred to us that if we wanted layers of flavor, we needed to have layers of barbecue sauce. When the chicken was mostly cooked through over the indirect heat, we moved the pieces out on both sides (nearer to the coals, but not over them) and introduced sauce in several applications. Constant turning and moderate heat allowed us to sauce the chicken continually for about 20 minutes while it finished cooking. This worked well, because just as one layer of sauce was drying, we added another coat on top of it, creating a thick, complex, multi-layered "skin" of barbecue flavor.

Wanting to finish this chicken with a bang, we moved the pieces directly over the coals, which were fading but still relatively hot, and continued to flip them and slather them with sauce for the final five minutes of cooking. This created a robust, crusty char that tasters loved. We finally had perfectly cooked chicken with intense barbecue flavor—summer never tasted so sweet.

Charcoal-Grilled Barbecued Chicken

SERVES 4 TO 6

You can use a mix of chicken breasts, thighs, and drumsticks, making sure they add up to about 10 pieces. Any more than that and you won't be able to line them up on the grill. Although our classic barbecue sauce is best, you can substitute 3 cups of plain store-bought sauce; our favorite brand is Bull's-Eye. If using kosher chicken, skip the brining process. To use kosher salt in the brine, see page 12 for conversion information and more tips on brining. For more information on setting up a grill, see page 180.

- ½ cup table salt (see note)
- ½ cup sugar
- 3 pounds bone-in, skin-on chicken pieces (breasts, whole legs, thighs, and/or drumsticks), trimmed (see note)
- 1 teaspoon ground black pepper
- ¼ teaspoon cayenne pepper
- 1 recipe Barbecue Sauce (page 209)

1. Dissolve the salt and sugar in 2 quarts cold water in a large container. Submerge the chicken in the brine, cover, and refrigerate for 30 minutes. Mix the pepper and cayenne in a small bowl; set aside. Remove the chicken from the brine, rinse well, and pat dry with paper towels. Rub the spice mixture all over the chicken pieces. Transfer half of the barbecue sauce (about 1½ cups) to a serving bowl and set aside.

2. Meanwhile, light a large chimney starter filled with charcoal (about 6 quarts) and allow to burn until the coals are fully ignited and partially covered with a thin layer of ash, 20 to 25 minutes. Open the bottom vent on the grill. Build a double-banked fire by arranging the coals in two even piles banked on opposite sides of the grill, leaving the middle third of the grill empty (see the illustration on page 181). Set the cooking grate in place, cover the grill with the lid, and let the grate heat up, about 5 minutes. Use a grill brush to scrape the cooking grate clean. Dip a wad of paper towels in oil; holding the wad with tongs, oil the cooking grate.

3. Place the chicken in the center of the grill, skin-side down. Open the grill lid vents completely and cover, positioning the vents over the chicken. Grill until the chicken begins to brown and the thickest part of the breast registers 140 degrees and/or the thickest part of the thigh and drumstick registers 160 degrees on an instant-read thermometer, 20 to 25 minutes.

4. Move the chicken close to any of the coals. Continue to grill, uncovered, flipping the chicken and brushing with the remaining barbecue sauce (about 1½ cups) every 2 minutes until sticky, 10 to 12 minutes. Move the chicken directly over the hot coals and continue to brush and flip the chicken until the sauce on the chicken is crusted and the thickest part of the breast registers 160 to 165 degrees and/or the thickest part of the thigh and drumstick registers 170 to 175 degrees on an instant-read thermometer, 5 to 8 minutes longer. Transfer the chicken to a platter and let rest for 10 minutes. Serve, passing the reserved barbecue sauce separately.

VARIATION

Gas-Grilled Barbecued Chicken

Follow the recipe for Charcoal-Grilled Barbecued Chicken through step 1. Turn all the burners to high and heat the grill with the lid down until very hot, about 15 minutes. Use a grill brush to scrape the cooking grate clean. Dip a wad of paper towels in oil; holding the wad with tongs, oil the cooking grate. Leave the primary burner on high and turn off the other burner(s). Place the chicken in the center of the cooler side of the grill, skin-side down, cover, and proceed with the recipe from step 3, grilling with the lid down.

Tomato and Cucumber Salad

SERVES 6

This cool and refreshing salad is a nice accompaniment to most any of our grilled chicken recipes.

- 2 medium cucumbers, seeded, sliced, salted, and drained (see the illustrations on page 213)
- Salt
- 4–5 large ripe tomatoes
- 3 tablespoons extra-virgin olive oil
- 3 tablespoons juice from 1 lemon
- ¼ cup finely chopped red onion
- ¼ cup chopped fresh mint leaves
- Ground black pepper

1. Let the salted cucumbers drain, weighted, in a colander for at least 1 hour and up to 3 hours.
2. Core and halve the tomatoes, then cut each half into 4 or 5 wedges. Toss the wedges with ½ teaspoon salt in a large bowl; let rest until a small pool of liquid accumulates, 15 to 20 minutes.
3. Meanwhile, whisk the oil, lemon juice, red onion, mint, and pepper to taste in a small bowl. Pour the mixture over the tomatoes and accumulated liquid and toss to coat. Set aside to allow the flavors to blend, about 5 minutes.
4. Add the drained cucumber pieces and toss to combine. Season with salt and pepper to taste and serve immediately.

Grilled Alabama Barbecued Chicken

WHILE MOST PEOPLE THINK OF BARBECUE sauce as red, sweet, and tomatoey, there are dozens of regional barbecue sauces that don't contain either tomato or a lot of sugar. For example, mustard-and-vinegar-based sauces are common in the Carolinas, and a mayonnaise-based sauce is a specialty in northern Alabama. Although we have been fortunate enough to sit down to a plate of this mayonnaise-style barbecue, we have never come across a good recipe for it. We went into the test kitchen and got to work.

While the origins of many recipes can be hazy, it's easy to trace the history of Alabama chicken and white barbecue sauce to one place: the Big Bob Gibson Bar-B-Q Restaurant in Decatur. This barbecue mecca (the *Birmingham News* calls it the best barbecue in the state) has been around since 1925. Bob Gibson started his barbecue career by digging a smoke pit in his backyard. Soon he opened his first restaurant, the descendant of which his grandchildren and great-grandchildren run today. According to grandson Don McLemore, Big Bob (he was 6 feet, 4 inches tall and weighed 300 pounds) was best known for his white barbecue sauce.

The recipe (a family secret) has not changed in more than 80 years. Although Big Bob used the sauce mostly on hickory-smoked chicken, McLemore says nowadays people put it on everything from pork to potato chips. Before starting on the white barbecue sauce, we wanted to figure out the best way to smoke the chicken and determine if there was a way we could fit two birds on the grill.

When cooking a whole bird, we usually bank the charcoal on opposite sides of the grill and place the bird right in the center. At Big Bob's, hickory chips are added for great smoky flavor, and we saw no reason to change this part of the recipe. We found that 2 cups of hickory chips placed directly on the coals gave the chickens a nice smoky flavor. Unfortunately, it took nearly two hours to grill two whole chickens, and our fire was beginning to peter out. We didn't want to add more coals, so we looked for ways to reduce the cooking time. Splitting the chickens in half not only cut the barbecue time to less than an hour and exposed more of the meat to the smoke, it also allowed us to place two whole chickens on the grill easily. By moving the chickens to the hotter portion of the grill toward the end of cooking, the skin became slightly crisp and turned a beautiful golden brown. Finally, adding a simple spice rub of ground black pepper and cayenne to the chicken before grilling gave the meat a bold flavor that stood up nicely to the flavorful sauce.

It was time to work on the sauce. We started by ordering a bottle from Big Bob's. The sauce was creamy and tart, with a hint of sweetness and decent heat. Clearly, the sauce started with mayonnaise that was thinned out with vinegar to reach a loose consistency not unlike that of salad dressing. Tasters preferred the sweet-tart flavor of cider vinegar to bland white vinegar, and a little granulated sugar reinforced the subtle sweetness in the sauce. For heat, we relied on black pepper, just like Big Bob. But tasters wanted more heat. A little cayenne and horseradish punched up the sauce without making the heat too overpowering.

According to McLemore, at Big Bob's each smoked chicken is "baptized" by being dunked in a 2-gallon vat of white sauce that is continually replenished. We didn't want to make a vat of sauce. Fortunately, we found that brushing the chickens with the sauce twice—once when they came off the grill and again 10 minutes later—was sufficient. We served extra sauce on the side for dipping the chicken—and maybe some potato chips, too.

ARRANGING CHICKEN ON THE GRILL

Place the chicken halves skin-side down in the center of the grill, alternating the direction of the chicken halves to allow all four to fit snugly on a standard grill.

Charcoal-Grilled Alabama Barbecued Chicken

SERVES 6

If using a kosher bird, skip the brining process. To use kosher salt in the brine, see page 12 for conversion information and more tips on brining. For more information on setting up a grill, see page 180. Use hickory chips or chunks for this recipe.

CHICKEN AND BRINE

- 1 cup table salt
- 1 cup sugar
- 2 (3½- to 4-pound) whole chickens, giblets discarded and split (see the illustrations on page 9) (see note)
- 2 (3-inch) wood chunks or 2 cups wood chips (see note)
- 1 teaspoon ground black pepper
- ½ teaspoon cayenne pepper

WHITE BARBECUE SAUCE

- ¾ cup mayonnaise
- 2 tablespoons cider vinegar
- 2 teaspoons sugar
- ½ teaspoon prepared horseradish
- ½ teaspoon salt
- ½ teaspoon ground black pepper
- ¼ teaspoon cayenne pepper

1. For the chicken and brine: Dissolve the salt and sugar in 1 gallon cold water in a large container. Submerge the chickens in the brine, cover, and refrigerate for 1 hour. Soak the wood chunks to cover for 1 hour and drain. If using wood chips, divide them between 2 aluminum foil packets according to the instructions on page 183. Mix the pepper and cayenne together in a small bowl; set aside.

2. Remove the chickens from the brine, rinse well, and pat dry with paper towels. Rub the spice mixture over the chicken halves.

3. FOR THE SAUCE: Meanwhile, puree all of the sauce ingredients in a blender until smooth, about 1 minute. Transfer to an airtight container and refrigerate for at least 1 hour and up to 2 days.

4. Light a large chimney starter filled with charcoal (about 6 quarts) and allow to burn until the coals are fully ignited and partially covered with a thin layer of ash, 20 to 25 minutes. Open the bottom vent on the grill. Build a double-banked fire by arranging the coals in two even piles banked on opposite sides of the grill, leaving the middle third of the grill empty (see the illustration on page 181). Nestle 1 soaked wood chunk or 1 foil packet with chips on top of each pile. Set the cooking grate in place, cover the grill with the lid, and let the grate heat up, about 5 minutes. Use a grill brush to scrape the cooking grate clean. Dip a wad of paper towels in oil; holding the wad with tongs, oil the cooking grate.

5. Place the split chickens in the center of the grill, skin-side down (see the illustration on page 187). Open the grill lid vents completely and cover, positioning the vents over the chickens. Grill until the chicken is browned and an instant-read thermometer inserted in the thickest part of the breast reaches 140 degrees, 35 to 40 minutes. Move the chicken out over the hot coals, cover, and continue to grill until both sides are golden brown and the thickest part of the breast registers 160 to 165 degrees and the thickest part of the thigh registers 170 to 175 degrees on an instant-read thermometer, 15 to 20 minutes longer.

6. Transfer the chicken to a cutting board, brush with 2 tablespoons of the sauce, tent loosely with foil, and let rest for 10 minutes. Remove the foil and brush the chicken with 1 more tablespoon of the sauce. Carve the chicken (see the illustrations on page 11) and serve, passing the remaining sauce separately.

➢ VARIATION

Gas-Grilled Alabama Barbecued Chicken

Use wood chips rather than chunks for this recipe.

Follow the recipe for Charcoal-Grilled Alabama Barbecued Chicken through step 3. In step 1, instead of making foil packets for the wood chips, soak 2 cups wood chips for 30 minutes in cold water to cover and drain. Place the wood chips in a foil tray (see page 183). Place the foil tray on top of the primary burner and position the cooking grate. Turn all the burners to high and heat the grill with the lid down until the wood chips begin to smoke, about 15 minutes. (If the chips ignite, use a water-filled spray bottle to extinguish.) Use a grill brush to scrape the cooking grate clean. Dip a wad of paper towels in oil; holding the wad with tongs, oil the cooking grate. Leave the primary burner on high and turn off all the other burner(s). Place the chicken in the center of the cooler side of the grill skin-side down, cover, and proceed with the recipe from the grilling time and temperature instructions as directed in step 5, grilling with the lid down.

Grilled Barbecued Pulled Chicken

THE PULLED CHICKEN SANDWICH IS A LESSER staple of Dixieland barbecue shacks, where the ribs and pulled pork usually take center stage. But from a business standpoint, it's a very practical choice for the pitmaster, who no doubt has plenty of extra barbecued chicken on hand. The tender, smoky meat is simply pulled off the bone in moist, soft shreds, tossed with tangy, sweet sauce, and piled high on soft white bread with pickle chips and coleslaw. To us, this is the ultimate example of taking leftovers to another level. We have tried to make it at home, but our leftover chicken is more often merely boneless and bland, and a bottle of barbecue sauce offers little help. If we wanted some great pulled chicken barbecue, we'd have to start from scratch.

Most of the recipes we researched were no more than footnotes to recipes for barbecued chicken that treated pulled chicken sandwiches as mere leftovers. The few exceptions were pale, "quick and easy" imitations of the ideal, instructing us to grill a few boneless chicken breasts and then toss them with sauce. This approach was so inferior to the real thing—no smoke or fall-apart texture, just pasty bottled sauce—that it reminded us of the crimes committed every day by Northerners in the name of Southern cornbread. We wanted, at the very least, to take the pulled chicken sandwich seriously. And, like most Northerners, we didn't have all day.

Tasters loved the smoky flavor of a whole chicken, which spent about an hour on the grill, but there were two problems. First, coordinating the doneness between breasts and legs seemed like overkill for pulled chicken. Also, there was something heartbreaking about taking a whole grill-roasted chicken with crisp, mahogany skin and chopping it down into a sandwich. Using parts would solve both problems: It would give us more control over cooking, and we would avoid having to deconstruct the perfect barbecued bird.

We tried grilling both whole leg quarters and bone-in breasts; the latter tended to dry out, so we went with the legs. These quarters took only 30 minutes to cook through when cooked over direct heat—not enough time to develop much smoky flavor. Instead, we turned to indirect heat and a "low and slow" grill temperature. During this longer cooking time, the meat turned deliciously smoky and was moist and tender as well. (Unlike breast meat, dark leg meat can cook for more than an hour without drying out.) We tested various setups for the charcoal and finally settled on two piles of coals on opposite sides of the grill, with the legs in the middle. (Putting all of the coals on one side of the grill produced uneven heat, cooking the legs closest to the coals too quickly.) Without any direct heat to sear the meat, there was no need to flip the legs during cooking. In fact, there were advantages to keeping the legs skin-side up for the duration: The rendered fat from the skin basted the meat, keeping it juicy and preventing it from turning dry and leathery from the heat and smoke. With two moderate piles of charcoal (about 40 briquettes each) and two good-sized chunks of hickory or mesquite, the legs cooked gently but thoroughly in about an hour and absorbed plenty of smoke flavor along the way.

Whole chicken leg quarters (thighs and drumsticks attached) have great flavor and are cheap (especially when purchased in giant supermarket "family packs"), and dark meat is nearly impossible to overcook. On the downside, they are riddled with connective tissue, blood vessels, and interior veins of fat, none of which are appetizing. And while the breast is basically one big muscle, the leg is made up of a dozen or so smaller muscles, with fibers running every which way. Also, pulling and shredding breast meat is a snap; handling leg meat is a chore. We discovered a partial solution to this problem when we accidentally overcooked the chicken one afternoon. The internal temperature had shot up to around 185 degrees (15 degrees past "done" for legs), but the meat was still moist. In addition, more of the connective tissue had dissolved, so with only a gentle tug the meat now fell off the bone in large pieces. More fat had rendered out as well, making the chicken less greasy.

Always impatient, we wanted a shortcut to the shredding work once the meat was off the bone, so we tried pulsing the meat in the food processor. This raised a few eyebrows in the test kitchen. "I prefer to chew my own food," quipped one colleague when we placed a bowl of the sauced, machine-chopped chicken in front of her. It may have looked like cat food, but tasters liked the flavor, and this processed chicken was able to absorb more sauce than the hand-pulled did.

We then made a serendipitous discovery while packing up the leftovers from this test. We tossed together the hand-pulled and machine-processed batches of chicken, and right away we noticed that the combination of the two textures looked more appetizing than either of the two alone—it looked, in fact, just like pulled pork. In addition to the flavor boost, the chopped chicken helped to bind the mixture and made it stiffer, so it piled nicely on the bun instead of sliding off onto the plate.

The next day, with this 50/50 mixture in mind, we began separating the chicken into two piles as we pulled it off the bones. The intact larger pieces were set aside for hand-shredding, while the smaller, crustier bits went into the food processor for a few quick pulses. Not only did this result in the perfect texture, but it also saved us some preparation time.

We experimented with different types of barbecue sauce, including thin vinegar-and-mustard-based "Carolina-style" sauces—the traditional complements for the rich, full flavor of pulled pork. Tasters, however, found these sauces too overpowering for relatively lean, mild chicken. They much preferred our existing recipe for barbecue sauce, which has a base of ketchup and juice from pureed onions and can be made in less than 30 minutes. We made just a few adjustments to the consistency, as the existing sauce was too thick for properly coating the finer shreds of chicken.

Our last problem was that the pulled chicken had cooled to room temperature once all the shredding work was done. To reheat the pulled chicken, we tossed it back into the pan with the sauce, and the meat also softened nicely in the steam generated by the sauce. At last, we had barbecued pulled chicken that was bun-worthy.

Charcoal-Grilled Barbecued Pulled Chicken

SERVES 6 TO 8

We like hickory or mesquite wood for this recipe. Chicken leg quarters consist of drumsticks attached to thighs; often also attached are backbone sections that must be trimmed away (see the illustrations on page 7). Supermarkets may also refer to these pieces as chicken legs, which are chicken leg quarters with the backbone sections already removed; they require less trimming and may weigh less than leg quarters. Serve the pulled chicken with hamburger rolls or sandwich bread, pickles, and coleslaw. For more information on setting up a grill, see page 180.

CHICKEN

- 2 (3-inch) wood chunks or 2 cups wood chips (see note)
- 8 bone-in, skin-on chicken leg quarters (about 7 pounds total), trimmed (see the illustrations on page 7)
- Salt and ground black pepper

SAUCE

- 1 large onion, peeled and quartered
- ¼ cup water
- 1½ cups ketchup
- 1½ cups apple cider
- 3 tablespoons Worcestershire sauce
- 3 tablespoons Dijon mustard
- ¼ cup light or dark molasses
- ½ teaspoon ground black pepper
- 4 tablespoons apple cider vinegar
- 1 tablespoon vegetable oil
- 2 medium garlic cloves, minced or pressed through a garlic press (about 2 teaspoons)
- 1½ tablespoons chili powder
- ½ teaspoon cayenne pepper
- Hot sauce

1. FOR THE CHICKEN: Soak the wood chunks in cold water to cover for 1 hour and drain. If using wood chips, divide them between 2 aluminum foil packets according to the instructions on page 183.

2. Meanwhile, light a large chimney starter ¾ filled with charcoal (about 4½ quarts) and allow to burn until the coals are fully ignited and partially covered with a thin layer of ash, 20 to 25 minutes. Open the bottom vent on the grill. Build a double-banked fire by arranging the coals in two even piles banked on opposite sides of the grill, leaving the middle third of the grill empty (see the illustration on page 181). Nestle 1 soaked wood chunk or one foil packet with chips on top of 1 pile of coals (reserve the remaining wood chunk or packet). Set the cooking grate in place, cover the grill with the lid, and let the grate heat up, about 5 minutes. Use a grill brush to scrape the cooking grate clean. Dip a wad of paper towels in oil; holding the wad with tongs, oil the cooking grate.

3. Meanwhile, pat the chicken dry with paper towels and season with salt and pepper. Place the chicken legs in a single layer in the center of the grill over the roasting pan, skin-side up. Open the grill lid vents halfway and cover, positioning the vents over the chicken. Grill for 30 minutes (the internal grill temperature should register about 325 degrees after 30 minutes).

4. Working quickly, remove the lid and, using tongs, rotate each leg so that the side facing inward now faces the coals; do not flip the chicken pieces. Add the second wood chunk or foil packet to either pile of coals; cover and continue to grill until the thickest part of the thigh registers about 185 degrees on an instant-read thermometer, 30 to 40 minutes longer (the internal grill temperature should register about 310 degrees). Transfer the chicken to a cutting board and let rest until cool enough to handle.

5. FOR THE SAUCE: While chicken is cooking or cooling, process the onion with the water in a food

processor until pureed and the mixture resembles slush, about 30 seconds. Strain the mixture through a fine-mesh strainer into a liquid measuring cup, pressing on the solids with a rubber spatula to obtain ¾ cup juice. Discard the solids.

6. Whisk the onion juice, ketchup, apple cider, Worcestershire, mustard, molasses, pepper, and 3 tablespoons of the cider vinegar together in a medium bowl.

7. Heat the oil in a large saucepan over medium heat until shimmering. Add the garlic, chili powder, and cayenne and cook until fragrant, about 30 seconds. Whisk in the ketchup mixture and bring to a boil. Reduce the heat to medium-low and simmer until the flavors meld and the sauce is slightly thickened, about 15 minutes. Transfer about 2 cups of the sauce to a serving bowl.

8. When the chicken is cool enough to handle, remove and discard the skin from the chicken legs. Using your fingers, pull the meat off the bones, dividing larger pieces (which should fall off the bones easily) and smaller, drier pieces into two equal piles.

9. Place the smaller chicken pieces in a food processor and pulse until coarsely chopped, three to four 1-second pulses. Transfer the chicken to the saucepan with the remaining sauce. Using your fingers or two forks, pull the larger chicken pieces into long shreds and add to the saucepan. Stir in the remaining tablespoon cider vinegar, cover, and cook over medium-low heat, stirring occasionally, until heated through, about 10 minutes. (Up to this point, the chicken and sauce can be transferred to a 13 by 9-inch glass baking dish, covered with foil, and placed in a 250-degree oven for up to an hour.) Season with hot sauce to taste and serve, passing the remaining barbecue sauce separately.

VARIATION

Gas-Grilled Barbecued Pulled Chicken

Use wood chips rather than chunks for this recipe.

Soak 2 cups wood chips for 30 minutes in cold water to cover and drain. Place the wood chips in a foil tray (see page 183). Place the foil tray on top of the primary burner and position the cooking grate. Turn all the burners to high and heat the grill with the lid down until the wood chips begin to smoke, about 15 minutes. (If the chips ignite, use a water-filled spray bottle to extinguish.) Use a grill brush to scrape the cooking grate clean. Dip a wad of paper towels in oil; holding the wad with tongs, oil the cooking grate. Leave the primary burner on high and turn off all the other burner(s). Follow the recipe for Charcoal-Grilled Barbecued Pulled Chicken from step 3, placing the chicken legs in a single layer on the cooler side of the grill, skin-side up, and grilling with the lid down. Proceed as directed, omitting the wood chunks and extending the cooking time in step 3 to 35 minutes and the cooking time in step 4 to 45 minutes.

EQUIPMENT: Barbecue Mitts

For a dedicated outdoor cook, a good barbecue mitt is an invaluable grilling accessory. But you can pay anywhere from $5 for a simple cotton barbecue mitt to $33 for a high-tech model. Does advanced technology equal advanced performance? We took eight mitts outside to find out.

Testers were asked to hold mitt-clad hands three inches over a 600-degree grill. The Grill Life Leather Grill Glove showed the best performance; its thick leather provided superior protection. The cotton mitts also did a fine job of protecting hands from the heat of the grill, but thin mitts of any material fared poorly. The silicone mitt was flatly rejected—we were surprised at how warm (and sweaty) our hands got while using the mitt for just 30 seconds, as its outside surfaces became almost too hot to touch.

Next, we evaluated the mitts' effect on testers' dexterity when flipping zucchini slices with tongs and reaching to the back of the grill to turn potatoes. In most cases, we found that heavy, thick fabrics significantly impaired agility. The exception among thick gloves was the Grill Life Leather Grill Glove, whose five-fingered shape was surprisingly comfortable and nimble.

Last, we briefly (and carefully) inserted each mitt directly into a flame to simulate a flare-up. The Grill Life Leather Grill Glove was the only one to ace the test, braving the fire unscathed. The others emerged scorched and charred.

THE BEST BARBECUE MITTS

Grill Life Leather Grill Gloves' heavy leather and 18-inch length keep hands and arms cool, and the glove shape provides a surprising amount of control.

GRILL LIFE

TANDOORI CHICKEN

TO MOST PEOPLE, TANDOORI CONJURES images of unnaturally red-dyed chicken from Indian restaurants. What they often don't realize is that the red dye has long taken the place of a fiery coating of red pepper, and that tandoori is not really a dish at all, but a cooking method. A tandoor oven is a beehive-shaped structure that cooks both meats and breads at a very high temperature in a very short amount of time. The bottom of the tandoor contains a pile of red-hot coals that can crank the internal temperature of the tandoor in excess of 900 degrees. Meats, such as chicken and lamb, are skewered on long metal stakes that resemble thin-bladed swords. The tips of the skewers rest on the bottom of the tandoor, and the heat circulates freely around the roasting meat.

Hoping to avoid the dry and flavorless meat that often arrives when you order restaurant tandoori, we started out by testing a variety of recipes from noted Indian chefs. These recipes took us from the grill to the oven to the broiler and back again, as we tried to find a way to mimic the tandoor's searing heat and coal-roasted flavor. We used various spice rubs and marinades, but, in the end, most of these recipes resulted in tough, overcooked meat that was either charred black or boiled-looking and wan. The marinades for most of these recipes, despite their laundry list of spices, yielded a flavor that was bland and chalky at best. Our goals were to replicate the intense heat of a tandoor oven at home, create a universal tandoori marinade base, and infuse our meat with some serious spice.

Focusing first on recreating a tandoor oven at home, we concluded that the most logical place to begin our testing was the grill, because it could best replicate the tandoor's intense, coal-fired heat and the flavor the tandoor oven produces. We began our testing with bone-in chicken breasts (common tandoori fare) and a simple yogurt-based tandoori marinade. Right from the start, unfortunately, grilling posed a few problems. It was difficult to prevent the marinade from burning on the outside before the chicken achieved the proper doneness on the inside. (Sure, a little char adds nice flavor, but too much overpowers the flavors of the spice and meat.)

As with many of our grilled chicken recipes, we wondered whether an indirect cooking method on the grill would help solve our problems. For the next round, we set up a double-banked fire, with coals banked evenly on opposite sides of the grill, leaving the center empty. This has the advantage of creating a more moderate cooking zone in the center of the grill, with even heat coming from both sides. We placed the chicken skin-side down in the center of the grill, covered the grill, and waited patiently for our results. After about 20 to 25 minutes, we flipped the chicken as it was just starting to turn golden brown—no black char in sight. We then moved the chicken out over the hot coals on either side of the grill and finished off the cooking there. This prevented the skin from burning but allowed it to achieve the slightly charred, crisp appearance we were looking for. Better yet, the meat was juicy and moist—nothing like the dried-out pieces of chicken from our local Indian takeout. We then decided to spoon on some extra marinade in the final stages of cooking. This enhanced our crisp, golden crust and added the flavor of the marinade to each bite.

With our cooking methods in place, we focused next on the flavor of the marinade—the vehicle for infusing the meat with flavor and spice. Most tandoori marinades use yogurt for its tang and also as a cool background for the pungent aromatics and spices. We used a generous amount of minced aromatics to flavor our marinade, but the pieces of garlic, ginger, and onion seemed to just float in the marinade without contributing much flavor. It was then that we decided to puree all the marinade ingredients in a blender. This simple step allowed for maximum flavor extraction from the aromatics, creating an intensely flavorful marinade. The spice mix we created started with coriander, cumin, garam masala, nutmeg, cinnamon, and pepper. We then found that the marinade benefited from a few additions—the zing of lemon zest and the earthiness of turmeric.

Many of the marinade recipes we researched contained a liquid in the form of either water or oil. We tried both and, for a few reasons, found it especially beneficial to add vegetable oil to the marinade. First, since the spices are oil-soluble, the oil in the marinade allowed them to bloom when heated. Next, the oil enriched the yogurt. And finally, the oil helped the exterior of the meat to crisp and brown. In terms of marinating time, we found it necessary to marinate the meat for at least 4 hours and noted that its flavor continued to increase when the meat was allowed to sit in the marinade for up to 24 hours. Going longer than 24 hours didn't increase the flavor further, but rather turned the texture of the meat a bit mushy.

At last we had achieved what we had set out to accomplish; deeply flavored meat from a home-made "tandoor" that was not only juicy, but also had the slightly charred appearance of meat pulled directly from an authentic tandoor.

Charcoal-Grilled Tandoori Chicken

SERVES 4

For even cooking, the chicken breasts should be of comparable size. Try to purchase split bone-in, skin-on breasts that weigh about 12 ounces each. Whole milk, low-fat, and nonfat yogurt all work equally well here. Serve with Basic Pilaf-Style Rice (page 114) and a spicy mango chutney or Yogurt-Mint Cucumber Sauce (page 212). For more information on setting up a grill, see page 180.

- 1 tablespoon ground coriander
- 1 teaspoon ground cumin
- 1 teaspoon ground turmeric
- 1 teaspoon garam masala
- ½ teaspoon ground nutmeg
- ½ teaspoon ground cinnamon
- ¼ teaspoon ground black pepper
- 1 cup plain yogurt (see note)
- ¼ cup vegetable oil
- 1 medium onion, chopped coarse
- 5 medium garlic cloves, peeled
- 1 (2-inch) piece fresh ginger, peeled and chopped coarse
- 1 tablespoon grated zest from 1 lemon
- 2 teaspoons salt
- 4 bone-in, skin-on split chicken breasts (10 to 12 ounces each), trimmed

1. Puree the spices, yogurt, oil, onion, garlic, ginger, lemon zest, and salt in a blender (or food processor) until smooth, about 30 seconds. Transfer ¼ cup of the mixture to an airtight container and refrigerate. Transfer the remaining marinade to a large zipper-lock bag along with the chicken breasts. Seal shut, toss to coat, and refrigerate for at least 4 hours and up to 24 hours.

2. Meanwhile, light a large chimney starter filled with charcoal (about 6 quarts) and allow to burn until the coals are fully ignited and partially covered with a thin layer of ash, 20 to 25 minutes. Open the bottom vent on the grill. Build a double-banked fire by arranging the coals in two even piles banked on opposite sides of the grill, leaving the middle third of the grill empty (see the illustration on page 181). Set the cooking grate in place, cover the grill with the lid, and let the grate heat up, about 5 minutes. Use a grill brush to scrape the cooking grate clean. Dip a wad of paper towels in oil; holding the wad with tongs, oil the cooking grate.

3. Remove the chicken from the zipper-lock bag and place it in the center of the grill, skin-side down. Open the grill lid vents completely and cover, positioning the vents over the chicken. Grill until the chicken begins to brown and the thickest part of the breast registers 140 degrees on an instant-read thermometer, 20 to 25 minutes.

4. Flip the chicken over, brush the ¼ cup reserved marinade evenly over the top, and move the chicken out directly over the hot coals. Continue to grill, uncovered, flipping occasionally, until both sides are golden brown and the thickest part of the breast registers 160 to 165 degrees on an instant-read thermometer, 5 to 10 minutes longer. Let the chicken rest for 10 minutes before serving.

VARIATION

Gas-Grilled Tandoori Chicken

Follow the recipe for Charcoal-Grilled Tandoori Chicken through step 1. Turn all the burners to high and heat the grill with the lid down until very hot, about 15 minutes. Use a grill brush to scrape the cooking grate clean. Dip a wad of paper towels in oil; holding the wad with tongs, oil the cooking grate. Leave the primary burner on high and turn off all the other burner(s). Place the chicken in the center of the cooler side of the grill, skin-side down, cover, and proceed with the recipe from step 3, grilling with the lid down.

Grilled Thai-Style Chicken Breasts

THAI GRILLED CHICKEN IS CLASSIC STREET fare. This herb-and-spice-rubbed chicken is served in small pieces and eaten as finger food, along with a sweet and spicy dipping sauce. Thai flavors are wonderfully aromatic and complex, making this dish a refreshing change of pace from typical barbecue fare. But is it possible to bring the flavors of Thailand into the American kitchen (or backyard) without using an ingredient list as long as your arm and making several trips to Asian specialty stores?

An initial sampling of recipes made us wonder if this dish ought to remain indigenous street food. Among the hard-to-find ingredients were cilantro root and lemon grass, and there was a profusion of odd mixtures, including an unlikely marriage of peanut butter and brown sugar. In the end, the simplest version won out: a rub made only with cilantro, black pepper, lime juice, and garlic. We would use this as our working recipe.

Because tasters preferred white meat, we decided to go with bone-in breasts. Brined chicken was vastly preferred to unbrined, and tasters liked the addition of sugar along with salt, which complemented the sweetness of the sauce. We settled on ½ cup of each in 2 quarts of water.

Tasters liked the working rub recipe, but they wanted more complexity of flavor. Our first step was to reduce the amount of cilantro, as it had been overpowering the other ingredients. Curry powder made the chicken taste too much like Indian food, and coconut milk turned the chicken milky and soggy and made the skin flabby. The earthy flavor of coriander was welcome, and fresh ginger worked well to balance the garlic. Tasters praised this blend as more complex but complained that it still lacked bite, so we added more garlic.

The skin on the chicken was now crisp and flavorful, but not much rub was getting through to the meat. Test cooks offered suggestions ranging from slicing pockets in the meat and stuffing them with the rub to butterflying the breasts and placing the rub inside. In the end, the best alternative proved to be the easiest: We took some of the rub and placed it in a thick layer under the skin as well as on top of it. Now not only was the crisp skin flavorful, but so was the moist flesh beneath it as well.

Most recipes call for grilling the chicken over a single-level fire, but, as we suspected, this resulted in a charred exterior and an uncooked interior. We had a head start on the cooking method, as we had already grilled hundreds of pounds of chicken in the test kitchen. As we had learned from our tandoori chicken (see page 192) and barbecued chicken (see page 184), placing raw chicken over a hot (or even medium-hot) fire causes too many flare-ups, resulting in burnt skin. We had much better luck starting the chicken over lower heat to render the fat slowly and completely, without the danger of flare-ups. We set up a double-banked fire with coals piled high on opposite sides of the grill, leaving the center empty, creating a cooler cooking zone in the center of the grill on which to start the chicken, skin-side down. This worked like a charm with our Thai chicken, allowing the flavors of the Thai rub to develop rather than burn.

The true Thai flavors of this dish come through in the sauce, a classic combination of sweet and spicy. Most recipes suffered from one extreme or the other. In our working recipe, we had tried to create a balance of flavors: 2 teaspoons of red pepper flakes, ⅓ cup of sugar, ¼ cup of lime juice, ¼ cup of white vinegar, and 3 tablespoons of fish sauce. But tasters found even this sauce to be overwhelmingly sweet and spicy.

Reducing the red pepper flakes was a step in the right direction, as it allowed the other flavors to come through. Everyone liked garlic, but not too much of it; there was already a lot of garlic on the chicken. A decrease in the amount of fish sauce was welcomed, reducing the fishy flavor of the sauce but not its salty complexity. We found it best to mix the sauce right after the chicken goes into the brine, which gives the flavors time to meld.

Traditionally, this dish is cut into small pieces and eaten as finger food. But our version is just as good (and a whole lot neater) when served whole with a knife and fork.

Charcoal-Grilled Thai-Style Chicken Breasts with Sweet and Sour Dipping Sauce

SERVES 4

For even cooking, the chicken breasts should be of comparable size. Try to purchase split bone-in, skin-on breasts that weigh about 12 ounces each. If using kosher chicken, skip the brining process. To use kosher salt in the brine, see page 12 for conversion information and more tips on brining. For more information on setting up a grill, see page 180.

CHICKEN AND BRINE

- ½ cup table salt
- ½ cup sugar
- 4 bone-in, skin-on split chicken breasts (10 to 12 ounces each), trimmed (see note)

SPICE MIXTURE

- ⅔ cup minced fresh cilantro leaves
- ¼ cup juice from 2 limes
- 12 medium garlic cloves, minced or pressed through a garlic press (about ¼ cup)
- 2 tablespoons minced or grated fresh ginger
- 2 tablespoons ground black pepper
- 2 tablespoons ground coriander
- 2 tablespoons vegetable oil

DIPPING SAUCE

- ⅓ cup sugar
- ¼ cup distilled white vinegar
- ¼ cup juice from 2 limes
- 2 tablespoons fish sauce
- 1 medium garlic clove, minced or pressed through a garlic press (about 1 teaspoon)
- 1 teaspoon red pepper flakes

1. FOR THE CHICKEN AND BRINE: Dissolve the salt and sugar in 2 quarts cold water in a large container. Submerge the chicken in the brine, cover, and refrigerate for 30 minutes.

2. Mix the cilantro, lime juice, garlic, ginger, pepper, coriander, and oil together in a small bowl; set aside. Remove the chicken from the brine, rinse well, and pat dry with paper towels. Following the illustrations on page 105, use your fingers to gently loosen the skin covering the chicken pieces. Place about 1 tablespoon of the spice mixture under the skin, directly on the meat in the center of each breast. Gently press on the skin to distribute the mixture over the meat. Rub the spice mixture all over the outside of the chicken pieces. Cover with plastic wrap and refrigerate while preparing the grill.

3. FOR THE DIPPING SAUCE: Meanwhile, whisk the ingredients in a small bowl until the sugar dissolves. Let stand at room temperature to allow the flavors to meld, about 1 hour.

4. Meanwhile, light a large chimney starter filled with charcoal (about 6 quarts) and allow to burn until the coals are fully ignited and partially covered with a thin layer of ash, 20 to 25 minutes. Open the bottom vent on the grill. Build a double-banked fire by arranging the coals in two even piles banked on opposite sides of the grill, leaving the middle third of the grill empty (see the illustration on page 181). Set the cooking grate in place, cover the grill with the lid, and let the grate heat up, about 5 minutes. Use a grill brush to scrape the cooking grate clean. Dip a wad of paper towels in oil; holding the wad with tongs, oil the cooking grate.

5. Place the chicken in the center of the grill, skin-side down. Open the grill lid vents completely and cover, positioning the vents over the chicken. Grill until the chicken begins to brown and the thickest part of the breast registers 140 degrees on an instant-read thermometer, 20 to 25 minutes. Move the chicken out over the hot coals and continue to grill, uncovered, until both sides are golden brown and the thickest part of the breast registers 160 to 165 degrees on an instant-read thermometer, 5 to 10 minutes longer. Let the chicken rest for 10 minutes. Serve, passing the dipping sauce separately.

VARIATION

Gas-Grilled Thai-Style Chicken Breasts with Sweet and Sour Dipping Sauce

Follow the recipe for Charcoal-Grilled Thai-Style Chicken Breasts with Sweet and Sour Dipping Sauce through step 3. Turn all the burners to high and heat the grill with the lid down until very hot, about 15 minutes. Use a grill brush to scrape the cooking grate clean. Dip a wad of paper towels in oil; holding the wad with tongs, oil the cooking grate. Leave the primary burner on high and turn off all the other burner(s). Place the chicken in the center of the cooler side of the grill, skin-side down, cover, and proceed with the recipe from step 5, grilling with the lid down.

Grilled Jamaican Jerk Chicken

JAMAICA, A MOUNTAINOUS ISLAND IN THE Caribbean Sea, has a rich culture and a colorful cuisine, including a style of cooking all its own. Called jerk, this style of cooking can be traced back to the native inhabitants of the island, the Carib-Arawak Indians, who cooked meat over green wood, which added a distinctive smoky flavor. The Indians also "jerked" the meat before cooking it, which meant making deep slashes in the meat and stuffing them with herbs and spices. From this seemingly primitive technique, Jamaican jerk has evolved into one of Jamaica's most famous exports.

Traditionally made with pork, jerk today increasingly is made with chicken or fish. Focusing on chicken (chicken parts in particular), we gathered some recipes from a variety of cookbooks and headed into the kitchen. While Jamaican jerk seasoning can be found in almost any supermarket spice aisle, it often tastes dusty and stale and barely penetrates the meat. After just one test, we knew we would be making a paste instead of simply using dried spices for the jerk seasoning. The challenges would be to create a jerk paste that was well balanced—not too spicy, too harsh, or too bland—and to figure out how to apply the paste so that it flavored the chicken, not just the skin.

We began by making our jerk paste with Scotch bonnets, the most popular hot chile of Jamaica, which we liked for its great flavor and slow, steady heat. We then added some allspice, garlic, thyme, and scallions. To temper the heat and spice, we added vegetable oil and dark, smoky molasses, both of which had the added benefit of making the paste smoother and more cohesive—perfect for adhering to the chicken.

In our research, we found that many recipes call for marinating the chicken for days—a step we wanted to skip. After much trial and error with "quick" marinating techniques, we realized that if we wanted the jerk seasonings to flavor the meat more quickly, we would have to rub the paste directly on the meat. This technique produced dramatic results, cutting the marinating time from 24 hours to two. Now we were ready to fire up the grill.

To keep the skin from burning before the meat near the bone was cooked through, we built a double-banked fire on the grill. We began by placing the chicken, skin-side down, over the cooler center of the grill to render the skin and cook the chicken until it was almost done. We then slid the chicken out over the hot coals to finish cooking, which allowed the jerk paste on the exterior of the bird to char slightly—just enough to create an authentic smoky flavor. We now had moist, flavorful meat with perfectly charred skin.

When serving the chicken, we passed around some lime wedges and a grilled fruit salsa (see page 197), an accompaniment common to Jamaican cuisine that we thought would complement the chicken nicely. The tart flavor of the lime, along with the sweetness of the salsa, mingled with the jerk beautifully, providing the perfect finishing touch.

Charcoal-Grilled Jamaican Jerk Chicken with Grilled Banana Salsa

SERVES 4

This recipe is pretty spicy; for a milder version, use the lesser amount of Scotch bonnets and discard the seeds and ribs before processing the chiles. If you cannot find Scotch bonnets, substitute an equal amount of habaneros or 4 to 6 jalapeños. Wear disposable latex gloves when handling the chiles, as Scotch bonnets are particularly potent and can cause a burning sensation. For more information on setting up a grill, see page 180.

- 1 bunch scallions, chopped coarse
- 1/4 cup vegetable oil
- 2 tablespoons light or dark molasses
- 2–3 Scotch bonnet chiles, stemmed (and seeded, if desired; see note)

3 medium garlic cloves, peeled
1 tablespoon dried thyme
2 teaspoons ground allspice
2 teaspoons salt
3 pounds bone-in, skin-on chicken pieces (split breasts, drumsticks, and/or thighs), trimmed
1 recipe Grilled Banana Salsa (below)
1 lime, cut into wedges (for serving)

1. Puree the scallions, oil, molasses, chiles, garlic, thyme, allspice, and salt in a food processor (or blender) until almost smooth, about 15 seconds. Wearing latex gloves, and following the illustrations on page 105, use your fingers to gently loosen the skin covering the chicken pieces. Place about 1 tablespoon of the spice mixture under the skin, directly on the meat in the center of each breast. Gently press on the skin to distribute the mixture over the meat. Transfer the chicken to a large zipper-lock bag. Pour the remaining spice mixture over the chicken. Seal shut, toss to coat, and refrigerate for at least 2 hours and up to 24 hours.

2. Meanwhile, light a large chimney starter filled with charcoal (about 6 quarts) and allow to burn until the coals are fully ignited and partially covered with a thin layer of ash, 20 to 25 minutes. Open the bottom vent on the grill. Build a double-banked fire by arranging the coals in two even piles banked on opposite sides of the grill, leaving the middle third of the grill empty (see the illustration on page 181). Set the cooking grate in place, cover the grill with the lid, and let the grate heat up, about 5 minutes. Use a grill brush to scrape the cooking grate clean. Dip a wad of paper towels in oil; holding the wad with tongs, oil the cooking grate.

3. Place the chicken in the center of the grill, skin-side down. Open the grill lid vents completely and cover, positioning the vents over the chicken. Grill until the chicken begins to brown and the thickest part of the breast registers 140 degrees and/or the thickest part of the thigh and drumstick registers 160 degrees on an instant-read thermometer, 20 to 25 minutes. Move the chicken out over the hot coals and continue to grill, uncovered, until both sides are dark brown and the thickest part of the breast registers 160 to 165 degrees and/or the thickest part of the thigh and drumstick registers 170 to 175 degrees on an instant-read thermometer, 5 to 10 minutes longer. Transfer the chicken to a platter and let rest for 10 minutes. Serve, passing the salsa and lime wedges separately.

VARIATION

Gas-Grilled Jamaican Jerk Chicken with Grilled Banana Salsa

Follow the recipe for Charcoal-Grilled Jamaican Jerk Chicken with Grilled Banana Salsa through step 1. Turn all the burners to high and heat the grill with the lid down until very hot, about 15 minutes. Use a grill brush to scrape the cooking grate clean. Dip a wad of paper towels in oil; holding the wad with tongs, oil the cooking grate. Leave the primary burner on high and turn all the other burner(s) off. Place the chicken in the center of the cooler side of the grill, skin-side down, and proceed with the recipe from step 3, grilling with the lid down.

Grilled Banana Salsa

MAKES ABOUT 3 CUPS

Use the grill setup in the recipe for Charcoal- or Gas-Grilled Jamaican Jerk Chicken for this recipe. We like the starchy sweetness of bananas here, but other thickly sliced, sweet tropical fruits such as mango, papaya, or even pineapple will work as well.

3 firm but ripe bananas, peeled and halved lengthwise
1 large red onion, peeled and sliced into ½-inch-thick rounds
2 tablespoons vegetable oil
½ teaspoon ground cumin
Salt and ground black pepper
2 tablespoons juice from 1 lime
2 tablespoons minced fresh mint leaves
1 tablespoon light brown sugar
1 tablespoon dark rum (optional)

1. Brush the banana halves and onion rounds with the oil and season with the cumin and salt and pepper. Lay the onion directly over the hot coals and grill on both sides until well browned, 3 to 4 minutes per side. Transfer the onion to the cooler part of the

grill and cook until softened, about 4 minutes. Lay the bananas directly over the hot coals and grill on both sides until browned in spots, about 2 minutes per side. Transfer the onion and bananas to a cutting board and cool slightly.

2. Coarsely chop the grilled bananas and onion, then toss with the lime juice, mint, brown sugar, and rum (if using) in a medium bowl. Season with salt and pepper to taste and serve.

GRILLED BUTTERFLIED CHICKEN

REMOVING THE BACKBONE FROM A WHOLE chicken—a process known as butterflying—may seem like an unnecessary and time-consuming process. But we have found that this relatively quick and simple procedure provides many benefits, because it leaves the bird with a more even thickness. Basically, butterflying lets you grill a whole chicken in much the same way that you grill parts.

A flattened 3-pound chicken cooks in a little over a half hour, whereas a whole grill-roasted bird requires over one hour of cooking. In addition, because the breast isn't sticking out and exposed to the heat while the legs are tucked under and away from the heat, all the parts of a flattened bird get done at the same time. Finally, unlike a whole roasted chicken, the butterfly cut is a breeze to separate into sections when carving. One cut down the breast with the kitchen shears, a quick snip of the skin holding the legs, and the job is done.

Most recipes for butterflied chicken call for weighting the bird on the grill to promote fast, even cooking. The chicken is covered with a baking sheet and weighed down with heavy cans or bricks. We grilled butterflied chicken with and without weights and found that while the weighted bird cooked slightly quicker, weighting is an added step that can be a bit of an annoyance. Lifting the weights on and off the chicken proved cumbersome, and we found that the skin often stuck to the pan. With a few more tests, we decided that the ease of grilling an unweighted bird outweighed the shorter cooking time and slightly more attractive appearance of a weighted bird.

Many recipes call for turning the chicken several times on the grill. However, the chicken skin was quick to tear when overhandled, so we wanted to devise a cooking method that involved minimal flipping. When we placed the chicken on the charcoal grill, skin-side down, over a single-level hot fire, the skin burned long before the chicken had cooked through. Borrowing from the method we use for grill-roasting whole chickens, which involves grilling over indirect heat, we banked the coals evenly on opposite sides of the grill, leaving the center empty. This creates a cooler cooking zone on which to grill meat that requires a longer cooking time. The chicken's skin was then able to render more slowly, allowing both it and the chicken to reach perfection at the same time. We also tested flipping the chicken—from just once to three times—and realized that this, likewise, was an unnecessary step with our butterflied bird. This recipe was getting easier and easier.

We still had a couple questions about butterflying and grilling. Did we really need to pound the chicken after we butterflied it, or was it enough to just flatten it with our hands? Finally, we wanted to know if we could season the chicken with herbs and garlic without them burning on the grill.

We thought pounding the chicken might decrease cooking time, but it made no noticeable difference. Flattening the bird with our hands was all we needed to do. In the end, the simplest method proved to be the best—no pounding, weighting, or flipping—simply place the butterflied chicken on the cooler part of the grill, skin-side down, cover, and grill to perfection.

Seasoning the outside of the chicken with herbs or garlic proved to be pointless—the herbs charred, and the garlic burned. But a butterflied chicken is especially easy to season under the skin. Since the back is removed, access to the legs and thighs is simple. Barbecue sauces and glazes can be brushed onto the skin once the chicken is nearly done. After just two or three minutes on the grill, the glaze will caramelize nicely and give the skin excellent flavor.

Charcoal-Grilled Butterflied Chicken

SERVES 2 TO 3

If using a kosher bird, skip the brining process. To use kosher salt in the brine, see page 12 for conversion information and more tips on brining. For more information on setting up a grill, see page 180.

- ½ cup table salt
- ½ cup sugar
- 1 (3½- to 4-pound) whole chicken, giblets discarded, butterflied (see the illustrations on page 8)
- Ground black pepper

1. Dissolve the salt and sugar in 2 quarts cold water in a large container. Submerge the chicken in the brine, cover, and refrigerate for 1 hour. Remove the chicken from the brine, rinse well, and pat dry with paper towels. Season with pepper.

2. Meanwhile, light a large chimney starter filled with charcoal (about 6 quarts) and allow to burn until the coals are fully ignited and partially covered with a thin layer of ash, 20 to 25 minutes. Open the bottom vent on the grill. Build a double-banked fire by arranging the coals in two even piles banked on opposite sides of the grill, leaving the middle third of the grill empty (see the illustration on page 181). Set the cooking grate in place, cover the grill with the lid, and let the grate heat up, about 5 minutes. Use a grill brush to scrape the cooking grate clean. Dip a wad of paper towels in oil; holding the wad with tongs, oil the cooking grate.

3. Place the chicken on the center of the grill, skin-side down. Open the grill lid vents completely and cover, positioning the vents over the chicken. Grill the chicken until the skin is crisp and golden brown and the thickest part of the breast registers 160 to 165 degrees and the thickest part of the thigh registers 170 to 175 degrees on an instant-read thermometer, about 45 minutes.

4. Transfer the chicken to a cutting board and let rest for 10 minutes. Carve the chicken (see the illustrations on page 11) and serve.

VARIATIONS

Gas-Grilled Butterflied Chicken

Follow the recipe for Charcoal-Grilled Butterflied Chicken through step 1. Turn all the burners to high and heat the grill with the lid down until very hot, about 15 minutes. Use a grill brush to scrape the cooking grate clean. Dip a wad of paper towels in oil; holding the wad with tongs, oil the cooking grate. Turn all the burners to medium-low. Place the chicken on the grill, skin-side down, and cook with the lid down until the skin is crisp and golden and the thickest part of the breast registers 160 to 165 degrees and the thickest part of the thigh registers 170 to 175 degrees on an instant-read thermometer, about 45 minutes. (If after 35 minutes the skin is not crisp and golden, turn the burners up to medium for the final 10 minutes of cooking.)

Grilled Butterflied Chicken with Chipotle, Honey, and Lime

For this recipe, a spicy paste (made with smoky chipotle chiles) is rubbed under the chicken skin before cooking, and a sweet and sour honey–lime juice glaze is applied once the chicken is almost done.

Mix together 3 tablespoons minced chipotle chiles in adobo sauce, 2 teaspoons minced cilantro leaves, and ½ teaspoon grated lime zest in a small bowl. Whisk together 3 tablespoons juice from 2 limes and 2 tablespoons honey in another small bowl. Follow the recipe for Charcoal-Grilled or Gas-Grilled Butterflied Chicken, brining, rinsing, and drying the chicken as directed. Rub the chile mixture under the skin of the breast, thighs, and legs. Reposition the chicken parts and season with pepper. Grill as directed, brushing both sides of the chicken with the honey–lime juice glaze during the last 2 minutes of grilling.

Grilled Butterflied Chicken with Pesto

Classic basil pesto is delicious, but feel free to use almost any herb paste, including pesto made with cilantro, arugula, or mint. If you are pressed for time, store-bought pesto works well in this recipe.

Follow the recipe for Charcoal-Grilled or Gas-Grilled Butterflied Chicken, brining, rinsing, and drying the chicken as directed. Rub ½ cup Classic Basil Pesto (page 213) under the skin of the breast, thighs, and legs. Reposition the chicken parts and season with pepper. Grill as directed.

Grilled Butterflied Chicken with Green Olive Tapenade

The tapenade is fairly salty, so make sure to rinse the chicken very thoroughly after brining.

Pulse 10 large pitted Spanish green olives, 1 chopped garlic clove, 2 anchovy fillets, 1 teaspoon drained capers, and 3 tablespoons extra-virgin olive oil in a food processor until the mixture becomes a slightly chunky paste (do not overprocess). Follow the recipe for Charcoal-Grilled or Gas-Grilled Butterflied Chicken, brining, rinsing, and drying the chicken as directed. Rub the olive mixture under the skin of the breast, thighs, and legs. Reposition the chicken parts and season with pepper. Grill as directed.

Grilled Butterflied Chicken with Lemon and Rosemary

This recipe is an Italian classic. Try other herbs, including oregano, sage, thyme, or marjoram, in place of the rosemary.

Mix together 2 teaspoons grated zest from 1 lemon, 2 medium garlic cloves, minced or pressed through a garlic press (about 2 teaspoons), and 1 teaspoon minced fresh rosemary in a small bowl. Whisk together 3 tablespoons lemon juice and 3 tablespoons extra-virgin olive oil in another small bowl. Follow the recipe for Charcoal-Grilled or Gas-Grilled Butterflied Chicken, brining, rinsing, and drying the chicken as directed. Rub the lemon zest mixture under the skin of the breast, thighs, and legs. Reposition the chicken parts and season with pepper. Grill as directed, brushing both sides of the chicken with the lemon-oil mixture during the last 2 minutes of grilling.

Grilled Butterflied Chicken alla Diavola

This spicy version is excellent served with lemon wedges.

Heat ¼ cup olive oil, 4 medium garlic cloves, minced or pressed through a garlic press (about 4 teaspoons), 2 teaspoons ground black pepper, and 2 teaspoons red pepper flakes in a small saucepan over medium heat until fragrant, about 3 minutes. Remove from the heat, let cool to room temperature, and divide the mixture between two small bowls. Follow the recipe for Charcoal-Grilled or Gas-Grilled Butterflied Chicken, brining, rinsing, and drying the chicken as directed. Rub half of the garlic mixture under the skin of the breast, thighs, and legs. Reposition the chicken parts and season with pepper. Grill as directed. Drizzle with the remaining garlic mixture just before serving.

Grilled Butterflied Chicken with Barbecue Sauce

Although our barbecue sauce is best, this recipe works with plain store-bought sauce; our favorite brand is Bull's-Eye.

Follow the recipe for Charcoal-Grilled or Gas-Grilled Butterflied Chicken, brushing both sides of the chicken with ⅓ cup Barbecue Sauce (page 209) in the last 5 minutes of grilling.

Grill-Roasted Whole Chicken

EVERY YEAR MILLIONS OF COOKS GRILL ALL manner of chicken parts, from breasts and thighs to drumsticks. But chicken parts don't spend enough time on the grill to pick up much smoke flavor. When serious smoky taste is what we're after, we grill-roast a whole chicken. When grilled over indirect heat (coals banked to the side, with the chicken over the cooler part of a covered grill), the bird cooks in about an hour, giving it plenty of time to pick up a good hit of smoke.

Grill-roasting a whole chicken turns out to be a fairly straightforward matter. On reading through various recipes while researching this topic, however, we did notice some variations in technique. Wanting to determine the very best technique, we decided to test the important variables, including how to arrange the coals, whether to use a V-rack, when and how to turn the bird, and how to flavor it.

When grill-roasting large birds (such as turkeys) or big cuts of meat (such as prime rib), the standard setup is to fill half of a kettle grill with charcoal and to leave the other half empty. The food is placed on the cooler side of the grill, and the kettle is covered. Because one side of the food faces the lit coals, the bird or meat will cook unevenly unless it is rotated at least once. Rotating is simple enough, but the heat dissipates when the lid is removed, and you often have to add more coals, which is a pain. Since a chicken is much smaller than a turkey or prime rib, we wondered if the lit coals could be banked on opposite sides of the kettle grill and the chicken cooked in the middle. After several tests, we concluded that this arrangement works fine, with some caveats.

First, the coals must be piled fairly high on opposite sides to form relatively tall but narrow piles. We split the coals between opposite sides of the grill and ended up piling the lit briquettes three or four levels high. If the coals are arranged in wider, shorter piles, the cooler spot in the middle of the grill won't be large enough to protect the bird from direct heat. Second, you must use a relatively small chicken. We found that the skin on a large roaster scorches long before the meat cooks through. Last, keep the vents in the lid halfway open so that the fire burns at a fairly even pace. If the vents are open all the way, the fire burns too hot at the outset—thereby scorching the bird's skin—and then peters out before the chicken has cooked through.

With the heat attacking the chicken from two sides, the bird cooks evenly, so there's no need to rotate it. (On gas grills, where just one lit burner is used to cook by indirect heat, you will need to rotate the bird.) After our initial tests, however, we did conclude that it was necessary to flip the bird once during the hour-long cooking process. The skin on top of the bird cooks faster than the skin touching the grate. (Although this seems counterintuitive, repeated tests confirmed this observation.) Because the side of the bird that finishes right-side up tends to look better (grill marks fade and the skin bronzes more evenly), we decided to start the chicken breast-side down.

When we cook a turkey on the grill, we always cradle it in a V-rack, which keeps the skin from scorching and promotes even cooking. We prepared several chickens with and without V-racks and found that those placed directly on the cooking grate browned better and cooked just fine. Again, because a chicken is small, the bird spends much less time than a turkey on the grill, and the skin is less likely to burn.

With our technique perfected, we focused on the flavoring options. As expected, we found that brining the chicken helps it retain moisture while cooking and is therefore recommended. The one exception is a kosher bird, which is salted during processing and cooks up moist—and perfectly seasoned—without brining.

During the course of our testing, we tried brushing the chicken with melted butter and olive oil before and during grilling. Although a buttered bird browned marginally better than an oiled one, we don't recommend using either. Birds coated with a spice rub cooked up crispier and were better looking than greased birds.

Charcoal Grill–Roasted Whole Chicken

SERVES 2 TO 3

If using a kosher bird, skip the brining process. To use kosher salt in the brine, see page 12 for conversion information and more tips on brining. For more information on setting up a grill, see page 180.

- ½ cup table salt
- ½ cup sugar
- 1 (3½- to 4-pound) whole chicken, giblets discarded (see note)
- 3 tablespoons spice rub (see page 203)
- 4 (3-inch) wood chunks or 4 cups wood chips

1. Dissolve the salt and sugar in 2 quarts cold water in a large container. Submerge the chicken in the brine, cover, and refrigerate for 1 hour. Remove the chicken from the brine, rinse well, and pat dry with paper towels. Massage the spice rub all over the chicken, inside and out, gently lifting the skin to distribute the spice rub underneath but leaving the skin attached to the chicken.

2. Meanwhile, soak the wood chunks in cold water to cover for 1 hour and drain. If using wood

chips, divide them between 2 aluminum foil packets according to the instructions on page 183.

3. Light a large chimney starter filled with charcoal (about 6 quarts) and allow to burn until the coals are fully ignited and partially covered with a thin layer of ash, 20 to 25 minutes. Open the bottom vent on the grill. Build a double-banked fire by arranging the coals in two even piles banked on opposite sides of the grill, leaving the middle third of the grill empty (see the illustration on page 181). Nestle 2 soaked wood chunks or 1 foil packet with chips on top of each pile. Set the cooking grate in place, cover the grill with the lid, and let the grate heat up, about 5 minutes. Use a grill brush to scrape the cooking grate clean. Dip a wad of paper towels in oil; holding the wad with tongs, oil the cooking grate. (The internal grill temperature should register about 375 degrees.)

4. Place the chicken in the center of the grill, breast-side down. Open the grill lid vents halfway and cover, positioning the vents over the chicken. Grill the chicken for 30 minutes. (The internal grill temperature should register about 325 degrees after 30 minutes.)

5. Working quickly, remove the lid and, using two large wads of paper towels, turn the chicken breast-side up. Cover and continue to grill until the thickest part of the breast registers 160 to 165 degrees and the thickest part of the thigh registers 170 to 175 degrees on an instant-read thermometer, 25 to 35 minutes longer.

6. Transfer the chicken to a cutting board and let rest 10 minutes. Carve the chicken (see the illustrations on page 11) and serve.

VARIATIONS

Gas Grill–Roasted Whole Chicken

While grill-roasting, adjust the lit burner as necessary to maintain a temperature of 350 to 375 degrees inside the grill. Use wood chips rather than chunks for this recipe.

Follow the recipe for Charcoal Grill–Roasted Whole Chicken through step 1. In step 2, instead of making foil packets for the wood chips, soak 2 cups wood chips for 30 minutes in cold water to cover and drain. Place the wood chips in a foil tray (see page 183). Place the foil tray on top of the primary burner and position the cooking grate. Turn all the burners to high and heat the grill with the lid down until the wood chips begin to smoke, about 15 minutes. (If the chips ignite, use a water-filled spray bottle to extinguish.) Use a grill brush to scrape the cooking grate clean. Dip a wad of paper towels in oil; holding the wad with tongs, oil the cooking grate. Leave the primary burner on high and turn off all the other burner(s). Place the chicken on the cooler side of the grill, skin-side down. Cover and grill for 35 minutes. Using two large wads of paper towels, turn the chicken breast-side up so that the leg and wing that were facing away from the lit burner are now facing toward it. Close the lid and continue to grill until the thickest part of the breast registers 160 to 165 degrees and the thickest part of the thigh registers 170 to 175 degrees on an instant-read thermometer, 30 to 40 minutes longer. Transfer the chicken to a cutting board and let rest for 10 minutes. Carve the chicken (see the illustrations on page 11) and serve.

Grill-Roasted Whole Chicken with Barbecue Sauce

If you like, you can use the 3 tablespoons of our Pantry Spice Rub (page 202); it goes nicely with our Barbecue Sauce (page 209). Although our classic barbecue sauce is best, this recipe also works with plain store-bought sauce; our favorite brand is Bull's-Eye.

Follow the recipe for Grill-Roasted Whole Chicken (charcoal or gas). After rotating the chicken breast-side up, roast just until an instant-read thermometer inserted into the thickest part of the thigh registers 160 degrees, 15 to 30 minutes longer. Working quickly, brush the outside and inside of the chicken with ½ cup of Barbecue Sauce (page 209). Cover and continue to grill until the thickest part of the breast registers 160 to 165 degrees and the thickest part of the thigh registers 170 to 175 degrees on an instant-read thermometer, 10 to 15 minutes longer. Transfer the chicken to a cutting board and let rest for 10 minutes. Carve the chicken (see the illustrations on page 11) and serve.

Pantry Spice Rub for Chicken

MAKES ABOUT ½ CUP

- 2 tablespoons ground cumin
- 2 tablespoons curry powder
- 2 tablespoons chili powder
- 1 tablespoon ground allspice
- 1 tablespoon ground black pepper
- 1 teaspoon ground cinnamon

Combine all of the ingredients in a small bowl. Use as directed. (The rub can be stored in an airtight container at room temperature for up to 1 month.)

Cajun Spice Rub

MAKES ABOUT ½ CUP

- ¼ cup sweet paprika
- 1 tablespoon kosher salt
- 1 tablespoon garlic powder
- 1½ teaspoons dried thyme
- 1 teaspoon ground celery seeds
- 1 teaspoon ground black pepper
- 1 teaspoon cayenne pepper

Combine all of the ingredients in a small bowl. Use as directed. (The rub can be stored in an airtight container at room temperature for up to 1 month.)

Grill-Roasted Beer Can Chicken

BEER CAN CHICKEN HAS BEEN A REGULAR ON the barbecue cook-off circuit for some time. The bird is rubbed with spices and then an open, partly full beer can is inserted into the main cavity of the chicken. The chicken is grill-roasted as it "sits" on the can, which functions as a vertical roaster. For cooking a whole chicken on the grill, we already knew that grill-roasting was the way to go. The coals are banked on each side of the grill and the chicken is placed in the center. With the heat attacking the chicken from two sides, the bird cooks evenly. (Otherwise, if the bird is cooked over direct heat, the drippings cause unwelcome flare-ups and charred skin.) Adding a can of beer to the mix sounded downright odd, but we were willing to give it a try, since barbecue masters claim it turns out smoky chicken with incredibly moist, tender meat.

First, we started with our fire. As we do with grill-roasting, we arranged the hot coals in piles on opposite sides of the grill. After adding some soaked wood chips to the coals, we had even heat and lots of smoke. We next moved on to the chicken. We found 3½-pound birds to be an ideal size to accommodate a beer can. Larger birds are doable but tricky—they take longer to cook, which is a nuisance, and not everyone has a grill large enough to fit a big bird.

We decided that we wanted the beer to pull triple duty, not only as stand and steamer but also as flavor container. After our first round of tests, we found that, by itself, the beer didn't impart a whole lot of flavor, and we found no discernible difference among various types of beer, whether pricey or cheap. However, a few crumbled bay leaves added to the can did the trick, infusing the meat with potent herbal flavor. For another test, we emptied a soda can and filled it with water (and crumbled bay leaves). Although the difference was not dramatic, the flavor was a bit washed out and less appealing. Evidently, the beer was contributing something to the bird. We then replaced the beer with white wine in one test and lemonade in another. The white wine did nothing for flavor, but tasters were able to detect a lightly sweet lemon flavor in the bird cooked over lemonade, so if you prefer not to cook with beer, lemonade is a good option.

Now that we had the smoke from the grill and the flavorful steam from the can, it was time to spice things up with a spice rub. At the same time, we wanted to figure out how to achieve a crisp skin. We tried oiling the chickens before rubbing on the spices, but these birds ended up flabby and flavorless. We tried patting the chicken dry with paper towels before rubbing on the spices, and this time we rubbed them not just on the skin but under it and inside the chicken cavity as well.

SETTING UP BEER CAN CHICKEN

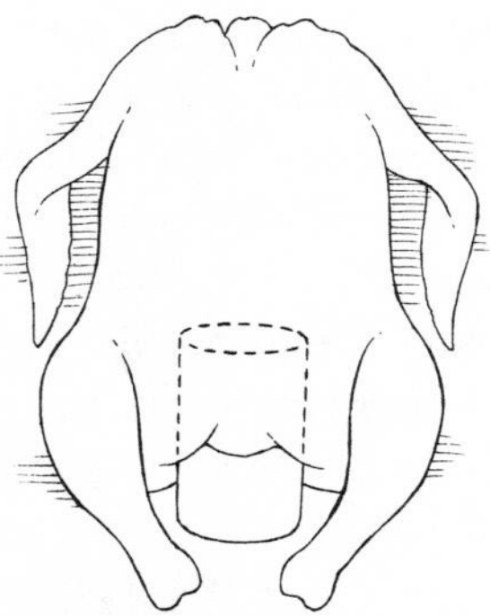

With the legs pointing down, slide the chicken over the open beer can. The two legs and the beer can form a tripod that steadies the chicken on the grill.

This was a big improvement, although the skin was still turning out a bit on the thick side, especially around the thighs.

Hoping to help drain the excess fat, we used a skewer to poke holes all over the skin. This worked perfectly, rendering out the fat in those hard-to-reach places and leaving an extra-crisp skin. An unexpected benefit of this technique was that the skewer captured and deposited small amounts of the rub deep into the meat. In essence, the skewer was injecting the seasonings into the chicken, making for the fullest-flavored, juiciest grill-roasted chicken we'd ever eaten.

Charcoal Grill–Roasted Beer Can Chicken

SERVES 2 TO 3

If you prefer, use lemonade instead of beer; fill an empty 12-ounce soda or beer can with 10 ounces (1¼ cups) lemonade and proceed as directed. You will need a 13 by 9-inch disposable foil roasting pan for this recipe.

- 4 (3-inch) wood chunks or 4 cups wood chips
- 1 (12-ounce) can beer (see note)
- 2 bay leaves
- 3 tablespoons Cajun Spice Rub (page 203)
- 1 (3½- to 4-pound) whole chicken, giblets discarded

1. Soak the wood chunks in cold water to cover for 1 hour and drain. If using wood chips, divide them between 2 aluminum foil packets according to the instructions on page 183.

2. Open the beer can and pour out (or drink) about ¼ cup. With a church key can opener, punch two more large holes in the top of the can (for a total of three holes). Crumble the bay leaves into the beer. Massage the spice rub all over the chicken, inside and out. Gently lift up the skin over the breast and rub the spice rub directly onto the meat (see page 8). Using a skewer, poke the skin all over. Slide the chicken over the beer can so that the drumsticks reach down to the bottom of the can and the chicken stands upright; set aside at room temperature.

3. Meanwhile, light a large chimney starter filled with charcoal (about 6 quarts) and allow to burn until the coals are fully ignited and partially covered with a thin layer of ash, 20 to 25 minutes. Open the bottom vent on the grill. Place a 13 by 9-inch disposable foil roasting pan in the center of the grill. Build a double-banked fire by arranging the coals in two even piles banked on opposite sides of the grill, leaving the middle third of the grill empty (see page 181). Nestle 2 soaked wood chunks or 1 foil packet with chips on top of each pile. Set the cooking grate in place, cover the grill with the lid, and let the grate heat up, about 5 minutes. Use a grill brush to scrape the cooking grate clean. (The internal grill temperature should register about 375 degrees.)

4. Place the chicken (with the can) in the center of the cooking grate, with the wings facing the coals (the ends of the drumsticks will help steady the chicken). Open the grill lid vents halfway and cover. Grill-roast until the thickest part of the breast registers 160 to 165 degrees and the thickest part of the thigh registers 170 to 175 degrees on an instant-read thermometer, 65 to 85 minutes. (The internal grill temperature should register about 325 degrees after 30 minutes.)

5. Using two large wads of paper towels, transfer the chicken to a platter or tray, making sure to keep the can upright; let rest for 15 minutes. With a wad of paper towels, carefully lift the chicken

off the can and onto a cutting board. Discard the remaining beer and can. Carve the chicken (see the illustrations on page 11) and serve.

VARIATION

Gas Grill–Roasted Beer Can Chicken

Be sure not to open the lid of the gas grill too often during cooking; the temperature of the grill will drop significantly each time you do so. Use wood chips rather than chunks for this recipe.

In step 1, instead of making a foil packet for the wood chips, soak 2 cups wood chips for 30 minutes in cold water to cover and drain. Place the wood chips in a foil tray (see page 183). Place the foil tray on top of the primary burner and position the cooking grate. Turn all the burners to high and heat the grill with the lid down until the wood chips begin to smoke, about 15 minutes. (If the chips ignite, use a water-filled spray bottle to extinguish.) Use a grill brush to scrape the cooking grate clean. Leave the primary burner on high and turn off all the other burner(s). Meanwhile, follow the recipe for Charcoal Grill–Roasted Beer Can Chicken through step 2. Place the chicken over the cooler part of the grill with a wing side facing the primary burner. Cover and grill-roast for 35 minutes, adjusting the lit burner as needed to maintain a temperature of 325 to 350 degrees inside the grill. Rotate the chicken so that the drumstick and wing that were facing away from the lit burner are now facing toward it. Cover and continue to grill-roast until the thickest part of the breast registers 160 to 165 degrees and the thickest part of the thigh registers 170 to 175 degrees on an instant-read thermometer, 25 to 40 minutes longer. Proceed as directed from step 5.

American Potato Salad

SERVES 6 TO 8

For best results, do not substitute sweet pickle relish for the minced sweet pickles.

- 3 pounds red potatoes (10 medium), scrubbed and cut into ¾-inch chunks
- ½ cup red wine vinegar
- Salt and pepper
- ¾ cup mayonnaise
- ½ cup minced sweet pickles (see note)
- 1 tablespoon Dijon mustard
- 4 hard-cooked eggs, peeled and chopped coarse (see page 35)
- 2 celery ribs, chopped fine
- 3 tablespoons minced red onion
- 3 tablespoons minced fresh parsley

Place the potatoes in a large pot filled with 4 quarts water, bring to a simmer, and cook until tender, about 10 minutes. Drain the potatoes and transfer to a large bowl. Gently toss the warm potatoes with the vinegar, ½ teaspoon salt, and ½ teaspoon pepper and refrigerate for 20 minutes. Meanwhile, mix the mayonnaise, pickles, and mustard together in a small bowl and set aside. Toss the chilled potatoes with the mayonnaise mixture, eggs, celery, onion, and parsley. Season with salt and pepper to taste.

Grill-Roasted Cornish Game Hens

THESE SINGLE-SERVING BIRDS PROVIDE crisp skin and delicate meat—with no postcooking butchering. But just because they're small doesn't mean that Cornish game hens are easy to grill. Cornish game hens look good on the plate, and since one hen makes a single serving, everyone gets portions of both white and dark meat with little or no butchering. We also find that the meat is more delicate and tender than that of standard chicken. Most home cooks roast these elegant birds, but grilling has the potential to add smoky flavor and deliver really crisp skin.

We started our testing by trying to adapt the test kitchen's method for grilling whole chickens. After the chicken is treated to a short brine—soaking the meat in salted water for an hour—and a spice rub,

BUTTERFLYING AND SKEWERING GAME HENS

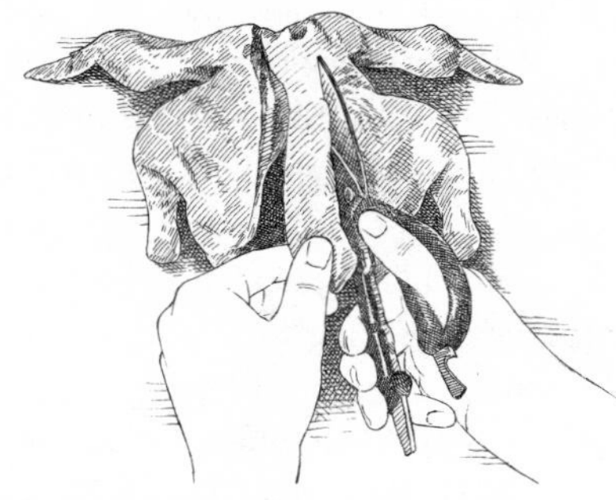

1. Remove the Backbone: Use poultry shears to cut through the bones on either side of the backbone.

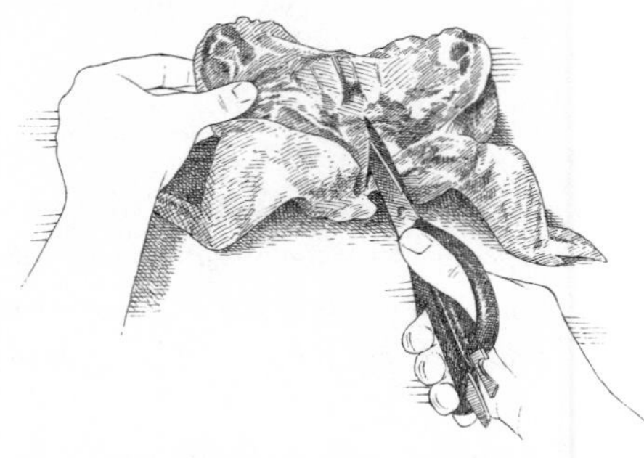

2. Cut the Breastbone: With the skin side down, make a ¼-inch cut into the bone separating the thickest part of the breast halves.

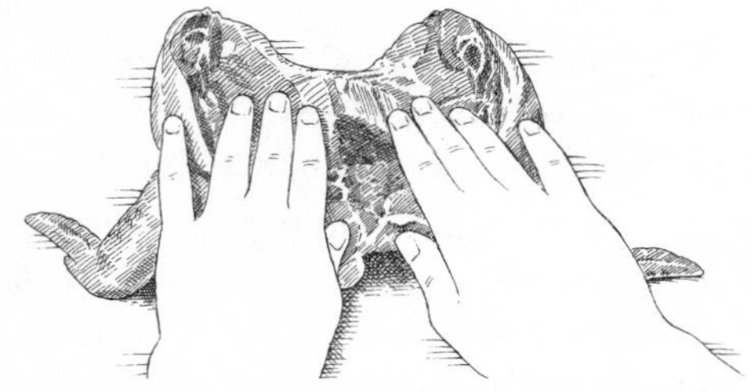

3. Flatten the Bird: Lightly press on the ribs with your fingers to flatten the game hen.

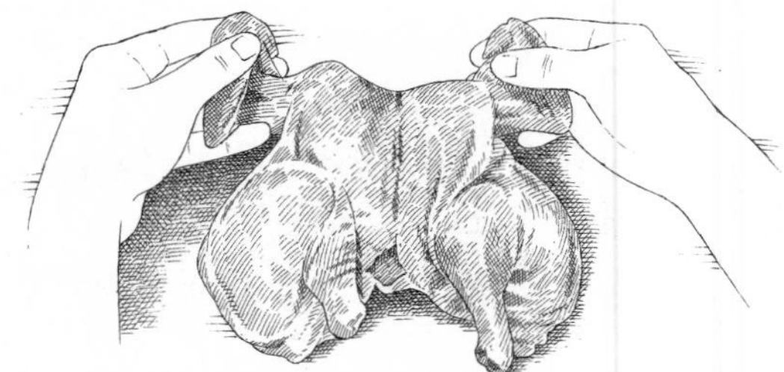

4. Tuck the Wings: With the skin facing up, fold the wingtips behind the bird in order to secure them. Brine the birds.

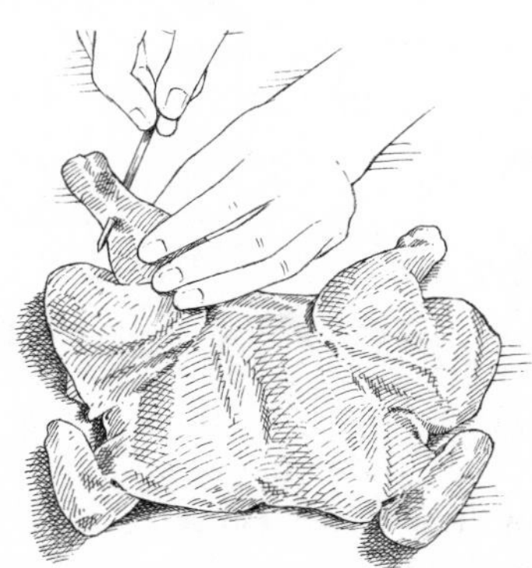

5. Insert the Skewer: Insert the flat metal skewer ½ inch from the end of the drumstick through the skin and meat and out the other side.

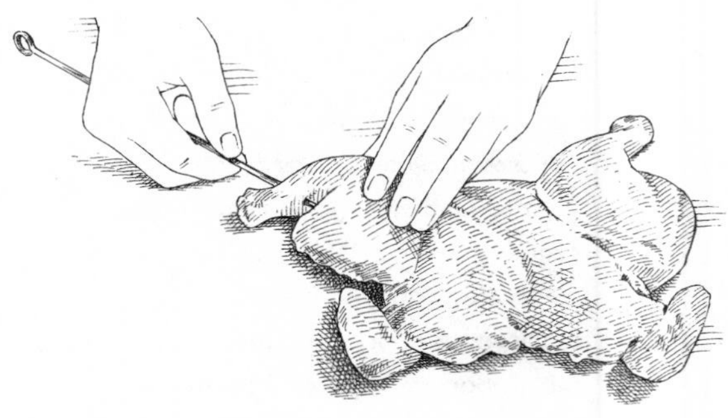

6. Skewer the Thigh: Turn the leg so that the end of the drumstick faces the wing, then insert the tip of the skewer into the meaty section of the thigh under the bone.

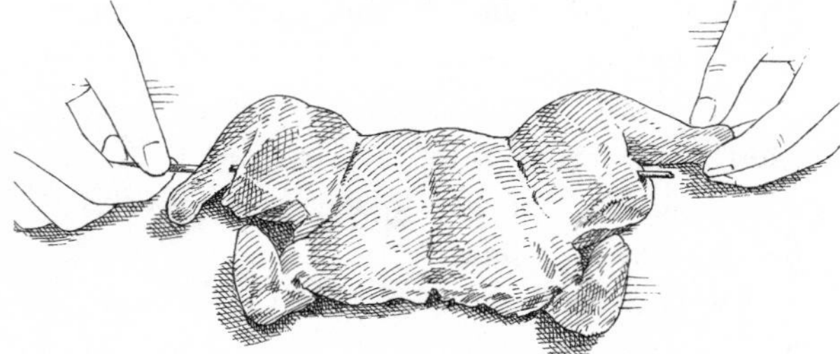

7. Skewer Across: Press the skewer all the way through the breast and second thigh. Fold the end of the drumstick toward the wing and insert the skewer ½ inch from the end.

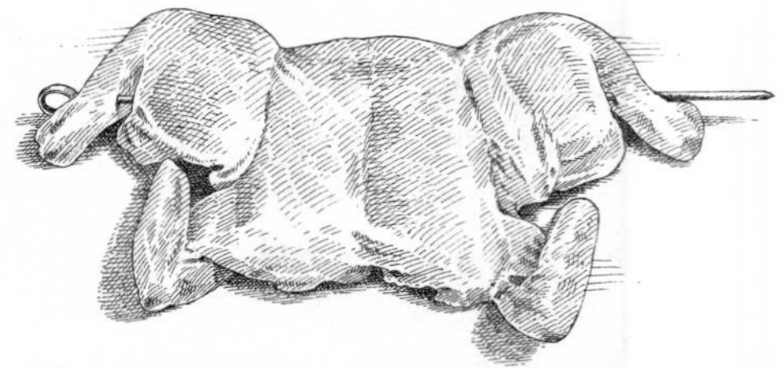

8. Stretch the Skin: Press the skewer so that the blunt end rests against the bird, and stretch the skin tight over the legs, thighs, and breast halves.

it's placed in the middle of a hot grill with coals and soaked wood chunks banked on opposite sides. An hour later, the chickens emerge beautifully bronzed. We thought we could easily translate this method to game hens. Not quite.

Our first modification was to put a drip pan under the hens to catch the rendered fat while also creating defined banks for the coals. This helped create a larger cooking area in the center of the grill, allowing all four hens to fit. Getting crisp skin without overcooking the delicate breast meat was trickier. The closest our initial testing came was spotty patches of browned and flabby skin, mostly between the breast and the thighs. Clearly, this was a hurdle we'd have to clear before worrying about the spice rub and finishing glaze that would give these birds the special treatment they call for.

Whereas grill-roasting larger birds for an hour produces a mahogany skin and a perfect interior, keeping the game hens on the grill for that length of time made for bone-dry meat. Many recipes for grilled game hens call for removing the backbone (this process is called butterflying). This would put all of the skin on one side, which could face the coals and thus crisp more quickly. Butterflying also makes each bird a uniform thickness, which promotes even cooking. We used a pair of scissors to remove the delicate backbone and to cut the bone dividing the breast halves.

Although these splayed-open birds browned evenly and cooked uniformly, presentation was a whole other matter. As a result of turning backbone-less birds, the legs flipped over the breast, and the scant piece of skin holding the breast to the thighs tore. Securing the legs to the body seemed like our best option. We used metal skewers to poke and stick a dozen hens into various contortionist positions before we landed on a method that worked. This kebab-like presentation also made it easier to fit the birds on the grates.

In flavor, texture, and appearance, tasters agreed that these Cornish game hens were finally in a class by themselves. But we still thought they could benefit from a last blast of intense heat to make the skin crispier. To avoid charred birds, we found it best to sear them last, not first, as is traditionally the case with grilled meats. Grill-roasting the birds with the lid down to an internal temperature of 160 to 165 degrees before finishing them over the now-cooler coals resulted in crisp skin—and just the right amount of browning.

All we had left to do was build upon the grilled, smoky flavor via a rub and a glaze. After trying rubs with up to 20 ingredients, we settled on a seven-part version that gave the hens a sweet and savory complexity. The rub helped crisp the skin even further, giving it a gorgeous mahogany hue. Finishing the birds with a quick glaze of ketchup, brown sugar, and soy sauce provided the crowning touch to such a handsome presentation.

Charcoal Grill–Roasted Cornish Game Hens

SERVES 4

If your supermarket just has hens that weigh 1½ to 2 pounds, buy 3 instead of 4, brine them for an extra 15 minutes, and extend the cooking time in step 5 by 10 to 15 minutes. Thaw frozen game hens in the refrigerator for 36 to 48 hours before brining. You can substitute your favorite barbecue sauce for the glaze or use the Asian Barbecue Glaze (recipe follows). You will need a 16 by 12-inch disposable aluminum roasting pan for this recipe. If using kosher birds, skip the brining process. To use kosher salt in the brine, see page 12 for conversion information and more tips on brining. For more information on setting up a grill, see page 180.

HENS AND BRINE

- **1 cup table salt**
- **4 Cornish game hens (1¼ to 1½ pounds each), butterflied (see the illustrations on page 206; see note)**
- **2 tablespoons brown sugar**
- **1 tablespoon paprika**
- **2 teaspoons garlic powder**
- **2 teaspoons chili powder**
- **1 teaspoon ground black pepper**
- **1 teaspoon ground coriander**
- **⅛ teaspoon cayenne pepper**
- **2 (3-inch) wood chunks or 2 cups wood chips (optional)**

BARBECUE GLAZE

- ½ cup ketchup
- 2 tablespoons brown sugar
- 1 tablespoon soy sauce
- 1 tablespoon white vinegar
- 1 tablespoon prepared yellow mustard
- 1 medium garlic clove, minced or pressed through a garlic press (about 1 teaspoon)

1. FOR THE HENS AND BRINE: Dissolve the salt in 4 quarts cold water in a large container. Submerge the hens in the brine, cover, and refrigerate for 1 hour. Combine the brown sugar and spices in a small bowl and set aside. Soak the wood chunks (if using) in cold water to cover for 1 hour and drain. If using wood chips, divide them between 2 aluminum foil packets according to the instructions on page 183.

2. Remove the chicken from the brine, rinse well, and pat dry with paper towels. Following the illustrations on page 206, use a 10 to 12-inch flat metal skewer to secure each hen. Rub each hen evenly with the spice mixture and then refrigerate them while preparing the grill.

3. FOR THE GLAZE: Cook all the ingredients in a small saucepan over medium heat, stirring occasionally, until thickened and slightly reduced, about 5 minutes.

4. Meanwhile, light a large chimney starter filled with charcoal (about 6 quarts) and allow to burn until the coals are fully ignited and partially covered with a thin layer of ash, 20 to 25 minutes. Open the bottom vent on the grill. Build a double-banked fire by arranging a 16 by 12-inch disposable foil roasting pan in the center of the grill, with the coals evenly divided and banked on opposite sides (see the illustration on page 181). Nestle 1 soaked wood chunk or 1 foil packet with chips on top of each pile. Set the cooking grate in place, cover the grill with the lid, and let the grate heat up, about 5 minutes. Use a grill brush to scrape the cooking grate clean. Dip a wad of paper towels in oil; holding the wad with tongs, oil the cooking grate.

5. Place the hens on the center of the grill over the aluminum pan, skin-side down. Open the grill lid vents completely and cover, positioning the vents over the hens. Grill the hens until the skin has started to turn golden brown and the thickest part of the thigh registers 160 to 165 degrees on an instant-read thermometer, 20 to 30 minutes.

6. Flip the hens and move them out over the hot coals (2 hens per side). Cover and continue to grill until browned, about 5 minutes. Brush the hens with half of the glaze, then flip and grill for 2 minutes. Brush the remaining glaze over the hens; flip and continue to grill until the thickest part of the breast registers 160 to 165 degrees and the thickest part of the thigh registers 170 to 175 degrees on an instant-read thermometer, 1 to 3 minutes longer.

7. Transfer the hens to a cutting board and let rest for 10 minutes. Remove the skewers, cut the hens in half through the breastbone, and serve.

VARIATION

Gas Grill–Roasted Cornish Game Hens

Use wood chips rather than chunks for this recipe.

1. Follow the recipe for Charcoal Grill–Roasted Cornish Game Hens through step 3. In step 1, instead of making a foil packet for the wood chips (if using), soak 2 cups wood chips for 30 minutes in cold water to cover and drain. Place the wood chips in a foil tray (see page 183). Place the foil tray on top of the primary burner and position the cooking grate. Turn all the burners to high and heat the grill with the lid down until the chips begin to smoke, about 15 minutes. (If the chips ignite, use a water-filled spray bottle to extinguish.) Use a grill brush to scrape the grate clean. Dip a wad of paper towels in oil; holding the wad with tongs, oil the cooking grate. Turn all of the burners to medium.

2. Place the hens on the grill, skin-side down, cover, and grill until the skin is deeply browned and shows grill marks, 10 to 15 minutes. (If you have hot spots, you might have to move the hens on the grill.) Flip the hens; cover and continue to grill until the thickest part of thigh registers 160 to 165 degrees on an instant-read thermometer, 10 to 15 minutes more.

3. Brush the hens with half of the glaze. Flip the hens and cook until the glaze is thick and the hens

are deep brown, 2 to 3 minutes. Brush the bone side of the hens with the remaining glaze and flip. Cook the second side until deeply browned and the thickest part of the breast registers 160 to 165 degrees and the thickest part of the thigh registers 170 to 175 degrees on an instant-read thermometer, 2 to 3 minutes more.

4. Transfer the hens to a cutting board and let rest for 10 minutes. Remove the skewers, cut the hens in half through the backbone, and serve.

Asian Barbecue Glaze

MAKES ABOUT ½ CUP

If you like, replace the Barbecue Glaze in the recipe with this variation while using the same spice mixture.

- ¼ cup ketchup
- ¼ cup hoisin sauce
- 2 tablespoons rice wine vinegar
- 1 tablespoon soy sauce
- 1 tablespoon toasted sesame oil
- 1 tablespoon minced or grated fresh ginger

Cook all the ingredients in a small saucepan over medium heat, stirring occasionally, until thickened and reduced, about 5 minutes; set aside.

Salsas, Relishes, and Sauces

THE CONDIMENT-LIKE SALSAS, RELISHES, AND sauces in this section can be served at the table with many of our grilled chicken recipes. Most are made with raw ingredients; the rest are lightly cooked. Almost all of them can be made in advance, refrigerated for several days, and then brought to room temperature before serving.

The terms "salsa" and "relish" can be used interchangeably, although salsas are usually made with Latin ingredients or flavors.

Barbecue Sauce

MAKES 3 CUPS

Brush this sauce onto chicken parts during the final stages of grilling and serve extra at the table. For more heat, add additional hot sauce to taste. This sauce is used for our Classic Barbecued Chicken (page 184), but would also be great with Chicken Wings (page 176).

- 2 medium onions, peeled and quartered
- ½ cup water
- 2 cups ketchup
- ½ cup plus 2 tablespoons light or dark molasses
- ¼ cup cider vinegar
- ¼ cup Worcestershire sauce
- ¼ cup Dijon mustard
- 1 tablespoon liquid smoke (optional)
- 1 teaspoon hot sauce (see note)
- ½ teaspoon ground black pepper
- ¼ cup vegetable oil
- 2 medium garlic cloves, minced or pressed through a garlic press (about 2 teaspoons)
- 1 teaspoon chili powder

1. Process the onions and water in a food processor until pureed and the mixture resembles slush, about 30 seconds. Strain the mixture through a fine-mesh strainer into a liquid measuring cup, pressing on the solids with a rubber spatula to obtain ½ cup juice. Discard the solids.

2. Whisk the onion juice, ketchup, molasses, vinegar, Worcestershire, mustard, liquid smoke (if using), hot sauce, and black pepper together in a medium bowl.

3. Heat the oil in a large saucepan over medium heat until shimmering. Add the garlic and chili powder and cook until fragrant, about 30 seconds. Whisk in the ketchup mixture and bring to a boil. Reduce the heat to medium-low and simmer until the flavors meld and the sauce is thickened, about 25 minutes. (The sauce can be refrigerated in an airtight container for up to 1 week.)

Red Pepper–Jícama Relish

MAKES ABOUT 3½ CUPS

This crunchy, refreshing, slawlike relish is mildly sweet, making it a nice foil for spicy foods. Serve with Southwestern Chicken Kebabs (page 175) or in place of the Grilled Banana Salsa for Jamaican Jerk Chicken (page 196).

- 3 tablespoons vegetable oil
- 1½ tablespoons juice from 1 lime
- 2 teaspoons honey
- ¼ teaspoon ground cumin
- ¼ teaspoon chili powder
- Salt and ground black pepper
- 1 red bell pepper, stemmed, seeded, and cut into thin strips
- ½ small jícama (8 ounces), tough outer skin removed, cut into matchsticks (see the illustrations below)
- 1 medium Granny Smith apple, cored, quartered, and cut into ¼-inch dice
- 2 scallions, sliced thin

1. Whisk together the oil, lime juice, honey, cumin, chili powder, ¼ teaspoon salt, and ⅛ teaspoon pepper to taste in a large bowl.

2. Add the red pepper, jícama, apple, and scallions to the dressing and toss to coat. Season with salt and pepper to taste. Serve. (The relish can be refrigerated in an airtight container for up to 4 hours.)

Guacamole

MAKES 2½ TO 3 CUPS

Very ripe Hass avocados are key to this recipe. For more heat, include the jalapeño ribs and seeds when mincing. To minimize the risk of discoloration, prepare the minced ingredients first so that they are ready to mix with the avocados as soon as they are cut. Like our Tomato Salsa (page 211), our guacamole makes a great accompaniment to a variety of dishes such as Chicken Fajitas (page 169).

- 3 ripe Hass avocados, peeled, pitted, and cut into ½-inch cubes
- Salt
- 2 tablespoons minced red onion
- ¼ cup minced fresh cilantro leaves
- 2 tablespoons juice from 1 lime
- 1 small jalapeño chile, seeds and ribs removed, chile minced (see note)
- 1 medium garlic clove, minced or pressed through a garlic press (about 1 teaspoon)

Using a fork, mash two of the avocados and ¼ teaspoon salt to a relatively smooth puree in a medium bowl. Fold in the remaining diced avocado and all of the remaining ingredients. Season with salt to taste and serve. (The guacamole can be covered with plastic wrap pressed directly onto the surface of the mixture and refrigerated for up to 1 day; bring to room temperature before serving.)

PREPARING JÍCAMA

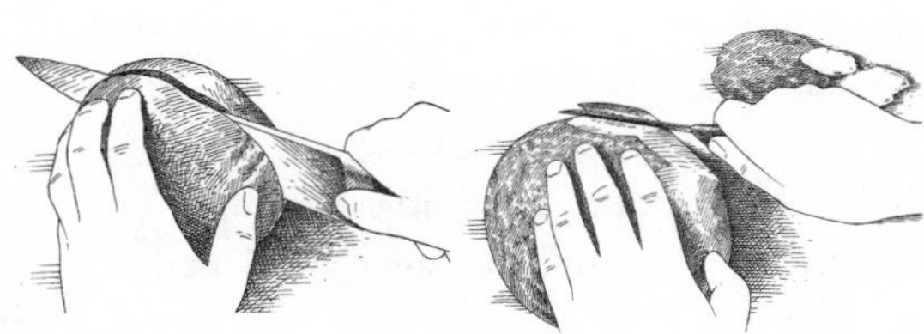

1. Slice the jícama in half through the equator.

2. Use a paring knife to peel the brown outer skin.

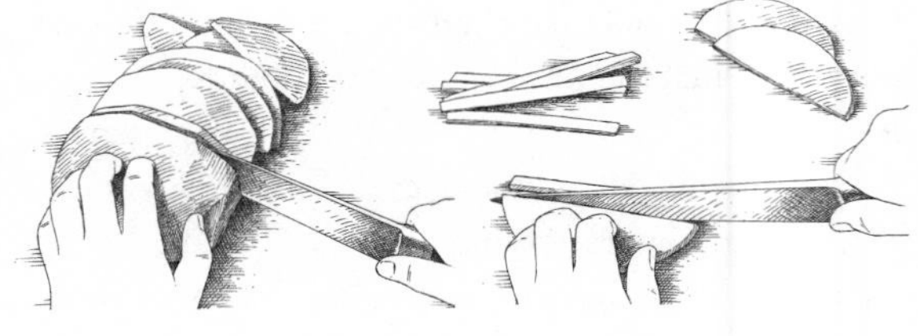

3. Place each half flat-side down on a cutting board and slice into half circles ⅛ inch thick.

4. Stack the half circles and slice lengthwise into matchsticks.

Tomato Salsa

MAKES ABOUT 3 CUPS

For more heat, include the jalapeño ribs and seeds when mincing. The amount of sugar and lime juice to use depends on the ripeness of the tomatoes. The salsa can be made 2 to 3 hours in advance, but hold off adding the salt, lime juice, and sugar until just before serving. The salsa is a nice accompaniment to Chicken Enchiladas (page 290), Chicken Tacos (page 315), Chicken Fajitas (page 169), and simple grilled chicken.

- 1½ pounds firm, ripe tomatoes, cut into ⅜-inch dice (about 3 cups)
- 1 large jalapeño chile, seeds and ribs removed, chile minced (see note)
- ½ medium red onion, minced (about ½ cup)
- 1 small garlic clove, minced or pressed through a garlic press (about ½ teaspoon)
- ¼ cup minced fresh cilantro leaves
- ½ teaspoon salt
- Pinch ground black pepper
- 2–6 teaspoons juice from 1 lime
- Sugar

1. Set a large colander in a large bowl. Place the tomatoes in the colander and let them drain for 30 minutes. As the tomatoes drain, layer the jalapeño, onion, garlic, and cilantro on top. Shake the colander to drain off the excess tomato juice; discard the juice and wipe out the bowl.

2. Transfer the contents of the colander to the now-empty bowl. Add the salt, pepper, and 2 teaspoons of the lime juice and toss to combine. Season with sugar and additional lime juice to taste. Serve.

Salsa Verde

MAKES ABOUT ¾ CUP

A slice of sandwich bread pureed into the sauce keeps the flavors balanced and gives the sauce body. Toasting the bread rids it of excess moisture that might otherwise make for a gummy sauce. This sauce is best served immediately after it is made. It makes a nice accompaniment to Grilled Chicken Breasts (page 166) or Grill-Roasted Whole Chicken (page 201).

- 1 slice high-quality white sandwich bread
- ½ cup extra-virgin olive oil
- 2 tablespoons juice from 1 lemon
- 2 cups lightly packed fresh parsley leaves
- 2 medium anchovy fillets
- 2 tablespoons drained capers
- 1 small garlic clove, minced or pressed through a garlic press (about ½ teaspoon)
- ⅛ teaspoon salt

1. Toast the bread in a toaster at the lowest setting until the surface is dry but not browned, about 15 seconds. Remove the crust and cut the bread into rough ½-inch pieces (you should have about ½ cup).

2. Process the bread pieces, oil, and lemon juice in a food processor until smooth, about 10 seconds. Add the parsley, anchovies, capers, garlic, and salt. Pulse until the mixture is finely chopped (the mixture should not be smooth), about five 1-second pulses, scraping down the bowl with a rubber spatula after 3 pulses. Transfer the mixture to a small bowl and serve.

CUTTING TOMATOES FOR SALSA

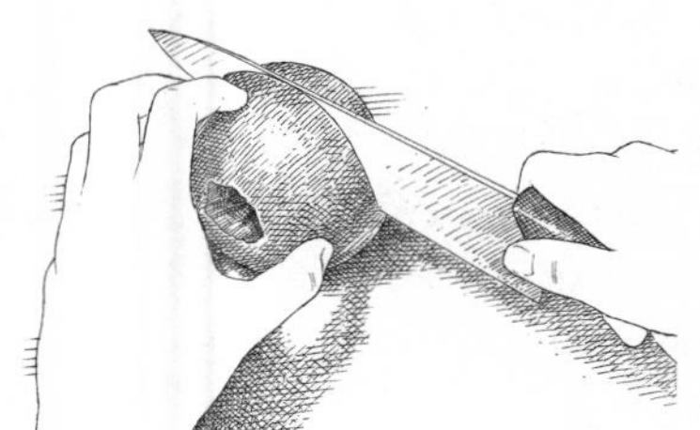

1. Cut each cored tomato in half through the equator.

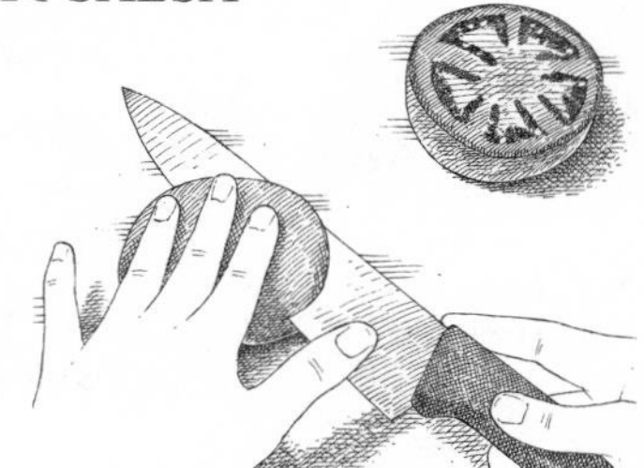

2. Cut each half into ⅜-inch-thick slices.

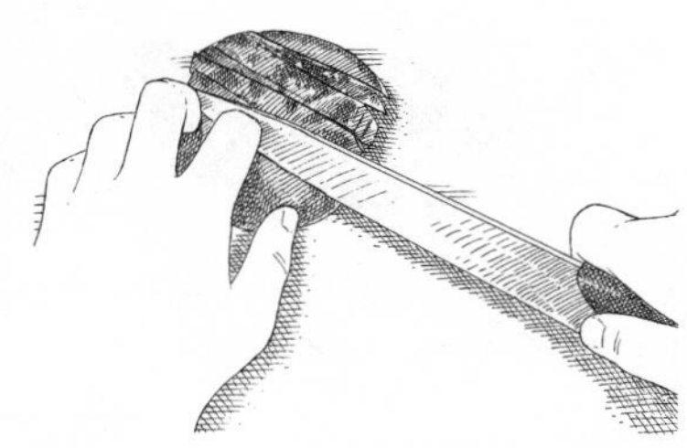

3. Stack two slices; cut them into ⅜-inch strips and then into ⅜-inch dice.

PEELING A MANGO

Because of their odd shape and slippery texture, mangoes are notoriously difficult to peel. Here's how we handle this task.

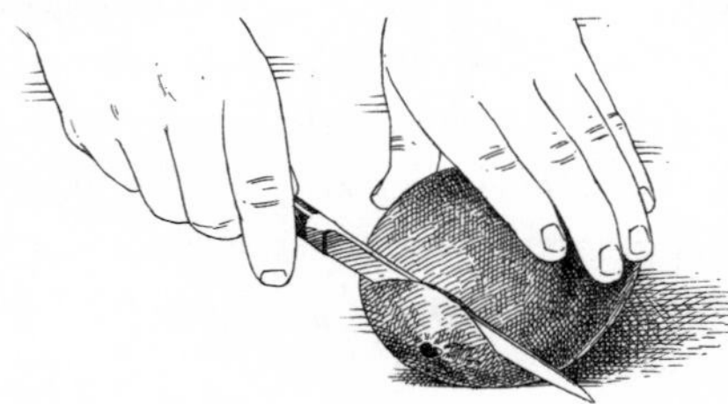

1. Remove a thin slice from one end of the mango so that it sits flat on a work surface.

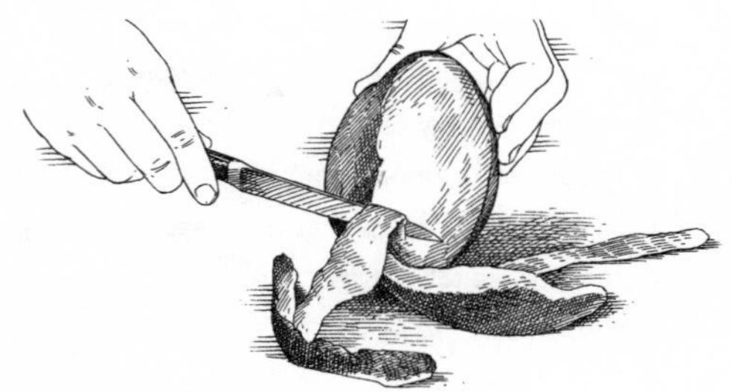

2. Hold the mango cut-side down and remove the skin in thin strips using a sharp paring knife, working from top to bottom.

3. Cut down along the side of the flat pit to remove the flesh from one side of the mango. Do the same on the other side of the pit.

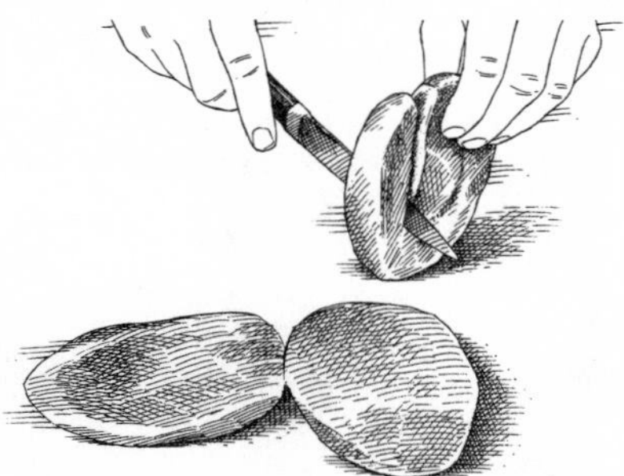

4. Trim around the pit to remove any remaining flesh. The mango flesh can now be chopped or sliced as desired.

Black Bean and Mango Salsa

MAKES ABOUT 2½ CUPS

This Caribbean-inspired mixture is great with grilled chicken. For more heat, add the jalapeño ribs and seeds when mincing. Serve with Chicken Fajitas (page 169), Caribbean Chicken Kebabs (page 173), or Chipotle-Lime Chicken Breasts (page 167).

- 1 medium mango, peeled, pitted, and cut into ¼-inch dice (see the illustrations at left)
- ½ cup cooked black beans
- ¼ red bell pepper, stemmed, seeded, and chopped small
- ¼ green bell pepper, stemmed, seeded, and chopped small
- ¼ medium red onion, chopped small
- 6 tablespoons pineapple juice
- ¼ cup juice from 2 limes
- ¼ cup minced fresh cilantro leaves
- 1 tablespoon ground cumin
- ½ jalapeño chile, seeds and ribs removed, chile minced (see note)
- Salt and ground black pepper

Mix all of the ingredients, including salt and pepper to taste, together in a medium bowl. Transfer to an airtight container and refrigerate to blend the flavors for at least 1 hour and up to 4 days.

Yogurt-Mint Cucumber Sauce

SERVES 4

Known as raita, this creamy salad is traditionally served as a cooling contrast to curry dishes. It is a natural pairing with our Curry Chicken Kebabs (page 174), Tandoori Chicken (page 193), or Chicken Biryani (page 376).

- 3 medium cucumbers, peeled, seeded, sliced, salted, and drained (see the illustrations on page 213)
- 1 cup plain low-fat yogurt
- ¼ cup minced fresh mint leaves
- 2 tablespoons extra-virgin olive oil

- 1 medium garlic clove, minced or pressed through a garlic press (about 1 teaspoon)
- Salt and ground black pepper

Let the salted cucumbers drain, weighted, in a colander for at least 1 hour and up to 3 hours. Whisk together the yogurt, mint, oil, garlic, ¼ teaspoon salt, and ⅛ teaspoon pepper in a medium bowl. Add the drained cucumbers and toss to coat. Transfer to an airtight container and refrigerate for at least 1 hour and up to 2 days. Season with salt and pepper to taste before serving.

PREPARING THE CUCUMBERS

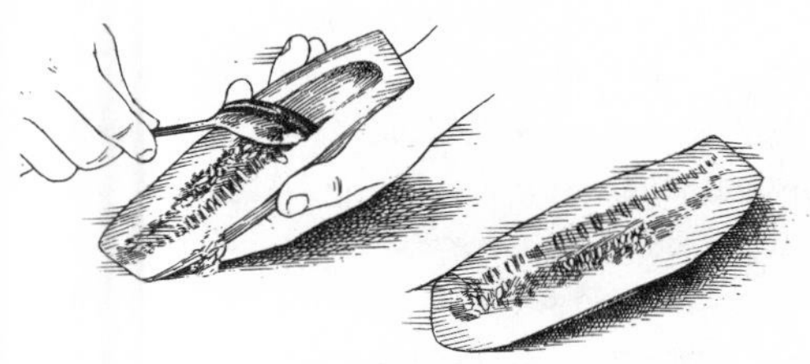

1. Peel and halve each cucumber lengthwise. Use a small spoon to remove the seeds and surrounding liquid from each cucumber half.

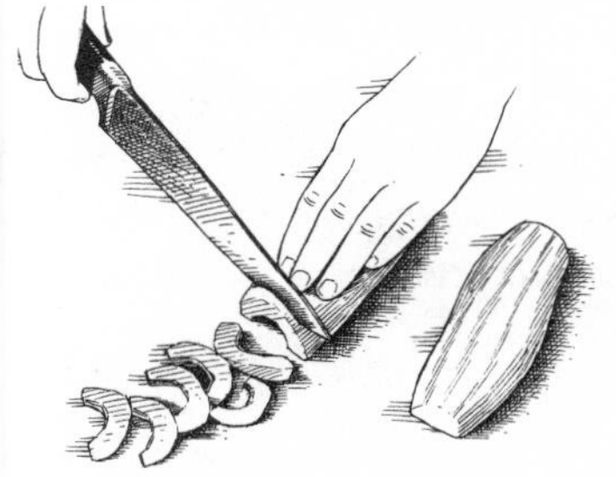

2. Lay the cucumber halves flat-side down on a work surface and slice them on the diagonal into ¼-inch-thick pieces. Toss the cucumbers and salt (1 teaspoon for each cucumber) in a colander set in a bowl.

3. Place a gallon-size zipper-lock plastic bag filled with water on top of the cucumbers to weigh them down and force out the liquid. Drain for at least 1 hour and up to 3 hours.

Classic Basil Pesto

MAKES ABOUT ¾ CUP

Pounding the basil releases its flavorful oils into the pesto more readily. Basil often darkens in pesto, but you can boost the color by adding the parsley. Pesto is great to have on hand and is terrific on grilled chicken.

- ¼ cup pine nuts, walnuts, or almonds
- 3 medium cloves garlic, unpeeled
- 2 cups packed fresh basil leaves
- 2 tablespoons packed fresh parsley leaves (optional; see note)
- 7 tablespoons extra-virgin olive oil
- Salt
- ¼ cup finely grated Parmesan or Pecorino Romano cheese
- Ground black pepper

1. Toast the nuts in a small, heavy skillet over medium heat, stirring frequently, until just golden and fragrant, about 5 minutes; set aside. Add the garlic to the empty skillet and toast over medium heat, shaking the pan occasionally, until fragrant and the color of the cloves deepens slightly, about 7 minutes. Let the garlic cool slightly, then peel and chop coarsely.

2. Place the basil and parsley (if using) in a heavy-duty 1-gallon zipper-lock plastic bag. Pound the bag with the flat side of a meat pounder or rolling pin until all the leaves are bruised.

3. Process the nuts, garlic, herbs, oil, and ½ teaspoon salt in a food processor until smooth, stopping as necessary to scrape down the sides of the bowl, about 1 minute. Stir in the Parmesan and season with salt and pepper to taste. (The pesto can be refrigerated in an airtight container for up to 4 days.)

BRUISING BASIL

Place the basil leaves in a zipper-lock plastic bag and bruise with a meat pounder or rolling pin.

INGREDIENTS: High-End Extra-Virgin Olive Oils

In 2001, we tasted inexpensive supermarket oils and proclaimed DaVinci ($12.99 per liter) our favorite. In subsequent tastings, DaVinci has continued its dominance over other mass-market brands. But what if price isn't your first consideration? Does more money buy better olive oil?

When Americans want extra-virgin olive oil, we generally buy Italian. But a growing number of extra-virgin olive oils from other countries now fill store shelves, including more offerings from Spain, the top olive-growing nation, and Greece. There are even oils from California. Gathering 10 best-selling boutique extra-virgin olive oils from a variety of countries, priced at $20 to $56 per liter, we stripped them of their stylish labels and put them through the rigors of a blind tasting.

Sipped straight up from little cups, the extra-virgin olive oils in our lineup offered a pleasingly wide range of flavors, from fruity and "olive-y" to mild, buttery, and mellow to powerfully green, grassy, and pungent. Why does olive oil have such a wide-ranging flavor profile? Experts agree that the type of olive, the time of harvest (earlier means greener, more bitter, and pungent; later, more mild and buttery), and the processing are the biggest factors. As one expert pointed out, olive oil is really just olive juice, and the quickest, gentlest extraction yields the truest flavors. The best-quality oil comes from olives picked at their peak and processed as quickly as possible without heat (which can coax more oil from the olives but at the expense of flavor).

The big loser in our tasting was DaVinci, our favorite inexpensive oil, which finished dead last. Although disappointed, we weren't really surprised. This oil may be better than the other inexpensive options, but it couldn't compete with high-end products. At least when it comes to olive oil, high prices buy more than just pretty bottles.

We were surprised, however, that tasters were not impressed with the high-end Italian oils, which finished in fifth through eighth place. Our two top finishers came from Spain, the third from Greece. We needed to explain these unexpected findings.

As we tallied our tasting results, we realized that our two favorite oils—both praised by tasters for their fairly assertive yet well-balanced flavor—were made with a blend of olives. The Columela and Núñez de Prado oils are a mix of intense Picual and mild Hojiblanca olives (the Núñez also adds delicate-flavored Picudo olives), creating a "fruity" olive oil with no elements that were perceived as too strong-tasting—or too mild. By contrast, the other two Spanish oils we tasted, L'Estornell and Pons, were made with only the mild-mannered Arbequina olive, and they rated much less favorably.

Darrell Corti, owner of the Corti Brothers store in Sacramento, California, and chairman of olive-oil judging at the Los Angeles County Fair (the top domestic and international olive-oil competition in the United States), told us that producers often blend extra-virgin oils from olives with distinct flavors to create the overall flavor profile they want. According to Corti, the best oil is often made from a blend of varietals; the blend may consist of several oils, each one made from a single varietal (known as monocultivar, or single-olive, oils), or from a "field blend," in which different types of olives are picked and then processed together to create a single oil.

Was blending the answer we sought? Maybe not. Ranking nearly as high as the top Spaniards was a Greek oil, Terra Medi, made only with Koroneiki olives. It is not a blend, yet its balanced character and fruity, rounded flavor, with no harsh notes, made it similar in profile to the two top oils. Additionally, while some of the so-so Italian oils were made from single varietals, others were blends. So blending alone doesn't guarantee great oil.

The choice of olives is one factor that makes a particular oil more or less appealing. With their characteristic green, intense olive flavor and peppery aftertaste, the Italian oils had a few vocal supporters, but the majority of tasters felt that the oils' harsh pungency overwhelmed the olive flavor.

In the end, balance turned out to be the key factor that determined the winners of our tasting, and we found it in Spanish oils, not Italian oils. Our tasters preferred oils of medium-fruity intensity. Italian oils generally fall into the high-intensity category.

For everyday use (particularly for recipes where olive oil is heated or must compete with strong flavors), we'll stick with DaVinci, but for drizzling over foods just before serving, the test kitchen is ready for an oil change. The top-ranked Columela is our new test-kitchen favorite when we want an extra-virgin olive oil with high-end flavor, but don't want to break the bank to pay for it.

THE BEST EXTRA-VIRGIN OLIVE OIL

A blend of intense Picual and mild Hojiblanca olives, Columela Extra-Virgin Olive Oil took top honors for its fruity flavor and excellent balance.

COLUMELA

CLASSIC COBB SALAD **PAGE 36**

WHITE CHICKEN CHILI **PAGE 64**

WARM ROAST CHICKEN AND BREAD SALAD WITH ARUGULA **PAGE 340**

CHICKEN AREPAS WITH AVOCADO AND CILANTRO **PAGE 399**

CHICKEN ENCHILADAS **PAGE 290**

STIR-FRIED CHICKEN, GREEN BEANS, AND SHIITAKES WITH TERIYAKI SAUCE **PAGE 239**

BREADED STUFFED CHICKEN BREASTS WITH GOAT CHEESE AND THYME FILLING **PAGE 371**

CHARCOAL-GRILLED CHICKEN FAJITAS **PAGE 169**

CHARCOAL-GRILLED JAMAICAN JERK CHICKEN **PAGE 196**

COQ AU VIN **PAGE 357**

ORANGE-HONEY GLAZED CHICKEN BREASTS **PAGE 98**

LATINO-STYLE CHICKEN AND RICE **PAGE 285**

PAN-ROASTED CHICKEN BREASTS WITH POTATOES **PAGE 307**

SAUTÉED CHICKEN WITH CHERRY TOMATOES, OLIVES, FETA, AND MINT **PAGE 305**

ROAST CHICKEN WITH ROOT VEGETABLES **PAGE 127**

KORE AN FRIED CHICKEN **PAGE 157**

8
STIR-FRIES

Stir-Fries

Chicken Stir-Fries

A CHICKEN STIR-FRY SHOULD BE THE ULTIMATE quick and easy weeknight meal—the meat and vegetables are quickly cooked over high heat, tossed together with a flavorful sauce, and served over rice. But cooking the chicken just right isn't always so easy—with its relatively small amount of fat, chicken inevitably becomes dry and stringy when cooked over high heat. Perfection in a chicken stir-fry, then, requires split-second timing to avoid chicken that's either dry all the way through or cooked perfectly on the outside while still raw on the inside. We were after a stir-fry that featured tender, juicy, bite-sized pieces of chicken paired with just the right combination of vegetables in a simple-to-prepare yet complex-flavored sauce.

Our first decision was to use boneless, skinless breasts for ease of preparation and because white meat cooks more quickly than dark. In addition, tasters found dark meat to be chewy when stir-fried, with bits of connective tissue and fat still attached. But chicken breasts do have a downside: They are notoriously bland and very easy to overcook.

In the past, we've used a marinade to impart flavor to meat destined for stir-fries, and chicken is no exception. Tossing the pieces of chicken in a simple soy sauce–rice wine mixture for 10 minutes before cooking added much-needed flavor, but did nothing to improve the texture.

The obvious solution to dry chicken was brining, our favorite method for keeping poultry moist. But a half hour or more of brining time followed by 10 minutes of marinating was out of the question; this was supposed to be a quick midweek stir-fry. It seemed redundant to soak the chicken first in one salty solution (brine) and then another (marinade), so we decided to combine the two, using the soy sauce to provide the high salt level in the brine. This turned out to be a key secret to great chicken stir-fry. Now we were turning out highly flavored, juicy pieces of chicken—most of the time. (Given the finicky nature of high-heat cooking, some batches of chicken still occasionally turned out tough because of overcooking.)

Looking for ways to further protect the chicken and keep it from drying out, we turned to a traditional Chinese technique called velveting, which involves coating chicken pieces in a thin cornstarch and egg white or oil mixture, then parcooking in moderately heated oil. The coating forms a barrier around the chicken that keeps precious moisture inside; that extra juiciness makes the chicken seem more tender. Cornstarch mixed with egg white yielded a cakey coating; tasters preferred the more subtle coating provided by cornstarch mixed with oil. This velveted chicken was supple, but it was also pale, and, again, this method seemed far too involved for a quick weeknight dinner.

We wondered if the same method—coating in a cornstarch mixture—would still work if we eliminated the parcooking step. It did. This chicken was not only juicy and tender, but it also developed an attractive golden brown coating. Best of all, the entire process took less than five minutes. The only problem was that the coating, which was more of an invisible barrier than a crust, became soggy and slimy when cooked in the sauce.

Our science editor explained that the cornstarch was absorbing liquid from the sauce, which resulted in the slippery finish. We cut the cornstarch with flour, which created a negligible coating—not too thick, not too slimy—that also managed to seal in the chicken juices. Substituting sesame oil for peanut oil added a welcome depth of flavor.

After trying everything from pounding to cubing the chicken, tasters liked simple, thin slices best. We found the breasts were easiest to cut after freezing them for 15 minutes. These wide, flat slices of chicken browned easily; we cooked them in two batches, first browning one side without stirring, and then stirring them once to quickly brown the second side, rather than constantly stirring, as many recipes suggest. Although choosing not to "stir-fry" seemed counterintuitive, we found that the constant motion of that method detracted from the browning of the chicken.

After the chicken was cooked, we removed it from the pan and added the vegetables in batches. By adding just a small volume of food at a time, the intense heat in the pan is maintained. Slow-cooking vegetables such as onions and mushrooms go into the pan first, followed by quicker-cooking items such as celery and snow peas. Leafy greens and herbs go in last.

To cook vegetables that won't soften even after several minutes of stir-frying, we steamed them by adding a bit of water to the pan and covering it. This method works especially well with broccoli and green beans. Once the vegetables are crisp-tender, the cover comes off so that excess water can evaporate. We found the combinations and variations of vegetables to be limitless, from broccoli and red bell pepper to green beans and shiitake mushrooms, and even to kimchi and bean sprouts, one of our more exotic pairings. Once you become comfortable with the techniques of stir-frying and learn how long each vegetable takes to cook, you can mix and match most any vegetables to your liking.

Most stir-fry recipes add the aromatics (typically garlic, ginger, and scallions) at the outset of the cooking process, when the pan is empty. But by the time the stir-fry is done, the aromatics that have been added to the empty pan have burned and become harsh-tasting. In our testing, we found it best to cook the aromatics after the vegetables. When the vegetables are done, we push them to the sides of the pan, add the aromatics mixed with some oil to the center, and cook until the aromatics are fragrant but not colored, about 20 seconds. We then stir the fragrant aromatics into the vegetables. At this point, the chicken is returned to the pan along with the sauce.

For the sauce, we found that chicken broth (or orange or tangerine juice when appropriate flavor-wise) makes the best base because it is not overpowering. Soy sauce, hoisin, oyster sauce, black bean sauce, and fish sauce are all potent flavor enhancers. We also tested the addition of a little cornstarch to the sauce to help it coat the meat and vegetables, and found that a small amount is a good thing in most sauces (the amount varies depending on the viscosity of the other ingredients in the sauce). Otherwise, the sauce will be too thin and will not adhere properly to the solids. Once the chicken and sauce are added back to the pan with the vegetables, the whole dish is cooked just until the sauce is thickened.

In the end, a great chicken stir-fry doesn't really take more time to prepare than a bad one. It does, however, require more attention to detail and knowledge of a few quick tricks. Note that the recipes in this chapter are designed to serve four as a main course with rice.

Stir-Fried Chicken and Bok Choy with Spicy Hoisin Sauce

SERVES 4

To make slicing the chicken easier, first freeze it for 15 minutes. See page 242 for more information on stir-frying. Stir-fries cook quickly, so have everything prepped before you begin cooking. Serve with Sticky White Rice (page 242).

SAUCE

- ¼ cup hoisin sauce
- 1½ tablespoons soy sauce
- 1½ tablespoons Chinese rice cooking wine or dry sherry
- 2 teaspoons Asian chili-garlic sauce

STIR-FRY

- 1 pound boneless, skinless chicken breasts (about 2 large breasts), trimmed and sliced thin (see page 242)
- 2 tablespoons toasted sesame oil
- 1 tablespoon cornstarch
- 1 tablespoon unbleached all-purpose flour
- 2 teaspoons soy sauce
- 2 teaspoons Chinese rice cooking wine or dry sherry
- 3 medium garlic cloves, minced or pressed through a garlic press (about 1 tablespoon)
- 1 tablespoon minced or grated fresh ginger
- 2 scallions, minced
- 2 tablespoons plus 1 teaspoon vegetable oil
- 1 small head bok choy (about 1 pound), stalks and greens separated, stalks sliced crosswise into ¼-inch-wide strips and greens cut into ½-inch-wide strips (see the illustrations at right)

1. For the sauce: Whisk all of the ingredients together; set aside.

2. For the stir-fry: Toss the chicken with the sesame oil, cornstarch, flour, soy sauce, and rice wine in a small bowl and let marinate for 10 minutes, or up to 1 hour. In a separate bowl, mix together the garlic, ginger, scallions, and 1 teaspoon of the vegetable oil; set aside.

3. Heat 1½ teaspoons more of the vegetable oil in a 12-inch nonstick skillet over high heat until

just smoking. Add half of the chicken, break up any clumps, then cook without stirring until the meat is browned at the edges, 2 to 3 minutes. Stir the chicken and continue to cook until cooked through, 1 to 2 minutes longer. Transfer the chicken to a medium bowl and repeat with 1½ teaspoons more of the vegetable oil and the remaining chicken; transfer to the bowl, cover with foil, and set aside.

4. Add the remaining 1 tablespoon vegetable oil to the skillet and return to high heat until just smoking. Add the bok choy stalks and cook for 1 minute.

5. Clear the center of the pan, add the garlic mixture, and cook, mashing the mixture, until fragrant, 15 to 20 seconds. Stir the garlic mixture into the bok choy.

6. Stir in the bok choy greens and the chicken, along with any accumulated juices. Whisk the sauce to recombine, then add to the skillet and cook, tossing constantly, until the sauce is thickened, about 30 seconds. Transfer to a serving platter and serve.

PREPARING BOK CHOY

1. Trim the bottom inch from the head of bok choy. Wash and pat dry the leaves and stalks. With a chef's knife, cut the leafy green portion away from either side of the white stalk.

2. Cut each white stalk in half lengthwise and then crosswise into thin strips.

3. Stack the leafy greens and then slice them crosswise into thin strips. Keep the sliced stalks and leaves separate.

Stir-Fried Chicken and Broccoli with Oyster Sauce

SERVES 4

To make slicing the chicken easier, first freeze it for 15 minutes. See page 242 for more information on stir-frying. Stir-fries cook quickly, so have everything prepped before you begin cooking. Serve with Sticky White Rice (page 242).

SAUCE

- 5 tablespoons oyster sauce
- 2 tablespoons low-sodium chicken broth
- 1 tablespoon Chinese rice cooking wine or dry sherry
- 1 tablespoon light brown sugar
- 1 teaspoon toasted sesame oil
- 1 teaspoon cornstarch

STIR-FRY

- 1 pound boneless, skinless chicken breasts (about 2 large breasts), trimmed and sliced thin (see page 242)
- 2 tablespoons toasted sesame oil
- 1 tablespoon cornstarch
- 1 tablespoon unbleached all-purpose flour
- 2 teaspoons soy sauce
- 2 teaspoons Chinese rice cooking wine or dry sherry
- 6 medium garlic cloves, minced or pressed through a garlic press (about 2 tablespoons)
- 1 tablespoon minced or grated fresh ginger
- 2 scallions, minced
- 2 tablespoons plus 1 teaspoon vegetable oil
- 1¼ pounds broccoli, florets and stems separated, florets cut into bite-sized pieces, stems trimmed, peeled, and sliced ⅛ inch thick (see the illustration on page 279)
- ⅓ cup water
- 1 red bell pepper, stemmed, seeded, and sliced into ¼-inch-wide strips

1. FOR THE SAUCE: Whisk all of the ingredients together; set aside.

2. FOR THE STIR-FRY: Toss the chicken with the sesame oil, cornstarch, flour, soy sauce, and rice wine in a small bowl and let marinate for 10 minutes, or up to 1 hour. In a separate bowl, mix together the garlic, ginger, scallions, and 1 teaspoon of the vegetable oil; set aside.

3. Heat 1½ teaspoons more of the vegetable oil in a 12-inch nonstick skillet over high heat until just smoking. Add half of the chicken, break up any clumps, then cook without stirring until the meat is browned at the edges, 2 to 3 minutes. Stir the chicken and continue to cook until cooked through, 1 to 2 minutes longer. Transfer the chicken to a medium bowl and repeat with 1½ teaspoons more of the vegetable oil and the remaining chicken; transfer to the bowl, cover with foil, and set aside.

4. Add the remaining 1 tablespoon vegetable oil to the skillet and return to high heat until just smoking. Add the broccoli florets and stems and cook for 30 seconds. Add the water, cover, and reduce the heat to medium. Steam the broccoli until tender-crisp, about 2 minutes. Remove the lid, add the bell pepper, and continue to cook until the vegetables are crisp-tender, about 2 minutes.

5. Clear the center of the skillet, add the garlic mixture, and cook, mashing the mixture, until fragrant, 15 to 20 seconds. Stir the garlic mixture into the vegetables.

6. Stir in the chicken, along with any accumulated juices. Whisk the sauce to recombine, then add to the skillet and cook, tossing constantly, until the sauce is thickened, about 30 seconds. Transfer to a serving platter and serve.

Stir-Fried Chicken, Scallions, and Bell Peppers with Hoisin-Sesame Sauce

SERVES 4

To make slicing the chicken easier, first freeze it for 15 minutes. See page 242 for more information on stir-frying. The scallions are used as a vegetable in this stir-fry, rather than as simply a garnish. Stir-fries cook quickly, so have everything prepped before you begin cooking. Serve with Sticky White Rice (page 242).

SAUCE

- ½ cup low-sodium chicken broth
- ¼ cup Chinese rice cooking wine or dry sherry
- 3 tablespoons hoisin sauce
- 1 tablespoon soy sauce
- 2 teaspoons cornstarch
- 1 teaspoon toasted sesame oil

STIR-FRY

- 1 pound boneless, skinless chicken breasts (about 2 large breasts), trimmed and sliced thin (see page 242)
- 2 tablespoons toasted sesame oil
- 1 tablespoon cornstarch
- 1 tablespoon unbleached all-purpose flour
- 2 teaspoons soy sauce
- 2 teaspoons Chinese rice cooking wine or dry sherry
- 6 medium garlic cloves, minced or pressed through a garlic press (about 2 tablespoons)
- 1 tablespoon minced or grated fresh ginger
- ⅛ teaspoon red pepper flakes
- 2 tablespoons plus 1 teaspoon vegetable oil
- 12 medium scallions, white and green parts separated, both sliced on the bias into 1-inch lengths
- 2 red bell peppers, stemmed, seeded, and sliced into ¼-inch-wide strips

1. FOR THE SAUCE: Whisk all of the ingredients together; set aside.

2. FOR THE STIR-FRY: Toss the chicken with the sesame oil, cornstarch, flour, soy sauce, and rice wine in a small bowl and let marinate for 10 minutes, or up to 1 hour. In a separate bowl, mix together the garlic, ginger, red pepper flakes, and 1 teaspoon of the vegetable oil; set aside.

3. Heat 1½ teaspoons more of the vegetable oil in a 12-inch nonstick skillet over high heat until just smoking. Add half of the chicken, break up any clumps, then cook without stirring until the meat is browned at the edges, 2 to 3 minutes. Stir the chicken and continue to cook until cooked through, 1 to 2 minutes longer. Transfer the chicken to a medium bowl and repeat with 1½ teaspoons more of the vegetable oil and the remaining chicken; transfer to the bowl, cover with foil, and set aside.

4. Add the remaining 1 tablespoon vegetable oil to the skillet and return to high heat until just smoking. Add the scallion whites and cook for 1 minute. Add the bell peppers and cook, stirring occasionally, until crisp-tender, 2 minutes.

5. Clear the center of the skillet, add the garlic mixture, and cook, mashing the mixture, until fragrant, 15 to 20 seconds. Stir the garlic mixture into the vegetables.

6. Stir in the scallion greens and the chicken, along with any accumulated juices. Whisk the sauce to recombine, then add to the skillet and cook, tossing constantly, until the sauce is thickened, about 30 seconds. Transfer to a serving platter and serve.

Stir-Fried Chicken, Asparagus, and Carrots with Spicy Orange Sauce

SERVES 4

To make slicing the chicken easier, first freeze it for 15 minutes. See page 242 for more information on stir-frying. Use a vegetable peeler to peel strips of zest, but take care to avoid the bitter pith beneath the skin. If the asparagus spears are very thick, slice each stalk in half lengthwise before cutting into 2-inch lengths. Stir-fries cook quickly, so have everything prepped before you begin cooking. Serve with Sticky White Rice (page 242).

SAUCE

- 2 (2-inch-long) strips orange zest from 1 orange (see note)
- ½ cup juice from 2 oranges
- ¼ cup Chinese rice cooking wine or dry sherry
- 2 tablespoons soy sauce
- 1 tablespoon sugar
- 2 teaspoons cornstarch
- 1 teaspoon toasted sesame oil
- ½ teaspoon red pepper flakes

STIR-FRY

- 1 pound boneless, skinless chicken breasts (about 2 large breasts), trimmed and sliced thin (see page 242)
- 2 tablespoons toasted sesame oil
- 1 tablespoon cornstarch
- 1 tablespoon unbleached all-purpose flour
- 2 teaspoons soy sauce
- 2 teaspoons Chinese rice cooking wine or dry sherry
- 3 medium garlic cloves, minced or pressed through a garlic press (about 1 tablespoon)
- 1 tablespoon minced or grated fresh ginger
- 2 scallions, minced
- 2 tablespoons plus 1 teaspoon vegetable oil
- 1 pound asparagus (about 1 bunch), tough ends trimmed and sliced on the bias into 2-inch lengths (see note)
- 2 carrots, peeled and cut into 2-inch-long matchsticks (see the illustration on page 238)

1. FOR THE SAUCE: Whisk all of the ingredients together; set aside.

2. FOR THE STIR-FRY: Toss the chicken with the sesame oil, cornstarch, flour, soy sauce, and rice wine in a small bowl and let marinate for 10 minutes, or up to 1 hour. In a separate bowl, mix together the garlic, ginger, scallions, and 1 teaspoon of the vegetable oil; set aside.

3. Heat 1½ teaspoons more of the vegetable oil in a 12-inch nonstick skillet over high heat until just smoking. Add half of the chicken, break up any clumps, then cook without stirring until the meat is browned at the edges, 2 to 3 minutes. Stir the chicken and continue to cook until cooked through, 1 to 2 minutes longer. Transfer the chicken to a

TRIMMING TOUGH ENDS FROM ASPARAGUS

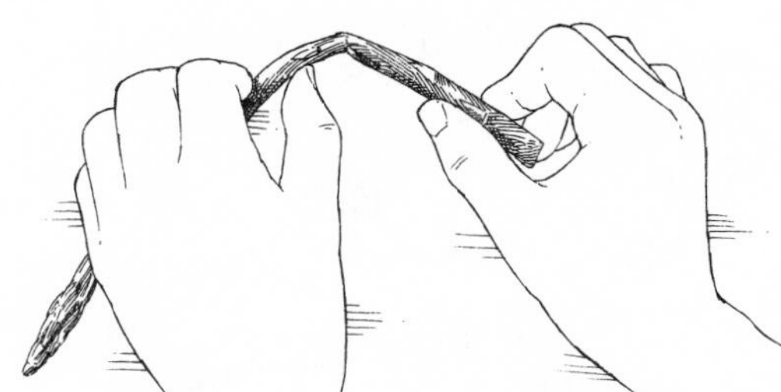

In our tests, we found that the tough, woody part of the stem will break off in just the right place if you hold the spear the right way. With one hand, hold the asparagus about halfway down the stalk; with the thumb and index fingers of the other hand, hold the spear about an inch up from the bottom. Bend the stalk until it snaps.

medium bowl and repeat with 1½ teaspoons more of the vegetable oil and the remaining chicken; transfer to the bowl, cover with foil, and set aside.

4. Add the remaining 1 tablespoon vegetable oil to the skillet and return to high heat until just smoking. Add the asparagus and carrots and cook until crisp-tender, 2 to 3 minutes.

5. Clear the center of the skillet, add the garlic mixture, and cook, mashing the mixture, until fragrant, 15 to 20 seconds. Stir the garlic mixture into the vegetables.

6. Stir in the chicken, along with any accumulated juices. Whisk the sauce to recombine, then add it to the skillet and cook, tossing constantly, until the sauce has thickened, about 30 seconds. Transfer to a serving platter and serve.

CUTTING CARROTS INTO MATCHSTICKS

1. Slice the carrot on the bias into ¼-inch-thick rounds.

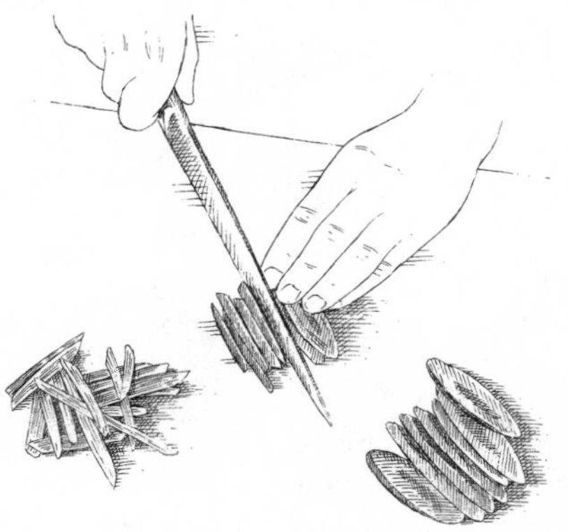

2. Fan the rounds and cut them into strips that measure about 2 inches long and ¼ inch thick.

Stir-Fried Chicken, Snow Peas, and Cabbage with Oyster Sauce

SERVES 4

To make slicing the chicken easier, first freeze it for 15 minutes. See page 242 for more information on stir-frying. Stir-fries cook quickly, so have everything prepped before you begin cooking. Serve with Sticky White Rice (page 242).

SAUCE

- 1 cup low-sodium chicken broth
- 3 tablespoons oyster sauce
- 1 tablespoon soy sauce
- 1 tablespoon cornstarch
- 2 teaspoons toasted sesame oil

STIR-FRY

- 1 pound boneless, skinless chicken breasts (about 2 large breasts), trimmed and sliced thin (see page 242)
- 2 tablespoons toasted sesame oil
- 1 tablespoon cornstarch
- 1 tablespoon unbleached all-purpose flour
- 2 teaspoons soy sauce
- 2 teaspoons Chinese rice cooking wine or dry sherry
- 3 medium garlic cloves, minced or pressed through a garlic press (about 1 tablespoon)
- 1 tablespoon minced or grated fresh ginger
- 2 scallions, minced
- 2 tablespoons plus 1 teaspoon vegetable oil
- 1 cup snow peas, stems and strings removed (see the illustration on page 240)
- ¼ cup water
- 1 pound green cabbage (about ½ medium head), cored and cut into 2-inch squares
- 1 tablespoon sesame seeds, toasted (optional)

1. For the sauce: Whisk all of the ingredients together; set aside.

2. For the stir-fry: Toss the chicken with the sesame oil, cornstarch, flour, soy sauce, and rice wine in a small bowl and let marinate for 10 minutes, or up to 1 hour. In a separate bowl, mix together the garlic, ginger, scallions, and 1 teaspoon of the vegetable oil; set aside.

3. Heat 1½ teaspoons more of the vegetable oil in a 12-inch nonstick skillet over high heat until just smoking. Add half of the chicken, break up any clumps, then cook without stirring until the meat is browned at the edges, 2 to 3 minutes. Stir the chicken and continue to cook until cooked through, 1 to 2 minutes longer. Transfer the chicken to a medium bowl and repeat with 1½ teaspoons more of the vegetable oil and the remaining chicken; transfer to the bowl, cover with foil, and set aside.

4. Add the remaining 1 tablespoon vegetable oil to the skillet and return to high heat until just smoking. Add the snow peas and cook until beginning to brown and soften, 1 to 2 minutes. Add the water, cover, and reduce the heat to medium. Steam the peas until crisp-tender, about 2 minutes. Remove the lid, add the cabbage, and continue to cook until the cabbage is wilted, about 3 minutes.

5. Clear the center of the skillet, add the garlic mixture, and cook, mashing the mixture, until fragrant, 15 to 20 seconds. Stir the garlic mixture into the vegetables.

6. Return the chicken, along with any accumulated juices, to the skillet. Whisk the sauce to recombine, then add to the skillet and cook, tossing constantly, until the sauce is thickened, about 30 seconds. Transfer to a serving platter, sprinkle with sesame seeds (if using), and serve.

Stir-Fried Chicken, Green Beans, and Shiitakes with Teriyaki Sauce

SERVES 4

You can substitute 1 tablespoon white wine or sake mixed with 1 teaspoon sugar for the mirin. To make slicing the chicken easier, first freeze it for 15 minutes. See page 242 for more information on stir-frying. Stir-fries cook quickly, so have everything prepped before you begin cooking. Serve with Sticky White Rice (page 242).

SAUCE

- ¾ cup low-sodium chicken broth
- 2 tablespoons soy sauce
- 2 tablespoons sugar
- 1 tablespoon mirin (see note)
- 2 teaspoons cornstarch
- ⅛ teaspoon red pepper flakes

STIR-FRY

- 1 pound boneless, skinless chicken breasts (about 2 large breasts), trimmed and sliced thin (see page 242)
- 2 tablespoons toasted sesame oil
- 1 tablespoon cornstarch
- 1 tablespoon unbleached all-purpose flour
- 2 teaspoons soy sauce
- 2 teaspoons Chinese rice cooking wine or dry sherry
- 3 medium garlic cloves, minced or pressed through a garlic press (about 1 tablespoon)
- 1 tablespoon minced or grated fresh ginger
- 2 scallions, minced
- 2 tablespoons plus 1 teaspoon vegetable oil
- 1 pound green beans, ends trimmed (see the illustration on page 106) and cut on the bias into 1-inch pieces
- ¼ cup water
- 8 ounces shiitake mushrooms, stems discarded, caps wiped clean and sliced ¼ inch thick

1. For the sauce: Whisk all of the ingredients together; set aside.

2. For the stir-fry: Toss the chicken with the sesame oil, cornstarch, flour, soy sauce, and rice wine in a small bowl and let marinate for 10 minutes, or up to 1 hour. In a separate bowl, mix together the garlic, ginger, scallions, and 1 teaspoon of the vegetable oil; set aside.

3. Heat 1½ teaspoons more of the vegetable oil in a 12-inch nonstick skillet over high heat until just smoking. Add half of the chicken, break up any clumps, then cook without stirring until the meat is browned at the edges, 2 to 3 minutes. Stir the chicken and continue to cook until cooked through, 1 to 2 minutes longer. Transfer the chicken to a medium bowl and repeat with 1½ teaspoons more of the vegetable oil and the remaining chicken; transfer to the bowl, cover with foil, and set aside.

4. Add the remaining 1 tablespoon vegetable oil to the skillet and return to high heat until just

smoking. Add the green beans and cook until beginning to brown and soften, 1 to 2 minutes. Add the water, cover, and reduce the heat to medium. Steam the green beans until crisp-tender, about 2 minutes. Remove the lid, add the mushrooms, and continue to cook until browned, about 3 minutes.

5. Clear the center of the skillet, add the garlic mixture, and cook, mashing the mixture, until fragrant, 15 to 20 seconds. Stir the garlic mixture into the vegetables.

6. Return the chicken, along with any accumulated juices, to the skillet. Whisk the sauce to recombine, then add to the skillet and cook, tossing constantly, until the sauce is thickened, about 30 seconds. Transfer to a serving platter and serve.

Stir-Fried Chicken, Snap Peas, and Bell Pepper with Sesame Sauce

SERVES 4

To make slicing the chicken easier, first freeze it for 15 minutes. See page 242 for more information on stir-frying. Stir-fries cook quickly, so have everything prepped before you begin cooking. Serve with Sticky White Rice (page 242).

SAUCE

- ¾ cup low-sodium chicken broth
- ¼ cup soy sauce
- 2 tablespoons Chinese rice cooking wine or dry sherry
- 1 tablespoon cornstarch
- 1 tablespoon Asian chili sauce
- 1 tablespoon sugar
- 2 teaspoons toasted sesame oil

STIR-FRY

- 1 pound boneless, skinless chicken breasts (about 2 large breasts), trimmed and sliced thin (see page 242)
- 2 tablespoons toasted sesame oil
- 1 tablespoon cornstarch
- 1 tablespoon unbleached all-purpose flour
- 2 teaspoons soy sauce
- 2 teaspoons Chinese rice cooking wine or dry sherry
- 3 medium garlic cloves, minced or pressed through a garlic press (about 1 tablespoon)
- 1 tablespoon minced or grated fresh ginger
- 2 scallions, minced
- 2 tablespoons plus 1 teaspoon vegetable oil
- 1 pound snap peas, stems and strings removed (see the illustration below)
- ¼ cup water
- 1 red bell pepper, stemmed, seeded, and sliced into ¼-inch-wide strips
- 2 tablespoons sesame seeds, toasted

1. FOR THE SAUCE: Whisk all of the ingredients together; set aside.

2. FOR THE STIR-FRY: Toss the chicken with the sesame oil, cornstarch, flour, soy sauce, and rice wine in a small bowl and let marinate for 10 minutes, or up to 1 hour. In a separate bowl, mix together the garlic, ginger, scallions, and 1 teaspoon of the vegetable oil; set aside.

3. Heat 1½ teaspoons more of the vegetable oil in a 12-inch nonstick skillet over high heat until just smoking. Add half of the chicken, break up any clumps, then cook without stirring until the meat is browned at the edges, 2 to 3 minutes. Stir the chicken and continue to cook until cooked through, 1 to 2 minutes longer. Transfer the chicken to a medium bowl and repeat with 1½ teaspoons more of the vegetable oil and the remaining chicken; transfer to the bowl, cover with foil, and set aside.

4. Add the remaining 1 tablespoon vegetable oil to the skillet and return to high heat until just smoking. Add the snap peas and cook until beginning to brown and soften, 1 to 2 minutes. Add the

STRINGING SNOW PEAS AND SNAP PEAS

Snap off the tip of the snow pea or snap pea while pulling down along the flat side of the pod to remove the string.

water, cover, and reduce the heat to medium. Steam the snap peas until crisp-tender, about 2 minutes. Remove the lid, add the bell pepper, and continue to cook until browned, about 3 minutes.

5. Clear the center of the skillet, add the garlic mixture, and cook, mashing the mixture, until fragrant, 15 to 20 seconds. Stir the garlic mixture into the vegetables.

6. Return the chicken, along with any accumulated juices, to the skillet. Whisk the sauce to recombine, then add to the skillet and cook, tossing constantly, until the sauce is thickened, about 30 seconds. Transfer to a serving platter, sprinkle with sesame seeds, and serve.

Stir-Fried Chicken, Onion, and Snow Peas with Tangerine Sauce

SERVES 4

Oranges can be used in place of the tangerines. Use a vegetable peeler to peel strips of zest, but take care to avoid the bitter pith beneath the skin. To make slicing the chicken easier, first freeze it for 15 minutes. See page 242 for more information on stir-frying. Stir-fries cook quickly, so have everything prepped before you begin cooking. Serve with Sticky White Rice (page 242).

SAUCE

- 2 (2-inch-long) strips tangerine zest from 1 tangerine (see note)
- ¾ cup juice from 3 to 4 tangerines (see note)
- 2 tablespoons soy sauce
- 2 tablespoons Chinese black bean sauce
- 1 tablespoon sugar
- 1 teaspoon cornstarch
- 1 teaspoon toasted sesame oil
- ¼ teaspoon red pepper flakes

STIR-FRY

- 1 pound boneless, skinless chicken breasts (about 2 large breasts), trimmed and sliced thin (see page 242)
- 2 tablespoons toasted sesame oil
- 1 tablespoon cornstarch
- 1 tablespoon unbleached all-purpose flour
- 2 teaspoons soy sauce
- 2 teaspoons Chinese rice cooking wine or dry sherry
- 3 medium garlic cloves, minced or pressed through a garlic press (about 1 tablespoon)
- 1 tablespoon minced or grated fresh ginger
- 2 scallions, minced
- 2 tablespoons plus 1 teaspoon vegetable oil
- 1 large onion, halved and sliced ½ inch thick
- 1 pound snow peas, stems and strings removed (see the illustration on page 240)
- ¼ cup water

1. For the sauce: Whisk all of the ingredients together; set aside.

2. For the stir-fry: Toss the chicken with the sesame oil, cornstarch, flour, soy sauce, and rice wine in a small bowl and let marinate for 10 minutes, or up to 1 hour. In a separate bowl, mix together the garlic, ginger, scallions, and 1 teaspoon of the vegetable oil; set aside.

3. Heat 1½ teaspoons more of the vegetable oil in a 12-inch nonstick skillet over high heat until just smoking. Add half of the chicken, break up any clumps, then cook without stirring until the meat is browned at the edges, 2 to 3 minutes. Stir the chicken and continue to cook until cooked through, 1 to 2 minutes longer. Transfer the chicken to a medium bowl and repeat with 1½ teaspoons more of the vegetable oil and the remaining chicken; transfer to the bowl, cover with foil, and set aside.

4. Add the remaining 1 tablespoon vegetable oil to the skillet and return to high heat until just smoking. Add the onion and cook until beginning to brown and softened, 3 to 5 minutes. Add the snap peas and water, cover, and reduce the heat to medium. Steam the snow peas until crisp-tender, 1 to 2 minutes. Remove the lid and continue to cook until browned, 1 to 2 minutes.

5. Clear the center of the skillet, add the garlic mixture, and cook, mashing the mixture, until fragrant, 15 to 20 seconds. Stir the garlic mixture into the vegetables.

6. Return the chicken, along with any accumulated juices, to the skillet. Whisk the sauce to recombine, then add to the skillet and cook, tossing constantly, until the sauce is thickened, about 30 seconds. Transfer to a serving platter and serve.

Stir-Fry 101

Stir-fries are naturally quick. The key is to have all your chicken and vegetables prepped before you begin cooking. They should be cut into even pieces so that they all cook at the same rate.

SLICING CHICKEN FOR STIR-FRIES

It is better to take five minutes and cut up your own chicken than to buy packages labeled "for stir-fry," since the pieces can be unevenly cut. To make it easier to slice the chicken, place it in the freezer for 15 minutes. Boneless, skinless breasts work best for stir-fries and are easy to cut into thin strips. In the world of stir-frying, chicken requires a fairly long time to cook through and brown slightly—at least 3 to 5 minutes.

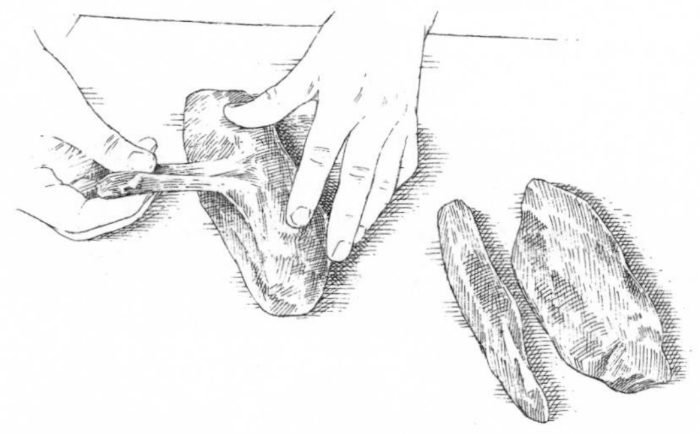

1. To produce uniform pieces of chicken, separate the tenderloins from the partially frozen boneless, skinless breasts.

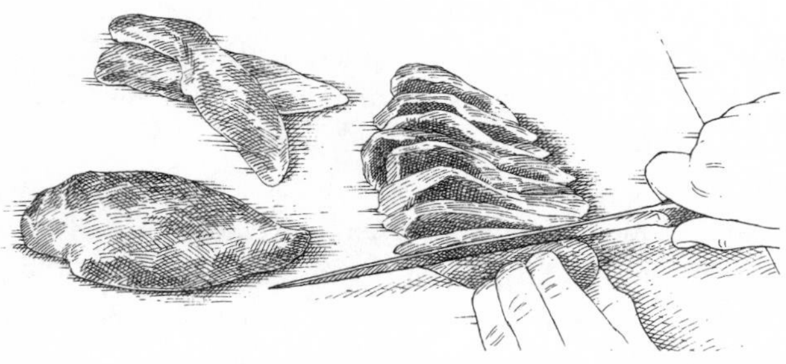

2. Slice the breasts across the grain into thin strips that are 1½ to 2 inches long. Center pieces need to be cut in half so that they are approximately the same length as the end pieces.

3. Cut tenderloins on the diagonal to produce pieces about the same size as the strips of breast meat.

ESSENTIAL TOOLS FOR STIR-FRYING SUCCESS

Stir-frying requires only a couple of pieces of basic equipment (you probably already own them). Woks are the traditional cooking vessel for stir-frying in China. Conically shaped, a wok rests in a cylindrical pit containing the fire. Flames lick the bottom and sides of the pan so that food cooks remarkably quickly. A wok, however, is not designed for stovetop cooking, where heat comes only from the bottom. Therefore, we prefer a **12- or 14-inch nonstick skillet** for stir-frying. This pan requires a minimum of oil and prevents food from burning and sticking to the surface as it stir-fries. We tested several major brands of nonstick skillets (see our testing on page 246) and particularly liked pans that were sturdy but not overly heavy, with a good nonstick performance.

Our second choice for stir-frying is a regular 12- or 14-inch traditional skillet (see page 263 for our testing of traditional skillets). Without the nonstick coating, you will need to use slightly more oil. However, this pan will deliver satisfactory results. If you do not own a large skillet of any kind, do not substitute a smaller size. A 10-inch skillet is not large enough to accommodate all the ingredients in a stir-fry recipe for four. The ingredients will steam rather than stir-fry.

Chinese cooks use long-handled, **shovel-like spatulas** to move food around woks. The same tool works well in a nonstick skillet, although, to protect the pan's surface, you should use only plastic or wooden implements. We prefer a large spatula with a wide, thin blade and a long, heat-resistant handle.

STICKY WHITE RICE

SERVES 4 TO 6

Do not stir the rice as it cooks. The finished rice can stand off the heat, covered, for up to 15 minutes. Serve with any of the recipes in this chapter.

- **2 cups long-grain white rice**
- **3 cups water**
- **½ teaspoon salt**

1. Place the rice in a fine-mesh strainer set over a bowl. Rinse under running water, swishing with your hands until the water runs clear. Drain thoroughly.

2. Bring the rinsed rice, the water, and salt to a boil in a saucepan over medium-high heat. Cook, uncovered, until the water level drops below the surface of the rice and small holes form, about 5 minutes.

3. Reduce the heat to low, cover, and cook until the rice is tender and the water is fully absorbed, about 15 minutes. Serve.

STIR-FRYING STEP-BY-STEP

Here are the four key steps to making a stir-fry. (Be sure to use a 12- or 14-inch nonstick skillet and cook over high heat.)

1. Start by cooking the chicken. After the chicken has browned and cooked through, remove it from the pan and cover with foil to keep warm.

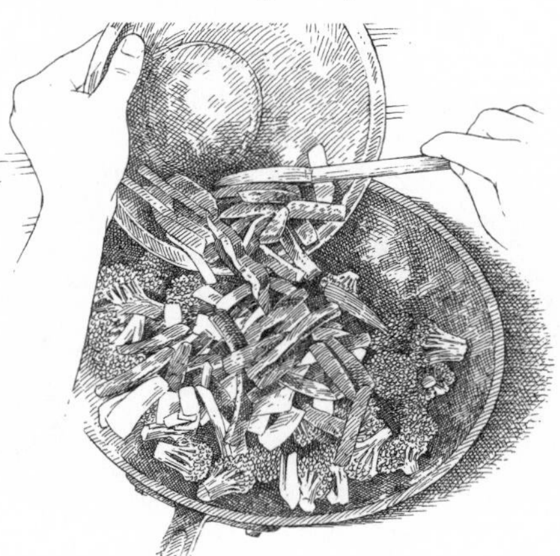

2. Next, cook the vegetables in batches, adding the tougher vegetables first and the more delicate vegetables later. This ensures that each vegetable will be perfectly cooked.

3. Push the vegetables to the edges of the skillet, clearing a spot in the middle. Add the garlic, ginger, and a little oil to the cleared spot and cook, mashing them until they are fragrant, about 30 seconds.

4. Return the cooked chicken to the skillet, add the sauce, and toss to combine. Continue to cook until the sauce has thickened.

TWO WAYS OF PREPARING GINGER

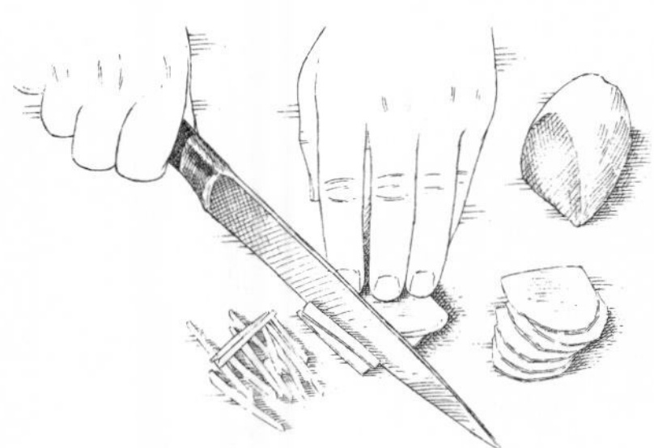

1a. Slice the peeled knob of ginger into thin rounds, then fan the rounds out and cut them into thin, matchsticklike strips.

1b. Chop the matchsticks crosswise into a fine mince.

2. Peel a small section of a large piece of ginger. Grate the peeled portion, using the rest of the ginger as a handle to keep fingers safely away from the grater.

ASIAN INGREDIENTS

WITH THE INCREASED INTEREST IN AUTHENTIC ASIAN COOKING, SUPERMARKETS ARE CARRYING a wider array of Asian ingredients. The following list includes common Asian ingredients that you'll find in our stir-fries.

ASIAN CHILI SAUCE

Used both in cooking and as a condiment, this sauce comes in many different forms, each with varying degrees of heat. You'll find jars of chili sauce labeled "sambal oelek," "sriracha," and "chili garlic sauce" in the international aisle of larger supermarkets. You can use them interchangeably whenever a recipe calls for Asian chili sauce—just remember, a little goes a long way with these fiery sauces. Consisting of chiles, sugar, vinegar, salt, and sometimes garlic, Asian chili sauce will keep indefinitely when refrigerated.

COCONUT MILK

Coconut milk is widely available in cans. It adds richness and a mild coconut flavor to soups, curries, and stir-fries. Be sure to shake the can well before using to distribute the coconut cream that will have solidified at the top of the can. Do not confuse coconut milk with cream of coconut, which is much sweeter.

FISH SAUCE

Fish sauce, or *nam pla* or *nuoc mam,* is a salty, amber-colored liquid made from fermented fish. It is used as both an ingredient and a condiment in many Asian cuisines, most commonly in the foods of Southeast Asia. Used in very small amounts, it adds a well-rounded, salty flavor to sauces, soups, and marinades. Fish sauce will keep indefinitely without refrigeration.

HOISIN SAUCE

Also called Peking sauce, hoisin sauce is a mixture of soybeans, garlic, chile peppers, and spices, the most predominant of which is five-spice powder. This thick, dark-brown sauce has a complex flavor that forms the base of many stir-fries. It is also used as a table condiment, much like ketchup. This sauce will keep indefinitely when refrigerated.

MIRIN

Mirin is a sweet rice wine used for cooking. Made from glutinous rice, mirin—which is typically used in Japanese cooking—can also contain corn syrup, water, alcohol, and salt. We use mirin to brighten the flavor of stir-fries, teriyaki, and other Asian dishes. If you cannot find mirin, substitute 1 tablespoon white wine and ½ teaspoon sugar for every 1 tablespoon of mirin.

CHINESE RICE COOKING WINE

Rice wine is a rich-flavored liquid that is made from fermented glutinous rice or millet. Aged for 10 years or more, rice wine is used both for drinking and cooking (the cooking rice wine has a lower alcohol content than the other). Technically, rice wine should be called rice "beer," since it's fermented from a grain and not a fruit. It ranges in color from clear to amber and tastes slightly sweet and aromatic.

SESAME OIL

Raw sesame oil, which is very mild and light in color, is used mostly for cooking, while toasted sesame oil, which has a deep amber color, is primarily used for seasoning because of its intense, nutty flavor. For the biggest hit of sesame flavor, we prefer to use toasted sesame oil. Just a few drops of this oil will give stir-fries or noodle dishes a deep, nutty flavor—but too much will be overpowering.

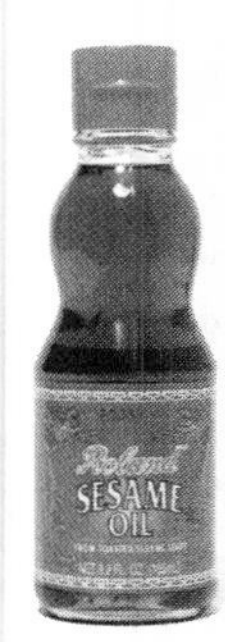

SOY SAUCE

Available everywhere, soy sauce is made from fermented soybeans with roasted wheat or barley added. We prefer naturally brewed soy sauces to synthetic sauces, which are very salty (and include hydrolyzed vegetable protein in their ingredient lists). "Lite" or lower-sodium soy sauces are widely available and may be used in any recipe. Tamari is a Japanese soy sauce that contains little or no wheat, and is typically richer and stronger in flavor than regular soy sauce.

Stir-Fried Chicken and Eggplant with Red Curry Sauce

SERVES 4

To make slicing the chicken easier, first freeze it for 15 minutes. See page 242 for more information on stir-frying. Stir-fries cook quickly, so have everything prepped before you begin cooking. For increased heat, use the higher amount of the red curry paste. Serve with Sticky White Rice (page 242).

SAUCE

- ½ cup low-sodium chicken broth
- ¼ cup coconut milk
- 2 tablespoons light brown sugar
- 1 tablespoon fish sauce
- 1 tablespoon juice from 1 lime
- 1 teaspoon cornstarch

STIR-FRY

- 1 pound boneless, skinless chicken breasts (about 2 large breasts), trimmed and sliced thin (see page 242)
- 2 tablespoons toasted sesame oil
- 1 tablespoon cornstarch
- 1 tablespoon unbleached all-purpose flour
- 2 teaspoons soy sauce
- 2 teaspoons Chinese rice cooking wine or dry sherry
- 3 medium garlic cloves, minced or pressed through a garlic press (about 1 tablespoon)
- 1 tablespoon minced or grated fresh ginger
- 2 scallions, minced
- 1–1½ teaspoons red curry paste (see note)
- 2 tablespoons plus 1 teaspoon vegetable oil
- 1 medium eggplant (about 1 pound), peeled and cut into ¾-inch cubes
- 2 cups basil leaves
- Lime wedges for serving (optional)

1. For the sauce: Whisk all of the ingredients together; set aside.

2. For the stir-fry: Toss the chicken with the sesame oil, cornstarch, flour, soy sauce, and rice wine in a small bowl and let marinate for 10 minutes, or up to 1 hour. In a separate bowl, mix together the garlic, ginger, scallions, red curry paste, and 1 teaspoon of the vegetable oil; set aside.

3. Heat 1½ teaspoons more of the vegetable oil in a 12-inch nonstick skillet over high heat until just smoking. Add half of the chicken, break up any clumps, then cook without stirring until the meat is browned at the edges, 2 to 3 minutes. Stir the chicken and continue to cook until cooked through, 1 to 2 minutes longer. Transfer the chicken to a medium bowl and repeat with 1½ teaspoons more of the vegetable oil and the remaining chicken; transfer to the bowl, cover with foil, and set aside.

4. Add the remaining 1 tablespoon vegetable oil to the skillet and return to high heat until just smoking. Add the eggplant and cook until beginning to brown and no longer spongy, 5 to 7 minutes.

5. Clear the center of the skillet, add the garlic mixture, and cook, mashing the mixture, until fragrant, 15 to 20 seconds. Stir the garlic mixture into the vegetables.

6. Return the chicken, along with any accumulated juices, to the skillet. Whisk the sauce to recombine, then add to the skillet with the basil leaves and cook, tossing constantly, until the sauce is thickened, about 30 seconds. Transfer to a serving platter and serve with lime wedges, if desired.

Stir-Fried Chicken, Kimchi, and Bean Sprouts with Korean-Style Sauce

SERVES 4

Kimchi is a Korean pickled vegetable condiment and commonly contains napa cabbage, scallions, garlic, and ground chiles in brine. It varies in heat intensity, flavor, and pungency. If possible, avoid brands with strong fish or shrimp flavor that can overpower the chicken. If the kimchi you purchase is made from green cabbage and not napa cabbage, extend the cooking time by 1 to 2 minutes. To make slicing the chicken easier, first freeze it for 15 minutes. See page 242 for more information on stir-frying. Stir-fries cook quickly, so have everything prepped before you begin cooking. Serve with Sticky White Rice (page 242).

SAUCE
- ¾ cup low-sodium chicken broth
- 3 tablespoons soy sauce
- 1 tablespoon sugar
- 2 teaspoons cornstarch
- 1 teaspoon sesame oil

STIR-FRY
- 1 pound boneless, skinless chicken breasts (about 2 large breasts), trimmed and sliced thin (see page 242)
- 2 tablespoons toasted sesame oil
- 1 tablespoon cornstarch
- 1 tablespoon unbleached all-purpose flour
- 2 teaspoons soy sauce
- 2 teaspoons Chinese rice cooking wine or dry sherry
- 3 medium garlic cloves, minced or pressed through a garlic press (about 1 tablespoon)
- 1 tablespoon minced or grated fresh ginger
- 2 tablespoons plus 1 teaspoon vegetable oil
- 1 cup drained kimchi (from a 16-ounce jar), cut into 1-inch pieces
- 5 scallions, white and green parts separated, both sliced on the bias into 1-inch lengths
- 4 ounces mung bean sprouts (about 2 cups)

1. For the sauce: Whisk all of the ingredients together; set aside.

2. For the stir-fry: Toss the chicken with the sesame oil, cornstarch, flour, soy sauce, and rice wine in a small bowl and let marinate for 10 minutes, or up to 1 hour. In a separate bowl, mix together the garlic, ginger, and 1 teaspoon of the vegetable oil; set aside.

3. Heat 1½ teaspoons more of the vegetable oil in a 12-inch nonstick skillet over high heat until just smoking. Add half of the chicken, break up any clumps, then cook without stirring until the meat is browned at the edges, 2 to 3 minutes. Stir the chicken and continue to cook until cooked through, 1 to 2 minutes longer. Transfer the chicken to a medium bowl and repeat with 1½ teaspoons more of the vegetable oil and the remaining chicken; transfer to the bowl, cover with foil, and set aside.

4. Add the remaining 1 tablespoon vegetable oil to the skillet and return to high heat until just smoking. Add the kimchi and scallion whites and cook until aromatic, 1 to 2 minutes. Stir in the bean sprouts.

5. Clear the center of the skillet, add the garlic mixture, and cook, mashing the mixture, until fragrant, 15 to 20 seconds. Stir the garlic mixture into the vegetables.

6. Return the chicken, along with any accumulated juices, to the skillet. Whisk the sauce to recombine, then add to the skillet with the scallion greens and cook, tossing constantly, until the sauce is thickened, about 30 seconds. Transfer to a serving platter and serve.

EQUIPMENT:
Inexpensive Nonstick Skillets

Nothing takes the challenge out of cooking stir-fries and delicate foods, like eggs, better than a slick nonstick skillet. The downside is that the nonstick coating is easily damaged, so we find it best to buy inexpensive nonstick skillets. We tested nine 12-inch nonstick skillets ranging in price from $8.99 to $49.99. Our main criticisms focused on pan construction, because some of the pans turned out to be downright flimsy. However, the Cuisinart Chef's Classic Nonstick Hard Anodized Omelet Pan ($41.95) was our favorite, with the Wearever Hard-Anodized Nonstick Skillet ($29.99) coming in a close second.

THE BEST NONSTICK SKILLETS

The Cuisinart Chef's Classic Nonstick Hard Anodized Omelet Pan and Wearever Hard-Anodized Nonstick Skillet offer the best combination of nonstick performance and solid construction.

9 CHICKEN MEETS PASTA

Chicken Meets Pasta

FEW FOODS RIVAL PASTA IN TERMS OF SPEED or convenience. Pasta is almost always on hand, cooks in minutes, and can serve as the basis for literally hundreds of meals. And chicken has virtually the same appeal—quick, convenient, and available in a variety of forms (ground, sausage, boneless, skinless, bone-in, skin-on, etc.). So it only makes sense that the marriage of pasta and chicken is a reliable one that yields a seemingly endless number of flavorful pairings.

When it comes to incorporating chicken into a pasta dish, we have found that it truly is recipe-specific, as the type of chicken varies from recipe to recipe. For some recipes in this chapter, we took a basic method for cooking the chicken (sliced thin and cooked in a skillet) and combined it with a simple chicken broth–based sauce (which we then simmered in the same skillet) and the pasta. Then we came up with a whole host of combinations using different vegetables, cheeses, and herbs. Chicken and broccoli is one of the classic pairings, but we also developed some more inventive ones, like bacon, peas, and Gorgonzola, and mushrooms and pine nuts with Pecorino Romano.

In addition, we have developed our own version of the classic orecchiette, broccoli rabe, and sausage, but for this recipe we used sweet Italian chicken sausage instead of pork. Because the chicken sausage is leaner than its pork cousin, we have boosted the dish with onion, garlic, and red pepper flakes, and we stirred in flavorful extra-virgin olive oil before serving.

And in looking for more ways to use ground chicken, we developed recipes for chicken Bolognese and big "Little Italy–sized" chicken meatballs with marinara. We found that we were able get the Bolognese on the table in under an hour because, unlike the traditional trio of beef, pork, and veal, the chicken did not need such a long simmering time to become tender. To develop rich, deep flavor in our sauce, we added porcini mushrooms and pancetta, along with the traditional aromatics. For the meatballs, we combined the ground chicken with sweet Italian chicken sausage and added lots of Parmesan cheese, herbs, onions, and garlic. To keep the meatballs tender, we made a panade (or paste) using sandwich bread and milk.

Last but not least, we have included recipes for pasta salad with chicken (and vegetables)—the perfect light summer dinner. Like our chicken salads (see pages 28–31), we found that a whole roast chicken provided the perfect amount of meat for our recipes. (We like to make our own fuss-free bird, but a rotisserie chicken works as well.) While we normally like to cook our pasta until al dente, we found that for cold pasta we liked the pasta completely tender. Instead of rinsing the pasta to cool it, we tossed it with oil and spread it out on a baking sheet. This kept the starches intact, which allowed the pasta to hold on to the dressing. For the dressings, we developed a creamy pesto and a lemony vinaigrette that generously coated both the shredded chicken and the pasta.

We designed this chapter to offer a wide range of recipes for the pasta- and chicken-loving cook. Because the possibilities really are endless, you can come up with your own flavor and vegetable combinations—consult "Cooking Pasta 101" on page 254 for more general information on cooking pasta.

Pasta with Chicken and Vegetables

CHICKEN AND PASTA ARE A GREAT MATCH. Add some vegetables to the mix and you have the perfect weeknight dinner. Unfortunately, this simple pairing often produces disappointing results—tough meat, bland pasta, and drab-looking vegetables are usually hiding beneath a fatty cream sauce with little flavor. We knew we could do better. We wanted to develop a foolproof method for cooking the chicken, pair it with a clean-flavored sauce that complements the other elements without overwhelming them, and then develop a whole slew of recipes with vegetable, cheese, and flavor variations.

Right off the bat, we decided that boneless,

skinless chicken breasts were the best choice (they're easy to prepare and an ideal choice for what should be a relatively quick weeknight meal) and tested various cooking methods, including microwaving, broiling, sautéing, and poaching (simmering in a liquid). Not surprisingly, microwaving produced bland chicken with a steamed taste, and the timing was tricky. Broiling and sautéing produced meat with the most flavor, but the nicely seared edges of the chicken turned tough and stringy after being tossed with the pasta and sauce. Poaching the chicken—in the pasta water or the simmering sauce—produced meat that was tender and juicy, but the flavor was washed out.

Wanting the flavor provided by a sauté and the tenderness that comes with poaching, we focused on combining these methods. Lightly cooking the chicken with a little butter in a skillet until it just began to turn golden, we removed it from the pan when it was still underdone. After building a sauce in the now-empty skillet, we returned the chicken to the pan and let it simmer in the sauce until fully cooked. That did the trick; we now had chicken that was tender and flavorful.

Turning our attention next to the additional ingredients, we found that some, such as mushrooms, bacon, and caramelized onions, could be cooked in the pan before building the sauce. When it came to the green vegetables, namely broccoli, asparagus, and kale, we found that it was best to blanch them, given that there was already a pot of boiling water going for the pasta. We simply transferred them to a paper towel–lined plate to drain while we boiled the pasta.

Up until now, we had been making a sauce by thickening heavy cream with flour and butter (called a roux), and we had determined that garlic, pepper flakes, fresh herbs, and white wine were all crucial for flavor. But tasters wanted more. We tried omitting the roux and letting the cream simmer and thicken on its own, but this produced a sauce that was much too fatty. We then tried replacing portions of the cream with chicken broth and were relieved to finally hear positive comments from tasters.

The flavors of the wine, garlic, and herbs were no longer muted by the heavy sauce, and, as an added bonus, the broth gave our dish a significant boost in chicken flavor. Incrementally increasing the amount of broth and decreasing the amount of cream, we made sauce after sauce, each one better than the last, until the cream was entirely eliminated. Instead, we rounded out each dish with a few tablespoons of butter, cream, or olive oil, a handful of cheese, and some fresh herbs. Now the sauce finally carried some serious flavor, and we had a simple chicken and pasta dish that was bound to be a crowd-pleaser.

Chicken and Pasta with Broccoli and Sun-Dried Tomatoes

SERVES 4

Be sure to use low-sodium chicken broth in this recipe; regular chicken broth will make the dish extremely salty. The broccoli is blanched in the same water that is later used to cook the pasta. Remove the broccoli when it is tender at the edges but still crisp at the core—it will continue to cook with residual heat. If you can't find Asiago cheese, you can substitute Parmesan.

- 4 tablespoons (½ stick) unsalted butter
- 1 pound boneless, skinless chicken breasts (about 2 large breasts), trimmed and sliced thin (see the illustrations on page 242)
- 1 medium onion, minced
- Salt
- 6 medium garlic cloves, minced or pressed through a garlic press (about 2 tablespoons)
- 2 teaspoons minced fresh thyme leaves
- 2 teaspoons unbleached all-purpose flour
- ¼ teaspoon red pepper flakes
- 2 cups low-sodium chicken broth
- 1 cup dry white wine
- 1½ pounds broccoli (about 1 large bunch), florets cut into 1-inch pieces and stalks discarded (see illustration 1 on page 279) (see note)
- 8 ounces ziti or penne (about 2½ cups)
- 2 ounces Asiago cheese, grated (about 1 cup), plus more for serving (see note)

- 1 (7- to 8½-ounce) jar oil-packed sun-dried tomatoes, rinsed, patted dry, and cut into ¼-inch strips (about 1 cup)
- 1 tablespoon minced fresh parsley leaves
- Ground black pepper

1. Bring 4 quarts water to a boil in a large pot for the broccoli and the pasta.

2. Meanwhile, heat 1 tablespoon of the butter in a 12-inch nonstick skillet over high heat until beginning to brown. Add the chicken, break up any clumps, and cook without stirring until beginning to brown, about 1 minute. Stir the chicken and continue to cook until almost cooked through, about 2 minutes longer. Transfer the chicken to a medium bowl, cover with foil, and set aside.

3. Add 1 tablespoon more of the butter, the onion, and ¼ teaspoon salt to the skillet and cook over high heat until browned on the edges, 2 to 3 minutes. Stir in the garlic, thyme, flour, and pepper flakes and cook until fragrant, about 30 seconds. Add the chicken broth and wine, bring to a simmer, and cook over medium heat until the sauce has thickened slightly and reduced to 1¼ cups, about 15 minutes.

4. Meanwhile, stir 1 tablespoon salt and the broccoli into the boiling water and cook, stirring often, until the broccoli florets are crisp-tender, about 2 minutes (do not overcook). Using a slotted spoon, transfer the broccoli to a paper towel–lined plate and set aside.

5. Return the water to a boil, stir in the pasta, and cook, stirring often, until the pasta is al dente. Reserve 1 cup of the pasta cooking water, then drain the pasta and return it to the pot. Return the chicken to the skillet along with the remaining 2 tablespoons butter, the Asiago, and sun-dried tomatoes. Continue to simmer until the chicken is cooked through, about 1 minute.

6. Pour the chicken and sauce mixture over the pasta and add the reserved broccoli and the parsley. Toss gently to combine, adding the reserved pasta cooking water as needed to loosen the sauce. Season with salt and pepper to taste and serve, passing additional Asiago separately.

Chicken and Pasta with Caramelized Onions and Red Bell Peppers

SERVES 4

Be sure to use low-sodium chicken broth in this recipe; regular chicken broth will make the dish extremely salty. If you can't find Asiago cheese, you can substitute Parmesan.

- 6 tablespoons (¾ stick) unsalted butter
- 1 pound boneless, skinless chicken breasts (about 2 large breasts), trimmed and sliced thin (see the illustrations on page 242)
- 3 medium onions, halved and sliced thin
- Salt
- 2 red bell peppers, stemmed, seeded, and sliced into ¼-inch strips
- 6 medium garlic cloves, minced or pressed through a garlic press (about 2 tablespoons)
- 2 teaspoons minced fresh thyme leaves
- 2 teaspoons unbleached all-purpose flour
- ¼ teaspoon red pepper flakes
- 2 cups low-sodium chicken broth
- 1 cup dry white wine
- 8 ounces ziti or penne (about 2½ cups)
- 2 ounces Asiago cheese, grated (about 1 cup), plus more for serving
- ½ cup shredded fresh basil leaves (see the illustrations on page 252)
- Ground black pepper

1. Bring 4 quarts water to a boil in a large pot for the pasta.

2. Meanwhile, heat 1 tablespoon of the butter in a 12-inch nonstick skillet over high heat until beginning to brown. Add the chicken, break up any clumps, and cook without stirring until beginning to brown, about 1 minute. Stir the chicken and continue to cook until almost cooked through, about 2 minutes longer. Transfer the chicken to a medium bowl, cover with foil, and set aside.

3. Add 2 tablespoons more of the butter, the onions, and ¼ teaspoon salt to the skillet and cook over medium heat until softened and golden brown, about 15 minutes. Add the bell peppers and cook until softened, about 5 minutes. Transfer to

the bowl with the chicken.

4. Add 1 tablespoon more of the butter, the garlic, thyme, flour, and pepper flakes to the skillet and cook over medium heat until fragrant, about 30 seconds. Add the chicken broth and wine, bring to a simmer, and cook over medium heat until the sauce has thickened slightly and reduced to 1¼ cups, about 15 minutes.

5. Meanwhile, stir 1 tablespoon salt and the pasta into the boiling water and cook, stirring often, until the pasta is al dente. Reserve 1 cup of the pasta cooking water, then drain the pasta and return it to the pot. Return the chicken, onions, and bell peppers to the skillet along with the remaining 2 tablespoons butter and the Asiago. Continue to simmer until the chicken is cooked through, about 1 minute.

6. Pour the chicken and sauce mixture over the pasta and add the basil. Toss gently to combine, adding the reserved pasta cooking water as needed to loosen the sauce. Season with salt and pepper to taste and serve, passing additional Asiago separately.

SHREDDING BASIL

For larger herb leaves such as basil or mint, a cut called a chiffonade is the most attractive and bruise-free way to shred them.

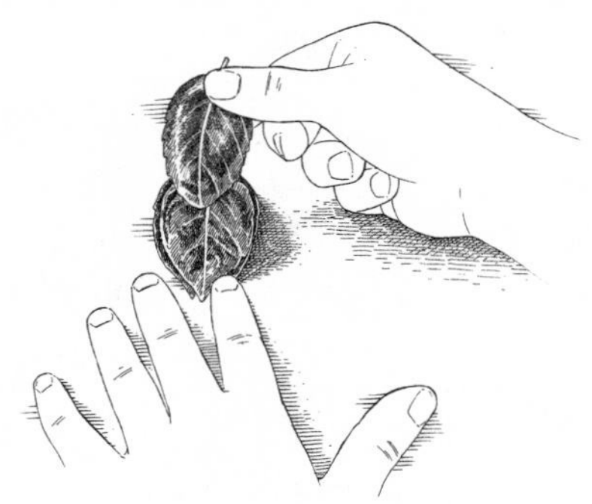

1. Stack three or four clean, dry leaves.

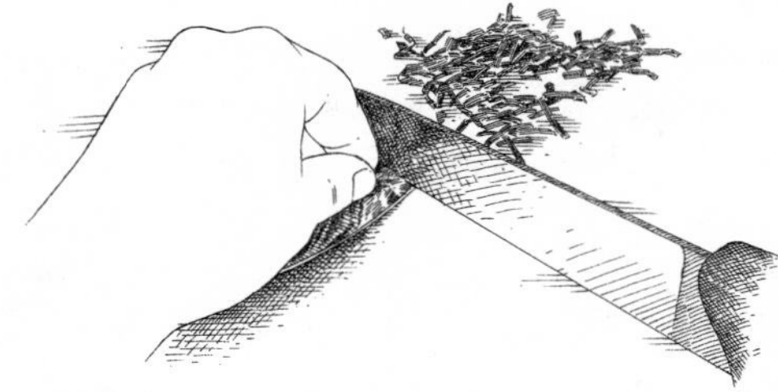

2. Roll the stack up tightly, like a cigar, and slice thin.

Chicken and Pasta with Greens and Beans

SERVES 4

Be sure to use low-sodium chicken broth in this recipe; regular chicken broth will make the dish extremely salty.

- 2 tablespoons unsalted butter
- 1 pound boneless, skinless chicken breasts (about 2 large breasts), trimmed and sliced thin (see the illustrations on page 242)
- 1 medium onion, minced
- Salt
- 6 medium garlic cloves, minced or pressed through a garlic press (about 2 tablespoons)
- 2 teaspoons minced fresh thyme leaves
- 2 teaspoons unbleached all-purpose flour
- ¼ teaspoon red pepper flakes
- 2 cups low-sodium chicken broth
- 1 cup dry white wine
- 1½ pounds kale (about 1 large bunch), thick stems trimmed and leaves sliced thin (see the illustration on page 58)
- 8 ounces cavatappi or campanelle (about 3 cups)
- 1 (15-ounce) can cannellini beans, drained and rinsed
- 2 ounces Parmesan cheese, grated (about 1 cup), plus more for serving
- 2 tablespoons extra-virgin olive oil
- Ground black pepper

1. Bring 4 quarts water to a boil in a large pot for the kale and the pasta.

2. Meanwhile, heat 1 tablespoon of the butter in a 12-inch nonstick skillet over high heat until beginning to brown. Add the chicken, break up any clumps, and cook without stirring until beginning to brown, about 1 minute. Stir the chicken and continue to cook until almost cooked through, about 2 minutes longer. Transfer the chicken to a medium bowl, cover with foil, and set aside.

3. Add the remaining 1 tablespoon butter, the onion, and ¼ teaspoon salt to the skillet and cook over high heat until browned on the edges, 2 to 3 minutes. Stir in the garlic, thyme, flour, and pepper

flakes and cook until fragrant, about 30 seconds. Add the chicken broth and wine, bring to a simmer, and cook over medium heat until the sauce has thickened slightly and reduced to 1¼ cups, about 15 minutes.

4. Meanwhile, stir 1 tablespoon salt and the kale into the boiling water and cook, stirring often, until the kale is almost tender, about 2 minutes (do not overcook). Using a slotted spoon, transfer the kale to a paper towel–lined plate and set aside.

5. Return the water to a boil, stir in the pasta, and cook, stirring often, until the pasta is al dente. Reserve 1 cup of the pasta cooking water, then drain the pasta and return it to the pot. Return the chicken to the skillet along with the beans, Parmesan, and oil. Continue to simmer until the chicken is cooked through, about 1 minute.

6. Pour the chicken and sauce mixture over the pasta and add the reserved kale. Toss gently to combine, adding the reserved pasta cooking water as needed to loosen the sauce. Season with salt and pepper to taste and serve, passing additional Parmesan separately.

Chicken and Pasta with Bacon, Peas, and Gorgonzola

SERVES 4

Be sure to use low-sodium chicken broth in this recipe; regular chicken broth will make the dish extremely salty. If you like, you can substitute 4 ounces Fontina, shredded (about 1 cup), for the Gorgonzola.

- **3 tablespoons unsalted butter**
- **1 pound boneless, skinless chicken breasts (about 2 large breasts), trimmed and sliced thin (see the illustrations on page 242)**
- **4 ounces (about 4 slices) bacon, chopped medium**
- **1 medium onion, minced**
- **Salt**
- **6 medium garlic cloves, minced or pressed through a garlic press (about 2 tablespoons)**
- **2 teaspoons minced fresh thyme leaves**
- **2 teaspoons unbleached all-purpose flour**
- **¼ teaspoon red pepper flakes**
- **2 cups low-sodium chicken broth**
- **1 cup dry white wine**
- **8 ounces cavatappi or campanelle (about 3 cups)**
- **1 cup frozen peas**
- **2 ounces Gorgonzola cheese, crumbled (about ½ cup) (see note)**
- **2 tablespoons minced fresh chives**
- **Ground black pepper**

1. Bring 4 quarts water to a boil in a large pot for the pasta.

2. Meanwhile, heat 1 tablespoon of the butter in a 12-inch nonstick skillet over high heat until beginning to brown. Add the chicken, break up any clumps, and cook without stirring until beginning to brown, about 1 minute. Stir the chicken and continue to cook until almost cooked through, about 2 minutes longer. Transfer the chicken to a medium bowl, cover with foil, and set aside.

3. Add the bacon to the skillet and cook over medium-low heat until the fat is rendered and the bacon is crisp, about 9 minutes. Transfer to a paper towel–lined plate, leaving 1 tablespoon of the fat behind in the pan. Add the onion and ¼ teaspoon salt to the skillet and cook over high heat until browned on the edges, 2 to 3 minutes. Stir in the garlic, thyme, flour, and pepper flakes and cook until fragrant, about 30 seconds. Add the chicken broth and wine, bring to a simmer, and cook over medium heat until the sauce has thickened slightly and reduced to 1¼ cups, about 15 minutes.

4. Meanwhile, stir 1 tablespoon salt and the pasta into the boiling water and cook, stirring often, until the pasta is al dente. Reserve 1 cup of the pasta cooking water, then drain the pasta and return it to the pot. Return the chicken to the skillet along with the remaining 2 tablespoons butter and the peas. Continue to simmer until the chicken is cooked through, about 1 minute.

5. Pour the chicken and sauce mixture over the pasta and add the reserved bacon, the Gorgonzola, and chives. Toss gently to combine, adding the reserved pasta cooking water as needed to loosen the sauce. Season with salt and pepper to taste and serve.

Cooking Pasta 101

Cooking pasta seems simple—just boil water and wait—but cooking perfect pasta takes some finesse. Here's how we do it.

CHOOSING PASTA

You have two basic choices—dried or fresh. Dried pasta is made from high-protein durum wheat flour, so it cooks up springy and firm and is suitable for thick tomato and meat sauces as well as concentrated oil-based sauces. Fresh pasta is made from softer all-purpose flour and is quite delicate. Its rough, porous surface pairs well with dairy-based sauces.

DRIED SEMOLINA PASTA

No longer gummy and bland, American brands of semolina (which is coarsely ground durum wheat) pasta have improved so much that many bested their pricey Italian counterparts in our tasting.

Cooking Tip: When cooked to al dente, pasta retains some chew but is neither hard nor gummy at the center.

DRIED PASTA WINNER: RONZONI

FRESH EGG PASTA

While your best bet for fresh pasta is still homemade, there are a few serviceable supermarket options. Our favorite brand is found in the refrigerator case, sealed in spoilage-retardant packaging and made from pasteurized eggs.

Cooking Tip: Fresh pasta is easily overcooked, so test early. Drain the pasta a few minutes before it reaches al dente, return it to the empty pot, and then cook with the sauce for another minute or two. The underdone pasta will absorb flavor from the sauce, and the starch from the pasta will help thicken the sauce.

FRESH PASTA WINNER: BUITONI

WHOLE WHEAT AND GRAIN PASTAS

Most of the whole wheat pastas we tried were gummy, grainy, or lacking in "wheaty" flavor, but there were a few that we really liked. Our favorite is made from a blend of whole wheat and regular flours. We were less thrilled about the alternative-grain pastas we tried. Made from rice, corn, quinoa, and spelt, these products were plagued by shaggy, mushy textures and off flavors. If you're desperate to avoid wheat, try Tinkyáda Organic Brown Rice Pasta.

Cooking tip: Cook and use as you would dried semolina pasta.

WHOLE WHEAT PASTA WINNER: RONZONI HEALTHY HARVEST

MATCHING PASTA SAUCES AND SHAPES

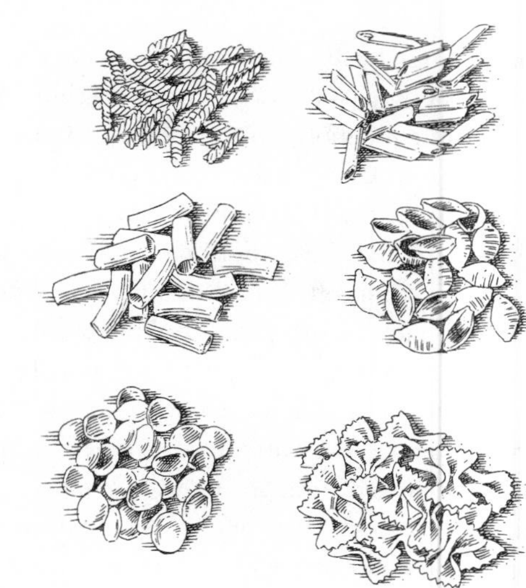

SHORT PASTAS

Short tubular or molded pasta shapes do an excellent job of trapping chunky sauces. Sauces with very large chunks are best with rigatoni or other large tubes. Sauces with small chunks make more sense with fusilli or penne. Clockwise from top right, the shapes shown are: penne, shells, farfalle, orecchiette, rigatoni, and fusilli.

STRAND PASTAS

Long strands are best with smooth sauces or sauces with very small chunks. In general, wider noodles, such as pappardelle and fettuccine, can support slightly chunkier sauces than can very thin noodles. Clockwise from top right, the shapes shown are: fettuccine, linguine, spaghetti, capellini, and pappardelle.

AT A GLANCE

COOKING PASTA

1. Add salt and pasta to water at a rolling boil.
2. Stir immediately to prevent sticking.
3. Cover and return to boil, stirring often.
4. Check early and often for doneness.
5. Reserve some cooking water and drain.
6. Sauce, season, and serve immediately.

THE SETUP

Pasta cooks quickly and should be served immediately, so have all the necessary ingredients and utensils assembled before you begin—as well as your family or dinner guests. As the Italians say, "People wait for pasta, not the other way around."

Water and Pot: You'll need 4 quarts of water to cook ½ to 1 pound of dried pasta. Any less and the noodles may stick. Pasta leaches starch as it cooks. Without plenty of water to dilute it, the starch coats the noodles, making them sticky.

The pot should be large, with at least a 6-quart capacity—to guard against boilovers. But forget expensive metal pots and fancy mesh inserts. A lightweight, inexpensive stockpot with sturdy handles and a lid does the job just fine.

Oil: Unless you're serving a butter- or cream-based sauce, keep some extra-virgin olive oil on hand for drizzling over the sauced pasta for a final burst of flavor. Just don't waste it in the cooking water: It won't prevent the pasta from sticking (not a problem if you use enough water), but it will prevent the sauce from coating the pasta.

Pasta: One pound of dried pasta generally serves four to six people as a main course, depending on whether the sauce is light (tomato sauce), rich (creamy Alfredo or hearty Bolognese), or bulked up with other ingredients, such as vegetables or seafood.

Liquid Measuring Cup: In that last flurry of activity before saucing the pasta and getting dinner on the table, it's easy to forget to reserve some cooking water to thin the sauce, if needed. We often place a measuring cup in the colander as a reminder when we start to cook.

Colander: Once the pasta is drained, give the colander a shake or two, but don't shake the pasta bone-dry. The little bit of hot cooking water clinging to the pasta will help the sauce coat it.

Sauce: Don't drop the pasta into the water until the sauce is nearly ready. Smooth sauces and sauces with very small bits, such as garlic and oil, are best with long strands of pasta. Chunkier sauces are best matched with short tubular or molded shapes.

Salt: Properly seasoned cooking water is crucial for good flavor—use 1 tablespoon table salt (or 2 tablespoons kosher salt) per 4 quarts of water.

Serving Bowls and Ladle: We like to serve pasta in wide soup bowls, as the edge provides an easy place to twirl noodles on a fork. To warm, before serving the pasta (especially important with cream sauces, which cool quickly and congeal) add a few extra cups of water to the pasta pot. When it boils, ladle about ½ cup of boiling water into each bowl and let stand while the pasta cooks.

Pasta Fork: Of the countless items of pasta paraphernalia we've tested over the years, the only one we recommend is a pasta fork—a long-handled, perforated spoon with ridged teeth. The wood variety is clunky and prone to splitting, but the plastic and stainless-steel versions are great. Not essential—basic tongs work fine—but we're glad we bought one.

QUICK TIP

WARM THE SERVING BOWL

If you're using a large serving bowl, try placing it underneath the colander while draining the pasta. The hot water heats up the bowl, which keeps the pasta warm longer.

Chicken and Pasta with Mushrooms and Pine Nuts

SERVES 4

Be sure to use low-sodium chicken broth in this recipe; regular chicken broth will make the dish extremely salty.

- 3 tablespoons unsalted butter
- 1 pound boneless, skinless chicken breasts (about 2 large breasts), trimmed and sliced thin (see the illustrations on page 242)
- 1 pound white mushrooms, wiped clean and sliced thin
- 1 medium onion, minced
- Salt
- 6 medium garlic cloves, minced or pressed through a garlic press (about 2 tablespoons)
- 2 teaspoons minced fresh thyme leaves
- 2 teaspoons unbleached all-purpose flour
- ½ ounce dried porcini mushrooms, rinsed and minced
- 2 cups low-sodium chicken broth
- 1 cup dry white wine
- 8 ounces cavatappi or campanelle (about 3 cups)
- 2 ounces Pecorino Romano cheese, grated (about 1 cup), plus more for serving
- 2 tablespoons heavy cream
- ¼ cup pine nuts, toasted
- 1 tablespoon minced fresh parsley leaves
- Ground black pepper

1. Bring 4 quarts water to a boil in a large pot for the pasta.

2. Meanwhile, heat 1 tablespoon of the butter in a 12-inch nonstick skillet over high heat until beginning to brown. Add the chicken, break up any clumps, and cook without stirring until beginning to brown, about 1 minute. Stir the chicken and continue to cook until almost cooked through, about 2 minutes longer. Transfer the chicken to a medium bowl, cover with foil, and set aside.

3. Add 1 tablespoon more of the butter and the mushrooms to the skillet and cook over medium-high heat until the mushrooms release their liquid and are browned, about 12 minutes. Transfer to the bowl with the chicken.

4. Add the remaining tablespoon of the butter, the onion, and ¼ teaspoon salt to the skillet and cook over high heat until browned on the edges, 2 to 3 minutes. Stir in the garlic, thyme, flour, and porcini and cook until fragrant, about 30 seconds. Add the chicken broth and wine, bring to a simmer, and cook over medium heat until the sauce has thickened slightly and reduced to 1¼ cups, about 15 minutes.

5. Meanwhile, stir 1 tablespoon salt and the pasta into the boiling water and cook, stirring often, until the pasta is al dente. Reserve 1 cup of the pasta cooking water, then drain the pasta and return it to the pot. Return the chicken and mushrooms to the skillet along with the Pecorino Romano and cream. Continue to simmer until the chicken is cooked through, about 1 minute.

6. Pour the chicken and sauce mixture over the pasta and add the pine nuts and parsley. Toss gently to combine, adding the reserved pasta cooking water as needed to loosen the sauce. Season with salt and pepper to taste and serve, passing additional Pecorino Romano separately.

Chicken and Pasta with Asparagus and Lemon

SERVES 4

Be sure to use low-sodium chicken broth in this recipe; regular chicken broth will make the dish extremely salty.

- 4 tablespoons (½ stick) unsalted butter
- 1 pound boneless, skinless chicken breasts (about 2 large breasts), trimmed and sliced thin (see the illustrations on page 242)
- 1 leek, white and light green parts only, minced and rinsed thoroughly (see the illustrations on page 45)
- Salt
- 6 medium garlic cloves, minced or pressed through a garlic press (about 2 tablespoons)
- 2 teaspoons minced fresh thyme leaves
- 2 teaspoons unbleached all-purpose flour
- 2 cups low-sodium chicken broth

- 1 cup dry white wine
- 1 pound asparagus (about 1 bunch), tough ends trimmed and cut into 1-inch lengths
- 8 ounces penne or ziti (about 2½ cups)
- 2 ounces Parmesan cheese, grated (about 1 cup), plus more for serving
- 2 teaspoons grated zest and ¼ cup juice from 1 lemon
- 2 tablespoons shredded fresh basil leaves (see the illustrations on page 252)
- Ground black pepper

1. Bring 4 quarts water to a boil in a large pot for the asparagus and the pasta.

2. Meanwhile, heat 1 tablespoon of the butter in a 12-inch nonstick skillet over high heat until beginning to brown. Add the chicken, break up any clumps, and cook without stirring until beginning to brown, about 1 minute. Stir the chicken and continue to cook until almost cooked through, about 2 minutes longer. Transfer the chicken to a medium bowl, cover with foil, and set aside.

3. Add 1 tablespoon more of the butter, the leek, and ¼ teaspoon salt to the skillet and cook over high heat until browned on the edges, 2 to 3 minutes. Stir in the garlic, thyme, and flour and cook until fragrant, about 30 seconds. Add the chicken broth and wine, bring to a simmer, and cook over medium heat until the sauce has thickened slightly and reduced to 1¼ cups, about 15 minutes.

4. Meanwhile, stir 1 tablespoon salt and the asparagus into the boiling water and cook, stirring often, until the asparagus is crisp-tender, about 1 minute (do not overcook). Using a slotted spoon, transfer the asparagus to a paper towel–lined plate and set aside.

5. Return the water to a boil, stir in the pasta, and cook, stirring often, until the pasta is al dente. Reserve 1 cup of the pasta cooking water, then drain the pasta and return it to the pot. Return the chicken to the skillet along with the remaining 2 tablespoons butter, the Parmesan, lemon zest, and lemon juice. Continue to simmer until the chicken is cooked through, about 1 minute.

6. Pour the chicken and sauce mixture over the pasta and add the reserved asparagus and the basil. Toss gently to combine, adding the reserved pasta cooking water as needed to loosen the sauce. Season with salt and pepper to taste and serve, passing additional Parmesan separately.

Orecchiette with Broccoli Rabe

BROCCOLI RABE IS NATIVE TO THE Mediterranean region, and although it was once a wild herb it is now widely grown throughout southern Italy. Broccoli rabe looks much like long-stemmed broccoli, but it has a spicy, bitter flavor that is commonly paired with sausage, garlic, and orecchiette (an ear-shaped pasta) for a simple and satisfying meal.

If you are not familiar with broccoli rabe, it can seem tricky to cook. Broccoli rabe contains thick stalks, tender leaves, and small florets. If all the stalks were removed, there would be little left to this plant. We had to devise a cooking method that would soften the stalks but keep the florets and leaves from becoming mushy.

We tested boiling and steaming and found that steaming is not ideal—it cooks this tough green unevenly. By the time the thick stalks softened, the tender florets were mushy. Boiling does a better job of cooking the various parts of this plant evenly, if only because it is faster and there is less time for the florets to become mushy. But the thick ends of each stalk never softened properly, even when boiled, so we decided that they should be trimmed before cooking. The remaining portion of the stalks and the florets should be cut into bite-sized pieces (about 1½ inches long).

Using the same pot of water for boiling the broccoli rabe and the pasta made for a streamlined method; we simply boiled the broccoli rabe first, then removed it with a slotted spoon or spider, and then boiled the pasta. Vegetables are often dunked in ice water after being quickly boiled to prevent any further cooking from residual heat (a process called blanching), but we found this step unnecessarily cumbersome for such a simple dish. Rather,

INGREDIENTS: Parmesan Cheese

The buttery, nutty, slightly fruity taste and crystalline crunch of genuine Parmigiano-Reggiano cheese is a one-of-a-kind experience. Produced using traditional methods for the past 800 years in one government-designated area of northern Italy, this premium Parmesan has a distinctive flavor that is said to come as much from the region's own geography as from the production process. But is all of this regional emphasis for real, or can really good Parmesan be made anywhere? Recently, many more brands of American-made Parmesan have been appearing in supermarkets. They're sold at a fraction of the price of the authentic stuff, which can cost up to $33 a pound. But what are you giving up when you buy American?

To see how they stacked up, we bought eight nationally distributed brands at the supermarket: six domestic Parmesans and two imported Parmigiano-Reggianos, ranging in price from $8.49 to $17.17 per pound.

In Italy, the making of Parmesan is highly codified. In brief, raw, partly skimmed milk from cows that graze in a small area of Emilia-Romagna in northern Italy is warmed and combined with a starter culture to begin the curdling process. Eventually, the curds are formed into wheels that weigh about 80 pounds, and the words "Parmigiano-Reggiano" are stenciled on the exterior. The cheese is submerged in brine (salty water) for several days. Finally, the cheese is aged. The process is laborious and time-consuming, which explains the high price tag for this cheese. There are also plenty of places to cut corners, which is one reason why domestic Parmesans are less expensive. But that's not the whole story.

What the cows eat will affect the flavor of their milk and the resulting cheese. In Italy, the cows designated for Parmigiano-Reggiano graze outdoors; in the United States, most cows are not pastured but are given a concentrated feed. Additionally, the American practice of pasteurization kills microorganisms (such as microflora and yeasts) that are retained in Italian raw milk, where they add unique flavor components. Similarly, the starter cultures differ, with Italians using the whey left from the cheese-making of the day before, and Americans generally purchasing starters from enzyme manufacturers.

Given all the differences in the manufacturing process on each side of the Atlantic, it shouldn't come as much of a surprise that our tasters easily picked out the imports in our lineup of eight supermarket cheeses. The two genuine Parmigiano-Reggianos, sold in supermarkets under brand names Boar's Head and Il Villaggio, were the panel's clear favorites.

So what made the imported cheeses stand out? Interestingly, though our test kitchen tasters usually like salty foods, the imports had the lowest salt content. Texture was another big factor. The Italian imports had a drier, crumblier texture and crystalline crunch. Nearly all of the American cheeses were perceptibly moister, some even to the point of bounciness, with few or no crystals.

While Italian Parmesans are all aged at least 12 and usually 24 months, for domestic Parmesan the federal standard is 10 months, though a few manufacturers, including Kraft, petitioned (and got temporary permission) to shorten the aging standard to six months. The Kraft products in our lineup performed poorly. (Kraft also now produces our previous favorite domestic Parmesan, Digiorno, using this new shorter aging period, which may help explain why it rated so poorly with our tasters this time.)

While our tasters clearly preferred Italian Parmigiano-Reggiano, they also praised the top two domestic cheeses for their pleasingly "nutty" flavor. BelGioioso and SarVecchio were two of the longer-aged of the domestic cheeses, at 10 months and 20 months, respectively. While these cheeses can't really compete with our top-ranked imports, BelGioioso offered "lovely, delicate flavor" for just more than half the price.

THE BEST SUPERMARKET PARMESAN CHEESE

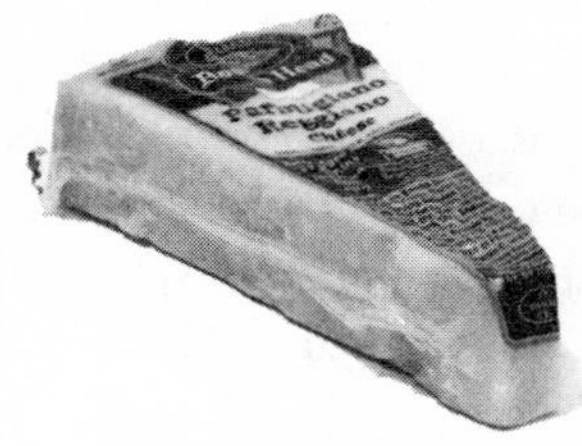

BOAR'S HEAD

IL VILLAGGIO

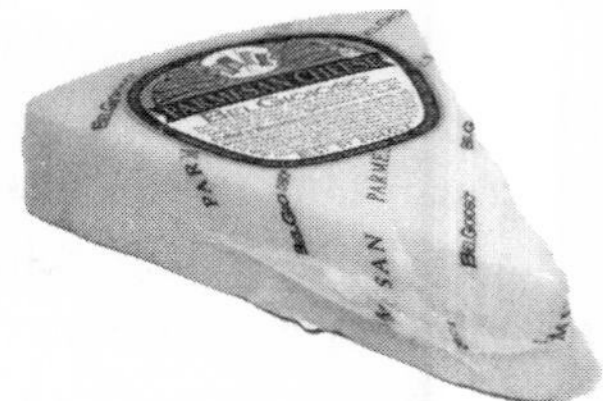

BELGIOIOSO

Real Parmigiano-Reggiano was tasters' clear favorite; both Boar's Head and Il Villaggio can be found in supermarkets. Priced at just $9 per pound, domestically made BelGioioso Parmesan is surprisingly good and is our best buy.

we undercooked the broccoli rabe by a few seconds, then let the residual heat finish cooking it through while the pasta boiled.

Sweet sausage is a classic pairing with broccoli rabe and pasta—its flavor balances the bitterness of the greens. This dish is typically made with pork sausage, but we found chicken sausage to be a great substitute—it is widely available in supermarkets and is a lighter alternative to pork sausage. We found it best to remove the sausage from its casing and break it into small, bite-sized pieces so that its flavor could be evenly distributed throughout the dish. A generous dose of sautéed garlic and a pinch of spicy red pepper flakes also pumped up the flavor of the dish nicely.

As for the sauce, tasters preferred a combination of a little olive oil and cheese, rather than a broth-based sauce, to lightly coat the pasta. The additional flavors of the broth (we tried both chicken and vegetable broth) were unwelcome and overwhelmed this otherwise fresh-tasting dish. Some recipes we found used a combination of butter and oil for the sauce, and tasters agreed that a little butter in the sauce tasted good; stirring the butter into the pasta with the sauce preserved its fresh, clean, dairy flavor. When dealing with a simple olive oil–based sauce where only a small amount of oil is used, we noted that it is important to reserve some of the pasta water to help keep the finished dish from appearing dry. The pasta water has a seasoned flavor and a slightly starchy consistency that are ideal for keeping the dish fresh and moist without adding any unwelcome flavors.

Orecchiette with Chicken Sausage and Broccoli Rabe

SERVES 4

Ziti or penne can be substituted for the orecchiette. If you prefer to use broccoli instead of broccoli rabe, use 2 pounds broccoli cut into 1-inch florets, and increase the boiling time to 2 minutes in step 3.

- **2 tablespoons extra-virgin olive oil**
- **8 ounces sweet Italian chicken sausage, casings removed**
- **1 medium onion, minced**
- **9 garlic cloves, minced or pressed through a garlic press (about 3 tablespoons)**
- **½ teaspoon red pepper flakes**
- **Salt**
- **1 bunch broccoli rabe (about 1 pound), ends trimmed, cut into 1½-inch lengths (see the illustrations below) (see note)**
- **1 pound orecchiette (see note)**
- **2 ounces Parmesan or Asiago cheese, grated (about 1 cup), plus more for serving**
- **2 tablespoons unsalted butter**
- **Ground black pepper**

1. Bring 4 quarts water to a boil in a large pot for the broccoli rabe and the pasta.

2. Meanwhile, heat the oil in a 12-inch nonstick skillet over medium-high heat until shimmering. Add the sausage and onion and cook until the sausage is lightly browned, breaking the meat up with a wooden spoon, 6 to 8 minutes. Stir in the garlic

PREPARING BROCCOLI RABE

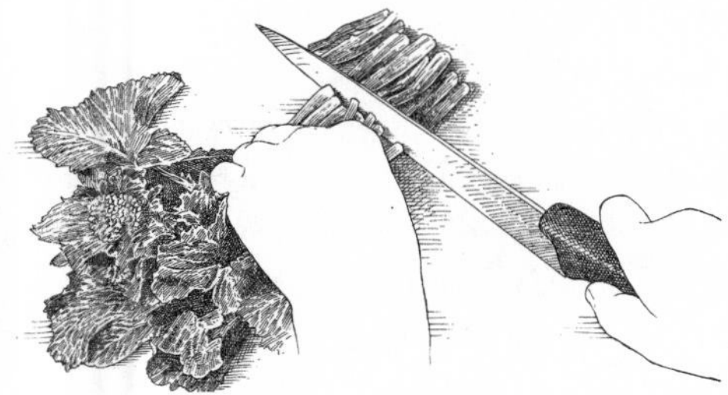

1. The thick stalk ends of broccoli rabe should be trimmed and discarded. Use a sharp knife to cut off the thickest part (usually the bottom 2 inches) of each stalk.

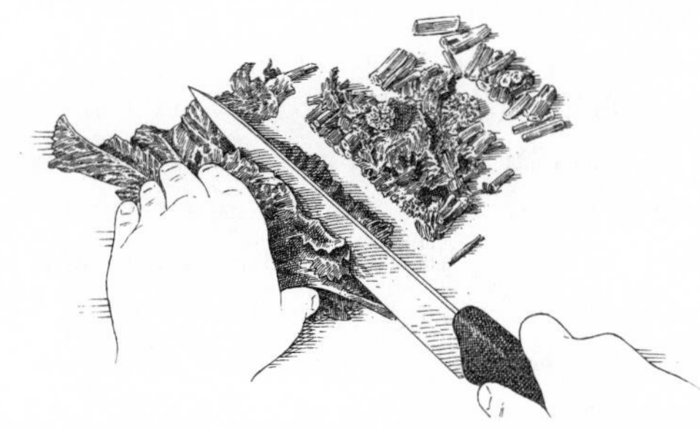

2. Cut the remaining stalks and florets into bite-sized pieces, about 1½ inches long.

and pepper flakes and cook until fragrant, about 30 seconds; set aside off the heat.

3. Stir 1 tablespoon salt and the broccoli rabe into the boiling water and cook, stirring often, until the broccoli rabe stems are crisp-tender, about 1½ minutes (do not overcook). Using a slotted spoon, transfer the broccoli rabe to the skillet with the sausage mixture and set aside.

4. Return the water to a boil, stir in the pasta, and cook, stirring often, until the pasta is al dente. Reserve 1 cup of the pasta cooking water, then drain the pasta and return it to the pot. Stir in ⅓ cup of the pasta cooking water, the sausage–broccoli rabe mixture, Parmesan, and butter until well combined. Add the remaining reserved pasta cooking water as needed to loosen the sauce. Season with salt and pepper to taste and serve, passing additional Parmesan separately.

Quick Cheesy Breadsticks

MAKES 6 BREADSTICKS

These soft breadsticks are a nice accompaniment to many of the recipes in this chapter.

- **1 pound store-bought pizza dough**
- **2 tablespoons olive oil, plus more for greasing the baking sheet**
- **1 ounce Parmesan cheese, grated (about ½ cup)**
- **½ teaspoon kosher salt**
- **½ teaspoon ground black pepper**

Adjust an oven rack to the middle position and heat the oven to 400 degrees. Roll out the pizza dough into a 9 by 6-inch rectangle. Cut the dough into six 1-inch-wide strips and lay them on a well-oiled baking sheet. Brush with 2 tablespoons olive oil and sprinkle with the Parmesan, salt, and pepper. Bake until golden brown, about 15 minutes. Let cool slightly on a wire rack and serve warm.

Pasta with Chicken Bolognese

HERE IN THE TEST KITCHEN WE ARE ALWAYS looking for new ways to use ground chicken, so when we stumbled on a recipe for chicken Bolognese, we were both excited and intrigued. Traditional Bolognese gets its big flavor and tender texture from braising ground meat (usually beef, pork, and veal) and softened vegetables in slowly reduced milk, wine, and tomatoes for upward of three hours. Could we achieve the same rich flavor and tender texture from ground chicken? More importantly, would using ground chicken, which is more tender than ground meat, speed up the simmering time and transform this Sunday night supper into a quick weeknight dinner? We had a hunch that it would; however, a few batches in the kitchen had us thinking otherwise—we were left with rubbery and somewhat bland chicken floating in a subpar tomato sauce. If we were going to do this, it had to be everything that we expected from a long-cooked meaty sauce.

Off the bat, we tried adding other ingredients to boost the flavor of the chicken, such as pancetta, prosciutto, and even porcini mushrooms. Prosciutto was out, owing to its overly salty flavor, but pancetta was a perfect fit—a little went a long way, adding a

SCIENCE:
Why Does Milk Make Meat Tender?

Browning adds flavor, but it also causes the protein molecules in ground meat to denature (unwind). As the proteins unwind, they link up to create a tighter network and squeeze out some of the water in the meat. Long simmering allows some of that liquid to be reabsorbed. But if you skip the browning and cook the meat in milk (or any other liquid), you limit the temperature of the meat to about 212 degrees (browning occurs in dry heat and at higher temperatures). As a result, meat cooked in milk does not dry out and toughen but remains tender. This means you can simmer the sauce just until the liquid has reduced to the right consistency, rather than waiting for the meat to soften.

subtle depth of flavor. And porcini mushrooms had such an amazingly beefy impact on the sauce that we just couldn't refuse them.

Vegetables were next under the microscope. Our favorite three-hour recipe called for celery, carrots, and onion, but we that found celery could go by the wayside. Garlic found a home, but tasters thought herbs were distracting. Either butter or olive oil could be used to sauté the vegetables, but we chose butter for its richer flavor.

Tomatoes add sweetness to the sauce, and their juice is used to braise the meat. We tried all kinds—whole, crushed, diced, sauce—and in the end liked the juicy canned diced tomatoes pulsed briefly in the food processor. To provide deeper, slow-cooked tomato flavor, we added some tomato paste.

In a true Bolognese, liquids are reduced slowly, one at a time, to tenderize the meat and develop the characteristic sweetness of the sauce. Because chicken is so lean, we knew that we had to find a quicker method—the chicken wouldn't withstand the half day of simmering time required to achieve such sweetness. To sweeten the sauce, we added a teaspoon of sugar. But it wasn't until we started thinking outside the box and tried sweeter white wines like Riesling and Gewürztraminer in place of the traditional dry Sauvignon Blanc that our sauce achieved the proper flavor. We even tried a white Zinfandel—the "other" white wine—often snubbed for its grapey-sweet flavor. Guess what? It worked beautifully. To cut the simmering time down even more, we reduced the wine on the side in a separate skillet; 1¼ cups went down to 2 tablespoons in 20 minutes.

Now meaty, sweet, and fast, this 45-minute sauce had everything going for it—well, almost. The chicken still presented itself in the form of little rubber pellets, and no sauce, however good, could mask that.

A hint of an answer came when we thought about the milk. In Italian cooking, milk and meat are often braised together, producing very tender results. What if we soaked the ground chicken in milk before cooking? We tried it. After sautéing the vegetables, we added the milk-soaked chicken to the hot pan and watched as it disintegrated into grainy, mushy bits. OK, this was not the perfect solution, but at least the chicken wasn't tough.

THE PAN MATTERS

When the sauce is simmered in a Dutch oven, it doesn't reduce quickly enough, and the consistency is watery (left). When the sauce is simmered in a 12-inch skillet, the texture is thicker, and the sauce reduces more quickly (right).

Next, we added the chicken directly to the pan along with the milk (no soaking). Same as before, the chicken fell apart into bits, but this time, no mush. Sure that we were on the right track, the next time we added the chicken to the pan, we quickly broke it into large pieces with a wooden spoon (letting it spend no more than a minute in the pan alone) and then added the milk. We stirred the two together to break up the meat and—success! This chicken was incredibly tender. Because we weren't browning the chicken, it never obtained that tough crust that takes hours upon hours to return to its tender state and, as a result, made a sauce that was rich and meaty, sweet and bold, luxuriously tender, and on the table in 45 minutes.

Pasta with Chicken Bolognese

SERVES 4 TO 6

Sweet white wines such as Gewürztraminer, Riesling, and even white Zinfandel work especially well with this sauce. For the best texture in the finished sauce, it is important to mince the vegetables. If desired, use a food processor, pulsing each vegetable separately until finely minced. Be diligent about breaking the chicken into small pieces in step 3, or the sauce will be too chunky. Any shape of pasta will work in this recipe, although fettuccine and rigatoni are our favorites. For more information on buying ground chicken, *see page 3.*

- 1 (28-ounce) can diced tomatoes
- 1¼ cups sweet white wine (see note)
- 4 tablespoons (½ stick) unsalted butter
- 4 ounces pancetta, cut into ¼-inch pieces
- ½ carrot, peeled and minced
- ½ medium onion, minced (about ½ cup)
- ½ ounce dried porcini mushrooms, rinsed and minced
- Salt
- 1 medium garlic clove, minced or pressed through a garlic press (about 1 teaspoon)
- 1 teaspoon sugar
- 1¼ pounds ground chicken
- 1½ cups whole milk
- 2 tablespoons tomato paste
- Ground black pepper
- 1 pound pasta (see note)
- Parmesan cheese, grated (for serving)

1. Pulse the tomatoes with their juice in a food processor until chopped fine, about eight 1-second pulses; set aside. Simmer the wine in a 10-inch nonstick skillet over medium-low heat until reduced to 2 tablespoons, about 20 minutes; set aside.

2. Meanwhile, melt the butter in a 12-inch skillet over medium-high heat. Add the pancetta and cook, stirring frequently, until well browned, about 2 minutes. Reduce the heat to medium; add the carrot, onion, porcini, and ¼ teaspoon salt and cook, stirring frequently, until the vegetables are softened, about 4 minutes. Stir in the garlic and sugar and cook until fragrant, about 30 seconds.

3. Add the chicken and cook for 1 minute, breaking the meat into small pieces with a wooden spoon. (Some of the chicken will still be pink.) Stir in the milk and bring to a simmer. Reduce the heat to medium and continue to simmer, breaking up the meat into small pieces, until most of the liquid has evaporated and the meat begins to sizzle, about 14 minutes.

4. Stir in the tomato paste and cook for 1 minute. Add the tomatoes, ¼ teaspoon salt, and ⅛ teaspoon pepper. Bring to a simmer over medium-high heat, then reduce heat to medium and simmer until the sauce is thickened but still moist, 12 to 15 minutes. Stir in the reduced wine and simmer until the flavors are blended, about 5 minutes.

5. Meanwhile, bring 4 quarts water to a boil in a large pot for the pasta. Stir in 1 tablespoon salt and the pasta and cook, stirring often, until the pasta is al dente. Reserve 1 cup of the pasta cooking water, then drain the pasta and return it to the pot. Stir in 2 cups of the sauce and 2 tablespoons of the pasta water until well combined. Add the remaining pasta cooking water as needed to loosen the sauce. Season with salt and pepper to taste and serve, passing the remaining sauce and Parmesan separately.

PANCETTA

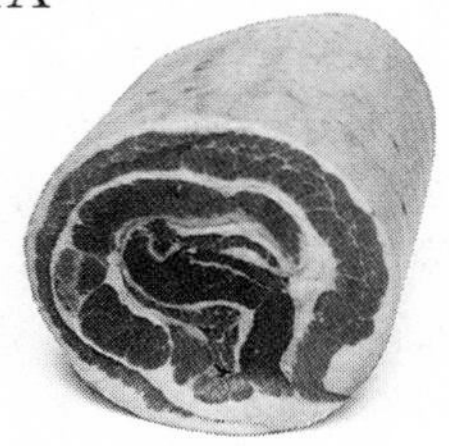

Just like bacon, pancetta comes from the belly of the pig, but it has a very different flavor. American bacon is cured with salt, sugar, and spices and then smoked. Pancetta is not smoked, and the cure does not contain sugar—just salt, pepper, and, usually, cloves. As a result, pancetta has a richer, meatier flavor than bacon. Pancetta is rolled tightly, packed in a casing, and then sliced thin or thick, as desired.

Chicken Meatballs and Marinara

ON THE HUNT FOR SOME INTERESTING WAYS to use ground chicken, we decided to develop a recipe for big, "Little Italy–sized" meatballs. We quickly found out that while making big meatballs is easy, making big meatballs with chicken that are also flavorful, tender, and moist, with enough structure to hold their shape, is difficult. Traditional meatball recipes rely on fatty meats like ground pork, beef, and veal to give their meatballs structure and flavor. As soon as we made our first few batches of chicken meatballs, we could see that we were in trouble. The meatballs were either dry and grainy, or moist and pasty—not to mention flavorless.

To start, we focused on the binders that were necessary to keep the meatballs tender and prevent them from falling apart during cooking. We started with the egg. Wondering if we could eliminate it, we made batches both with and without an egg, and it was clear that the egg added much-needed moisture. We tried using different amounts until we settled on two whole eggs. These meatballs were a breeze to handle.

As for remaining binders, the possibilities included dried bread crumbs, fresh bread crumbs, ground crackers, and bread (or bread crumbs) soaked in milk. We found that dried bread and cracker crumbs soaked up any available moisture, making the meatballs harder and drier when cooked. By comparison, the meatballs made with fresh bread crumbs soaked in milk were moist, creamy, and rich. Milk was clearly an important part of the equation. After trying various amounts, we settled on ¼ cup milk mixed with four slices of bread (processed into bread crumbs) to form a panade, or paste.

This drier, leaner mixture held its shape well and cooked up easily in the pan, but still, without all the fat that beef and pork provide, we were

EQUIPMENT: Traditional Skillets

The choices in material, weight, brand, and price of skillets—from $10 to $140—are dizzying. Preliminary tests on a lightweight discount store special selling for $10 confirmed our suspicions that cheap was not the way to go. But how much do you need to spend on this vital piece of kitchen equipment? To find out what more money buys, we zeroed in on a group of eight pans from well-known manufacturers, ranging in price from $60 to more than twice that.

All of the pans tested had flared sides, a design that makes it easier to flip foods in the pan (accomplished by jerking the pan sharply on the burner). Oddly, this design feature has created some confusion when it comes to nomenclature. Different manufacturers have different names for their flare-sided pans, including sauté pan, skillet, frypan, chef's pan, and omelette pan. In the test kitchen, we refer to flare-sided pans as skillets and to pans with straight sides (and often lids as well) as sauté pans. All of the pans tested also fall into a category we refer to as traditional—that is, none of the pans were nonstick. Most had uncoated stainless steel cooking surfaces, which we prize for promoting a fond (the browned, sticky bits that cling to the interior of the pan when food is sautéed and that help flavor sauces).

The pans tested measured 12 inches in diameter (across the top) or as close to that as we could get from each manufacturer. We like this large size in a skillet because it can accommodate a big steak or all of the pieces of a cut-up 3-pound chicken. Because the pan walls slope inward, the cooking surface of each pan measures considerably less than 12 inches. In fact, we found that even ¼ inch less cooking space could determine whether all of the chicken pieces fit without touching and therefore how well they would brown. (If a pan is too crowded, the food tends to steam rather than brown.)

Skillet construction also varies, and our group included two popular styles: clad and disk bottom. Clad means that the whole pan body, from the bottom up through the walls, is made from layers of the same metal that have been bonded under intense pressure and heat. These layers often form a sandwich, with the "filling" made of aluminum—which has the third-highest thermal conductivity of all metals, behind silver and copper—and each slice of "bread" made of stainless steel—which is attractive, durable, and nonreactive with acidic foods, but is a lousy heat conductor on its own.

In the disk-bottom construction style, only the pan bottom is layered, and so the walls are thinner than the bottom. We found the clad versus nonclad construction to be less important than weight. A lightweight (1 pound, 1 ounce) aluminum budget pan was the quickest to reach 361 degrees, at an average of 2.8 minutes, but the lightweight pan performed poorly in kitchen tests.

We concluded that a range of three to four pounds is ideal in a 12-inch skillet. These medium-weight pans brown foods beautifully, and most testers handled them comfortably. These pans have enough heft for heat retention and structural integrity, but not so much that they are difficult to lift or manipulate.

Which skillet should you buy? For its combination of excellent performance, optimum weight and balance, and overall ease of use, the All-Clad was the hands-down winner.

THE BEST TRADITIONAL SKILLET

ALL-CLAD

The All-Clad Stainless 12-Inch Frypan ($135) browns food perfectly and is spacious and easy to handle.

losing much of the flavor. Adding sautéed onion, garlic, red pepper flakes, dried oregano, and fresh parsley helped. A handful of Parmesan contributed welcome richness. Our meatballs were getting close, but there was still something missing. We tried different herbs and cheeses to no avail. Then a colleague suggested substituting raw Italian chicken sausage for some of the ground chicken. Our tasters loved the flavor boost the sausage added.

When we started cooking the meatballs, our progress came to a grinding halt. Even the largest frying pan in the test kitchen could handle only five or six meatballs at a time. What's more, the meatballs were so big that they turned crusty and charred on the outside before they were cooked through. Getting frustrated, we turned to the oven. Lower temperatures produced flabby, gray meatballs; we turned up the heat and our luck began to change. At 475 degrees, the meatballs were baking to a nice golden brown. This method was easy and much less messy then frying.

We could now focus on the marinara sauce. As we sautéed the onions, garlic, oregano, and red pepper flakes for the sauce, we were reminded of the batch that we had just sautéed for the meatballs. In our busy lives, we hate cooking the same thing twice for one recipe. Instead, we decided to sauté the mixture, transferring half of it to the bowl with the remaining meatball ingredients, and leaving the other half behind in the pot to continue making the marinara sauce.

To build rich tomato flavor, we added tomato paste to the sauce along with the aromatics and cooked it until fragrant. All that was left was to add crushed tomatoes and wine and simmer the entire mixture. The resulting sauce had a deep crimson color, a hearty texture, and the complex flavor of a slow-cooked sauce—all in just one hour. Served over a bowl of steaming-hot spaghetti, or eaten with a slice of crusty bread to sop up the sauce, these tender meatballs offer a big taste of Little Italy.

Rosemary-Olive Focaccia

SERVES 6

This recipe is great alongside pasta, but it's also good with many soups and stews.

- **1 pound store-bought pizza dough**
- **Extra-virgin olive oil, for oiling the baking dish and brushing the dough**
- **¼ cup olives, pitted and chopped**
- **½ teaspoon minced fresh rosemary**
- **½ teaspoon kosher salt**
- **½ teaspoon ground black pepper**

Adjust an oven rack to the middle position and heat the oven to 400 degrees. Press the pizza dough into a well-oiled 13 by 9-inch baking pan or 10-inch pie dish and dimple the surface with your fingers. Brush the dough liberally with extra-virgin olive oil and sprinkle with the olives, rosemary, salt, and pepper. Bake until golden brown, about 30 minutes. Cool on a wire rack, cut into pieces, and serve warm.

Chicken Meatballs and Marinara

SERVES 8 (MAKES ENOUGH TO COAT 2 POUNDS OF SPAGHETTI)

The meatballs and sauce both use the same onion mixture. Serve with spaghetti, or your favorite long pasta shape, and grated Parmesan cheese. For more information on buying ground chicken, see page 3.

ONION MIXTURE

- **¼ cup olive oil**
- **3 medium onions, minced**
- **9 medium garlic cloves, minced or pressed through a garlic press (about 3 tablespoons)**
- **1 tablespoon dried oregano**
- **¾ teaspoon red pepper flakes**

MARINARA

- **¼ cup tomato paste**
- **1 cup dry red wine**
- **4 (28-ounce) cans crushed tomatoes**
- **1 cup water**
- **1 ounce Parmesan cheese, grated (about ½ cup)**

¼ cup shredded fresh basil leaves
Salt
Sugar

MEATBALLS

4 slices high-quality white sandwich bread, torn into pieces
¼ cup whole milk
½ pound sweet Italian chicken sausage, casings removed
2 ounces Parmesan cheese, grated (about 1 cup)
½ cup minced fresh parsley leaves
2 large eggs
3 medium garlic cloves, minced or pressed through a garlic press (about 1 tablespoon)
1½ teaspoons salt
2½ pounds ground chicken

1. FOR THE ONION MIXTURE: Heat the oil in a large Dutch oven over medium-high heat until shimmering. Add the onions and cook until golden brown, 10 to 15 minutes. Stir in the garlic, oregano, and pepper flakes and cook until fragrant, about 30 seconds. Transfer half of the onion mixture to a large bowl and set aside.

2. FOR THE MARINARA: Add the tomato paste to the remaining onion mixture in the pot and cook until fragrant, about 1 minute. Add the wine and cook until thickened slightly, about 2 minutes. Stir in the tomatoes and water and simmer over low heat until the sauce is no longer watery, 45 to 60 minutes. Stir in the cheese and basil and season with salt and sugar to taste.

3. FOR THE MEATBALLS: Adjust an oven rack to the upper-middle position and heat the oven to 475 degrees. Process the bread in a food processor to fine crumbs, about 10 seconds. Transfer to the bowl with the reserved onion and stir in the milk to moisten. Add the sausage, Parmesan, parsley, eggs, garlic, and salt and mash to combine. Add the ground chicken and knead with your hands until well combined. Form the mixture into 2½-inch meatballs (you should have about 16 meatballs), place on a rimmed baking sheet, and bake until lightly browned, about 20 minutes.

4. Transfer the meatballs to the pot with the sauce and simmer for 10 minutes. Serve. (The meatballs and marinara sauce can be refrigerated in an airtight container for up to 2 days, or frozen for up to 1 month.)

INGREDIENTS: Tomato Paste

A celebrated ingredient in its post-WWII heyday, when the long-cooked tomato sauce was king, tomato paste has fallen by the wayside as discerning cooks have favored fresher, more brightly flavored tomato sauces. These days, our use of tomato paste comes with a more conservative hand. We reserve it for occasions when a deep tomato flavor is warranted, such as in a chili or our Bolognese sauce.

Given this limited use, we wondered if it mattered which brand we used. To find out, we went to local supermarkets to gather seven brands for a tasting: six American brands in small cans and an Italian import in a toothpaste-like tube. We asked our tasters to taste the tomato paste as is—no cooking, no sauce.

Every brand did well in providing a big tomato punch, but the Amore brand, imported from Italy, was the unanimous winner, owing to its "intense" and "fresh" flavor. Amore is the only tomato paste tested that contains fat, which could account for its bigger flavor. The Amore brand also scored points because of its tube packaging. Just squeeze out what you need and store the rest in the refrigerator. No fuss, no waste.

How did the flavor of this tomato paste hold up in cooking? We tasted it, along with Hunt's, the brand that came in last, in our Bolognese recipe, to see if we could detect a difference. We did indeed pick out (and downgrade) the distinct dried herb flavor of the Hunt's paste. On the other hand, we liked the sauce made with the Amore tomato paste for its deep, round tomato flavor.

THE BEST TOMATO PASTE

An Italian import, Amore was our tasters' favorite brand. They described this paste-in-a-tube as "intense" and "fresh." The no-fuss, no-waste packaging is also appealing.

Pasta Salad

HERE IN THE TEST KITCHEN, WE HAVE certainly established that chicken and pasta are a top-notch combination—this entire chapter is evidence of that fact. We wanted to develop some cold pasta salad recipes with chicken (and vegetables) that made for the perfect weeknight dinner or a satisfying summer lunch. Instead of American-style mayonnaise-based pasta salads, we wanted to use lighter pesto- and vinaigrette-style dressings for these recipes.

Taking a cue from our chicken salad recipes (see pages 28–31), we decided to develop our recipes using shredded meat from a whole roasted bird with the knowledge that the slightly richer dark meat, combined with the white meat, made for more complex flavors. We developed a Simple Roast Chicken recipe (see page 120) for our chicken salads, but we also determined that, if you are short on time, substituting a supermarket rotisserie chicken is suitable (although we clearly preferred the flavor and texture of our chicken roasted at home).

With the chicken in place, we turned our attention to the pasta. The best pasta shapes for this type of dish have a textured surface with a concave nook or two that can trap the vinaigrette or pesto and keep it from sliding off. With its stubby form, indented center, and jagged edges, farfalle made an excellent partner, as did the spirals of fusilli.

Unlike hot pasta, which should generally be cooked until al dente, the pasta used in salads should cook slightly longer, until tender. (For tips on judging when shaped pasta is done, see page 267.) When the dressing was added straight to the just-cooked pasta, it took an hour to reach room temperature. The hot pasta also "cooked" the dressing, deadening its impact. Rinsing the pasta in cold water cooled it down quickly but made the surface of the pasta too slick to hold on to the dressing. The solution was to let the pasta cool in a single layer on a rimmed baking sheet, tossing in a splash of oil to prevent sticking, and then adding the dressing.

For the pesto-style dressing, we began by varying the ratios of the five integral ingredients: basil, garlic (blanched briefly to tame its harsh bite), Parmesan cheese, olive oil (extra-virgin), and pine nuts (toasted to enhance their nutty flavor). We found that we had to use a lot of basil (between three and four packed cups) to achieve decent herbal flavor and the bulk needed for the pesto to cling to the pasta. But when made even a few hours ahead of time, the basil turned dark and muddy.

Adding another green element that would better retain its vibrant color seemed the obvious solution.

EQUIPMENT: Food Processors

A food processor can make quick work out of any number of kitchen tasks, from slicing potatoes and shredding cheese to pureeing sauces and making pasta or tart doughs. After using a food processor repeatedly over the years, we have found two brands that have surpassed all others. The KitchenAid 12-Cup KFP750 ($249.99) and the 11-Cup Cuisinart Pro Custom 11 ($169) each have a large-capacity bowl and a powerful motor that excels at any kitchen task we throw at them. The KitchenAid was the hands-down winner with vegetable prep, but the Cuisinart performs all other tasks as well (or better) and costs less.

THE BEST FOOD PROCESSORS

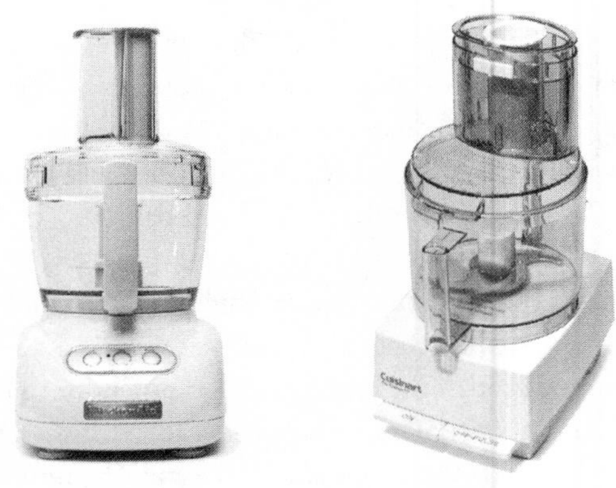

KITCHENAID CUISINART

KitchenAid and Cuisinart are our favorite food processors. If vegetable prep is important to you, buy the KitchenAid 12-Cup food processor. If you don't care too much about vegetable prep, the 11-Cup Cuisinart Pro Custom 11 performed all other tasks as well as (or better than) its pricier competition.

A small amount of fresh baby spinach (1 cup added to 3 cups of basil) provided a lovely bright green color and smooth texture without interfering with the basil flavor. While the relatively thin consistency of traditional pesto might be fine for hot noodles, a thicker, creamier pesto was in order for room-temperature pasta. We decided to borrow a standard ingredient used in many American pasta salads: mayonnaise. The creamy, tangy condiment served as the perfect binder—so long as it was used in moderation. Six tablespoons was enough to provide a creamy, luscious texture that coated the shredded chicken and pasta perfectly.

With the pesto dressing resolved, we moved on to the vinaigrette. We started with very simple vinaigrettes. Balsamic vinegar, white wine vinegar, red wine vinegar, and lemon juice seemed like the best choices to test in our vinaigrettes. The balsamic gave a lackluster performance; tasters disliked it for its sweetness, lack of bite, and the beige color it added to the pasta. Both white and red wine vinegars were nearly bordering on being too acidic, and they also lacked dimension. Lemon juice stole the show with its bright citrus acidity, and tasters agreed that it had a cohesive effect in the salad—it brought the flavors of the chicken and pasta together. We settled on 6 tablespoons of fresh lemon juice, which really came alive when combined with extra-virgin olive oil, grated lemon zest, one clove of garlic, and a bit of ground black pepper.

Our last task was to see what vegetables and add-ins we could agree on for our salads. Cherry tomatoes were a good choice for both the pesto- and vinaigrette-dressed salads, as they add great color and a perky tomato flavor, even out of season. A handful of toasted pine nuts brought out the nutty flavor of the pesto and added texture, while lightly cooked sugar snap peas (we simply cooked them in the pasta cooking water) had a subtle vegetal sweetness that we liked with the lemony vinaigrette, especially when paired with fresh mint and briny feta cheese. All in all, tasters were excited about combining room temperature pasta and chicken to create a new category of light and refreshing pasta and chicken dishes.

Pasta and Chicken Salad with Pesto

SERVES 6

This salad is best served the day it is made; if it's been refrigerated, bring it to room temperature before serving. We found that using a whole roast chicken for this salad yielded the right amount of both white and dark meat (see page 120 for our Simple Roast Chicken). For even less fuss, use a cooked supermarket rotisserie chicken. We like our pasta with a little bite (or al dente) when it is served hot, but for cool pasta salad we prefer pasta that is more tender than chewy. If a cut through the middle reveals a chalky white line (the color of uncooked pasta), the farfalle are not quite done and therefore need more cooking.

- 2 medium garlic cloves, unpeeled
- Salt
- 1 pound farfalle
- ¼ cup plus 1 tablespoon extra-virgin olive oil
- Ground black pepper
- ¾ cup pine nuts, toasted
- 3 cups packed fresh basil leaves (about 4 ounces)
- 1 cup packed baby spinach (about 1 ounce)
- 2 tablespoons juice from 1 lemon
- 1½ ounces Parmesan cheese, grated (about ¾ cup), plus more for serving
- 6 tablespoons mayonnaise
- 5 cups shredded roast chicken, at room temperature (see page 10) (see note)
- 1 pint cherry tomatoes, quartered, or grape tomatoes, halved

1. Bring 4 quarts water to a boil in a large pot for the pasta.

2. Add the garlic to the boiling water and cook for 1 minute. Remove the garlic with a slotted spoon and rinse under cold water to stop the cooking; set aside. Return the water to a boil, stir in 1 tablespoon salt and the pasta, and cook, stirring often, until the pasta is just past al dente. Reserve 1 cup of the pasta cooking water, drain the pasta, and return it to the pot. Pour 1 tablespoon of the oil over the pasta and

toss to combine. Season with salt and pepper to taste. Spread the pasta on a rimmed baking sheet and cool to room temperature, about 30 minutes.

3. When the garlic is cool, peel and mince it. Process ¼ cup of the pine nuts, the garlic, basil, spinach, lemon juice, remaining ¼ cup oil, 1 teaspoon salt, and ½ teaspoon pepper in a food processor until smooth, scraping the sides of the bowl as necessary, about 20 seconds. Add the Parmesan and mayonnaise and process until thoroughly combined, about 20 seconds. Transfer the mixture to a large serving bowl.

4. Add the cooled pasta and chicken and toss to combine, adding the reserved pasta cooking water as needed to loosen the pesto. Fold in the remaining ½ cup pine nuts and the tomatoes. Serve, passing additional Parmesan separately.

Pasta and Chicken Salad with Snap Peas, Feta, and Lemon Vinaigrette

SERVES 6

This salad is best served the day it is made; if it's been refrigerated, bring it to room temperature before serving. We found that using a whole roast chicken for this salad yielded the right amount of both white and dark meat (see page 120 for our Simple Roast Chicken). For even less fuss, use a fully cooked supermarket rotisserie chicken. We like our pasta with a little bite (or al dente) when it is served hot, but for cool pasta salad we prefer pasta that is more tender than chewy. If a cut through the middle reveals a chalky white line (the color of uncooked pasta), the fusilli are not quite done and therefore need more cooking. If desired, ½ pound asparagus (about ½ bunch), tough ends trimmed and cut into 1-inch lengths, can be substituted for the snap peas.

- 1 medium garlic clove, unpeeled
- Salt
- 8 ounces snap peas, stems and strings removed (see the illustration on page 240), halved crosswise (see note)
- 1 pound fusilli
- ½ cup plus 1 tablespoon extra-virgin olive oil
- Ground black pepper
- 6 tablespoons juice from 2 lemons
- 1 teaspoon grated zest from 1 lemon
- 5 cups shredded roast chicken, at room temperature (see page 10)
- 1 pint cherry tomatoes, quartered, or grape tomatoes, halved
- 4 ounces feta cheese, crumbled (about 1 cup)
- ¼ cup shredded fresh mint leaves

1. Bring 4 quarts water to a boil in a large pot for the snap peas and the pasta.

2. Add the garlic to the boiling water and cook for 1 minute. Remove the garlic with a slotted spoon and rinse under cold water to stop the cooking; set aside. Return the water to a boil, stir in 1 tablespoon salt and the snap peas, and cook until crisp-tender, 1 to 2 minutes. Remove from the water using a slotted spoon, transfer to a colander, and run under cold water to stop the cooking; set aside.

3. Return the water to a boil, add the pasta, and cook, stirring often, until the pasta is just past al dente. Drain the pasta and return it to the pot. Pour 1 tablespoon of the oil over the pasta and toss to combine. Season with salt and pepper to taste. Spread the pasta on a rimmed baking sheet and cool to room temperature, about 30 minutes.

4. When the garlic is cool, peel and mince it. Whisk the remaining ½ cup oil, the lemon juice, lemon zest, garlic, 1 teaspoon salt, and ½ teaspoon pepper together in a large bowl. Add the cooled snap peas, pasta, and chicken and toss to combine. Fold in the tomatoes, feta, and mint. Serve.

10 CASSEROLES

Casseroles

THE IDEA OF A SIMPLE BAKED, ONE-DISH MEAL is a satisfying one. Unfortunately, as processed convenience foods have become more widespread and people's devotion to spending time in the kitchen has waned, the classic casserole has taken a turn for the worse. What was once a comforting dish eagerly consumed at family events and potluck dinners has disintegrated all too often into a woeful amalgam of canned soup, frozen vegetables, and prepackaged meat topped with soggy bread crumbs. Our goal with this chapter, then, was to rescue the great American casserole.

Focusing on fresh ingredients and sound cooking principles, our recipes may require a little more effort and time than using the above-mentioned shortcuts, but we think you'll agree that the results are well worth it. We've provided recipes for casseroles that revive our old favorites, like Chicken Divan (page 278) and Chicken Tetrazzini (page 276). We have also included dishes like Lasagna Carnivale with Chicken Meatballs (page 298) that are sure to expand your casserole repertoire.

The biggest challenge we discovered when testing these recipes was bringing all the different ingredients together to form a cohesive and well-cooked dish, since we learned that each ingredient needed to be handled in a specific manner. For example, in the casseroles that contain pasta, such as Baked Penne and Chicken with Mushrooms (page 294), it was necessary to undercook the pasta so that it would be cooked just right when the casserole was fully baked. But in the case of the casseroles that contain rice, such as Chicken and Rice Casserole with Peas, Carrots, and Cheddar (page 281), we found that the rice needed to be fully cooked before going into the casserole, or else the rice would emerge from the oven crunchy and starchy. And in recipes such as Chicken Pot Pie (page 273) and Creamy Baked Four-Cheese Pasta with Chicken (page 292), we found that cooking the chicken directly in the sauce—and then removing it to cool and shred before adding it back to the casserole—enhanced the flavor of both the chicken and the sauce, and also allowed the shredded meat to meld with the other components of the casserole to become a cohesive one-dish meal.

We also discovered that we could throw out the notion that casseroles need to bake for a long period of time. Nothing ruins more casseroles than a long stay in the oven; ingredients will often become overcooked and insipid. We realized that since most of the ingredients that are going into these casseroles are already cooked, they don't need to be subjected to any more time in the oven than is absolutely necessary. By using a relatively hot oven (upward of 400 degrees), the casseroles don't take much time to heat through—and yet the flavors meld perfectly.

CHICKEN POT PIE

MOST EVERYONE LOVES A GOOD CHICKEN pot pie—juicy chunks of chicken, fresh vegetables, and a full-flavored sauce, all covered with warm pastry—though few seem to have the time or energy to make one. Like a lot of satisfying dishes, traditional pot pie takes time. Before the pie even makes it to the oven, the cook must poach a chicken, take the meat off the bone and cut it up, strain the stock, prepare and blanch the vegetables, make a sauce, and make and roll out the pie dough. Given the many time-consuming steps it can take to make a pot pie, our goal was to make the best one we could, as quickly as possible. Pot pie, after all, was intended as a weeknight supper.

We began by determining the best way to cook the chicken, using legs and thighs for the initial round of tests. Steaming the chicken took a lot of time, requiring about one hour, and the steaming liquid didn't make a strong enough stock for the pot-pie sauce. Roasting a chicken in the oven also required an hour, and by the time we took off the skin and mixed in the meat with the sauce and vegetables, the roasted flavor was lost. We had similar results with braised chicken. It lost its flavor once the browned skin was removed.

Next we tried poaching, the most traditional cooking method. Of the two poaching liquids we tried, we preferred the chicken poached in wine and broth to the one poached in broth alone. The wine infused the meat and made for a richer, fuller-flavored sauce. Now we were ready to test a cut-up chicken against simpler, quicker-cooking boneless, skinless chicken breasts.

Because boneless, skinless breasts cook so quickly, sautéing is generally a good cooking method for them. So before comparing poached parts versus poached breasts, we tried cooking the breasts three different ways. We cut raw breast meat into bite-sized pieces and sautéed them; we sautéed whole breasts, shredding the meat once it was cool enough to handle; and we poached whole breasts in broth, also shredding the meat. For simplicity's sake, we had hoped to like the sautéed whole breasts, but, once again, poaching was our favorite method. Sautéing caused the outer layer of meat to turn crusty, a texture we did not like in the pie. The sautéed chicken pieces also floated independently in the sauce, which couldn't adhere to them because of their smooth surface. By contrast, the tender poached and shredded chicken breasts mixed well with the vegetables, and their irregular shape enabled the sauce to cling.

Our only concern with the poached boneless, skinless breasts was the quality of the broth. In earlier tests, we found that bone-in parts could be poached in store-bought broth (rather than homemade stock) without much sacrifice in flavor. But we wondered how quick-cooking boneless, skinless breasts would fare in store-bought broth. The answer? Not as badly as we had feared. In our comparison of the pies made with boneless breasts poached in homemade stock as opposed to store-bought broth, we found little difference in quality. Evidently, it's not the cooking time of the chicken but the abundance of ingredients in a pot pie that makes it possible to use store-bought broth with no ill consequences.

Then we decided to make things even easier by poaching the chicken directly in the sauce. Not only was the sauce more flavorful—since it benefited from the juices the chicken yielded while cooking—but the chicken absorbed more flavor as well. Ultimately, we were able to shave almost half an hour off the cooking time (15 minutes to cook the breasts, compared with 40 minutes to cook the parts) and dirty one less dish by poaching directly in the sauce.

Turning our attention to the vegetables, we quickly realized that they have a tendency to overcook. A filling that is chock-full of bright, fresh vegetables going into the oven looks completely different after 40 minutes of high-heat baking under a blanket of dough. Carrots become mushy, while peas fade from spring green to drab olive. We wanted to find a way to preserve the vegetables' color and fresh flavor.

We began by making pies with the classic peas and carrots combination, using raw vegetables, frozen vegetables, and parboiled vegetables. After comparing the pies, we found that the frozen vegetables—the most convenient option—held their

INGREDIENTS:
Store-Bought Pie Dough

A flaky, buttery homemade pie crust is the ultimate crown for our Chicken Pot Pie (page 273), but it's also a fair amount of work. How much would we sacrifice by using a store-bought crust instead? To find out, we tried several types and brands—both dry mixes (just add water) and ready-made crusts, either frozen or refrigerated.

The dry mixes, including Betty Crocker ($1.69), Jiffy ($0.99), Krusteaz ($3.28), and Pillsbury ($1.39), all had problems. Some were too salty, some were too sweet, and all required both mixing and rolling—not much work saved. Frozen crusts, including Mrs. Smith's (also sold as Oronoque Orchards, $2.69) and Pillsbury Pet-Ritz ($2.69), required zero prep, but tasters found them pasty and bland, and it was nearly impossible to pry them from the flimsy foil "pie plate" in which they are sold. The one refrigerated contender, Pillsbury Just Unroll! Pie Crusts, wasn't bad. The crust baked up to an impressive flakiness. Better yet, this fully prepared product comes rolled up and is flexible enough to top a pie or line one of your own pie plates.

THE BEST STORE BOUGHT PIE DOUGH

While we prefer homemade crust, Pillsbury Just Unroll! Pie Crusts ($2.79 for two 9-inch crusts) are a solid alternative.

color and flavor best, the parboiled ones somewhat less so. The raw vegetables were not fully cooked at the end of the baking time and gave off too much liquid, watering down the flavor and thickness of the sauce.

Next, we wanted to develop a sauce that was flavorful and creamy, and that had the proper consistency. The sauce for chicken pot pie traditionally is based on a roux (a mixture of butter and flour sautéed together briefly), which is thinned with chicken broth and often enriched with cream. Because of the dish's inherent richness, we wanted to see how little cream we could get away with using. We tried three different pot-pie fillings, using 1½ cups cream, 2 cups half-and-half, and 2½ cups milk. Going into the oven, all of the fillings seemed to have the right consistency and creaminess; when they came out, however, it was a different story. Vegetable and meat juices diluted the consistency and creaminess of the milk and half-and-half sauces. To achieve a creamy-looking sauce, we needed to stick with cream. Next, we tested different amounts of cream: 1½ cups, 1 cup, and ¾ cup. The sauce made with ¾ cup wasn't rich enough; the 1½-cup filling was too heavy, while the cream overpowered the other flavors. The sauce made with 1 cup of cream was just right, with a silky consistency and a flavor that didn't overpower the other components of the dish.

Though our sauce was now the ideal consistency, it still tasted a little bland. We had been forced to abandon the wine in our sauce because it had a dulling effect on the color of the vegetables. Lemon juice, a flavor heightener we had seen in a number of recipes, created the same problem. We then tried vermouth, and it worked perfectly. Because vermouth is more intensely flavored than white wine, it gave us the flavor we were seeking without having to use a large amount.

We finally had a full-flavored yet streamlined chicken pot pie. One final note: As with any juicy pie, it's important to seal the sides so that the sauce doesn't leak out and make a mess of your oven. We also opted not to make ventilation holes for our chicken pie; that way, we could keep all the juices inside the pie—where they belong.

Chicken Pot Pie

SERVES 6 TO 8

While we think the best pot pies are those with a homemade pie crust, you can substitute store-bought pie dough (see page 272 for more information); you will need to buy 2 crusts. Most store-bought pie dough has already been rolled out and cut into a round shape that works great if you're making a round pie, but is very awkward if you want to top a 13 by 9-inch baking dish. You'll have to divide the filling between two 9-inch deep-dish pie plates. Lay the pie dough over the top and seal to the edges of the dishes, following the illustrations on page 274.

- 6 tablespoons (¾ stick) unsalted butter
- 3 celery ribs, sliced ¼ inch thick
- 2 medium onions, minced
- Salt
- ¾ cup unbleached all-purpose flour
- ¾ cup dry vermouth
- 4 cups low-sodium chicken broth
- 1 cup heavy cream
- 2 teaspoons minced fresh thyme leaves or ½ teaspoon dried
- 3 pounds boneless, skinless chicken breasts (about 8 medium), trimmed
- 1 (1-pound) bag frozen pea and carrot medley (about 3 cups; do not thaw)
- Ground black pepper
- 1 recipe Savory Pie Dough (page 274), chilled (see note)

1. Adjust an oven rack to the middle position and heat the oven to 375 degrees. Melt the butter in a Dutch oven over medium-high heat. Add the celery, onions, and 1 teaspoon salt and cook until softened and lightly browned, 5 to 7 minutes. Stir in the flour and cook, stirring constantly, until lightly browned, about 1 minute.

2. Gradually whisk in the vermouth and cook until evaporated, about 30 seconds. Slowly whisk in the broth, cream, and thyme. Add the chicken, partially cover, and bring to a simmer. Reduce the heat to low, cover completely, and cook until the thickest part of the breast registers 160 to 165 degrees on an instant-read thermometer, 10 to 15 minutes.

3. Transfer the chicken to a cutting board and set the Dutch oven aside, covered. When the chicken is cool enough to handle, shred into bite-sized pieces (see the illustration on page 10). Return the shredded chicken to the sauce with the peas and carrots. Season with salt and pepper to taste.

4. Pour the mixture into a 13 by 9-inch baking dish (or a shallow casserole dish of a similar size). Following the illustrations at right, roll out the pie dough, fit it over the baking dish, and crimp the edges tightly to seal. (At this point, the pot pie can be wrapped tightly in plastic wrap and then foil and refrigerated for up to 2 days or frozen for up to 1 month. If frozen, do not thaw before baking. Increase the baking time to 1¼ hours for refrigerated and 1¾ hours for frozen.)

5. Place the pot pie on a foil-lined rimmed baking sheet. Bake until the filling is hot and the crust is golden, about 1 hour. Let cool for 10 minutes before serving.

Savory Pie Dough

MAKES ENOUGH FOR 1 RECIPE CHICKEN POT PIE

For best results, be sure to use chilled vegetable shortening and chilled butter.

- **1½ cups (7½ ounces) unbleached all-purpose flour, plus more for the work surface**
- **½ teaspoon salt**
- **4 tablespoons vegetable shortening, chilled**
- **8 tablespoons (1 stick) unsalted butter, chilled and cut into ¼-inch cubes**
- **3–5 tablespoons ice water**

1. Process the flour and salt in a food processor until combined. Add the shortening and process until the mixture has the texture of coarse sand, about 10 seconds. Scatter the butter cubes over the top and pulse until the mixture is pale yellow and resembles coarse crumbs, with butter bits no larger than small peas, about ten 1-second pulses. Transfer the mixture to a medium bowl.

2. Sprinkle 3 tablespoons of the ice water over the mixture. With a rubber spatula, use a folding motion to mix. Press down on the dough with

ROLLING OUT AND ARRANGING DOUGH ON A POT PIE

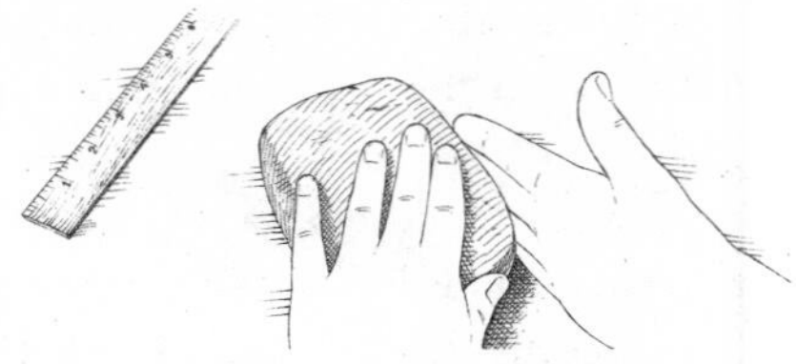

1. Press the dough into a 5 by 4-inch rectangle and wrap tightly with plastic wrap. Refrigerate until chilled, at least 30 minutes.

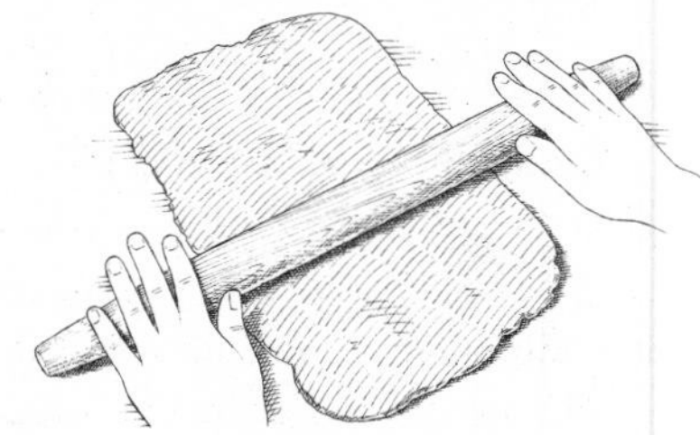

2. When the pot-pie filling is ready and the dough is chilled, roll the dough on a floured surface to a 15 by 11-inch rectangle, about ⅛ inch thick. (If making two 8-inch round casseroles, divide the dough into 2 portions before rolling it out.)

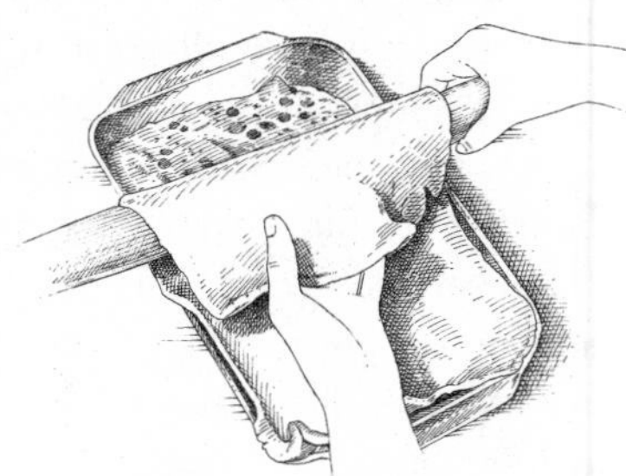

3. Roll the dough loosely over the rolling pin and unroll it evenly over the baking dish.

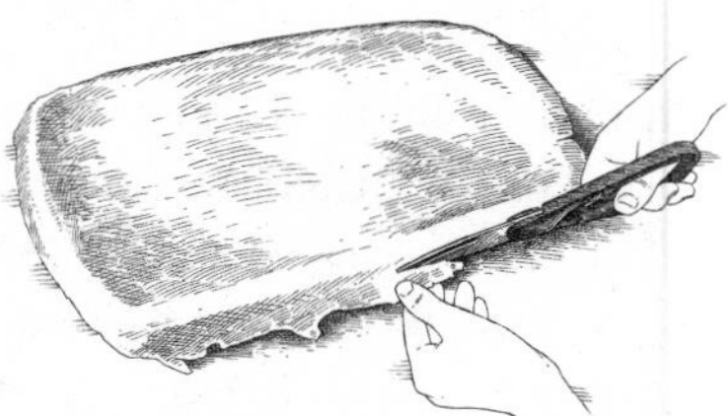

4. Trim the dough, leaving ½ inch hanging over the pan lip.

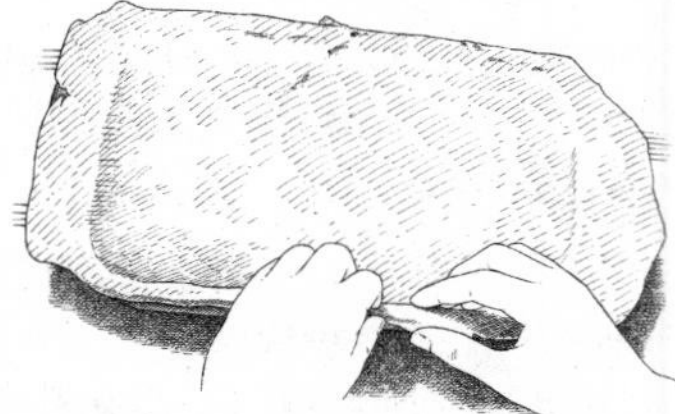

5. Press the dough firmly to seal it to the lip of the pan. (For a decorative border, press the edges of the pie with the tines of a fork.)

the broad side of the spatula until the dough sticks together, adding up to 2 tablespoons more ice water if necessary. Press the dough into a 5 by 4-inch rectangle (see the illustration on page 274) and wrap tightly in plastic wrap. Refrigerate until chilled, at least 30 minutes. Roll out the pie dough, top the pot pie, and seal the edges following the illustrations on page 274.

Chicken Tetrazzini

TETRAZZINI, WITH ITS BUTTERY BREAD crumbs, silky sauce, and tender noodles and meat, has the potential to be the ultimate comfort food. But the downside of many casseroles—flavors and textures become muted—holds true here. Add to that the fact that many tetrazzinis are made with subpar ingredients (such as canned soup, soggy noodles, leftover turkey or chicken, and a few stray vegetables from the crisper drawer), and it's no wonder that this American classic so often disappoints. Ready to give this hard-working casserole a well-deserved makeover, we began by shutting the cupboard door to all canned soups and focused on making a sauce from scratch.

A little research determined that cream of mushroom soup is the most commonly used sauce base. A mushroom-flavored sauce, therefore, was what we wanted. Testing both a béchamel (flour-thickened milk) and a velouté (flour-thickened broth), we found that neither was perfect. The béchamel sauce tasted too dairy-heavy, while the velouté was simply too light. A sauce made with a combination of milk and broth (thickened with flour) tasted better, but it still lacked some richness. Replacing the milk with half-and-half, we finally landed on the right basic flavor and heft. Four cups of liquid thickened with 4 tablespoons of flour produced enough sauce with the right texture to coat 1 pound of pasta, without being either soupy or gummy.

Focusing next on developing the mushroom flavor, we found it necessary to use a whopping 20 ounces of mushrooms. Any less just wouldn't do. Trying both cremini and white button mushrooms in the sauce, we noted that tasters could find no appreciable difference between them, so we went with the more available and less expensive white button mushrooms. The key to an intense mushroom flavor, we found, is to sauté the mushrooms until they release all their liquid and begin to brown. To round out the flavor of the sauce, onions, garlic, fresh thyme, cayenne, and Parmesan all proved to be absolutely necessary.

While most tetrazzini recipes call for using leftover chicken, we wanted a recipe that could be made from scratch. Borrowing a method from our Chicken Pot Pie (page 273), we gently poached boneless, skinless chicken breasts in the sauce, shredded them into bite-sized pieces, and then stirred the shredded chicken back into the sauce. We found the shredded chicken to be the right texture when paired with the noodles in the casserole. Furthermore, poaching the chicken directly in the sauce infused it with an extra layer of chicken flavor and enriched the final dish.

Moving on to the vegetables, we noted that many recipes use a lot of celery, which adds crunch but almost no flavor. Interestingly enough, our tasters preferred no celery at all. Bell peppers met a similar fate. We first tried green bell peppers, which were rejected immediately, and while red peppers performed slightly better, tasters preferred to do without them as well. Frozen peas and minced onion were the only vegetables given the thumbs-up by the test-kitchen staff. We found that the peas would not turn soggy if we added them right before baking.

Several recipes we researched called for elbow macaroni; however, we found this type of pasta too starchy and thick. We preferred fettuccine, linguine, or spaghetti instead, for texture and structural presence. Slightly undercooking the pasta prevents it from becoming mushy once baked. To make the dish easier to eat, we decided to break the long pasta in thirds so that there was no need to wind it around a fork.

As for the topping, we immediately rejected store-bought bread crumbs, which tasted too sandy. Instead, we found it easy to grind our own bread crumbs in the food processor with a little butter; they toast nicely in the oven while the casserole bakes.

Chicken Tetrazzini

SERVES 6 TO 8

Don't skimp on the salt and pepper; this dish needs generous seasoning. Underboiling the pasta in step 2 is important, or it will overcook in the oven and taste mushy.

TOPPING

- 4 slices high-quality white sandwich bread, torn into large pieces
- 2 tablespoons unsalted butter, melted and cooled

FILLING

- Salt
- 1 pound fettuccine, linguine, or spaghetti, broken into thirds
- 1 tablespoon olive oil
- 5 tablespoons unsalted butter
- 20 ounces white mushrooms, wiped clean, stems trimmed, and sliced ¼ inch thick
- 2 medium onions, minced
- 4 medium garlic cloves, minced or pressed through a garlic press (about 4 teaspoons)
- 1 tablespoon minced fresh thyme leaves
- ⅛ teaspoon cayenne pepper
- ¼ cup unbleached all-purpose flour
- 2 cups low-sodium chicken broth
- 2 cups half-and-half
- 2 pounds boneless, skinless chicken breasts (about 5 medium), trimmed
- 1½ cups frozen peas
- 2 ounces Parmesan cheese, grated (about 1 cup)
- Ground black pepper

1. FOR THE TOPPING: Pulse the bread and butter in a food processor until coarsely ground, about six 1-second pulses; set aside.

2. FOR THE FILLING: Adjust an oven rack to the middle position and heat the oven to 400 degrees. Bring 4 quarts water to a boil in a Dutch oven over high heat. Stir in 1 tablespoon salt and the pasta and cook, stirring occasionally, until just shy of al dente, about 8 minutes. Drain the pasta and toss with the oil; leave in the colander and set aside.

3. Wipe out the pot with paper towels. Add the butter to the pot and return to medium-high heat until melted. Add the mushrooms and ½ teaspoon salt and cook until the mushrooms have released their juices and are brown around the edges, 7 to 10 minutes. Add the onions and cook until softened, 5 to 7 minutes. Stir in the garlic, thyme, and cayenne and cook until fragrant, about 30 seconds. Add the flour and cook, stirring constantly, until golden, about 1 minute. Slowly whisk in the broth and half-and-half, bring to a simmer, and cook, whisking often, until lightly thickened, about 1 minute.

4. Add the chicken, partially cover, and bring to a simmer. Reduce the heat to low, cover completely, and cook until the thickest part of the breast registers 160 to 165 degrees on an instant-read thermometer, 10 to 15 minutes.

5. Transfer the chicken to a cutting board and set the Dutch oven aside, covered. When the chicken is cool enough to handle, shred into bite-sized pieces (see the illustration on page 10). Return the shredded chicken to the sauce with the pasta, peas, and Parmesan. Season with salt and pepper to taste.

6. Pour into a 13 by 9-inch baking dish (or a shallow casserole dish of a similar size) and sprinkle with the bread-crumb topping. Bake until the topping is browned and the sauce is bubbling, 10 to 15 minutes. Let cool for 10 minutes before serving.

Chicken Divan Casserole

CHICKEN, BROCCOLI, AND CHEDDAR CHEESE —beyond these three ingredients, there is some debate about what constitutes an authentic chicken Divan. We're not sure exactly how the dish was first served at the Paris restaurant for which it is named, but we're willing to wager it didn't include canned cream soup or processed cheese food, nor was it spooned out of a casserole dish tableside. Nevertheless, that's what the dish has become, according to recipes we sampled. After years of decline, chicken Divan has become the epitome of "dump and bake" cooking, in which simple, fresh ingredients are replaced with processed convenience products, smothered in cheesy cream sauces, and finally destroyed by eons of oven time, all in the name of a quick Tuesday night supper. We had no desire to restore chicken Divan to its original status as fancy French restaurant fare, but we hoped to develop an easy way to let those three basic ingredients anchor a simple one-dish meal.

Since many of the recipes we found for chicken Divan suggested serving the saucy dish over rice, we decided to save time and pots (always a major concern in the test kitchen) and include rice in the casserole to make a complete meal. Our first attempts resembled other chicken and rice casseroles we had developed: bite-sized chicken pieces tossed with rice and broccoli in a creamy cheddar sauce. It was a tried-and-true technique, but this time tasters were ambivalent. A broccoli spear simply dipped in the cheddar sauce tasted great, but when the florets were completely covered with the sauce and baked, even for a relatively short period of time, the broccoli turned limp and army green, and its fresh flavor was overwhelmed by the creamy sauce. We tried first blanching the broccoli in boiling water to set its vibrant green color, but even this reliable restaurant trick couldn't keep the broccoli from turning to mush.

We went back to the drawing board. How could we protect the broccoli from both the sauce and the withering heat of the oven? We decided to try a layering approach, spreading cooked rice on the bottom of a baking dish, covering the rice with a layer of broccoli, and placing whole chicken breasts on top. The sauce was then poured over the chicken and a bread-crumb topping was sprinkled over the sauce. The test failed, but not before we learned something. Long before the chicken breasts cooked through, the rice grains had completely overcooked. When we checked on the dish halfway through the cooking time, however, we noticed that the broccoli pieces directly under the chicken had remained bright green, while those in the spaces between the chicken breasts were drab and mushy. Clearly, the chicken had shielded the broccoli from the oven's heat.

Next, we tried slicing the breasts into thin cutlets, both to increase the surface area we could cover and to reduce the necessary cooking time. This worked quite well: The chicken cooked through in about 30 minutes, and the broccoli was pleasantly green and just tender. With the sauce confined to the top of the dish, we expected the rice to be dried out, but we found that the juices released by the chicken had kept it moist and had imparted a nice flavor to it as well.

This technique worked well, but the thinly sliced cutlets made for scant portions and were awkward to serve out of the casserole dish. We tried slicing the cutlets in half and overlapping them to fit more pieces into the dish. This required a few more minutes in the oven, but, when we served it up, the rice and broccoli were still in good shape. The chicken, rice, and broccoli had all come out of one dish, but each element was distinct, not smothered together in a heavy sauce. We made simple pilaf-style rice, sautéing chopped onion and chopped broccoli stalks for extra flavor, and undercooking the rice just slightly to allow for the carryover and oven cooking.

CUTTING CHICKEN CUTLETS FOR CHICKEN DIVAN

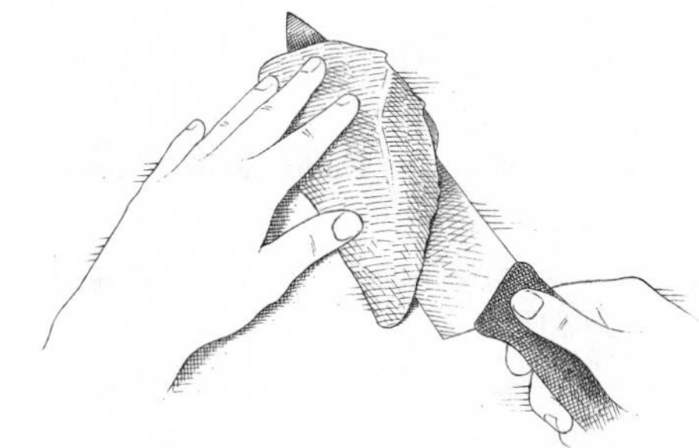

1. Slice the breasts in half horizontally into thin cutlets.

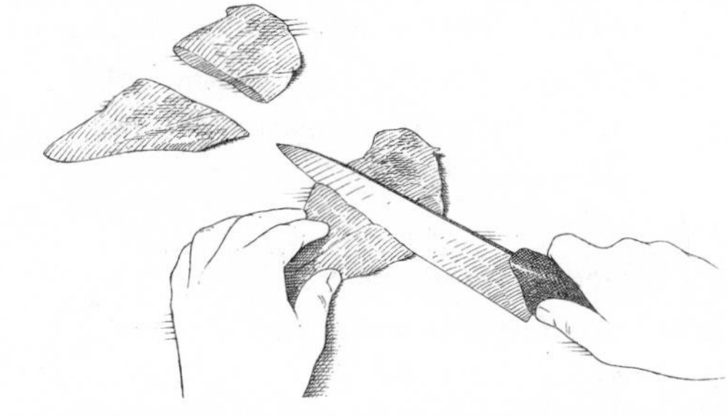

2. Cut the cutlets in half again crosswise into roughly 3 by 3-inch pieces.

For the cheese sauce, we stayed with the traditional cheddar, but tasters found that a small addition of grated Parmesan contributed a welcome nuttiness and, along with a pinch of cayenne pepper, gave the sauce a more grown-up flavor. Our first batches tasted great, but we forgot, again, to account for all the extra moisture the chicken released when it cooked. It thinned the sauce to the point where it puddled in the bottom of the dish, rather than coating the chicken as we had planned. We compensated by reducing the amount of liquid and holding the flour constant. Once the cheese was stirred into this sauce it looked too thick, but after the chicken had contributed its moisture, it was just right: creamy and thick, but not pasty. For the final touch, we found a combination of almonds and bread crumbs to be the ideal topping to finish this flavorful and satisfying dish.

Chicken Divan Casserole

SERVES 6 TO 8

You may use either sliced, slivered, or whole blanched almonds in the topping. Adjust the grinding time as necessary—the nuts should be in small pieces, not ground to a powder.

TOPPING

- 1 cup sliced, slivered, or whole blanched almonds (see note)
- 3 slices high-quality white sandwich bread, torn into large pieces
- 2 tablespoons unsalted butter, melted and cooled

FILLING

- Salt
- 1 medium bunch broccoli (about 1½ pounds), florets trimmed to 1-inch pieces, stalks peeled and chopped medium (see the illustrations on page 279)
- 1 tablespoon olive oil
- 1 medium onion, minced
- 1½ cups long-grain white rice
- 3½ cups water
- 4 tablespoons unsalted butter
- ¼ cup unbleached all-purpose flour
- 2 cups low-sodium chicken broth
- ¾ cup heavy cream
- 6 ounces sharp cheddar cheese, shredded (about 1½ cups)
- 1 ounce Parmesan cheese, grated (about ½ cup)
- ⅛ teaspoon cayenne pepper
- Ground black pepper
- 2 pounds boneless, skinless chicken breasts (about 5 medium), trimmed and prepared according to the illustrations on page 277
- 1 lemon, cut into wedges (for serving)

1. For the topping: Process the almonds in a food processor until coarsely ground, 5 to 10 seconds. Add the bread and butter and pulse to coarse crumbs, about six 1-second pulses; set aside.

2. For the filling: Adjust an oven rack to the middle position and heat the oven to 400 degrees. Bring 4 quarts water to a boil in a Dutch oven over high heat. Stir 1 tablespoon salt and the broccoli florets into the boiling water and cook, stirring often, until the broccoli florets are crisp and bright green, about 1 minute. Drain and transfer to a paper towel–lined baking sheet to cool; set aside.

3. Wipe out the pot with paper towels. Add the oil to the pot, return to medium heat, and heat the oil until shimmering. Add the broccoli stems, onion, and ½ teaspoon salt and cook until softened, about 7 minutes. Add the rice and cook, stirring to coat the grains with oil, for about 1 minute. Add the water and bring to a simmer. Cover, turn the

SHINGLING TECHNIQUE FOR CHICKEN DIVAN

Shingle the cutlets over the top of the casserole so that they overlap just slightly.

heat to low, and cook until the water is absorbed and the rice is just tender, about 16 minutes.

4. Meanwhile, melt the butter in a small saucepan over medium heat. Add the flour and cook, stirring constantly, until golden, about 1 minute. Slowly whisk in the chicken broth and cream; bring to a simmer, whisking often. Off the heat, whisk in the cheeses and cayenne until smooth. Season with salt and pepper to taste. Cover and set aside.

5. Spread the cooked rice into a 13 by 9-inch baking dish (or a shallow casserole dish of a similar size) and arrange the broccoli florets in an even layer over the rice. Following the illustration on page 278, shingle the chicken cutlets over the broccoli so that they overlap slightly. Pour about 2 cups of the sauce over the chicken and sprinkle with the bread-crumb topping. Bake until the chicken is no longer pink and the edges are bubbling, 30 to 35 minutes. Let cool for 10 minutes. Serve with the lemon wedges, passing the remaining sauce separately.

PREPARING THE BROCCOLI

1. Place the head of broccoli upside down on a cutting board and, with a large knife, trim off the florets very close to their heads. Cut the florets into bite-sized pieces.

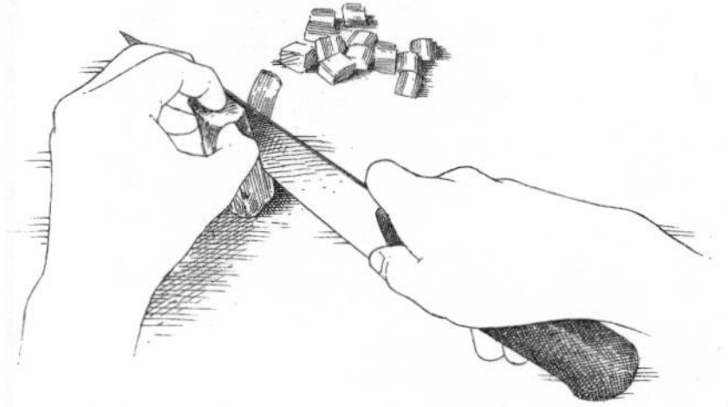

2. The stalks should also be trimmed and cooked. Stand each stalk up on the cutting board and square it off with a large knife. This will remove the outer ⅛ inch from the stalk, which is quite tough. Cut the trimmed stalk into ⅛-inch pieces.

Cheesy Chicken and Rice Bakes

LIKE A SEASONED PAIR OF HOLLYWOOD B-movie actors, chicken and rice get thrown together in all manner of ill-conceived projects and are expected to make it work. But this stick-to-your-ribs church supper staple is usually an uninspired performance, featuring bone-dry bits of chicken, "blown out" rice, army green vegetables, and a pasty, diet-busting sauce made with gobs of cheese and canned cream soups.

Our goal was to redesign this hearty and convenient weeknight casserole—to give it bright, fresh flavors and a lighter touch with the sauce while preserving its comforting richness. Existing recipes for this dish were vague and frustrating, calling for "cooked rice" and "cooked chicken," as if these initial cooking steps were trivial details. While we understood the desire to put leftovers to good use, we objected to this approach: It squanders an opportunity to build extra flavor into these ingredients, and it ignores the importance of making sure they're done at the same time. We checked the recommended cooking times and immediately saw why most recipes didn't bother to address the issue. In most cases, the casserole was doomed from the outset, sentenced to an hour or so in the oven. When it emerged, the rice had disintegrated and the chicken was unbearably tough—a significantly shorter spell in the oven would have to be a priority in developing our recipe.

For our first tests, we parboiled rice in one pot while we built a creamy sauce with chicken in another. Making a cooked, flour-thickened sauce from scratch allowed us to incorporate sautéed aromatics such as onion and garlic. The two elements were then combined in a casserole dish and baked in a hot oven until bubbling. The results were good—the chicken imparted a nice flavor to the sauce as it cooked, and vice versa—but did we really need two pots to make this dish? If the rice were likewise cooked directly in the sauce, we reasoned, it would also be more flavorful.

It was a good plan, but not a simple one, as we discovered when we considered how best to coordinate the various cooking times of the rice, chicken, and vegetables in the sauce. First, we tried tossing raw rice into the sauce once the chicken was cooked and then placing it in a hot oven. The results were beyond awful. After more than 45 minutes, the chicken was incredibly dry, the vegetables were mushy, the sauce was no more than a pasty residue, and the rice, amazingly, was still crunchy, with a few pockets of exploded grains near the edges. Numerous variations on this technique were attempted, with little success.

Why couldn't we get the rice to finish cooking properly in the oven? One problem was the uneven distribution of heat through the rectangular baking dish. Rice at the center of the dish was the slowest to cook, while grains around the edges blew apart. The problem was compounded by the fact that the cooking liquid was not water, but a thickened sauce. Rice cooks more slowly in a flour-bound sauce because much of the water is trapped by swollen starch granules, and so the rice grains are unable to absorb it.

We began to test recipes in which the rice was almost fully cooked in the sauce before the mixture was transferred to the oven, and immediately saw better results. At first we feared that the rice, already tender going into the oven, would quickly overcook. But the same principle that had prevented the rice from cooking in the oven now protected it from overcooking: There was not enough readily available moisture for the grains to absorb. Any lingering doubts about this theory were dispelled when we set out to determine just how much liquid we needed in order to fully cook the rice in the sauce. For just 1½ cups of raw rice, which would normally take about three cups of liquid to cook, it took a full 7 cups of liquid to both cook the rice and have enough left over for a creamy sauce to bind the casserole.

Another reason our casseroles tended to turn out pasty was the excessive amount of flour required to thicken that much liquid—as much as ½ cup or more. We knew that rice grains leached starch when cooked in an abundant quantity of water; now we could take advantage of that to thicken our sauce. Reducing the quantity of flour by half resulted in a sauce that started out quite thin—perfect for cooking rice—and thickened as it cooked, thanks to the extra starch released by the rice.

For the sauce, we experimented with chicken broth, milk, and cream in varying proportions and found that tasters preferred a 50/50 mix of milk and chicken broth, thickened with both a roux and a good melting cheese stirred in at the end. The addition of heavy cream made the sauce far too rich—the combined fat from the milk, butter, and cheese was more than sufficient.

Even with 7 full cups of liquid, the mixture looked thick and a little dry when we poured it into the casserole dish. But if we added any more liquid at the outset, the dish turned out soupy. The reason for this was the chicken. We had been adding the raw chicken (cut into small pieces) to the rice and sauce and allowing it to cook just until it was

CUTTING UP CHICKEN FOR CASSEROLES

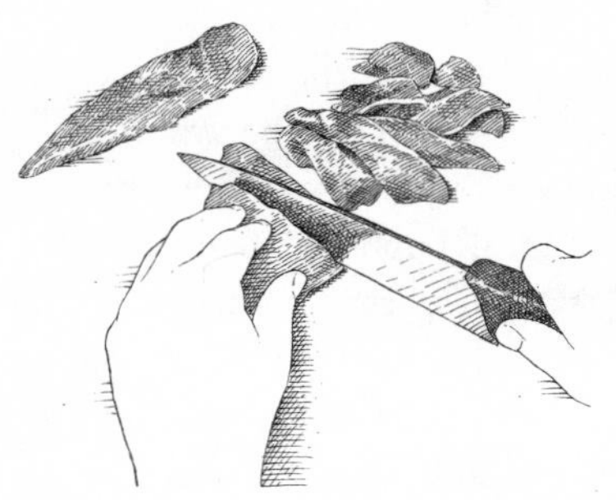

1. Separate the tenderloin from the breast. Starting at the thicker end, cut the breast into ¼-inch slices. Stop slicing when you reach the tapered triangle end.

2. With the flat side of a knife, press the tapered end to an even ¼-inch thickness and then cut the slices into 1-inch squares.

3. Use the same technique for the tenderloin, flattening it with the side of the knife and then cutting it into 1-inch pieces.

no longer pink. Then, as the entire dish went into the oven, the chicken continued to cook, releasing a lot of liquid, which thinned the sauce considerably. This also provided a handy visual cue for when the dish was done: When the bubbling vigorously around the edges, it meant the chicken had released all of its juices and was cooked through.

Chicken and Rice Casserole with Peas, Carrots, and Cheddar

SERVES 6 TO 8

After adding the rice, be sure to stir the sauce often for the first few minutes, using a heatsafe rubber spatula; this is when the rice is most likely to clump and stick to the bottom of the pot.

TOPPING

- 4 slices high-quality white sandwich bread, torn into large pieces
- 2 tablespoons unsalted butter, melted and cooled
- ½ ounce Parmesan cheese, grated (about ¼ cup)

FILLING

- 4 tablespoons unsalted butter
- 3 carrots, peeled and chopped medium
- 1 medium onion, minced
- Salt
- 3 medium garlic cloves, minced or pressed through a garlic press (about 1 tablespoon)
- ¼ cup unbleached all-purpose flour
- 3½ cups low-sodium chicken broth
- 3½ cups whole milk
- 1½ cups long-grain white rice
- Ground black pepper
- ⅛ teaspoon cayenne pepper
- 2 pounds boneless, skinless chicken breasts (about 5 medium), trimmed and prepared according to the illustrations on page 280
- 8 ounces sharp cheddar cheese, shredded (about 2 cups)
- 1½ cups frozen peas
- 2 tablespoons minced fresh parsley leaves
- 1 lemon, cut into wedges (for serving)

1. For the topping: Process the bread and butter in a food processor until coarsely ground, about six 1-second pulses. Transfer to a bowl and toss with the Parmesan; set aside.

2. For the filling: Adjust an oven rack to the middle position and heat the oven to 400 degrees. Melt the butter in a Dutch oven over medium heat. Add the carrots, onion, and 1 teaspoon salt and cook, stirring occasionally, until softened, 8 to 10 minutes. Stir in the garlic and cook until fragrant, about 30 seconds. Add the flour and cook, stirring constantly, until golden, about 1 minute. Slowly whisk in the broth and milk and bring to a simmer, whisking often. Stir in the rice, ⅛ teaspoon pepper, and the cayenne and return to a simmer. Turn the heat to medium-low, cover, and cook, stirring often, until the rice has absorbed much of the liquid and is just tender, 20 to 25 minutes.

3. Add the chicken and continue to cook uncovered over medium-low heat, stirring occasionally, until no longer pink, about 4 minutes. Off the heat, stir in the cheese and peas. Season with salt and pepper to taste.

4. Pour the mixture into a 13 by 9-inch baking dish (or a shallow casserole dish of a similar size) and sprinkle with the bread-crumb topping. Bake until the topping is browned and the casserole is bubbling, 20 to 25 minutes. Let cool for 10 minutes. Sprinkle with the parsley and serve with the lemon wedges.

Chicken and Rice Casserole with Sun-Dried Tomatoes and Spinach

SERVES 6 TO 8

Oil-packed sun-dried tomatoes are superior to the dried variety in both flavor and texture. Be sure to drain them well and pat them dry. After adding the rice, be sure to stir the sauce often for the first few minutes, using a heatsafe rubber spatula; this is when the rice is most likely to clump and stick to the bottom of the pot.

TOPPING

- 4 slices high-quality white sandwich bread, torn into large pieces
- 1 cup pine nuts
- 2 tablespoons unsalted butter, melted and cooled

- ½ ounce Parmesan cheese, grated (about ¼ cup)

FILLING

- 1 tablespoon olive oil
- 3 medium garlic cloves, minced or pressed through a garlic press (about 1 tablespoon)
- 1 (1-pound) bag curly-leaf spinach, stemmed and washed
- 4 tablespoons unsalted butter
- ¼ cup unbleached all-purpose flour
- 3½ cups low-sodium chicken broth
- 3½ cups whole milk
- 1½ cups long-grain white rice
- 1 teaspoon dried oregano
- Salt and ground black pepper
- 2 pounds boneless, skinless chicken breasts (about 5 medium), trimmed and prepared according to the illustrations on page 280
- 1 cup (one 8-ounce jar) oil-packed sun-dried tomatoes, drained, patted dry, and chopped coarse (see note)
- 8 ounces mozzarella cheese, shredded (about 2 cups)
- 2 tablespoons minced fresh parsley leaves
- 1 lemon, cut into wedges (for serving)

1. For the topping: Process the bread, pine nuts, and butter in a food processor until coarsely ground, about ten 1-second pulses. Transfer to a bowl and toss with the Parmesan; set aside.

2. For the filling: Adjust an oven rack to the middle position and heat the oven to 400 degrees. Heat the oil and garlic in a Dutch oven over medium-high heat and cook until the garlic is lightly golden, stirring often, about 2 minutes. Add the spinach by handfuls and stir to coat with oil until just wilted, about 4 minutes. Transfer the spinach to a colander set in the sink and, using tongs, gently squeeze the spinach to release the excess moisture. Coarsely chop the spinach and set aside.

3. Wipe out the pot with paper towels. Add the butter to the pot and return to medium heat until melted. Add the flour and cook, stirring constantly, until golden, about 1 minute. Slowly whisk in the broth and milk and bring to a simmer, whisking often. Stir in the rice, oregano, 1 teaspoon salt, and ⅛ teaspoon pepper and return to a simmer. Reduce the heat to medium-low, cover, and cook, stirring often, until the rice has absorbed much of the liquid and is just tender, 20 to 25 minutes.

4. Add the chicken and continue to cook uncovered over medium-low heat, stirring occasionally, until no longer pink, about 4 minutes. Off the heat, stir in the sun-dried tomatoes, cheese, and chopped spinach. Season with salt and pepper to taste.

5. Pour the mixture into a 13 by 9-inch baking dish (or a shallow casserole dish of a similar size) and sprinkle with the bread-crumb topping. Bake until the topping is browned and the casserole is bubbling, 20 to 25 minutes. Let cool for 10 minutes. Sprinkle with the parsley and serve with the lemon wedges.

Chicken and Rice Casserole with Chiles, Corn, and Black Beans

SERVES 6 TO 8

Don't skip the rinsing of the black beans, or the sauce will turn gray. Be sure to thaw and drain the corn thoroughly before stirring it into the filling. For more heat, include the jalapeño seeds and ribs when mincing. After adding the rice, be sure to stir the sauce often for the first few minutes, using a heatsafe rubber spatula; this is when the rice is most likely to clump and stick to the bottom of the pot.

TOPPING

- 8 ounces tortilla chips (about 2 cups)
- 2 tablespoons unsalted butter, melted and cooled

FILLING

- 4 tablespoons unsalted butter
- 2 red bell peppers, stemmed, seeded, and chopped medium
- 2 jalapeño chiles, seeds and ribs removed, chiles minced (see note)
- 1 medium onion, minced
- 1 teaspoon ground cumin
- Salt and ground black pepper
- ⅛ teaspoon cayenne pepper
- 3 medium garlic cloves, minced or pressed through a garlic press (about 1 tablespoon)

- ¼ cup unbleached all-purpose flour
- 3½ cups low-sodium chicken broth
- 3½ cups whole milk
- 1½ cups long-grain white rice
- 2 pounds boneless, skinless chicken breasts (about 5 medium), trimmed and prepared according to the illustrations on page 280
- 8 ounces pepper Jack cheese, shredded (about 2 cups)
- 1½ cups frozen corn, thawed and drained (see note)
- 1 (15.5-ounce) can black beans, drained and rinsed (see note)
- 2 tablespoons minced fresh cilantro leaves
- 1 lime, cut into wedges (for serving)

1. For the topping: Process the tortilla chips and butter in a food processor until coarsely ground, about 15 seconds; set aside.

2. For the filling: Adjust an oven rack to the middle position and heat the oven to 400 degrees. Melt the butter in a Dutch oven over medium heat. Add the bell peppers, jalapeños, onion, cumin, 1 teaspoon salt, ⅛ teaspoon pepper, and the cayenne and cook, stirring occasionally, until the vegetables are softened, about 10 minutes. Stir in the garlic and cook until fragrant, about 30 seconds. Add the flour and cook, stirring constantly, until golden, about 1 minute. Slowly whisk in the broth and milk and bring to a simmer, whisking often. Stir in the rice and return to a simmer. Turn the heat to medium-low, cover, and cook, stirring often, until the rice has absorbed much of the liquid and is just tender, 20 to 25 minutes.

3. Add the chicken and continue to cook uncovered over medium-low heat, stirring occasionally, until no longer pink, about 4 minutes. Off the heat, stir in the cheese, corn, and black beans. Season with salt and pepper to taste.

4. Pour the mixture into a 13 by 9-inch baking dish (or a shallow casserole dish of a similar size) and sprinkle with the tortilla-crumb topping. Bake until the topping is browned and the casserole is bubbling, 20 to 25 minutes. Let cool for 10 minutes. Sprinkle with the cilantro and serve with the lime wedges.

Latino-Style Chicken and Rice

THE BOLD-FLAVORED COUSIN OF AMERICAN-style chicken and rice, *arroz con pollo* (literally, "rice with chicken") is Latino comfort food at its most basic. Here in the test kitchen, we've had plenty of great versions: moist, tender chicken nestled in rice rich with peppers, onions, herbs, and deep chicken flavor—a satisfying one-dish meal.

Like most staples, however, arroz con pollo runs the gamut from the incredible to the merely edible, depending on how much time and effort you're willing to spend. The traditional method is to stew marinated chicken slowly with aromatic herbs and vegetables, creating a rich broth in which the rice is cooked once the chicken is fall-off-the-bone tender—terrific, yes, but also time-consuming. Quick versions speed things up by cooking the rice and chicken (often boneless) separately, then combining them just before serving. The trade-off is rice that's devoid of chicken flavor. Our goal was to split the difference: to streamline the more time-consuming, traditional recipes for arroz con pollo without sacrificing great taste.

If we wanted chicken-infused rice, it was clear the chicken and the rice would have to spend some time together. But how long was long enough? A few of the "quick" recipes we found called for simmering the chicken and rice together, chopping the chicken into small pieces that would be done in sync with the rice, in about half an hour. Was this our streamlined solution? The timing was right, but the results were not. The white meat and dark meat cooked unevenly, the skin was flabby, and, after 30 minutes, flavor infusion was minimal. Worse, the hacked-up chicken, replete with jagged bones, was wholly unappealing.

Regrouping, we decided to start with a traditional recipe and adjust things from there. We began, as we do with so many of our Spanish-influenced Latin dishes, with a sofrito, a mixture of chopped onions and green peppers sautéed in olive oil. Once the vegetables softened, we added the chicken and a few cups of water, turned the burner to low, and let the chicken poach for an hour. Removing the chicken, we added the rice to the pot, and 30 minutes later the rice had absorbed every drop of the rich broth the chicken had left behind. We added the chicken back to rewarm for 10 minutes, then lifted the lid. Now this was chicken-infused rice!

Unfortunately, it was also a two-hour project—and we hadn't even factored in the traditional marinade yet. What's more, while the dark meat was moist and tender, the leaner white meat was in bad shape. We recalled a recipe from our research that called for thighs only. Opting for all thighs meant uniform cooking times and shopping convenience (one big "value" pack).

A new problem emerged: Thighs are laden with fat, and this made the dish greasy. Removing the skin helped, but the meat near the surface dried out and the flavor suffered. The answer was to trim away visible pockets of waxy yellow fat and most of the skin, leaving just enough to protect the meat. We also replaced most of the water we were adding with an equal amount of store-bought chicken broth, which made up for lost chicken flavor. After almost an hour of stewing, the skin was pretty flabby, so we removed the chicken while the rice finished cooking. To make the chicken even more appealing, we took the additional step of removing the meat from the bones.

With the chicken resolved, we moved on to the rice. The two traditional rice choices for arroz con pollo are long grain and medium grain. While both were fine, tasters preferred the creamier texture of medium-grain rice. But medium-grain rice was not without its problems. The grains had a tendency to split and release too much starch, making the overall texture of the dish pasty. Giving the rice a stir partway through cooking helped keep any one layer from overcooking, as did removing the pot from the direct heat of the stovetop to the diffuse heat of the oven.

Traditionally, arroz con pollo has an orange hue that comes from infusing oil with achiote, a tropical seed also used for coloring cheddar cheese. Achiote is hard to find, so we experimented with substitutions. Turmeric and saffron looked right but tasted wrong—too much like curry or paella. (Achiote has no distinct flavor.) The solution was adding 8 ounces of canned tomato sauce to the broth.

A common method for infusing this dish with more flavor is to marinate the chicken for a few hours or even overnight. A nice idea, but we were hoping to make this a weeknight dish. Instead, we tried a quick, 15-minute marinade with garlic, oregano, and white vinegar. The results were a step in the right direction. We also tossed the chicken with olive oil, vinegar, and cilantro after pulling it off the bone—a postcooking "marinade"—to give it the additional boost it needed. Capers, red pepper flakes, pimientos, and briny olives rounded out the flavors.

All of our efforts at streamlining this dish had brought the cooking time down to 90 minutes—an hour to stew the chicken and half an hour to cook the rice—a far cry from the half-day affair we'd faced at the start. But was this the best we could do? To shave off still more time, we tried adding the rice to the pot when the chicken still had half an hour to go. The chicken was fine, but the rice near the chicken pieces cooked unevenly. The solution to this problem was easy: Instead of giving the rice only one stir during cooking, we gave it a second stir to redistribute the ingredients. Now both the rice and the chicken were perfectly cooked, and we finally had a rich, flavorful, authentic-tasting dish in just over an hour.

TAKING THE MEAT OFF THE BONE

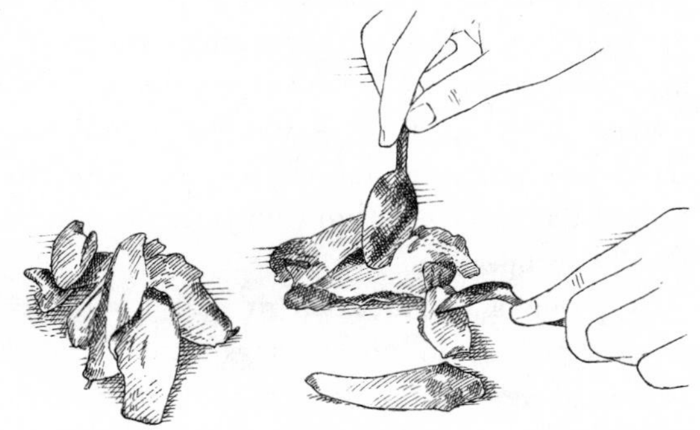

Removing the meat from the bone isn't hard when there's plenty of time for it to cool, but for our Latino-Style Chicken and Rice, we wanted it fast. To spare our fingertips, we tried using two forks, but they tended to shred the meat rather than pull it apart intact. Our solution? Two spoons, which were much more gentle—and just as effective.

Latino-Style Chicken and Rice

SERVES 4 TO 6

To keep the dish from becoming greasy, remove excess fat from the chicken thighs and trim the skin. To use long-grain rice instead of medium-grain, increase the amount of water added in step 3 from ¼ to ¾ cup and add the additional ¼ cup water in step 4 as needed. When removing the chicken from the bone in step 5, we found it better to use two spoons rather than two forks; forks tend to shred the meat, while spoons pull it apart in chunks.

- 6 medium garlic cloves, minced or pressed through a garlic press (about 2 tablespoons)
- 5 teaspoons distilled white vinegar
- Salt and ground black pepper
- ½ teaspoon dried oregano
- 4 pounds bone-in, skin-on chicken thighs (about 10 thighs), trimmed (see note)
- 2 tablespoons olive oil
- 1 medium onion, minced
- 1 green bell pepper, stemmed, seeded, and chopped fine
- ¼ teaspoon red pepper flakes
- ¼ cup minced fresh cilantro leaves
- 1¾ cups low-sodium chicken broth
- 1 (8-ounce) can tomato sauce
- ½ cup water
- 3 cups medium-grain white rice
- ½ cup green Manzanilla olives, pitted (see the illustration on page 101) and halved
- 1 tablespoon capers, rinsed
- ½ cup jarred whole pimientos, drained and cut into 2 by ¼-inch strips
- 1 lemon, cut into wedges (for serving)

1. Adjust an oven rack to the middle position and heat the oven to 350 degrees. Combine the garlic, 3 teaspoons of the vinegar, 1 teaspoon salt, ½ teaspoon black pepper, and the oregano in a large bowl. Add the chicken, coat it evenly with the marinade, and set aside for 15 minutes.

2. Heat 1 tablespoon of the oil in a Dutch oven over medium heat until shimmering. Add the onion, bell pepper, and pepper flakes and cook, stirring occasionally, until the vegetables begin to soften, 5 to 7 minutes. Stir in 2 tablespoons of the cilantro.

3. Push the vegetables to the sides of the pot and increase the heat to medium-high. Add the chicken to the center of the pot, skin-side down. Cook until the outer layer of the meat becomes opaque, 2 to 4 minutes per side, reducing the heat if the chicken begins to brown. Stir in the broth, tomato sauce, and ¼ cup of the water. Bring to a simmer, cover, reduce the heat to medium-low, and simmer for 20 minutes.

4. Stir in the rice, olives, capers, and ¾ teaspoon salt and bring to a simmer. Cover, transfer to the oven, and cook, stirring every 10 minutes, until the thickest part of the thigh registers 170 to 175 degrees on an instant-read thermometer, about 30 minutes. If, after 20 minutes of cooking, the rice appears dry and the bottom of the pot begins to scorch, stir in the remaining ¼ cup water.

5. Transfer the chicken to a cutting board and set the Dutch oven aside, covered. Following the illustration on page 284, pull the meat off the bones into large chunks using two spoons; discard the skin and bones. Place the chicken in a large bowl and toss with the remaining tablespoon oil, the remaining 2 teaspoons vinegar, the remaining 2 tablespoons cilantro, and the pimientos. Season with salt and pepper to taste. Place the chicken on top of the rice, cover, and let stand until warmed through, about 5 minutes. Serve with the lemon wedges.

VARIATION

Latino-Style Chicken and Rice with Breast Meat

Follow the recipe for Latino-Style Chicken and Rice, substituting 4 pounds bone-in, skin-on split chicken breasts (about 6 medium), trimmed and cut in half crosswise, for the chicken thighs. Remove the chicken from the pot in step 4 when the thickest part of the breast registers 160 to 165 degrees on an instant-read thermometer (after about 20 minutes). Transfer the chicken to a cutting board, tent loosely with foil, and set aside. In step 4, cook the rice mixture until the rice has absorbed all the liquid and is tender but still holds its shape, about 30 minutes.

Latino-Style Chicken and Rice with Bacon and Roasted Red Peppers

SERVES 4 TO 6

To keep the dish from becoming greasy, remove excess fat from the chicken thighs and trim the skin. To use long-grain rice instead of medium-grain, increase the amount of water added in step 3 from ¼ to ¾ cup and add the additional ¼ cup water in step 4 as needed. When removing the chicken from the bone in step 5, we found it better to use two spoons rather than two forks; forks tend to shred the meat, while spoons pull it apart in chunks.

- 6 medium garlic cloves, minced or pressed through a garlic press (about 2 tablespoons)
- 5 teaspoons distilled sherry vinegar
- 2 teaspoons sweet paprika
- Salt and ground black pepper
- 4 pounds bone-in, skin-on chicken thighs (about 10 thighs), trimmed (see note)
- 4 ounces (about 4 slices) bacon, cut into ½-inch pieces
- 1 medium onion, minced
- 1 red bell pepper, stemmed, seeded, and chopped fine
- 1 carrot, peeled and chopped fine
- ¼ teaspoon red pepper flakes
- ¼ cup minced fresh parsley leaves
- 1¾ cups low-sodium chicken broth
- 1 (8-ounce) can tomato sauce
- ½ cup water
- 3 cups medium-grain rice
- 1 tablespoon olive oil
- ½ cup jarred roasted red peppers, drained and cut into 2 by ¼-inch strips
- 1 lemon, cut into wedges (for serving)

1. Adjust an oven rack to the middle position and heat the oven to 350 degrees. Combine the garlic, 3 teaspoons of the sherry vinegar, paprika, 1 teaspoon salt, and ½ teaspoon black pepper in a large bowl. Add the chicken, coat it evenly with the marinade, and set aside for 15 minutes.

2. Fry the bacon in a large Dutch oven over medium heat until crisp, 6 to 8 minutes. Using a slotted spoon, transfer the bacon to a paper towel–lined plate and set aside. Pour off all but one tablespoon of the bacon fat, return to the stove over medium heat, and heat the fat until shimmering. Add the onion, bell pepper, carrot, and pepper flakes and cook, stirring occasionally, until the vegetables begin to soften, 5 to 7 minutes. Stir in 2 tablespoons of the parsley.

3. Push the vegetables to the sides of the pot and increase the heat to medium-high. Add the chicken to the center of the pot, skin-side down. Cook until the outer layer of the meat becomes opaque, 2 to 4 minutes per side, reducing the heat if the chicken begins to brown. Stir in the broth, tomato sauce, and ¼ cup of the water. Bring to a simmer, cover, reduce the heat to medium-low, and simmer for 20 minutes.

4. Stir in the rice and ¾ teaspoon salt and bring to a simmer. Cover, transfer to the oven, and cook, stirring every 10 minutes, until the thickest part of the thigh registers 170 to 175 degrees on an instant-read thermometer, about 30 minutes. If, after 20 minutes of cooking, the rice appears dry and the bottom of the pot begins to scorch, stir in the remaining ¼ cup water.

5. Transfer the chicken to a cutting board and set the Dutch oven aside, covered. Following the illustration on page 284, pull the meat off the bones into large chunks using two spoons; discard the skin and bones. Place the chicken in a large bowl and toss with the remaining 2 teaspoons sherry vinegar, the remaining 2 tablespoons parsley, the oil, and roasted red peppers. Season with salt and pepper to taste. Place the chicken on top of the rice, cover, and let stand until warmed through, about 5 minutes. Sprinkle with the reserved bacon and serve with the lemon wedges.

VARIATION

Latino-Style Chicken and Rice with Breast Meat, Bacon, and Roasted Red Peppers

Follow the recipe for Latino-Style Chicken and Rice with Bacon and Roasted Red Peppers, substituting 4 pounds bone-in, skin-on split chicken breasts (about 6 medium), trimmed and cut in half crosswise, for the chicken thighs. Remove the chicken from the pot in step 4 when the thickest part of the breast registers 160 to 165 degrees on an instant-read thermometer (after about 20 minutes). Transfer the chicken to a cutting board, tent loosely with foil, and set aside. In step 4, cook the rice mixture until the rice has absorbed all the liquid and is tender but still holds its shape, about 30 minutes.

King Ranch Casserole

KING RANCH JUST MIGHT BE THE MOST famous casserole in Texas. Layers of tender chicken, corn tortillas, and spicy tomatoes are bound together in a rich, cheesy sauce. Favored by home cooks and Junior Leaguers, this subtly spicy casserole dates back to the 1950s. This dish became popular for its mildly spicy Southwestern flavors as well as for its convenience (most recipes start with one can each of cream of chicken and cream of mushroom soup).

After a disappointing round of tests, we wondered if our Texan friends had been telling us tall tales about this dish. The tortillas were soggy, the chicken was tough and dry as a bone, and the sauce was made gloppy and bland by the undiluted canned soup. Given the outsized reputation of this dish, we had to do better. We found a few modern recipes that called for a freshly poached chicken and homemade cheese sauce, but their instructions seemed overly fussy for such a simple casserole. Could we find a middle road that lost the canned soup, but didn't create multiple unnecessary steps?

Starting with the sauce, we cooked onions and chiles in butter, then added ground cumin and Ro-Tel tomatoes, the Texas brand of spicy canned tomatoes that are the hallmark of this recipe. Instead of draining the tomatoes and discarding the flavorful juice (as most recipes instructed), we reduced the liquid to intensify the tomato flavor. Then we stirred in flour for thickening, cream for richness, and chicken broth for flavor. Twenty minutes of kitchen work yielded a silky, flavorful sauce that put canned soup to shame.

To assemble the casserole, we layered the sauce with corn tortillas and cooked chicken, then topped it with cheese before baking. It smelled fantastic coming out of the oven, but the chicken was leathery and the tortillas had disintegrated into corn mush. To solve the chicken problem, we tried layering raw chicken in between the tortillas, but it failed to cook through. The solution was to partially poach the chicken in the sauce before assembling the casserole, which guaranteed perfectly cooked, well-seasoned meat.

We tried replacing the soggy tortillas with store-bought tortilla chips, but tasters complained about the extra grease in the middle of the casserole. Crisping the tortillas in the oven (in effect, making homemade chips) kept them from turning to mush in the casserole and cut out the greasiness. All our casserole needed now was a crisp topping. Having abandoned store-bought tortilla chips inside the casserole, we decided to give them a shot as a crushed-up crunchy topping. The flavor and texture were fine, and after trying different brands to find the perfect fit, we finally hit on one that everyone loved: Fritos corn chips. They crowned this Texas classic with just the right amount of saltiness, corn flavor, and crunch.

King Ranch Casserole

SERVES 6 TO 8

If you can't find Ro-Tel tomatoes, substitute one 14.5-ounce can diced tomatoes and one 4-ounce can chopped green chiles. Cojack is a creamy blend of colby and Monterey Jack cheeses. Monterey Jack cheese can be used in its place. For more heat, include the jalapeño seeds and ribs when mincing.

- **12 (6-inch) corn tortillas**
- **1 tablespoon unsalted butter**
- **2 medium onions, minced**
- **2 jalapeño chiles, seeds and ribs removed, chiles minced (see note)**
- **2 teaspoons ground cumin**

- 2 (10-ounce) cans Ro-Tel tomatoes (see note)
- 5 tablespoons unbleached all-purpose flour
- 2½ cups low-sodium chicken broth
- ½ cup heavy cream
- 1½ pounds boneless, skinless chicken breasts (about 4 medium), trimmed, halved lengthwise, and cut crosswise into ½-inch slices
- 1 pound Cojack cheese, shredded (about 4 cups) (see note)
- 2 tablespoons minced fresh cilantro leaves
- Salt and ground black pepper
- 2¼ cups Fritos corn chips, crushed

1. Adjust two oven racks to the upper-middle and lower-middle positions and heat the oven to 450 degrees. Lay the tortillas on two baking sheets, lightly coat both sides with nonstick cooking spray, and bake until slightly crisp and browned, about 12 minutes. Cool slightly and then break into bite-sized pieces. Adjust the top oven rack to the middle position.

2. Melt the butter in a Dutch oven over medium-high heat. Add the onions, chiles, and cumin and cook until lightly browned, about 8 minutes. Add the tomatoes and cook until most of the liquid has evaporated, about 10 minutes. Add the flour and cook, stirring constantly, for 1 minute. Slowly whisk in the broth and cream and bring to a simmer, whisking often. Cook until thickened, 2 to 3 minutes. Stir in the chicken and cook until no longer pink, about 4 minutes. Off the heat, stir in the cheese and cilantro until the cheese is melted. Season with salt and pepper to taste.

3. Scatter half of the tortilla pieces in a 13 by 9-inch baking dish (or a shallow casserole dish of a similar size). Spoon half of the filling evenly over the tortillas. Scatter the remaining tortillas over the filling and top with the remaining filling. Place the casserole on a foil-lined rimmed baking sheet.

4. Bake until the filling is bubbling, about 15 minutes. Sprinkle the Fritos evenly over the top and bake until lightly browned, about 10 minutes. Let cool for 10 minutes before serving.

Chicken Enchiladas

ENCHILADAS ARE QUITE POSSIBLY THE MOST popular Mexican casserole; softened tortillas rolled around a savory, cheesy filling (often containing chicken) and baked in a spicy chili sauce. Traditional methods require a whole day of preparation. Could we streamline the preparation and still retain the authentic flavor of the real thing?

We began by preparing various simplified recipes. All of them produced disappointing results. Mushy tortillas, bland or bitter sauces, uninspired fillings, too much cheese, and lackluster flavor left tasters yearning for something tastier and more authentic. We had our work cut out for us.

To start, we did a side-by-side tasting of corn and wheat-flour tortillas. Tasters came out clearly in favor of the corn, with its more substantial texture that held up better when made in advance. Tasters also preferred the small 6-inch corn tortillas to the larger 8-inch size. The smaller size provided the best proportion of tortilla to filling and sauce, and fit neatly into a 9-inch baking pan.

We tried rolling the corn tortillas around the filling straight out of the package, but they were tough and cracked easily (see photo on page 290). Most recipes prep the tortillas before rolling in order to make them soft and pliable. The traditional approach is to dip each tortilla in hot oil (to create a moisture barrier) and then in the sauce (to add flavor) prior to assembly. Although this technique works well, it is time-consuming, tedious, and messy. Heating a stack of tortillas in the microwave also proved disappointing. The tortillas had softened, but the resulting enchiladas were mushy. Next, we tried wrapping the tortillas in foil and steaming them on a plate over boiling water. These tortillas turned wet and soggy when baked.

Thinking back to the traditional first step of dipping the tortilla in oil gave us an idea. Using the modern-day convenience of oil in a spray can, we placed the tortillas in a single layer on a baking sheet, sprayed both sides lightly with vegetable oil, and warmed them in a moderate oven. This proved to be the shortcut we were hoping to find. The oil-sprayed, oven-warmed tortillas were pliable, and their texture—after being filled, rolled, and baked—was just perfect.

Moving onto the sauce next, we prepared a half dozen traditional recipes and compared them to store-bought cans of enchilada sauce. Convenience was the only thing the store-bought sauces had going for them; the tasters hated their harsh, tinny flavors. The homemade sauces, on the other hand, were smooth and somewhat thick, with a truly satisfying, deep chile flavor. The only problem was that whole dried chiles played a central role in all of these homemade sauces. Not only are whole chiles difficult to find in some areas, but they also require substantial preparation time, including toasting, seeding, stemming, rehydrating, and processing in a blender. Our sauce would need to depend on store-bought chili powder if we wanted to keep the recipe streamlined.

The obvious question now was how to augment the flavor of the usually bland chili powder available in the supermarket. Our first thought was to heat the chili powder in oil, a technique that intensifies flavors. We began by sautéing onions and garlic and then added the chili powder to the pan. This indeed produced a fuller, deeper flavor. We enhanced the flavor further by adding ground cumin, coriander, and sugar—tasters gave this combo a thumbs-up.

Many traditional recipes incorporate tomatoes for substance and flavor. Keeping convenience in mind, we explored canned tomato products first. We tried adding diced tomatoes and then pureeing the mixture. The texture was too thick and too tomatoey. Canned tomato sauce—which has a very smooth, slightly thickened texture and a mild tomato flavor—turned out to be a better option.

We knew we wanted a chicken-based filling, but it wasn't clear to us how we should cook the chicken. We tried the common method of poaching in broth or water, but tasters said this chicken tasted bland and washed out. We tried roasting both white and dark meat and, although it was extremely time-consuming, tasters really liked the flavor of the dark meat. Obsessed with speed and flavor, we had an idea. Why not use boneless, skinless thighs

ASSEMBLING ENCHILADAS

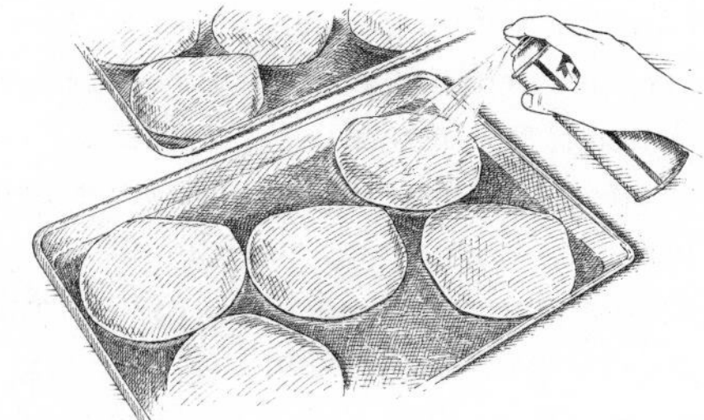

1. Place the tortillas on two baking sheets. Lightly coat both sides with vegetable oil spray. Bake until the tortillas are soft and pliable.

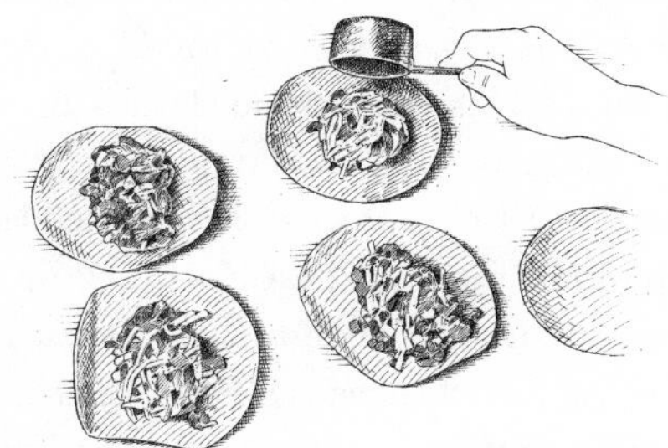

2. Place the warm tortillas on a work surface. Place a heaping ⅓ cup filling onto the center of each tortilla.

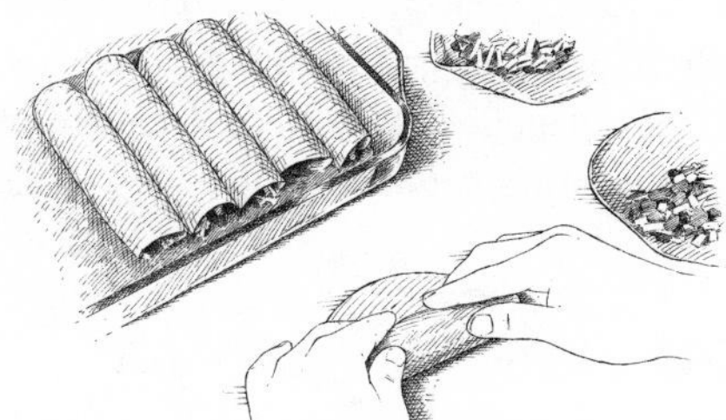

3. Hand-roll each tortilla tightly. Place them in a baking dish, side by side, seam-side down.

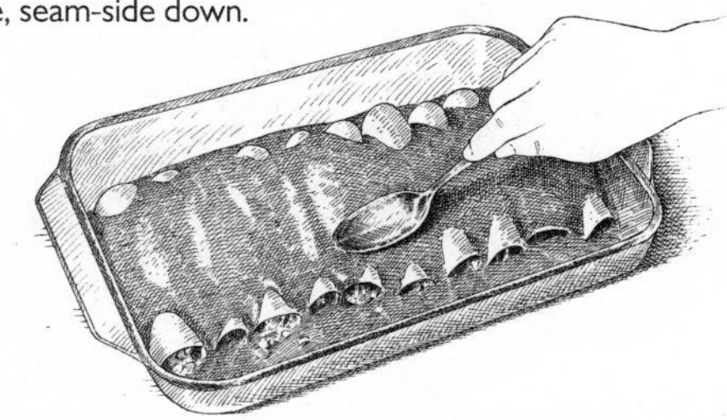

4. Pour the sauce over the enchiladas. Use the back of a spoon to spread the sauce to completely coat the top of each tortilla.

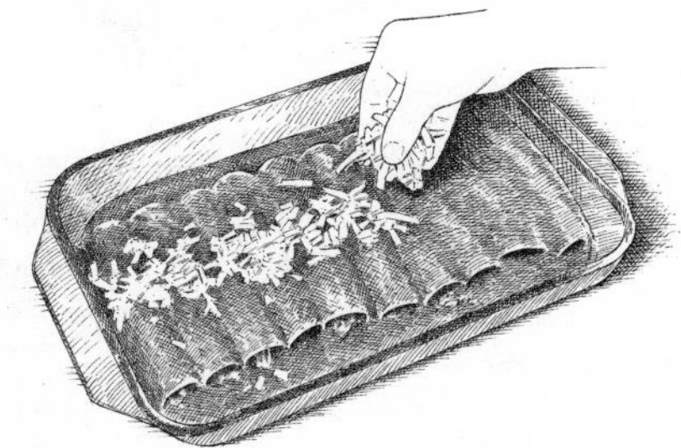

5. Sprinkle the remaining ½ cup cheese down the center.

and poach them right in the sauce? The thighs cooked quickly and were nicely seasoned. Cooking the chicken in the sauce also lent the sauce a wonderful richness. And shredding the chicken once it was cooked gave it just the right texture to bind nicely with the other filling ingredients.

We strained the sauce and added its flavorful solids to the chicken for the filling. Cheese was next on our list. Queso fresco, the traditional choice, is an unripened cheese with a creamy color, mild flavor, and crumbly texture. But because it is not readily available in many parts of the United States, we tried farmer's cheese instead. Tasters liked this cheese for its creamy texture and mellow flavor, but it was Monterey Jack and sharp white cheddar that made the top of the list. The Jack is mellow while the cheddar adds a sharp, distinctive flavor. In the end, tasters preferred the sharp flavor of the cheddar. (Cheese, we discovered, also helps to bind the filling ingredients.)

Looking for more heat, we taste-tested the addition of fresh jalapeños, chipotles in adobo sauce, and pickled jalapeños. The fresh jalapeños were too mild. Chipotles (smoked jalapeños stewed in a seasoned sauce) added a distinctive, warm heat and smoky flavor that some tasters enjoyed but that most found too spicy and overwhelmingly smoky. Everyone was surprised to find that the very convenient pickled jalapeños (sold in both cans and jars) were the favorite. The vinegar pickling solution added spicy, bright, and sour notes to the filling. We now had authentic-tasting enchiladas that didn't take all day to make.

ROLLING TORTILLAS EASILY

Straight from the refrigerator, a corn tortilla is too stiff to roll and will tear at the edges, as seen in the top photograph. Spraying the tortilla with oil and heating it for 2 to 4 minutes in a 300-degree oven will make the tortilla pliable and easy to manage, as shown in the bottom photograph.

Chicken Enchiladas

SERVES 4 TO 6

If you prefer, Monterey Jack can be used instead of cheddar, or, for a mellower flavor and creamier texture, try substituting an equal amount of farmer's cheese. Serve with sour cream, diced avocado, shredded romaine lettuce, and lime wedges.

- 2 tablespoons vegetable oil
- 1 medium onion, minced
- 3 tablespoons chili powder
- 3 medium garlic cloves, minced or pressed through a garlic press (about 1 tablespoon)
- 2 teaspoons ground coriander
- 2 teaspoons ground cumin
- 2 teaspoons sugar
- Salt
- 2 (8-ounce) cans tomato sauce
- ⅓ cup water
- 1 pound boneless, skinless chicken thighs (about 4 thighs), trimmed
- 10 ounces sharp cheddar cheese, shredded (about 2½ cups) (see note)
- ½ cup minced fresh cilantro leaves
- 1 (4-ounce) can pickled jalapeños, drained and chopped (about ¼ cup)
- 10 (6-inch) corn tortillas

1. Adjust an oven rack to the middle position and heat the oven to 300 degrees. Heat the oil in a large saucepan over medium-high heat until shimmering. Add the onion and cook until softened and lightly browned, 5 to 7 minutes. Stir in the chili powder, garlic, coriander, cumin, sugar, and

½ teaspoon salt and cook, stirring constantly, until fragrant, about 30 seconds. Stir in the tomato sauce and water and bring to a simmer.

2. Add the chicken thighs, partially cover, and bring to a simmer. Reduce the heat to low, cover completely, and cook until the thickest part of the thigh registers 170 to 175 degrees on an instant-read thermometer, about 13 minutes. Transfer the chicken to a cutting board. When the chicken is cool enough to handle, shred into bite-sized pieces (see the illustration on page 10) and transfer to a large bowl.

3. Pour the sauce through a medium-mesh strainer and into a medium bowl, pressing on the solids to extract as much sauce as possible. Set the sauce aside and transfer the solids to the bowl with the shredded chicken. Stir 2 cups of the cheese, the cilantro, and jalapeños into the chicken mixture. Season with salt to taste and set aside.

4. Following the illustrations on page 289, lightly coat both sides of the tortillas with vegetable oil spray. Place the tortillas on two baking sheets. Place one baking sheet in the oven and bake until the tortillas are soft and pliable, 2 to 4 minutes. Transfer the tortillas to a clean work surface. Place a heaping ⅓ cup filling onto the center of each warm, softened tortilla and roll it up tightly, following the illustrations on page 289. Arrange the enchiladas, seam-side down, in a single layer in a 13 by 9-inch baking dish (or a shallow casserole dish of a similar size). Repeat with the remaining tortillas, increasing the oven temperature to 400 degrees after they are removed from the oven.

5. Pour the sauce over the enchiladas, covering the tortillas completely, then sprinkle the remaining ½ cup cheese down the center of the enchiladas, following the illustrations on page 289. Cover the dish with aluminum foil that has been coated with nonstick cooking spray and bake until the sauce is bubbling and the cheese is melted, 20 to 25 minutes.

6. Remove the foil and continue to bake until the cheese on top is browned in spots, about 5 minutes longer. Let cool for 10 minutes before serving.

Creamy Baked Four-Cheese Pasta with Chicken

IN ITALIAN, *AL FORNO* MEANS "FROM THE oven," so, logically, *pasta al forno* means "pasta from the oven." Here in the test kitchen we are quite familiar with al forno pastas—lasagna, baked ziti, and baked macaroni and cheese are among the most popular versions in this country. In our reading of authentic Italian cookbooks, however, we came across an array of pasta al forno recipes, with various pasta shapes, sauces, and flavorings—in Italy, when it comes to pasta al forno, it seems as though the sky is the limit.

We decided to marry the pasta al forno technique with the flavors of *pasta ai quattro formaggi*, the classic Italian pasta dish with four cheeses and heavy cream. And to make it even more substantial, we wanted to add chicken to our dish. This combination of baked pasta and a creamy cheese sauce is a classic example of simple Italian cooking. Our goal was to discover how to make this dish a great one, delivering a pasta dinner that was silky-smooth and rich, with a golden brown crust on top and chicken flavor throughout.

Of course, we found that the cheese was the first issue in terms of both flavor and texture. We were committed to Italian cheeses, but this barely diminished our choices—the recipes we found called for varying combinations and amounts. Recipes contained anywhere from 1 cup to 6½ cups of cheese for 1 pound of pasta, and the selection of cheeses was just as dizzying: Asiago, fontina, Taleggio, Pecorino Romano, mascarpone, mozzarella, Gorgonzola, Parmesan, and ricotta all turned up in our research. However, some initial testing reduced the scope quickly: Mascarpone and ricotta added neither flavor nor texture, and Asiago was bland. Pasta tossed with mozzarella was gooey and greasy, whereas Taleggio was not only difficult to obtain, but also made the pasta too rich and gluey. Tasters favored a combination of Italian fontina (which is creamier and better-tasting than versions of this cheese made elsewhere), Gorgonzola, Pecorino Romano, and Parmesan.

With our winning cheese combination settled, we turned our attention to incorporating it into the other ingredients of the dish. Both heating the cheeses and cream together and adding the cheeses separately to the hot pasta produced nasty messes. Each attempt caused the cheeses to curdle, separate, and/or turn greasy. Some recipes solve this problem by starting with a white sauce—a béchamel—which is made by cooking butter and flour together (to make a roux), then whisking in milk or cream, followed by the cheese. The flour in the sauce works as a type of binder that helps prevent the cheese from separating. This approach worked great, and we found that basing the sauce on cream was better than basing it on milk. Unlike milk, cream thickens and stabilizes on its own as it simmers and reduces, and therefore a sauce made with cream requires less flour than one made with milk. And the less flour you use in the sauce, the silkier the texture of the final dish.

In order to sauce 1 pound of pasta well, the béchamel needed to yield about 3 cups. Not wanting to load up the sauce with 3 cups of heavy cream, we borrowed a technique we use in many of our other pasta recipes and added some of the pasta cooking water to the sauce. Combining 1½ cups of the pasta cooking water with 1½ cups of cream yielded a creamy, light-tasting sauce.

Yet we were still bothered by the notion of stirring the cheeses into the béchamel. In theory, the less the cheeses are cooked, the more flavor you'll get from them. With this in mind, we tried mixing the cheeses into the hot pasta with the hot béchamel just before the casserole went into the oven. This worked wonderfully, and the final dish was the most flavorful yet.

Incorporating the chicken into the pasta dish was the next challenge. Boneless, skinless breasts seemed to be the easiest option, but preventing them from overcooking and turning tough was the hurdle. As we had learned in our Chicken Tetrazzini (page 276), poaching the chicken was the best method in terms of incorporating the chicken, as well as the easiest, with no need to dirty an extra pot. First we tried simply poaching the chicken in the pasta water, but tasters found the resulting chicken to be bland and washed-out. We then tried poaching the chicken right in the sauce. This method worked wonders—the chicken took on some of the sauce's flavor and also enriched the sauce, thus maximizing the chicken flavor. Rather than cutting the raw chicken into pieces before poaching, we found it best to poach the boneless breasts whole and then shred them into bite-sized pieces. When the chicken was poached and then shredded, it remained moist and kept its tender texture.

Tubular pasta shapes and large shells allow the sauce to coat the pasta inside and out and are the best choice here. Many al forno recipes suggest cooking the pasta fully and then baking it for 30 minutes, but we found that this method resulted in mushy pasta. To keep the pasta from overcooking in the oven, we found it necessary to undercook it by a few minutes, and then minimize the baking time. Just 15 minutes in a 500-degree oven (in a shallow baking dish so that it heats more quickly) is enough to turn the pasta and sauce into pasta al forno—the beautifully browned top contrasts nicely with the creamy pasta and helps balance the richness of the sauce.

Creamy Baked Four-Cheese Pasta with Chicken

SERVES 6 TO 8

If you do not like the flavor of Gorgonzola, omit it and increase the fontina to 7 ounces. Underboiling the pasta in step 1 is important, or it will overcook in the oven and become mushy. Be careful when seasoning the sauce with salt in step 2, as the cheeses tend to be quite salty. If you use shell pasta, be sure to buy the large variety and not the jumbo size.

- Salt
- 1 pound penne, ziti, or large shells (see note)
- 1 tablespoon olive oil
- 2 tablespoons unsalted butter
- 2 tablespoons unbleached all-purpose flour
- 2 medium garlic cloves, minced or pressed through a garlic press (about 2 teaspoons)
- 1½ cups heavy cream

- Ground black pepper
- 2 pounds boneless, skinless chicken breasts (about 5 medium), trimmed
- 4 ounces Italian fontina cheese, shredded (about 1 cup)
- 3 ounces Gorgonzola cheese, crumbled (about ¾ cup) (see note)
- 2 ounces Parmesan cheese, grated (about 1 cup)
- 1 ounce Pecorino Romano cheese, grated (about ½ cup)
- 2 tablespoons minced fresh parsley leaves

1. Adjust an oven rack to the middle position and heat the oven to 500 degrees. Bring 4 quarts water to a boil in a Dutch oven over high heat. Stir in 1 tablespoon salt and the pasta and cook, stirring often, until just shy of al dente, about 8 minutes. Reserve 1½ cups of the pasta cooking water. Drain the pasta and toss with the oil; leave in the colander and set aside.

2. Wipe out the pot with paper towels. Add the butter to the pot, return to medium-low heat, and heat the butter until melted. Add the flour and cook, stirring constantly, until golden, about 1 minute. Stir in the garlic and cook until fragrant, about 30 seconds. Slowly whisk in the cream and reserved pasta cooking water. Bring to a simmer and cook, whisking often, until slightly thickened, about 1 minute. Season with salt and pepper to taste.

3. Add the chicken breasts, partially cover, and bring to a simmer. Reduce the heat to low, cover completely, and cook until the thickest part of the breast registers 160 to 165 degrees on an instant-read thermometer, 10 to 15 minutes.

4. Transfer the chicken to a cutting board and set the Dutch oven aside, covered. When the chicken is cool enough to handle, shred into bite-sized pieces (see the illustration on page 10). Return the shredded chicken to the sauce and toss with the pasta, fontina, Gorgonzola, ½ cup of the Parmesan, and the Pecorino. Season with salt and pepper to taste. Transfer to a 13 by 9-inch baking dish (or a shallow casserole dish of a similar size) and sprinkle with the remaining ½ cup Parmesan. Bake until the top is golden, about 15 minutes. Let cool for 10 minutes. Sprinkle with the parsley and serve.

Creamy Baked Penne, Chicken, and Vegetables

PASTA AND CHICKEN ARE SUCH POPULAR ingredients on their own that we figured teaming them up in a casserole would be a smash hit. Initially, we were wrong. Dry, rubbery chicken, mushy pasta, and bland sauce turned out to be the downsides of this casserole. We'd need to develop a chicken and pasta casserole that turned out juicy chunks of chicken and tender (not mushy!) pasta, all bound together with a creamy, well-seasoned sauce.

We started off with a basic cream sauce—we sautéed aromatics (such as onions and garlic), then added cream and allowed the sauce to simmer, thicken, and reduce before we finished it with cheese. This type of sauce worked great at binding the pasta and chicken together, but it tasted a little too rich. After all, we had just developed a rich, cheesy version of baked pasta in the Creamy Baked Four-Cheese Pasta with Chicken (page 292). For this baked pasta dish, we wanted a slightly lighter version with vegetables. We tried replacing some of the heavy cream with chicken broth and found that it not only made the sauce taste lighter, but it boosted the chicken flavor, too. A little white wine also helped cut through the sauce's heaviness without diluting its flavor. These additions of broth and wine, however, made the texture of the sauce a bit too thin. Unlike cream, chicken broth and wine don't become dramatically thicker as they reduce. In order to make the sauce thick enough to coat the chicken and penne properly, we found it necessary to add some flour.

We then tried flavoring the sauce with several different types of cheese and noted that Italian cheeses fit the bill. Giving Parmesan, Italian fontina, and Pecorino Romano a whirl, we found that we didn't care for a sauce flavored with just one type of cheese (too boring and one-dimensional), but rather preferred a sauce flavored with a combination of cheeses. We opted for a combination of fontina and Parmesan—the fontina had good melting qualities, and the Parmesan contributed a distinctive nutty flavor that tasters enjoyed.

Up to this point, we had been cooking the pasta to an al dente consistency, tossing it with some cooked chicken and the cream sauce, and then spreading it into a casserole dish. The casserole was sprinkled with a little extra cheese and baked until bubbling and browned. By serving time, unfortunately, the al dente pasta overcooked to a mushy consistency. To solve this problem, we undercooked the pasta, testing a variety of boiling times to get it just right. In the end, we found that the pasta required only about 8 minutes of boiling, at which point it was just shy of al dente. After draining it, we tossed the pasta with the remaining ingredients and baked the casserole. In the oven, the pasta absorbed some of the sauce and cooked through, but still retained some of its texture.

While the casserole baked, we surveyed the two pots on the stove—one to boil the pasta and one to prepare the cream sauce. To cut out a pot, we found we could boil the pasta in one pot, then set the pasta aside in a colander while we used the same pot for the sauce. To prevent the pasta from sticking together as the sauce cooked, we tossed it with a little oil. We had been using ziti in these initial casseroles (chicken and ziti is a classic combo), but luckily we ran out of it one day and substituted penne. The tasters raved about the smaller, more elegant size of the penne and found it to be a more appropriate pairing with the chicken and cream sauce.

Moving next to the chicken, we found it easiest to use boneless, skinless breasts. Wanting to prevent the chicken from overcooking and turning tough, we first tried tossing small pieces of raw chicken with the sauce and undercooked penne and letting it cook through in the oven. This method, unfortunately, didn't work. It took far too long for the chicken to cook through in the oven, by which time the pasta was overdone and the sauce had dried out. Testing a variety of ways to precook the chicken, we tried broiling, sautéing, and poaching it in the pasta water. Broiling turned the edges of the chicken unappealingly crisp, while poaching in water resulted in a bland, washed-out flavor. Sautéing the chicken in a skillet with a little oil worked well, but it required an extra pan, which we were loathe to use. Working with the poaching idea, we then tried poaching the chicken right in the sauce. This method worked like a charm—the chicken took on some of the sauce's flavor, and vice versa.

During our final chicken cooking tests, we learned that how the chicken is cut is nearly as important as how it is cooked. Rather than cutting the raw chicken into pieces before poaching, we found it best to poach the boneless breasts whole and then shred them into bite-sized pieces. When the chicken was poached and then shredded, it tasted much more moist and kept its tender texture.

Now we just needed to fine-tune the casserole's flavors. Although everything was perfectly cooked, the dish was a bit bland. We tried adding some herbs but, although good-tasting (we kept them in the recipe), alone they weren't enough. Turning to mushrooms, we found that their distinctive, earthy flavor shone through and gave this casserole some much-needed oomph. A combination of both fresh mushrooms (we like cremini mushrooms for their color and flavor) and dried porcinis worked perfectly. In developing a variation, we found that artichoke hearts with lemon and tarragon also worked nicely with the pasta, chicken, and cream sauce and made for an elegant, company-worthy casserole.

Baked Penne and Chicken with Mushrooms

SERVES 6 TO 8

Underboiling the pasta in step 1 is important, or it will overcook in the oven and become mushy.

- Salt
- 1 pound penne
- 4 tablespoons olive oil
- 1½ pounds cremini mushrooms, wiped clean and sliced ¼ inch thick
- 1 medium onion, minced
- ½ ounce dried porcini mushrooms, rinsed and minced

- 8 medium garlic cloves, minced or pressed through a garlic press (about 8 teaspoons)
- 1 tablespoon minced fresh thyme leaves or 1 teaspoon dried
- ¼ cup unbleached all-purpose flour
- 2 cups low-sodium chicken broth
- 1 cup dry white wine
- 1 cup heavy cream
- 2 pounds boneless, skinless chicken breasts (about 5 medium), trimmed
- 6 ounces Italian fontina cheese, shredded (about 1½ cups)
- 2 ounces Parmesan cheese, grated (about 1 cup)
- Ground black pepper
- 2 tablespoons minced fresh parsley leaves

1. Adjust an oven rack to the middle position and heat the oven to 400 degrees. Bring 4 quarts water to a boil in a Dutch oven over high heat. Stir in 1 tablespoon salt and the pasta and cook, stirring often, until just shy of al dente, about 8 minutes. Drain the pasta and toss with 1 tablespoon of the oil; leave in the colander and set aside.

2. Wipe out the pot with paper towels. Add the remaining 3 tablespoons oil to the pot, return to medium-low heat, and heat the oil until shimmering. Add the cremini mushrooms, onion, porcini mushrooms, and 1 teaspoon salt. Cover and cook, stirring often, until the mushrooms have released their liquid, about 10 minutes. Uncover, increase the heat to medium-high, and continue to cook, stirring often, until the mushrooms are dry and browned, 5 to 10 minutes.

3. Stir in the garlic and thyme and cook until fragrant, about 30 seconds. Stir in the flour and cook, stirring constantly, until golden, about 1 minute. Slowly whisk in the broth, wine, and cream.

4. Add the chicken breasts, partially cover, and bring to a simmer. Reduce the heat to low, cover completely, and cook until the thickest part of the breast registers 160 to 165 degrees on an instant-read thermometer, 10 to 15 minutes.

5. Transfer the chicken to a cutting board and set the Dutch oven aside, covered. When the chicken is cool enough to handle, shred into bite-sized pieces (see the illustration on page 10). Return the shredded chicken to the sauce with the pasta, ¾ cup of the fontina, and ½ cup of the Parmesan. Season with salt and pepper to taste. Transfer to a 13 by 9-inch baking dish (or a shallow casserole dish of a similar size). Toss the remaining ¾ cup fontina and remaining ½ cup Parmesan together in a small bowl and sprinkle over the top of the casserole.

6. Bake, uncovered, until the top is browned and the sauce is bubbling, 25 to 35 minutes. Let cool for 10 minutes. Sprinkle with the parsley and serve.

Baked Penne and Chicken with Artichokes and Tarragon

SERVES 6 TO 8

If you can't find frozen artichokes, you can substitute 3 (14-ounce) cans artichoke hearts; you will need to thoroughly drain, rinse, and pat them dry before using. Underboiling the pasta in step 1 is important, or it will overcook in the oven and become mushy.

- Salt
- 1 pound penne
- 4 tablespoons olive oil
- 3 (9-ounce) boxes frozen artichokes, thawed, patted dry, and chopped coarse (see note)
- 1 medium onion, minced
- 8 medium garlic cloves, minced or pressed through a garlic press (about 8 teaspoons)
- ¼ teaspoon grated zest from 1 lemon
- ¼ cup unbleached all-purpose flour
- 2 cups low-sodium chicken broth
- 1 cup dry white wine
- 1 cup heavy cream
- 2 pounds boneless, skinless chicken breasts (about 5 medium), trimmed
- 3 bay leaves
- 1½ cups frozen peas
- 6 ounces Italian fontina cheese, shredded (about 1½ cups)

- 2 ounces Parmesan cheese, grated (about 1 cup)
- 3 tablespoons juice from 1 lemon
- Ground black pepper
- 3 tablespoons minced fresh tarragon leaves

1. Adjust an oven rack to the middle position and heat the oven to 400 degrees. Bring 4 quarts water to a boil in a Dutch oven over high heat. Stir in 1 tablespoon salt and the pasta and cook, stirring often, until just shy of al dente, about 8 minutes. Drain the pasta and toss with 1 tablespoon of the oil; leave in the colander and set aside.

2. Wipe out the pot with paper towels. Add the remaining 3 tablespoons oil to the pot, return to medium heat, and heat the oil until shimmering. Add the artichokes, onion, and 1 teaspoon salt and cook until the artichokes are lightly browned, 8 to 10 minutes.

3. Stir in the garlic and lemon zest and cook until fragrant, about 30 seconds. Stir in the flour and cook, stirring constantly, until golden, about 1 minute. Slowly whisk in the broth, wine, and cream.

4. Add the chicken breasts and bay leaves, partially cover, and bring to a simmer. Reduce the heat to low, cover completely, and cook until the thickest part of the breast registers 160 to 165 degrees on an instant-read thermometer, 10 to 15 minutes.

5. Transfer the chicken to a cutting board, discard the bay leaves, and set the Dutch oven aside, covered. When the chicken is cool enough to handle, shred into bite-sized pieces (see the illustration on page 10). Return the shredded chicken to the sauce and toss with the pasta, peas, ¾ cup of the fontina, ½ cup of the Parmesan, and the lemon juice. Season with salt and pepper to taste. Transfer to a 13 by 9-inch baking dish (or a shallow casserole dish of a similar size). Toss the remaining ¾ cup fontina and remaining ½ cup Parmesan together in a small bowl and sprinkle over the top of the casserole.

6. Bake, uncovered, until the top is browned and the sauce is bubbling, 25 to 35 minutes. Let cool for 10 minutes. Sprinkle with the tarragon and serve.

Lasagna Carnivale with Chicken Meatballs

IN ITALY, *CARNIVALE* IS A FESTIVAL THAT takes place just before Lent, the period of time before Easter during which observant Roman Catholics do not eat meat. Traditionally, Carnivale was a time to consume all of the meat that remained in the village before the fast, but these days it is a great public celebration that entails dressing up in costumes, wearing decorative masks, and partying all day and night. In Naples, a city in southern Italy, a lasagna with tiny meatballs, tomato sauce, and mozzarella cheese is traditionally made to celebrate Carnivale. Appropriately, it is called *lasagna de Carnivale.*

We have eaten more than our share of lasagna, which is often nothing more than mushy noodles swimming in a sea of red sauce and cheese. We wanted to try the Neapolitan style of lasagna, with its distinct layers, moderate amount of deeply flavored sauce, and tender meatballs, but we would never make it at home—it contains around 25 ingredients and takes an entire day to prepare. Starting from the idea that less sauce and more pasta is better, we wanted to devise a recipe with these classic tastes, but without the backbreaking labor. To top it off, while the Italians make their lasagna with beef, we wanted to try making ours with chicken.

Our first task was to make sense of the cheese component. Various Italian recipes call for mozzarella, ricotta (sometimes mixed with whole eggs or egg yolks), and/or a hard grating cheese (usually Parmesan, but sometimes Pecorino Romano). After trying the various combinations, we realized that ricotta was responsible for what we call "lasagna meltdown"—the loss of shape and distinct layering. Even with the addition of whole eggs or yolks as a thickener, we found that ricotta is too watery to use in lasagna that includes meatballs, and usually leads to a sloppy mess.

Mozzarella provides plenty of creaminess, and its stringiness binds the layers to each other and helps keep them from slipping apart when served.

Fresh mozzarella, however, has too much moisture to be effective. When it melts, it releases so much liquid that the lasagna becomes mushy and watery. In addition, the delicate flavor of expensive fresh mozzarella is lost in the baking. After a few disastrous attempts with fresh mozzarella, we turned to its shrink-wrapped cousin, whole-milk mozzarella, and had much better results. We also found that adding either Parmesan or Pecorino Romano provides a pleasantly sharp contrast to the somewhat mild mozzarella.

With the cheese question resolved, we next focused on the meatballs. Here again we looked to traditional Italian recipes for inspiration, then tried to simplify. We seasoned ground chicken with herbs, cheese, egg yolks, and bread crumbs. However, instead of rolling out real meatballs, which would be too large to rest snugly between the layers of pasta, we pinched off small bits of the mixture. We tried pinching them off directly into hot oil, which worked fine, but this required us to stand over the oil frying upward of four batches. Instead, we placed the meatballs on a baking sheet and, after just eight to 10 minutes in a 450-degree oven, they were done.

Since our aim was to simplify matters, we decided to add the meatballs to a quick-cooking tomato sauce made with crushed tomatoes. Many traditional recipes simmer whole tomatoes or tomato puree for hours to make a rich, complex sauce. However, since lasagna has so many competing elements, we found that little was gained by this lengthy process. Simmering canned, crushed tomatoes just long enough to make a sauce—about 10 minutes—was sufficient.

Next, we focused our attention on the choice of noodles and layering tricks. Here in the test kitchen we often make lasagna with no-boil noodles. They really simplify the process and produce great results, so we thought we would give them a try here. We made our working recipe with no-boil noodles, only to find out that they did not work—they emerged from the oven with a tough, cardboard-like texture. Thinking that soaking the noodles in hot water would help them to soften, we gave it a try. No luck. Our lightly sauced lasagna simply did not have enough moisture for the noodles to absorb and become tender as the lasagna cooked. This type of lasagna requires a more traditional type of noodle.

Many Italian lasagna recipes call for fresh pasta. Tasters liked the thinness of the fresh noodles, but voted unanimously against making them from scratch—after all, we were trying to simplify our lasagna-making process, not complicate it. We then tried several brands of fresh pasta from our local markets, but they varied dramatically, not only in thickness and dimensions, but also in quality. Traditional dried lasagna noodles—the type that require being boiled before assembling the lasagna—turned out to be our favorite, in part because they were the most reliable, but also because tasters were most satisfied with the lasagna they produced. The key to working with these noodles is boiling them until soft and then rinsing them with cold water; this stops them from cooking further and becoming mushy, and also rinses away some of the starch, preventing them from sticking together.

In terms of the actual layering procedure, we found it helpful to grease the baking pan with cooking spray. We then spread a small amount of tomato sauce (without any meatballs) over the pan to moisten the bottom layer of pasta and added the first layer of noodles. After that, we spread the sauce and meatballs evenly over the noodles, covered them with shredded mozzarella, and then sprinkled on grated Parmesan. We then built more layers by this same process. We realized that the tomato sauce and meatballs tended to dry out when not covered by pasta, so the final layer we covered with only the two cheeses, which brown during baking to give an attractive appearance.

After just 20 minutes in a 400-degree oven, the lasagna was ready to eat (although we do recommend letting it cool for 10 minutes before serving). This lasagna is certainly just as satisfying as traditional Neapolitan versions and quicker to assemble. The best part is that you don't have to wait for Carnivale to enjoy it!

Lasagna Carnivale with Chicken Meatballs

SERVES 8

Do not substitute no-boil noodles; they do not work in this dish. The size of the noodles will depend on the brand; if the noodles are short (such as DeCecco), you will layer them crosswise in the dish, but if they are long (such as Barilla and Ronzoni), you will layer them lengthwise. Regardless of which brand of noodle you are using, there should be 3 noodles per layer. For more information on buying ground chicken, see page 3.

MEATBALLS AND SAUCE

- 1 pound ground chicken (see note)
- 2 ounces Parmesan or Pecorino Romano cheese, grated (about 1 cup)
- ½ cup store-bought plain dried bread crumbs
- 2 large eggs, lightly beaten
- ½ cup minced fresh basil or parsley leaves
- Salt and ground black pepper
- 3 tablespoons olive oil
- 2 medium garlic cloves, minced or pressed through a garlic press (about 2 teaspoons)
- 1 (28-ounce) can crushed tomatoes

NOODLES AND CHEESE

- 1 tablespoon salt
- 12 dried lasagna noodles (see note)
- 1 pound whole-milk mozzarella cheese, shredded (about 4 cups)
- 4 ounces Parmesan or Pecorino Romano cheese, grated (about 2 cups)

1. For the meatballs and sauce: Adjust an oven rack to the middle position and heat the oven to 450 degrees. Coat a rimmed baking sheet with nonstick cooking spray; set aside. Mix together the chicken, cheese, bread crumbs, eggs, 5 tablespoons of the basil, 1 teaspoon salt, and ½ teaspoon pepper until uniform. Pinch off scant teaspoon-sized pieces of the mixture (about the size of a small grape) and arrange on the prepared baking sheet. Bake the meatballs until just cooked through and lightly browned, 8 to 10 minutes. Decrease the oven temperature to 400 degrees.

2. Heat the oil and garlic in a medium saucepan over medium heat until the garlic starts to sizzle, about 2 minutes. Stir in the tomatoes, bring to a simmer, and cook until the sauce thickens slightly, 10 to 15 minutes. Off the heat, stir in the remaining 3 tablespoons basil and season with salt and pepper to taste. Stir the meatballs into the sauce and set aside, covered.

3. For the noodles and cheese: Meanwhile, bring 4 quarts water to a boil in a large pot. Stir in the salt and noodles and cook, stirring often, until the pasta is al dente. Drain the noodles and rinse them under cold water until cool. Spread the noodles out in a single layer over clean kitchen towels. (Do not use paper towels; they will stick to the pasta.)

4. Coat a 13 by 9-inch baking dish with nonstick cooking spray. Smear 3 tablespoons of the tomato sauce (without any meatballs) over the bottom of the pan. Line the pan with a layer of pasta, making sure that the noodles touch but do not overlap. Spread about 1½ cups of the tomato sauce with meatballs evenly over the pasta. Sprinkle evenly with 1 cup of the mozzarella and ½ cup of the Parmesan. Repeat the layering of pasta, tomato sauce with meatballs, and cheeses 2 more times. For the fourth and final layer, cover the pasta with the remaining 1 cup mozzarella and sprinkle with the remaining ½ cup Parmesan.

5. Bake until the cheese on top is browned in spots and the sauce is bubbling, 20 to 25 minutes. Let cool for 10 minutes before serving.

11 EXPRESS LANE CHICKEN

Express Lane Chicken

CHICKEN HAS LONG BEEN A SIMPLE AND convenient dinner option, and its mild flavor can play host to a variety of flavors, so it never gets boring. Chicken is widely available and, better yet, quick cooking, so no matter how tired you are after a long day, or pressed for time on a busy weeknight, it can easily make a satisfying, family-pleasing meal. For these reasons, this chapter contains both naturally speedy chicken recipes and streamlined longer-cooking ones to help you get dinner on the table in about 30 minutes. Now, we're not talking about whole roasted birds, braised thighs, or barbecued chicken here—this chapter features quick-cooking chicken breasts (both boneless and bone-in), cutlets, chicken sausage, and ground chicken.

This chapter is home to basic recipes, like sautéed boneless, skinless chicken breasts or cutlets and pan-roasted bone-in, skin-on chicken breasts, any of which makes the perfect centerpiece to a delicious and quick meal. An added bonus in sautéing and pan-roasting are the browned bits, called fond, left behind in the skillet. They are the perfect building block for a quick, flavorful pan sauce. Pan sauces provide endless variety, turning a simple sautéed piece of chicken into something truly special. (See pages 303–305 for more information on pan sauces.)

Here in the test kitchen we believe that quick cooking isn't only about the time it takes to cook a meal. It can also involve streamlining the number of pots and pans used in a recipe, as each one requires attention (and washing). A complete meal often means pulling out one pan for the meat, at least one for the vegetables, another for the starch, and so on. For many of the recipes in this chapter, we realized we could reduce the number of pans we use to the bare essentials—primarily just a skillet. In some cases, we use a two-track approach, relying on a skillet and a baking dish. In these cases, we start by pan-searing meat in the skillet and then transfer it to the baking dish to finish cooking in the oven. Why? Because this frees up the skillet for cooking side dishes, allowing us to develop a wider variety of meals.

The recipes in this chapter aim to choreograph these sorts of issues while delivering tasty one-dish meals in just about 30 minutes. In addition to adapting some unmistakable skillet classics, like tacos and Sloppy Joes, we found that, as we developed new recipes, we could free ourselves to be more inventive by rotating ingredients in and out of the skillet. This flexibility enabled us to create dishes like Chicken and Couscous with Fennel and Orange (page 308).

Note that you will need either a nonstick or a traditional 12-inch skillet for the recipes in this chapter (see pages 246 and 263 for recommended brands of nonstick and traditional skillets). In addition, some recipes require an ovensafe skillet, but if you do not have one, you can instead transfer the mixture to a shallow 2-quart casserole dish before baking or broiling. Similarly, if a recipe calls for a lid and you don't have one that fits your skillet, simply lay a sheet of foil over the skillet and crimp the edges to seal.

Sautéed Chicken

BONELESS, SKINLESS CHICKEN BREASTS ARE like a blank canvas just waiting to be transformed—in this case, into a quick, convenient dinner. But they are not without challenges. We've all been on the receiving end of poorly cooked chicken breasts. As innocuous as they may look, if they are cooked poorly, no amount of pan sauce can camouflage their dry, leathery meat.

To cook chicken breasts correctly, the first thing to consider is size. Be sure to select chicken breasts of equal size so that they will cook evenly and at the same rate. And be sure to remove the tenderloin from each breast—they tend to fall off when cooking and dramatically affect the cooking time (you can reserve them for another use such as a stir-fry). Turning the heat down when browning the second side of the breasts is crucial to keep the pan from scorching while the chicken cooks through and helps to prevent a leathery, stringy exterior. Chicken cutlets (thinner than chicken breasts) are prone to overcooking. The key to cutlets is to use high heat and cook them quickly.

Whether cooking breasts or cutlets, we found that flouring the chicken prior to sautéing protected the meat from drying out and helped to prevent it from sticking to the skillet. For optimum browning, we found it absolutely essential to use a large 12-inch traditional skillet, and we like to use vegetable oil for its high smoke point and neutral flavor. Sautéed chicken breasts and cutlets are great on their own, but they can easily be elevated to company-worthy status with the addition of a quick pan sauce (see pages 303–305).

Simple Sautéed Chicken Breasts

SERVES 4

If you like, serve the chicken with a pan sauce—see the recipes on pages 303–305.

½ cup unbleached all-purpose flour
4 boneless, skinless chicken breasts (5 to 6 ounces each), tenderloins removed and breasts trimmed (see the illustrations on page 6)
Salt and ground black pepper
2 tablespoons vegetable oil

1. Place the flour in a shallow dish. Pat the chicken dry with paper towels and season with salt and pepper. Working with 1 chicken breast at a time, dredge in the flour, shaking off the excess.

2. Heat the oil in a 12-inch skillet over medium-high heat until just smoking. Add the chicken and cook until well browned on one side, 6 to 8 minutes.

3. Flip the chicken over, reduce the heat to medium-low, and continue to cook until the thickest part of the breast registers 160 to 165 degrees on an instant-read thermometer, 6 to 8 minutes longer.

4. Transfer the chicken to a plate, tent loosely with foil, and let rest for at least 5 minutes (or while making a pan sauce) before serving.

Simple Sautéed Chicken Cutlets

SERVES 4

Be careful not to overcook the cutlets—they really do cook through in just 4 minutes. If you like, serve the cutlets with a pan sauce—see the recipes on pages 303–305.

4 boneless, skinless chicken breasts (5 to 6 ounces each), tenderloins removed and breasts trimmed (see the illustrations on page 6)
½ cup unbleached all-purpose flour
Salt and ground black pepper
¼ cup vegetable oil

1. Following the illustrations on page 6, slice each chicken breast in half horizontally and pound each cutlet as directed between two sheets of plastic wrap to a uniform ¼-inch thickness.

2. Place the flour in a shallow dish. Pat the chicken dry with paper towels and season with salt and pepper. Working with 1 cutlet at a time, dredge in the flour, shaking off the excess.

3. Heat 2 tablespoons of the oil in a 12-inch skillet over medium-high heat until just smoking. Add 4 of the cutlets and cook until lightly browned on both sides, about 4 minutes. Transfer to a plate and tent loosely with foil.

4. Add the remaining 2 tablespoons oil to the skillet and repeat with the remaining cutlets. (Tent loosely with foil if making a pan sauce.) Serve.

Pan-Roasted Chicken Breasts

PAN-ROASTING, A RESTAURANT TECHNIQUE in which food is browned on the stovetop in a skillet that is then placed directly in the oven, is a great technique for quick weeknight cooking. The bonus of pan-roasting is that the skillet is left with caramelized drippings, or fond, which is ideal for making a rich, flavorful pan sauce to accompany the chicken (see pages 303–305 for more information on pan sauces).

When it came to browning, we heated 1 tablespoon vegetable oil in the skillet until it was smoking and then browned both sides of the chicken before transferring the skillet to the lowest rack in the oven. We tried oven temperatures ranging from 375 up to 500 degrees. The highest temperatures caused profuse smoking and, sometimes, singed drippings. Temperatures on the lower end meant protracted cooking times. At 450 degrees, however, the skin was handsomely browned and crackling crisp, and the chicken cooked swiftly to the internal temperature of 160 degrees, which translated to about 18 minutes for 12-ounce breasts.

Pan-Roasted Chicken Breasts

SERVES 4

Remember to preheat your oven before assembling your ingredients. If the split breasts are of different sizes, check the smaller ones a few minutes early to see if they are cooking more quickly, and remove them from the oven if they are done. If you like, serve the chicken with a pan sauce—see the recipes on pages 303–305.

- 4 bone-in, skin-on split chicken breasts (10 to 12 ounces each), trimmed
- Salt and ground black pepper
- 1 tablespoon vegetable oil

1. Adjust an oven rack to the lowest position and heat the oven to 450 degrees.
2. Pat the chicken dry with paper towels and season with salt and pepper. Heat the oil in an ovensafe 12-inch skillet over medium-high heat until just smoking. Add the chicken, skin-side down, and cook until deep golden, about 5 minutes. Flip the chicken over and cook until golden on the second side, about 3 minutes longer.
3. Flip the chicken skin-side down and place the skillet in the oven. Roast until the thickest part of the breast registers 160 to 165 degrees on an instant-read thermometer, 15 to 18 minutes.
4. Using a potholder or oven mitt, remove the skillet from the oven. Transfer the chicken to a plate, tent loosely with foil, and let rest for at least 5 minutes (or while making a pan sauce) before serving.

Quick Pan Sauces

THE BASE OF A PAN SAUCE IS THE FOND, OR browned bits, clinging to the bottom of the skillet after sautéing chicken (or meat or fish). Once the protein is removed from the skillet, aromatics such as minced shallots can be sautéed; then, in a process called deglazing, liquid—usually wine, broth, or both—is added to help dissolve the fond into a flavorful sauce. The sauce is then simmered to concentrate flavors and thicken. We found that the addition of 1 teaspoon of flour reduced the simmering time by helping to thicken the sauce. These pan sauces work great with our Simple Sautéed Chicken Breasts (page 302), Simple Sautéed Chicken Cutlets (page 303), or Pan-Roasted Chicken Breasts (this page).

Vermouth, Leek, and Tarragon Pan Sauce

MAKES ENOUGH FOR 4 CHICKEN BREASTS OR 8 CHICKEN CUTLETS

- 2 teaspoons vegetable oil (if needed)
- 1 medium leek, white part only, halved lengthwise, sliced ¼ inch thick, and rinsed thoroughly (see the illustrations on page 45)
- 1 teaspoon unbleached all-purpose flour
- ¾ cup low-sodium chicken broth
- ½ cup dry vermouth or white wine
- 1 tablespoon cold unsalted butter
- 2 teaspoons minced fresh tarragon leaves
- 1 teaspoon whole-grain mustard
- Salt and ground black pepper

1. After removing the chicken from the skillet, add the oil (if needed) and the leek and cook over medium-high heat until softened, about 2 minutes. Stir in the flour and cook for 30 seconds.
2. Stir in the broth and vermouth, scraping up any browned bits. Bring to a simmer and cook until the sauce measures ¾ cup, 3 to 5 minutes. Stir in any accumulated chicken juices, return to a simmer, and cook for 30 seconds.
3. Off the heat, whisk in the butter, tarragon, and mustard. Season with salt and pepper to taste.

Lemon, Caper, and Parsley Pan Sauce

MAKES ENOUGH FOR 4 CHICKEN BREASTS OR 8 CHICKEN CUTLETS

- 2 teaspoons vegetable oil (if needed)
- 1 medium shallot, minced (about 3 tablespoons)

- 1 teaspoon unbleached all-purpose flour
- ¾ cup low-sodium chicken broth
- 1 tablespoon cold unsalted butter
- 1 tablespoon capers, rinsed and chopped
- 1 tablespoon minced fresh parsley leaves
- 2 teaspoons juice from 1 lemon
- Salt and ground black pepper

1. After removing the chicken from the skillet, add the oil (if needed) and the shallot and cook over medium-high heat until softened, about 2 minutes. Stir in the flour and cook for 30 seconds.

2. Stir in the broth, scraping up any browned bits. Bring to a simmer and cook until the sauce measures ½ cup, 2 to 3 minutes. Stir in any accumulated chicken juices, return to a simmer, and cook for 30 seconds.

3. Off the heat, whisk in the butter, capers, parsley, and lemon juice. Season with salt and pepper to taste.

Sherry, Red Pepper, and Toasted Garlic Pan Sauce

MAKES ENOUGH FOR 4 CHICKEN BREASTS OR 8 CHICKEN CUTLETS

- 2 teaspoons vegetable oil (if needed)
- 3 medium garlic cloves, minced or pressed through a garlic press (about 1 tablespoon)
- 1 teaspoon unbleached all-purpose flour
- ¼ teaspoon paprika
- ¾ cup low-sodium chicken broth
- ½ cup plus 1 teaspoon dry sherry
- ¼ cup jarred roasted red peppers, patted dry and cut into ¼-inch pieces
- 1 tablespoon cold unsalted butter
- ½ teaspoon minced fresh thyme leaves
- Salt and ground black pepper

1. After removing the chicken from the skillet, add the oil (if needed) and the garlic and cook over medium-high heat until lightly browned, about 30 seconds. Stir in the flour and paprika and cook for 30 seconds.

2. Stir in the broth and ½ cup of the sherry, scraping up any browned bits. Bring to a simmer and cook until the sauce measures ¾ cup, 3 to 5 minutes. Stir in any accumulated chicken juices, return to a simmer, and cook for 30 seconds.

3. Off the heat, whisk in the peppers, butter, thyme, and the remaining 1 teaspoon sherry. Season with salt and pepper to taste.

Sweet-Tart Red Wine Sauce

MAKES ENOUGH FOR 4 CHICKEN BREASTS OR 8 CHICKEN CUTLETS

- 2 teaspoons vegetable oil (if needed)
- 1 medium shallot, minced (about 3 tablespoons)
- 1 teaspoon unbleached all-purpose flour
- ¾ cup low-sodium chicken broth
- ½ cup dry red wine
- 1 tablespoon cold unsalted butter
- 1 tablespoon light brown sugar
- 1 teaspoon minced fresh thyme leaves
- 1 teaspoon red wine vinegar
- Salt and ground black pepper

1. After removing the chicken from the skillet, add the oil (if needed) and the shallot and cook over medium-high heat until softened, about 2 minutes. Stir in the flour and cook for 30 seconds.

2. Stir in the broth and wine, scraping up any browned bits. Bring to a simmer and cook until the sauce measures ¾ cup, 3 to 5 minutes. Stir in any accumulated chicken juices, return to a simmer, and cook for 30 seconds.

3. Off the heat, whisk in the butter, sugar, thyme, and vinegar. Season with salt and pepper to taste.

Chipotle Chile and Orange Sauce

MAKES ENOUGH FOR 4 CHICKEN BREASTS OR 8 CHICKEN CUTLETS

- 2 teaspoons vegetable oil (if needed)
- 1 medium shallot, minced (about 3 tablespoons)
- 1 teaspoon unbleached all-purpose flour
- ¾ cup orange juice
- ½ cup low-sodium chicken broth
- 1 tablespoon cold unsalted butter

1 tablespoon minced fresh cilantro leaves
1 teaspoon minced chipotle chile in adobo sauce
Salt and ground black pepper

1. After removing the chicken from the skillet, add the oil (if needed) and the shallot and cook over medium-high heat until softened, about 2 minutes. Stir in the flour and cook for 30 seconds.

2. Stir in the orange juice and broth, scraping up any browned bits. Bring to a simmer and cook until the sauce measures ¾ cup, 3 to 5 minutes. Stir in any accumulated chicken juices, return to a simmer, and cook for 30 seconds.

3. Off the heat, whisk in the butter, cilantro, and chipotle. Season with salt and pepper to taste.

Easy Sautéed Chicken with Cherry Tomatoes

HAVING SOLVED THE PROBLEMS OF SAUTÉED chicken breasts (see page 302)—mainly dry, leathery meat—and having mastered some basic pan sauces (see pages 303–305), we decided to figure out how else we might transform plain, sautéed chicken breasts. We came across a magazine photo of perfectly browned boneless, skinless breasts topped with a fresh-looking mixture of tomatoes, olives, and feta cheese. This dish was colorful and inviting, and we thought it would make the perfect meal on a hot summer night.

We followed our basic recipe for sautéed chicken breasts (see page 302); while the chicken rested, we put the remainder of the dish together in a flash. We started with a little olive oil and garlic in the skillet and then added cherry tomatoes and olives and cooked them just until the tomatoes began to wilt. The tomato juices mingled with the fond in the pan and created a mixture that was part sauce, part side dish. Instead of adding the feta cheese to the hot pan (where it would melt), we poured the tomato-olive mixture over the chicken once it was off the heat, and then sprinkled the cheese over the top. The cool, creamy, tangy cheese was the perfect contrast to the warm, sweet tomatoes and briny olives. The finishing touch: a sprinkling of shredded mint leaves to add color and freshness.

Tasters liked this dish so much that we came up with a slightly heartier variation using tomatoes, bacon, blue cheese, and scallions.

Sautéed Chicken with Cherry Tomatoes, Olives, Feta, and Mint

SERVES 4

If desired, basil can be used instead of the mint.

½ cup unbleached all-purpose flour
4 boneless, skinless chicken breasts (5 to 6 ounces each), tenderloins removed and breasts trimmed (see the illustrations on page 6)
Salt and ground black pepper
4 tablespoons olive oil, plus 2 more teaspoons (if needed)
2 medium garlic cloves, minced or pressed through a garlic press (about 2 teaspoons)
1 pint cherry tomatoes, halved
½ cup kalamata olives, pitted (see the illustration on page 101) and halved
1–2 tablespoons water (if needed)
2 ounces feta cheese, crumbled (about ½ cup)
¼ cup shredded fresh mint leaves

1. Place the flour in a shallow dish. Pat the chicken dry with paper towels and season with salt and pepper. Working with 1 chicken breast at a time, dredge in the flour, shaking off the excess.

2. Heat 2 tablespoons of the oil in a 12-inch skillet over medium-high heat until just smoking. Add the chicken and cook until well browned on one side, 6 to 8 minutes.

3. Flip the chicken over, reduce the heat to medium-low, and continue to cook until the thickest part of the breast registers 160 to 165 degrees on an instant-read thermometer, 6 to 8 minutes longer. Transfer the chicken to a serving

platter, tent loosely with foil, and let rest while making the sauce.

4. Add 2 more teaspoons of the oil (if needed) and the garlic to the skillet and cook over medium-high heat until fragrant, about 30 seconds. Stir in the tomatoes and olives, scraping up any browned bits. (If necessary, add enough of the water to help loosen the browned bits from the bottom of the pan.) Cook until the tomatoes are just softened, about 2 minutes. Stir in any accumulated chicken juices and season with salt and pepper to taste.

5. Off the heat, stir in the remaining 2 tablespoons olive oil and pour the tomatoes over the chicken. Sprinkle with the feta and mint. Serve.

➢ VARIATION

Sautéed Chicken with Cherry Tomatoes, Bacon, Blue Cheese, and Scallions

If you do not like blue cheese, goat cheese makes an excellent substitution.

- ½ cup unbleached all-purpose flour
- 4 boneless, skinless chicken breasts (5 to 6 ounces each), tenderloins removed and breasts trimmed (see the illustrations on page 6)
- Salt and ground black pepper
- 2 tablespoons vegetable oil
- 4 ounces (about 4 slices) bacon, chopped medium
- 2 medium garlic cloves, minced or pressed through a garlic press (about 2 teaspoons)
- 1 pint cherry tomatoes, halved
- 1–2 tablespoons water (if needed)
- 2 ounces blue cheese, crumbled (about ½ cup)
- 2 scallions, sliced thin

1. Place the flour in a shallow dish. Pat the chicken dry with paper towels and season with salt and pepper. Working with 1 chicken breast at a time, dredge in the flour, shaking off the excess.

2. Heat the vegetable oil in a 12-inch skillet over medium-high heat until just smoking. Add the chicken and cook until well browned on one side, 6 to 8 minutes.

3. Flip the chicken over, reduce the heat to medium-low, and continue to cook until the thickest part of the breast registers 160 to 165 degrees on an instant-read thermometer, 6 to 8 minutes longer. Transfer the chicken to a serving platter, tent loosely with foil, and let rest while making the sauce.

4. Add the bacon to the skillet and cook over medium-low heat until browned and crisp, 6 to 8 minutes. Using a slotted spoon, transfer the bacon to a paper towel–lined plate. Pour off all but 1 tablespoon fat from the skillet, stir in the garlic, and cook over medium-high heat until fragrant, about 30 seconds. Stir in the tomatoes, scraping up any browned bits. (If necessary, add enough of the water to help loosen the browned bits from the bottom of the pan.) Cook until the tomatoes are just softened, about 2 minutes. Stir in any accumulated chicken juices and season with salt and pepper to taste.

5. Off the heat, pour the tomatoes over the chicken. Sprinkle with the bacon, blue cheese, and scallions. Serve.

Pan-Roasted Chicken Breasts with Potatoes

ROASTED CHICKEN AND POTATOES IS A classic combination, but you can forget about getting it on the table in around 30 minutes, right? For starters, a whole chicken needs to see at least one hour of oven time, and potatoes take somewhere in that time range to get golden brown and crisp. Nevertheless, we were determined to turn this tasty dinner into a simple weeknight standby.

We decided early on that bone-in chicken breasts would take the place of a whole chicken. By starting the chicken breasts in a skillet, as we did in our Pan-Roasted Chicken Breasts (page 303), we were able to get the skin nicely browned and crisp. We then transferred the chicken to a baking dish to finish cooking in a hot oven, thereby freeing up the skillet for our potatoes. We used red potatoes because their tender skin doesn't require peeling. In our initial tests, we had trouble getting the potatoes simultaneously golden and crisp on the outside and tender on the inside; there just wasn't enough time. We got a jump-start on the potatoes by microwaving them while the chicken browned and then adding them to the skillet in a single layer to achieve a deeply caramelized exterior and creamy, moist interior.

As a final flourish, we mimicked the tasty pan juices of a traditional roast chicken by infusing olive oil with lemon juice, garlic, red pepper flakes, and thyme. Drizzled over the chicken and potatoes just before serving, it lent the same moistness and bright flavors as traditional pan juices.

Pan-Roasted Chicken Breasts with Potatoes

SERVES 4

Remember to preheat your oven before assembling your ingredients. If the split breasts are of different sizes, check the smaller ones a few minutes early to see if they are cooking more quickly, and remove them from the oven if they are done.

- **4 bone-in, skin-on split chicken breasts (10 to 12 ounces each), trimmed**
- **Salt and ground black pepper**
- **6 tablespoons olive oil**
- **1½ pounds red potatoes (4 to 5 medium), cut into 1-inch wedges**
- **2 tablespoons juice from 1 lemon**
- **1 medium garlic clove, minced or pressed through a garlic press (about 1 teaspoon)**
- **1 teaspoon minced fresh thyme leaves**
- **Pinch red pepper flakes**

1. Adjust an oven rack to the lowest position and heat the oven to 450 degrees.

2. Pat the chicken dry with paper towels and season with salt and pepper. Heat 1 tablespoon of the oil in a 12-inch nonstick skillet over medium-high heat until just smoking. Add the chicken, skin-side down, and cook until deep golden, about 5 minutes.

3. Meanwhile, toss the potatoes with 1 tablespoon more oil, ½ teaspoon salt, and ¼ teaspoon pepper in a microwave-safe bowl. Cover tightly with plastic wrap. Microwave on high until the potatoes begin to soften, 5 to 7 minutes, shaking the bowl (without removing the plastic) to toss the potatoes halfway through.

4. Transfer the chicken, skin-side up, to a baking dish and bake until the thickest part of the breast registers 160 to 165 degrees on an instant-read thermometer, 18 to 20 minutes. Tent loosely with foil and let rest for 5 minutes.

5. While the chicken bakes, pour off any grease in the skillet, add 1 more tablespoon oil, and return to medium heat until shimmering. Drain the microwaved potatoes, then add to the skillet and cook, stirring occasionally, until golden brown and tender, about 10 minutes.

6. Whisk the remaining 3 tablespoons oil, the lemon juice, garlic, thyme, and pepper flakes together. Drizzle the lemon-thyme oil over the chicken and potatoes before serving.

Chicken and Couscous

COUSCOUS, MADE FROM SEMOLINA AND water, is a mainstay on Moroccan tables and has become increasingly popular in the United States in recent years. Offering a change from the same old chicken and rice, and naturally quick-cooking, it seemed perfect for an exotic and flavorful meal that could be easily prepared for dinner on a busy weeknight.

First, we browned chicken breasts and transferred them to the oven to finish cooking, which freed up the skillet for the vegetables. Red onion and fennel form the base of the dish, providing body, texture, and a clean vegetal sweetness. We stirred the couscous into the vegetables along with garlic and a pinch of cayenne. Instead of using straight chicken broth for the cooking liquid, we also added orange juice, which is sweet and slightly acidic, helping to pull the fennel flavor to the fore and brighten the entire dish. We then brought the liquid to a simmer and let the mixture sit off the heat until the couscous absorbed the broth and was evenly plump and tender—which took just 5 minutes! For our final step, we made a fragrant oil using orange juice, cayenne, and cilantro—all ingredients we had already used in the recipe—and drizzled it over the chicken and couscous before serving. In addition, we developed a variation with chickpeas, dried apricots, and cinnamon. The dried, chopped apricots soften during cooking and lend a pleasant sweetness to the dish.

Chicken and Couscous with Fennel and Orange

SERVES 4

Be sure to use chicken breasts that are roughly the same size to ensure even cooking. Use regular fine-grain couscous in this dish. Large-grain couscous, often labeled Israeli-style, takes much longer to cook and won't work in this recipe.

- ½ cup unbleached all-purpose flour
- 4 boneless, skinless chicken breasts (5 to 6 ounces each), tenderloins removed and breasts trimmed (see the illustrations on page 6)
- Salt and ground black pepper
- ½ cup olive oil
- 1 red onion, halved and sliced thin
- 1 fennel bulb, trimmed, cored, and sliced thin (see the illustrations on page 100)
- 1 cup couscous (see note)
- 3 medium garlic cloves, minced or pressed through a garlic press (about 1 tablespoon)
- Cayenne pepper
- 1 cup orange juice
- ¾ cup low-sodium chicken broth
- ¼ cup minced fresh cilantro leaves

1. Adjust an oven rack to the lower-middle position, place a baking dish on the rack, and heat the oven to 300 degrees.

2. Place the flour in a shallow dish. Pat the chicken dry with paper towels and season with salt and pepper. Working with 1 chicken breast at a time, dredge in the flour, shaking off the excess.

3. Heat 2 tablespoons of the oil in a 12-inch nonstick skillet over medium-high heat until just smoking. Add the chicken and cook until lightly browned on both sides, about 5 minutes. Transfer the chicken to the dish in the oven and cook until the thickest part of the breast registers 160 to 165 degrees on an instant-read thermometer, 8 to 12 minutes.

4. While the chicken bakes, add 1 more tablespoon of the oil to the skillet and return to medium-high heat until shimmering. Add the onion, fennel, and ½ teaspoon salt and cook until the onion is softened, 5 to 7 minutes. Stir in the couscous, garlic, and a pinch cayenne and cook until fragrant, about 30 seconds.

5. Stir in ¾ cup of the orange juice and the broth, scraping up any browned bits. Bring to a simmer, cover, and let sit off the heat until the liquid is absorbed, about 5 minutes.

6. In a bowl, whisk together the remaining 5 tablespoons oil, remaining ¼ cup orange juice, 2 tablespoons of the cilantro, and a pinch cayenne.

7. Gently fold the remaining 2 tablespoons cilantro into the couscous with a fork and season with salt and pepper to taste. Drizzle the orange-cilantro oil over the chicken and couscous before serving.

VARIATION

Chicken and Couscous with Chickpeas and Apricots

Follow the recipe for Chicken and Couscous with Fennel and Orange, omitting the fennel and substituting ½ teaspoon ground cinnamon for the cayenne in step 4. Add 1 (15-ounce) can chickpeas, drained and rinsed, and 1 cup roughly chopped dried apricots with the orange juice in step 5. Substitute a pinch ground cinnamon for the cayenne in step 6.

Sopa Seca

THIS SKILLET SUPPER IS BASED ON THE traditional Mexican dish *sopa seca*, which translates literally as "dry soup." It begins with an aromatic broth built in a skillet (the soup part), which is poured over thin strands of pasta in a baking dish and baked until the liquid is absorbed and the pasta is tender (the dry part). It's not a difficult dish to make, but we hoped to streamline it further by getting rid of the baking time and cooking the entire dish on the stovetop. Authentic versions of the dish often require specialty ingredients, and frankly none of these recipes are substantial enough to serve as a main dish. For our quick version, we wanted a dish that relied on easily accessible ingredients, and we also wanted to add some chicken for a truly satisfying meal.

Traditionally, this dish is prepared with *fideos*, thin strands of coiled, toasted noodles, which lend a distinctive background flavor. These noodles are great, but they are not found at our local market. We found that vermicelli, toasted in a skillet until golden brown, was the closest match in terms of texture and depth of flavor. After toasting the vermicelli, we browned thinly sliced boneless, skinless chicken breasts and then transferred the chicken to a bowl while we built the sauce.

We browned sliced chorizo—a Mexican sausage that's found in many supermarkets—along with onion, garlic, and a jalapeño chile, which are traditional in sopa seca. But the fresh jalapeño gave this quick-cooking interpretation too much of a raw chile flavor. Instead, we turned to canned chipotles in adobo, which are smoked jalapeños in a vinegary sauce—they were perfect. They still pack a punch in terms of spice, but without the rawness of the fresh chile. We then added canned diced tomatoes with their juices, along with chicken broth, to make a rich base. To add additional heft to the dish, canned black beans went into the mixture. Lastly, we added the vermicelli back in and simmered the mixture until most of the liquid was absorbed and the pasta was tender. We then returned the chicken to the pan and sprinkled shredded Monterey Jack cheese over the noodles; the cheese melted to form a gooey layer. A little minced cilantro added freshness, color, and authenticity and put the finishing touches on the dish.

BREAKING LONG-STRAND PASTA IN HALF

Though we don't normally recommend breaking pasta strands in half, this step makes it easier to toast vermicelli in a skillet.

1. To keep the pasta from flying every which way in the kitchen, roll up the bundle of pasta in a kitchen towel that overlaps the pasta by 3 or 4 inches at both ends.

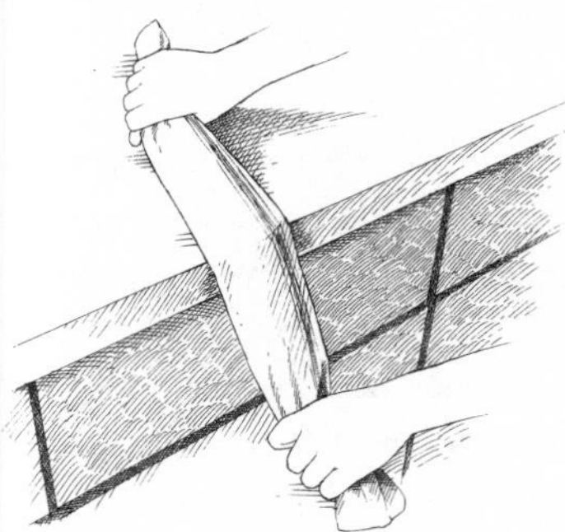

2. Firmly holding both ends of the rolled bundle, center it over the edge of a table or counter. Push down with both hands to break the pasta in the middle of the bundle.

Skillet Vermicelli with Chicken, Chorizo, and Black Beans

SERVES 4

If you like your food spicy, increase the chipotle in adobo to 1 tablespoon. Serve with sour cream, if desired.

- 8 ounces vermicelli, broken in half (see the illustrations at left)
- 3 tablespoons vegetable oil
- 1 pound boneless, skinless chicken breasts (about 2 large), trimmed (see the illustration on page 6) and sliced thin
- 4 ounces chorizo, halved lengthwise and sliced ¼ inch thick
- 1 medium onion, minced
- Salt
- 2 medium garlic cloves, minced or pressed through a garlic press (about 2 teaspoons)
- 2 teaspoons minced chipotle chile in adobo sauce (see note)
- 1 (14.5-ounce) can diced tomatoes
- 2 cups low-sodium chicken broth
- 1 cup canned black beans, drained and rinsed
- Ground black pepper
- 2 ounces Monterey Jack cheese, shredded (about ½ cup)
- ¼ cup minced fresh cilantro leaves

1. Cook the vermicelli with 1 tablespoon of the oil in a 12-inch nonstick skillet over medium-high

heat, stirring frequently, until toasted and golden, about 4 minutes. Transfer to a paper towel–lined plate and set aside.

2. Add 1 more tablespoon of the oil to the skillet and return to medium-high heat until just smoking. Add the chicken, break up any clumps, and cook without stirring until beginning to brown, about 1 minute. Stir the chicken and continue to cook until cooked through, about 2 minutes longer. Transfer the chicken to a medium bowl, cover with foil, and set aside.

3. Add the remaining 1 tablespoon oil to the skillet along with the chorizo, onion, and ½ teaspoon salt and cook over medium heat until the onion is softened, 5 to 7 minutes. Stir in the garlic and chipotle and cook until fragrant, about 30 seconds.

4. Stir in the tomatoes, broth, beans, and toasted vermicelli. Cover and cook, stirring often and adjusting the heat as necessary to maintain a vigorous simmer, until all the liquid is absorbed and the vermicelli is tender, about 10 minutes.

5. Return the chicken to the skillet and season with salt and pepper to taste. Off the heat, sprinkle the cheese over the top. Cover and let sit off the heat until the cheese melts, about 1 minute. Sprinkle with cilantro before serving.

Skillet Chicken and Pasta Suppers

HAVING MASTERED SEVERAL CHICKEN AND pasta dishes in Chapter 9 (see page 247), we turned our attention to developing expeditious one-pan skillet chicken and pasta dishes that were still hearty enough to be a complete meal. We found that small amounts of pasta (about 8 ounces) cook very well in a 12-inch skillet with a brothy sauce. And because we were cooking the pasta in the same skillet used to cook the other elements—chicken, vegetables, and sauce—it absorbed maximum flavor.

When developing these recipes, we weighed our pasta, which we find to be the most accurate way to measure it. If you do not have a scale on hand, be sure to measure the pasta by thoroughly packing it in a dry measuring cup. Using the specified amount of pasta is important to the success of these recipes—if you use more than indicated, there won't be enough liquid to cook it through. And, conversely, if you use less, the resulting sauce will be too thin or soupy. Pasta shape is important, too—use the shape specified for best results.

We began with the classic combination of penne with sausage (chicken sausage) and spinach. We started by browning the sausage in the skillet and then added garlic, chicken broth, water, and penne. (In an earlier test, we found that using all chicken broth overwhelmed the other flavors of the dish, which is why we decided to dilute it with water.) We found it necessary to crank the heat to high and really let it simmer so that the pasta absorbed the liquid and became tender. The dish was good but not as flavorful as we would have liked, so we added finely chopped sun-dried tomatoes to perk things up. Once the pasta was done, we stirred in handfuls of spinach and cooked the mixture just until the spinach wilted. To finish things off, we stirred in grated Parmesan, which not only added flavor, but also mixed with what was left of the pasta cooking liquid to create a light sauce that perfectly coated the pasta. Crunchy toasted pine nuts provided the final touch to this hearty skillet supper. We then made a version with broccoli in place of the spinach and thinly sliced chicken breasts instead of the sausage. For this variation, a splash of white wine rounds out the sauce a bit, giving the dish a sophisticated flavor in a short amount of time.

Skillet Penne with Sausage and Spinach

SERVES 4

Use either hot or sweet Italian-style chicken sausage here. The spinach may seem like a lot at first, but it wilts down substantially. Ziti can be used instead of penne.

- 1 tablespoon olive oil
- 1 pound Italian-style chicken sausage, casings removed
- 3 medium garlic cloves, minced or pressed through a garlic press (about 1 tablespoon)
- 2¼ cups low-sodium chicken broth

- 2¼ cups water
- 8 ounces penne (about 2½ cups)
- ½ cup oil-packed sun-dried tomatoes, rinsed and chopped fine
- Salt
- 1 (6-ounce) bag baby spinach
- 2 ounces Parmesan cheese, grated (about 1 cup), plus more for serving
- ¼ cup pine nuts, toasted
- Ground black pepper

1. Heat the oil in a 12-inch nonstick skillet over medium-high heat until just smoking. Add the sausage, breaking it up with a spoon, and cook until lightly browned, about 3 minutes. Stir in the garlic and cook until fragrant, about 30 seconds.

2. Stir in the broth, water, pasta, sun-dried tomatoes, and ½ teaspoon salt. Increase the heat to high and cook, stirring often, until the pasta is tender and the liquid has thickened, 15 to 18 minutes.

3. Stir in the spinach, one handful at a time, and cook until wilted. Off the heat, stir in the Parmesan and pine nuts. Season with salt and pepper to taste. Serve, passing additional Parmesan separately.

VARIATION

Skillet Chicken, Broccoli, and Ziti

Asiago or Pecorino Romano can be substituted for the Parmesan, if desired. Penne can also be used here.

- 4 tablespoons olive oil
- 1 pound boneless, skinless chicken breasts (about 2 large), trimmed and sliced thin (see the illustrations on page 10)
- 1 medium onion, minced
- Salt
- 6 medium garlic cloves, minced or pressed through a garlic press (about 2 tablespoons)
- ¼ teaspoon red pepper flakes
- 2 cups low-sodium chicken broth
- 2 cups water
- ½ cup dry white wine
- 8 ounces ziti (about 2½ cups)
- 8 ounces broccoli florets (about 3 cups)
- 2 ounces Parmesan cheese, grated (about 1 cup), plus more for serving
- Ground black pepper

1. Heat 1 tablespoon of the oil in a 12-inch nonstick skillet over medium-high heat until just smoking. Add the chicken, break up any clumps, and cook without stirring until beginning to brown, about 1 minute. Stir the chicken and continue to cook until cooked through, about 2 minutes longer. Transfer the chicken to a medium bowl, cover with foil, and set aside.

2. Add 1 more tablespoon of the oil to the skillet along with the onion and ¼ teaspoon salt and cook over medium heat until the onion is softened, 5 to 7 minutes. Stir in the garlic and pepper flakes and cook until fragrant, about 30 seconds. Stir in the broth, water, wine, pasta, and ¼ teaspoon salt. Increase the heat to high and cook, stirring often, for 12 minutes. Add the broccoli and continue to simmer until the pasta and broccoli are tender and the liquid has thickened, about 5 minutes longer.

3. Return the chicken to the skillet to warm through. Off the heat, stir in the remaining 2 tablespoons oil and the Parmesan. Season with salt and pepper to taste. Serve, passing additional Parmesan separately.

Weeknight Chicken Pot Pie

MOST RECIPES FOR QUICK CHICKEN POT PIE are lousy. The filling is not much more than canned, condensed cream-of-you-name-it soup, leftover chicken, and a paltry amount of vegetables. These versions are far from the comforting dinner that's always been a family favorite. As for the pastry topping, most quick recipes rely on refrigerated pie dough or refrigerated biscuits baked on top of the stew, but even with this shortcut we had trouble getting this oven-baked dinner on the table in a reasonable amount of time. We knew we could create a quick and fresh-tasting pot pie that relied on neither bad shortcuts nor the talents of an Olympic sprinter.

Sautéing boneless, skinless breasts in butter is not only quick (much faster than cutting up a whole chicken and roasting the parts), but it also gave us fond, the flavorful browned bits left behind that would add substantial flavor to our sauce. After we browned the chicken, we removed it from the skillet and added celery and onion, which we sautéed in more butter. Vermouth, chicken broth, cream, and thyme were then thickened with flour to form the sauce; then we added the chicken back to the skillet to finish cooking through—allowing the chicken to flavor the sauce and the sauce to flavor the chicken. Once the chicken was cooked through, we shredded it and mixed it back into the sauce with peas and carrots for a fresh burst of flavor and color.

We found that baking a round of refrigerated pie dough or refrigerated biscuits, while assembling a flavorful skillet chicken stew, allows you to pull this dinner together in record time. Just before serving, simply slide the pie crust right onto the stew (or place the biscuits on top). No one will know the difference.

Weeknight Chicken Pot Pie

SERVES 4

Remember to preheat your oven before assembling your ingredients. We prefer the flavor of Pillsbury Golden Homestyle Biscuits or Pillsbury Just Unroll! Pie Crusts, but you can use your favorite brand (you will need anywhere from 4 to 8 biscuits depending on their size). Because these products all bake at different temperatures, baking times will vary, so bake them according to the package instructions. To make homemade biscuits, see page 313. Serve this pot pie right from the skillet or transfer the mixture to a large pie dish and top with the biscuits or pie crust.

- 1 package refrigerated biscuits or 1 refrigerated pie crust (see note)
- 1½ pounds boneless, skinless chicken breasts (about 4 medium), trimmed
- Salt and ground black pepper
- 4 tablespoons unsalted butter
- 1 medium onion, minced
- 1 celery rib, sliced thin
- ¼ cup unbleached all-purpose flour
- ¼ cup dry vermouth or dry white wine
- 2 cups low-sodium chicken broth
- ½ cup heavy cream
- 1½ teaspoons minced fresh thyme leaves
- 2 cups frozen pea and carrot medley, thawed

1. Adjust an oven rack to the middle position and heat the oven according to the biscuit or pie crust package instructions.

2. Pat the chicken dry with paper towels and season with salt and pepper. Heat 2 tablespoons of the butter in a 12-inch skillet over medium heat until melted. Add the chicken and cook until lightly browned on both sides, about 5 minutes. Transfer the chicken to a plate.

3. Add the remaining 2 tablespoons butter to the skillet and return to medium heat until melted. Add the onion, celery, and ½ teaspoon salt and cook until the onion is softened, 5 to 7 minutes. Stir in the flour and cook, stirring constantly, until incorporated, about 1 minute.

4. Stir in the vermouth and cook until evaporated,

SHAPING BISCUITS

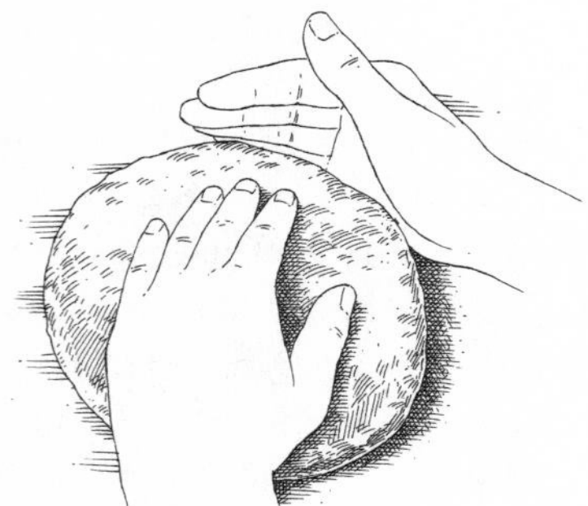

1. Pat the dough on a lightly floured work surface into a ¾-inch-thick circle.

2. Use a 2½-inch biscuit cutter to punch out rounds. Push together the remaining pieces of dough, pat into a ¾-inch-thick circle, and punch out more rounds. Discard the remaining scraps.

about 30 seconds. Slowly whisk in the broth, cream, and thyme and bring to a simmer. Nestle the chicken into the pan, cover, and cook over medium-low heat until the thickest part of the breast registers 160 to 165 degrees on an instant-read thermometer, about 10 minutes.

5. While the sauce simmers, bake the biscuits according to the package instructions or unfold the pie dough onto a parchment paper–lined baking sheet and bake according to the package instructions.

6. Transfer the chicken to a clean plate. Stir the peas and carrots into the sauce and simmer until heated through, about 2 minutes. When the chicken is cool enough to handle, cut or shred it into bite-sized pieces (see the illustration on page 10) and return to the skillet.

7. Season the filling with salt and pepper to taste. If using a pie crust, carefully slide it onto the filling and serve. If using biscuits, place on top of the filling and serve.

Quick Homemade Biscuits

MAKES 8 BISCUITS, ENOUGH FOR 1 POT PIE

These easy biscuits come together in just 20 minutes.

- **2 cups (10 ounces) unbleached all-purpose flour, plus more for the work surface**
- **2 teaspoons sugar**
- **2 teaspoons baking powder**
- **½ teaspoon salt**
- **1½ cups heavy cream**

1. Adjust an oven rack to the upper-middle position and heat the oven to 450 degrees.

2. Whisk the flour, sugar, baking powder, and salt together in a large bowl. Stir in the cream with a wooden spoon until a dough forms, about 30 seconds. Turn the dough out onto a lightly floured work surface and gather into a ball. Knead the dough briefly until smooth, about 30 seconds.

3. Pat the dough into a ¾-inch-thick circle. Cut the biscuits into rounds using a 2½-inch biscuit cutter (see the illustrations on page 312).

4. Place the biscuits on a parchment paper–lined baking sheet. Bake until golden brown, about 15 minutes.

Skillet Tamale Pie

THERE ARE MANY TRULY AWFUL RECIPES OUT there for quick tamale pie. Many feature over-spiced or bland meat dumped together with a can of creamed corn and topped with cornbread mix, which is, incidentally, the best part. When the test kitchen prepared various incarnations of this recipe, not a cornbread crumb was left on tasters' plates—but we can't say the same for the fillings we tried. Many recipes relied on a packet of stale and dusty taco seasoning mix for flavor, while others merely seasoned the meat with salt and pepper. We set out to make a quick tamale pie containing a juicy, spicy mixture of ground chicken (rather than the usual ground beef) and vegetables. Seasoned with onion, garlic, chili powder, and a little fresh cilantro, the tamale filling tasted fresh and spicy. We then stirred cheddar cheese into the filling, not only for flavor and richness, but also to help bind the mixture together. With the filling in place, we zeroed in on the topping. We had already decided that nothing beats the convenience of cornbread mix—just pour into a bowl, add milk (and sometimes egg), mix, and bake. As we expected, the moist, tender crumb, subtle sweetness, and corn flavor was the perfect complement to the spicy filling.

Skillet Tamale Pie

SERVES 4

Remember to preheat your oven before assembling your ingredients. Cornbread mixes vary from brand to brand; we liked Betty Crocker Golden Corn Muffin and Bread Mix and Jiffy Corn Muffin Mix. You may need a few additional ingredients to make this recipe, depending on the cornbread mix you are using. Serve with sour cream.

- **2 tablespoons vegetable oil**
- **1 medium onion, minced**

- 2 tablespoons chili powder
- Salt
- 3 medium garlic cloves, minced or pressed through a garlic press (about 1 tablespoon)
- 1 pound ground chicken
- 1 (15-ounce) can black beans, drained and rinsed
- 1 (14.5-ounce) can diced tomatoes, drained
- 1 (6.5- to 8.5-ounce) package cornbread mix (see note)
- 4 ounces cheddar cheese, shredded (about 1 cup)
- 2 tablespoons minced fresh cilantro
- Ground black pepper

1. Adjust an oven rack to the middle position and heat the oven to 450 degrees.

2. Heat the oil in a 12-inch skillet over medium heat until shimmering. Add the onion, chili powder, and ½ teaspoon salt and cook until the onion is softened, 5 to 7 minutes. Stir in the garlic and cook until fragrant, about 30 seconds.

3. Stir in the chicken, beans, and tomatoes and cook, breaking up the meat with a wooden spoon, until the meat is no longer pink, about 5 minutes.

4. Meanwhile, mix the cornbread batter according to the package instructions.

5. Stir the cheddar and cilantro into the filling and season with salt and pepper to taste. Dollop the cornbread batter evenly over the filling and spread into an even layer. Bake until the cornbread is cooked through in the center, 10 to 15 minutes. Serve.

Homemade Cornbread Topping

MAKES ENOUGH FOR 1 RECIPE SKILLET TAMALE PIE

If you don't have a cornbread mix on hand for Skillet Tamale Pie (or if you simply want to make the topping from scratch), use this easy recipe instead. It's a bit sweet, like the cornbread mixes we recommend, but tasters found its mild sweetness a good complement to the tangy meat filling.

- ¾ cup (3¾ ounces) unbleached all-purpose flour
- ¾ cup yellow cornmeal
- 3 tablespoons sugar
- ¾ teaspoon baking powder
- ¼ teaspoon baking soda
- ¾ teaspoon salt
- ¾ cup buttermilk
- 1 large egg
- 3 tablespoons unsalted butter, melted and cooled

1. Whisk the flour, cornmeal, sugar, baking powder, baking soda, and salt together in a large bowl.

2. In a separate bowl, whisk the buttermilk and egg together. Stir the buttermilk mixture into the flour mixture until uniform, then stir in the butter until just combined. Use as directed in step 5 of Skillet Tamale Pie.

Chicken Sloppy Joes

SLOPPY JOES, WHILE POPULAR AND QUICK, are often little more than a can of sweet sauce dumped over greasy, third-rate burger meat. And though the base for Sloppy Joes is pretty constant among most published recipes—onion, garlic, spices, something sweet, something sour, and something tomato—many of the recipes we tried were either greasy, dry, crumbly, bland, too sweet, too sour, or even too saucy. Not this version. Our recipe uses leaner ground chicken, and the key proved to be finding the right balance of meat and sauce.

For the meat, ground chicken was a given, although we soon discovered that the way we cooked the meat was just as important as its fat content. For soft, tender meat, it's important to cook it until just pink (no further), then add the remaining ingredients and finish cooking the meat through.

Because Sloppy Joes are essentially for kids, we wanted to keep the spices to a minimum. Just ½ teaspoon of chili powder and a dash or two of hot sauce added subtle heat. Ketchup combined with tomato puree and a little brown sugar struck the perfect sweet/sour balance. Ten minutes of simmering was all this mixture needed to transform it from a runny meat sauce to a nicely thickened, saucy meat dish—ideal for sitting on a soft burger bun.

Chicken Sloppy Joes

SERVES 4

Serve this kid-friendly favorite with pickles.

- 2 tablespoons vegetable oil
- 1 medium onion, minced
- ½ teaspoon chili powder
- Salt
- 3 garlic cloves, minced or pressed through a garlic press (about 1 tablespoon)
- 1 pound ground chicken
- 1 cup tomato puree
- ½ cup ketchup
- ¼ cup water
- 1 teaspoon brown sugar
- Hot sauce
- 4 hamburger buns

1. Heat the oil in a 12-inch skillet over medium heat until shimmering. Add the onion, chili powder, and ½ teaspoon salt and cook until the onion is softened, 5 to 7 minutes. Stir in the garlic and cook until fragrant, about 30 seconds.

2. Add the chicken and cook, breaking up the meat with a wooden spoon, until almost cooked through but still slightly pink, about 2 minutes.

3. Stir in the tomato puree, ketchup, water, brown sugar, and ¼ teaspoon hot sauce. Simmer until the sauce is slightly thicker than ketchup, 8 to 10 minutes.

4. Season with salt and hot sauce to taste. Spoon the meat mixture onto the hamburger buns and serve.

Chicken Tacos

FORGET THE TACO KIT—OUR TACOS TASTE far better and are just as quick to make. In this chapter, we have included two popular types of tacos: the classic ground meat variety in a fried tortilla shell, as well as a version with shredded meat wrapped up in a warm, soft tortilla.

For ground meat tacos, many recipes use stale, dusty, salty spice blends; however, we made our own bright, fresh-tasting blend. Instead of dumping a laundry list of raw spices onto the meat, we first bloomed our spices (chili powder and dried oregano) with the onion and garlic in oil to bring out their complex flavors. Tomato sauce conveniently made the meat saucy and rich, while cider vinegar and brown sugar provided the characteristic sweet and sour tang.

For the shredded chicken tacos, we lightly browned boneless, skinless breasts on one side, added chicken broth, covered the pan, and poached the breasts until they were done. This method produced meat that was moist and tender, even when shredded. With the chicken cooked, we built the seasoning base. Cumin added depth, while chipotle chile in adobo sauce added a rich smokiness and some heat. We returned the shredded chicken to the pan, along with a hefty amount (¼ cup) of minced fresh cilantro, sliced scallions, and lime juice for the fresh flavor and color that's missing from taco kits.

When it came to garnishes, shredded cabbage or iceberg lettuce, shredded cheese, diced avocado, salsa, sour cream, and lime wedges were the perfect accompaniments to both types of tacos.

Ground Chicken Tacos

SERVES 4

Shredded iceberg lettuce, shredded cheese, salsa, and sour cream are particularly worthy accompaniments for this recipe. We use canned plain tomato sauce (sold in 8-ounce cans) for this recipe.

- 1 tablespoon vegetable oil
- 1 medium onion, minced
- Salt
- 3 medium garlic cloves, minced or pressed through a garlic press (about 1 tablespoon)
- 2 tablespoons chili powder
- 1 teaspoon dried oregano
- 1 pound ground chicken
- ½ cup plain tomato sauce (see note)
- 2 teaspoons cider vinegar
- 1 teaspoon light brown sugar
- Ground black pepper
- 8–12 store-bought taco shells, warmed

INGREDIENTS:
Store-Bought Taco Shells

Frying your own taco shells from fresh corn tortillas can't be beat, but when you're in a hurry, store-bought taco shells are a quick and convenient alternative. We tasted our way through six brands of taco shells (warmed according to package instructions). Old El Paso Taco Shells came out ahead.

THE BEST STORE-BOUGHT TACO SHELLS
Old El Paso Taco Shells finished first among the brands we tested.

1. Heat the oil in a 12-inch nonstick skillet over medium-high heat until shimmering. Add the onion and ¼ teaspoon salt and cook until softened, 5 to 7 minutes. Stir in the garlic, chili powder, and oregano and cook until fragrant, about 30 seconds.

2. Add the chicken and cook, breaking up the meat with a wooden spoon, until almost cooked through but still slightly pink, about 2 minutes.

3. Stir in the tomato sauce, vinegar, and sugar and simmer over medium-low heat until thickened, about 4 minutes. Season with salt and pepper to taste. Divide the filling evenly among the taco shells and serve, passing any desired accompaniments separately.

Chicken Soft Tacos

SERVES 4

There are many possible accompaniments for these tacos; however, shredded cabbage or iceberg lettuce, shredded cheese, diced avocado, salsa, sour cream, and lime wedges are our favorites.

- 8–12 (6-inch) corn or flour tortillas
- 1½ pounds boneless, skinless chicken breasts (about 3 large), trimmed
- Salt and ground black pepper
- 2 tablespoons vegetable oil
- ¾ cup low-sodium chicken broth
- 1 medium onion, minced
- 3 medium garlic cloves, minced or pressed through a garlic press (about 1 tablespoon)
- 2 teaspoons minced chipotle chile in adobo sauce
- ¼ teaspoon ground cumin
- ¼ cup minced fresh cilantro leaves
- 2 scallions, sliced thin
- 2 tablespoons juice from 1 lime

1. Adjust an oven rack to the middle position and heat the oven to 200 degrees. Wrap the tortillas in foil and warm on a baking sheet in the oven.

2. Pat the chicken dry with paper towels and season with salt and pepper. Heat 1 tablespoon of the oil in a 12-inch nonstick skillet over medium-high heat until just smoking. Add the chicken and cook until browned on one side, about 3 minutes. Flip the chicken over, add ½ cup of the chicken broth, and cover. Reduce the heat to medium and continue to cook until the thickest part of the breast registers 160 to 165 degrees on an instant-read thermometer, 5 to 7 minutes longer. Transfer to a cutting board. When the chicken is cool enough to handle, shred into bite-sized pieces (see the illustration on page 10).

3. Wipe out the skillet with paper towels. Heat the remaining 1 tablespoon oil in the skillet over medium heat until shimmering. Add the onion and ½ teaspoon salt and cook until softened, 5 to 7 minutes. Stir in the garlic, chipotle, and cumin and cook until fragrant, about 30 seconds. Add the remaining ¼ cup chicken broth and bring to a simmer. Return the shredded chicken to the skillet and cook until warmed through, about 30 seconds.

4. Stir in the cilantro, scallions, and lime juice. Season with salt and pepper to taste. Place the chicken and tortillas on a platter and serve, passing any desired accompaniments separately.

12
LIGHT AND LEAN

Light and Lean

MANY COOKS TODAY ARE LOOKING FOR ways to incorporate healthier meals into their repertoire. For this reason, we decided to create a chapter on chicken that takes fat and calories into account—but without abandoning our quest for quality. We wanted to include both recipes that are naturally lower in fat and high-fat favorites like fried chicken that we could make over into a lighter dish.

Like most people, when we think of "healthy" chicken recipes, what comes to mind is the image of a Spartan serving of broiled chicken with nary a sauce in sight. We wanted to create lighter recipes that worked within the context of a full meal—meaning a reasonable portion of meat prepared in a way that didn't break the calorie bank.

We wanted to see if we could find a way to make "light" recipes taste just as good as every other recipe we make here in the test kitchen. We also wanted to come up with recipes for "real" food—food that most people eat for dinner on a typical weeknight, such as cheesy chicken enchiladas or oven-fried chicken breasts. Often, the key to success was not as simple as substituting a low-fat (or nonfat) ingredient for a full-fat one. Sometimes a different technique was the key (like using just a teaspoon of oil and covering the pot when sweating vegetables, which saves lots of calories at the outset).

In this chapter, you will find a range of recipes that start with the basics, including simple sautéed chicken breasts and cutlets. Many people have trouble cooking these leaner cuts of meat at home. The meat can be bland and dry because these cuts don't have much fat, which provides flavor and moisture. Sauces and glazes help solve both of these problems, but you must also pay attention to how you cook lean cutlets. To build flavor in the meat itself, it must have a nicely browned exterior. This can be achieved by using a large skillet (to minimize crowding) and by preheating the skillet.

As for the sauces, we found a couple of ways to create light versions that were as rich-tasting as their high-fat counterparts that rely on butter and cream. After much testing, we learned that a couple of tablespoons of light cream cheese, along with broth, wine, and aromatics, gave some sauces a deceptive richness, while milk mixed with cornstarch thickened and finished others. Along with sauces such as Mushroom-Sherry Sauce and Creamy Whole-Grain Mustard and Dill Sauce (both page 322), we created a relish-like "sauce" using fresh and dried fruit and plenty of spices, which added lots of flavor.

We also found that cooking boneless breasts *en papillote*—essentially steaming them in foil packets in the oven—was yet another way to take advantage of the virtues of naturally lean boneless, skinless chicken breasts (see Chicken and Vegetables en Papillote on page 323). The secret to making this technique successful (rather than bland and boring) is to toss the vegetables with a little oil, fresh herbs, and aromatics and to layer heartier vegetables below the chicken (so that they cook through) and juicier fruits and vegetables on top (so that they release their juices into the chicken and form a sauce).

But that's not all. While we improved on naturally lean chicken dishes, we also successfully made over several high-fat chicken dishes. From Light Chicken Parmesan (where we toasted the crumbs before coating the chicken, instead of pan-frying breaded chicken—see page 329) to Light Chicken Enchiladas (where light cheese and vegetable oil spray came to the rescue—see page 333) we found ways to cut a significant amount of fat and calories from these favorites without sacrificing flavor.

SAUTÉED CHICKEN BREASTS

FOR ANYONE WHO WANTS TO EAT HEALTHIER, boneless, skinless chicken breasts are a requisite ingredient. Virtually fat free and packed with protein, boneless chicken breasts also have the added bonus of being exceptionally easy to prepare. And while you can certainly broil or bake chicken, sautéing is the only way to achieve that beautiful golden brown exterior. The major problem with sautéing, however, is that it tends to dry out the chicken—especially if you're trying to cook with little fat in the pan. And when the chicken dries out, you might as well be eating cardboard in terms of flavor. We also wanted to develop a handful of pan sauces that would add flavor to simple chicken breasts, without relying on butter and heavy cream.

To begin, we investigated different pan choices, knowing that the type of pan we used would be crucial to a successful sauté. We found that a large, 12-inch, traditional skillet was absolutely necessary to promote the best browning. Crowding the chicken into a smaller pan produced steam, which resulted in a pale and unappetizing-looking crust. Also, we noted that a nonstick skillet did not work as well as a traditional skillet. While this may seem counterintuitive for healthier cooking (because nonstick pans allow you to cook with less fat), we found that, regardless of skillet type, a certain amount of fat is necessary for a good sauté. Without enough fat, the crust turns out spotty—burnt in some spots and completely pale in others.

Although we knew we needed to use oil in order to achieve a golden, evenly sautéed crust, we had to determine which type of oil was best and exactly how much of it we needed. Many light recipes use olive oil because of its reputation for promoting good health; however, we prefer vegetable oil here. Not only does it have a higher smoke point but, unlike olive oil, the flavor of vegetable oil is neutral and will pair with anything. Cooking our way through nearly 12 pounds of chicken, we found the optimum amount of vegetable oil for a sauté to be 4 teaspoons. Chicken sautéed with less (including vegetable oil sprays) resulted in unattractive, spotty crusts (as well as slightly scorched pans).

We also experimented with various heat levels. When we sautéed the chicken over high heat, it became too dark too quickly while remaining underdone on the inside. On the other hand, cooking the chicken very slowly over low heat made it chewy and didn't produce that all-important golden crust. Working between these two ranges, we determined that the optimal heat level was a combination of medium-high and medium-low. First we achieved a golden crust on one side over medium-high heat, and then we flipped the chicken over, turned the heat to medium-low, and continued to cook the chicken through. This way, the chicken achieved a gorgeous, sautéed crust while its interior remained tender.

Up to this point we had been using unfloured breasts. We were curious whether flouring the breasts would make a difference in the outcome. Indeed, it did prove to be beneficial. Flour promoted a more even browning on the exterior of the chicken. More important, however, it seemed to protect both the crust and the interior of the chicken. It prevented the crust from turning tough and stringy while keeping the interior more moist. In a side-by-side test, we found that floured chicken seemed more moist when cooked for the same amount of time as unfloured chicken.

Now that we felt we had mastered the techniques for sautéing chicken breasts, we wanted to see how they would transfer to cutlets (breasts that have been sliced in half horizontally to yield two pieces). Using the same skillet, we found we could cut out 1 teaspoon of the oil (per batch) without any ill effects. This is because cutlets are essentially half as thick as breasts, and consequently they cook more than twice as fast. More oil is needed when cooking chicken breasts in order to prevent the pan from scorching during the longer cooking time, but this is not the case with the quick-cooking cutlets—the cutlets cook through before anything has a chance to burn. Also, we found we needed to have the heat at medium-high for the entire cooking time so that the cutlets would lightly brown on both sides. This method produced a nicely cooked chicken cutlet, with sufficient flavor from the browning but without the rubbery texture of overcooked meat. That said, since the cutlets took up more space in the pan, we had to cook them in two batches (using 1 tablespoon of oil per batch).

Topping off our perfectly sautéed chicken with a pan sauce, we uncovered a few tricks to keep these sauces low in fat without losing any flavor. Pan sauces are typically finished with some sort of fat—cream or butter—to add richness and help emulsify the sauce. We tried many substitutes for the butter and cream, including low-fat sour cream, buttermilk, yogurt, yogurt cheese, milk, and half-and-half. The winning substitutes turned out to be a whole milk–cornstarch slurry for the butter, and light cream cheese for the heavy cream. We also came across some relish-style sauces using fruit, which is naturally low in fat. Finally, we enhanced the flavor of each sauce by making good use of those flavorful browned bits left in the pan.

Sautéed Chicken Breasts

SERVES 4

If you like, serve the chicken with a pan sauce—see the recipes on pages 321–322.

- ½ cup unbleached all-purpose flour
- 4 boneless, skinless chicken breasts (5 to 6 ounces each), tenderloins removed and breasts trimmed (see the illustrations on page 6)
- Salt and ground black pepper
- 4 teaspoons vegetable oil

1. Place the flour in a shallow dish. Pat the chicken dry with paper towels and season with salt and pepper. Working with 1 chicken breast at a time, dredge in the flour, shaking off the excess.

2. Heat the oil in a 12-inch skillet over medium-high heat until just smoking. Add the chicken and cook until well browned on one side, 6 to 8 minutes.

3. Flip the chicken over, reduce the heat to medium-low, and continue to cook until the thickest part of the breast registers 160 to 165 degrees on an instant-read thermometer, 6 to 8 minutes longer.

4. Transfer the chicken to a plate, tent loosely with foil, and let rest for at least 5 minutes (or while making a pan sauce) before serving.

PER SERVING: **Cal** 240; **Fat** 7g; **Sat fat** 1g; **Chol** 100mg; **Carb** 0g; **Protein** 40g; **Fiber** 0g; **Sodium** 260mg

Sautéed Chicken Cutlets

SERVES 4

Be careful not to overcook the cutlets—they really do cook through in just 4 minutes. If you like, serve the cutlets with a pan sauce—see the recipes on pages 321–322.

- 4 boneless, skinless chicken breasts (5 to 6 ounces each), tenderloins removed and breasts trimmed (see the illustrations on page 6)
- ½ cup unbleached all-purpose flour
- Salt and ground black pepper
- 2 tablespoons vegetable oil

1. Following the illustrations on page 6, slice each chicken breast in half horizontally and pound each cutlet as directed between two sheets of plastic wrap to a uniform ¼-inch thickness.

2. Place the flour in a shallow dish. Pat the chicken dry with paper towels and season with salt and pepper. Working with 1 chicken cutlet at a time, dredge in the flour, shaking off the excess.

3. Heat 1 tablespoon of the oil in a 12-inch skillet over medium-high heat until just smoking. Add 4 of the cutlets and cook until lightly browned on both sides, about 4 minutes. Transfer to a plate and tent loosely with foil.

4. Add the remaining tablespoon oil to the skillet and repeat with the remaining 4 cutlets. (Tent loosely with foil if making a pan sauce.) Serve.

PER SERVING: **Cal** 270; **Fat** 9g; **Sat fat** 1.5g; **Chol** 100mg; **Carb** 5g; **Protein** 40g; **Fiber** 0g; **Sodium** 260mg

Low-Fat Pan Sauces and Relishes

WE COOKED UP LOTS OF LOW-FAT PAN SAUCES in the test kitchen, and here are a few of our favorites for chicken. Simply follow the master recipe for Sautéed Chicken Breasts or Cutlets and continue with any of the pan sauces listed below. Be sure not to wash out the pan after browning the chicken—those browned bits remaining on the bottom of the skillet add important flavor. All of the recipes that follow yield enough sauce for four chicken breasts or eight cutlets.

Piccata Sauce

MAKES ENOUGH FOR 4 CHICKEN BREASTS OR 8 CHICKEN CUTLETS

We prefer the flavor of whole milk in the sauce; however, 2 percent milk or half-and-half will also work. Do not use 1 percent or skim milk.

- 1 medium shallot, minced (about 3 tablespoons)
- Salt
- 2 medium garlic cloves, minced or pressed through a garlic press (about 2 teaspoons)
- 1½ cups low-sodium chicken broth
- ½ lemon, end trimmed, sliced thin

- 2 tablespoons whole milk
- 1 teaspoon cornstarch
- 2 tablespoons juice from 1 lemon
- 2 tablespoons capers, rinsed and patted dry
- 1 tablespoon minced fresh parsley leaves
- Ground black pepper

1. After removing the chicken from the skillet, add the shallot and ¼ teaspoon salt to the oil left in the skillet and cook over medium-low heat until softened, about 2 minutes. Stir in the garlic and cook until fragrant, about 30 seconds.

2. Stir in the broth and lemon slices, scraping up any browned bits. Bring to a simmer and cook until the mixture measures 1 cup, about 5 minutes. Stir in any accumulated chicken juices and return to a simmer. Whisk the milk and cornstarch together in a small bowl, then whisk into the simmering sauce. Continue to simmer the sauce until it has thickened, about 1 minute.

3. Off the heat, stir in the lemon juice, capers, and parsley and season with salt and pepper to taste. Spoon the sauce over the chicken before serving.

PER SERVING: **Cal** 25; **Fat** 0.5g; **Sat fat** 0g; **Chol** 0mg; **Carb** 4g; **Protein** 1g; **Fiber** 0g; **Sodium** 490mg

Mushroom-Sherry Sauce

MAKES ENOUGH FOR 4 CHICKEN BREASTS OR 8 CHICKEN CUTLETS

We prefer the flavor of whole milk in the sauce; however, 2 percent milk or half-and-half will also work. Do not use 1 percent or skim milk.

- 10 ounces white mushrooms, wiped clean and sliced thin
- 1 medium shallot, minced (about 3 tablespoons)
- 1 teaspoon sugar
- 2 medium garlic cloves, minced or pressed through a garlic press (about 2 teaspoons)
- 1 teaspoon minced fresh thyme leaves
- ¼ cup plus 1 teaspoon dry sherry
- 1½ cups low-sodium chicken broth
- 2 tablespoons whole milk
- 1 teaspoon cornstarch
- 1 tablespoon minced fresh parsley leaves
- Salt and ground black pepper

1. After removing the chicken from the skillet, add the mushrooms, shallot, and sugar to the oil left in the skillet, cover, and cook over medium-low heat until the mushrooms have released their liquid, about 7 minutes. Stir in the garlic and thyme and continue to cook, uncovered, until the mushroom juices have evaporated and the mushrooms are golden brown, about 2 minutes.

2. Stir in ¼ cup of the sherry, scraping up any browned bits. Add the broth, bring to a simmer, and cook until the mixture measures 1½ cups, about 5 minutes. Stir in any accumulated chicken juices and return to a simmer. Whisk the milk and cornstarch together in a small bowl, then whisk into the simmering sauce. Continue to simmer the sauce until it has thickened, about 1 minute.

3. Off the heat, stir in the remaining 1 teaspoon sherry and the parsley and season with salt and pepper to taste. Spoon the sauce over the chicken before serving.

PER SERVING: **Cal** 50; **Fat** 0.5g; **Sat fat** 0g; **Chol** 0mg; **Carb** 7g; **Protein** 2g; **Fiber** 0g; **Sodium** 230mg

Creamy Whole-Grain Mustard and Dill Sauce

MAKES ENOUGH FOR 4 CHICKEN BREASTS OR 8 CHICKEN CUTLETS

- 1 medium shallot, minced (about 3 tablespoons)
- Salt
- 2 medium garlic cloves, minced or pressed through a garlic press (about 2 teaspoons)
- ¼ cup dry white wine
- 1½ cups low-sodium chicken broth
- 3 tablespoons light cream cheese
- ¼ cup whole-grain mustard
- 1 tablespoon minced fresh dill
- Ground black pepper

1. After removing the chicken from the skillet, add the shallot and ¼ teaspoon salt to the oil left in the skillet and cook over medium-low heat until softened, about 2 minutes. Stir in the garlic and cook until fragrant, about 30 seconds.

2. Stir in the wine, scraping up any browned bits. Add the broth, bring to a simmer, and cook

until the mixture measures ¾ cup, about 5 minutes. Stir in any accumulated chicken juices and return to a simmer. Whisk in the cream cheese, and continue to simmer until the sauce has thickened, about 1 minute.

3. Off the heat, stir in the mustard and dill and season with salt and pepper to taste. Spoon the sauce over the chicken before serving.

PER SERVING: **Cal** 70; **Fat** 3g; **Sat fat** 1.5g; **Chol** 5mg; **Carb** 5g; **Protein** 3g; **Fiber** 1g; **Sodium** 720mg

Apricot-Orange Relish with Chipotle

MAKES ENOUGH FOR 4 CHICKEN BREASTS OR 8 CHICKEN CUTLETS

- 1 medium shallot, minced (about 3 tablespoons)
- Salt
- 2 medium garlic cloves, minced or pressed through a garlic press (about 2 teaspoons)
- ½ teaspoon minced chipotle chile in adobo sauce
- 1 cup orange juice
- ½ cup dried apricots, chopped medium
- 1 orange, peeled, quartered, and cut crosswise into ¼-inch wedges (see the illustrations on page 102)
- 1 tablespoon minced fresh cilantro leaves
- Ground black pepper

1. After removing the chicken from the skillet, add the shallot and ¼ teaspoon salt to the oil left in the skillet and cook over medium-low heat until softened, about 2 minutes. Stir in the garlic and chipotle and cook until fragrant, about 30 seconds.

2. Stir in the orange juice and apricots, scraping up any browned bits. Bring to a simmer and cook until the apricots are plump and the juice has thickened, about 2 minutes. Stir in any accumulated chicken juices and return to a simmer.

3. Off the heat, stir in the orange and cilantro and season with salt and pepper to taste. Spoon the sauce over the chicken before serving.

PER SERVING: **Cal** 130; **Fat** 0g; **Sat fat** 0g; **Chol** 0mg; **Carb** 30g; **Protein** 2g; **Fiber** 3g; **Sodium** 150mg

MINCING A SHALLOT

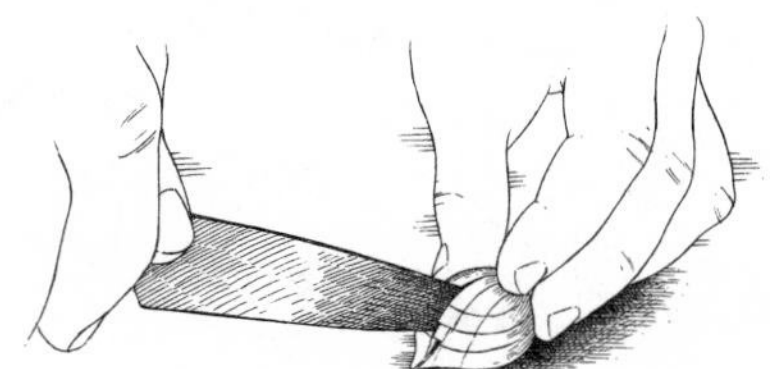

1. Place the peeled bulb flat-side down and make several slices parallel to the work surface, almost to (but not through) the root end. Then make a number of very closely spaced parallel cuts through the top of the shallot down to the work surface.

2. Finish the mincing by making very thin slices perpendicular to the lengthwise cuts.

Chicken and Vegetables en Papillote

COOKING *EN PAPILLOTE* IS A CLASSIC FRENCH method that involves baking food in a tightly sealed parchment paper packet. In effect, the food—often a protein—steams in its own juices, developing a delicate texture and an intense, clean flavor. Unlike many other classic French cooking methods, which usually feature butter and cream, cooking en papillote is naturally light and healthy. Since there is so much moisture and concentrated flavor sealed in the packet, little added fat is needed. And with the addition of vegetables, you get a well-rounded main course. Best of all, this dish takes little work outside of assembly; there's no stovetop cooking and little mess. Our goal in the test kitchen was to develop an easy, more contemporary version of this French classic, with perfectly moist and tender pieces of chicken, well-seasoned vegetables, and flavorful juices.

Traditional French methods for cooking en papillote are somewhat arcane. Pieces of parchment must be trimmed to an exact size, and folding patterns reminiscent of origami are employed to ensure a tight seal. Admittedly, the results make for a dramatic presentation—the paper balloons and browns in the oven and is slit open at the table by the diner. Because many home kitchens do not have parchment paper on hand, however, we opted to use aluminum foil as a more convenient, modern upgrade. While it lacks the dramatic presentation of the parchment, aluminum foil works just as effectively and doesn't require labor-intensive folding. The seams can simply be crimped together.

We quickly settled on using naturally low-fat boneless, skinless breasts and then turned our attention to the vegetables. We needed to find vegetables that were both suitable for steaming, without becoming flavorless and mushy, and compatible with the cooking time of the chicken. After a lot of trial and error, we found that using two types of vegetables was best. Firmer vegetables like carrots, fennel, cabbage, squash, and artichokes provided a sturdy base for the chicken and protected it from the direct heat of the oven. In addition, these firm vegetables, when properly cut, matched the cooking time of the chicken perfectly. We also found it essential to use juicy vegetables and fruit like tomatoes and oranges. These ingredients, which we placed on top of the chicken, exuded a lot of moisture and created the steam needed for cooking; as an added benefit, their flavorful juices also seeped into the chicken.

The overall flavor of this dish was still rather bland, but we found that we could make it more potent simply by mixing a little olive oil with garlic, shallots, crushed red pepper flakes, and assertive herbs such as oregano, and then tossing this mixture with the vegetables and fruit before placing them in the foil packets. And while we were reluctant to add the fat and calories of oil, it was essential for creating a satisfying sauce around the chicken.

MAKING FOIL PACKETS

1. Arrange the vegetables and seasoned chicken in the center of a 14 by 12-inch sheet of heavy-duty aluminum foil.

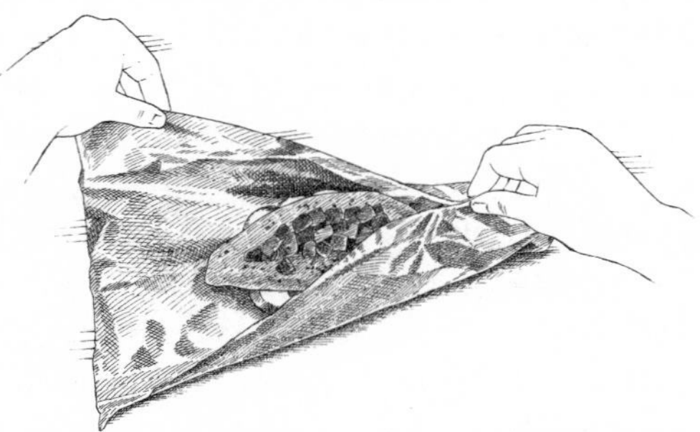

2. Bring the longer sides of the foil up to meet over the chicken. Crimp the edges together in a ¼-inch fold and then fold over three more times. Fold the open edges at either end of the packets together in a ¼-inch fold, then fold over twice again to seal.

Chicken with Zucchini and Tomatoes en Papillote

SERVES 4

The packets can be assembled several hours ahead of time and refrigerated, but they should be baked just before serving. To prevent overcooking, open each packet promptly after baking. Serving this dish on warmed dinner plates is a nice touch.

- 4 boneless, skinless chicken breasts (5 to 6 ounces each), tenderloins removed and breasts trimmed (see the illustrations on page 6)
- Salt and ground black pepper
- 2 tablespoons extra-virgin olive oil
- 2 medium garlic cloves, minced or pressed through a garlic press (about 2 teaspoons)
- 1 teaspoon minced fresh oregano leaves
- ¼ teaspoon red pepper flakes
- 3 medium plum tomatoes (about 12 ounces), cored, seeded, and chopped medium
- 2 medium zucchini (about 12 ounces), sliced ¼ inch thick
- ¼ cup shredded fresh basil leaves (see the illustrations on page 252)

1. Adjust an oven rack to the middle position and heat the oven to 450 degrees. Following the illustrations on page 6, pound each breast as directed between two sheets of plastic wrap to a uniform ½-inch thickness. Pat the chicken dry with paper towels and season with salt and pepper.

2. Combine the oil, garlic, oregano, pepper flakes, ¼ teaspoon salt, and ⅛ teaspoon pepper in a medium bowl. Spoon half of the oil mixture into a separate medium bowl and gently toss with the tomatoes. Add the zucchini to the remaining olive oil mixture and toss to coat.

3. Cut four 14 by 12-inch rectangles of heavy-duty foil and lay them flat on a work surface. Following illustration 1 on page 324, shingle the zucchini in the center of each piece of foil. Place the chicken on top of the zucchini, then top with the tomatoes. Tightly crimp the foil into packets following illustration 2 on page 324.

4. Set the packets on a rimmed baking sheet and bake until the thickest part of the breast registers 160 to 165 degrees on an instant-read thermometer, about 25 minutes.

5. Carefully open the packets, allowing the steam to escape away from you, and let cool briefly. Smooth out the edges of the foil and, using a spatula, gently transfer the chicken, vegetables, and any accumulated juices onto warmed dinner plates. Sprinkle with the basil before serving.

PER SERVING: **Cal** 280; **Fat** 9g; **Sat fat** 1.5g; **Chol** 100mg; **Carb** 7g; **Protein** 41g; **Fiber** 2g; **Sodium** 270mg

VARIATION

Chicken with Artichokes, Lemon, and Tomatoes en Papillote

Follow the recipe for Chicken with Zucchini and Tomatoes en Papillote, substituting thyme for the oregano, 1 tablespoon grated lemon zest for the red pepper flakes, and 2 (9-ounce) boxes frozen artichoke hearts, thawed and patted dry with paper towels, for the zucchini. In step 2, add 2 medium shallots, sliced thin, to the artichokes and toss with the remaining olive oil mixture. Proceed with the recipe as directed.

PER SERVING: **Cal** 300; **Fat** 10g; **Sat fat** 1.5g; **Chol** 100mg; **Carb** 12g; **Protein** 42g; **Fiber** 5g; **Sodium** 290mg

Chicken with Fennel, Carrots, and Oranges en Papillote

SERVES 4

The packets can be assembled several hours ahead of time and refrigerated, but they should be baked just before serving. To prevent overcooking, open each packet promptly after baking. Serving this dish on warmed dinner plates is a nice touch.

- **4 boneless, skinless chicken breasts (5 to 6 ounces each), tenderloins removed and breasts trimmed (see the illustrations on page 6)**
- **Salt and ground black pepper**
- **2 tablespoons extra-virgin olive oil**
- **1 medium shallot, sliced thin**
- **1 teaspoon minced fresh tarragon leaves**
- **2 medium oranges, peeled, quartered, and cut crosswise into ¼-inch wedges (see the illustrations on page 102)**
- **2 carrots, peeled and cut into matchsticks (see the illustrations on page 238)**
- **1 medium fennel bulb (about 1 pound), trimmed, halved, cored, and sliced into ¼-inch strips (see the illustrations on page 100)**
- **2 scallions, sliced thin**

1. Adjust an oven rack to the middle position and heat the oven to 450 degrees. Following the illustrations on page 6, pound each breast as directed between two sheets of plastic wrap to a uniform ½-inch thickness. Pat the chicken dry with paper towels and season with salt and pepper.

2. Combine the oil, shallot, tarragon, ¼ teaspoon salt, and ⅛ teaspoon pepper in a medium bowl. Spoon half of the oil mixture into a separate medium bowl and gently toss with the oranges. Add the carrots and fennel to the remaining olive oil mixture and toss to coat.

3. Cut four 14 by 12-inch rectangles of heavy-duty foil and lay them flat on a work surface. Following illustration 1 on page 324, mound the fennel and carrots in the center of each piece of foil. Place the chicken on top of the vegetables, then top with the oranges. Tightly crimp the foil into packets following illustration 2 on page 324.

4. Set the packets on a rimmed baking sheet and bake until the thickest part of the breast registers 160 to 165 degrees on an instant-read thermometer, about 25 minutes.

5. Carefully open the packets, allowing the steam to escape away from you, and let cool briefly. Smooth out the edges of the foil and, using a spatula, gently transfer the chicken, vegetables, and any accumulated juices onto warmed dinner plates. Sprinkle with the scallions before serving.

PER SERVING: **Cal** 330; **Fat** 9g; **Sat fat** 1.5g; **Chol** 100mg; **Carb** 18g; **Protein** 41g; **Fiber** 5g; **Sodium** 310mg

VARIATION

Chicken with Green Cabbage, Carrots, and Ginger en Papillote

Follow the recipe for Chicken with Fennel, Carrots, and Oranges en Papillote, substituting 2 medium garlic cloves, minced or pressed through a garlic press, and 2 tablespoons minced or grated fresh ginger for the shallot, and 1 tablespoon low-sodium soy sauce for the salt in step 2. Omit the tarragon. Substitute 1 pound green cabbage (about ½ head), cored and sliced thin, for the fennel in step 2. Proceed with the recipe as directed.

PER SERVING: **Cal** 340; **Fat** 9g; **Sat fat** 1.5g; **Chol** 100mg; **Carb** 20g; **Protein** 42g; **Fiber** 6g; **Sodium** 440mg

Oven-Baked Brown Rice

SERVES 6

Brown rice takes roughly twice as long to cook as white rice; the oven's heat is gentler than that of a stovetop burner, so there is less risk of scorching. To minimize any loss of water through evaporation, cover the saucepan as the water is heating, and use the water as soon as it reaches a boil. If you own an 8-inch ceramic baking dish with a lid, use it instead of the glass baking dish and foil. To double the recipe, use a 13 by 9-inch baking dish; the baking time need not be increased.

- 1½ cups long-, medium-, or short-grain brown rice
- 2⅓ cups water
- 1 tablespoon olive oil
- ½ teaspoon salt

1. Adjust an oven rack to the middle position and heat the oven to 375 degrees. Spread the rice in an 8-inch-square glass baking dish.

2. Bring the water and oil to a boil, covered, in a medium saucepan over high heat. Once the water is boiling, immediately stir in the salt and pour the water over the rice. Cover the baking dish tightly with a double layer of foil and bake until the rice is tender, about 1 hour.

3. Remove the baking dish from the oven, uncover, and fluff the rice with a fork. Cover the dish with a clean kitchen towel and let stand for 5 minutes. Uncover and let the rice stand for 5 minutes longer before serving.

PER SERVING: **Cal** 190; **Fat** 3.5g; **Sat fat** 0.5g; **Chol** 0mg; **Carb** 36g; **Protein** 4g; **Fiber** 2g; **Sodium** 200mg

Oven-Fried Chicken Breasts

FRIED CHICKEN RANKS HIGH ON THE LIST OF forbidden foods for those watching calories and fat, which is why there is no shortage of recipes for oven-fried chicken. But much to our dismay, a lot of the oven-fried chicken recipes we found were equally as fatty as the real thing. It looked like we had some work to do to find a recipe for light oven-fried chicken.

After gathering up the most promising low-fat oven-fried chicken recipes we could find, we headed into the test kitchen. Right away, we knew the crust would pose our major challenge. Most recipes turned out either greasy or dry chicken coated with a wide array of different "crusts," none of which even began to approximate that of real fried chicken.

Determined to investigate every possible crust alternative, we gathered together a host of possible ingredients and tried them all (or what felt like all). We tested cereals such as cornflakes and Grape-Nuts, but the distinct flavor of these cereals (among others) overpowered the chicken. Cracker crumbs did not work, because they either had too much fat or produced bland and dry coatings. Flour or cornmeal failed to provide the crunch we sought and often flaked off the chicken during (or shortly after) cooking.

We finally tried some different crackers (sometimes found in the specialty aisle in the grocery store): Melba toast. Melba toast is super-crunchy and has a good (but subtle) flavor and zero fat. Alone, the toast was too dry and had a tendency to flake off the chicken. We needed to add something to its crumbs to form a cohesive coating. So we tried a bit of oil, which gave it a touch of "fried" flavor without adding a lot of fat. A light spray of vegetable oil also gave the chicken an appealing deep bronze color.

But we were still stuck on how to adhere our coating to the chicken. Up to this point we had been using eggs in all of our tests, but we knew they added too much fat. So we substituted several low-fat dairy products, such as buttermilk, low-fat milk, sour cream, and yogurt. All of these dairy bases made the coating too soggy; it lacked the crispness that is the hallmark of fried chicken. Additionally, low-fat mayonnaise was too greasy, causing the coating to just fall off the chicken before it reached our mouths. Eggs were really the best choice. And then it hit us: What if we just used egg whites? This turned out to be the answer. The tackiness of the egg whites helped the crumbs adhere, but they produced a very thin coating that didn't become soggy, and, best of all, the whites added no fat.

Now that we had resolved the coating, we turned our attention to the best way to oven-fry the chicken. We found that a moderately hot oven (450 degrees) was helpful in browning the coating while also allowing the chicken to cook through perfectly in 40 minutes and to remain moist and tender. Also, it's important to put the chicken on a rack set on a baking sheet—this helps keep the coating uniformly crunchy (otherwise, the bottom of the pieces will be soft).

Some of us sought a spicy fried chicken while others wanted it gently seasoned, so for flavoring we added a bit of Dijon, plus some garlic, thyme, and cayenne. This balance of seasonings satisfied those of us who wanted a richer-tasting fried chicken and those who wanted some heat. The spiced, extra-crunchy coating was a wonderful complement to the juicy, sweet chicken fresh out of the oven. With less mess and a lot less fat than fried chicken, we'll take this satisfying alternative any day of the week.

Oven-Fried Chicken Breasts

SERVES 4

Although we like to use bone-in chicken for this recipe, you can substitute 4 boneless, skinless chicken breasts and reduce the cooking time to 25 minutes.

- 1 (5-ounce) box plain Melba toast, broken into 1-inch pieces
- 2 tablespoons vegetable oil
- 3 large egg whites
- 1 tablespoon Dijon mustard
- 2 teaspoons minced fresh thyme leaves
- ¼ teaspoon garlic powder
- ⅛ teaspoon cayenne pepper
- 4 bone-in, skin-on split chicken breasts (10 to 12 ounces each), trimmed (see the illustrations on page 7) and skin removed
- Salt and ground black pepper
- Nonstick cooking spray

1. Adjust an oven rack to the upper-middle position and heat the oven to 450 degrees. Cover a baking sheet with foil and place a wire rack on top. Pulse the Melba toast in a food processor into coarse crumbs, about twelve 1-second pulses. Spread the crumbs in a shallow dish and toss with the oil.

2. Whisk the egg whites, mustard, thyme, garlic powder, and cayenne together in a separate shallow dish.

3. Pat the chicken dry with paper towels and season with salt and pepper. Working with 1 chicken breast at a time, dip into the egg white mixture, allowing the excess to drip off. Coat with the Melba crumbs, pressing gently so that the crumbs adhere. Lay the chicken on the prepared wire rack and lightly coat the tops with nonstick cooking spray.

4. Bake until the coating is golden and the thickest part of the breast registers 160 to 165 degrees on an instant-read thermometer, about 40 minutes. Serve immediately.

PER SERVING: Cal 460; **Fat** 11g; **Sat fat** 1.5g; **Chol** 130mg; **Carb** 28g; **Protein** 59g; **Fiber** 2g; **Sodium** 720mg

Light Chicken Parmesan

THE BEST PART OF CHICKEN PARMESAN—composed of breaded, fried chicken cutlets topped with tomato sauce, Parmesan cheese, and melted mozzarella—is the crisp, golden coating on the cutlets. Unfortunately, this terrific breaded coating is the result of frying the cutlets in a good amount of oil. Sure, there are lots of recipes for low-fat or "un-fried" chicken Parmesan that bake the breaded cutlets rather than frying them, but none that we tried even came close to the flavor, color, or crispness of a traditional fried recipe. They literally paled by comparison, with their flavorless, washed-out-looking crusts. We wondered if we couldn't develop a better low-fat version, one actually worth eating.

Setting aside the issue of the sauce and cheese, we started with how to cook the breaded cutlets. Obviously deep-frying and pan-frying the cutlets were both out—these methods simply used too much oil. That left us with just the oven, but simply breading the cutlets (using the classic breading of flour, then egg—in this case egg whites—then bread crumbs) and baking them on a baking sheet didn't work. The breading never turned brown or crisp, the bottoms became soggy, the breading tasted stale, and the chicken was rubbery and dry—a real loser on all counts. We had our work cut out for us.

Focusing on oven temperature, we found that baking the cutlets for 15 minutes at 475 degrees produced the most tender and juicy chicken. To encourage browning, we tried lightly coating the baking sheet with oil and heating it in the oven before adding the breaded chicken, but the bread crumbs soaked up the oil and turned greasy. Baking the chicken on a wire rack set over a baking sheet solved the soggy bottom issue, and spraying the tops with vegetable oil helped the breading on top of the cutlets crisp up nicely. We still, however, had issues with their bland flavor and pale color.

Then it hit us—why didn't we toast the bread crumbs to a golden color before breading the cutlets? We toasted the bread crumbs in a skillet over medium heat until golden, then breaded the cutlets, sprayed the tops with vegetable oil, and baked them on the rack. These cutlets were a big improvement, with an even golden color and crisp fried texture. The flavor of the breading, however, still needed help. Adding a tablespoon of olive oil to the crumbs before they toasted gave them a nice "fried" flavor without turning them greasy or adding too many calories, and tossing them with some grated Parmesan cheese once they cooled helped boost their flavor dramatically. The cutlets now actually tasted like traditional chicken Parmesan—we were getting somewhere.

Testing the difference between store-bought dried bread crumbs, fresh bread crumbs, and panko (Japanese-style bread crumbs), the test kitchen universally disliked the "old," "ground cardboard" flavor of the store-bought dried bread crumbs. Both the fresh bread crumbs and the panko were well liked; however, tasters preferred the neutral flavor and ultra-crisp texture of panko over that of the fresh bread crumbs, which had a sweeter flavor and sandy texture.

INGREDIENTS: Panko

The incredibly light, shatteringly crisp texture of panko (Japanese-style bread crumbs) is a far cry from the dusty, fine dry bread crumbs familiar to most cooks in the U.S. The crumbs of panko are larger than standard bread crumbs and thoroughly dried. As panko has become more popular in the U.S., more brands have made their way to grocery store shelves.

To see if there really is a difference among brands, we picked up four samples—Wel-Pac, Dynasty, Kikkoman, and Ian's—at Boston-area supermarkets and tested them with our Light Chicken Parmesan. Each brand worked fine for this application, but with slightly different textural qualities. While the Wel-Pac, Dynasty, and Kikkoman brands possessed a delicate crispness, the oil-free Ian's provided a much more substantial crunch. In the end, if a super-crunchy—rather than delicate and crisp—texture is what you're aiming for, choose Ian's.

THE BEST PANKO BREAD CRUMBS

If you're looking for crumbs with substantial crunch, tasters deemed Ian's brand of panko the best of the bunch.

Now that we had flavorful, crisp, golden, "oven-fried" cutlets, we tried layering them in a casserole dish with some tomato sauce and low-fat shredded mozzarella. Returning the casserole dish to the oven so that the mozzarella could melt, we were disappointed at how quickly the crisp breading turned soggy. Any area of breading that touched the sauce, cheese, or other cutlets lost its crispness. Looking for a better method, we decided to leave the cutlets right on the rack and spoon just a small portion of the sauce and mozzarella onto the center of each piece of chicken, leaving the edges uncovered. Returning the rack to the oven, we found that the uncovered edges and the bottoms of the breaded cutlets remained crisp while the mozzarella cheese melted. Bingo!

Tasters were pleased with our makeover of this classic dish—we were successfully able to toast the bread crumbs with a touch of oil to give them flavor and color, bake the cutlets in a hot oven on a rack rather than frying them in excess oil, and, finally, replace the full-fat mozzarella with low-fat mozzarella. Served with a little extra sauce and grated Parmesan on the side, these oven-baked chicken Parmesan cutlets not only knock 14 grams of fat and 100 calories per serving off the traditional recipe, but they really do taste just as good.

Light Chicken Parmesan

SERVES 6

If you are tight on time, you can substitute 2 cups of your favorite plain tomato sauce for the Simple Tomato Sauce. Two cups of fresh bread crumbs can be substituted for the panko (they will shrink as they toast). Because these cutlets are breaded, we found that 1 cutlet per person was plenty—but buy the largest chicken breasts you can find to ensure good-sized portions.

- 3 large boneless, skinless chicken breasts (7 to 8 ounces each), tenderloins removed and breasts trimmed (see the illustrations on page 6) (see note)
- Salt and ground black pepper
- 1½ cups panko (Japanese-style bread crumbs) (see note)
- 1 tablespoon olive oil
- 1 ounce Parmesan cheese, grated (about ½ cup), plus extra for serving
- ½ cup unbleached all-purpose flour
- 1½ teaspoons garlic powder
- 3 large egg whites
- 1 tablespoon water
- Nonstick cooking spray
- 1 recipe Simple Tomato Sauce for Chicken Parmesan (page 330), warmed
- 3 ounces low-fat mozzarella cheese, shredded (about ¾ cup)
- 1 tablespoon shredded fresh basil leaves (see the illustrations on page 252)

1. Adjust an oven rack to the middle position and heat the oven to 475 degrees. Following the illustrations on page 6, slice each chicken breast in half horizontally and pound each cutlet as directed between two sheets of plastic wrap to a uniform ¼-inch thickness. Pat the chicken dry with paper towels and season with salt and pepper.

2. Combine the bread crumbs and oil in a 12-inch skillet and toast over medium heat, stirring often, until golden, about 10 minutes. Spread the bread crumbs in a shallow dish and let cool, then stir in the Parmesan.

3. Combine the flour, garlic powder, 1 teaspoon salt, and ½ teaspoon pepper in a second shallow dish and whisk the egg whites and water in a third shallow dish.

4. Line a rimmed baking sheet with foil, place a wire rack on top, and spray the rack with nonstick cooking spray. Working with 1 chicken cutlet at a time, lightly dredge in the flour, shaking off the excess, then coat with the egg white mixture, allowing the excess to drip off. Finally, coat with the bread crumbs, pressing gently so that the crumbs adhere. Place the breaded chicken on the wire rack.

5. Lightly coat the tops of the cutlets with nonstick cooking spray. Bake until the chicken is no longer pink in the center and feels firm when pressed with a finger, about 15 minutes.

6. Remove the chicken from the oven. Spoon 2 tablespoons of the sauce onto the center of each cutlet and top the sauce with 2 tablespoons of the mozzarella. Return the chicken to the oven and

continue to bake until the cheese has melted, about 5 minutes. Sprinkle with the basil and serve, passing the remaining sauce and Parmesan separately.

PER SERVING: **Cal** 310; **Fat** 8g; **Sat fat** 2.5g; **Chol** 75mg; **Carb** 20g; **Protein** 38g; **Fiber** 1g; **Sodium** 790mg

Simple Tomato Sauce for Chicken Parmesan

MAKES ABOUT 2 CUPS

This easy sauce also works well with pasta.

- 1 (28-ounce) can diced tomatoes
- 4 medium garlic cloves, minced or pressed through a garlic press (about 4 teaspoons)
- 1 tablespoon tomato paste
- 1 teaspoon olive oil
- ⅛ teaspoon red pepper flakes
- 1 tablespoon minced fresh basil leaves
- Salt and ground black pepper

Pulse the tomatoes with their juices in a food processor until mostly smooth, about ten 1-second pulses; set aside. Cook the garlic, tomato paste, oil, and pepper flakes in a medium saucepan over medium heat until the tomato paste begins to brown, about 2 minutes. Stir in the pureed tomatoes and cook until the sauce is thickened and measures 2 cups, about 20 minutes. Off the heat, stir in the basil and season with salt and pepper to taste. Cover and set aside until needed.

PER ⅓-CUP SERVING: **Cal** 35; **Fat** 1g; **Sat fat** 0g; **Chol** 0mg; **Carb** 7g; **Protein** 1g; **Fiber** 0g; **Sodium** 360mg

Light Chicken and Rice

GETTING A FULL MEAL ON THE TABLE FOR a family is not an easy task. Getting a nutritious, healthy meal on the table can be even tougher. When cooking for a family, casseroles and one-dish meals are perfect. They require a minimum of fuss, and everything is on the table in one fell swoop. But most of these dishes are filled with fatty, calorie-dense ingredients, making them a poor choice for those watching their diet. In search of healthier one-dish meals, we experimented with dishes that were inherently healthy or could be reconfigured to be healthy.

One dish came to mind immediately: chicken and rice. We thought the combination of juicy chicken and tender grains of rice was a sure winner, and if we selected our ingredients carefully and perfected our cooking techniques, this dish had the potential to be a perfect low-fat, one-dish meal. This feat, however, was not as easy as we had hoped. After several tests, we found that consistently cooked chicken and rice was hard to achieve. Add a vegetable to the mix and things got even trickier. Somewhat taken aback by our difficulties, we were even more determined to develop a healthy and streamlined one-pot chicken and rice dish.

Instead of trying to figure out the three variables (chicken, rice, and vegetables) all at once, we started by focusing on the chicken and rice components, hoping that the vegetables would fall in line later. The type of chicken to use was our first concern. Normally, we would use chicken thighs because of their moistness and because their cooking time closely matches that of the rice. But in this particular case, we knew that they would add too much fat. With thighs out of the question, we felt bone-in breasts were an attractive alternative, because the rib bones would provide some protection and keep the meat from drying out. But the flavor of bone-in breasts was not much better than that of boneless, skinless breasts, which are virtually fat-free. The challenge with boneless breasts, however, was that they would cook too quickly—likely before the rice was done.

We knew it would be tricky to work out the timing. Cooking the chicken and the rice together from the start did not work. The rice cooked unevenly and the chicken was inevitably overcooked. We hit on the idea of staggering the cooking of the two ingredients but using the same pot. We first seared the chicken, then removed it from the heat. Next we sautéed the aromatics (onion and garlic) and added the rice and broth. Once the mixture came to a simmer, we cooked the rice for 10 minutes. Without the chicken, the rice had room to cook and wasn't weighed down by the meat. Once the rice had absorbed the broth, we could add the chicken back to the pot so that it would both flavor the rice and finish cooking.

Last, we focused on the vegetables. Now that we had an established cooking routine for the rice, we identified several stages during which we could add vegetables. We tried to add the vegetables to the pot in the first 10 minutes but found that, like the chicken, the vegetables inhibited the rice from absorbing water, and the result was unevenly cooked rice. Next, we tried adding the vegetables to the pot with the chicken but found that there was too much food in the pan, which again led to uneven cooking. Finally, we tried adding thawed frozen vegetables at the very end of the cooking time, after we removed the chicken from the pot to allow the rice to sit off the heat. This turned out to be the perfect solution, and, much to our surprise, the frozen vegetables tasted great and retained their vibrant color and crisp texture after just a few minutes in the pot.

To finish the dish, we wanted to elevate the flavor and richness with a little cheese; since we had used so little oil or other fat in the cooking, we had room to indulge without ruining the healthy aspects of our finished dish. We found that low-fat cheddar contributed both flavor and creaminess to a version that included frozen broccoli, while Parmesan, which is a low-fat cheese, added a nice depth of flavor to a variation with carrots and peas.

Light Chicken and Rice with Broccoli and Cheddar

SERVES 6

When adding the chicken to the pot, lay it gently on top of the rice without pressing down. If the chicken is pressed too deeply into the rice, the rice will cook unevenly.

- **6** **boneless, skinless chicken breasts (5 to 6 ounces each), tenderloins removed and breasts trimmed (see the illustrations on page 6)**
- **Salt and ground black pepper**
- **4** **teaspoons vegetable oil**
- **1** **medium onion, minced**
- **4** **medium garlic cloves, minced or pressed through a garlic press (about 4 teaspoons)**
- **1** **teaspoon minced fresh thyme leaves**
- **⅛** **teaspoon red pepper flakes**
- **1½** **cups long-grain white rice**
- **3¼** **cups low-sodium chicken broth**
- **½** **cup dry white wine**
- **12** **ounces frozen broccoli florets, thawed**
- **4** **ounces 50 percent light cheddar cheese, shredded (about 1 cup)**

1. Pat the chicken dry with paper towels and season with salt and pepper. Heat 1½ teaspoons of the oil in a large Dutch oven over medium-high heat until just smoking. Brown half of the chicken on both sides, 5 to 8 minutes per side, reducing the heat if the pan begins to scorch. Transfer the chicken to a plate and set aside. Return the pot to medium-high heat and repeat with 1½ more teaspoons of the oil and the remaining 3 chicken breasts; transfer the chicken to the plate.

2. Add the remaining teaspoon oil, the onion, garlic, thyme, pepper flakes, and ½ teaspoon salt to the pot. Cover and cook over medium-low heat, stirring often, until the onion is softened, 8 to 10 minutes. Stir in the rice, increase the heat to medium, and cook, uncovered, until the edges turn translucent, about 3 minutes. Stir in the broth and wine and bring to a simmer, scraping up any browned bits. Cover, reduce the heat to low, and cook for 10 minutes.

3. Gently lay the chicken on top of the rice and continue to cook, covered, until the thickest part of the breast registers 160 to 165 degrees on an instant-read thermometer, 10 to 15 minutes.

4. Transfer the chicken to a plate and tent loosely with foil. Stir the broccoli into the rice, cover, and let the pot stand off the heat until the rice is tender and the broccoli has warmed through, about 10 minutes. Stir in the cheese, season with salt and pepper to taste, and serve with the chicken.

PER SERVING: **Cal** 460; **Fat** 9g; **Sat fat** 3g; **Chol** 110mg; **Carb** 42g; **Protein** 50g; **Fiber** 2g; **Sodium** 840mg

VARIATION

Light Chicken and Rice with Carrots, Peas, and Parmesan

Follow the recipe for One-Pot Chicken and Rice with Broccoli and Cheddar, omitting the red pepper flakes. Substitute 12 ounces frozen pea and carrot medley, thawed, for the broccoli and replace the cheddar with ½ cup grated Parmesan cheese.

PER SERVING: Cal 450; **Fat** 8g; **Sat fat** 2g; **Chol** 105mg; **Carb** 41g; **Protein** 48g; **Fiber** 1g; **Sodium** 890mg

Light Chicken Enchiladas

WE LOVE ENCHILADAS FOR ALL OF THE things that make them a calorie- and fat-laden nightmare: the gooey cheese, the juicy chicken, and the heavy, rich sauce. This recipe was in definite need of some overhauling.

We started with the chicken filling, determining right off the bat that dark meat would have to go; it was too fatty. But when we tried substituting roasted or sautéed boneless breasts, we found that they made the filling dry, chewy, and flavorless.

Now that we knew that boneless breasts couldn't just be substituted for chicken thighs, we turned to cooking technique as a possible solution. Instead of sautéing or roasting the chicken and then adding shredded chicken to the filling, we decided to make a flavorful sauce and then poach the chicken in it. This approach had several benefits: It moistened and flavored the chicken, and it flavored the sauce. The chicken retained much of the sweet and spicy taste of the sauce, and the sauce developed a deeper, richer flavor from the stewing chicken.

To capitalize on this process, we developed a sauce that was well spiced and would impart its flavors efficiently to the meat. We settled on chili powder and cumin to flavor the tomatoey sauce and reduced the amount of oil to half a teaspoon.

Now that we had solved the issue of the filling, we turned our attention to the tortillas, which are traditionally heated quickly in oil prior to being rolled so that they will not crack or break. Because tortillas soak up a lot of oil, this step adds significant fat to the dish. So we had to come up with an alternative method that accomplished the same goal. We borrowed a trick from our recipe for classic chicken enchiladas. Using the modern-day convenience of oil in a spray can, we placed the tortillas in a single layer on a baking sheet, sprayed both sides very lightly with vegetable oil, and warmed them in a moderate oven. This proved to be the alternative we were hoping to find. The oil-sprayed, oven-warmed tortillas were pliable, and their texture after being filled, rolled, and baked was just perfect.

Dealing with the cheese was our last hurdle. Surprisingly, it turned out to be the easiest to surmount. Full-fat enchiladas call for upward of a pound of cheese. Obviously, we couldn't use this

INGREDIENTS:
Light Cheddar Cheese

High in fat and calories, cheese is an ingredient we usually use with a very light hand when developing lower-fat recipes. But cutting back on or omitting cheese entirely is simply not an option in recipes where cheese takes center stage, so we decided to look at the variety of light cheddars out there. There are many options, ranging from cheeses made with 2 percent milk to those labeled fat-free, 75 percent light, and 50 percent light. We tasted all of these options on their own with crackers and in our Light Chicken Enchiladas.

The fat-free cheese was immediately out of the running for being rubbery and overly sweet. The 2 percent reduced-fat cheese won high marks, but it was still a little high in fat for our purposes. The 75 percent light cheddar produced a filling that was grainy, with a bitter aftertaste. The 50 percent light cheddar, on the other hand, worked well; Cabot 50% Light Cheddar was the favorite of the tasters for its sharp tanginess.

THE BEST LIGHT CHEDDAR

Though it doesn't quite stack up against fine aged cheddar when eaten on a cracker, tasters liked the creaminess and cheesy flavor that Cabot 50% Light Cheddar lent to our light dishes.

much cheese. We tried many different amounts and found that if we used less than half a pound, the enchiladas lacked the quintessential cheesiness that we all desired. But a half pound of cheese still added too much fat to the dish. So we turned to low-fat cheddar cheese and were pleased by the satisfying flavor and texture. We found that with half in the filling and half sprinkled on top, we were satisfied with the rich, cheesy flavor of the dish, and in the process we had reduced the fat content per serving by 24 grams.

In the end, the chicken, combined with the piquant sauce and the melted cheese, required little else to make this a delicious dish. We added only pickled jalapeños and ½ cup cilantro to give this lightened Mexican dish brightness and punch.

Light Chicken Enchiladas

SERVES 6

Make sure that the cooked chicken is finely shredded, or the edges of large pieces will tear through the tortillas. Serve these enchiladas with lime wedges, low-fat sour cream, diced avocado, shredded lettuce, and hot sauce.

- 1 medium onion, minced
- ½ teaspoon vegetable oil
- Salt
- 3 medium garlic cloves, minced or pressed through a garlic press (about 1 tablespoon)
- 3 tablespoons chili powder
- 2 teaspoons ground cumin
- 2 teaspoons sugar
- 2 (8-ounce) cans tomato sauce
- 1 cup water
- 1 pound boneless, skinless chicken breasts (about 2 large), trimmed
- 8 ounces 50 percent light cheddar cheese, shredded (2 cups)
- 1 (4-ounce) can pickled jalapeño chiles, drained and chopped
- ½ cup minced fresh cilantro leaves
- 12 (6-inch) corn tortillas
- Nonstick cooking spray
- 1 lime, cut into wedges (for serving)

1. Adjust an oven rack to the middle position and heat the oven to 300 degrees. Combine the onion, oil, and ½ teaspoon salt in a large saucepan. Cover and cook over medium-low heat, stirring often, until the onion is softened, 8 to 10 minutes. Stir in the garlic, chili powder, cumin, and sugar and cook until fragrant, about 30 seconds. Stir in the tomato sauce and water, bring to a simmer, and cook until thickened slightly, about 5 minutes.

2. Add the chicken breasts, partially cover, and bring to a simmer. Reduce the heat to low, cover completely, and cook until the thickest part of the breast registers 160 to 165 degrees on an instant-read thermometer, 10 to 15 minutes. Transfer the chicken to a cutting board. When the chicken is cool enough to handle, shred into bite-sized pieces (see the illustration on page 10) and transfer to a large bowl.

3. Pour the sauce through a medium-mesh strainer into a medium bowl, pressing on the solids to extract as much sauce as possible. Set the sauce aside and transfer the solids to the bowl with the shredded chicken. Stir ½ cup of the sauce, 1 cup of the cheddar, the jalapeños, and cilantro into the chicken mixture. Season with salt to taste and set aside.

4. Following the illustrations on page 289, lightly coat both sides of the tortillas with nonstick cooking spray. Place the tortillas on two baking sheets. Place one baking sheet in the oven and bake until the tortillas are soft and pliable, 2 to 4 minutes. Transfer the tortillas to a clean work surface. Place a heaping ⅓ cup filling onto the center of each warm, softened tortilla and roll it up tightly following the illustrations on page 289. Arrange the enchiladas, seam-side down, in a single layer in a 13 by 9-inch baking dish (or a shallow casserole dish of a similar size). Repeat with the remaining tortillas, increasing the oven temperature to 400 degrees after they are removed from the oven.

5. Pour 1 cup of the sauce over the enchiladas, covering the tortillas completely, then sprinkle the remaining 1 cup cheese down the center of the enchiladas, following the illustrations on page 289. Cover the dish with aluminum foil that has been coated lightly with nonstick cooking spray and bake until the sauce is bubbling and the cheese is melted, 20 to 25 minutes.

6. Remove the foil and continue to bake until the cheese on top is browned in spots, about 5 minutes longer. Let cool for 10 minutes before serving, passing the remaining 1 cup sauce and the lime wedges separately.

PER SERVING: **Cal** 350; **Fat** 10g; **Sat fat** 4.5g; **Chol** 65mg; **Carb** 37g; **Protein** 33g; **Fiber** 7g; **Sodium** 980mg

Chicken Meat Loaf

THERE ARE FEW DISHES MORE HOMEY AND satisfying than meat loaf, with its deep meaty flavor and hearty but light texture. Like most comfort meals, however, meat loaf is packed with fat and calories. We wondered if it was possible to use ground chicken in place of beef to make a meat loaf that was just as good—but lower in fat.

We began our testing with the ground chicken itself. We typically recommend buying ground chicken made from dark meat for its superior flavor and texture, but it's so high in fat and calories that ground beef might as well be used. Ground chicken made from all white meat was so dry and stiff that it resembled a foam block in both taste and texture. A combination of ground dark and white meat was the solution. This chicken produced a moist loaf that would satisfy even the most avid beef lover. Now that we had settled on the kind of ground chicken for our meat loaf, we began experimenting with binders.

Most meat loaf has some sort of binder. When trying various recipes, we learned that those prepared without a binder were coarse-textured and dense, like a big hamburger. We tried a wide range of binders, from cereal and oatmeal to crackers and bread crumbs. After trying them all, we found that bread crumbs provided the best texture without adding an off-flavor or superfluous fat. We also found that a little bit of whole milk and several eggs helped to bind the meat loaf together and provided some added richness.

In addition to bread crumbs, milk, and eggs, the tasters unanimously approved of sautéed onion and a couple cloves of garlic to flavor the mixture. Although these aromatics added time to the preparation, their contribution to the overall flavor was undeniable. We found it was important to sweat these ingredients in a sauté pan before adding them to the meat mixture—otherwise they would become overpowering in the dish. In addition to onion and garlic, a healthy dose of chopped parsley and thyme gave our low-fat meat loaf a fuller, more complex flavor.

Now that we were satisfied with the flavor of our meat loaf, all that was left was to determine the best cooking method. We tried baking the meat loaf in a traditional loaf pan, but this produced an unappealing meat loaf, since the sides of the loaf steamed rather than baked. We therefore made a free-form loaf and baked it on a wire rack set on a baking sheet that was covered in foil. This method allowed the top as well as the sides to get brown, creating a delicious caramelized exterior. As for oven temperatures, we tried a wide range of heat levels (and times) and learned that it was optimal to cook the loaf at a lower temperature for a longer period of time, since this helped ensure a juicy meat loaf.

We thought we were done at this point, but tasters asked for more in the form of a sauce or a glaze to complement the meat. So we returned to the kitchen and experimented with a number of sweet and sticky ingredients, such as honey, syrup, jams, and preserves. Good old ketchup mixed with brown sugar and vinegar turned out to be the winner. Brushed on the loaf toward the end of the baking and left for a short stay under the broiler, this glaze hugged the loaf and reminded us of the best home-cooked full-fat meat loaf we had ever tasted.

Chicken Meat Loaf with Brown Sugar–Ketchup Glaze

SERVES 8

If you can't find a blend of ground chicken, buy one package each of white and dark meat.

MEAT LOAF

- **2** **slices high-quality white sandwich bread, torn into large pieces**
- **1** **medium onion, minced**

- 2 medium garlic cloves, minced or pressed through a garlic press (about 2 teaspoons)
- 1 teaspoon vegetable oil
- Salt
- 3 tablespoons milk or plain yogurt
- 2 large eggs
- 2 teaspoons Dijon mustard
- 2 teaspoons Worcestershire sauce
- 1 teaspoon minced fresh thyme leaves
- ½ teaspoon ground black pepper
- ¼ teaspoon hot pepper sauce
- 2 pounds ground chicken (see note)
- ¼ cup minced fresh parsley leaves

GLAZE

- ½ cup ketchup
- ¼ cup packed light brown sugar
- 4 teaspoons cider or white vinegar

1. FOR THE MEAT LOAF: Process the bread in a food processor until coarsely ground, about six 1-second pulses; set aside.

2. Adjust an oven rack to the middle position and heat the oven to 350 degrees. Line a rimmed baking sheet with foil and place a wire rack on top; set aside. Fold a piece of heavy-duty foil into a 10 by 6-inch rectangle; set aside.

3. Combine the onion, garlic, oil, and ⅛ teaspoon salt in a medium skillet. Cover and cook over medium-low heat, stirring often, until the onion is softened, 8 to 10 minutes; set aside to cool. Whisk the milk, eggs, mustard, Worcestershire, thyme, pepper, hot sauce, and ¼ teaspoon salt together in a medium bowl.

4. Mix the chicken, bread crumbs, parsley, cooked onion mixture, and egg mixture together in a large bowl with your hands until uniformly combined. Press the mixture together into a compact mass, then turn it out onto the foil rectangle. Using your hands, press the meat into an evenly thick loaf about 2 inches tall and 1 inch from the edge of the foil on all sides.

5. Transfer the foil and meat loaf to the center of the prepared wire rack. Bake the meat loaf until the center of the loaf registers 145 to 150 degrees on an instant-read thermometer, 50 to 55 minutes. Remove from the oven and turn on the broiler.

6. FOR THE GLAZE: While the meat loaf cooks, combine the ingredients for the glaze in a small saucepan and bring to a simmer over medium heat. Cook, stirring occasionally, until thick and syrupy, about 5 minutes; set aside.

7. Brush the cooked meat loaf with half of the ketchup glaze and broil until the glaze bubbles and begins to brown around the edges, 3 to 5 minutes. Remove the meat loaf from the oven and brush with the remaining glaze; continue to broil until the center of the loaf registers 160 to 165 degrees on an instant-read thermometer, 3 to 5 minutes longer. Let cool for 10 minutes. Slice into 1-inch-thick pieces and serve.

PER SERVING: **Cal** 240; **Fat** 11g; **Sat fat** 3g; **Chol** 130mg; **Carb** 16g; **Protein** 21g; **Fiber** 1g; **Sodium** 400mg

CHICKEN BURGERS

WHETHER GRILLED, FRIED, OR BROILED, burgers are one of America's favorite foods. Unfortunately, a good hamburger is usually made with the fattiest meat you can find (about 34 grams of fat for a 5-ounce burger). To satisfy a burger craving, you can try a low-fat chicken burger. But in our experience, these burger substitutes are pretty bad—dry, tasteless, and colorless. We set out to develop a chicken burger that would satisfy us whenever the craving for a burger struck.

We first struggled with the type of ground chicken to use. The chicken burgers we made from ground dark meat cooked up juicy and flavorful, but they did not save us much on fat or calories, considering that, like typical all-beef burgers, they were between 15 and 20 percent fat. The burgers made with white chicken meat were as dry as could be. There was so little fat in them that they tended to burn when cooking, and boy, were they bland. The burgers made with a combination of dark and white ground chicken were promising. They had a decent, meaty flavor and were relatively juicy. We figured this was a good start and, with a little help, we knew this meat would make a flavorful burger.

We noticed first that our patties lacked heft and moistness. We began to correct this by adding a combination of milk and bread (also called a panade) to the chicken meat—the same mixture we use to lend moisture to meatballs. The resulting burgers tasted, well, like meatballs, and the patties had an unattractive pale color. We tried a whole host of other ingredients (mashed beans, rehydrated mushrooms, and minced tempeh among them), but they were no better. All of these ingredients either gave the burgers a strong flavor that overshadowed the chicken or failed to add any moistness to the patties. Then we stumbled onto fat-free ricotta. It was exactly what we were looking for. The ricotta gave the burgers a moist, chewy texture, and its mildness allowed the chicken flavor to stand out.

Flavoring the chicken patties was tricky. We tried every ingredient in the test kitchen that we thought would add a meaty flavor to the burgers, from teriyaki sauce and fermented black beans to olive paste. After eating a lot of bad (and some good) burgers, we found two ingredients that gave our chicken burgers optimal flavor: Worcestershire sauce and Dijon mustard.

Because chicken must be cooked to well-done for safety reasons, figuring out how to maintain a juicy burger was difficult. Too high a heat and the burgers burn before they're done; too low and they are pale and virtually steam-cooked (and very unappealing). We experimented with several different cooking methods, including broiling and roasting, but nothing beat the simplicity of browning in a heavy-bottomed skillet. We found the best way to cook the chicken burgers without drying them out was to sear them over medium heat, then cook them partially covered over low heat until they reached an internal temperature of 160 degrees. This resulted in a burger that had a rich crust and remained moist inside (and required a minimal amount of fat to cook). This burger was now so good that if we closed our eyes we would swear we were eating a real, full-fat hamburger.

Chicken Burgers

SERVES 4

The ricotta cheese can burn easily, so keep a close watch on the burgers as they cook. If you can't find a blend of ground chicken, buy one package each of white and dark meat.

- 1¼ **pounds ground chicken (see note)**
- ¼ **cup fat-free ricotta cheese**
- 2 **teaspoons Worcestershire sauce**
- 2 **teaspoons Dijon mustard**
- ½ **teaspoon salt**
- ¼ **teaspoon ground black pepper**
- 1 **tablespoon vegetable oil**

1. Mix the chicken, ricotta, Worcestershire, mustard, salt, and pepper together in a large bowl with your hands until uniformly combined. Divide the mixture into 4 portions. Lightly toss one portion from hand to hand to form a ball, then lightly flatten the ball with your fingertips into a 1-inch-thick patty. Repeat the process with the remaining portions.

2. Heat the oil in a 12-inch nonstick skillet over medium heat until just smoking. Lay the burgers in the skillet and cook until light brown and crusted, 3 to 4 minutes. Flip the burgers over and continue to cook until the second side is light brown, 3 to 4 minutes longer.

3. Reduce the heat to low, partially cover, and continue to cook until the thickest part of the burger registers 160 to 165 degrees on an instant-read thermometer, 8 to 10 minutes longer, flipping once more if necessary for even browning. Serve.

PER SERVING: Cal 240; **Fat** 15g; **Sat fat** 3.5g; **Chol** 95mg; **Carb** 2g; **Protein** 24g; **Fiber** 0g; **Sodium** 480mg

13 CHICKEN DINNERS FOR TWO

Chicken Dinners for Two

CHICKEN IS WELL SUITED TO COOKING FOR two. Individual breasts and thighs can be purchased from most butchers' cases, or you can buy them in family-sized packs that can easily be divided into portions for two and frozen. For this chapter, we had several goals in mind: We wanted to uncover some new and interesting chicken dinners, and we wanted to scale the recipes to yield two servings—for those with smaller families who don't want to be eating roast chicken or stew for the entire week. Most importantly, we wanted our recipes to be complete meals.

As it turns out, cooking for two isn't always as simple as halving a recipe. Spices can become dulled or too potent, there is never enough sauce, and then there is the question of the proper-size pan to use. Not to mention you end up with lots of odds and ends in your refrigerator—half an onion, a quarter of a red bell pepper, two-thirds of a can of tomatoes, and a half-empty carton of chicken broth. Sure, some of these remnants are unavoidable when cooking, but we have developed the recipes in this chapter specifically with this predicament in mind (our recipes use a shallot instead of half an onion, for instance), while at the same time taking all the guesswork out of cooking for two.

When developing recipes for this chapter, we kept in mind that sometimes leftovers simply aren't very good. Take paella, for example—most recipes yield enough to serve a crowd, and reheating it produces an inedible mess of rubbery shrimp, mushy rice, and dry shreds of chicken. Our recipe combines everything we love about paella—spicy chorizo, saffron-infused rice, plump shrimp, and tender chicken—but in a 10-inch skillet and without leftovers (unless, of course, you are cooking for one).

As we learned with the paella, rice, grains, and beans can be among the most difficult ingredients to scale down for two—finding the right balance of liquid to rice is key. Sure, it seems easy—just add water or broth to the rice and simmer—but all too often there is too much liquid, or worse, not enough, and the rice burns on the bottom. For this chapter, we developed noteworthy recipes—for example, chicken with Israeli couscous, orzo, or lentils—that take the anxiety out of the equation. Each recipe combines chicken with a perfectly cooked starch and vegetable all in one pan and precisely times the addition of each ingredient.

Lastly, an added bonus to cooking for two: with fewer vegetables to prep, not as many batches of chicken to brown, and less sauce to reduce, cooking for two is inherently quicker than cooking for more.

Roast Chicken and Bread Salad

THE IDEA OF USING BREAD IN A SALAD MAY be unfamiliar to some, but bread salad is not uncommon in Italy. There, stale bread is typically combined with fresh ingredients (such as tomatoes, onions, and herbs) and a dressing made from oil, vinegar, and seasonings to create a flavorful and satisfying salad. We wanted to take this idea one step further and create a complete one-dish meal by pairing cubes of rustic bread with juicy roast chicken, fresh arugula, ripe tomato, and shaved Parmesan. This recipe gets its inspiration from a recipe for Roast Chicken with Bread Salad in the *Zuni Café Cookbook,* by Judy Rogers, in which a perfect roast chicken and its drippings are served over a bread and arugula salad. We thought this would be the perfect dinner for two.

We knew from the start that using a whole chicken for this recipe wasn't an option—it would yield too much meat for two people. Instead, we decided to use bone-in, skin-on chicken breasts. Taking a cue from our pan-roasted chicken breasts, we pan-seared the chicken until it was golden brown. Then, instead of transferring the entire skillet to the oven as we normally do, we set the chicken in a baking dish, thereby freeing up the skillet to make the dressing.

For the bread, we found that sliced white bread or airy supermarket bread that is highly refined and becomes rock-hard within a few days won't do. Ideally, the proper bread for bread salads should not contain sugar or sweeteners of any kind, which would conflict with the savory nature of the other ingredients. Nor should the loaf have raisins or nuts. What the bread should have is a sturdy texture and a good wheaty flavor. Because many people don't typically have stale bread on hand, we wanted our recipe to work with fresh bread. Instead of toasting the bread in the oven in a separate pan, we placed it in the baking dish, underneath the chicken. This way, the bread toasted and at the same time absorbed the flavorful drippings from the chicken as it cooked.

The dressing came together quickly. We added garlic and thyme to the skillet for background and depth. Then, to mimic the pan drippings of a whole chicken, we stirred in chicken broth and scraped the bottom of the skillet to release the flavorful fond. To finish the dressing and provide some acidity, we stirred in a little red wine vinegar.

We tossed the dressing with the bread and pieces of tender chicken, adding arugula, tomatoes, Parmesan shavings, and a sprinkling of toasted pine nuts—typical Mediterranean ingredients that highlight the origins of this dish. The warm juices saturate the bread cubes and wilt the arugula, creating a flavorful and cohesive dish.

Warm Roast Chicken and Bread Salad with Arugula

SERVES 2

If the split breasts are of different sizes, check the smaller one a few minutes early; if it is done, remove it from the oven while the larger one finishes cooking. Drizzle the salad with high-quality extra-virgin olive oil before serving, if desired.

- 6 ounces French or Italian bread, cut or torn into 1-inch cubes (about 4 cups)
- 3 tablespoons olive oil
- Salt and ground black pepper
- 2 bone-in, skin-on split chicken breasts (10 to 12 ounces each), trimmed
- 1 medium garlic clove, minced or pressed through a garlic press (about 1 teaspoon)
- ½ teaspoon minced fresh thyme leaves
- ⅔ cup low-sodium chicken broth
- 1 tablespoon red wine vinegar
- 4 ounces baby arugula (about 7 cups lightly packed)
- 1 medium ripe tomato, cored, seeded, and chopped medium
- 1 tablespoon pine nuts, toasted
- Shaved Parmesan cheese (for serving)

1. Adjust an oven rack to the lowest position and heat the oven to 450 degrees. Toss the bread cubes with 1 tablespoon of the oil, ¼ teaspoon salt, and a pinch pepper. Place the bread in an 8-inch-square baking dish in an even layer and set aside.

2. Pat the chicken dry with paper towels and season with salt and pepper. Heat 1 more tablespoon of the oil in a 10-inch skillet over medium-high heat until just smoking. Add the chicken, skin-side down, and cook until deep golden, about 5 minutes.

3. Transfer the chicken, skin side up, to the baking dish on top of the bread cubes and bake until the thickest part of the breast registers 160 to 165 degrees on an instant-read thermometer and the bread is browned in spots, 18 to 20 minutes. Transfer the chicken to a cutting board. When the chicken is cool enough to handle, remove the meat from the bones and cut into 1-inch chunks; discard the bones.

4. While the chicken bakes, pour off any fat in the skillet, add the remaining 1 tablespoon oil, the garlic, and thyme and cook over medium heat until fragrant, about 30 seconds. Stir in the broth, scraping up any browned bits. Bring to a simmer and cook until thickened slightly, about 3 minutes. Stir in the vinegar, cover, and remove from the heat.

5. Transfer the bread cubes to a large bowl. Pour all but 2 tablespoons of the broth mixture over the bread cubes and toss to coat. Gently fold the chicken, along with any accumulated juices, the arugula, tomato, pine nuts, and reserved 2 tablespoons broth mixture into the bread cubes. Season with salt and pepper to taste, garnish with the Parmesan, and serve.

MAKING PARMESAN SHAVINGS

Thin shavings of Parmesan can be used to garnish a variety of dishes. Simply run a sharp vegetable peeler along the length of a piece of cheese to remove paper-thin curls.

Chicken Stew

A BIG POT OF STEW IS GREAT IF YOU ARE feeding a crowd or want ample leftovers, but there are times when you get a hankering for stew and you don't want to make a big batch. In addition to making more servings than a family of two wants, most stew recipes require hours of preparation and simmering—due in part to the large quantity they yield. We've taken a recipe for chicken stew and scaled it down to feed two people. This stew gets its inspiration from a hearty Portuguese-style soup, *caldo verde*, which is typically made with greens, potatoes, and sausage. We added chicken to our recipe to make our stew even heartier and more deeply flavored.

Focusing on the chicken first, we settled on bone-in, skin-on chicken thighs. We browned the thighs with the skin on, as the rendered fat from the skin meant we could use less oil, allowing the chicken flavor to have a strong presence. After browning the thighs, we set them aside while we sautéed aromatics (shallot, garlic, and oregano). We then added chicken broth and simmered the thighs until cooked through. The meat was shredded and returned to the pot. We did find, however, that it was best to remove the skin before shredding the chicken and returning it to the stew; otherwise, our stew became greasy.

For the sausage, we selected hot, pungent chorizo—its potent spices contributed to a rich and full-flavored broth. And for the greens, we settled on kale, which, unlike more delicate greens, resisted wilting and provided a forgiving window of time in which it could cook. The kale also imparted a sweet cabbage flavor to the soup that was both delicious and authentic.

Traditionally, caldo verde is thickened by breaking down or mashing potato in the soup. Tasters liked stew in which the potato was not broken down completely. Two medium-sized red potatoes, cut into 1-inch chunks, were all that this recipe needed, and we had a hearty dinner for two that can be made any night of the week.

Chicken Stew with Potatoes, Chorizo, and Kale

SERVES 2

If you can't find chorizo sausage, use tasso, andouille, or linguiça. In step 1, season the chicken only lightly with salt, as some brands of chorizo can be quite salty.

- **1½ pounds bone-in, skin-on chicken thighs (about 4 thighs), trimmed**
- **Salt and ground black pepper**
- **2 tablespoons olive oil**
- **3 ounces chorizo, halved lengthwise and cut crosswise into ¼-inch pieces (see note)**
- **1 medium shallot, minced (about 3 tablespoons)**
- **2 medium garlic cloves, minced or pressed through a garlic press (about 2 teaspoons)**
- **½ teaspoon minced fresh oregano leaves or ⅛ teaspoon dried**
- **3 cups low-sodium chicken broth**
- **8 ounces kale (about ½ bunch), stems removed and leaves cut crosswise into ¼-inch strips (about 4 packed cups)**
- **2 medium red potatoes (about 10 ounces), scrubbed and cut into 1-inch chunks**

1. Pat the chicken dry with paper towels and season with salt and pepper. Heat 1 tablespoon of the oil in a large saucepan over medium-high heat until just smoking. Add the chicken and cook until well browned on both sides, about 5 minutes. Transfer the chicken to a plate, leaving the fat in the pot, and set aside.

2. Add the chorizo to the pot and cook over medium heat, stirring occasionally, until browned, about 4 minutes. Stir in the shallot, garlic, and oregano and cook until fragrant, about 30 seconds. Stir in the broth, scraping up any browned bits.

3. Nestle the chicken, along with any accumulated juices, into the pot and bring to a simmer. Cover, reduce the heat to medium-low, and simmer until the thickest part of the thigh registers 170 to 175 degrees on an instant-read thermometer, 20 to 25 minutes.

4. Transfer the chicken to a cutting board. Stir the kale and potatoes into the stew, cover, and cook

over medium heat until the potatoes are tender, 10 to 15 minutes. When the chicken is cool enough to handle, remove the meat from the bones and shred into bite-sized pieces (see the illustration on page 10); discard the skin and bones. Return the shredded chicken to the stew and add the remaining 1 tablespoon oil. Continue to cook until heated through, about 2 minutes. Season with salt and pepper to taste and serve.

Skillet Chicken Dinners

IT'S NO WONDER THAT BONELESS, SKINLESS chicken breasts are so popular—they are widely available, easy to prepare, and quick-cooking. They can be purchased individually, but they are most often sold in packs of four, so you can cook two and freeze two for another night. We wanted to incorporate this convenient cut of chicken into a simple but satisfying skillet supper. Recalling our quick recipes for Chicken and Couscous (page 308), which were such a hit in the test kitchen, we aimed to follow a similar approach but scale it down to feed two people instead of a family of four.

We began by browning lightly floured breasts, and then we transferred them to the oven to cook through. Next to go into the pan was the couscous, but for this recipe we decided to use Israeli couscous, which is larger than traditional couscous and therefore must be simmered (like pasta). We found that toasting the small pearls before simmering them kept the grains distinct and added a pleasant nuttiness. Next, we simmered the couscous with an aromatic combination of shallot, garlic, red pepper flakes, lemon zest, and chicken broth.

Now we needed only some sort of vegetable to complete the dish, so we stirred in baby spinach just until it wilted. A little lemon juice and tangy feta cheese added brightness and put the finishing touch on this simple recipe.

We liked this recipe so much that we developed a version with orzo, asparagus, and Parmesan cheese that is equally easy and tasty.

Chicken with Israeli Couscous, Spinach, and Feta

SERVES 2

Israeli couscous is larger than traditional couscous and therefore must be simmered (like pasta). Orzo can be substituted for the couscous.

- ¼ cup unbleached all-purpose flour
- 2 boneless, skinless chicken breasts (5 to 6 ounces each), tenderloins removed and breasts trimmed (see the illustrations on page 6)
- Salt and ground black pepper
- 3 tablespoons olive oil
- ¾ cup Israeli couscous (see note)
- 1 medium shallot, minced (about 3 tablespoons)
- 3 medium garlic cloves, minced or pressed through a garlic press (about 1 tablespoon)
- ½ teaspoon grated zest plus 2 tablespoons juice from 1 lemon
- ¼ teaspoon red pepper flakes
- 1½ cups low-sodium chicken broth
- 1 (6-ounce) bag baby spinach
- 2 ounces feta cheese, crumbled (about ½ cup)

1. Adjust an oven rack to the lower-middle position, place a baking dish on the rack, and heat the oven to 300 degrees.

2. Place the flour in a shallow dish. Pat the chicken dry with paper towels and season with salt and pepper. Working with 1 chicken breast at a time, dredge in the flour, shaking off the excess.

3. Heat 1 tablespoon of the oil in a 10-inch nonstick skillet over medium-high heat until just smoking. Add the chicken and cook until well browned on both sides, about 5 minutes. Transfer the chicken to the dish in the oven and cook until the thickest part of the breast registers 160 to 165 degrees on an instant-read thermometer, 8 to 12 minutes.

4. While the chicken bakes, add 1 more tablespoon of the oil and the couscous to the skillet and toast over medium heat until light golden, about 2 minutes. Stir in the shallot, 2 teaspoons of the garlic, ¼ teaspoon of the lemon zest, and ⅛ teaspoon of the pepper flakes and cook until fragrant, about 30 seconds.

5. Stir in the broth, scraping up any browned bits. Bring to a simmer and cook over medium-low heat, stirring frequently, until the liquid is absorbed and the couscous is al dente, 8 to 10 minutes. Stir in the spinach, one handful at a time, and cook until wilted.

6. In a small bowl, whisk 1 tablespoon of the lemon juice with the remaining 1 tablespoon oil, 1 teaspoon garlic, ¼ teaspoon lemon zest, and ⅛ teaspoon pepper flakes.

7. Off the heat, stir the cheese and remaining 1 tablespoon lemon juice into the couscous and season with salt and pepper to taste. Divide the couscous between two plates and top with the chicken. Drizzle with the garlic-oil mixture and serve.

Chicken with Orzo, Asparagus, and Parmesan

SERVES 2

Israeli couscous can be substituted for the orzo.

- ¼ cup unbleached all-purpose flour
- 2 boneless, skinless chicken breasts (5 to 6 ounces each), tenderloins removed and breasts trimmed (see the illustrations on page 6)
- Salt and ground black pepper
- 3 tablespoons olive oil
- ¾ cup orzo (see note)
- 1 medium shallot, minced (about 3 tablespoons)
- 3 medium garlic cloves, minced or pressed through a garlic press (about 1 tablespoon)
- 1 teaspoon minced fresh thyme leaves
- ½ teaspoon grated zest plus 2 tablespoons juice from 1 lemon
- 1½ cups low-sodium chicken broth
- 8 ounces asparagus (about ½ bunch), tough ends trimmed, cut into 1-inch lengths
- 1 ounce Parmesan cheese, grated (about ½ cup)

1. Adjust an oven rack to the lower-middle position, place a baking dish on the rack, and heat the oven to 300 degrees.

2. Place the flour in a shallow dish. Pat the chicken dry with paper towels and season with salt and pepper. Working with 1 chicken breast at a time, dredge in the flour, shaking off the excess.

3. Heat 1 tablespoon of the oil in a 10-inch nonstick skillet over medium-high heat until just smoking. Add the chicken and cook until well browned on both sides, about 5 minutes. Transfer the chicken to the dish in the oven and cook until the thickest part of the breast registers 160 to 165 degrees on an instant-read thermometer, 8 to 12 minutes.

4. While the chicken bakes, add 1 more tablespoon of the oil and the orzo to the skillet and toast over medium heat until light golden, about 2 minutes. Stir in the shallot, 2 teaspoons of the garlic, ½ teaspoon of the thyme, and ¼ teaspoon of the lemon zest and cook until fragrant, about 30 seconds.

5. Stir in the broth, scraping up any browned bits. Bring to a simmer and cook over medium-low heat, stirring frequently, for 4 minutes. Stir in the asparagus, cover, and continue to cook until the liquid is absorbed, the orzo is al dente, and the asparagus is crisp-tender, 4 to 6 minutes longer.

6. Meanwhile, in a small bowl, whisk 1 tablespoon of the lemon juice with the remaining 1 tablespoon oil, 1 teaspoon garlic, ½ teaspoon thyme, and ¼ teaspoon lemon zest.

7. Off the heat, stir the cheese and remaining 1 tablespoon lemon juice into the orzo and season with salt and pepper to taste. Divide the orzo between two plates and top with the chicken. Drizzle with the garlic-oil mixture and serve.

Chicken Ragù

A TRADITIONAL RAGÙ RECIPE YIELDS ENOUGH to serve the whole neighborhood, and it takes an entire Sunday to make. We wanted to develop a scaled-down recipe for quick ragù that nonetheless tasted like it had cooked for hours.

Ragù is a rich, thick meat sauce that often contains beef short ribs or pork spareribs. But since we were going to be using chicken in ours, we decided that thighs would be the best choice for their rich flavor and meaty texture. We started by browning the thighs, and then we set them aside while we built the sauce. The fond from the browned chicken, along with shallot and garlic, formed the base of the sauce, and we added some oregano and red wine for further complexity. We then pulsed canned diced tomatoes until chopped fine and added them to the pot. (Crushed tomatoes vary widely from brand to brand, so we've found that it's usually best to buy canned diced tomatoes and crush them yourself.) To cut the acidity of the tomatoes and wine, we added some chicken broth.

Our sauce was close, but it needed more of that deep, rich flavor that is characteristic of a long-simmered stew. We took a cue from our Pasta with Chicken Bolognese (page 261) and added dried porcini mushrooms. Their earthy flavor and meaty texture complemented the chicken so well that we also decided to add thinly sliced white mushrooms.

After just 15 minutes of simmering, we had a hearty and rich chicken ragù. We tossed the sauce with some rigatoni and finished the dish with a touch of butter and a little minced parsley.

Rigatoni with Braised Chicken and Mushroom Ragù

SERVES 2

Other shapes of pasta can be used instead of rigatoni.

- 1 (14.5-ounce) can diced tomatoes
- 8 ounces boneless, skinless chicken thighs (about 2 thighs), trimmed
- Salt and ground black pepper
- 2 tablespoons unsalted butter
- 4 ounces white mushrooms, wiped clean and sliced thin
- 1 medium shallot, minced (about 3 tablespoons)
- 3 medium garlic cloves, minced or pressed through a garlic press (about 1 tablespoon)
- ¼ ounce dried porcini mushrooms, rinsed and minced
- ¼ teaspoon dried oregano
- ½ cup low-sodium chicken broth
- ¼ cup dry red wine
- 8 ounces rigatoni (about 3 cups)
- 1 tablespoon minced fresh parsley leaves
- Parmesan cheese, grated (for serving)

1. Pulse the tomatoes with their juice in a food processor until chopped fine, eight 1-second pulses; set aside.

2. Pat the chicken dry with paper towels and season with salt and pepper. Heat 1 tablespoon of the butter in a large saucepan over medium-high heat until melted. Add the chicken and cook until well browned on both sides, about 5 minutes. Transfer the chicken to a plate and set aside.

3. Add the white mushrooms and ¼ teaspoon salt to the skillet and cook over medium heat until the mushrooms have released their juices and are brown around the edges, about 5 minutes. Stir in the shallot, garlic, porcini, and oregano and cook until fragrant, about 30 seconds.

4. Add the tomatoes, broth, and wine, scraping up any browned bits. Add the chicken and bring to a simmer. Reduce the heat to medium-low and cook until the thickest part of the thigh registers 170 to 175 degrees on an instant-read thermometer, about 15 minutes. Transfer the chicken to a cutting board. When the chicken is cool enough to handle, shred into bite-sized pieces (see the illustration on page 10). Return the shredded chicken to the sauce and continue to cook until heated through, about 2 minutes. Season with salt and pepper to taste.

5. Meanwhile, bring 4 quarts water to a boil in a large pot. Stir in 1 tablespoon salt and the pasta and cook, stirring often, until the pasta is al dente. Reserve ½ cup of the pasta cooking water, then drain the pasta and return it to the pot. Stir in 1 cup of the sauce, the remaining 1 tablespoon butter, and the parsley until well combined. Add the pasta cooking water as needed to loosen the sauce. Serve, passing the remaining sauce and Parmesan separately.

PAELLA

PAELLA, ONCE FOUND PRIMARILY ON RESTaurant menus, is making a bit of a comeback in the home kitchen. As is true of many classic dishes, however, paella made the traditional Spanish way serves a crowd, can take hours of preparation, and requires a laundry list of ingredients, ranging from artichokes and green beans to chicken, pork, lobster, and calamari. But, with some adjustments to technique and ingredients, we were confident we could make paella for two in no time.

The hallmarks of paella are the saffron-infused rice and the chorizo, so we weren't going to forgo either. In an attempt to slim down the ingredient list, however, we decided to feature chicken thighs and quick-cooking shrimp and save the pork, clams, and lobster for a larger feast. Spanish cuisine uses a trio of onion, garlic, and tomatoes sautéed in olive oil—called a sofrito—as the foundation for its rice dishes, and we followed suit, using a shallot in place of the onion. We also threw in green peas for sweetness and color. And for rice that is flavorful and not mushy, we used the traditional short-grain rice, like Valencia or Arborio, and we first coated the grains in the oil and aromatics before adding the cooking liquid. Using water for the cooking liquid made the dish taste bland, and clam broth was overpowering. Because chicken was to be one of the primary flavors in the dish, chicken broth proved the best choice.

To serve paella, it is customary to bring the pan to the table and allow diners to serve themselves. Even though our version was less than authentic, it looked the part, and so we saw no reason to break with this serving tradition.

Paella

SERVES 2

If you can't find chorizo sausage, use tasso, andouille, or linguiça. Serve with lemon wedges, if desired.

- 8 ounces extra-large (21 to 25 per pound) shrimp, peeled and deveined
- Salt and ground black pepper
- 8 ounces boneless, skinless chicken thighs (about 2 thighs), trimmed
- 2 tablespoons olive oil
- 4 ounces chorizo, halved lengthwise and cut crosswise into ¼-inch pieces (see note)
- 1 medium shallot, minced (about 3 tablespoons)
- ⅛ teaspoon saffron threads, crumbled, or saffron powder
- ¾ cup Valencia or Arborio rice
- 3 medium garlic cloves, minced or pressed through a garlic press (about 1 tablespoon)
- 1½ cups low-sodium chicken broth
- 1 medium ripe tomato, cored and chopped medium
- ¼ cup frozen peas, thawed
- 1 tablespoon minced fresh parsley leaves

1. Pat the shrimp dry with paper towels, season with salt and pepper, and set aside. Pat the chicken dry with paper towels and season with salt and pepper. Heat 1 tablespoon of the oil in a 10-inch skillet over medium-high heat until just smoking. Add the chicken and cook until well browned on both sides, about 5 minutes. Transfer the chicken to a plate and set aside.

2. Add the remaining 1 tablespoon oil, the chorizo, shallot, saffron, and ½ teaspoon salt to the skillet and cook until the shallot is softened and the chorizo is browned, about 4 minutes. Stir in the rice and garlic and cook until fragrant, about 30 seconds.

3. Add the broth and tomato, scraping up any browned bits. Add the chicken and bring to a simmer. Reduce the heat to medium-low, cover, and cook until the thickest part of the thigh registers 170 to 175 degrees on an instant-read thermometer and most of the liquid is absorbed, about 15 minutes. Transfer the chicken to a cutting board. When it is cool enough to handle, shred the chicken into bite-sized pieces (see the illustration on page 10).

4. Scatter the shrimp over the rice and continue to cook, covered, until the rice is tender and the shrimp are cooked through, about 5 minutes. Off the heat, return the chicken to the skillet, sprinkle the peas and parsley over the rice, cover, and let warm through, about 2 minutes. Season with salt and pepper to taste and serve.

Skillet Chicken Fajitas

FAJITAS, A COMBINATION OF GRILLED MEAT, onions, and peppers tucked into flour tortillas, are simple at heart and quick-cooking by design. That said, we wanted to develop a scaled-down fajita recipe that could be made without lugging out the grill.

For the meat we chose boneless, skinless chicken breasts. Traditionally, the chicken (or meat) for fajitas is marinated in lime juice, then grilled. But we were staying indoors. Pan-searing the chicken seemed like the obvious alternative, so we started the chicken on the stovetop and then transferred it to the oven to finish cooking. However, we found that lime-marinated chicken had a tendency to steam, not sear. Our solution was to wait until the chicken was cooked and then toss the sliced chicken with a zesty seasoning mixture of lime juice, cilantro, Worcestershire, and brown sugar.

As the chicken finished cooking in the oven, we sautéed the pepper and onion in the same skillet, taking advantage of the flavorful fond left behind by the chicken. As the pepper and onion cooked, the fond was effectively deglazed and lent the vegetables a full flavor that needed little enhancement, except for a sprinkling of chili powder, which added a characteristically Southwestern touch to the mix.

Skillet Chicken Fajitas

SERVES 2

If you like your fajitas spicy, add a sliced jalapeño along with the bell pepper. Serve with salsa, sour cream, chopped avocado, shredded cheese, shredded lettuce, and lime wedges.

- 12 ounces boneless, skinless chicken breasts (about 2 medium), tenderloins removed and breasts trimmed (see the illustrations on page 6)
- Salt and ground black pepper
- 2 tablespoons vegetable oil
- 1 red, yellow, or orange bell pepper, stemmed, seeded, and sliced thin
- 1 small red onion, halved and sliced thin
- 2 tablespoons water
- 1 teaspoon chili powder
- 2 tablespoons juice from 1 lime
- 1 tablespoon minced fresh cilantro leaves
- 1 teaspoon Worcestershire sauce
- ½ teaspoon brown sugar
- 6 (6-inch) flour tortillas

1. Adjust an oven rack to the lower-middle position, place a baking dish on the rack, and heat the oven to 300 degrees. Pat the chicken dry with paper towels and season with salt and pepper.

2. Heat 1 tablespoon of the oil in a 10-inch nonstick skillet over medium-high heat until just smoking. Add the chicken and cook until well browned on both sides, about 5 minutes. Transfer the chicken to the dish in the oven and cook until the thickest part of the breast registers 160 to 165 degrees on an instant-read thermometer, 8 to 12 minutes.

3. While the chicken bakes, add the bell pepper, onion, water, chili powder, and ¼ teaspoon salt to the skillet and cook over medium heat, scraping up any browned bits, until the onion is softened, 5 to 7 minutes. Transfer to a serving bowl and tent loosely with foil.

4. Mix the remaining 1 tablespoon oil, the lime juice, cilantro, Worcestershire, brown sugar, and ¼ teaspoon salt together in large bowl and set aside. Stack the tortillas on a plate and cover with plastic wrap. Microwave until soft and hot, 30 seconds to 2 minutes.

5. Cut the chicken into ¼-inch slices, add to the bowl with the marinade, and toss to combine. Arrange the chicken on a platter and serve with the tortillas and vegetables.

Chicken Kebabs

MAKING CHICKEN KEBABS CAN BE A LENGTHY process. Cutting and skewering the meat and vegetables takes time. Preparing kebabs for two is less labor-intensive for sure—you have to prepare only a fraction of the meat and vegetables—but could our kebabs be even less time consuming if we employed the broiler instead of the grill?

We borrowed some tips from our existing chicken kebab recipe, such as using thighs, which are less prone to drying out than white meat. We cut the thighs into 1½-inch chunks and marinated them in a mixture of olive oil, garlic, fresh herbs, salt, and pepper. As in our traditional kebab recipe, we reserved some of the marinade to mix with lemon juice and pour over the chicken and vegetables for a fresh hit of flavor after they cooked.

For the vegetables, we chose a red bell pepper and shallots, which we peeled and quartered. To give some heft to our skewers, and round out this recipe to become a full meal, we turned to baby red potatoes. While we would normally steer away from potatoes when making kebabs (they must be precooked, which can be a hassle), with such a small number of potatoes required for this recipe it was easy—and no cutting was required! We simply zapped the potatoes in the microwave until they began to soften, and then we skewered them.

The kebabs should be broiled 5 inches from the heat element. For the juiciest meat with the strongest broiled flavor, we found that the skewers should be cooked for 13 to 15 minutes. Check for doneness by cutting into one of the chicken pieces with a small knife, and remove the skewers from the broiler as soon as there is no sign of pink at the center.

A final note on skewering—chicken pieces cooked on a round skewer tended to spin when we lifted them from the broiler, inhibiting even cooking. A flat skewer worked best and proved more effective at holding the meat in place.

Indoor Chicken and Vegetable Kebabs

SERVES 2

You will need four 12-inch skewers for this recipe. See page 171 for more information about skewers. Although white breast meat can be used, we prefer the juicier, more flavorful dark thigh meat for these kebabs. Whichever you choose, do not mix white and dark meat on the same skewer, since they cook at different rates. If you cannot find baby red potatoes, substitute 2 medium red potatoes (about 10 ounces), scrubbed and cut into 1-inch chunks.

CHICKEN AND MARINADE

- ¼ cup olive oil
- 2 tablespoons minced fresh mint leaves
- ¾ teaspoon minced fresh rosemary or ¼ teaspoon dried
- 2 medium garlic cloves, minced or pressed through a garlic press (about 2 teaspoons)
- 1 teaspoon grated zest plus 1 tablespoon juice from 1 lemon
- ½ teaspoon salt
- Pinch ground black pepper
- 12 ounces boneless, skinless chicken thighs (about 3 thighs), trimmed and cut into 1½-inch chunks

VEGETABLES

- 12 baby red potatoes (about 10 ounces), scrubbed (see note)
- 1 tablespoon olive oil
- ¼ teaspoon salt
- Pinch ground black pepper
- 1 red, yellow, or orange bell pepper, stemmed, seeded, and cut into 1-inch pieces
- 3 medium shallots, peeled, root end left intact, and quartered

1. FOR THE CHICKEN AND MARINADE: Whisk the olive oil, mint, rosemary, garlic, lemon zest, salt, and pepper together in a medium bowl. Transfer 2 tablespoons of the marinade to an airtight container, stir in the lemon juice, and set aside. Add the remaining marinade to a large zipper-lock bag along with the chicken. Seal shut, toss to coat, and refrigerate for at least 2 hours and up to 24 hours. (If you marinate the chicken for more than 2 hours, refrigerate the reserved marinade until you are ready to cook the chicken; bring to room temperature before using.)

2. Adjust an oven rack 5 inches from the broiler element and heat the broiler. Line a broiler-pan bottom with foil and cover with the broiler-pan top; coat the broiler-pan top with nonstick cooking spray.

3. FOR THE VEGETABLES: Toss the potatoes with the oil, salt, and pepper in a microwave-safe bowl. Cover tightly with plastic wrap. Microwave on high until the potatoes begin to soften, 3 to 5 minutes, shaking the bowl (without removing the plastic) to toss the potatoes halfway through. Let the potatoes cool slightly.

4. Using four 12-inch metal skewers, thread each skewer with 1 piece of pepper, 1 potato, 1 shallot quarter, and 1 cube of meat. Repeat this sequence two more times.

5. Broil until the meat and vegetables are spotty brown, 8 to 10 minutes. Flip the kebabs and continue to broil until spotty brown on the second side, about 5 minutes longer. Transfer the kebabs to a platter, pour the reserved marinade over the kebabs, tent loosely with foil, and let sit for 5 minutes. Serve.

Tortilla Casserole

THERE IS A CLASSIC MEXICAN CASSEROLE called *chilaquiles* in which tortillas are layered with sauce, chicken, and vegetables—think of it as Mexican lasagna. Like lasagna, this dish can take a long time to assemble and makes enough to fill a 13 by 9-inch baking dish. We wanted to simplify the classic recipe and turn it into a quick weeknight skillet dinner for two.

We first browned boneless, skinless chicken breasts in a skillet and then set them aside while we worked on the sauce. We cooked shallot and garlic with chipotle chile in adobo sauce, which lent the dish smokiness and heat, and then added chicken broth to form the base of the sauce. Instead of using tortillas—which, we discovered, became soggy in the sauce—we turned to store-bought tortilla chips. We stirred half of the tortilla chips into the sauce, nestled in the chicken breasts, and simmered the mixture until the chicken was cooked through and the tortilla chips broke down and thickened the sauce. We then shredded the chicken and stirred it back into the sauce, along with shredded cheese, chopped tomato, cilantro, and the remaining tortilla chips. The sauce coated the newly added tortilla chips just enough to moisten them, while at the same time enabling them to keep some of their texture and crunch.

Lastly, we topped the casserole with more shredded cheese and broiled it briefly to melt the cheese quickly but not dry out the casserole. To bring a little color to the finished dish, we added a sprinkling of fresh cilantro.

Skillet Tortilla Casserole

SERVES 2

Monterey Jack can be substituted for the cheddar if desired. For a spicier dish, add the greater amount of chipotle chile. In step 2, season the chicken only lightly with salt, as some brands of tortilla chips can be quite salty. Serve with sour cream. If you don't have an ovensafe skillet, you can transfer the casserole to a baking dish before broiling.

- 2 boneless, skinless chicken breasts (5 to 6 ounces each), trimmed
- Salt and ground black pepper
- 2 tablespoons vegetable oil
- 1 medium shallot, minced (about 3 tablespoons)
- 2 medium garlic cloves, minced or pressed through a garlic press (about 2 teaspoons)
- 1–2 teaspoons minced chipotle chile in adobo sauce (see note)
- 1½ cups low-sodium chicken broth
- 5 ounces tortilla chips, broken into 1-inch pieces (about 5 cups)
- 1 medium ripe tomato, cored, seeded, and chopped medium
- 4 ounces sharp cheddar cheese (about 1 cup), shredded
- 2 tablespoons minced fresh cilantro leaves

1. Adjust an oven rack to 5 inches from the broiler element and heat the broiler.

2. Pat the chicken dry with paper towels and season with salt and pepper. Heat 1 tablespoon of the oil in an ovensafe 10-inch skillet over medium heat until just smoking. Add the chicken and cook until well browned on both sides, about 5 minutes. Transfer to a plate and set aside.

3. Add the remaining 1 tablespoon oil, the shallot, garlic, chipotle, and ¼ teaspoon salt to the skillet and cook over medium heat until fragrant, about 30 seconds. Add the broth and bring to a simmer, scraping up any browned bits. Stir in 2½ cups of the tortilla chips. Nestle the chicken into the broth and chips, cover, and cook over medium-low heat until the thickest part of the breast registers 160 to 165 degrees on an instant-read thermometer, about 10 minutes. Transfer the chicken to a cutting board. When the chicken is cool enough to handle, shred it into bite-sized pieces (see the illustration on page 10).

4. Return the chicken to the skillet along with the tomato, ½ cup of the cheese, and 1 tablespoon of the cilantro. Stir in the remaining 2½ cups tortilla chips until moistened.

5. Sprinkle the remaining ½ cup cheese over the top and broil until golden brown, 5 to 10 minutes. Let cool for 5 minutes. Sprinkle with the remaining 1 tablespoon cilantro and serve.

Sausage with Lentils

FAST-COOKING LEGUMES, LIKE LENTILS, ARE ready within one hour and are a perfect foil to hearty chicken sausage. Because of the meat's assertive flavor, the dish requires few additional ingredients, which minimizes both shopping and preparation time. Moreover, sausages are a great option when cooking for two, because you can buy them either individually from your butcher's case, or in bulk and freeze them in twos.

We tried a wide range of readily available chicken sausages, including apple and sage, hot and sweet Italian, and lemon and thyme. Italian chicken sausages were the most widely available in our local markets, so we decided to call for them in our recipe. As for cooking the sausages, we simply browned them in a skillet and transferred them to a plate while we focused on the lentils.

Glossy green lentils du Puy were our lentil of choice. Their firm texture—they retain their shape better than other lentils—and hearty flavor are ideal when paired with sausage. For the fullest flavor, we simmered them in diluted chicken broth flavored with shallot and thyme. In 35 minutes, the lentils were just shy of tender—the perfect state.

We then nestled the sausages into the lentils to finish cooking. In about eight minutes, the lentils were glossy, the cooking liquid had evaporated, and the sausages were cooked through but still juicy.

To round out the dish, we made a last-minute decision to add chard to our recipe. We cooked the stems with the shallot and stirred in the leaves before nestling the sausages into the lentils. Our final touch was a tablespoon of olive oil for its fruity finish, and fresh lemon juice for brightness.

Sausage with Lentils and Chard

SERVES 2

Lentils du Puy are small, dark-green lentils that hold their shape when cooked. We use sweet Italian chicken sausages in this recipe, but you can substitute your favorite variety.

- **3 tablespoons olive oil**
- **2 sweet Italian chicken sausages (about 8 ounces) (see note)**
- **8 ounces chard (about ½ bunch), stems and leaves separated, stems chopped fine, leaves chopped medium**
- **1 medium shallot, minced (about 3 tablespoons)**
- **1 teaspoon minced fresh thyme leaves**
- **1½ cups low-sodium chicken broth**
- **4 ounces (½ cup) lentils du Puy, picked over and rinsed (see note)**
- **2 teaspoons juice from 1 lemon**
- **Salt and ground black pepper**

1. Heat 1 tablespoon of the oil in a 10-inch skillet over medium-high heat until just smoking. Add the sausages and cook until browned on all sides, about 4 minutes. Transfer to a plate.

2. Add 1 more tablespoon of the oil, the chard stems, shallot, and thyme to the skillet and cook until the chard stems are softened, about 4 minutes.

3. Add the broth and lentils and bring to a simmer, scraping up any browned bits. Reduce the heat to low, cover, and cook, stirring occasionally, until the lentils are mostly tender but still slightly crunchy, about 35 minutes.

4. Stir in the chard leaves, one handful at a time. Nestle the sausages into the lentils and chard, cover, and continue to cook until the lentils are completely tender and the sausage registers 160 to 165 degrees on an instant-read thermometer, 6 to 8 minutes. Transfer the sausages to a cutting board. When the sausages are cool enough to handle, slice on the bias into ½-inch-thick pieces.

5. Stir the lemon juice and the remaining 1 tablespoon oil into the lentils and season with salt and pepper to taste. Arrange the sausages over the lentils and serve.

Stuffed Bell Peppers

STUFFED PEPPERS ARE THE PERFECT WEEKnight dinner for two—they are made from pantry ingredients, they come together quickly, and they combine vegetable, starch, and protein all in one dish. We have certainly had more than our share of bad stuffed peppers—a drab green shell crammed with leftovers from the school cafeteria. This recipe is different. We developed a version using ground chicken, based on the classic 1950s-style stuffed pepper, with rice, ground meat, and ketchup.

For peppers that had a tender bite yet retained enough structure to stand up on the plate, we found that a 3-minute dip in boiling water followed by a cooling period worked best—it yielded the perfect balance of structure and chew.

Even with a pepper that's cooked to perfection, everyone knows that the stuffing is the real star of the show in this dish. Our recipe uses long-grain white rice. Sautéed onion and garlic round out the flavors, while tomatoes add a fresh note and some color. Bound together with a little cheese and topped with ketchup, this pepper is not only a model of make-it-from-what-you-have-in-the-pantry simplicity, but it also can be varied easily just by switching a few ingredients.

The first trick to streamlining the technique is to use the boiling water from the blanched peppers to cook the rice. While the peppers cool and the rice cooks, the onions, garlic, and chicken can be sautéed. Then filling and peppers can be assembled and heated through in the oven. The result? Stuffed peppers that take only 45 minutes from start to finish—and that are truly worth eating.

Classic Stuffed Bell Peppers with Chicken

SERVES 2

Choose bell peppers with broad bases that will allow the peppers to stand up on their own. For information about buying ground chicken, see page 3.

- Salt
- 4 medium red, yellow, or orange bell peppers (about 6 ounces each), ½ inch trimmed off the tops, stemmed and seeded
- ½ cup long-grain white rice
- 2 tablespoons olive oil
- 1 medium onion, minced
- 12 ounces ground chicken
- 3 medium garlic cloves, minced or pressed through a garlic press (about 1 tablespoon)
- 1 (14.5-ounce) can diced tomatoes, drained with ¼ cup juice reserved
- 5 ounces Monterey Jack cheese, shredded (about 1¼ cups)
- 2 tablespoons minced fresh parsley leaves
- Ground black pepper
- ¼ cup ketchup

1. Adjust an oven rack to the middle position and heat the oven to 350 degrees. Bring 4 quarts water to a boil in a large pot over high heat.

2. When the water boils, add 1 tablespoon salt and the bell peppers. Cook until the peppers just begin to soften, about 3 minutes. Remove the peppers from the water, allowing any excess water to drain back into the pot. Place the peppers, cut-side up, on a paper towel–lined plate.

3. Return the water to a boil. Add the rice and cook until tender, about 13 minutes. Drain the rice, transfer to a large bowl, and set aside.

4. Meanwhile, heat the oil in a 12-inch skillet over medium-high heat until shimmering. Add the onion and cook, stirring occasionally, until softened, 5 to 7 minutes. Stir in the chicken and cook, breaking it into small pieces, until no longer pink, about 4 minutes. Stir in the garlic and cook until fragrant, about 30 seconds. Transfer the mixture to the bowl with the rice. Stir in the tomatoes, 1 cup of the cheese, and the parsley. Season with salt and pepper to taste. Stir the ketchup and reserved tomato juice together in a small bowl.

5. Place the peppers, cut-side up, in an 8-inch-square baking dish (or a shallow casserole of a similar size). Divide the filling evenly among the peppers. Spoon about 2 tablespoons of the ketchup mixture over each filled pepper, then sprinkle each with 1 tablespoon of the remaining cheese. Bake until the cheese is browned and the filling is heated through, about 30 minutes. Serve.

VARIATION

Stuffed Bell Peppers with Currants and Feta Cheese

Follow the recipe for Classic Stuffed Bell Peppers with Chicken through step 3, adding 1 tablespoon minced or grated fresh ginger, 1 teaspoon garam masala, and ¼ cup currants with the garlic in step 4. Substitute feta cheese for the Monterey Jack. Omit the ketchup mixture.

14
DRESSING UP CHICKEN

Dressing Up Chicken

CHICKEN HAS A REPUTATION FOR BEING SIMPLE and straightforward fare—we tend to think of it as a quick weeknight dish or perhaps as part of a homey and satisfying casserole. But chicken is well suited to an endless variety of preparations and flavors, and with a little extra time and ingredients you can dress up chicken for a special occasion or meal.

Dressing up chicken doesn't need to take hours of preparation, however. We focused first on Coq au Vin (page 357), a restaurant classic known as a *fricassee,* which is a dish that is part sauté, part stew. Chicken parts are browned and then stewed along with mushrooms, onions, and a boldly flavored sauce for a refined yet uncomplicated meal. We then turned our attention to some classic special-occasion dishes such as Chicken Piccata (page 359), Chicken Marsala (page 360), and Chicken Saltimbocca (page 362). These dishes are also restaurant favorites that can translate easily to the home kitchen. They each call for thin chicken cutlets, and we found that slicing a chicken breast in half horizontally and gently pounding the halves to a ¼-inch thickness was the best way to ensure uniform cutlets that cooked quickly and evenly. Cutlets this thin need just a few minutes to cook through, so the majority of your time can be spent preparing the sauce. The pan sauces that accompany these dishes are what define them, and each one is packed with flavorful ingredients that make it stand out from the crowd.

When you do have a little extra time to spend on dinner, we also offer a variety of dishes that call for slightly more involved or unique preparations, making them perfect for an intimate dinner gathering. For example, breading and stuffing chicken makes for an attractive presentation, but it is also a time-consuming process, making this type of dish ideal for a special occasion. The challenge of our Breaded Stuffed Chicken Breasts (see page 371) was finding the right way to encase the stuffing in the chicken, in order to prevent it from leaking out and making a mess. By butterflying boneless, skinless chicken breasts, we achieved the perfect shape for rolling up the chicken around the filling. With a short stay in the refrigerator, the chicken bundle edges sealed together, making it easy to flour and coat the chicken. Finally, we opted to bake the chicken rather than fry it, producing a crunchy, evenly browned coating every time.

We also developed a recipe for Chicken with Parmesan Risotto (page 369). Risotto is a dish fit for company, and our goal was to figure out how to incorporate chicken in an elegant presentation that was complex and flavorful. This meant we were not going to simply toss in shredded chicken. Instead, we chose to brown bone-in, skin-on chicken pieces, and then remove them from the pot and finish them in the oven while we built the risotto in the same pot, utilizing the flavorful fond as our base for the rich creamy risotto. We then sliced the chicken off the bone and shingled it on top of the risotto for an attractive presentation.

Here you'll also find a modern favorite, Chicken Biryani (page 376). Because this dish employs slightly more time-consuming techniques, it isn't ideal for a Tuesday night dinner. But with just a little more time on your hands, you can create a meal that's sure to impress.

Finally, we turned to the whole bird. Since whole roast chickens are usually reserved for family-style meals and regarded as simple fare, we turned to Cornish game hens for dressing up whole birds. These small birds are the perfect size for individual servings, so each guest gets their own bird. We stuff and then roast the hens, brushing them several times with a balsamic glaze for a flavorful, crisp skin that makes this dish ideal for entertaining.

Chicken Fricassee

THE NAME OF THIS DISH COMES FROM AN old French word, *fricasser* (to fry), but the dish fricassee is a bit confusing. It is often mistaken for a sauté (where no liquid is included in the cooking) or a stew (where the meat is simmered in liquid for the entire process). But in a fricassee, the meat, usually chicken, is sautéed in butter or sometimes oil before being stewed with vegetables. The meat, carved into pieces before cooking, is served surrounded by the vegetables, along with a pan sauce bound with egg yolks and cream. In other words, it's exactly in between the two, neither sauté nor stew—it's a fricassee. When made properly, this dish is meaty, rich, and satisfying. Unfortunately, we've had versions where the sauce is thin and insipid and the chicken is dry despite being cooked in a lot of liquid. For such a simple dish, there is a lot of room for improvement.

First taking a glance at our array of authentic fricassee recipes, we noticed a few things they had in common. First, they all use a whole chicken cut into pieces. Second, each recipe starts by browning the chicken in fat, then adding liquid to finish the dish as a stew. Finally, the resulting sauce is finished with an egg yolk liaison, or beaten egg yolks with heavy cream. For this dish, these three characteristics had to be put to the test.

We first addressed the issue of the chicken itself. Since we like a choice of white or dark meat, we prefer chicken parts (such as thighs or breasts). You can use skinless chicken parts if you like, but we suggest chicken parts with the skin on, as the skin helps to contribute flavor to the sauce from the browning process.

Next, we focused on technique. With the basic model in place (brown the chicken in butter or oil, then add liquid and cook), we started by browning our chicken in vegetable oil, as early tests revealed that the chicken burned in places when browned in butter. We next tested the stewing liquid. Many traditional French recipes simmer the chicken in equal amounts of chicken stock and white wine. Tasters judged this sauce too acidic, a result of the generous amount of wine, we reasoned. For our next version, we cut out the wine and used chicken broth only, but the sauce tasted too flat. A bit of wine was definitely in order. Adding the wine back in incremental amounts, we found that ½ cup of dry white wine with 1½ cups of chicken broth yielded the right balance of meaty richness and bright flavors. To this liquid base we added our vegetable garnish. We tested carrots, celery, mushrooms, pearl onions, yellow onions, shallots, garlic, and all combinations of the above. Our favorite grouping was onions and

Glazed Carrots

SERVES 4

We like using a nonstick skillet here because it makes cleanup a breeze; however, a regular 12-inch skillet will also work. If you don't have a lid that fits your skillet, use a baking sheet or cover the skillet with a large sheet of foil and crimp it carefully around the edge of the skillet.

- **1 pound carrots (about 6 medium), peeled and sliced ¼ inch thick on the bias (see the illustration at right)**
- **½ cup low-sodium chicken broth**
- **3 tablespoons sugar**
- **Salt**
- **1 tablespoon unsalted butter**
- **2 teaspoons juice from 1 lemon**
- **Ground black pepper**

1. Bring the carrots, broth, 1 tablespoon of the sugar, and ½ teaspoon salt to a simmer, covered, in a 12-inch nonstick skillet over medium-high heat. Reduce the heat to medium and cook until the carrots are almost tender when pierced with the tip of a paring knife, about 5 minutes. (Be careful not to let the knife penetrate all the way through the carrots as it can damage the nonstick surface.)

2. Uncover, increase the heat to high, and simmer rapidly until the liquid is reduced to about 2 tablespoons, 1 to 2 minutes.

3. Stir the butter and the remaining 2 tablespoons sugar into the skillet and continue to cook, stirring frequently, until the carrots are completely tender and the glaze is light gold, about 3 minutes. Off the heat, stir in the lemon juice, season with salt and pepper to taste, and serve.

SLICING CARROTS ON THE BIAS

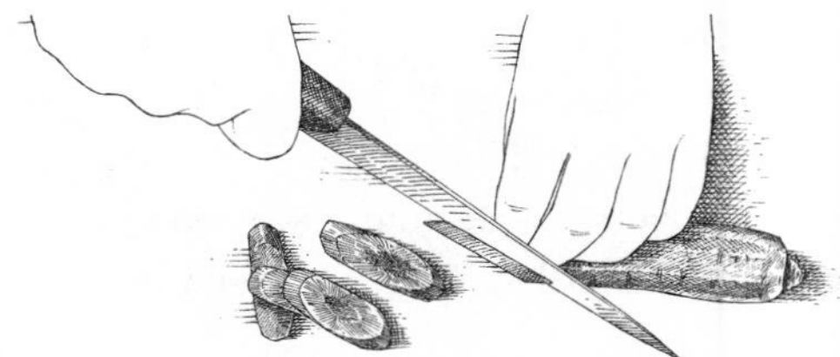

Cutting carrots on the bias is not just for looks (although they do look prettier this way). The bias slice ensures that all the pieces are about the same size (roughly ¼ inch thick) so that they will cook quickly and evenly.

mushrooms, with a little minced garlic, thyme, and bay leaves added for flavor.

With our flavors in place, it was time to get the timing down. We browned two batches of chicken, one lightly and the other to a deep golden brown on both sides. The more caramelization in the pan, the richer the sauce, so browning to a deep golden brown is our preference. Once the chicken was nicely browned, we removed it from the pan to cook our garnish. We had planned to caramelize the onion before adding the mushrooms, but with 30 minutes already gone by, we decided to save time by cooking the two vegetables together. From there we added our aromatic flavorings and some flour for thickening, and then we deglazed the pan with white wine and chicken broth. We were now ready to return the chicken to finish cooking.

With the chicken pieces nestled in the stewing liquid, we started our timer. Twenty minutes later the breast meat was perfectly cooked, but the thighs were still undercooked and tough. Another 20 minutes later, the thighs were approaching perfection while the breasts were now dry and overcooked. We were going to have to stagger the timing for the meat going into the pan if we wanted a perfect fricassee. Simple enough; once our stewing liquid was simmering and ready for the chicken, we added only the thighs and cooked them, covered, for 40 minutes. At that point, we added the breast meat and cooked the entire dish for an additional 20 minutes. All the meat was perfectly cooked, and it was time to finish the sauce.

Traditional recipes call for egg yolks and cream to finish this sauce, but we didn't want an extremely rich sauce, and trying to prevent the egg yolks from curdling in the pan seemed too fussy for this simple meal. We omitted the eggs and focused on the cream, adding various amounts to find the perfect balance of richness and meatiness. Tasters were stuck between ⅓ cup and ½ cup cream, some citing the more generous amount as too rich, while others expressing that it was just right. We went with ⅓ cup, knowing we could always add more if necessary. Either way, this chicken fricassee was everything we wanted it to be: rich and deeply flavored. It's essential to serve the fricassee over rice or noodles, or to offer crusty bread to soak up the delicious sauce.

Chicken Fricassee

SERVES 4 TO 6

If using both chicken breasts and legs/thighs, we recommend cutting the breast pieces in half so that each person can have some white meat and some dark meat. The two types of meat do not cook at the same rate; if using both, note that the breast pieces are added partway through the cooking time. Rice, pasta, or crusty bread is a good accompaniment to this saucy dish.

- 4 pounds bone-in, skin-on chicken pieces (split breasts cut in half, drumsticks, and/or thighs), trimmed
- Salt and ground black pepper
- 2 tablespoons vegetable oil
- 2 tablespoons unsalted butter
- 10 ounces white mushrooms, wiped clean and quartered
- 1 medium onion, minced
- 2 medium garlic cloves, minced or pressed through a garlic press (about 2 teaspoons)
- 2 teaspoons minced fresh thyme leaves
- 2 tablespoons unbleached all-purpose flour
- 1½ cups low-sodium chicken broth
- ½ cup dry white wine
- 2 bay leaves
- ⅓ cup heavy cream
- 2 teaspoons juice from 1 lemon
- 2 tablespoons minced fresh parsley leaves

1. Pat the chicken dry with paper towels and season with salt and pepper. Heat the oil in a large Dutch oven over medium-high heat until just smoking. Brown half of the chicken on both sides, 5 to 8 minutes per side, reducing the heat if the pan begins to scorch. Transfer the chicken to a plate, leaving the fat in the pot. Return the pot with the fat to medium-high heat and repeat with the remaining half of the chicken; transfer the chicken to the plate.

2. Pour off all of the fat from the pot, add the butter, and return to medium-high heat until melted. Add the mushrooms, onion, and ¼ teaspoon salt and cook, stirring occasionally, until the liquid released by the mushrooms evaporates and the mushrooms and onion are lightly

browned, 8 to 10 minutes. Stir in the garlic and thyme and cook until fragrant, about 30 seconds. Stir in the flour and cook for 1 minute. Whisk in the broth, wine, and bay leaves, scraping up any browned bits.

3. Nestle the chicken, along with any accumulated juices, into the pot and bring to a simmer. Cover, turn the heat to medium-low, and simmer until the chicken is fully cooked and tender, about 20 minutes for the breasts (160 to 165 degrees on an instant-read thermometer) or 1 hour for the thighs and drumsticks (170 to 175 degrees on an instant-read thermometer). (If using both types of chicken, simmer the thighs and drumsticks for 40 minutes before adding the breasts.)

4. Transfer the chicken to a serving dish, tent loosely with foil, and let rest while finishing the sauce. Remove and discard the bay leaves. Skim as much fat as possible off the surface of the sauce and return to a simmer until the sauce has thickened slightly, 4 to 6 minutes. Off the heat, stir in the cream, lemon juice, and parsley. Season with salt and pepper to taste. Pour the sauce over the chicken and serve.

Coq au Vin

THIS CLASSIC FRICASSEE OF CUT-UP CHICKEN is cooked in a red wine sauce and finished with a garnish of bacon, tiny glazed pearl onions, and sautéed mushrooms. At its best, coq au vin is hugely tasty, the acidity of the wine rounded out by rich, salty bacon and sweet, caramelized onions and mushrooms. The chicken soaks up those same dark, compelling flavors. We set about creating a recipe that would satisfy our appetite for a really great coq au vin.

We started out by cooking and tasting a number of recipes from French cookbooks. As we cooked, we noticed that the recipes fell into two categories: those that were simple and rustic in character, and those that were a bit more complicated but promised a more refined dish. The recipes in the first category were versions of a straightforward brown fricassee. Tasting these simpler versions, we recognized them as the serviceable renditions of recent memory: The sauces were good but not extraordinary; the chicken tasted mostly like chicken, without absorbing additional flavors. In short, the recipes weren't special enough to merit the time they demanded.

We moved on to testing a handful of much more complicated recipes. One of them, also a brown fricassee, was a two-day affair with an elaborate sauce. The recipe began by combining red wine with veal stock and browned vegetables and reducing this mixture by about half. The chicken was then browned and the pan deglazed with the reduced wine mixture. Once the chicken was cooked, the sauce was strained, bound first with beurre manié (a paste of mashed butter and flour) and then with a bit of chicken liver pureed with heavy cream, and finished with flambéed cognac.

Although this particular recipe was built on the same basic model as the others, the resulting dish was in a whole different league. It was what a good coq au vin ought to be—the sauce was beautifully textured, clean-flavored, and rich without being heavy or murky. The chicken was drenched in flavor. Though we were able to make it in just one day instead of two, the recipe unquestionably demanded more time, more last-minute fussing, and a lot more dishes (in addition to a blender) than the other recipes we'd made.

In trying to simplify this recipe, two techniques stood out when we compared it with the others. First, our working recipe bound the sauce differently, using a beurre manié and chicken liver rather than sprinkling the meat or vegetables with flour at the beginning. This recipe also used all chicken legs instead of both legs and breasts, which is traditional.

We first tested a coq au vin bound with beurre manié and compared it with one in which the vegetables were sprinkled with flour. We liked the streamlined method of sprinkling the flour over the vegetables to give the sauce some viscosity, but felt that the richness of the butter in the beurre manié was missing in this leaner sauce. To make our sauce richer, we whisked cold butter into the finished sauce, which rounded out the flavors with the added benefit of thickening the sauce.

Traditionally an entire bird is used in coq au vin,

so when we tasted the version that used legs only, many tasters missed the white meat. Other tasters felt that all dark meat made sense for gauging the cooking time, since white meat and dark meat cook at a different rate. The bottom line: Use the cuts you like. As long as the thighs and legs get a head start before the breasts are added to the pot, the end result is just as good either way.

Having determined that sprinkling flour on the vegetables and finishing the sauce with butter were two important keys to the success of this dish, we ran some final tests to find out if the addition of cognac, chicken liver, or tomato paste improved the sauce enough to merit the extra trouble. Only tomato paste made the cut, as it's easy to whisk in and adds extra body and flavor.

Coq au Vin

SERVES 4 TO 6

Regular bacon can be substituted for the thick-cut. Use any $10 bottle of fruity, medium-bodied red wine such a Pinot Noir, Côtes du Rhône, or Zinfandel. If using both chicken breasts and legs/thighs, we recommend cutting the breast pieces in half so that each person can have some white meat and some dark meat. The two types of meat do not cook at the same rate; if using both, note that the breast pieces are added partway through the cooking time. Serve with buttered egg noodles.

- **6 ounces thick-cut bacon (about 5 slices), chopped medium (see note)**
- **Vegetable oil, as needed**
- **4 pounds bone-in, skin-on chicken pieces (split breasts cut in half, drumsticks, and/or thighs), trimmed**
- **Salt and ground black pepper**
- **10 ounces white mushrooms, wiped clean and quartered**
- **5 ounces frozen pearl onions, thawed (about 2 cups)**
- **1 tablespoon tomato paste**
- **2 medium garlic cloves, minced or pressed through a garlic press (about 2 teaspoons)**
- **3 tablespoons unbleached all-purpose flour**
- **1 (750-milliliter) bottle medium-bodied red wine (about 3 cups; see note)**
- **2½ cups low-sodium chicken broth**
- **1 teaspoon minced fresh thyme leaves or ¼ teaspoon dried**
- **2 bay leaves**
- **2 tablespoons unsalted butter**
- **2 tablespoons minced fresh parsley leaves**

1. Fry the bacon in a large Dutch oven over medium heat until crisp, 5 to 7 minutes. Transfer the bacon to a paper towel–lined plate, leaving the fat in the pot. (You should have about 2 tablespoons fat; if necessary, add vegetable oil to equal 2 tablespoons.)

2. Pat the chicken dry with paper towels and season with salt and pepper. Return the pot with the bacon fat to medium-high heat until just smoking. Brown half of the chicken on both sides, 5 to 8 minutes per side, reducing the heat if the pan begins to scorch. Transfer the chicken to a plate, leaving the fat in the pot. Return the pot with the fat to medium-high heat and repeat with the remaining half of the chicken; transfer the chicken to the plate.

3. Pour off all but 1 tablespoon fat from the pot. (Add additional oil to equal 1 tablespoon, if needed.) Add the mushrooms and pearl onions and cook over medium heat, stirring occasionally, until lightly browned, about 10 minutes. Stir in the tomato paste and garlic and cook until fragrant, about 30 seconds. Stir in the flour and cook for 1 minute. Whisk in the wine, broth, thyme, and bay leaves, scraping up any browned bits.

4. Nestle the chicken, along with any accumulated juices, into the pot and bring to a simmer. Cover, turn the heat to medium-low, and simmer until the chicken is fully cooked and tender and the thickest part of the breasts registers 160 to 165 degrees (about 20 minutes) and the thickest part of the thighs and drumsticks registers 170 to 175 degrees (about 1 hour) on an instant-read thermometer. (If using both types of chicken, simmer the thighs and drumsticks for 40 minutes before adding the breasts.)

5. Transfer the chicken to a serving dish, tent loosely with foil, and let rest while finishing the sauce. Remove and discard the bay leaves. Skim as much fat as possible off the surface of the sauce and return to a simmer until the sauce is thickened and measures about 2 cups, about 20 minutes. Off the

heat, whisk in the butter, 1 tablespoon at a time, and season with salt and pepper to taste. Pour the sauce over the chicken, sprinkle with the reserved bacon and the parsley, and serve.

Chicken Piccata

CHICKEN PICCATA—SAUTÉED CUTLETS WITH a lemon-caper sauce—is a restaurant classic that translates easily to the home kitchen. We imagined that piccata would be easy to perfect, and it was, after we realized that most recipes miss the point. To begin with, many cookbook authors add extraneous ingredients and thereby ruin the pure simplicity of the dish. The other major problem is blandness. Many recipes contain just a tablespoon of lemon juice and a teaspoon of capers, neither of which provides much flavor. Our goals were simple: to cook the chicken properly and to make a streamlined sauce that really tastes of lemon and capers.

Focusing first on the chicken, we found that most packaged chicken cutlets we bought were shabby at best. The edges were shaggy and uneven, causing them to dry out and toughen before the rest of the cutlet was cooked through. Cutting our own cutlets from boneless, skinless chicken breasts proved to be a better option, and we were able to get an even thickness with a quick pounding, which produced cutlets with a more delicate texture and uniform thinness. Although this step did take a few extra minutes, the results were far superior to any we got with supermarket cutlets.

Many piccata recipes call for flouring or breading the cutlets. As in past tests, we found that floured cutlets browned better and were less likely to stick to the pan. Tasters did not like breaded cutlets; what's the point of developing a crisp crust only to douse it with sauce? We also tried dipping the cutlets in milk as well as in beaten eggs before flouring them. Although the crust was a bit thicker when cooked, tasters felt that there was little advantage to this extra step.

With our chicken tests completed, we turned our attention to the sauce. We wanted a strong lemon flavor that wasn't harsh or overly acidic. We also wanted a sauce that was thick enough to nap the sautéed cutlets. We knew we wanted to deglaze the empty skillet used to cook the chicken to loosen the flavorful browned bits, then reduce the liquid and thicken it.

Most of the recipes we uncovered in our research called for 1 to 2 tablespoons of lemon juice. All of our tasters agreed that these sauces weren't lemony enough. We found that ¼ cup of juice delivered a nice lemon punch. Recipes that instructed the cook to deglaze the hot pan with lemon juice and then simmer the sauce for several minutes tasted flat. Adding the lemon juice toward the end of the cooking time helped keep it tasting fresh.

Our caper testing led us to a similar conclusion. You need to use a lot of capers—we think 2 tablespoons is just right—and they should be added when the sauce is nearly done so that they retain their shape.

We next focused on the liquid for deglazing the pan. Chicken broth and white wine were the most obvious candidates. The wine seemed like a good idea, but it contributed more acid to the sauce, which it did not need. Broth proved a more neutral base for the lemon juice and capers.

Before deglazing the pan, we sautéed some aromatics in the pan drippings. We tested shallot, onion, scallion, and garlic separately. All were fine, although tasters preferred the shallot. Just make sure to watch the pan carefully so that the aromatics don't burn. Add the broth to the pan as soon as the shallot starts to color.

At this point, our sauce was quite good, but we wondered if there was another way to add lemon flavor. In our research we uncovered several recipes that called for lemon slices. We halved a lemon, then cut it into very thin half circles. We tried adding the lemon slices with the lemon juice, but the slices were too crunchy and numerous. For the next test, we used just half a lemon and added the slices with the broth. They simmered for about four minutes and softened considerably. The longer simmering time also allowed oils from the peel to flavor the sauce. We tried replacing the sliced lemon with grated zest, but found the slices more appealing and less work.

The last remaining issue was thickening the

sauce. Some recipes called for a roux (a combination of flour and fat), while others added either softened butter or softened butter mixed with flour once the sauce was cooked. A roux made the sauce too thick. Thickening the sauce at the end seemed more practical. The butter-flour paste gave the sauce a floury taste that dulled the flavors of the lemon and capers. Plain butter proved best. Parsley, added with the butter, gave the sauce some nice color.

Chicken Piccata

SERVES 4

Be careful not to overcook these thin cutlets—they really do cook in just 2½ to 3 minutes. However, if your cutlets are thicker than ¼ inch, you will need to extend the cooking time on the second side by about 1 minute.

- 2 large lemons
- 4 boneless, skinless chicken breasts (5 to 6 ounces each), tenderloins removed and breasts trimmed (see the illustrations on page 6)
- ½ cup unbleached all-purpose flour
- Salt and ground black pepper
- ¼ cup vegetable oil
- 1 small shallot, minced (about 2 tablespoons)
- 1 cup low-sodium chicken broth
- 2 tablespoons small capers, rinsed
- 3 tablespoons unsalted butter
- 2 tablespoons minced fresh parsley leaves

1. Halve 1 lemon pole to pole. Trim the ends from one half and cut it crosswise into ⅛-inch-thick slices; set aside. Juice the remaining half and the whole lemon to obtain ¼ cup juice and reserve.

2. Following the illustrations on page 6, slice each chicken breast in half horizontally and pound each cutlet as directed between two sheets of plastic wrap to a uniform ¼-inch thickness.

3. Place the flour in a shallow dish. Pat the chicken dry with paper towels and season with salt and pepper. Working with 1 chicken cutlet at a time, dredge in the flour, shaking off the excess.

4. Heat 2 tablespoons of the oil in a 12-inch skillet over medium-high heat until just smoking. Add 4 of the cutlets and cook until lightly browned on one side, about 2 minutes. Flip the chicken over and continue to cook until no longer pink, 30 seconds to 1 minute. Transfer the chicken to a plate and tent loosely with foil. Add the remaining 2 tablespoons oil to the skillet and repeat with the remaining 4 cutlets. Transfer to the plate and tent loosely with foil while making the sauce.

5. Add the shallot to the skillet and cook over medium heat until softened, about 2 minutes. Stir in the broth and lemon slices, scraping up any browned bits. Bring to a simmer and cook until the sauce reduces to ⅓ cup, about 4 minutes. Add the reserved lemon juice, the capers, and any accumulated chicken juices and simmer until the sauce reduces again to ⅓ cup, about 1 minute.

6. Off the heat, whisk in the butter, 1 tablespoon at a time, followed by the parsley. Season with salt and pepper to taste. Spoon the sauce over the chicken and serve.

VARIATIONS

Chicken Piccata with Prosciutto

Follow the recipe for Chicken Piccata, adding 2 ounces thinly sliced prosciutto, cut into 1 by ¼-inch pieces, along with the shallot. Cook until the prosciutto is just lightly crisped, about 45 seconds, and proceed with the recipe as directed.

Chicken Piccata with Black Olives

Follow the recipe for Chicken Piccata, adding ¼ cup pitted and chopped black olives along with the lemon juice and capers and proceeding with the recipe as directed.

Chicken Marsala

CHICKEN MARSALA IS A CLASSIC ITALIAN restaurant staple. Ideally, this dish should feature tender chicken cutlets napped in a silky Marsala wine–enriched pan sauce. But, after several disappointing encounters with this dish that involved watery sauces, soggy mushrooms, and pale chicken, we realized that chicken Marsala was in need of a rescue.

While all of the recipes we found listed the same three ingredients—chicken breasts, mushrooms, and Marsala—the cooking methods differed. Some called for simmering the chicken and mushrooms in Marsala, which resulted in flavors that were waterlogged and bland. Others recommended cooking everything in separate pans, creating not only a messy kitchen but a dish with disjointed flavors. Yet others had the cook sauté everything in the same pan, but sequentially. The clear winner turned out to be the classic approach, in which the meat is sautéed first, while the browned bits left in the pan are splashed with wine and enriched with butter to create a sauce. With this decided, we focused on perfecting the sautéed chicken and developing the sauce.

When sautéing, the most important steps include getting the skillet as hot as possible and patting the chicken dry with paper towels before dusting it with a light coating of flour. Using these pointers as a guide, we sautéed with a variety of oils and with butter, finding that vegetable oil was the least likely to burn or splatter.

Our next task was to figure out how to get the mushrooms crisp and brown without burning the drippings left from the sautéed chicken. One way to do this, we thought, would be to add more fat to the pan and scrape the browned bits off the bottom before cooking the mushrooms. We tried adding both fat and flavor by cooking small pieces of pancetta (Italian bacon that has been cured but not smoked) right after the chicken. Just as we thought, the fat rendered from the pancetta prevented the chicken drippings from burning while providing the oil necessary for sautéing the mushrooms—not to mention adding a meaty, pepper-flavored punch to the sauce.

Because several types and grades of Marsala wine can be found on the market, we conducted a taste test before doing any cooking, trying imported and California brands of both the sweet and dry varieties. We favored an imported wine, Sweet Marsala Fine, for its depth of flavor, smooth finish, and reasonable price. By reducing the wine, we found the silky, plush texture we were looking for in the final sauce. Knowing that stock or broth is traditionally added to pan sauces for depth of flavor and body, we tested a variety of broth-to-Marsala ratios. Again and again, tasters preferred a sauce made only from wine, slightly reduced. The stock simply got in the way of the Marsala's distinctive zip.

All we had to do now was round out the final flavors. Lemon juice tempered the Marsala's sweetness, while a garlic clove and a teaspoon of tomato paste rounded out the sauce. Last, we found that half a stick of unsalted butter, whisked in at the end, made for a rich, silky finish.

Chicken Marsala

SERVES 4

Be careful not to overcook these thin cutlets—they really do cook in just 2½ to 3 minutes. However, if your cutlets are thicker than ¼ inch, you will need to extend the cooking time on the second side by about 1 minute. Our wine of choice for this dish is Sweet Marsala Fine, an Italian wine that gives the sauce body, soft edges, and a smooth finish.

- **4 boneless, skinless chicken breasts (5 to 6 ounces each), tenderloins removed and breasts trimmed (see the illustrations on page 6)**
- **½ cup unbleached all-purpose flour**
- **Salt and ground black pepper**
- **¼ cup vegetable oil**
- **2½ ounces (about 3 slices) pancetta, cut into 1 by ⅛-inch pieces**
- **8 ounces white mushrooms, wiped clean and sliced thin**
- **1 medium garlic clove, minced or pressed through a garlic press (about 1 teaspoon)**
- **1 teaspoon tomato paste**
- **1½ cups sweet Marsala (see note)**
- **4 tablespoons (½ stick) unsalted butter**
- **2 tablespoons minced fresh parsley leaves**
- **1½ tablespoons juice from 1 lemon**

1. Following the illustrations on page 6, slice each chicken breast in half horizontally and pound each cutlet as directed between two sheets of plastic wrap to a uniform ¼-inch thickness.

2. Place the flour in a shallow dish. Pat the chicken dry with paper towels and season with salt and pepper. Working with 1 chicken cutlet at a time, dredge in the flour, shaking off the excess.

3. Heat 2 tablespoons of the oil in a 12-inch skillet over medium-high heat until just smoking.

Add 4 of the cutlets and cook until lightly browned on one side, about 2 minutes. Flip the chicken over and continue to cook until no longer pink, 30 seconds to 1 minute. Transfer the chicken to a plate and tent loosely with foil. Add the remaining 2 tablespoons oil to the skillet and repeat with the remaining 4 cutlets. Transfer to the plate and tent loosely with foil while making the sauce.

4. Return the skillet to low heat and add the pancetta. Cook, stirring occasionally, until the pancetta is browned and crisp, about 4 minutes. With a slotted spoon, transfer the pancetta to a paper towel–lined plate to drain.

5. Add the mushrooms to the pan and increase the heat to medium-high. Cook, stirring occasionally, until the liquid released by the mushrooms evaporates and the mushrooms begin to brown, about 8 minutes. Stir in the garlic, tomato paste, and cooked pancetta and cook until fragrant, about 30 seconds.

6. Off the heat, add the Marsala and any accumulated juices from the chicken. Return the pan to medium heat and simmer, scraping up any browned bits, until the sauce is slightly syrupy and reduced to 1¼ cups, about 5 minutes.

7. Off the heat, whisk in the butter, 1 tablespoon at a time, followed by the parsley and lemon juice. Season with salt and pepper to taste. Spoon the sauce over the chicken and serve.

Chicken Saltimbocca

SALTIMBOCCA, A SIMPLE VARIATION ON A basic veal scaloppine, hails from Rome. The traditional version has long been a standard menu item in the trattorias of Italy as well as Italian restaurants in this country. Made by sautéing veal cutlets with prosciutto and sage, this simple yet elegant dish promises, literally, to "jump in your mouth" with its distinctive blend of flavors. Needless to say, when we came across a new chicken spin on this old Italian classic, we were immediately intrigued.

But as happens all too often when cooks start to meddle with a perfectly good thing, most chicken adaptations we found took the dish too far from its roots. Many added unnecessary stuffing, breading, and cheese. Others fiddled with the proportions, allowing a thick slab of prosciutto to share equal billing with the chicken and knock the balance of flavors out of whack. Perfecting chicken saltimbocca, then, would be a matter of avoiding the temptation to overcomplicate the dish with extraneous ingredients and figuring out how to give each of the three key elements—chicken, prosciutto, and sage—its due.

Most of the chicken saltimbocca recipes we came across followed the traditional practice of threading a toothpick through the prosciutto and a whole sage leaf to attach them to the cutlet, then dredging the entire package in flour before sautéing it on both sides. We found this method to be problematic. Flour got trapped in the small gaps where the ham bunched up around the toothpick, leaving sticky, uncooked spots. We wondered if we could skip the flouring and sauté the chicken and prosciutto without any coating. This worked fine for the ham, which crisped nicely without help from the flour. The chicken, on the other hand, browned unevenly and tended to stick to the pan. Surprisingly, flouring only the cutlet—before attaching the ham—proved to be the solution. And by sautéing the cutlet prosciutto-side down first, we were able to keep the flour under the prosciutto from turning gummy.

With our flouring method under control, it was time to turn our attention to proportions. While we liked imported prosciutto for the rich flavor it added to the overall dish, if the slice was too thick, the taste overwhelmed everything else and the ham had trouble staying put; if the slice was too thin, however, it fell apart when separated from another. The ideal slice was just thick enough to hold its shape—about the thickness of two or three sheets of paper. Though some recipes folded the slice to make it fit on the cutlet, this resulted in ham that was only partially crisped and overpowered the chicken with its flavor. We found trimming the ham to fit the cutlet in a single layer worked best on all counts.

While the prosciutto needed to be tamed, the sage flavor needed a boost. In the traditional dish, each cutlet features a single sage leaf (fried in oil before being attached), so that the herbal flavor imparted is very subtle. Perhaps the sage of yore boasted far bigger leaves than are grown today, but this was one aspect of the original that we found lacking. Tethering additional leaves to the cutlet with the toothpick, however, was cumbersome and still resulted in adding flavor only to bites that actually contained sage.

We wanted a more even distribution of herbal flavor. Would infusing the cooking oil with sage be a way to diffuse—and heighten—its flavor? We tossed a handful of leaves into the cooking oil before sautéing the cutlets, removing the herbs before they burned. Tasters, however, detected only a very slight flavor boost in the finished dish. The way to more intense and evenly distributed sage flavor turned out to be as simple as chopping the leaves and sprinkling them over the floured cutlet before adding the ham. The only thing missing was the pretty look of the fried sage leaf. While not necessary, frying enough sage leaves to place on the cooked cutlets is an elegant finishing touch.

The only aspect of the dish we had not yet examined was the toothpick. After skewering prosciutto to 150 cutlets in the course of our testing, we decided enough was enough. What would happen if we just dropped the toothpick from the routine? After flouring the cutlet, sprinkling it with sage, and placing the prosciutto on top, we carefully lifted the bundle and placed it as we had been doing, prosciutto-side down, in the hot oil. Once the edges of the chicken on the bottom had browned, we flipped the cutlet, revealing ham that seemed almost hermetically sealed to the chicken.

A quick pan sauce made from vermouth, lemon juice, butter, and parsley was all we needed to accentuate the perfect balance of flavors. At last we had a dish that was both incredibly simple and elegant.

INGREDIENTS: Dry Vermouth

Though it's often used in cooking, and even more often in martinis, dry vermouth is a potable that is paid very little attention. Its base is a white wine, presumably not of particularly high quality, as evidenced by the relatively low prices of most vermouths. The wine is fortified with neutral grape spirits that hike the alcohol level up a few percentage points to 16 to 18 percent, and it is "aromatized," or infused, with "botanicals" such as herbs, spices, and fruits. Dry vermouth, also called extra-dry vermouth, is imported from France and Italy or is made domestically in California.

We rounded up eight brands and tasted the vermouths straight (chilled) and in simple pan sauces for chicken. Our favorites were Gallo Extra Dry and Noilly Prat Original French Dry.

THE BEST DRY VERMOUTHS

GALLO

NOILLY PRAT

Gallo Extra Dry is floral and fruity, creating a balanced, complex, and smooth pan sauce. Noilly Prat Original French Dry is herbaceous, with faint anise notes, which resulted in a balanced and fresh-tasting pan sauce.

Chicken Saltimbocca

SERVES 4

Although whole sage leaves make a beautiful presentation, they are optional and can be left out of step 3. Make sure to buy prosciutto that is thinly sliced, not shaved; also avoid slices that are too thick, as they won't stick to the chicken. The prosciutto slices should be large enough to fully cover one side of each cutlet.

- 4 boneless, skinless chicken breasts (5 to 6 ounces each), tenderloins removed and breasts trimmed (see the illustrations on page 6)
- ½ cup unbleached all-purpose flour
- Ground black pepper
- 1 tablespoon minced fresh sage leaves, plus 8 large leaves (optional)
- 8 thin prosciutto slices (about 3 ounces) (see note)
- 4 tablespoons olive oil
- 1¼ cups dry vermouth or white wine
- 2 teaspoons juice from 1 lemon
- 4 tablespoons unsalted butter, cut into 4 pieces and chilled
- 1 tablespoon minced fresh parsley leaves
- Salt

1. Following the illustrations on page 6, slice each chicken breast in half horizontally and pound each cutlet as directed between two sheets of plastic wrap to a uniform ¼-inch thickness.

2. Combine the flour and 1 teaspoon pepper in a shallow dish. Pat the chicken dry with paper towels. Dredge the chicken in the flour, shaking off any excess. Lay the cutlets flat and sprinkle evenly with the minced sage. Place 1 prosciutto slice on top of each cutlet, pressing lightly to adhere; set aside.

3. Heat 2 tablespoons of the oil in a 12-inch skillet over medium-high heat until beginning to shimmer. Add the sage leaves (if using) and cook until the leaves begin to change color and are fragrant, 15 to 20 seconds. Using a slotted spoon, transfer the sage to a paper towel–lined plate and set aside. Add 4 of the cutlets to the pan, prosciutto-side down, and cook until lightly browned on one side, about 2 minutes. Flip the chicken over and continue to cook until no longer pink, 30 seconds to 1 minute. Transfer the chicken to a plate and tent loosely with foil. Add the remaining 2 tablespoons oil to the skillet and repeat with the remaining 4 cutlets. Transfer to the plate and tent loosely with foil while making the sauce.

4. Pour off the excess fat from the skillet. Stir in the vermouth, scraping up any browned bits, and simmer until reduced to about ⅓ cup, 5 to 7 minutes. Stir in the lemon juice. Turn the heat to low and whisk in the butter, 1 tablespoon at time. Off the heat, stir in the parsley and season with salt and pepper to taste. Spoon the sauce over the chicken, place a sage leaf on each cutlet (if using), and serve.

Chicken Francese

YOU MIGHT NOT HAVE HEARD OF CHICKEN francese. This simple but refined dish consists of pan-fried chicken cutlets with a light but substantial eggy coating and a bright, lemony sauce. Although its name hints at a rich pedigree—one account claims that Italians once made this dish for Napoleon Bonaparte—there is no classical French or Italian version. Instead, chicken francese is most strongly identified with Italian-American cooking in and around New York City.

Hazy background aside, we found that chicken francese was related to the familiar but loosely defined group of thin-cut chicken (and sometimes veal) dishes that includes scaloppine, parmigiana, Milanese, piccata, and Marsala. But francese also has much in common with a well-known egg-coated breakfast dish: French toast. While many of the other thin-cut chicken dishes are dusted with flour or shrouded in crisp bread crumbs, chicken francese has a soft, rich, eggy coating. The silky lemon sauce nestles into nooks in this soft coating so that each bite reveals just the right balance of chicken, coating, and sauce.

For the chicken, we started with untrimmed and unpounded chicken breast halves. These proved too thick; the egg coating burned before the meat cooked through. Store-bought cutlets (roughly half the thickness of breast halves) were ragged and uneven, causing the edges of the cutlets and the coating to dry out by the time the chicken cooked through. We decided to trim and pound the breast halves into cutlets ourselves to get the evenness and thickness we wanted. By trimming off the tenderloins and slicing the breasts in half horizontally, we were able to get the thickness close to our desired ¼ inch. A few whacks with a meat pounder got us all the way there. Yes, this step did take about five minutes, but the results were far superior to any of the supermarket cutlets.

In all the recipes we could find, some combination of eggs and flour was used to create the soft coating. With the ingredients set, we now turned to the method. Some recipes dredged the chicken in flour first, some in egg first, and still others combined the eggs and flour to create a batter. The batter approach seemed promising because it was simpler, but the resulting coating was tough and rubbery. To solve this problem, we first tried adding baking soda and/or baking powder to the mixture for lightness, but they also added uncharacteristic crispness and an off-flavor. Next we tried using milk instead of water (some batter recipes called for using either). Milk made the coating more tender, but the batter became too thin and dripped off the chicken. It was time to abandon the batter approach and test the other options. In the end, dredging the cutlets in flour, dipping them in beaten egg, and then adding a second coating of flour worked best. This technique guaranteed that the coating would stay put, and, because the final coating consisted of flour (as opposed to bread crumbs, for instance), the finished cutlets were delicate and soft. We wondered if the eggs would benefit from a little milk (something that had worked in our tests with a batter coating). Sure enough, just a couple of tablespoons all but guaranteed a tender—not rubbery—coating.

Tasters enjoyed the sauces made with fresh lemon juice augmented with vermouth and chicken broth. We also tested garlic, onion, and shallot, even though they are not traditional in chicken francese. Only shallot made the cut, providing a mellow, sweet background flavor that balanced the lemon while still letting the citrus lead the way.

Thin, watery sauces saturated the coating, making it peel right off; a thicker sauce, we reasoned, would cling to (but not penetrate) the coating we had worked so hard to attain. Reducing the vermouth, broth, and lemon juice mixture was not sufficient. Finishing the sauce with butter or cornstarch helped to thicken it, but neither was perfect. The best solution was to make a classic roux of flour and butter. The roux was a more reliable thickener than either butter or cornstarch alone.

Cutlets sautéed in butter tasted better than cutlets sautéed in oil, but the butter burned. Adding some oil to the butter raised its smoke point without diluting its flavor impact. By using a nonstick skillet, we could get away with just a tablespoon each of oil and butter for each batch of cutlets. To make sure that the second batch looked as nice as the first, we wiped out the pan between batches. Once the second batch was done and in the oven, we wiped out the pan again and used it to finish our lemon sauce.

At this point we thought we were done. Tasters loved our sauce and the chicken. Maybe they loved the sauce too much—they wanted more of it. At first we thought, no problem, just make more sauce. But additional lemon juice, vermouth, and broth needed additional time to simmer and reduce. By the time the sauce was done, the cutlets were cold and had dried out. The solution was to switch the recipe around and start with the sauce, then cook the chicken. Is it unconventional to make the sauce before cooking the chicken? You bet. But now we could deliver on the promise of this "lost" recipe—quick, fresh chicken cutlets with a soft, eggy coating and a generous amount of silky, well-balanced lemon sauce.

Chicken Francese

SERVES 4

Be careful not to overcook these thin cutlets—they really do cook in just under 4 minutes. However, if your cutlets are thicker than ¼ inch, you will need to extend the cooking time on the second side by about 1 minute. The sauce is very lemony—for less tartness, reduce the amount of lemon juice by about 1 tablespoon.

SAUCE

- 3 tablespoons unsalted butter
- 1 large shallot, minced (about 4 tablespoons)
- 1 tablespoon unbleached all-purpose flour
- 2¼ cups low-sodium chicken broth
- ½ cup dry vermouth or white wine
- ⅓ cup juice from 2 lemons
- Salt and ground black pepper

CHICKEN

- 4 boneless, skinless chicken breasts (5 to 6 ounces each), tenderloins removed and breasts trimmed (see the illustrations on page 6)
- Salt and ground black pepper
- 1 cup unbleached all-purpose flour
- 2 large eggs
- 2 tablespoons milk
- 2 tablespoons unsalted butter
- 2 tablespoons olive oil
- 2 tablespoons minced fresh parsley leaves

1. Adjust an oven rack to the middle position and heat the oven to 200 degrees.

2. FOR THE SAUCE: Melt 1 tablespoon of the butter in a medium nonreactive saucepan over medium heat. Add the shallot and cook, stirring occasionally, until softened, about 2 minutes. Stir

in the flour and cook until light golden brown, about 1 minute. Whisk in the broth, vermouth, and lemon juice and bring to a simmer. Cook, whisking occasionally, until the sauce measures 1½ cups, about 15 minutes. Strain the sauce through a fine-mesh strainer. Return the sauce to the saucepan and set aside, discarding the solids.

3. FOR THE CHICKEN: Following the illustrations on page 6, slice each chicken breast in half horizontally and pound each cutlet as directed between two sheets of plastic wrap to a uniform ¼-inch thickness. Pat the chicken dry with paper towels and season with salt and pepper.

4. Combine the flour, 1 teaspoon salt, and ¼ teaspoon pepper in a shallow dish and whisk the eggs and milk together in a medium bowl. Working with 1 chicken cutlet at a time, dredge in the flour, shaking off the excess, then coat with the egg mixture, allowing the excess to drip off. Finally, coat with the flour again, shaking off the excess. Place the coated chicken in a single layer on a wire rack set over a rimmed baking sheet.

5. Heat 1 tablespoon each of the butter and oil in 12-inch nonstick skillet over medium-high heat until the foaming subsides. Add 4 of the cutlets and cook until lightly browned on one side, 2 to 3 minutes. Flip the chicken over and continue to cook until no longer pink and lightly browned on the second side, about 1 minute. Transfer the chicken to a clean wire rack set over a rimmed baking sheet and keep warm in the oven. Wipe out the skillet with paper towels. Add the remaining 1 tablespoon each of the butter and oil to the skillet and repeat with the remaining cutlets, then transfer to the oven. Wipe out the skillet with paper towels.

6. TO FINISH THE SAUCE AND SERVE: Transfer the sauce to the now-empty skillet and cook over medium-low heat until warmed, about 2 minutes. Whisk in the remaining 2 tablespoons butter, 1 tablespoon at a time, and season with salt and pepper to taste. Transfer 4 of the chicken cutlets to the skillet, turn to coat with sauce, then transfer each serving (2 cutlets) to individual plates. Repeat with the remaining cutlets. Spoon 2 tablespoons of the sauce over each serving and sprinkle with the parsley. Serve, passing the remaining sauce separately.

VARIATION

Chicken Francese with Tomato and Tarragon

Follow the recipe for Chicken Francese, adding 1 sprig fresh parsley and 1 sprig fresh tarragon to the sauce along with the broth, vermouth, and lemon juice in step 2. Add 1 medium tomato, seeded and chopped medium, to the sauce before spooning it over each serving in step 6. Substitute fresh tarragon for the parsley.

Chicken with 40 Cloves of Garlic

POULET À QUARANTE GOUSSES D'AIL, OR chicken with 40 cloves of garlic, is a classic Provençal dish that entered the American culinary consciousness several decades ago, when our interest in French gastronomy was sparked. But since its introduction, chicken with 40 cloves of garlic has failed to make it onto many dinner tables or into many cooks' repertoires—and not without reason.

Recipes for chicken with 40 cloves of garlic involve a whole or cut-up chicken. Sometimes the chicken is browned, sometimes not. It is put into a pot along with raw garlic cloves (most often unpeeled), some liquid (usually wine and/or chicken broth), and sometimes onions and other aromatic vegetables and herbs, and then the lot is cooked, covered, for an hour or more. The garlic becomes soft and spreadable, but its flavor is spiritless, not like that of sweet, sticky roasted garlic. With such prolonged cooking, the chicken becomes tender, but the breast meat takes on a dry, chalky quality, and the flavor of the chicken in general is vapid, as if it has been washed out into the liquid. In addition, as cannot be helped in moist-heat cookery, the chicken skin is soggy, flabby, and wholly unappealing, even if the chicken has first been browned.

A diagnostic test of several recipes found all tasters in agreement. We all sought richer, more concentrated flavors like those imparted by roasting, not braising. We wanted the chicken browned, full-flavored, and crisp-skinned and the garlic browned, sweet, and nutty. And we wanted a savory sauce to unite the elements.

Our first decision was to use a cut-up chicken rather than a whole bird, because it cooks faster and more evenly. We brined the chicken, browned it in a large skillet, tossed in the unpeeled garlic cloves from three medium heads (42 cloves, so pretty true to the name), and slipped the skillet into a hot oven. About 12 minutes later, the chicken was fully cooked; we removed the chicken pieces, leaving the garlic in the skillet, and made a pan sauce with the drippings, wine, chicken broth, and butter. The gravest offense of this attempt came from the garlic: The cloves were far from done. Although they were browned, they were neither creamy nor spreadable, and they had a raw, fiery flavor. The second problem was that the chicken, though flavorful and crisp-skinned, seemed divorced from the other elements. Third, the sauce lacked depth and tasted of neither chicken nor garlic. Despite its demerits, this technique showed enough promise that we were compelled to pursue it.

We grappled with the garlic first. We knew that to soften and gain color, the cloves would have to roast in dry heat, but they would require considerably more time to roast than was built into the pan-roasting technique. Hence, they would need to be at least partially roasted by the time they joined the chicken. Some tests later, we arrived at roasting the garlic cloves, tossed with a little olive oil, salt, and pepper, in a small baking dish for 40 minutes in a 400-degree oven. For the first 30 minutes, they cooked under foil to speed things along. For the final 10 minutes, they went uncovered to finish browning. At this point, the garlic cloves were soft, sweet, and mellow, but could still withstand some additional cooking with the chicken and sauce. Because the garlic could be roasted while the chicken was being brined and browned, this step did not add time to the recipe.

We then focused on refining the cooking technique. In a braise, the chicken cooks half-submerged in simmering liquid and an exchange of flavors thereby occurs, to the benefit of both the chicken and the liquid that becomes the sauce. This made us decide to modify the pan-roasting technique. After we browned the chicken, we poured off the rendered fat, added chicken broth and dry vermouth (we came to use vermouth because it is herbaceous, slightly sweet, and more flavorful than most white wines of the same price), added the roasted garlic cloves, returned the chicken skin-side up, and then put the skillet in the 400-degree oven from which the garlic had emerged. Things were slightly improved with this pan-roasting/braising technique. The sauce had better flavor (although it was still mousy, especially in texture), and the chicken seemed to be more a part of the dish. The skin, however, had turned soggy from the moisture.

To counter the effects of the moisture, we tried increasing the oven temperature to 450 degrees. This produced acceptably crisp skin. The ultimate solution, however, was a quick blast of broiler heat, which crisped the skin very nicely in less than five minutes. Because cooks with drawer-type gas broilers might find this step inconvenient, if not impossible, we made it optional. We were nonetheless pleased with the results of this hybrid pan-roasting/braising technique.

Now a different issue came into play. The brined chicken, cooked in the liquid that eventually becomes the sauce, seemed to exude juices that resulted in an overseasoned sauce, even for those tasters who love salt. We pulled back on the salt in the brine until we were using only ¼ cup of table salt per 2 quarts of water. Unsure that this small amount was of any benefit to the dish as a whole, we compared it with a batch made with unbrined chicken. Even this weak brine improved the flavor and juiciness of the cooked chicken.

Finally, we worked on the flavor of the sauce. Inspired by those recipes that included onions, we roasted some shallots—milder in flavor than onions—with the garlic cloves to see if they would affect the flavor of the sauce. Indeed they did: The sauce tasted fuller and rounder. Some tasters even found the roasted shallots to be good eating. Herbs—thyme, rosemary, and bay leaves—all had pleasing effects on the flavor of the sauce, offering depth and complexity.

One recipe we saw recommended mashing a few of the garlic cloves and adding them back to the sauce. We squeezed the cloves from their skins into a bowl and then mashed them to a paste with a rubber spatula. What an extraordinarily good idea. The garlic paste endowed the sauce with the velvety texture of a well-made gravy, and the sauce was now richly flavored with garlic in addition to the chicken and wine. Last, several tablespoons of butter to enrich the sauce met with applause.

Chicken with 40 Cloves of Garlic

SERVES 4 TO 6

Try not to purchase heads of garlic that contain enormous cloves; if unavoidable, increase the foil-covered baking time to 40 to 45 minutes so that the largest cloves soften fully. A large Dutch oven can be used in place of a skillet. If using kosher chicken, skip the brining process. To use kosher salt in the brine, see page 12 for conversion information and more tips on brining. Serve the dish with slices of crusty baguette; you can dip the bread into the sauce and use the roasted garlic cloves as a spread.

- **Table salt**
- **4 pounds bone-in, skin-on chicken pieces (split breasts cut in half, drumsticks, and/or thighs) (see note)**
- **Ground black pepper**
- **3 medium garlic heads, outer papery skins removed, cloves separated and unpeeled**
- **2 medium shallots, peeled and quartered**
- **3 tablespoons olive oil**
- **2 sprigs fresh thyme**
- **1 sprig fresh rosemary**
- **2 bay leaves**
- **¾ cup low-sodium chicken broth**
- **¾ cup dry vermouth or white wine**
- **2 tablespoons unsalted butter**

1. Adjust an oven rack to the middle position and heat the oven to 400 degrees. Dissolve ¼ cup salt in 2 quarts cold water in a large container. Submerge the chicken in the brine, cover, and refrigerate for 30 minutes. Remove the chicken from the brine, rinse well, and pat dry with paper towels. Season the chicken with pepper.

2. Meanwhile, toss the garlic and shallots with 1 tablespoon of the oil in a 9-inch pie plate (or a shallow dish of similar size) and season with salt and pepper. Cover tightly with foil and roast until softened and beginning to brown, about 30 minutes, shaking the dish after 15 minutes to toss the contents (the foil can be left on during tossing). Uncover, stir, and continue to roast, uncovered, until browned and fully tender, about 10 minutes longer, stirring once or twice. Remove from the oven and increase the oven temperature to 450 degrees.

3. Tie the thyme, rosemary, and bay leaves together with kitchen twine; set aside. Heat the remaining 2 tablespoons oil in an ovensafe 12-inch skillet over medium-high heat until just smoking. Brown half of the chicken on both sides, 5 to 8 minutes per side, reducing the heat if the pan begins to scorch. Transfer the chicken to a plate, leaving the fat in the skillet. Return the skillet with the fat to medium-high heat and repeat with the remaining half of the chicken; transfer the chicken to the plate. Pour off any fat left in the skillet.

4. Add the broth, vermouth, garlic-shallot mixture, and herb bundle to the skillet and bring to a simmer over medium heat, scraping up any browned bits. Nestle the chicken, skin-side up, along with any accumulated juices, into the skillet and bring to a simmer. Transfer the skillet to the oven and roast until the thickest part of the breast registers 160 to 165 degrees and the thickest part of the thighs and drumsticks registers 170 to 175 degrees on an instant-read thermometer, 10 to 12 minutes. If desired, increase the heat to broil and broil to crisp the skin, 3 to 5 minutes.

5. Transfer the chicken to a serving dish, tent loosely with foil, and let rest while finishing the sauce. Using a slotted spoon, reserve 10 to 12 garlic cloves in a small bowl and set aside. Scatter the remaining garlic cloves and shallots around the chicken and discard the herbs. When the reserved garlic is cool enough to handle, squeeze the garlic from the skins into a bowl, then mash the garlic to a paste with a rubber spatula. Discard the skins.

6. Whisk the garlic paste into the sauce in the skillet and simmer over medium-high heat until incorporated, about 2 minutes. Off the heat, whisk in the butter, 1 tablespoon at a time, and season with salt and pepper to taste. Transfer the sauce to a serving dish and serve with the chicken.

Chicken with Risotto

RISOTTO IS A CLASSIC PREPARATION OF Italian rice in which the rice is simmered—along with judicious amounts of wine and broth—and stirred until the starch in the rice is transformed into a velvety, creamy sauce that coats the grains of rice, which are cooked to an al dente texture. It is rich, satisfying, and perfect for company. Though it is often served as a side dish or first course, our goal was to incorporate chicken into creamy risotto for an elegant one-dish meal.

Starting with the chicken, we opted for pan-roasting, a restaurant technique in which food is browned on the stovetop in a skillet that is then placed in the oven to finish cooking. However, instead of placing the skillet in the oven, we transferred the chicken to a separate dish to finish cooking in the oven, while we then cooked the risotto in the skillet to take advantage of the fond (browned, caramelized bits) left behind by the chicken. We tested oven temperatures ranging from 375 to 500 degrees and discovered that the highest temperature caused profuse smoking and singed drippings, while temperatures on the lower end meant protracted cooking times. At 450 degrees, however, the skin was handsomely browned and crackling crisp, and the chicken cooked swiftly to an internal temperature of 160 degrees. With our chicken cooked to perfection, we moved on to the risotto.

Risotto is one of the highlights of Italian cooking and, unsurprisingly, myths surrounding it abound. What's more, everyone has a firm opinion in matters of cooking technique and equipment, so we set out to separate fact from fiction and get to the heart of risotto.

Obviously, the rice is the key element to a texturally flawless risotto. We found that medium-grain rice is the best choice, as it provides some starchiness but not too much. But not all medium-grain rice is the same. In our kitchen tests, we found that the risotto technique may be used with non-Italian medium-grain rice, but the finished texture will pale in comparison to risotto made with Italian rice, which provides the best contrast between supple sauce and firm rice. We think Italian rice is a must.

Italian rice comes in four varieties: superfino, fino, semifino, and commune. The top two grades include Arborio (the most widely available), Carnaroli, and Vialone Nano. There are even more varieties, like Baldo and the quick-cooking Poseidone, but they can be difficult to find outside of Italy. In a side-by-side taste test of Arborio, Carnaroli, and Vialone Nano, tasters were split evenly between the Arborio and Carnaroli; those liking firmer rice grains chose Arborio, and those liking softer, creamier rice chose Carnaroli. Vialone was deemed too soft, and it had a pasty texture; the grains lacked a firm center.

Having good-quality rice is only half the battle; cooking it successfully is the other half. After countless batches with minute variations, we were certain about a few points. First, slowly cooking diced onion until it softened and yielded its juices was imperative for the dish's final flavor and texture, while its sweetness lent depth. The next step was sautéing the rice, which prompted its starches to turn translucent—a good visual clue for adding liquid. When we did not cook the rice prior to adding liquid, the risotto was mushy and chalky, and the rice grains lacked their distinctive chew.

Once the rice was sautéed, it was time to add the liquids. The wine must be added before the broth so that the boozy flavor has a chance to cook off. Virtually all risottos are made with a light, dry white wine, although some regional specialties are made with red wine. Risotto made without wine lacks dimension and tastes bland, so don't skip this ingredient.

The recipes we researched offered a wide range of options for broth, from plain water to veal stock. Water didn't impress us, and veal stock is rare in all but the best-provisioned professional kitchen. Straight chicken broth proved too intense, but diluting chicken broth with roughly an equal amount of water was just right—the combination added richness and depth without taking over.

Contrary to conventional wisdom and the instructions in most cookbooks, we discovered that constant stirring is unnecessary. We added half the broth once the wine had cooked off and allowed the rice to simmer for about 10 minutes, or half the cooking time, with little attention. The rice floated freely, individual grains suspended by the bubbling broth. During this period, we stirred the rice infrequently—about every three minutes—to ensure that it was not sticking to the bottom of the pan. Once all the broth was absorbed by the rice, we added more, a half cup at a time. For this period, stirring every minute or so was important; if we did not, the rice stuck to the bottom of the pan.

There is quite a bit of controversy surrounding the doneness of risotto. Some insist it should have a chalky, solid bite, while others feel it should be soft to the core. Tasters expressed individual preferences quite strongly, so you must taste as the rice nears completion and decide for yourself. Generally, we began tasting our rice after about 20 minutes of cooking; you can always cook it longer for a softer texture, but you can never bring back bite.

For the final touch, Parmesan goes in at the very end to preserve its distinctive flavor and aroma. Grated cheese proved best, as it melted almost instantaneously. Because its taste is so prominent, the quality of the cheese is paramount. This is the perfect occasion for buying authentic Parmesan freshly cut from the wheel, which boldly displays its branded trademark on the rind. For the most attractive presentation, we found it best simply to slice the chicken off the bone and shingle it over the risotto before serving.

Chicken with Parmesan Risotto

SERVES 4

Don't worry if you have broth left over once the rice is finished cooking; each brand of rice cooks differently, and we prefer to err on the side of slightly too much broth rather than too little. If you do use all the broth and the rice still has not finished cooking, add hot water. Garnish with shaved Parmesan cheese, if desired.

- 3½ cups low-sodium chicken broth, plus more as needed
- 3 cups water
- 4 bone-in, skin-on split chicken breasts (10 to 12 ounces each), trimmed
- Salt and ground black pepper
- 1 tablespoon olive oil
- 4 tablespoons (½ stick) unsalted butter
- 1 medium onion, minced
- 2 cups Arborio or Carnaroli rice
- 1 cup dry white wine
- 2 ounces Parmesan cheese, grated (about 1 cup)
- 2 tablespoons minced fresh parsley leaves

1. Adjust an oven rack to the lowest position and heat the oven to 450 degrees. Bring the broth and water to a simmer in a medium saucepan over medium-high heat. Reduce the heat to the lowest possible setting to keep the broth warm.

2. Pat the chicken dry with paper towels and season with salt and pepper. Heat the oil in a Dutch oven over medium-high heat until just smoking. Add the chicken, skin-side down, and cook until deep golden, about 5 minutes.

3. Transfer the chicken, skin-side up, to a baking dish and bake until the thickest part of the breast registers 160 to 165 degrees on an instant-read thermometer, 18 to 20 minutes. Tent loosely with foil and let rest until ready to serve.

4. While the chicken bakes, pour off any fat in the Dutch oven, add the butter, onion, and ½ teaspoon salt, and cook over medium heat, stirring occasionally, until softened, 5 to 7 minutes. Add the rice and cook, stirring frequently, until the edges of the grains are transparent, about 4 minutes.

5. Add the wine and cook, stirring frequently and scraping up any browned bits, until the wine is completely absorbed by the rice, about 2 minutes. Add 3 cups of the warm broth and simmer over medium-low heat, stirring infrequently (about every 3 minutes), until the liquid is absorbed and the bottom of the pan is dry, 10 to 12 minutes.

6. Continue to cook, stirring frequently and adding more broth, ½ cup at a time, every 3 to 4 minutes as needed to keep the pan bottom from drying out, until the grains of rice are cooked through but still somewhat firm in the center, 8 to 10 minutes. Off the heat, stir in the Parmesan cheese, season with salt and pepper to taste, and cover until ready to serve.

7. Meanwhile, remove the chicken from the

bones and carve into ½-inch-thick slices (see the illustration on page 10); discard the bones. Add additional warm broth as needed to loosen the risotto. Portion the risotto into warmed shallow bowls, shingle the sliced chicken over the top, and sprinkle with the parsley. Serve.

VARIATIONS

Chicken with Porcini Mushroom Risotto

Follow the recipe for Chicken with Parmesan Risotto, substituting 3 large shallots, minced (about ¾ cup), for the onion. Add ½ ounce dried porcini mushrooms, rinsed and minced, to the pan with the shallots in step 4. Substitute Pecorino Romano cheese for the Parmesan.

Chicken with Spring Vegetable Risotto

Follow the recipe for Chicken with Parmesan Risotto, substituting 1 leek, white and light green parts only, minced and rinsed thoroughly, for the onion and tarragon for the parsley. Snap off the tough ends from 8 ounces asparagus (about ½ bunch) and cut the spears on the bias into ½-inch lengths. In step 6, add the broth as directed. After about 2 minutes, stir in the asparagus and ½ cup frozen peas and continue as directed.

Stuffed Chicken Breasts

CHICKEN BREASTS THAT ARE BREADED AND stuffed with the right filling are a most impressive dish—a true special-occasion entrée. When the breasts are sliced, the filling oozes out into a creamy, tasty sauce and the crust makes a crunchy counterpoint. We wanted to create the ultimate stuffed chicken breasts for the perfect dinner party main course.

Stuffed chicken breasts have three distinct components: the chicken, the filling, and the coating. Typically, the stuffed chicken breast is rolled in a coating, then fried up crisp. However, as was clear from the many recipes we tried, getting the filling to survive cooking without leaking was key. So we started there.

Some recipes call for cutting a slit in the thickest part of the breast and inserting the filling. That was easy, but it was impossible to get the pocket deep enough to accommodate more than a paltry amount of filling, and it became clear that giving the filling any path of egress (even the smallest opening) wasn't a good idea. One false move and the hot filling came streaming out during cooking—a dangerous proposition when frying.

We needed to find a way to encase the filling completely. Some recipes we came across in our research called for pounding the chicken thin, putting the filling on top, then rolling the chicken around it to form a compact package. This method worked much better, but it was hard to pound the chicken thin and wide enough to encase the filling without accidentally tearing the flesh—or leaving awkward ragged edges in the process. Borrowing a trick the test kitchen has used for other recipes, we butterflied the breasts lengthwise first (giving us cutlets twice as wide but half as thick as the original), then pounded them just to make them even. Much better—less pounding meant less damage. Experimenting with various thicknesses, we decided ¼ inch was optimal.

Flattened, our chicken cutlets resembled large teardrops. Following the rolling-and-folding technique used in some recipes, we placed the filling just above the tapered end of the "teardrop" and proceeded as if wrapping a burrito: rolling the tapered end completely over the filling, folding in the sides toward the center, and then continuing to roll up from the tapered end until we had a fairly tight bundle.

We were on the right track, but occasionally the folded-in sides refused to stay put. We quickly diagnosed the problem. The ¼-inch-thick sides, once folded over, were double the thickness of the rest of the bundle. Easy enough: We simply pounded the outer edges of the cutlets a little thinner (⅛ inch) than the rest. Obsessive precision? Yes, we'll admit it. But the foolproof results—no leaks—were worth it. (That said, getting the cutlets to a uniform ¼-inch thickness is almost as reliable.)

Now, with four compact chicken bundles at the ready, we could focus on the exterior. We began the coating process as most recipes do, by using a standard breading procedure: dusting each stuffed chicken breast with seasoned flour, dipping it in beaten egg, and rolling it in bread crumbs. But breading the chicken immediately after stuffing was a hazardous affair: The seam sometimes opened up and, while the filling didn't actually fall out, the entire package became less compact (thus undoing the previous antileak-protection work). We caught a break when, at one point, we happened to leave the unbreaded, uncovered, stuffed chicken in the refrigerator for an hour while we tended to other tasks. We noticed that the edges had begun to stick together, nearly gluing shut. Much sturdier. From then on, we purposely left the stuffed chicken in the refrigerator to set up.

We moved on to the coating. No matter what type of crumbs we used—fresh or dried, coarse or fine—we found that deep-frying gave the chicken a thin, homogeneous quality. This was not the texture we were after. By the time the chicken was fully cooked, the exterior was a hard, tan-colored shell that had to be drained thoroughly to prevent greasiness. We wanted to do away with deep-frying altogether. We tried pan-frying the chicken in a small amount of oil just until the crumbs became delicately crisp. Once the breasts were browned, we finished cooking them to the proper internal temperature in the oven. So far, so good—well, mostly. While the tops and bottoms of the chicken were nicely browned, it was hard to get the sides evenly colored without manhandling the chicken, which often resulted in unraveling.

That's when we made the decision that would finally and effectively transform our chicken into an elegant dinner showpiece: baking our chicken. To achieve a crunchy, golden coating, we tossed fresh bread crumbs, vegetable oil, and salt and pepper onto a baking sheet. The crumbs baked up tasty and crisp. We then simply dredged the chicken rolls in seasoned flour, dipped them in egg, coated them with the browned bread crumbs, and then transferred them to a baking sheet to bake. No more frying, no more skillet, no more spotty browning. The crisp (but not oily) crust was now a perfect foil for the creamy interior.

All we had left to do was to perk up the plain filling. Traditional recipes stuff the chicken with butter or cream cheese spiked with nothing more than parsley. Between the two, tasters preferred the cream cheese for its creaminess and tang. Sautéed onion and garlic provided the rich cheese with welcome savory notes. Once we had the basics down, we used this mixture as a base to host other flavor combinations, like goat cheese and thyme, ham and cheddar, gorgonzola with walnuts and figs, and mushrooms with provolone. Lastly, a teaspoon of Dijon mustard whisked into the egg wash (for coating the chicken) provided another layer of flavor to our chicken bundles.

After batches and batches of mediocre stuffed chicken breasts, we were happy with the outcome—beautifully browned, crisp, stuffed chicken breasts with fragrant, herb-speckled filling. Moreover, these visually appealing chicken breasts can be assembled entirely ahead of time and simply popped into the oven before serving—a surefire way to impress your family and friends.

Breaded Stuffed Chicken Breasts

SERVES 4

While homemade bread crumbs taste best, you can substitute 2 cups panko (Japanese bread crumbs), toasted as directed in the recipe. Don't skimp on the chicken chilling time in step 3, or else the chicken will unravel when breading in step 5. Serve with lemon wedges, if desired.

- 4 boneless, skinless chicken breasts (5 to 6 ounces each), tenderloins removed and breasts trimmed (see the illustrations on page 6)
- Salt and ground black pepper
- 1 recipe filling (see pages 372–374)
- 4–5 slices high-quality white sandwich bread, torn into large pieces (see note)
- 2 tablespoons vegetable oil

½ cup unbleached all-purpose flour
3 large eggs, lightly beaten
1 teaspoon Dijon mustard

1. Adjust an oven rack to the lower-middle position and heat the oven to 300 degrees.

2. Following the illustrations on page 373, butterfly each chicken breast and pound as directed between two sheets of plastic wrap. Pat the chicken dry with paper towels and season with salt and pepper.

3. Place the cutlets, cut-side up, on a clean work surface. Following the illustration on page 373, place a quarter of the filling near the tapered end of the cutlet. Roll the chicken over the filling to form a neat, tight package, pressing on the seam to seal. Repeat with the remaining stuffing and chicken. Refrigerate the chicken, seam-side down, uncovered, to allow the edges to seal further, about 1 hour.

4. Meanwhile, pulse half of the bread in a food processor until coarsely ground, about sixteen (1-second) pulses. Repeat with the remaining half of the bread (you should have about 3½ cups of crumbs). Toss the crumbs with the oil, ⅛ teaspoon salt, and ⅛ teaspoon pepper and spread out over a rimmed baking sheet. Bake the crumbs, stirring occasionally, until golden brown and dry, about 25 minutes. Transfer the crumbs to a shallow dish and let cool to room temperature. Increase the oven temperature to 350 degrees.

5. Combine the flour, ¼ teaspoon salt, and ⅛ teaspoon pepper in a second shallow dish and whisk the eggs and Dijon together in a third shallow dish. Working with 1 chicken roll at a time, dredge in the flour, shaking off the excess, then coat with the egg mixture, allowing the excess to drip off. Finally, coat with the bread crumbs, pressing gently so that the crumbs adhere. (Up to this point, the chicken can be refrigerated in an airtight container for up to 24 hours. Increase the baking time by 5 to 10 minutes.)

6. Place the chicken rolls at least 1 inch apart on a wire rack set over a foil-lined rimmed baking sheet. Bake until the center of the chicken registers 160 to 165 degrees on an instant-read thermometer, 35 to 40 minutes. Let rest for 5 minutes before serving.

Goat Cheese and Thyme Filling

MAKES ENOUGH TO STUFF 4 BONELESS, SKINLESS CHICKEN BREASTS

Parsley or tarragon can be substituted for the thyme.

1 tablespoon unsalted butter
1 small onion, minced
2 teaspoons minced fresh thyme leaves (see note)
1 small garlic clove, minced or pressed through a garlic press (about ½ teaspoon)
3 ounces cream cheese, softened (about ⅓ cup)
2 ounces goat cheese, softened (about ¾ cup)
⅛ teaspoon salt
⅛ teaspoon ground black pepper

1. Melt the butter in a medium skillet over medium heat. Add the onion and cook, stirring occasionally, until well browned, about 10 minutes. Stir in the thyme and garlic and cook until fragrant, about 30 seconds; set aside to cool.

2. Mix the cooled onion mixture, cream cheese, goat cheese, salt, and pepper together until uniform. Spoon the cheese mixture onto the chicken as directed on page 373.

Gorgonzola, Walnut, and Fig Filling

MAKES ENOUGH TO STUFF 4 BONELESS, SKINLESS CHICKEN BREASTS

Two tablespoons dried cherries or cranberries can be substituted for the figs.

1 tablespoon unsalted butter
1 small onion, minced
1 teaspoon minced fresh thyme leaves
1 small garlic clove, minced or pressed through a garlic press (about ½ teaspoon)
2 ounces gorgonzola cheese, crumbled (about ½ cup)
2 ounces cream cheese, softened (about ¼ cup)
¼ cup walnuts, toasted and chopped
3 medium dried figs, chopped (about 2 tablespoons) (see note)

1	tablespoon dry sherry
1/8	teaspoon salt
1/8	teaspoon ground black pepper

1. Melt the butter in a medium skillet over medium heat. Add the onion and cook, stirring occasionally, until well browned, about 10 minutes. Stir in the thyme and garlic and cook until fragrant, about 30 seconds; set aside to cool.

2. Mix the cooled onion mixture, gorgonzola cheese, cream cheese, walnuts, figs, sherry, salt, and pepper together until uniform. Spoon the cheese mixture onto the chicken as directed below.

Ham and Cheddar Filling

MAKES ENOUGH TO STUFF 4 BONELESS, SKINLESS CHICKEN BREASTS

You can substitute Swiss for the cheddar cheese for a cordon bleu–style stuffed chicken breast. If you don't plan on using the filling right away, be sure to store the ham separately from the cream cheese mixture.

1	tablespoon unsalted butter
1	small onion, minced
1	teaspoon minced fresh thyme leaves
1	small garlic clove, minced or pressed through a garlic press (about ½ teaspoon)
4	ounces cheddar cheese, shredded (about 1 cup) (see note)
4	ounces cream cheese, softened (about ½ cup)
1/8	teaspoon salt
1/8	teaspoon ground black pepper
4	slices (about 4 ounces) thin-sliced cooked deli ham

1. Melt the butter in a medium skillet over medium heat. Add the onion and cook, stirring occasionally, until well browned, about 10 minutes. Stir in the thyme and garlic and cook until fragrant, about 30 seconds; set aside to cool.

2. Mix together the cooled onion mixture, cheddar cheese, cream cheese, salt, and pepper until uniform. Place a slice of ham onto each chicken breast, then top with the cheese mixture as directed below.

Mushroom and Provolone Filling

MAKES ENOUGH TO STUFF 4 BONELESS, SKINLESS CHICKEN BREASTS

If you don't plan on using the filling right away, be sure to store the mushrooms separately from the cream cheese mixture.

3	tablespoons unsalted butter
10	ounces white mushrooms, wiped clean and quartered
	Salt and ground black pepper

BUILDING A STUFFED AND BREADED CHICKEN BREAST

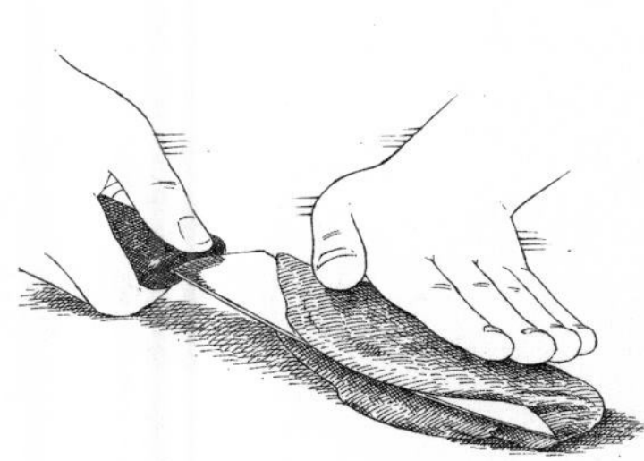

1. Starting on the thinner side, butterfly the breast by slicing it lengthwise almost in half. Open the breast up to create a single flat cutlet.

2. With the cutlet between sheets of plastic wrap, pound (starting at the center) to ¼ inch thick. Pound the outer perimeter to ⅛ inch.

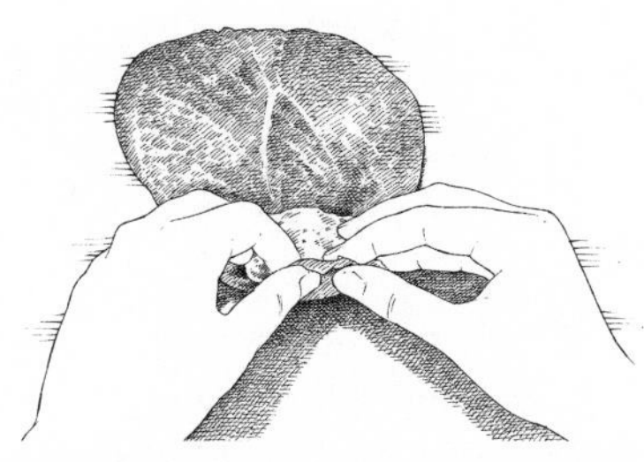

3. Place the stuffing near the tapered end of the cutlet and roll up the end to completely enclose the stuffing. Fold in the sides and continue rolling to form a cylinder.

- 1 small onion, minced
- 1 tablespoon minced fresh rosemary
- 1 teaspoon minced fresh thyme leaves
- 1 small garlic clove, minced or pressed through a garlic press (about ½ teaspoon)
- 4 ounces provolone cheese, shredded (about 1 cup)
- 4 ounces cream cheese, softened (about ½ cup)

1. Melt 2 tablespoons of the butter in a medium skillet over medium-high heat. Add the mushrooms and cook until the liquid has evaporated and the mushrooms are golden brown, 10 to 15 minutes. Season with salt and pepper to taste; transfer the mushrooms to a medium bowl and set aside to cool.

2. Add the remaining 1 tablespoon butter and the onion to the now-empty skillet and cook over medium heat, stirring occasionally, until well browned, about 10 minutes. Stir in the rosemary, thyme, and garlic and cook until fragrant, about 30 seconds; set aside to cool.

3. Mix together the cooled onion mixture, provolone cheese, cream cheese, ⅛ teaspoon salt, and ⅛ teaspoon pepper until uniform. Spread the mushroom mixture onto the chicken, then spoon the cheese mixture on top as directed on page 373.

Herb-Butter Filling

MAKES ENOUGH TO STUFF 4 BONELESS, SKINLESS CHICKEN BREASTS

Use this filling to make Chicken Kiev.

- 8 tablespoons (1 stick) unsalted butter, softened
- 1 tablespoon minced shallot
- 1 tablespoon minced fresh parsley leaves
- ½ teaspoon minced fresh tarragon leaves
- 1 tablespoon juice from 1 lemon
- ⅜ teaspoon salt
- ⅛ teaspoon ground black pepper

Pan-Roasted Asparagus

SERVES 4 TO 6

This recipe works best with asparagus that is at least ½ inch thick near the base. Do not use pencil-thin asparagus because it cannot withstand the heat and will overcook.

- 1 tablespoon olive oil
- 1 tablespoon unsalted butter
- 2 pounds (about 2 bunches) thick asparagus, tough ends trimmed
- Salt and ground black pepper
- ½ lemon

1. Heat the oil and butter in a 12-inch skillet over medium-high heat. When the butter has melted, add half of the asparagus to the skillet with the tips pointed in one direction and the remaining spears with the tips pointed in the opposite direction. Using tongs, distribute the spears in an even layer (the spears will not quite fit into a single layer). Cover and cook until the spears are bright green but still crisp, about 5 minutes.

2. Uncover, increase the heat to high, and continue to cook until the spears are tender and well browned along one side, 5 to 7 minutes, using tongs to move the spears from the center of the pan to the edge of the pan, to ensure that all are browned.

3. Transfer the asparagus to a serving dish, season with salt and pepper to taste, and squeeze the lemon half over the spears. Serve.

VARIATION

Pan-Roasted Asparagus with Toasted Garlic and Parmesan

Before cooking the asparagus in step 1, cook 3 sliced garlic cloves with 2 tablespoons olive oil over medium heat until crisp and golden, about 5 minutes. Transfer the garlic to a paper towel–lined plate and proceed with step 1, adding the butter to the oil left in the skillet. Sprinkle the toasted garlic and 2 tablespoons grated Parmesan cheese over the asparagus before serving.

1. Mix together the butter, shallot, parsley, tarragon, lemon juice, salt, and pepper in a medium bowl with a rubber spatula until thoroughly combined. Form into a 3-inch square on a sheet of plastic wrap. Wrap tightly and refrigerate until firm, about 1 hour.

2. Unwrap the butter and cut into four pieces. Place one piece of the butter mixture onto the chicken as directed on page 373.

Chicken Biryani

THE POPULAR INDIAN CHICKEN DISH MURGH biryani has about as much in common with American-style chicken and rice as naan does with Wonder bread. They both share the same major ingredients but diverge widely from there. In biryani, long-grain basmati rice takes center stage, enriched with butter, saffron, and a variety of fresh herbs and pungent spices. Pieces of tender chicken and browned onions are layered with the rice and baked until the flavors have mingled. This is India in a pot.

But it comes at a stiff price. Traditional biryani recipes are long in both ingredients and labor. The chicken is rubbed with spices and marinated before being browned; the rice is soaked, blanched, and mixed with a complex masala, or blend, of innumerable spices; the onions are deep-fried. Finally, everything is layered (chicken, onions, rice) into a cooking vessel and baked or steamed until the flavors have blended. In addition, most biryani recipes we tested were made greasy by the deep-fried onions, and the rice had overcooked by the time the chicken was done. We set out to find a middle path between the extremes of dull simplicity and epicurean complexity.

We prepared a few classic biryani recipes to better acquaint ourselves with the dish, a task that required a full day in the test kitchen and produced a huge pile of dirty dishes. We made three timesaving discoveries. First, we learned that we could skip the step of marinating the chicken (too much time, too little flavor enhancement). Second, we could finish the rice in the oven, eliminating the need for constant monitoring on the stovetop. Third, it was possible to cook the onions and the chicken in the same Dutch oven, saving a pan. The streamlined recipe, in its working form, now consisted of browning the chicken, cooking the onions, parboiling the rice, and then steaming the layered biryani until done.

The best-tasting biryani from our recipe tests was made with an abundant layer of deep-fried onions, but they inevitably turned the dish greasy. Onions sautéed in a tablespoon of fat (oil or butter) failed to brown properly. More fat was clearly necessary, but how much could we add without turning the dish greasy? We started with ½ cup of fat for two sliced onions and reduced it 1 tablespoon at a time. In the end, 3 tablespoons proved sufficient. A combination of butter and rendered chicken fat prevailed over oil, adding more flavor and color. Garlic and ginger were added to the onions for further complexity, and mincing the garlic and grating the ginger intensified their flavor.

Tasters preferred dark meat chicken—it was more flavorful and juicy than white meat, which ended up dry. Bone-in thighs are the test kitchen favorite because they are so meaty. Having already eliminated marinating, we followed test kitchen protocol for braising chicken pieces. (Biryani is, in essence, a braise, because it uses moist, low heat for cooking.) To eke out as much flavor as we could, we browned the chicken deeply, with the skin on for protection. Before layering the pieces with the

SLICING ONIONS THIN

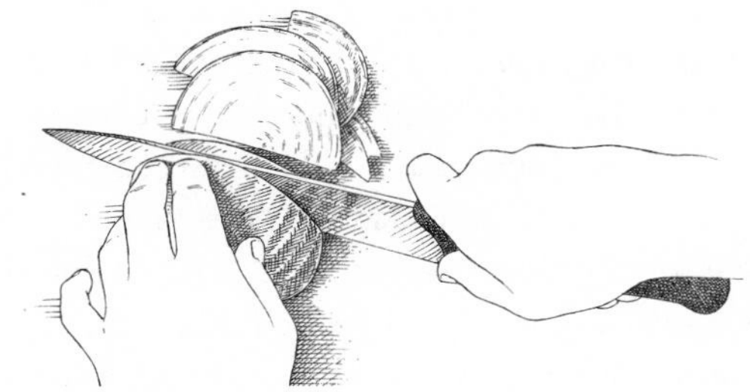

To slice an onion thin, halve it pole to pole, peel it, set it on a cut side, and then slice crosswise.

rice, we stripped off the skin. With this last step, the greasiness issue was finally put to rest.

Biryani's subtle, delicate flavor and aroma are largely derived from the masala of whole spices blended into the rice. Before serving, we diligently fished out the spices from the rice, as tasters strongly objected to unexpectedly biting down on whole cardamom pods, but this nitpicky task grew tiresome. To save ourselves from fishing out cardamom pods and coriander seeds in our finished biryani, we opted for ground versions of these two spices. To keep the ground spices from tasting raw, we bloomed them, along with the whole spices, in the butter to both develop their flavor and infuse the butter. Tasters approved of ground cardamom and coriander, cinnamon stick, and whole cumin seeds. The cumin seeds added contrast to the soft, fluffy rice, as well as a burst of flavor. In the end, the only "fishing" we had to do was for two pieces of cinnamon stick, a reasonable task for the reward. Sweet, earthy, sharp, and musky, the spices paired well together.

Most of the recipes we found parboiled the rice before building the biryani. This was usually done by tossing the rice into a pot of boiling water and simmering for 5 minutes. In an effort to streamline this process, we decided to prepare our rice in the same manner as our pilafs: we sautéed the rice in butter and spices until the edges of the grains began to turn translucent, about three minutes. Next, we added an equal amount of water to the rice and allowed this mixture to simmer until all the water had evaporated, at which point we stirred in the currants, covered the pot, and set it aside until we were ready to layer our biryani. This process left the rice perfectly parcooked and well seasoned.

Saffron is mixed with the rice as both a coloring and flavoring agent. But we quickly found out that any more than a pinch turned the rice Day-Glo orange and made it taste medicinal. To incorporate the saffron, we used a technique that we found in our research. We bloomed the saffron in warm milk and swirled it on top of the rice layer. This left a visually appealing spiral design on top of the biryani, and when the rice was fluffed after cooking, gave a checkered appearance to the rice with specks of both yellow and white.

Tasters demanded a fair amount of heat to round out the flavor of the biryani. We added one jalapeño, along with some of its seeds for additional fire. A little sweetness from currants (you could use raisins in a pinch) helped to temper the heat and accent the warm spices. Fresh cilantro sprinkled on just before serving gave the dish a shot of freshness, while a dollop of raita, a refreshing yogurt sauce (see page 212), was the perfect accompaniment.

Chicken Biryani

SERVES 4 TO 6

We recommend using a medium or large Dutch oven for this recipe. For more heat, include the jalapeño seeds and ribs when mincing. Serve this dish with our Yogurt-Mint Cucumber Sauce (page 212).

SPICES

- 1 cinnamon stick, broken in half
- 1 teaspoon ground coriander
- 1 teaspoon cumin seeds
- ⅛ teaspoon ground cardamom

BIRYANI

- 3 tablespoons unsalted butter
- 2 cups basmati rice, rinsed
- Salt and ground black pepper
- 2¾ cups water
- ¼ cup currants
- 8 bone-in, skin-on chicken thighs (about 3 pounds), trimmed
- 1 teaspoon vegetable oil, plus more as needed
- 2 medium onions, halved and sliced thin
- 6 medium garlic cloves, minced or pressed through a garlic press (about 2 tablespoons)
- 1 tablespoon minced or grated fresh ginger
- 1 jalapeño chile, seeds and ribs removed, chile minced
- ½ teaspoon saffron threads, lightly crumbled
- 2 tablespoons milk, warmed
- ¼ cup minced fresh cilantro leaves

1. For the spices: Adjust an oven rack to the lower-middle position and heat the oven to 350 degrees. Combine the spices in a small bowl and set aside.

2. For the biryani: Melt the butter in a medium saucepan over medium-high heat. Add the spices and cook until fragrant, about 10 seconds. Stir in the rice, 1 teaspoon salt, and ¼ teaspoon pepper and cook, stirring frequently, until the edges of the grains begin to turn translucent, about 3 minutes. Stir in 2 cups of the water and cook, uncovered, until all the water has evaporated. Remove the rice from the heat, stir in the currants, cover, and set aside until needed.

3. Meanwhile, pat the chicken dry with paper towels and season with salt and pepper. Heat the oil in a medium Dutch oven over medium-high heat until just smoking. Brown the chicken on both sides, 5 to 8 minutes per side, reducing the heat if the pan begins to scorch. Transfer the chicken to a plate, remove and discard the skin, and tent loosely with foil to keep warm.

4. Pour off all but 3 tablespoons of fat from the pot. (Add additional oil to equal 3 tablespoons, if needed.) Add the onions and cook over medium heat, stirring often, until softened and dark brown, 10 to 12 minutes. Stir in the garlic, ginger, and jalapeño and cook until fragrant, about 30 seconds. Transfer the onion mixture to a bowl, season with salt to taste, and set aside.

5. Add the remaining ¾ cup water to the pot, scraping up the browned bits. Place the chicken in the pot, skinned-side up, and sprinkle the browned onions over the top. Pour the rice on top of the onions and smooth into an even layer with a rubber spatula (neither the onions nor the chicken should be visible). Stir the saffron into the warm milk, then pour the mixture over the rice in a spiral pattern.

6. Cover and bake until the rice is tender, about 45 minutes. Remove from the oven and let rest for 5 to 10 minutes. Fluff the rice with a fork, then portion the biryani into individual bowls, scooping from the bottom of the pot. Sprinkle the individual servings with cilantro before serving.

Roast Cornish Game Hens

EVEN THOUGH CORNISH HENS ARE CHEAP enough (two for five bucks in our grocery store) and cook quickly enough for a weeknight supper (less than 30 minutes unstuffed), most people think of them as festive fare. And for good reason. They make a stunning presentation, and they stuff beautifully. Cooking a large number of Cornish hens to perfection, however, is not an easy task, as problems abound: the white meat and dark meat cook at different rates, browning can be difficult (these small birds cook quickly), and stuffing them can be a challenge. One final problem: After roasting a few batches, we realized that these birds didn't taste superb. Because most Cornish hens are mass-produced and not premium quality, we were faced with the added challenge of trying to deepen their flavor. Despite these challenges, we were determined to develop a recipe for really good roast Cornish game hens that would be perfect for a special-occasion meal.

You may as well steam Cornish hens as roast six of them in a high-sided roasting pan. The pan sides shield the birds from oven heat, and their snug fit in the pan further prevents browning. So our first move was to get the birds out of the roasting pan and onto a wire rack set over the pan. Our second step in the right direction was to space the birds as far apart as possible. Just as chicken pieces won't brown if overcrowded in the frying pan, Cornish hens won't brown if arranged too close together on the rack.

From our initial testing, we determined that rotating the birds was crucial for moist and juicy breast meat. Though the unturned birds were more deeply browned, their breast meat was indeed drier than that of the birds that were rotated. But because Cornish hens are in the oven for such a relatively short time, and because there are so many of them, multiple turns are out of the question. One turn, from breast-side down to breast-side up, was our limit.

After roasting Cornish hens at temperatures

ranging from 350 degrees to 500 degrees, as well as roasting at a high temperature to start and then finishing low—and starting low and finishing high—we found that all oven temperatures had their problems. We finally settled on 400 degrees, cranking up the oven to 450 degrees during the last few minutes of roasting. This hotter roasting temperature was high enough to encourage browning, while low enough to keep the oven from smoking dramatically. Adding water to the roasting pan once the fat starts to render and the juices start to flow further ensures a smokeless kitchen at even 450 degrees. Another perk: The pan is automatically deglazed in the oven. Once the birds are roasted, you can pour the pan juices into a saucepan without having to deglaze the roasting pan over two burners.

Even roasted at a relatively high 400 degrees with a 450-degree finish, Cornish hens simply don't spend enough time in the oven to develop the deep mahogany color we sought. We needed some sort of glaze to fix the color problem. Testing three different glazes, we roasted six more birds, brushing two with soy sauce, two with balsamic vinegar, and two with jam thinned with a little soy sauce. We applied the glaze twice: right before they were turned, and once again after the oven temperature was increased to 450 degrees. Because the high oven heat caramelized the sugar in these glazes, all of the birds colored more beautifully than any of our unglazed birds. But the balsamic vinegar glaze finished as our favorite, giving the hens a pleasant spotty brown, barbecued look.

But once we tasted them, disappointment loomed. Although our local grocery store sells premium-quality poussins (baby chickens), all of its Cornish hens are mass-produced. Just 2 hours in a saltwater bath, however, transformed these mediocre-tasting birds into something we would proudly serve to guests. Much like koshering, brining draws out the blood, giving the bird a clean, fresh flavor. The saltwater permeates the birds, making each bite, rather than just the skin, taste seasoned. No matter how you roast your Cornish hens, brining will improve them immensely.

Our final challenge was determining how to roast these birds, stuffed, without overcooking them (the stuffing can take longer than the birds to come up to a safe temperature). Although we're certain that slightly overcooking a stuffed bird is inevitable, two things help. Starting the birds breast-side down keeps the breast meat from drastically overcooking. And heating the stuffing before spooning it into the birds' cavities also reduces oven time. By stuffing the birds with microwave-hot stuffing, we were able to roast birds that registered 172 to 174 degrees in the breast and 176 to 178 degrees in the leg/thigh by the time the stuffing reached 165 degrees. Even though we thought breast meat at this temperature might be borderline dry (160 to 165 is ideal), we found this petite breast tender and juicy. Of course, the leg/thigh meat, which always tastes best at a higher temperature, was perfect.

Although we were aware that trussing would slow down the roasting of the hens' legs and thighs, we knew we had to do something. With its fragile, loose frame and dangling legs, a Cornish hen can be a bit unsightly. Stuffing the bird further increases the need to close the cavity. We quickly discovered that simply tying the hens' legs together was all that was needed to improve their looks and secure the stuffing without impeding the roasting.

Roast Stuffed Cornish Game Hens

SERVES 6

If you do not have a wire rack that will rest on top of your roasting pan, you can place the rack on a large rimmed baking sheet instead. Pouring a little broth into the roasting pan at the 25-minute mark, once the hens have been turned, both prevents them from smoking during cooking and makes instant jus, eliminating the need to deglaze the pan. To use kosher salt in the brine, see page 12 for conversion information and more tips on brining.

- Table salt
- 6 Cornish game hens (1¼ to 1½ pounds each), giblets removed and wings tucked (see the illustration on page 206)
- Ground black pepper
- 6 tablespoons balsamic vinegar
- 3 tablespoons olive oil
- 1 recipe stuffing (see pages 379–380)
- 1 cup low-sodium chicken broth
- ¼ cup dry vermouth or white wine

1. Dissolve 1 cup salt in 4 quarts cold water in a large container. Submerge the hens in the brine, cover, and refrigerate for 2 to 3 hours.

2. Adjust an oven rack to the middle position and heat the oven to 400 degrees. Remove the hens from the brine, rinse well, and pat dry with paper towels. Season the hens with pepper.

3. Whisk the vinegar and oil together in a small bowl and set aside. Cover the stuffing with plastic wrap and microwave on high until very hot, about 2 minutes. Spoon ½ cup of the hot stuffing into the cavity of each hen, then tie each hen's legs together with kitchen twine. Arrange the hens, breast-side down and with the wings facing out, on a wire rack set over a foil-lined rimmed baking sheet or roasting pan.

4. Roast the hens until the backs are golden brown, about 25 minutes. Remove the pan from the oven and brush each hen with the vinegar-and-oil glaze. Turn the hens, breast-side up and with the wings facing out, and brush with the glaze. Add ½ cup of the broth to the pan and continue to roast until the stuffed cavity registers 150 degrees on an instant-read thermometer, 15 to 20 minutes longer.

5. Remove the pan from the oven and increase the oven temperature to 450 degrees. Brush each hen with the glaze, add the remaining ½ cup broth to the pan, and continue to roast until the hens are spotty brown and the cavity registers 160 to 165 degrees on an instant-read thermometer, 5 to 10 minutes longer. Remove the hens from the oven, transfer to a cutting board, and let rest for 10 minutes.

6. Meanwhile, pour the cooking juices from the pan into a small saucepan and spoon off any excess fat. Add the vermouth and simmer over medium-high heat until the sauce thickens slightly and the flavors blend, 3 to 5 minutes. Season with salt and pepper to taste. Serve the hens, passing the sauce separately.

Couscous Stuffing with Dried Fruit and Pistachios

MAKES ABOUT 3 CUPS, ENOUGH FOR 6 CORNISH GAME HENS

Toasted slivered almonds can be substituted for the pistachio nuts.

- 2 tablespoons unsalted butter
- 1 small onion, minced
- 2 medium garlic cloves, minced or pressed through a garlic press (about 2 teaspoons)
- ¼ teaspoon ground cinnamon
- ⅛ teaspoon ground ginger
- ⅛ teaspoon ground turmeric
- 1 cup couscous
- 1⅓ cups low-sodium chicken broth
- ¼ cup shelled pistachio nuts, toasted and chopped coarse (see note)
- ¼ cup dried apricots, chopped fine
- 3 tablespoons currants
- 2 tablespoons minced fresh parsley leaves
- 1 teaspoon juice from 1 lemon
- Salt and ground black pepper

1. Melt the butter in a medium saucepan over medium heat. Add the onion and cook, stirring occasionally, until softened, 5 to 7 minutes. Stir in the garlic, cinnamon, ginger, and turmeric and cook until fragrant, about 30 seconds. Stir in the couscous and cook until well coated, 1 to 2 minutes.

2. Add the broth and bring to a simmer. Remove the saucepan from the heat, cover, and let stand for 5 minutes. Fluff the couscous with a fork and transfer to a medium microwave-safe bowl. Stir in the pistachios, apricots, currants, parsley, and lemon juice. Season with salt and pepper to taste. (The stuffing can be refrigerated in an airtight container for up to 24 hours.)

Wild Rice Stuffing with Carrot, Mushrooms, and Thyme

MAKES ABOUT 3 CUPS, ENOUGH FOR 6 CORNISH GAME HENS

The wild rice blend in this stuffing holds together when pressed with a fork. You can use wild rice, but the cooked grains will remain separate.

- 2 cups low-sodium chicken broth
- 1 cup wild rice blend (see note)
- 2 tablespoons unsalted butter
- 1 small onion, minced
- 1 carrot, peeled and chopped fine
- ½ celery rib, chopped fine
- 1 ounce dried porcini mushrooms, rinsed and minced
- 4 ounces shiitake mushrooms, stemmed, wiped clean, and sliced thin
- 2 tablespoons minced fresh parsley leaves
- 2 teaspoons minced fresh thyme leaves
- Salt and ground black pepper

1. Bring the broth to a boil in a medium saucepan. Add the rice and return to a boil. Reduce the heat to low, cover, and simmer until the rice is fully cooked, 40 to 50 minutes. Transfer the rice to a medium microwave-safe bowl and fluff with a fork.

2. Meanwhile, melt the butter in a 10-inch skillet over medium heat. Add the onion, carrot, celery, and porcini mushrooms and cook, stirring occasionally, until softened, 5 to 7 minutes. Add the shiitake mushrooms and cook until tender and the liquid evaporates, 8 to 10 minutes. Stir the mushroom mixture into the rice, along with the parsley and thyme. Season with salt and pepper to taste. (The stuffing can be refrigerated in an airtight container for up to 24 hours.)

Wild Rice Stuffing with Cranberries and Toasted Pecans

MAKES ABOUT 3 CUPS, ENOUGH FOR 6 CORNISH GAME HENS

The wild rice blend in this stuffing holds together when pressed with a fork. You can use wild rice, but the cooked grains will remain separate.

- 2 cups low-sodium chicken broth
- 1 cup wild rice blend (see note)
- 2 tablespoons unsalted butter
- 1 small onion, minced
- ½ celery rib, chopped fine
- ¼ cup pecans, toasted and chopped coarse
- ¼ cup dried cranberries
- 2 tablespoons minced fresh parsley leaves
- 2 teaspoons minced fresh thyme leaves
- Salt and ground black pepper

1. Bring the broth to a boil in a medium saucepan. Add the rice and return to a boil. Reduce the heat to low, cover, and simmer until the rice is fully cooked, 40 to 50 minutes. Transfer the rice to a medium microwave-safe bowl and fluff with a fork.

2. Meanwhile, melt the butter in a 10-inch skillet over medium heat. Add the onion and celery and cook, stirring occasionally, until softened, 5 to 7 minutes. Stir the onion mixture into the rice, along with the pecans, cranberries, parsley, and thyme. Season with salt and pepper to taste. (The stuffing can be refrigerated in an airtight container for up to 24 hours.)

15
SLOW COOKER

Slow Cooker

USING A SLOW COOKER TO PREPARE CHICKEN is a great idea when you want simply to prep the dish and then let it cook for several hours unattended—this method requires little to no hands-on time once everything goes into the pot. There is a catch, however: To extract a really good meal from your slow cooker, you can't just dump a bunch of raw ingredients in the crock and walk away; you must commit some time to prep work and building flavor. Our goal nevertheless was to develop hearty and practical recipes that would be packed with flavor, but would also minimize the amount of advance preparation.

The first task was cooking the chicken properly. After numerous tests, we found that, unlike tough cuts of meat, which typically need as many as 12 hours to become tender, chicken will overcook—even in a slow cooker. Many recipes called for eight hours of cooking on the low setting, but they resulted in chicken so soft that it literally fell off the bone and was altogether unappetizing. We found that four hours was a much better option, making these recipes more suitable for a day when you're around the house or have a half day's worth of errands. Finally, a word of hard-earned wisdom: Cooking on the high setting will yield tough, stringy meat. Our recommendation is to cook chicken in a slow cooker on the low setting only.

The next task was to decide between white and dark meat. Tasters unanimously favored thighs, which were moist and meaty. (That said, you can make these stews with breast meat, but the chicken will be a little dry.) We knew we had to use bone-in, skin-on thighs because, without skin to protect the meat during browning, the boneless, skinless thighs turned tough and stringy. The stews made with bone-in, skin-on thighs had moist, tender meat and a richer overall flavor. To avoid a mouthful of rubbery chicken skin, we removed it after browning, without sacrificing any flavor.

Now that we had decided on our method and timing for cooking the chicken, we turned our attention to the sauces and finishing the dishes. The biggest problem with slow-cooker recipes is the muddied, washed-out flavors of the finished dish—a problem created by the extensive cooking time—so our goal would be to build as much flavor as possible at the outset. We started with a basic slow-cooker chicken recipe (see our Slow-Cooker Chicken with White Wine, Tarragon, and Cream on page 385) to determine the best method for preparing and adding all the ingredients, then developed several variations following this basic process. We browned the chicken in a skillet with the skin on, removed the skin, and then transferred the chicken to the slow cooker while we built the sauce. We put the rendered chicken fat to work by using it to sauté the vegetables and herbs, adding more chicken flavor to the finished dish. The vegetables and herbs were added to the slow cooker, and then we deglazed the pan with a hefty dose of wine and chicken broth, which also went into the

PRACTICAL TIPS FOR SLOW-COOKER SUCCESS

- Use a 6-quart slow cooker to easily accommodate chicken and vegetables that will serve at least six people.
- Trim as much excess fat as possible from chicken.
- Brown chicken thoroughly in a heavy-bottomed skillet or Dutch oven first for maximum flavor.
- Feel free to assemble and brown the ingredients the day before. Just cover and refrigerate chicken and vegetables separately.
- Place hard or whole vegetables toward the edges of the cooker (where the heating elements reside) so that the vegetables will cook through, especially in chicken recipes (where the cooking time is short).
- Don't lift the lid during cooking: doing so extends the cooking time significantly.
- Stir in delicate fresh herbs at the end of the cooking time to preserve their flavor.
- Make sure the electrical cord of your slow cooker does not touch the outside of the base unit, since it gets very hot.

slow cooker—the fond left behind from browning the chicken added yet more flavor to the dish. Four hours later (on the low setting), we had moist, perfectly cooked chicken, but the larger vegetables hadn't cooked all the way through. The solution was to place larger vegetables (such as carrots or potatoes) along the outer edges of the slow cooker. Nestled next to the heating elements, they softened thoroughly while the chicken cooked.

We removed the chicken from the slow cooker and set it aside while we finished the flavorful sauce. A slurry of cream mixed with flour proved to be the best way to thicken the sauce, producing a creamy, luscious texture. You'll need to allow time for the sauce to thicken after adding the slurry at the end of the cooking process.

With our basic slow-cooker technique in place (brown the chicken to render fat, sauté the vegetables and herbs, deglaze the pan, and then thicken the sauce at the end with a flour-broth slurry), we ventured on to develop a variety of recipes that all use the same basic method. The key for each of these dishes was to use boldly flavored ingredients that stand up well to a long cooking time. We first turned to the "hunter-style" stews, Italy's chicken cacciatore and France's chicken chasseur, to adapt these flavors to our slow-cooker chicken. To help boost the flavor of the sauces in both dishes, we added dried porcini mushrooms, which brought a concentrated woodsy mushroom flavor. To complete the dishes, we added crushed tomatoes and roasted red peppers to the cacciatore, and in the chasseur we started by rendering bacon, which added a meaty depth that complemented the

EQUIPMENT: Slow Cookers

Part of the appeal of a slow cooker has always been price. But as slow cookers have gained popularity in recent years, manufacturers have added new features—and higher price tags. Does more money buy a better slow cooker? To find out, we rounded up seven models priced between $40 and $150. We chose slow cookers with oval inserts and capacities of 6 quarts or greater—traits we have found to be essential for any slow cooker.

The stovetop-safe inserts in the Rival VersaWare and the West Bend Versatility didn't brown meat very well—the recommended medium heat simply doesn't get the job done. A programmable timer was deemed a real asset, especially because all the machines with timers automatically switch to a warming mode when the timed cooking is done. This means that even if you're late coming home from work, your dinner won't be overcooked (or cold). The models without timers were downgraded.

Other features we found beneficial include an "on" light (so you don't accidentally leave it on overnight), insert handles (which make it easy to remove the insert), and a clear lid that allows you to see the food as it cooks.

The U.S. Department of Agriculture recommends that meat get out of the "danger zone" (that is, get above 140 degrees) within four hours. Every machine we tested was able to bring the meat up to temperature in the allotted time—even on low.

Although excess moisture is often a problem in slow-cooker dishes, most recipes are written assuming there will be little or no evaporation. The All-Clad, Hamilton Beach Stay or Go, Hamilton Beach Probe, Rival, and West Bend machines only allowed about 2 percent of their contents (3 quarts of 42-degree water) to evaporate after 3 hours of covered cooking on high. The two cookers that fared worst in this test, the KitchenAid and the Cuisinart, lost about 6 percent and 4 percent of their water, respectively.

All the slow cookers we tested did a good job with slow-cooking pot roast on both high and low and cooking chili and beans on high. But more important than the cooking tests were the features we deemed essential: timers that automatically shift to a "keep warm" setting at the end of cooking; a clear lid; an "on" indicator light; and handles on the insert. In the end, the All-Clad Stainless Steel Slow Cooker with Ceramic Insert came out ahead, providing slow, steady heat every time.

THE BEST SLOW COOKER

The All-Clad Stainless Steel Slow Cooker with Ceramic Insert ($149.95) aced all the cooking tests, and it has every feature we want, including insert handles and a clear lid.

ALL-CLAD

mushroom flavor. We then turned to a Provençal-style slow-cooker chicken, to which we added a whopping 12 cloves of garlic, a big dose of fresh herbs, and a handful of olives to conjure up the flavors of the Mediterranean.

Moving on to an Indian-style curry, we wanted a mild but flavor-packed dish with a light yet substantial sauce that would hold its own when served over rice or couscous. Frying the spices in a little oil encouraged their flavors to bloom and infused the stew with complex flavors, while coconut milk added an incredible richness.

Next we turned to Morocco for inspiration and sought to replicate a basic tagine (or stew). Characterized by a blend of sweet and savory, traditional tagines often have an extensive ingredient list—our plan was to try and duplicate the flavors of a traditional Moroccan tagine in the slow cooker while limiting the number of ingredients. Knowing that the choice of spices would be critical, we started with the three most common in Moroccan recipes: cardamom, cinnamon, and hot paprika. This trio provided just the right balance of warmth and spice. To temper the spices, we added apricots for their sweetness. For texture, we added canned chickpeas, but found their firmness was compromised by the long cooking period. We opted to stir them in for the final hour of cooking, enabling them to absorb the flavors of the stew yet maintain their integrity.

Country Captain Chicken was the last recipe we developed. We felt that this Georgia stew, rich with mango, raisins, tomatoes, and curry, would have flavors bold enough to withstand hours in a slow cooker. Yet with this dish, like many, the long, slow cooking took a toll on the seasonings. Bumping up the curry to a whopping 2 tablespoons was an easy fix, as was swapping the mango and raisins for a jar of mango chutney, which added just the right amount of sweet-tart flavor. Armed with a bowl of steamed rice and the full array of country captain garnishes (nuts, coconut, fruit), we were more than ready to dig into this new addition to our slow-cooker repertoire.

Slow-Cooker Chicken with White Wine, Tarragon, and Cream

SERVES 6

If cremini mushrooms (aka baby bellas) are unavailable, substitute portobello mushroom caps, cut into 1-inch pieces. Although we prefer the texture and flavor of chicken thighs here, you can substitute 6 bone-in, skin-on chicken breasts; the cooking time will remain the same, but the meat will be a bit drier. Serve with Simple Polenta (page 71) or Simple White Rice (page 386).

- 12 bone-in, skin-on chicken thighs (5 to 6 ounces each), trimmed (see note)
- Salt and ground black pepper
- 2 tablespoons vegetable oil, plus more as needed
- 1¼ pounds cremini mushrooms, wiped clean and quartered (see note)
- 1 medium onion, chopped medium
- 4 medium garlic cloves, minced or pressed through a garlic press (about 4 teaspoons)
- 1¾ cups dry white wine
- 1 cup low-sodium chicken broth
- 1 tablespoon minced fresh thyme leaves or 1 teaspoon dried
- 2 bay leaves
- 1 pound carrots (about 6 medium), peeled and cut into 3-inch lengths
- 1 cup heavy cream
- ¼ cup unbleached all-purpose flour
- ¼ cup minced fresh tarragon leaves
- 1 tablespoon juice from 1 lemon

1. Pat the chicken dry with paper towels and season with salt and pepper. Heat the oil in a 12-inch skillet over medium-high heat until just smoking. Brown half of the chicken on both sides, 5 to 8 minutes per side, reducing the heat if the pan begins to scorch. Transfer the chicken to a plate, leaving the fat in the pan. When cool enough to handle, remove the browned skin from the thighs and discard. Transfer the chicken to the slow cooker. Return the pan with

the fat to medium-high heat and repeat with the remaining half of the chicken.

2. Pour off all but 1 tablespoon fat from the pan. (Add additional oil to equal 1 tablespoon if needed.) Add the mushrooms, onion, and ¼ teaspoon salt to the pan, cover, and cook over medium heat, stirring occasionally, until the mushrooms have released their liquid, 8 to 10 minutes. Stir in the garlic and cook until fragrant, about 30 seconds. Stir in the wine, scraping up any browned bits, and simmer until reduced by half, about 5 minutes. Pour into the slow cooker.

3. Add the broth, thyme, and bay leaves to the slow cooker. Following the illustration on page 389, nestle the carrots into the slow cooker around the edges. Cover and cook on low until the chicken is tender, about 4 hours.

4. Transfer the chicken to a large serving dish and tent loosely with foil. Discard the bay leaves. Set the slow cooker to high. Whisk the cream and flour together until smooth, then stir into the slow cooker. Cover and continue to cook until the sauce is thickened and no longer tastes of flour, 15 to 30 minutes longer.

5. Stir in the tarragon and lemon juice and season with salt and pepper to taste. Spoon the vegetables and some of the sauce over the chicken and serve, passing the remaining sauce separately.

Simple White Rice

MAKES ABOUT 5 CUPS

To rinse the rice, you can either place it in a fine-mesh strainer and rinse under cool water, or place it in a medium bowl and repeatedly fill the bowl with water while swishing the rice around, then carefully drain off the water; in either case, you must rinse until the water runs clear.

- 2 cups long-grain or medium-grain white rice, rinsed
- 2½ cups water

1. Bring the rice and water to a boil in a large saucepan, then cover, reduce the heat to low, and cook until the water is just absorbed and there are small holes in the surface of the rice, about 10 minutes.

2. Remove the pot from the heat and let stand, covered, until the rice is tender, about 15 minutes longer. Serve.

Slow-Cooker Chicken Cacciatore

SERVES 6

If cremini mushrooms (aka baby bellas) are unavailable, substitute portobello mushroom caps, cut into 1-inch pieces. Although we prefer the texture and flavor of chicken thighs here, you can substitute 6 bone-in, skin-on chicken breasts; the cooking time will remain the same, but the meat will be a bit drier. Serve with pasta or Simple White Rice (at left).

- 12 bone-in, skin-on chicken thighs (5 to 6 ounces each), trimmed (see note)
- Salt and ground black pepper
- 2 tablespoons vegetable oil, plus more as needed
- 1¼ pounds cremini mushrooms, wiped clean and quartered (see note)
- 2 medium onions, halved and sliced thin
- 4 medium garlic cloves, minced or pressed through a garlic press (about 4 teaspoons)
- 1½ cups dry red wine
- 1 (28-ounce) can crushed tomatoes
- 2 cups low-sodium chicken broth
- ¼ ounce dried porcini mushrooms, rinsed and minced
- 2 tablespoons minced fresh thyme leaves or 2 teaspoons dried
- 2 bay leaves
- ½ teaspoon red pepper flakes
- ¼ cup unbleached all-purpose flour
- 1 (12-ounce) jar roasted red peppers, rinsed and cut into 1-inch strips (about 1½ cups)
- ¼ cup minced fresh parsley leaves

1. Pat the chicken dry with paper towels and season with salt and pepper. Heat the oil in a 12-inch skillet over medium-high heat until just smoking. Brown half of the chicken on both sides, 5 to 8 minutes per side, reducing the heat if the pan

begins to scorch. Transfer the chicken to a plate, leaving the fat in the pan. When cool enough to handle, remove the browned skin from the thighs and discard. Transfer the chicken to the slow cooker. Return the pan with the fat to medium-high heat and repeat with the remaining half of the chicken.

2. Pour off all but 1 tablespoon fat from the pan. (Add additional oil to equal 1 tablespoon if needed.) Add the cremini mushrooms, onions, and ¼ teaspoon salt to the pan, cover, and cook over medium heat, stirring occasionally, until the mushrooms have released their liquid, 8 to 10 minutes. Stir in the garlic and cook until fragrant, about 30 seconds. Stir in the wine, scraping up any browned bits, and simmer until reduced by half, about 5 minutes. Pour into the slow cooker.

3. Add the tomatoes, 1½ cups of the broth, the porcini mushrooms, thyme, bay leaves, and pepper flakes to the slow cooker. Cover and cook on low until the chicken is tender, about 4 hours.

4. Transfer the chicken to a large serving dish and tent loosely with foil. Discard the bay leaves. Set the slow cooker to high. Whisk the remaining ½ cup broth and the flour together until smooth, then stir into the slow cooker. Add the roasted red peppers, cover, and continue to cook until the sauce is thickened and no longer tastes of flour, 15 to 30 minutes longer.

5. Stir in the parsley and season with salt and pepper to taste. Spoon the vegetables and some of the sauce over the chicken and serve, passing the remaining sauce separately.

INGREDIENTS: Jarred Roasted Red Peppers

Jarred peppers are convenient, but are all brands created equal? To find out, we collected six brands from local supermarkets. The top two brands, Divina and Greek Gourmet, were preferred for their "soft and tender texture" (the Divina) and "refreshing," "piquant," "smoky" flavor (the Greek Gourmet). The other brands were marked down for their lack of "roasty flavor" and for the unpleasantly overpowering flavor of the brines. These peppers tasted as if they'd been "buried under brine and acid," or as if they had a "pepperoncini-like sourness" or a "sweet and acidic aftertaste." The conclusion? Tasters preferred peppers with a full, smoky, roasted flavor, a brine that was spicy and not too sweet, and a tender texture.

THE BEST JARRED ROASTED RED PEPPERS

DIVINA

GREEK GOURMET

Divina peppers were the top choice of tasters. Greek Gourmet peppers came in a close second.

Slow-Cooker Chicken Chasseur

SERVES 6

Chicken chasseur is a simple, peasant-style braise enriched by the deep, woodsy flavors of mushrooms and bacon. If cremini mushrooms (aka baby bellas) are unavailable, substitute portobello mushroom caps, cut into 1-inch pieces. Although we prefer the texture and flavor of chicken thighs here, you can substitute 6 bone-in, skin-on chicken breasts; the cooking time will remain the same, but the meat will be a bit drier. This dish is great served with pasta, polenta (see page 71), or a loaf of crusty bread.

- 8 ounces (about 8 slices) bacon, chopped fine
- 12 bone-in, skin-on chicken thighs (5 to 6 ounces each), trimmed (see note)
- Salt and ground black pepper
- Vegetable oil, as needed
- 1¼ pounds cremini mushrooms, wiped clean and quartered (see note)
- 1 medium red onion, chopped medium
- 4 medium garlic cloves, minced or pressed through a garlic press (about 4 teaspoons)
- 1½ cups dry white wine
- 2 tablespoons tomato paste
- 1 (14.5-ounce) can diced tomatoes, drained
- 2 cups low-sodium chicken broth
- ¼ ounce dried porcini mushrooms, rinsed and minced

- 1 tablespoon minced fresh thyme leaves or 1 teaspoon dried
- 2 bay leaves
- ½ teaspoon red pepper flakes
- ¼ cup unbleached all-purpose flour
- ¼ cup minced fresh parsley leaves

1. Cook the bacon in a 12-inch skillet over medium heat until crisp, about 8 minutes. Add the bacon to the slow cooker, leaving the bacon fat in the pan.

2. Pat the chicken dry with paper towels and season with salt and pepper. Pour off all but 2 tablespoons fat from the pan (add vegetable oil to equal 2 tablespoons if needed) and heat over medium-high heat until just smoking. Brown half of the chicken on both sides, 5 to 8 minutes per side, reducing the heat if the pan begins to scorch. Transfer the chicken to a plate, leaving the fat in the pan. When cool enough to handle, remove the browned skin from the thighs and discard. Transfer the chicken to the slow cooker. Return the pan with the fat to medium-high heat and repeat with the remaining half of the chicken.

3. Pour off all but 1 tablespoon fat from the pan. (Add additional vegetable oil to equal 1 tablespoon if needed.) Add the cremini mushrooms, onion, and ¼ teaspoon salt to the pan, cover, and cook over medium heat, stirring occasionally, until the mushrooms have released their liquid, 8 to 10 minutes. Stir in the garlic and cook until fragrant, about 30 seconds. Stir in the wine and tomato paste, scraping up any browned bits, and simmer until reduced by half, about 5 minutes. Pour into the slow cooker.

4. Add the tomatoes, 1½ cups of the broth, the porcini mushrooms, thyme, bay leaves, and pepper flakes to the slow cooker. Cover and cook on low until the chicken is tender, about 4 hours.

5. Transfer the chicken to a large serving dish and tent loosely with foil. Discard the bay leaves. Set the slow cooker to high. Whisk the remaining ½ cup broth and the flour together until smooth, then stir into the slow cooker. Cover and continue to cook until the sauce is thickened and no longer tastes of flour, 15 to 30 minutes longer.

6. Stir in the parsley and season with salt and pepper to taste. Spoon the vegetables and some of the sauce over the chicken and serve, passing the remaining sauce separately.

Slow-Cooker Chicken Provençal

SERVES 6

Although we prefer the texture and flavor of chicken thighs here, you can substitute 6 bone-in, skin-on chicken breasts; the cooking time will remain the same, but the meat will be a bit drier. This dish is often served with slices of crusty bread, but Simple Polenta (page 71) is also a good accompaniment.

- 12 bone-in, skin-on chicken thighs (5 to 6 ounces each), trimmed (see note)
- Salt and ground black pepper
- 2 tablespoons vegetable oil, plus more as needed
- 3 medium onions, chopped medium
- 12 medium garlic cloves, minced or pressed through a garlic press (about 4 tablespoons)
- 1½ cups dry white wine
- 1 (28-ounce) can crushed tomatoes
- 2 cups low-sodium chicken broth
- 1 tablespoon minced fresh thyme leaves or 1 teaspoon dried
- 1 tablespoon minced fresh oregano leaves or 1 teaspoon dried
- 2 bay leaves
- ¼ cup unbleached all-purpose flour
- ½ cup kalamata olives, pitted and chopped coarse (see the illustration on page 101)
- ¼ cup minced fresh parsley leaves
- 1 tablespoon grated zest from 1 lemon
- 1 lemon, cut into wedges (for serving)

1. Pat the chicken dry with paper towels and season with salt and pepper. Heat the oil in a 12-inch skillet over medium-high heat until just smoking. Brown half of the chicken on both sides, 5 to 8 minutes per side, reducing the heat if the pan begins to scorch. Transfer the chicken to a plate, leaving the fat in the pan. When cool enough to handle, remove the browned skin from the thighs and discard. Transfer the chicken to the slow cooker. Return the

pan with the fat to medium-high heat and repeat with the remaining half of the chicken.

2. Pour off all but 1 tablespoon fat from the pan. (Add additional oil to equal 1 tablespoon if needed.) Add the onions and ¼ teaspoon salt and cook until softened, 5 to 7 minutes. Stir in the garlic and cook until fragrant, about 30 seconds. Stir in the wine, scraping up any browned bits, and simmer until reduced by half, about 5 minutes. Pour into the slow cooker.

3. Add the tomatoes, 1½ cups of the broth, the thyme, oregano, and bay leaves to the slow cooker. Cover and cook on low until the chicken is tender, about 4 hours.

4. Transfer the chicken to a large serving dish and tent loosely with foil. Discard the bay leaves. Set the slow cooker to high. Whisk the remaining ½ cup broth and the flour together until smooth, then stir into the slow cooker. Cover and continue to cook until the sauce is thickened and no longer tastes of flour, 15 to 30 minutes longer.

5. Stir in the olives, parsley, and lemon zest and season with salt and pepper to taste. Spoon the vegetables and some of the sauce over the chicken and serve with lemon wedges, passing the remaining sauce separately.

Slow-Cooker Curried Chicken with Peas and Potatoes

SERVES 6

For more heat, include the jalapeño seeds and ribs when mincing. It is important that the potatoes be 2 to 3 inches in diameter (about 5 ounces each) so that they cook at the same rate as the other vegetables in the slow cooker. Although we prefer the texture and flavor of chicken thighs here, you can substitute 6 bone-in, skin-on chicken breasts; the cooking time will remain the same, but the meat will be a bit drier. Serve with Basic Rice Pilaf (page 114) or Perfect Couscous (page 80).

- 12 bone-in, skin-on chicken thighs (5 to 6 ounces each), trimmed (see note)
- Salt and ground black pepper
- 2 tablespoons vegetable oil, plus more as needed
- 1 pound carrots (about 6 medium), peeled and chopped medium
- 1 medium onion, halved and sliced thin
- 2 tablespoons minced or grated fresh ginger
- 2 jalapeño chiles, seeds and ribs removed, chiles minced (see note)
- 4 teaspoons curry powder
- ¼ teaspoon cayenne pepper
- 4 medium garlic cloves, minced or pressed through a garlic press (about 4 teaspoons)
- 1 cup canned crushed tomatoes
- 1 (14-ounce) can coconut milk
- 2½ cups low-sodium chicken broth
- ½ cup currants or golden raisins
- 2 bay leaves
- 1 cinnamon stick
- 2 pounds red potatoes (about 6 medium), scrubbed (see note)
- ¼ cup unbleached all-purpose flour
- 2 cups frozen peas
- ¼ cup minced fresh cilantro leaves
- 2 tablespoons juice from 1 lemon
- 1 lemon, cut into wedges (for serving)

1. Pat the chicken dry with paper towels and season with salt and pepper. Heat the oil in a 12-inch skillet over medium-high heat until just smoking. Brown half of the chicken on both sides, 5 to 8 minutes per side, reducing the heat if the pan begins to scorch. Transfer the chicken to a plate, leaving the fat in the pan. When cool enough to handle, remove the browned skin from the thighs and discard. Transfer the chicken to the slow cooker. Return the pan with the fat to

ARRANGING VEGETABLES IN A SLOW COOKER

In recipes where the meat is in the slow cooker for only four hours, it is important to arrange the vegetables around the edges of the slow cooker, near the heating elements, so that they will cook evenly.

medium-high heat and repeat with the remaining half of the chicken.

2. Pour off all but 1 tablespoon fat from the pan. (Add additional oil to equal 1 tablespoon if needed.) Add the carrots, onion, ginger, jalapeños, curry, cayenne, and ¼ teaspoon salt and cook until the vegetables are softened, 5 to 7 minutes. Stir in the garlic and cook until fragrant, about 30 seconds. Stir in the tomatoes, scraping up any browned bits, and bring to a simmer. Pour into the slow cooker.

3. Add the coconut milk, 2 cups of the broth, the currants, bay leaves, and cinnamon stick to the slow cooker. Following the illustration on page 389, nestle the potatoes into the slow cooker around the edges. Cover and cook on low until the chicken is tender, about 4 hours.

4. Transfer the chicken to a large serving dish and tent loosely with foil. Discard the bay leaves and cinnamon stick. Using a slotted spoon, remove the potatoes and transfer to a cutting board to cool slightly. Set the slow cooker to high. Whisk the remaining ½ cup broth and the flour together until smooth, then stir into the slow cooker. Quarter the potatoes and return them to the slow cooker, along with the peas. Cover and continue to cook until the sauce is thickened and no longer tastes of flour, 15 to 30 minutes longer.

5. Stir in the cilantro and lemon juice and season with salt and pepper to taste. Spoon the vegetables and some of the sauce over the chicken and serve with lemon wedges, passing the remaining sauce separately.

Slow-Cooker Moroccan-Spiced Chicken with Apricots

SERVES 6

Pitted prunes or raisins can be substituted for the apricots. If you are unable to find hot paprika, substitute sweet paprika mixed with ¼ teaspoon cayenne pepper. Although we prefer the texture and flavor of chicken thighs here, you can substitute 6 bone-in, skin-on chicken breasts; the cooking time will remain the same, but the meat will be a bit drier. Serve with Basic Rice Pilaf (page 114) or Perfect Couscous (page 80).

- 12 bone-in, skin-on chicken thighs (5 to 6 ounces each), trimmed (see note)
- Salt and ground black pepper
- 2 tablespoons vegetable oil, plus more as needed
- 2 medium onions, chopped medium
- 1½ teaspoons hot paprika (see note)
- ½ teaspoon ground cardamom
- 6 medium garlic cloves, minced or pressed though a garlic press (about 2 tablespoons)
- 3 cups low-sodium chicken broth
- 1 cup dried apricots, cut in half (see note)
- 1 cinnamon stick
- 1 (15-ounce) can chickpeas, drained and rinsed
- ¼ cup unbleached all-purpose flour
- ¼ cup minced fresh cilantro leaves
- 2 tablespoons juice from 1 lemon
- 1 lemon, cut into wedges (for serving)

1. Pat the chicken dry with paper towels and season with salt and pepper. Heat the oil in a 12-inch skillet over medium-high heat until just smoking. Brown half of the chicken on both sides, 5 to 8 minutes per side, reducing the heat if the pan begins to scorch. Transfer the chicken to a plate, leaving the fat in the pan. When cool enough to handle, remove the browned skin from the thighs and discard. Transfer the chicken to the slow cooker. Return the pan with the fat to medium-high heat and repeat with the remaining half of the chicken.

2. Pour off all but 1 tablespoon fat from the pan. (Add additional oil to equal 1 tablespoon if needed.) Add the onions, paprika, cardamom, and ¼ teaspoon salt and cook until the onions are softened, 5 to 7 minutes. Stir in the garlic and cook until fragrant, about 30 seconds. Stir in 2½ cups of the broth, the apricots, and cinnamon stick, scraping up any browned bits, and bring to a simmer. Pour into the slow cooker.

3. Cover and cook on low for 3 hours. Quickly stir in the chickpeas, replace the cover, and continue to cook until the chicken is tender, about 1 hour longer.

4. Transfer the chicken to a large serving dish and tent loosely with foil. Discard the cinnamon stick. Set the slow cooker to high. Whisk the

remaining ½ cup broth and flour together until smooth, then stir into the slow cooker. Cover and continue to cook until the sauce is thickened and no longer tastes of flour, 15 to 30 minutes longer.

5. Stir in the cilantro and lemon juice and season with salt and pepper to taste. Spoon the vegetables and some of the sauce over the chicken and serve with lemon wedges, passing the remaining sauce separately.

Slow-Cooker Cajun-Style Chicken with Sausage and Corn

SERVES 6

Although we prefer the texture and flavor of chicken thighs here, you can substitute 6 bone-in, skin-on chicken breasts; the cooking time will remain the same, but the meat will be a bit drier. Don't substitute frozen corn here, as it will have a mushy texture and will add little flavor. Serve this spicy Cajun stew with hot sauce and a crusty loaf of bread or Simple White Rice (page 386) to help sop up the sauce.

- 12 bone-in, skin-on chicken thighs (5 to 6 ounces each), trimmed (see note)
- Salt and ground black pepper
- 2 tablespoons vegetable oil, plus more as needed
- 2 medium onions, chopped medium
- 6 medium garlic cloves, minced or pressed though a garlic press (about 2 tablespoons)
- 2 cups low-sodium chicken broth
- 1 pound kielbasa, sliced into 1-inch pieces
- 1 tablespoon minced fresh thyme leaves or 1 teaspoon dried
- ½ teaspoon cayenne pepper
- 4 ears corn, husks and silk removed, cut into 2-inch lengths (see note)
- ¼ cup unbleached all-purpose flour
- 1 (12-ounce) jar roasted red peppers, rinsed and cut into 1-inch strips (about 1½ cups)
- ¼ cup minced fresh parsley leaves

1. Pat the chicken dry with paper towels and season with salt and pepper. Heat the oil in a 12-inch skillet over medium-high heat until just smoking. Brown half of the chicken on both sides, 5 to 8 minutes per side, reducing the heat if the pan begins to scorch. Transfer the chicken to a plate, leaving the fat in the pan. When cool enough to handle, remove the browned skin from the thighs and discard. Transfer the chicken to the slow cooker. Return the pan with the fat to medium-high heat and repeat with the remaining half of the chicken.

2. Pour off all but 1 tablespoon fat from the pan. (Add additional oil to equal 1 tablespoon if needed.) Add the onions and ¼ teaspoon salt and cook until softened, 5 to 7 minutes. Stir in the garlic and cook until fragrant, about 30 seconds. Stir in 1½ cups of the broth, scraping up any browned bits, and bring to a simmer. Pour into the slow cooker.

3. Add the kielbasa, thyme, and cayenne to the slow cooker. Cover and cook on low for 3 hours. Following the illustration on page 389, quickly nestle the corn into the slow cooker around the edges, replace the cover, and continue to cook until the chicken is tender, about 1 hour longer.

4. Transfer the chicken to a large serving dish and tent loosely with foil. Set the slow cooker to high. Whisk the remaining ½ cup broth and the flour together until smooth, then stir into the slow cooker. Add the roasted red peppers, cover, and continue to cook until the sauce is thickened and no longer tastes of flour, 15 to 30 minutes longer.

5. Stir in the parsley and season with salt and pepper to taste. Spoon the vegetables, sausage, and some of the sauce over the chicken and serve, passing the remaining sauce separately.

Slow-Cooker Country Captain Chicken

SERVES 6

Basic curry powder turns bitter after a few hours in a slow cooker, so stick with Madras curry powder—it's sweeter and hotter. Although we prefer the texture and flavor of chicken thighs here, you can substitute 6 bone-in, skin-on chicken breasts; the cooking time will remain the same, but the meat will be a bit drier. By tradition, this dish can be garnished with any or all of the following: sliced toasted almonds, shredded coconut, diced Granny Smith apples, and diced banana. For an accompaniment, either Basic Rice Pilaf (page 114) or Simple White Rice (page 386) is a must.

- 12 bone-in, skin-on chicken thighs (5 to 6 ounces each), trimmed (see note)
- Salt and ground black pepper
- 2 tablespoons vegetable oil, plus more as needed
- 2 medium onions, chopped medium
- 1 green bell pepper, stemmed, seeded, and chopped coarse
- 2 tablespoons Madras curry powder (see note)
- 4 medium garlic cloves, minced or pressed through a garlic press (about 4 teaspoons)
- 1 tablespoon minced fresh thyme leaves or 1 teaspoon dried
- 1½ teaspoons paprika
- ¼ teaspoon cayenne pepper
- 1 cup low-sodium chicken broth
- 1 (14.5-ounce) can diced tomatoes
- 5 tablespoons tomato paste
- 1 (9-ounce) jar mango chutney, such as Major Grey's

1. Pat the chicken dry with paper towels and season with salt and pepper. Heat the oil in a 12-inch skillet over medium-high heat until just smoking. Brown half of the chicken on both sides, 5 to 8 minutes per side, reducing the heat if the pan begins to scorch. Transfer the chicken to a plate, leaving the fat in the pan. When cool enough to handle, remove the browned skin from the thighs and discard. Transfer the chicken to the slow cooker. Return the pan with the fat to medium-high heat and repeat with the remaining half of the chicken.

2. Pour off all but 1 tablespoon fat from the pan. (Add additional oil to equal 1 tablespoon, if needed.) Add the onions, bell pepper, and ½ teaspoon salt and cook until the vegetables soften, 5 to 7 minutes. Stir in the curry powder, garlic, thyme, paprika, and cayenne and cook until fragrant, about 30 seconds. Stir in the broth, tomatoes, and tomato paste, scraping up any browned bits, and simmer until thick, about 2 minutes. Off the heat, stir in the chutney and pour the mixture into the slow cooker. Cover and cook on low until the chicken is tender, about 4 hours.

3. Transfer the chicken to a large serving dish and tent loosely with foil. Stir the sauce to recombine and season with salt and pepper to taste. Spoon the vegetables and some of the sauce over the chicken and serve, passing the remaining sauce separately.

INGREDIENTS: Mango Chutney

Mango chutney (sometimes called Major Grey's chutney) is a welcome accompaniment to many curries and roasted meats—it's also an essential component of our Slow-Cooker Country Captain Chicken (page 391). The name "Major Grey" is based on a fictional British soldier who supposedly enjoyed the sweet and sour punch of chutneys so much that he bottled his own. The name is not copyrighted and any bottled chutney can carry it.

Classic preparations cook unripe green mangoes with sugar, vinegar, and aromatic spices. But high levels of fructose corn syrup and caramel color cloud many store-bought varieties, and any natural mango flavors are often overshadowed by these additives. Many of the supermarket brands we tested were sickeningly sweet, with insipid, weak flavor. Tasters disliked the unnatural mango flavor in Crosse and Blackwell Major Grey's Chutney. A substantial dollop of ginger oil spiced Patak's Sweet Mango Chutney so heavily that tasters were torn; some appreciated the pungent, perfumed zing, while others complained about the ginger overload. Tasters liked the balanced sweetness and acidity of both Sharwood's Major Grey Mango Chutney and The Silver Palate Mango Chutney. In the end, the addition of lemon juice and peel gave The Silver Palate Mango Chutney a tangy boost that made it our favorite.

THE BEST MANGO CHUTNEY
A good mango chutney, like this one from The Silver Palate, offers a tangy, sweet, fruity complement to spicy curries.

16
STARTING WITH LEFTOVERS

Starting with Leftovers

WE KNOW THAT LEFTOVERS ARE A REAL SAVING grace for time-crunched cooks. But let's admit it: Who really wants to eat warmed-over sliced chicken? It's one thing to heat up a savory stew or casserole, but another thing altogether to transform leftover chicken into a new dish. So while we don't generally plan our cooking around recipes that incorporate leftovers, we think some of the ones in this chapter merit roasting an extra chicken on the weekend or sautéing a few extra breasts with your Tuesday night supper—just so you can make Chicken Arepas with Avocado and Cilantro or Moo Shu Chicken (both page 399).

We approached this chapter with the goal of providing specific recipes for leftover chicken. That said, we found that there are two key points to keep in mind when devising a new meal using leftover meat. The first trick is to make sure you have enough leftovers to work with. Although we've come across some recipes that claim you can stretch a 4-ounce piece of leftover chicken into dinner for four, it's just not true. All of the recipes in this chapter are based on 2 cups of shredded or thinly sliced chicken, which is plenty for four people.

The second and arguably most important trick is to understand that leftover chicken has already been cooked once, and additional cooking will only dry it out and ruin its flavor. Therefore, always add the leftover chicken to the new dish to warm it through just before serving.

How much meat can you expect to get from a cooked chicken? We roasted several chickens of varying weights and determined that you can get about 1 cup of cooked chicken per pound of raw chicken. If you're not using leftovers but purchasing a rotisserie chicken at the store, remember that chickens lose about 25 percent of their weight once cooked, so it will yield slightly more meat per pound than a raw chicken.

Chicken Panini

PANINI COME TO US FROM ITALY AND HAVE become extremely popular here in the United States. These pressed, grilled sandwiches, filled with any number of ingredients, can be found in upscale sandwich shops across the country. The bread should be golden brown and crisp and the filling hot, its ingredients melded together. We found that panini are the perfect way to use up leftover chicken, creating a delicious lunch or light dinner.

In restaurants, panini are cooked with a heavy cast-iron sandwich press that heats the sandwich from the top as it compresses the contents. While this item is standard issue in sandwich shops, it is not always found in home kitchens. To mimic the effects of a sandwich press, we used a preheated Dutch oven (or heavy pot) to weight the sandwiches. We came up with three combinations of ingredients for inspiration, but the possible flavor alternatives are limitless. These panini were so popular in the test kitchen that our tasters actually looked forward to these "leftovers."

Chicken and Roasted Red Pepper Panini

SERVES 4

Use sub rolls for this recipe (hearty sandwich bread will work, too); do not use bread that is really crusty or light and airy with a lot of holes. If your sub rolls are longer than 6 inches, cook the panini in 2 batches.

- **½ cup jarred roasted red peppers, rinsed, patted dry, and chopped**
- **½ cup kalamata olives, pitted (see the illustration on page 101)**
- **½ cup shredded fresh basil leaves (see the illustrations on page 252)**
- **2 tablespoons olive oil**
- **1 medium garlic clove, minced or pressed through a garlic press (about 1 teaspoon)**
- **4 (6-inch) sub rolls, halved lengthwise (see note)**
- **8 ounces thinly sliced deli provolone cheese**
- **2 cups shredded or thinly sliced cooked chicken**

1. Pulse the red peppers, olives, basil, 1 tablespoon of the oil, and the garlic in a food processor until coarsely chopped, about six 1-second pulses. Spread the pepper mixture evenly over both halves of the rolls. Layer 1 ounce of the cheese and ½ cup of the chicken over each roll bottom. Top with the remaining cheese and roll tops.

2. Heat the remaining 1 tablespoon oil in a 12-inch nonstick skillet over medium-low heat until shimmering. Meanwhile, heat a large Dutch oven (or heavy pot) over medium-low heat. Arrange the panini in the skillet and top with the preheated Dutch oven. Cook until the bottoms of the sandwiches are crisp and the cheese is beginning to melt, about 2 minutes. Remove the Dutch oven, flip the sandwiches over, replace the Dutch oven, and continue to cook until crisp on the second side and heated through, about 2 minutes. Serve.

VARIATIONS

Chicken, Arugula, and Fresh Mozzarella Panini

Follow the recipe for Chicken and Roasted Red Pepper Panini, substituting 2 ounces baby arugula (about 3½ lightly packed cups) for the roasted red peppers. Omit the basil. Substitute 8 ounces fresh mozzarella, thinly sliced, for the provolone.

Chicken, Caramelized Onion, and Goat Cheese Panini

Melt 2 tablespoons unsalted butter in a 12-inch nonstick skillet over medium heat. Add 2 medium onions, halved and thinly sliced, and ¼ teaspoon salt. Cook, stirring occasionally, until the onions are golden brown and caramelized, about 20 minutes. Follow the recipe for Chicken and Roasted Red Pepper Panini, substituting the caramelized onions for the roasted red peppers and ½ teaspoon minced fresh rosemary for the basil. Substitute 6 ounces goat cheese, crumbled, for the provolone.

Chicken Quesadillas

IN RECENT YEARS, QUESADILLAS HAVE EVOLVED into a version of bad Mexican pizza, becoming stale and soggy and unable to contain their oozing filling. We wanted to make quesadillas that were authentic in spirit (if not quite in substance) yet also quick enough to make for a weeknight dinner. We kept the tortillas crisp by lightly toasting them in a dry skillet. We then filled them, lightly coated them with oil and a sprinkling of salt, and returned them to the skillet until they were well browned and the cheese was fully melted. Using 8-inch tortillas and folding them in half around the filling allowed us to cook two at a time in the same skillet, and the fold also kept our generous cheese filling from leaking out.

Chicken Quesadillas

SERVES 2 TO 4

The skillet should be fairly hot, but it should never smoke; if it does, reduce the heat to medium-low. Serve with salsa, guacamole, and sour cream, if desired.

- 4 (8-inch) flour tortillas
- 2 cups shredded or thinly sliced cooked chicken
- 5½ ounces Monterey Jack or cheddar cheese, shredded (about 1⅓ cups)
- 4 teaspoons minced pickled jalapeños (optional)
- 4 teaspoons minced fresh cilantro leaves
- Vegetable oil
- Kosher salt

1. Adjust an oven rack to the middle position and heat the oven to 200 degrees.

2. Heat a 10-inch nonstick skillet over medium heat until hot, about 2 minutes. Toast the tortillas in the skillet, one by one, until soft and slightly puffed on both sides, about 1½ minutes per side; slide the tortillas onto a cutting board.

3. Sprinkle ½ cup of the chicken, ⅓ cup of the cheese, 1 teaspoon of the jalapeños (if using), and 1 teaspoon of the cilantro over half of each tortilla, leaving a ½-inch border around the edge. Fold the tortillas in half and press to flatten. Brush the tops generously with oil and sprinkle with salt; set aside.

4. Place 2 quesadillas in the skillet, oiled-sides down. Cook over medium heat until crisp and well browned, 1 to 2 minutes. Brush the tops with oil and sprinkle with salt. Flip the quesadillas over and continue to cook until the second sides are crisp and browned, 1 to 2 minutes longer. Transfer the quesadillas to a baking sheet and keep warm in the oven (they can be held for up to 20 minutes). Repeat with the remaining quesadillas. Let the quesadillas cool for 3 minutes before cutting and serving.

Cheesy Chicken Burritos

ANOTHER MEXICAN-INFLUENCED FAVORITE, burritos are well suited to the task of using up leftover chicken. Unlike other recipes that roll up canned refried beans, jarred salsa, and rice in a tortilla, we made a fresh-tasting and flavorful filling by simmering pinto beans and tomatoes with onion, garlic, and chipotle. Then we combined cooked rice with the leftover chicken, a generous amount of shredded cheddar, and cilantro. We mashed the bean mixture lightly and spread it over the tortillas, mounded the chicken and rice mixture on top, and rolled them up. To finish, we sprinkled our burritos with more cheddar and baked them in a 450-degree oven until the cheese melted and the filling was piping hot throughout.

Cheesy Chicken, Rice, and Bean Burritos

SERVES 4

Garnish with diced avocado and sour cream, if desired.

- 2 tablespoons vegetable oil
- 1 medium onion, minced
- 3 medium garlic cloves, minced or pressed through a garlic press (about 1 tablespoon)
- 2 teaspoons minced chipotle chile in adobo sauce
- 1 (15-ounce) can pinto beans, drained and rinsed
- 1 (14.5-ounce) can diced tomatoes
- ½ cup water
- Salt and ground black pepper
- 1 cup cooked rice
- 2 cups shredded or thinly sliced cooked chicken
- 8 ounces cheddar cheese, shredded (about 2 cups)
- ¼ cup minced fresh cilantro leaves
- 4 (10-inch) flour tortillas

1. Adjust an oven rack to the middle position and heat the oven to 450 degrees. Heat the oil in a 12-inch nonstick skillet over medium heat until shimmering. Add the onion and cook until softened, 5 to 7 minutes. Stir in the garlic and chipotle and cook until fragrant, about 30 seconds. Stir in the beans, tomatoes with their juice, and water and cook until the liquid has evaporated and the beans are softened, about 8 minutes. Mash the beans lightly using a potato masher. Season with salt and pepper to taste.

2. Place the rice in a medium microwave-safe bowl, cover with plastic wrap, and microwave on high until hot, about 90 seconds. Stir in the chicken, 1 cup of the cheese, and the cilantro.

3. Following the illustrations below, spread one-quarter of the bean mixture across each tortilla, leaving a 1½-inch border at the bottom edge and a 2-inch border on each side. Mound the rice mixture on the beans and fold the tortillas into burritos. Transfer the burritos, seam-side down, to

HOW TO ROLL A TIGHT BURRITO

1. Spread the bean mixture 1½ inches from the bottom of each tortilla, leaving a 2-inch border on either side, then mound the rice mixture on the beans.

2. Roll the bottom edge of the tortilla up over the filling to cover it completely. Using the tortilla for leverage, press the filling back onto itself into a tight, compact log.

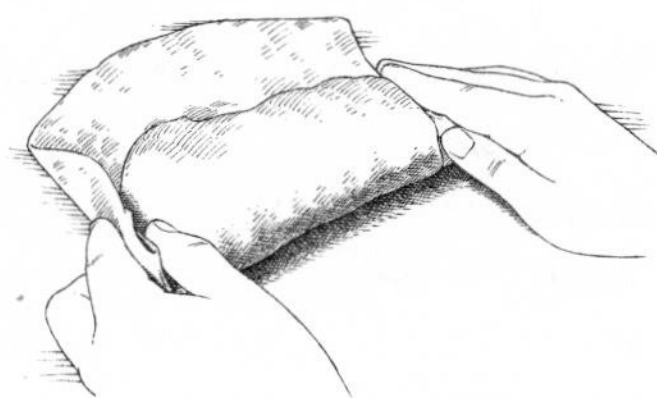

3. Fold the sides of the tortilla over the filling. Continue to roll the burrito into a tidy bundle. Place on a foil-lined baking sheet, seam-side down. If the ends come unfolded, simply tuck them under the burrito.

a baking sheet lined with foil, sprinkle with the remaining 1 cup cheese, and cover with a second large sheet of foil coated with cooking spray. Bake until the cheese is melted, 5 to 10 minutes. Serve immediately.

Chicken, Cheese, and Broccoli Calzone

CALZONES ARE USUALLY TOO BREADY—THIS one isn't. Each bite has the perfect ratio of tender crust to cheesy filling. However, with so much filling packed into the dough, our challenge was to prevent the crust from getting soggy. We found that, by using pesto instead of the traditional runny red sauce, we were able to pack flavor into the filling and keep it dry. (You can serve tomato sauce on the side.) Add to that chopped broccoli, shredded mozzarella, and shredded or thinly sliced chicken, and a complete meal is served. Store-bought pizza dough, dough from your local pizzeria, or one 12-ounce pop-up canister of pizza dough all work here, making this recipe quick and easy.

Chicken, Cheese, and Broccoli Calzone

SERVES 4

Store-bought pizza dough, dough from your local pizzeria, or one 12-ounce pop-up canister of pizza dough all work here. Although we prefer our Classic Pesto (page 213), you can substitute store-bought. Serve with a simple tomato sauce on the side.

1 (10-ounce) package frozen broccoli, thawed and chopped coarse
8 ounces part-skim mozzarella, shredded (about 2 cups)
2 cups shredded or thinly sliced cooked chicken
¼ cup pesto (see note)
Salt and ground black pepper
Unbleached all-purpose flour, for the work surface
1 pound pizza dough (see note)
Water, for sealing
2 tablespoons olive oil
Kosher salt (optional)

1. Adjust an oven rack to the middle position and heat the oven to 450 degrees. Pat the broccoli dry, place in a large bowl, and toss with the mozzarella, chicken, and pesto. Season with salt and pepper to taste.

2. On a lightly floured work surface, roll out the dough to a 12-inch round, about ¼ inch thick. Mound the filling over half of the dough, leaving a 1-inch border around the edge. Brush the edges of the dough with water. Fold the other half of the dough over the filling and press the edges to seal.

3. Grease a baking sheet with 1 tablespoon of the oil. Slide a wide spatula under the calzone and transfer to the baking sheet. Use a sharp knife or kitchen shears to cut five slits diagonally across the top. Brush the remaining 1 tablespoon oil over the top and sprinkle with kosher salt (if using). Bake until golden, 15 to 20 minutes. Cool briefly, cut into slices, and serve.

Chicken Arepas

AREPAS ARE A TYPE OF CORN CAKE POPULAR in Venezuela and Colombia. Variations also exist in other Latin countries, and in recent years they have even made their way to cosmopolitan areas in the United States. We decided to develop a recipe for Venezuelan arepas, which are split open and stuffed with a filling—anything from meat and cheese to eggs, corn, beans, or even fish—much like a sandwich. After all, many sources actually refer to arepas as the "hamburger" of Venezuela, where they are sold at fast-food joints called *areparias*. The idea of sandwich-style arepas appealed greatly to us, so we decided we would focus our attention there.

To make the chicken and avocado filling, a classic combination called *reina pepiada* in Venezuela, we bound tender shredded chicken together with rich chunks of avocado and added fresh cilantro, scallions, fresh lime juice, and a touch of chili powder to enliven the flavor. We could fit ¼ cup of filling into each arepa, which is plenty, considering that one arepa is perfect for a snack or light lunch, and two make a suitable dinner portion.

Chicken Arepas with Avocado and Cilantro

MAKES 8 FILLED AREPAS

Masarepa blanca, *a precooked white corn flour, is available in specialty Latin markets and often in the Latin American aisle at supermarkets. While we had the best results with masarepa, we found that white cornmeal can be substituted.*

AREPAS

- 2 cups (10 ounces) masarepa blanca (see note)
- 1 teaspoon salt
- 1 teaspoon baking powder
- 2½ cups warm water
- 2 tablespoons vegetable oil

FILLING

- 2 cups shredded cooked chicken
- 1 large, ripe avocado, halved, pitted, and cut into ½-inch chunks (see the illustrations on page 52 and 53)
- ¼ cup minced fresh cilantro leaves
- 2 scallions, sliced thin
- 3 tablespoons juice from 2 limes
- ½ teaspoon chili powder
- Salt and ground black pepper

1. For the arepas: Adjust an oven rack to the middle position and heat the oven to 400 degrees. Whisk the masarepa, salt, and baking powder together in a medium bowl. Gradually add the water and stir to form a dough. Using a generous ⅓ cup of dough for each, form eight 3-inch rounds, about ½ inch thick.

2. Heat 1 tablespoon of the oil in a 12-inch nonstick skillet over medium-high heat until shimmering. Add 4 of the arepas and cook until golden on both sides, about 4 minutes total. Transfer to a parchment paper–lined baking sheet and repeat with the remaining 1 tablespoon oil and the remaining 4 arepas. (The arepas can be refrigerated for up to 3 days or frozen for up to 1 month in a zipper-lock bag.)

3. Bake until the arepas sound hollow when tapped on the bottom, about 10 minutes. (If frozen, increase the baking time to 20 minutes.)

4. For the filling: While the arepas are in the oven, mix all the filling ingredients together in a medium bowl and season with salt and pepper to taste.

5. For serving: Split open the hot arepas using either a paring knife or two forks, as if they were English muffins, and stuff each with ¼ cup of the filling. Serve immediately.

Moo Shu Chicken

MOO SHU IS A STIR-FRIED DISH OF MEAT, shredded cabbage, and other vegetables that are rolled up in a thin crepe. While it is certainly easy enough to call in an order to your local Chinese takeout, why not make your own—especially if you've got some leftover chicken in the fridge?

Shredded cabbage is a given in moo shu, and we found that we liked the cabbage best when it still had a slightly crisp texture, so we added it with the chicken and cooked it just until it began to wilt. To intensify the flavor of the dish, we sautéed thinly sliced shiitake mushrooms and also included the classic Chinese combination of ginger, garlic, and scallions. A common problem with moo shu is that it is often oversauced, making the crepes soggy. Wary of this, we made just enough sauce to coat the vegetables—a simple mixture of chicken broth, soy sauce, cornstarch, and hoisin sauce for sweetness and depth. While Chinese crepes are available at specialty Asian markets, we were happy to roll up our moo shu in easy-to-find flour tortillas, which we quickly softened in the microwave while preparing the filling.

Moo Shu Chicken

SERVES 4

Shredded carrots, bean sprouts, or thinly sliced bamboo shoots can be stirred into the pan with the cabbage.

- ⅓ cup low-sodium chicken broth
- 6 tablespoons hoisin sauce
- 2 tablespoons soy sauce

- 2 teaspoons cornstarch
- 2 tablespoons vegetable oil
- 8 ounces shiitake mushrooms, stemmed, caps wiped clean and sliced thin
- 3 medium garlic cloves, minced or pressed through a garlic press (about 1 tablespoon)
- 1 tablespoon minced or grated fresh ginger
- 2 cups shredded or thinly sliced cooked chicken
- 12 ounces cabbage (½ small head), cored and shredded (about 4 cups)
- 5 scallions, sliced thin
- 8 (6-inch) flour tortillas

1. Mix the broth, 2 tablespoons of the hoisin sauce, the soy sauce, and cornstarch together in a small bowl and set aside.

2. Heat 1 tablespoon of the oil in a 12-inch nonstick skillet over high heat until just smoking. Add the mushrooms and cook until lightly browned, about 4 minutes.

3. Clear the center of the pan and add the remaining 1 tablespoon oil, the garlic, and ginger. Cook, mashing the garlic mixture into the pan until fragrant, about 30 seconds. Stir in the chicken, cabbage, and scallions and cook until the cabbage begins to wilt, about 1 minute.

4. Whisk the sauce to recombine, add it to the pan, and bring to a simmer. Cook until the sauce thickens and the mixture is hot, 1 to 2 minutes.

5. Meanwhile, stack the tortillas on a plate and cover with plastic wrap. Microwave until soft and hot, 30 seconds to 2 minutes. Serve the tortillas with the moo shu chicken and the remaining 4 tablespoons hoisin sauce.

Chicken Fried Rice

FRIED RICE SHOULD BE A SIMPLE DISH—AFTER all, it relies on leftover rice and naturally quick-cooking ingredients like eggs, frozen peas, and bean sprouts—but all too often it falls short. We've eaten our fair share of bad fried rice, from takeout containers of bland, greasy rice with rubbery meat and a meager amount of vegetables to recipes that rely on an overdose of soy sauce. We wanted to make simple, fresh, and flavorful fried rice.

To do so, we found it best to cook all the ingredients very quickly in stages over high heat, much like a stir-fry. To prevent the rice from getting mushy, we made sure that it was completely chilled before it went into the pan and then cooked it just until heated through. Garlic, soy sauce, and oyster-flavored sauce gave the rice complexity, while bean sprouts and scallions, stirred into the pan in the last minute, added freshness. This recipe comes together in under 10 minutes—faster than takeout and much fresher tasting.

Chicken Fried Rice

SERVES 4 TO 6

Don't try to make this dish with hot or even warm rice—it will turn out incredibly mushy. Use only cold or at least slightly chilled rice.

- 3 tablespoons vegetable oil
- 2 large eggs, lightly beaten
- 1 cup (6 ounces) frozen peas, thawed
- 2 medium garlic cloves, minced or pressed through a garlic press (about 2 teaspoons)
- 4 cups cooked white rice, chilled (see note)
- 2 cups shredded or thinly sliced cooked chicken
- 3 tablespoons low-sodium soy sauce
- 3 tablespoons oyster-flavored sauce
- 1 cup bean sprouts
- 5 medium scallions, sliced thin

1. Heat 1½ teaspoons of the oil in a 12-inch nonstick skillet over medium heat until shimmering. Add the eggs and cook without stirring until just beginning to set, about 20 seconds. Continue to cook, stirring constantly, until the eggs are cooked through but not browned, about 1 minute; transfer to a small bowl and set aside.

2. Add the remaining 2½ tablespoons oil to the skillet and return to high heat until just smoking. Add the peas and garlic and cook until fragrant, about 30 seconds. Add the rice, chicken, soy sauce, and oyster-flavored sauce and cook, stirring constantly, until the mixture is heated through, about 3 minutes.

3. Stir in the bean sprouts, scallions, and reserved cooked eggs and cook until heated through, about 1 minute. Serve immediately.

Cheesy Chicken and Rice Casserole

MOST FAST CHICKEN AND RICE CASSEROLES use canned soups or powdered soup packets—and they taste awful. We wanted to find a recipe that was just as easy to prepare but that actually tasted good. After testing several possibilities, we found that using long-grain white rice and a quick sauce made from chicken broth, cream, sautéed onion, and some garlic was the way to go. Partially cooking the rice in the sauce on the stovetop before mixing it with the vegetables and spreading it into the baking dish sped up the baking time significantly. Another trick we learned was to stir the leftover chicken into the casserole toward the end of the baking time so that it doesn't dry out.

Cheesy Chicken and Rice Casserole

SERVES 4

Don't add the chicken to the casserole until step 3; otherwise the chicken will dry out.

- 1 tablespoon vegetable oil
- 1 medium onion, minced
- 3 medium garlic cloves, minced or pressed through a garlic press (about 1 tablespoon)
- 1 teaspoon minced fresh thyme leaves
- 2½ cups low-sodium chicken broth
- ½ cup heavy cream
- 1 cup long-grain white rice
- 2 cups (8 ounces) frozen pea and carrot medley, thawed
- Salt and ground black pepper
- 2 cups shredded or thinly sliced cooked chicken
- 4 ounces cheddar cheese, shredded (about 1 cup)
- 20 Ritz crackers, crushed to coarse crumbs (about 1 cup)

1. Adjust an oven rack to the middle position and heat the oven to 450 degrees. Heat the oil in a 12-inch nonstick skillet over medium-high heat until shimmering. Add the onion and cook until softened, 5 to 7 minutes. Stir in the garlic and thyme and cook until fragrant, about 30 seconds. Add the broth and cream and bring to a simmer.

2. Stir in the rice, cover, and simmer over medium-low heat until the rice is almost tender, about 15 minutes. Stir in the peas and carrots and season with salt and pepper to taste. Pour the mixture into an 8-inch-square baking dish and bake for 5 minutes.

3. Stir in the chicken. Sprinkle the cheddar evenly over the top, then sprinkle with the cracker crumbs. Continue to bake until the crumbs are toasted, about 5 minutes. Serve.

Chicken Dinner Salads

MAKING CHICKEN SALAD IS THE OBVIOUS way to use up leftover chicken—our goal was to come up with some inspired flavors. One trick we found to making good chicken salad is to shred the meat rather than cut it up into cubes. The shreds of chicken get nicely coated with the dressing so that the salad is cohesive and flavorful; by contrast, the cubes taste dry and boring.

Chinese Chicken Salad includes shredded cabbage, bean sprouts, and chow mein noodles in a lively Asian-inspired vinaigrette. Romaine Salad with Chicken, Cheddar, Apple, and Spiced Pecans sports our favorite fall flavors pulled together with a tangy dried cranberry vinaigrette.

Chinese Chicken Salad

SERVES 4

La Choy is a widely available brand of chow mein noodles.

VINAIGRETTE

- ⅓ cup rice vinegar
- ¼ cup vegetable oil
- 3 tablespoons hoisin sauce
- 1½ tablespoons soy sauce
- 1 tablespoon minced or grated fresh ginger

SALAD

- ½ medium head napa cabbage, cored and shredded (about 4 cups)

- 1 red bell pepper, stemmed, seeded, and sliced thin
- 1 cup bean sprouts
- 2 scallions, sliced thin
- 2 cups shredded or sliced cooked chicken
- 1 cup chow mein noodles (see note)

1. For the vinaigrette: Whisk all the ingredients together in a medium bowl until well combined (alternatively, shake vigorously in a tight-lidded jar); set aside.

2. For the salad: In a large bowl, toss the cabbage, red pepper, sprouts, and scallions together with about two-thirds of the dressing. Divide the salad among individual plates. Place the shredded chicken in the bowl used to dress the cabbage and toss with the remaining dressing. Divide the dressed chicken evenly among the plates, sprinkle with the chow mein noodles, and serve.

Quick Spiced Pecans

MAKES ABOUT 2 CUPS

These nuts can be stored in a zipper-lock bag at room temperature for up to 1 week. If adding to a salad, be sure to shake off any extra sugar first.

- 2 tablespoons unsalted butter
- ½ teaspoon salt
- ¼ teaspoon ground black pepper
- ½ teaspoon ground cinnamon
- ⅛ teaspoon ground cloves
- ⅛ teaspoon ground allspice
- 2 cups pecan halves
- 1 tablespoon sugar

Melt the butter in a 12-inch nonstick skillet over medium-low heat. Stir in the salt, pepper, cinnamon, cloves, and allspice, followed by the pecans. Toast the nuts, stirring often, until the color of the nuts deepens slightly, 6 to 8 minutes. Transfer the nuts to a bowl and toss with the sugar. Spread the coated nuts on a plate to cool.

Romaine Salad with Chicken, Cheddar, Apple, and Spiced Pecans

SERVES 4

If the dressing seems thick, thin it with additional juice.

VINAIGRETTE

- ¼ cup cranberry juice (see note)
- ¼ cup dried cranberries
- ¼ cup raspberry vinegar
- 1 small shallot, peeled and quartered
- 2 teaspoons fresh thyme leaves
- 2 teaspoons Dijon mustard
- 1 small garlic clove, peeled
- ½ teaspoon salt
- ½ teaspoon ground black pepper
- ¾ cup extra-virgin olive oil

SALAD

- 1 large head romaine lettuce, torn into bite-sized pieces (about 10 cups)
- 8 ounces sharp cheddar cheese, cut into ½-inch cubes
- 1 Granny Smith apple, cored and sliced thin
- 1 cup spiced pecans (see recipe at left)
- ½ small red onion, sliced thin
- ¼ cup dried cranberries
- 2 cups shredded or sliced cooked chicken

1. For the vinaigrette: Combine the cranberry juice and dried cranberries in a microwave-safe bowl, cover with plastic wrap, and microwave on high until hot, about 1 minute. Puree the cranberry mixture, vinegar, shallot, thyme, mustard, garlic, salt, and pepper in a blender until the shallot and garlic are finely chopped, about 15 seconds. With the blender running, add the oil and continue to process until smooth and emulsified, about 15 seconds.

2. For the salad: Toss the lettuce, cheddar, apple, pecans, onion, and dried cranberries with ¾ cup of the vinaigrette. Divide the salad among individual plates. Place the shredded chicken in the bowl used to dress the lettuce and toss with ¼ cup of the dressing. Divide the dressed chicken evenly among the plates, arranging it on the lettuce. Serve, passing the remaining dressing separately.

Index

Note: *Italicized* page numbers refer to photographs.

C

N

O

P

T

A Note on Conversions

SOME SAY COOKING IS A SCIENCE AND AN art. We would say that geography has a hand in it, too. Flour milled in the United Kingdom and elsewhere will feel and taste different from flour milled in the United States. So we cannot promise that the loaf of bread you bake in Canada or England will taste the same as a loaf baked in the States, but we can offer guidelines for converting weights and measures. We also recommend that you rely on your instincts when making our recipes. Refer to the visual cues provided. If the bread dough hasn't "come together in a ball," as described, you may need to add more flour—even if the recipe doesn't tell you so. You be the judge. For more information on conversions and ingredient equivalents, visit our website at www.cooksillustrated.com and type "conversion chart" in the search box.

The recipes in this book were developed using standard U.S. measures following U.S. government guidelines. The charts below offer equivalents for U.S., metric, and Imperial (U.K.) measures. All conversions are approximate and have been rounded up or down to the nearest whole number. For example:

1 teaspoon = 4.9292 milliliters, rounded up to 5 milliliters
1 ounce = 28.3495 grams, rounded down to 28 grams

Volume Conversions

U.S.	METRIC
1 teaspoon	5 milliliters
2 teaspoons	10 milliliters
1 tablespoon	15 milliliters
2 tablespoons	30 milliliters
¼ cup	59 milliliters
⅓ cup	79 milliliters
½ cup	118 milliliters
¾ cup	177 milliliters
1 cup	237 milliliters
1¼ cups	296 milliliters
1½ cups	355 milliliters
2 cups	473 milliliters
2½ cups	592 milliliters
3 cups	710 milliliters
4 cups (1 quart)	0.946 liter
1.06 quarts	1 liter
4 quarts (1 gallon)	3.8 liters

Weight Conversions

OUNCES	GRAMS
½	14
¾	21
1	28
1½	43
2	57
2½	71
3	85
3½	99
4	113
4½	128
5	142
6	170
7	198
8	227
9	255
10	283
12	340
16 (1 pound)	454

Conversions for Ingredients Commonly Used in Baking

Baking is an exacting science. Because measuring by weight is far more accurate than measuring by volume, and thus more likely to achieve reliable results, in our recipes we provide ounce measures in addition to cup measures for many ingredients. Refer to the chart below to convert these measures into grams.

INGREDIENT	OUNCES	GRAMS
1 cup all-purpose flour*	5	142
1 cup whole wheat flour	5½	156
1 cup granulated (white) sugar	7	198
1 cup packed brown sugar (light or dark)	7	198
1 cup confectioners' sugar	4	113
1 cup cocoa powder	3	85
Butter†		
4 tablespoons (½ stick, or ¼ cup)	2	57
8 tablespoons (1 stick, or ½ cup)	4	113
16 tablespoons (2 sticks, or 1 cup)	8	227

* U.S. all-purpose flour, the most frequently used flour in this book, does not contain leaveners, as some European flours do. These leavened flours are called self-rising or self-raising. If you are using self-rising flour, take this into consideration before adding leavening to a recipe.

† In the United States, butter is sold both salted and unsalted. We generally recommend unsalted butter. If you are using salted butter, take this into consideration before adding salt to a recipe.

Oven Temperatures

FAHRENHEIT	CELSIUS	GAS MARK (IMPERIAL)
225	105	¼
250	120	½
275	130	1
300	150	2
325	165	3
350	180	4
375	190	5
400	200	6
425	220	7
450	230	8
475	245	9

Converting Temperatures from an Instant-Read Thermometer

We include doneness temperatures in many of our recipes, such as those for poultry, meat, and bread. We recommend an instant-read thermometer for the job. Refer to the table above to convert Fahrenheit degrees to Celsius. Or, for temperatures not represented in the chart, use this simple formula:

Subtract 32 degrees from the Fahrenheit reading, then divide the result by 1.8 to find the Celsius reading.

Example:

"Roast until the juices run clear when the chicken is cut with a paring knife or the thickest part of the breast registers 160 degrees on an instant-read thermometer." To convert:

$160°$ F – 32 = $128°$
$128° \div 1.8 = 71°$ C (rounded down from 71.11)